AN INTRODUCTION TO HUMAN FACTORS ENGINEERING

An Introduction to Human Factors Engineering

Christopher D. Wickens
University of Illinois at Champaign-Urbana

Sallie E. Gordon
University of Idaho

Yili Liu
University of Michigan

LONGMAN

An imprint of Addison Wesley Longman, Inc.

New York • Reading, Massachusetts • Menlo Park, California • Harlow, England
Don Mills, Ontario • Sydney • Mexico City • Madrid • Amsterdam

Editor-in-Chief: Priscilla McGeehon
Executive Editor: Rebecca J. Dudley
Marketing Manager: Jay O'Callaghan
Project Coordination and Text Design: Electronic Publishing Services Inc., NYC
Cover Designer: Kay Petronio
Art Studio: Electronic Publishing Services Inc., NYC
Photo Researcher: Mira Schachne
Full Service Production Manager: Valerie L. Zaborski
Manufacturing Manager: Hilda Koparanian
Electronic Page Makeup: Electronic Publishing Services Inc., NYC
Printer and Binder: The Maple-Vail Book Manufacturing Group
Cover Printer: Phoenix Color Corp.

For permission to use copyrighted material, grateful acknowledgment is made to the copyright holders throughout the text and is hereby made part of this copyright page.

Library of Congress Cataloging-in-Publication Data

Wickens, Christopher D.
    An introduction to human factors engineering / Christopher D.
Wickens, Sallie E. Gordon, Yili Liu.
        p.   cm.
    Includes bibliographical references and index.
    ISBN 0-321-01229-1
    1. Human engineering.   I. Gordon, Sallie E.   II. Liu, Yili.
III. Title.
TA166.W528   1997   97-40450
620.8'2—dc21   CIP

0-321-01229-1

12345678910—MA—00999897

Brief Contents

Detailed Contents

CHAPTER 9   **Control   259**

CHAPTER 12   Work Physiology   349

CHAPTER 13   Stress and Workload   377

CHAPTER 16   Automation   493

CHAPTER 17   Transportation Human Factors   513

Preface

We wrote this book because we saw a need for engineers and system designers and other professionals to understand how knowledge of human strengths and limitations can lead to better system design, more effective training of the user, and better assessment of the usability of a system. The knowledge and methods to accomplish these goals are embodied in the study of human factors engineering. As we point out in the early chapters, a *cost-benefit analysis* of human factors applications in system design usually provides a favorable evaluation of those applications.

Our intention in this book is to focus on the clear and intuitive explanation of human factors *principles*. We illustrate these principles with real-world design examples and, where relevent, show how these principles are based on understanding of the human's psychological, biological, and physical characteristics to give the reader an understanding of why the principles are formulated. Because of our focus on principles, we intentionally do not spend a great deal of time addressing psychological theory or research paradigms and experiments. We trust that the reader will know that the principles we describe are indeed based on valid research conclusions, and where relevent we provide citations as to where that research can be examined.

Also, we do not expect that this will be a stand-alone reference manual for applying human factors in design. Many specific numbers, values, and formulae, necessary for fabricating systems with human limitations in mind, were not included in this text in the interest of space. However, we point to ample references where designers can proceed to find these details.

Because of the way we have structured the book, emphasizing design principles and methodologies over theory and research, our primary target audience is the engineering undergraduate, who may well be participating in the design process. Hence we do not assume that the reader will necessarily have had an introductory course in psychology, and so we try to present some of the necessary psychological fundamentals. We also believe, however, that the book will be useful for applied psychology or undergraduate-level engineering psychology courses within a psychology department.

Human factors is a growing field. In many small industries, personnel are assigned to the position of human factors engineer who have no formal training in the discipline. Thus we hope that the book will not only reach the academic classroom in both engineering colleges and psychology departments but also be available as a reference for personnel and managers in the workplace.

We believe that the strengths of this book lie in its relatively intuitive and readable style, which attempts to illustrate principles clearly, with examples, and without excessive detail and which points to references where more information can be obtained. We have also tried to strike a balance between presenting the human factors associated with different aspects of human performance on the one hand (e.g., physical limitations, display processing, memory failures) and particularly important domains of current applications on the other. For example, there are separate chapters devoted to the human factors of transportation systems and of human computer interaction.

Acknowledgments

Several people have contributed to this endeavor. The following individuals provided valuable comments on earlier drafts of the work: Terence Andre, United States Air Force Academy; Mark Detweiler, Pennsylvania State University; John Casali, Virginia Polytechnical Institute; Joseph Meloy, Milwaukee School of Engineering; Edward Rinalducci, University of Central Florida; Joseph Goldberg, Pennsylvania State University; Philip Allen, Cleveland State University; and David Carkenord, Longwood College. Sallie Gordon wishes to thank Justin Hollands for his helpful suggestions, Nicki Jo Rich for her review/editing work, and Greg, Erin, and Shannon for their patience. The authors also gratefully acknowledge the great assistance of Margaret Dornfeld in the technical editing of the book, as well as the invaluable contributions of Mary Welborn for much of the administrative assistance in its preparation.

CHAPTER 1

Introduction to Human Factors

WHAT IS THE FIELD OF HUMAN FACTORS?

In a midwestern factory, a worker on an assembly line was required to reach to an awkward location and position a heavy component for assembly. Toward the end of a shift one day, after grabbing the component, he felt a twinge of pain in his lower back. A trip to the doctor revealed that the worker had suffered a ruptured disc, and he was laid off from work for several days. A lawsuit was brought against the company for requiring physical action that endangered the lower back.

In a household in the same city, an elderly resident encountered two problems. Examining the bottle of medicine she had been prescribed, she was unable to read the tiny print that listed the recommended dosage or even the red-printed safety warning beneath it. Ironically, a second difficulty prevented her from encountering harm caused by the first difficulty. She found herself unable to exert the combination of fine motor coordination and strength necessary for her to remove the "childproof" cap.

In a hurry to get a phone message through to a business, an unfortunate customer finds herself "talking" to an uncooperative electronic voice menu system. After impatiently hearing a long list of "If you want . . . , press #," she realizes that she accidentally pressed the number of the wrong option and now has no clue as to how to get back to the option she wanted, other than to hang up and repeat the lengthy process.

While all of the previous three episodes are generic in nature and repeated in many forms across the world, a fourth, which occurred in the Persian Gulf in 1987, was quite specific. The USS *Vincennes*, a U.S. Navy cruiser, was on patrol in the volatile conflict-ridden Persian Gulf when it received ambiguous information regarding an approaching aircraft. Characteristics of the radar system displays on board made it difficult for the crew to integrate the knowledge that the aircraft was approaching the ship with information about whether it was climbing or descending. Incorrectly diagnosing that the aircraft was descending, the crew tentatively identified it as a hostile approaching fighter. A combination of the short time to act in potentially life-threatening circumstances, further breakdowns in communication between people (both onboard the ship and from the aircraft itself), and crew expectancies that were driven by the hostile environment conspired to produce the captain's decision to fire at the approaching aircraft. Tragically, the aircraft was actually an Iranian passenger airline, which had been climbing rather than descending.

These four episodes all illustrate the role of *human factors*. In these cases human factors are graphically illustrated by breakdowns in the interactions between humans and the systems with which they work. Naturally there are many more times when these and other systems work well, often exceedingly so. However, it is characteristic of human nature that we notice when things go wrong more easily than when things go right. Furthermore, it is the situation when things go wrong that triggers the call for diagnosis and solution, and these are the key contributions of human factors to system design.

We may define the goal of human factors as making the human interaction with systems one that:

- Reduces error
- Increases productivity
- Enhances safety
- Enhances comfort

Human factors then involves the study of factors and development of tools that facilitate the achievement of these goals.

In the most general sense, these goals are accomplished through several procedures in the human factors cycle illustrated in Figure 1.1, which depicts the human operator (brain and body) and the system with which he or she is interacting, in the box at the left. First, (Fig. 1.1A) it is necessary to *diagnose* or identify the problems and deficiencies in the existing human-system interaction. To do this effectively, core knowledge of the nature of the physical body (its size, shape, and strength) and of the mind (its information-processing characteristics and limitations) must be coupled with a good understanding of the physical or information systems involved, and the appropriate *analysis* tools must be applied to clearly identify the cause of breakdowns. For example, why did the worker in our first story suffer the back injury? Was it the amount of the load or the awkward position required to lift it? Was this worker representative of others who also might suffer injury? Task analysis, statistical analysis, and incident and accident analysis are all critical here, and each of these will be discussed in later chapters of this book.

Having identified the problem, the five different approaches (Fig. 1.1B) may be directed toward implementing a solution (Booher, 1990), as shown at the bottom of the figure.

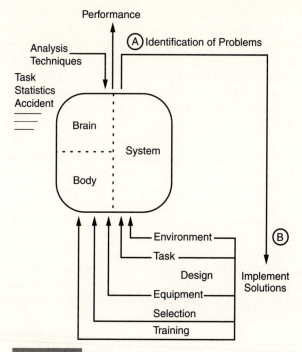

FIGURE 1.1

The cycle of human factors. Point A in the cycle identifies a cycle when human factors solutions are sought because a problem (e.g., accident or incident) has been observed in the human system interaction. Point B identifies a point where good human factors are applied at the beginning of a design cycle.

Equipment design changes the nature of the physical equipment with which humans must work. The medicine bottle in our example could be provided more readable labels and a better opening top. The radar display on the USS *Vincennes* might be redesigned to provide a more integrated representation of lateral and vertical motion of the aircraft.

Task design focuses more on changing what operators do, rather than the devices they use. The workstation for the assembly-line worker might have been redesigned so that the component did not need to be manually lifted, for example. Sometimes task design may involve assigning part or all of tasks to other workers or to *automated* components.

Environmental design implements changes—such as improved lighting, temperature control, and reduced noise—in the physical environment within which the task is carried out. A broader view of the environment could also include the organizational climate within which the work is carried out.

Training focuses on better preparing the worker for the conditions that he or she will encounter in the job environment by teaching and practicing the necessary physical or mental skills.

Selection is a technique that recognizes the individual differences across humans in almost every physical and mental dimension that is relevant for good system performance. Such performance can be optimized by selecting operators who possess the best profile of characteristics for the job. For example, the lower-back injury in our leading scenario might have been caused by asking a worker who had neither the necessary physical strength nor the body proportion to remove the component in a safe manner. The accident could have been prevented with a more stringent selection process.

As we see in the figure then, any and all of these approaches can be applied to "fix" the problems, and performance can be measured again to ensure that the fix was successful, an issue we address in the next chapter. It should be noted that our discussion up to this point has focused on *fixing* systems that are deficient, that is, intervening at Point A in Figure 1.1. In fact however, the practice of good human factors is just as relevant to *designing* systems that are effective and thereby to anticipating the human factors deficiencies before they are inflicted on system design. Thus, the role of human factors in the design loop can just as easily enter at Point B in Figure 1.1 as at Point A. Indeed if consideration for good human factors is given early in the design process, considerable savings in both money and possibly human suffering can be achieved (Booher, 1990; Hendrick, 1996). For example, early attention given to workstation design by the company in our first example, could have saved the several thousand dollars in legal costs resulting from the worker's law suite. In Chapter 3 of this book we talk in much greater detail about the role of human factors in the design process.

THE SCOPE OF HUMAN FACTORS

While the field of human factors originally grew out of a fairly narrow concern for human interaction with physical devices (usually military or industrial), its scope has broadened greatly during the last few decades. Membership in the primary North American professional organization of the *Human Factors and Ergonomics Society* has grown to 13,000, while in Europe, the *Ergonomics Society* has noted a corresponding growth. Furthermore, a recent survey indicates that these numbers may greatly underestimate the number of people in the workplace who actually consider themselves as doing human factors work (Williges et al., 1992).

This growth plus the fact that the practice of human factors is *goal oriented* rather than content oriented means that the precise boundaries of the discipline of human factors cannot be tightly defined. One way, however, of understanding what human factors professionals do is visualized in terms of the matrix shown in Figure 1.2. Across the top of the matrix is an (incomplete) list of the major categories of *systems* that define the contextual environments within which the human operates. On the left are those system environments in which the focus is the individual operator. Major categories here include the industrial environment (manufacturing and environments involving industrial processes, like nuclear power or chemical processes); the computer or information environment; the use of consumer products like watches, cameras, and VCRs; and vehicles (ground, water, or air based). On the right are depicted those environ-

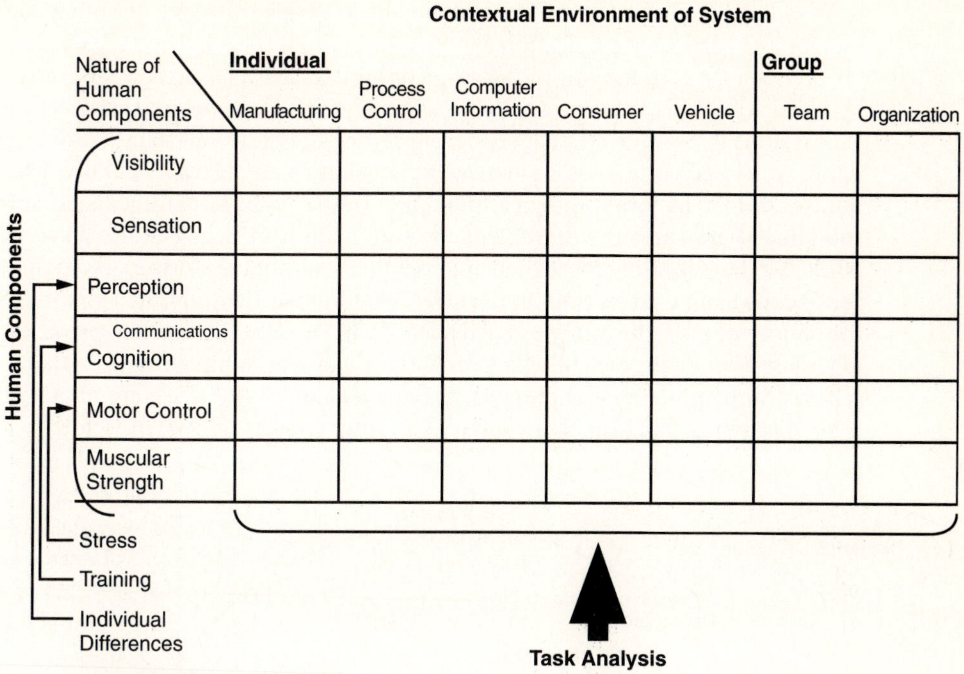

Contextual Environment of System

Nature of Human Components	Individual					Group	
	Manufacturing	Process Control	Computer Information	Consumer	Vehicle	Team	Organization
Visibility							
Sensation							
Perception							
Communications Cognition							
Motor Control							
Muscular Strength							

Human Components

Stress
Training
Individual Differences

Task Analysis

FIGURE 1.2

This matrix of human factors topics depicts human performance issues against contextual environments within which human factors may be applied. The study of human factors may legitimately belong within any cell or combination of cells in the matrix.

ments that focus on the interaction between two or more individuals. Here a distinction can be made between the focus on *teams* involved in a cooperative project and *organizations,* a focus that involves a wider concern with management structure.

Down the rows of Figure 1.2 are listed various components of the human user that are called on by the system in question. Is the information necessary to perform the task visible? Can it be sensed and adequately perceived? These components were inadequate for the elderly resident in the second example. What cognitive processes are involved in understanding the information and deciding what to do with it? Decisions on the USS *Vincennes* suffered because personnel did not correctly understand the situation. How are actions to be carried out, and what are the physical and muscular demands of those actions? This, of course, was the cause of the back injury for our worker in the example above. As shown at the far left of the figure, all of these processes may be influenced by *stresses* imposed on the human operator, by *training,* and by the *individual differences* in component skill and strength.

Thus, any given task environment across the top may impose on some subset of human components down the side, as defined by the cells within the matrix. A critical role of *task analysis* that we discuss in Chapter 3 is to identify the mapping from tasks to human components and thereby to define the scope of human factors for any particular application.

A second way of looking at the scope of human factors, is to consider the relationship of the discipline with other related domains of science and engineering. This is done within the circular rendering shown in Figure 1.3. Items within the figure are placed close to other items with which they are related. The core discipline of human factors is shown at the center of the circle, and immediately surrounding it are various subdomains of study within human factors; these are boldfaced. Surrounding these then are disciplines within the study of psychology (on the top) and engineering (at the sides) that intersect with human factors. At the bottom of the figure are presented a set of what we label as *domain-specific* engineering disciplines, each of which focuses on a particular kind of system that itself has human factors components. Finally, outside of the circle are identified other disciplines that also have overlap with some aspects of human factors.

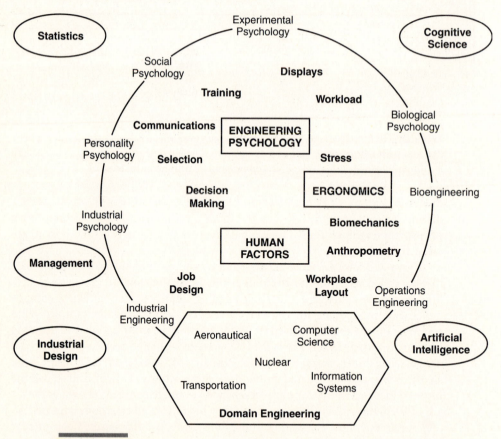

FIGURE 1.3

Illustrates the relationship between human factors, shown at the center, and other related disciplines of study. Those more closely related to psychology are shown at the top, and those related to engineering are shown toward the bottom.

While the figure depicts *human factors* at the center, there are two other closely related terms depicted in boxes within the circle whose relationship to human factors should be spelled out. Historically, the study of *ergonomics* has focused more directly on the aspect of human factors related to physical work (Grandjean, 1988): lifting, reaching, stress, and fatigue. This discipline is often closely related to aspects of human physiology, hence its closeness to the study of biological psychology and bioengineering. *Ergonomics* has also been the preferred label in Europe to describe all aspects of human factors. However, in practice the domains of human factors and ergonomics have been sufficiently blended on both sides of the Atlantic so that the distinction is often not maintained.

Engineering psychology, in contrast, is a discipline within psychology, whereas the study of human factors is a discipline within engineering. The distinction here is clear. The ultimate goal of the study of human factors is toward system design, accounting for those factors, psychological *and* physical, that are properties of the human component. In contrast, the ultimate goal of engineering psychology is in understanding the human mind, *as that understanding is relevant to the design of systems* (Wickens, 1992). In that sense, engineering psychology tends toward greater emphasis on discovering generalizable psychological principles and theory, while human factors tends toward greater emphasis on developing usable design principles. But this distinction is certainly not a hard and fast one.

The reader might also encounter the discipline of *cognitive engineering*. This discipline, also closely related to human factors, is slightly more complex in its definition (Rasmussen, Pejterson, & Goodstein, 1995) and cannot as easily be placed at a single region in the space of Figure 1.3. In essence it focuses on the complex, *cognitive* thinking and knowledge related aspects of system performance, independent of whether these operations are carried out by human or by machine agents, the latter dealing closely with elements of artificial intelligence and cognitive science.

THE STUDY OF HUMAN FACTORS AS A SCIENCE

Characteristics of human factors as a science (Meister, 1989) relate to the endeavor to seek *generalization* and *prediction*. On the one hand, in the problem diagnosis phase, shown in Figure 1.1, investigators wish to *generalize* across classes of problems that may have common elements. The problems of communications between an air traffic control center and the aircraft may have the same elements as the communications problems between workers on a noisy factory floor or between doctors and nurses in an emergency room, thus enabling similar solutions to be applied to all three. Such generalization is more effective when it is based on a deep understanding of the physical and mental components of the human operator. On the other hand, it is important to be able to *predict* that solutions that are envisioned to create good human factors will actually succeed when put into practice.

The critical element to achieving effective generalization and prediction is the nature of the *observation* or study of the human operator that we discuss in the next chapter. We will learn that there are a range of environments in which humans can be studied, which vary in the realism with which the environment simulates the relevant system. At one end of this range, the human factors researcher may fabricate certain elements of the system in the laboratory for highly controlled observations and experiments. At the other end, the researcher may examine human behavior (normal behavior, incidents, and accidents), as this is manifest by real users of real systems. In between, there is a category of *simulation* environments that vary in the degree of realism with which they capture elements of the real system. Researchers have learned that the most effective understanding, generalization, and prediction depends on the combination of observations along all levels of this continuum.

Thus, for example, the human factors engineer may couple an analysis of the events that led up to the USS *Vincennes* tragedy, with an understanding, based on laboratory research, of principles of decision making (Chapter 7), display integration (Chapter 8) and performance degradation under time stress (Chapter 13) and an analysis of communications patterns in a simulated emergency to gain a full appreciation of the causes of the *Vincennes'* incident and suggestions for remediation.

AN OVERVIEW OF THE BOOK

The following chapters are divided into four basic subsections. In the next two chapters (2, on research, and 3, on design), we describe different research techniques and design methodologies. The second subsection contains six chapters that address the nature of human information processing, in sensing (Chapters 4, on vision, and 5, on audition), perception and cognition (Chapter 6), decision making (Chapter 7), display processing (Chapter 8), and control (Chapter 9). The third subsection contains a set of five chapters that address many of the nonpsychological issues of human factors: workspace layout (Chapter 10), strength (Chapter 11), physiology (Chapter 12), stress (Chapter 13), and safety issues (Chapter 14). Chapters on safety and stress address psychological issues as well. The final subsection contains four chapters that focus on specific domains of application of human factors study—automation (Chapter 15), human computer interaction (Chapter 16), transportation (Chapter 17), training and selection (Chapter 18), and one chapter on group and organizational behavior (Chapter 19).

The reader is also directed to several other fine books covering similar and related material: Sanders & McCormick (1993), Bailey (1989), and Proctor & Van Zandt (1994) also offer comprehensive coverage of human factors. Norman (1988) examines human factors manifestations in the kinds of consumer systems that most of us encounter every day, and Meister (1989) addresses the science of human factors. Wickens (1992) provides a coverage of engineering psychology, foregoing treatment of those human components that are not related to psychology (e.g., visibility, reach, and strength). In complimentary fashion, Grandjean (1988) and Wilson & Corlett (1991) focus more on the physical aspects of human factors (i.e., classical "ergonomics"). Finally, a comprehensive treatment of nearly all aspects of human factors can be found in the 49 chapters contained within Salvendy's (1997) *Handbook of Human Factors and Ergonomics*.

There are several journals that address human factors issues, but probably the most important are *Ergonomics,* published by the International Ergonomics Society in the United Kingdom, and three publications offered by the Human Factors and Ergonomics Society in the United States: *Human Factors, Ergonomics in Design,* and the annual publication of the *Proceedings of the Annual Meeting of the Human Factors and Ergonomics Society.*

REFERENCES

Bailey, R.W. (1989). *Human performance engineering: Using human factors/ergonomics to achieve computer system usability* (2nd ed.). Englewood Cliffs, NJ: Prentice Hall.

Booher, H.R. (ed.) (1990). *MANPRINT: An approach to systems integration.* New York: Van Nostrand Reinhold.

Grandjean, E. (1988). *Fitting the task to the man* (4th ed.). London: Taylor & Francis.

Hendrick, H. (1996). The ergonomics of economics is the economics of ergonomics. *Proceedings of the 40th Annual Meeting of the Human Factors and Ergonomics Society* (pp. 1–10). Santa Monica, CA: Human Factors and Ergonomics Society.

Meister, D. (1989). *Conceptual aspects of human factors.* Baltimore: The Johns Hopkins University Press.

Norman, D.A. (1988). *The psychology of everyday things.* New York: Basic Books.

Proctor, R.W., and Van Zandt, T. (1994). *Human factors in simple and complex systems.* Needham Heights, MA: Allyn and Bacon.

Rasmussen, J., Pejtersen, A., and Goodstein, L. (1995). *Cognitive engineering: Concepts and applications.* New York: Wiley.

Salvendy, G. (1997). *Handbook of human factors and ergonomics* (2nd ed.). New York: Wiley.

Sanders, M.S., and McCormick, E.J. (1993). *Human factors in engineering and design* (7th ed.). New York: McGraw Hill.

Wickens, C.D. (1992). *Engineering psychology and human performance* (2nd ed.). New York: HarperCollins.

Williges, R., et al. (1992). *The education and training of human factors specialists.* Washington, DC: National Academy Press.

Wilson, J.R. and Corlett, E.N. (1991). *Evaluation of Human Work* London: Taylor and Francis.

CHAPTER 2

Research Methods

We saw in Chapter 1 that human factors is the application of scientific knowledge and principles to the design of products, systems, and/or environments. For example, we use our knowledge acquired from research on the human visual system to design VDTs or automotive display systems. Because human factors involves the application of science to system design, it is considered by many to be an *applied science*. While the ultimate goal is to establish principles that reflect performance of people in real-world contexts, the underlying scientific principles are gained through research conducted in both laboratory and real-world environments. People involved in human factors research may range from pure scientists doing basic laboratory research, to human factors engineers who apply the research findings of others to new designs.

Human factors researchers use standard methods for developing and testing scientific principles that have been developed over the years in traditional physical and social sciences. These methods range from the "true scientific experiment" conducted in highly controlled laboratory environments to less controlled but more realistic observational studies in the real world. Given this diversity of methods, a human factors researcher must be familiar with the range of research methods that are available, as well as know which methods are best for specific types of research questions. However, in addition to being well-versed in research methods, it is equally important for researchers to understand how the practitioner ultimately uses their findings. Ideally, this enables a researcher to direct his or her work in ways that are more likely to be useful to design, thus making the science applicable (Chapanis, 1991).

This chapter presents common ways that human factors researchers conduct studies to advance the scientific basis of their field. This will help you to understand descriptions of research studies covered later in this book, and other talks or publications in the field of human factors.

11

Knowledge of basic research methods is also necessary for human factors design work. That is, standard design methods are used during the first phases of product or system design. As alternative design solutions emerge, it is sometimes necessary to perform formal or informal studies to determine which design solutions are best for the current problem. At this point, designers must select and use appropriate research methods. Chapter 3 provides an overview of the more common design methods used in human factors and will refer you back to various research methods within the design context.

INTRODUCTION TO RESEARCH METHODS

What fields of science are applied in human factors work? We often think of human factors as an interdisciplinary field spanning psychology, engineering, and computer science. This would lead us to believe that human factors is the application of psychological theory and findings to product design, such as software interface design. This conclusion is partly true. There are many theories and principles developed in psychology that are applicable to system design. You will be reading about the most important of these in later chapters.

However, psychologists tend to study thought and behavior in a rather pure and context-free environment. Human factors, by definition, involve the interaction between humans and machine or environment. This occurs at both a psychological and a physical level. Thus, we must also rely on the science of anatomy and physiology so that systems "fit" the human (as will be described later in Chapters 10, 11, and 12). In addition, we need theories and principles that encompass the human-machine system as an *integrated unit*. Researchers in human factors study such integrated systems and attempt to develop scientific knowledge about the relationships between the system components. Put differently, human behavior affects design, but machine/environment design also affects behavior (Smith, 1993). For this reason, much of the scientific research performed in human factors is more specific in terms of the tasks and environments than that performed in basic subfields of psychology or physiology.

Basic and Applied Research

It should be apparent that scientific study relevant to human factors can range from basic to very applied research. *Basic research* can be defined as "the development of theory, principles, and findings that generalize over a wide range of people, tasks, and settings." An example would be a series of studies that tests the theory that as people practice a particular activity hundreds of times, it becomes automatic and no longer takes conscious, effortful cognitive processing. *Applied research* can be defined loosely as "the development of theory, principles, and findings that are relatively specific with respect to particular populations, tasks, products, systems, and/or environments." An example of applied research would be measuring the extent to which the use of a particular cellular phone while driving on an interstate highway takes driver attention away from primary driving tasks. Smith (1993) states that "applied research in human factors should be directed at delineating how performance is specifically influenced by particular design factors and/or combinations thereof."

While some specialists emphasize the dichotomy between basic and applied research, it is more accurate to say that there is a continuum, with all studies falling somewhere along the continuum depending on the degree to which the theory or findings generalize to other tasks, products, or settings. Both basic and applied research have complementary advantages and disadvantages. On the one hand, basic research tends to develop basic principles that have greater generality than applied research. It is conducted in rigorously controlled laboratory environments, an advantage because it prevents intrusions from other variables and allows us to be more confident in the cause-and-effect relationships we are studying. On the other hand, research in a laboratory environment is often simplistic and artificial and may bear little resemblance to performance in real-world environments. The point here is that caution is required in assuming that theory and findings developed through basic research will be applicable for a particular design problem (Kantowitz, 1990). For this reason, people doing basic research should strive to conduct controlled studies with a variety of tasks and within a variety of settings, some of which are conducted in the "field" rather than in the lab. This increases the likelihood that their findings are generalizable to new or different tasks and situations.

Given the discussion above, one might conclude that only applied research is valuable to the human factors designer. After all, applied research yields principles and findings specific to particular tasks and settings. Each designer need only find research findings corresponding to the particular combination of factors they are facing in the current design problem, and apply the findings. The problem with this view is that many, if not most, design problems are somehow different from those studied in the past. If, for example, you are designing a new and improved cellular phone, will the findings of previous work on attention be applicable? Probably not, because your new design may be much easier to use and take less attention. The advantage of applied research is also its downfall. It is more descriptive of real-world behavior, but it also tends to be much more narrow in scope.

In summary, basic research is useful for yielding principles of human behavior that can be applied in a variety of design contexts. This is especially important for the design of radically new products and environments, for example, interfaces for the Internet. However, applied research is also useful for human factors design for two reasons. First, there may be previous applied research that was conducted for similar tasks or environments, which can be used to guide system design. Second, the human factors specialist may come up with several alternative designs, and the methods described in this chapter can be used to evaluate the alternative designs.

Overview of Research Methods

The goal of scientific research is to describe, understand, and predict relationships between variables. In our example above, we were interested in the relationship between the variable of "using a cellular phone while driving" and "driving performance." More specifically, we might hypothesize that use of a cellular phone will result in poorer driving performance than not using the phone. This is an empirical question because it can be answered by conducting an experiment.

A variety of research methods are employed for human factors research. All are valuable in different contexts and for answering different types of questions. Both basic and applied research rely on two categories or types of research methods, experimental methods and descriptive methods.

The *experimental method* consists of deliberately producing a change in one or more causal or *independent variables* and measuring the effect of that change on one or more effect or *dependent variable.* In a true experiment, this manipulation is performed while keeping all other influential variables under control. The true experiment is technically the only way to infer cause-and-effect relationships. It is the most rigorous and well controlled of the research methods and is the standard to which other methods are held.

When researchers cannot control all of the other influential variables for one reason or another, they often conduct a "quasi-experiment." These look like experiments because causal variables are manipulated or set at different levels, and effect variables are measured. However, there are important differences that often reduce the validity of the study. These differences will be addressed below in our discussion of quasi-experiments.

The second major type of research design relies on *descriptive methods.* There are instances where researchers (or system designers) are interested in one or more theorized relationship between variables but cannot directly manipulate the casual variable(s). For example, a researcher may be interested in the relationship between years on the job at a manufacturing plant and risk-taking behavior. It is not feasible for the researcher to "set" the number of years on the job for each worker arbitrarily. Therefore, the researcher must simply measure both variables and evaluate the correlation or degree of relationship between them. Descriptive methods rely on measurement of variables such as performance, opinion, and so on and yield data describing the variables individually and in relationship to each other. If a researcher does this type of work, it is termed a study or research project but is technically not an experiment.

Basic research relies predominantly on the true experiment. This allows the most confidence in the cause-and-effect relationship being suggested by the research data. Applied research is often conducted in contexts that make a true experiment difficult or impossible to implement. In these cases, a quasi-experiment or descriptive study is conducted. Because these methods are less controlled than a true experiment, extra precautions should be taken to maximize the quality of the design. The following sections describe the major research methods in more detail and discuss methods for maximizing the quality of the studies, thereby increasing their validity. Keep in mind that in addition to being research tools, all of these methods are potentially used by human factors designers during one phase or another of the design process.

EXPERIMENTAL RESEARCH METHODS

An experiment involves looking at the relationship between causal independent variables and resulting changes in one or more dependent variables. The goal is to show that the independent variable, and no other variable, is responsible for causing any quantitative differences that we measure in the dependent variable. When we conduct an experiment or quasi-experiment, we proceed through a process of steps or stages.

Steps in Conducting an Experiment

There are roughly five steps in conducting an experiment, whether in the lab or the real world (Williges, 1995). The researcher begins with an idea or theory that yields a hypothesized relationship between the independent and dependent variables. Once we have an idea of the predicted relationship between variables, we specify the experimental plan, collect the data, analyze the data, and draw conclusions based on the statistical results.

> *Step 1. Define problem and hypotheses.* A researcher first hypothesizes the relationships between a number of variables and then sets up experimental designs to determine whether a cause-and-effect relationship does in fact exist. For example, we might hypothesize that changing peoples' work shifts back and forth between day and night produces more performance errors than having people on a constant day shift or on a constant night shift. Once the independent and dependent variables have been defined in an abstract sense (e.g., "fatigue" or "attention") and hypotheses have been stated, the researchers must develop more detailed experimental specifications.

> *Step 2. Specify the experimental plan.* Specifying the experimental plan consists of identifying all the details of the experiment to be conducted. The first step is to define each independent variable in terms of how it will be manipulated. For example, we would specify exactly what we mean by "alternating between day and night shifts." Is this a daily change or a weekly change? We next specify exactly what is meant by the dependent variable. What do we mean by "performance?" We must specify the concept in terms of some measurable variable. For example, we could define *performance* as the number of keystroke errors in data entry.

> The researcher next chooses an experimental design. There are a number of different possible designs that could be used to test the same hypothesis. The researcher must choose the design most appropriate for the problem (common designs are described below). The researcher determines equipment to be used, tasks to be performed (if any), the environment in which the study will take place, and the people who will participate in the study.

> *Step 3. Conduct the study.* The researcher obtains participants for the experiment, develops materials, and prepares to conduct the study. If he or she

is unsure of any aspects of the study, it is efficient to perform a very small experiment called a *pilot study* before conducting the entire "real" study. After checking everything through a pilot study, the experiment is carried out and data collected.

Step 4. Analyze the data. In an experiment, the dependent variable is measured and quantified for each subject (there may be more than one dependent variable). For the example described above, you would have a set of numbers representing the keystroke errors for the people who were on changing work shifts, a set for the people on day shift, and a set for the people on night shift. Data are analyzed using inferential statistics to see whether there are significant differences among the three groups.

Step 5. Draw conclusions. Based on the results of the statistical analysis, the researchers draws conclusions about the cause-and-effect relationships in the experiment. At the simplest level, this means determining whether hypotheses were supported. In applied research, it is often important to go beyond the obvious. For example, if we are evaluating various computer cursor control devices, we might obtain results showing a mouse to be superior to a trackball with respect to performance of certain tasks. Rather than just accepting that "the mouse was superior to the trackball," it is important for the researcher to go beyond the obvious and ask *why*. Is it because the devices require use of different types of muscle groups, or that one requires more fine motor control than the other? Identifying underlying reasons, whether psychological or physiological, allows for the development of principles and guidelines that are more likely to be useful to others.

Experimental Designs

Experiments can be conducted in a number of different ways. In a simple case, we might have only two groups of subjects and compare performance between the two groups. For example, we could have a study where one group of subjects uses a trackball for cursor control on a computer, and another group uses a mouse for cursor control. We evaluate the differences in performance to see which input device leads to more accurate performance. However, using a different type of experimental design, we could just as easily have the same group of subjects perform tasks alternatively with both a trackball and a mouse and then evaluate the differences. For any experiment, there are different designs that can be used to collect the data. Which design is best depends on the particular situation. The sections below describe the basic differences between experimental designs. However, it is beyond the scope of this text to outline how to select one design over another. Readers are referred to works such as Elmes, Kantowitz, and Roediger (1995), Keppel (1992), and Mitchell and Jolley (1996).

The Two-Group Design. In a *two-group design*, one independent variable or factor is tested with only two conditions or levels of the independent variable. In the classic two-group design, a *control* group of subjects gets no treatment (e.g., driving with no cellular car phone), and the *experimental* group of subjects gets some "amount" of the independent variable (e.g., driving while using a cellular phone). The dependent variable (driving performance) is compared for the two groups. However, in human factors it is frequently the case that we are comparing two different experimental treatment conditions, such as comparing performance using a trackball versus performance using a mouse. In these cases, it may not make sense to have a control group per se. Having a control group to compare with a mouse or trackball would mean having no cursor control at all, which does not really make sense.

Multiple Group Designs.   Sometimes the two-group design does not adequately test our hypothesis of interest. For example, if we want to assess the effects of VDT brightness on display perception, we might want to evaluate several different levels of brightness. We would be studying one independent variable (brightness) but would want to evaluate many *levels* of the variable. If we used five different brightness levels and therefore five groups, we would still be studying one independent variable, but would gain more information than if we only used two levels/groups. Similarly, we might want to test four different input devices for cursor control such as trackball, thumbwheel, traditional mouse, and keymouse. We would have four different experimental conditions but still only one independent variable (type of input device). Increasing the number of levels of an independent variable is especially important if we hypothesize a curvilinear relationship between the independent and dependent variables.

Factorial Designs.   In addition to increasing the number of levels used for manipulating an independent variable, we can expand the two-group design by evaluating more than one independent variable or factor in a single experiment. In human factors, we are often interested in complex systems and therefore in simultaneous relationships between many variables rather than just two. This makes research more complicated and difficult.

A multifactor design that evaluates two or more independent variables by combining the different levels of each independent variable is called a *factorial design.* The term *factorial* indicates that all possible combinations of the independent variable levels are combined and evaluated. Factorial designs allow the researcher to assess the effect of each independent variable by itself and also to assess how the independent variables interact with one another. Because much of human performance is complex and human-machine interaction is often complex, factorial designs are the most common research designs used in both basic and applied human factors research.

Factorial designs can be more complex than a 2×2 design in a number of ways. First, there can be multiple levels of each independent variable. For example, we could compare five different cellular phone designs with each other, and also with "no phone." And we might combine that first variable with a second variable consisting of four different driving conditions. This would result in a 6×4 factorial design.

Another way that factorial designs can become more complex is by increasing the number of independent variables. A design with three independent variables is called a three-way factorial design, for example, a $2 \times 2 \times 3$ factorial

EXAMPLE OF A SIMPLE FACTORIAL DESIGN:

To illustrate the logic behind factorial designs, we can first consider an example of the most simple factorial design. This is where two levels of one independent variable are combined with two levels of a second independent variable. Such a design is called a 2 × 2 factorial design. Imagine that a researcher wants to evaluate the effects of using a cellular phone on driving performance (and hence on safety). The researcher manipulates the first independent variable by comparing driving with and without use of a cellular phone. However, the researcher suspects that the driving impairment may only occur if the driving is taking place in heavy traffic. Thus, he or she may add a second independent variable consisting of light versus heavy traffic driving conditions. The experimental design would look like that illustrated in Figure 2.1: four groups of subjects derived from combining the two independent variables.

Imagine that we conducted the study, and for each of the subjects in the four groups shown in Figure 2.1, we counted the number of times the driver strayed outside of the driving lane. We can look at the general pattern of data by evaluating the cell means; that is, we combine the scores of all subjects within each of the four groups. Thus, we might obtain data such as that shown in Table 2.1.

If we only look at the effect of cellular phone use (combining the light and heavy traffic conditions), we might be led to believe that use of car

DRIVING CONDITIONS

	Light traffic	Heavy traffic
No car phone	No car phone while driving in light traffic	No car phone while driving in heavy traffic
Car phone	Use car phone while driving in light traffic	Use car phone while driving in heavy traffic

FIGURE 2.1
The four experimental conditions for a 2 × 2 factorial design.

TABLE 2.1 Hypothetical Data for Driving Study

Car Phone Use	Light traffic	Heavy traffic
No car phone	2.1	2.1
Car phone	2.2	5.8

phones impairs driving performance. But looking at the entire picture, as shown in Figure 2.2, we see that the use of a car phone only impairs driving in heavy traffic conditions (as defined in this particular study). When the lines connecting the cell means in a factorial study are not parallel, as in Figure 2.2, we know that there is some type of interaction between the independent variables. Factorial designs are popular for both basic research and applied questions because they allow researchers to evaluate interactions between variables.

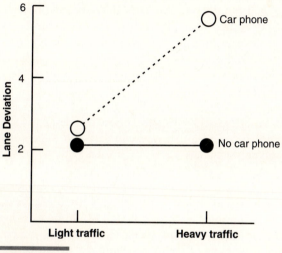

FIGURE 2.2

Illustration of interaction between cellular phone use and driving conditions.

design. Adding independent variables has two advantages: (1) It allows designers to vary more system features, and (2) it captures a greater part of the complexity found in the real world, making experimental results more likely to generalize.

Between-Subjects Design.   In most of the examples described above, the different levels of the independent variable were assessed using separate groups of subjects. For example, we might have one group of subjects use a cellular car phone in heavy traffic, another group use a cellular phone in light traffic, and so on. We compare the driving performance between groups of subjects, hence the term *between-subjects.* A between-subjects variable is an independent variable whereby different groups of subjects are used for each level or experimental condition.

A *between-subjects design* is a design in which all of the independent variables are between-subjects, and therefore each combination of independent variables is administered to a different group of subjects. Between-subjects designs are most commonly used when having subjects perform in more than one of the conditions would be problematic. For example, if you have subjects receive one type of training (e.g., on a simulator), they could not begin over again for another type of training because they would already know the material.

Within-Subject Designs.   In many experiments, it is feasible to have the same subjects participate in all of the experimental conditions. For example, in the driving study, we could have the same subjects drive for periods of time in each of the four conditions shown in Table 2.1. In this way, we could compare the performance of each person with him- or herself across the different conditions. This "within-subject" performance comparison illustrates where the method gets its name. When the same subject experiences all levels of an independent variable, it is termed a within-subjects variable. An experiment where all independent variables are within-subject variables is termed a *within-subjects design*. Using a within-subjects design is advantageous in a number of respects, including the fact that it is more sensitive and easier to find statistically significant differences between experimental conditions. Researchers usually choose this design over the between-subjects design unless it is not feasible, for example, when you are assessing a remedial program for job performance.

Mixed Designs.   In factorial designs, each independent variable can be either between-subjects or within-subjects. If both types are used, the design is termed a *mixed design*. An example of a mixed design would be learning to perform abdominal operations using a cadaver versus using a three-dimensional simulator. The independent variable of training equipment would be a between-subjects variable with two conditions. A second independent variable might be type of operation (aneurism versus appendectomy versus intestinal section removal). If all students in the study learned all three types of operation, this would be a within-subjects variable.

To summarize, an experiment where all of the independent variables are between-subjects variables is called a between-subjects design. Correspondingly, an experiment where all of the independent variables are within-subjects variables is called a within-subjects design. An experiment that has both between- and within-subjects variables is called a mixed design.

Multiple Dependent Variables

In the previous sections, we described several different types of experimental design that were variations of the same thing—multiple independent variables combined with a single dependent variable or "effect." However, the systems that we study, including the human, are very complex. We often want to measure how causal variables affect several *dependent variables* at once. For example, we might want to measure how use of a cellular phone affects a number of driving variables, including deviations from a straight path, reaction time to brake for cars or other objects in front of the vehicle, time to recognize objects in the driver's peripheral vision, speed, acceleration, and so forth. It is possible to perform an experiment and simultaneously measure multiple dependent variables. Determining the number of independent and dependent variables are relatively independent processes.

Selecting the Apparatus and Context

Once the experimental design has been specified with respect to independent and dependent variables, the researcher must decide what tasks the person will be performing, and under what context. For applied research, we try to identify tasks and environments that will give us the most generalizable results. This often means conducting the experiments under real-world or high-fidelity conditions.

Selecting Experimental Participants

Participants should represent the population or group in which the researcher is interested. For example, if we are studying pilot behavior, we would pick a sample of pilots who represent the pilot population in general. If we are studying the elderly, we define the population of interest (e.g., all people aged 65 and older who are literate); then we obtain a sample that is representative of that population. Notice that it would be difficult to find a sample that has all of the qualities of all elderly people. If lucky, we might get a sample that is representative of all elderly people living in the United States who are healthy, speak English, and so on.

Controls

In deciding how the study will be conducted, it is important to consider all variables that might impact the dependent variable. All of these extraneous variables have the potential to interfere in the causal relationship. Extraneous variables must be *controlled* so that they do not interfere. One group of extraneous variables is the wide range of ways participants differ from one another. These variables must be controlled, so it is important that the different groups of people in an experiment differ only with respect to the treatment condition and not on any other variable or category. For example, in the cellular phone study, you would not want elderly drivers using the car phone and young drivers using no phone. The easiest way to make sure all groups are equivalent is to take the entire set of subjects and randomly put them in one of the experimental conditions. That way, on the average, characteristics of the subjects will even out across the groups. This procedure is termed *random assignment.* Given a large enough number of participants, all the "subject variables" are automatically controlled just through the use of random assignment. True experiments rely on random assignment of participants so that researchers can make causal inferences.

Other variables in addition to subject variables must be controlled. For example, it would be a poor experimental design to have one condition where cellular car phones are used in a Jaguar and another condition where no phone is used in an Oldsmobile. There may be driving characteristics or automobile size differences that cause variations in driving behavior. The phone versus no-phone comparison should be carried out in the same vehicle (or same type of vehicle). Control of extraneous variables should be carried out for as many factors as is feasible. Thus, if it is a between-subjects design with four groups of subjects, all four groups should drive the same car, in the same place, with the same researcher(s), and so forth. If several cars are to be used, they should be balanced (used approximately equally) across all groups.

In summary, the researcher must control extraneous variables by making sure they do not covary along with the independent variable. If they do covary with the independent variable, they become *confounds* and make interpretation of the data impossible. This is because the researcher does not know which variable caused the differences in the dependent variable.

For within-subjects designs, there is another variable that must be controlled in addition to the extraneous variables relevant to between-subjects designs. This variable is called *order,* or order effects. When people participate in several treatment conditions, the dependent measure may show differences from one condition to the next simply because the treatments, or levels of the independent variable, are experienced in a particular order. For example, if participants use five different cursor control devices in an experiment, they might be fatigued by the fifth device and therefore exhibit more errors or slower times. This would be due to the order of devices used rather than the device per se. To keep order from confounding the independent variables, we use a variety of methods. For example, extensive practice can reduce learning effects. Time between conditions can reduce fatigue. Finally, researchers often use a technique termed *counterbalancing.* This simply means that different subjects receive the treatment conditions in different orders. For example, half of the participants in a study would use a trackball and then a mouse. The other half would use a mouse and then a trackball. There are specific techniques for counterbalancing order effects, with the most common one being a Latin-square design. Research methods books can be consulted for instruction on using these designs.

Conducting the Study

After designing the study and identifying a sample of participants, the researcher is ready to conduct the experiment actually and collect data (sometimes referred to as "running subjects"). Depending on the nature of the study, the experimenter may want to conduct a small pretest, or pilot study, to check that manipulation levels are set right, that participants (subjects) do not experience unexpected problems, and that the experiment will generally go smoothly.

When the experiment is being conducted, the experimenter should make sure that data collection methods remain constant. For example, an observer should not become more lenient over time; measuring instruments should remain calibrated. Finally, all participants should be treated ethically as described later.

Data Analysis

Once the experimental data have been collected, the researcher must determine whether the dependent variable(s) actually did change as a function of experimental condition. For example, did subjects take longer to perform tasks using a trackball as opposed to a mouse? To evaluate the research questions and hypotheses, the experimenter calculates two types of statistics, *descriptive* and *inferential statistics.* Descriptive statistics are a way to summarize the dependent variable for the different treatment conditions, while inferential statistics tell us the likelihood that any differences between our experimental groups are "real" and not just random fluctuations due to chance.

Descriptive Statistics.   Differences between experimental groups are usually described in terms of averages. Thus, the most common descriptive statistic is the *mean.* Research reports typically describe the mean scores on the dependent variable for each group of subjects (e.g., see the data shown in Table 2.1). This is a simple and easy-to-understand way of conveying the effects of the independent variable(s) on the dependent variable. Standard deviations are also sometimes given to convey the spread of scores.

Inferential Statistics.   While experimental groups may show different means for the various conditions, it is possible that such differences occurred solely on the basis of chance. Humans almost always show random variation in performance, even without manipulating any variables. It is not uncommon to get two groups of subjects who have different means on a variable, without the difference being due to any experimental manipulation. In fact, it is unusual to obtain means that are exactly the same. So the question becomes, Is the difference big enough that we can rule out chance and assume the independent variable had an affect? Inferential statistics give us the probability that the difference between the groups is due to chance. If we can rule out the "chance" explanation, then we infer that the difference was due to the experimental manipulation.

For a two-group design, the inferential statistical test usually used is a t-test. For more than two groups, we use an Analysis of Variance (ANOVA). Both tests yield a score; for a t-test, we get a value for a statistical term called t, and for ANOVA, we get a value for F. Most important, we also identify the probability, p, that the t or F value would be found by chance for that particular set of data.

Drawing Conclusions

Researchers usually assume that if p is less than .05, they can conclude that the results are not due to chance and therefore that there was an effect of the independent variable. Accidently concluding that independent or causal variables had an effect when it was really just chance is referred to as making a *Type I error.* If scientists use a .05 cutoff, they will be making a Type I error one in twenty times. In traditional sciences, a Type I error is considered a "bad thing" (Wickens, 1995). This makes sense if a researcher is trying to develop a cause-and-effect model of the physical or social world. It would lead to the development of false theories.

Researchers in human factors have accepted this implicit assumption that making a Type I error is bad. Research where the data result in inferential statistics with $p > .05$ is not accepted for publication in most journals. Experimenters studying the effects of system design alternatives must conclude that the alternatives made no difference. Program evaluation where introduction of a new program resulted in statistics of $p > .05$ must conclude that the new program did not work, all because there is greater than a one in twenty chance that spurious factors *could* have caused the results.

What is the cost of setting this arbitrary cutoff of $p = .05$? The cost is that researchers are more likely to make *Type II errors,* concluding that the experimental manipulation did not have an effect when in fact it *did*. This means a researcher evaluating a new display format may erroneously conclude that it does not help operator performance. A safety officer might conclude that a new piece of equipment is no easier to use under adverse environmental conditions when in fact it is easier. The likelihood of making Type I and Type II errors are inversely related.

The use of the $p = .05$ criterion is especially problematic in human factors because we frequently must conduct experiments and evaluations with relatively low numbers of subjects. Using a small number of subjects makes the statistical test less powerful and more likely to show "no significance," or $p > .05$. In addition, the difference in performance between different subjects or for the same subject but over time and conditions is also likely to be great. Again, these factors make it more likely that the results will show "no significance," or $p > .05$. The result is that human factors researchers frequently conclude that there is no difference in experimental conditions simply because there is more than a one in twenty chance that it *could* be caused by random variation in the data.

Statistical inference tests are always based on the law of averages. Take an example from medical research. We test a cancer drug and conduct a t-test for the drug versus a placebo. Imagine that we find $p = .20$. Statistically, this means there is a one-in-five chance that there was no effect of the drug, that the differences were simply due to random variation. Do we throw out the drug saying "No, it must not work"? We should not because there is too high of a risk that we have made a Type II error. We are better off doing more research. Did we fail to get a statistically significant effect because we did not have enough participants? Did it help some people but not others? If it helped four out of twenty people, we might do well to try to determine why it helped those four people.

Finally, consider a hypothetical example from the area of aviation research reported by Harris (1991). Earlier researchers had conducted statistical tests to compare the effects of two crew aircraft (pilot, copilot) versus three crew aircraft (pilot, copilot, flight engineer) on safety. Looking at accident rates, the researchers had concluded that while accident rates for two crew flights were higher, the differences were not statistically different. Harris evaluated the power of the statistical test and concluded that it was low enough that there was a 40 percent chance of a Type II error (there really was a difference but it went undetected). The point is that a researcher is likely to have made system design recommendations related to safety that were 40 percent likely to be incorrect. In human factors, where conclusions support design decisions and not just development and validation of theories, researchers must be more aware of the tradeoffs between Type I and Type II errors, and not blindly apply the traditional .05 cutoff.

New methods are being developed in order to avoid the pitfalls of using a single experiment to draw conclusions. Psychologists are using an analysis method called *meta-analysis,* a technique that combines the results of many studies into one analysis and overall conclusion. A meta-analysis can show the strength of a relationship between two variables across multiple studies. This means that we are less likely to make either a Type I or a Type II error and can be more confident in our conclusions.

Statistical Significance versus Practical Significance

Once chance is ruled out, meaning $p < .05$, researchers discuss the differences between groups as though they are a fact. However, it is important to remember that two groups of numbers can be statistically different from one another without the differences being very *large.* As an example, suppose we compare two groups of Army trainees. One group is trained in tank gunnery with a low-fidelity personal computer. Another group is trained with an expensive high-fidelity simulator. We might find that when we measure performance later, the mean percent correct for the personal computer group is 80 percent while the mean percent correct for the simulator group is 83 percent. If we used a large number of subjects, there may be a statistically significant difference between the two groups, and we would therefore conclude that the simulator is a better training system. However, especially for applied research, we must look at the difference between the two groups in terms of *practical* significance. Is it worth spending billions to place simulators on every military base to get an increase from 80 percent to 83 percent? This illustrates the tendency for some researchers to place too much emphasis on statistical significance and not enough emphasis on practical significance.

Quasi-Experiments

Quasi-experiments are conducted when the researcher cannot directly manipulate the independent variable(s). Quasi-experiments fall somewhere between "experimental" and "descriptive" research methods. While they are technically not experiments, we discuss them in this section because they use groups and statistical analyses that are similar to an experiment. There are a number of quasi-experimental designs (see Cook & Campbell, 1979), but the most common in human factors is the "non-equivalent control group design" with two variations, those that make use of existing groups and those that let subjects self-select their treatment conditions.

Existing Groups or Ex Post Facto Designs.   In many quasi-experiments, independent variables are selected which have different levels or conditions, but the levels were not explicitly created (and controlled) by the experimenter. Examples would include the variables of gender, age groups, levels of work experience, and weight. As an example, assume that we want to evaluate the hypothesis that workers with greater work experience (for example, over ten years) in a manufacturing plant exhibit lower risk-taking behavior. Our independent variable would be years on the job (e.g., <1, 1–10, and >10), and our dependent variable would be some measure of risk-taking. However, we cannot perform a true experiment. That would require obtaining a sample of workers, say ninety people from a local plant, and then randomly assigning them to one of the three levels of the experiment. We cannot assign workers to conditions because they already naturally occur within the conditions—they already have some number of years on the job. The problem with this design is that people who naturally fall into the different groups may vary on other dimensions as well. For example, people who have been on the job longer may have different personality characteristics than those who have worked less time. These personality characteristics may be responsible for any differences in risk-taking.

In applied research, we must often use such "existing groups" for experiments. These studies are called quasi-experiments because they look like true experiments but do not have the same level of control. Our inferences about cause and effect are much weaker because there may be competing causal factors that cannot be ruled out.

Subject Self-Selection to Condition.   Consider another example. We are evaluating the differences in cursor control for the trackball versus mouse example. We bring participants in and allow them to choose one device or the other for their work. We collect data and find that fewer errors were made with the trackball than with the mouse. Can we conclude that the input device was responsible for the difference? Only if we can assume that subjects choosing the trackball are the same on all characteristics as those choosing the mouse. Clearly we cannot make that assumption.

Using existing groups or letting subjects self-select their condition means introducing possible confounds that *cannot* be eliminated with any type of statistical analysis. Whenever possible, researchers should use a true experiment with random assignment of subjects to groups. This is true whether the study is being conducted for research purposes or for the support of system design and evaluation, as described in Chapter 3.

DESCRIPTIVE METHODS

While experimentation in a tightly controlled environment is valuable for uncovering basic laws and principles, there are often cases where research is better conducted in the real-world. In many respects, the use of complex tasks in a real-world environment results in data that are more generalizable because they capture more of the characteristics of a complex real-world environment. Unfortunately, conducting research in real-world settings often means that we must give up the "true" experimental design because we cannot directly manipulate and control variables. We have already seen one example of this in the quasi-experiment. Another case is *descriptive research,* where researchers simply measure a number of variables and possibly evaluate how they are related to one another.

One example of this type of research would be evaluating the driving behavior of local residents at various intersections. Another example would be measuring how people use a particular design of ATM (automatic teller machine). A third example would be observing workers in a manufacturing plant to identify the types and frequencies of unsafe behavior.

Observation

In many instances, human factors research consists of recording behavior during tasks performed under a variety of circumstances. For example, in studying naturalistic decision making, we might observe command and control personnel receiving information, asking for additional information, making decisions, and evaluating those decisions. This could be done for a wide range of tasks ranging from mundane everyday conditions to unusual emergency circumstances. Observational research can yield a great deal of information about human performance (including errors) under complex conditions.

In planning observational studies, a researcher identifies the variables to be measured, the methods to be employed for observing and recording each variable, conditions under which observation will occur, the observational time frame, and so forth. For example, if we are observing decision making and one variable is the type of information initially received, we must develop a taxonomy to classify the different types of information. Otherwise, observation will result in a large number of specific pieces of information that cannot be reduced into any meaningful descriptions or conclusions. It is usually most convenient to develop a taxonomy based on pilot data. This way, an observer can use a checklist to record and classify each instance of new information, condensing the information as it is collected.

In situations where a great deal of data is available, it may be more sensible to sample only a part of the behavioral data available or to sample behavior during different sessions rather than all at once. For example, a safety officer is better off sampling the prevalence of improper procedures or risk-taking behavior on the shop floor during several different sessions spread out over a period of time rather than all at once during one day. The goal is to get representative samples of behavior, and this is more easily accomplished by sampling over different days and during different conditions.

There are several other issues in observational research that are related to the quality of research and findings. First, researchers should consider the extent to which the process of observation is likely to affect the behavior being measured. This is particularly problematic for behaviors that violate company policy or are incompatible with prevalent social norms. A second issue is the reliability of the observer. Humans are notoriously unreliable in the sense that what they see and how they interpret it tends to change over time. Observer reliability can be increased by having two or more observers collect data for the same situation and then checking the percentage of observations in which they are in agreement. In addition, videotapes can be reviewed and discussed to increase interobserver reliability.

Surveys and Questionnaires

Both basic and applied research frequently rely on surveys or questionnaires to measure variables. Survey research is "the systematic gathering of information about people's beliefs, attitudes, values, and behavior" (Sommer & Sommer, 1986). An example would be conducting a survey of forest firefighters' beliefs, attitudes, values, and actual behavior with respect to safety and safety related procedures in firefighting. This information might be useful in developing new company policies, guidelines, training programs, and so forth to increase safety-oriented attitudes and behavior among firefighters.

A *questionnaire* is a set of written questions or scales used for both experimental and descriptive research. As an example, a true experiment might be conducted where participants are randomly assigned to one of five computer display conditions. After using the display for some period of time, they are given a questionnaire measuring several dependent variables such as subjective fatigue, beliefs about the effectiveness of the display, and so forth. Answers to the questionnaire would be quantified and submitted to statistical analyses, as described earlier in this chapter.

Questionnaires are also used in descriptive research where no independent variables are manipulated. They are extremely valuable in measuring perceptions, opinions, predictions, and other "mental phenomena" that affect the relationship between human and machine. There are two basic types of questionnaire: self-administered questionnaires where the respondent reads and fills out the questionnaire him- or herself, and interviewer-administered questionnaires where the researcher asks questions and records the answers. These are also known as *structured interviews*. Self-administered questionnaires are more common because they are faster and more efficient.

Content.   In developing a questionnaire, it is best to start with a definition of the variables of interest. For example, let us assume we are evaluating several alternative ergonomic designs for a computer workstation chair. We will probably measure several objective physiological and performance variables, but we are interested in people's subjective reactions as well. We might want to know if the chair feels comfortable, whether people had trouble making the various adjustments, and if people simply like the chair in general. However, in order to write the questionnaire assessing these variables, we must first develop a list of the exact variables we wish to measure. Thus, in identifying questionnaire content, it is better to start with a list of the dependent variables of interest. Often these will be grouped into categories, such as comfort (e.g., leg, back, arm, etc.), ease of use of the various controls, and overall appeal. Once the clusters of variables have been listed, specific questionnaire items are developed. The development of questionnaire items requires deciding on format for each question and then writing the question using clear and concise terms.

Format.   Question format can be either open-ended or closed. An open-ended question has a format where a question is asked and the respondents write their own answer (e.g., What did you like about the chair?). Open-ended questions are desirable when the researcher cannot foresee all possible answers, when the range of possible answers is too large to be practical, or when the researcher wants the respondent's own words for some reason (Sommer & Sommer, 1986).

Closed questions give respondents a limited choice of answers; examples are multiple choice questions or rating scales. An example would be:

In general, how easy was it to accomplish your goals using this ATM?

Extremely Difficult	1	2	3	4	5	6	7	Extremely Easy

There are numerous advantages to using closed questions. The predominant one is that they are much easier to convert to quantitative scores for the variables being studied. For example, a respondent could rate the overall appeal of a software interface design on a scale of 1 to 7. These values represent quantities that can be used as variables for descriptive or inferential statistical analyses.

Many analysts recommend using a combination of open-ended and closed questions so that each can overcome the disadvantages of the other. Some suggest that one put open-ended "reaction" questions at the beginning of a section or questionnaire, followed by the more specific closed questions. This helps to keep respondents from being biased by the content of specific questions.

Pretesting.   After the first draft of a questionnaire is written, it should be pretested. The researcher finds several respondents who are similar in characteristics to the ultimate group who will receive the questionnaire. These trial respondents are asked to fill out the questionnaire and give the researcher feedback regarding any problems that they note. This process is critical because the person writing the questionnaire is close to the subject and often will not be able to see when items are unclear or misleading. Pretesting can be done with a small number of respondents and usually no statistical analyses are needed.

Validity.   As with any other measure, questionnaires are only valid to the extent that they are well-designed and measure what they are intended to. Questionnaires often measure beliefs and behavior that are sensitive or open to judgment. Under most circumstances, respondents should be told that their answers will be both confidential and anonymous. It is common practice for researchers to place identifying numbers on the questionnaires rather than names. Employees are more likely to be honest if their name will never be directly associated with their answers.

Incident and Accident Analysis

Sometimes a human factors analyst needs to determine the overall functioning of a system, especially with respect to safety. There are a number of methods for evaluating safety, including the use of surveys and questionnaires. Another method is to evaluate the occurance of incidences, accidents, or both. An *incidence* is where a noticeable problem occurs during system operation, but an actual accident does not result from it. Some fields, such as the aerospace community, have formalized databases for recording reported incidents and accidents (Rosenthal & Reynard, 1991). The Aviation Safety Reporting Systems (ASRS) database is run by NASA and catalogs on the order of 30,000 incidents reported by pilots or air traffic controllers each year.

While this volume of information is potentially invaluable, there are certain difficulties associated with the database. First, just the sheer size of the qualitative database makes it difficult to search to develop or verify causal analyses. Second, even though people who submit reports are guaranteed anonymity, not all incidents are reported. Finally, a third problem is the fact that the reporting person may not give information that is necessary for identifying the root causes of the incident or accident. The more recent use of follow-up interviews has helped but not completely eliminated the problem.

Accident prevention is a major goal of the human factors profession, especially as humans are increasingly called upon to operate large and complex systems. Accidents can be systematically analyzed to determine the underlying root causes, whether they arose in the human, machine, or some interaction. Accident analysis has pointed to a multitude of cases where poor system design has resulted in "human error," including problems such as memory failures in the 1989 Northwest Airlines Detroit crash, training and decision errors in the 1987 Air Florida crash at Washington National Airport, high mental workload and poor decision making at Three-Mile Island, and attention tunneling in the 1972 Eastern Airlines Everglades crash. Accidents are usually the result of several coinciding breakdowns within a system. This means that most of the time, there are multiple unsafe elements such as training, procedures, controls and displays, system components, and so on that would ideally be detected *before* rather than after an accident. This requires a proactive approach to system safety analysis rather than a reactive one such as that provided by accident analysis. This topic will be addressed in greater length in Chapter 14.

Data Analysis for Descriptive Measures

Most descriptive research is conducted in order to evaluate the relationships between a number of variables. Whether the research data has been collected through observation or questionnaires, the goal is to (1) see whether relationships exist and (2) measure their strength. Relationships between variables can be measured in a number of ways. In this section, we briefly describe several of them.

Differences Between Groups. Researchers are frequently interested in how variables differ for different groups of people. For example, we might want to see how the attitudes and behavior of firefighters differ for people who are new on the job versus people who have extensive experience. Data for different groups of subjects can be evaluated using ANOVA just as it is done for true experiments. Data from questionnaires are frequently analyzed to see whether groups of subjects differ on one or more of the items. However, if you are analyzing more than a few variables, there are statistical adjustments that should be made in order to avoid increasing the chances of a Type I error (refer to a standard research methods and statistics text).

Relationships Between Continuous Variables. In the previous example, we grouped firefighters into novice versus experienced firefighters. However, it is also possible to see if there is a relationship between job experience and safety attitudes without grouping the subjects at all. This is done by performing a *correlational analysis*. The correlational analysis measures the extent to which two variables covary. For example, in a positive correlation, one variable increases as the values of another variable increase. In a negative correlation, the values of one variable increase as the other variable decreases. By calculating the correlation coefficient, *r*, we get a measure of the strength of the relationship. Statistical tests can be performed that determine the probability that the relationship is due to chance fluctuation in the variables. Thus we get information concerning whether a relationship exists (*p*) and a measure of the strength of the relationship (*r*).

One caution should be noted. When we find a statistically significant correlation, it is tempting to assume that one of the variables caused the changes seen in the other variable. This causal inference is unfounded for two reasons. First, the direction of causation could actually be in the opposite direction. For example, we might find that years on the job is negatively correlated with risk-taking. While it is possible that staying on the job makes an employee more cautious, it is also possible that being more cautious results in a lower likelihood of injury or death. This may therefore cause people to stay on the job. Second, a third variable might cause changes in both variables. For example, people who try hard to do a good job may be encouraged to stay on and may also be cautious as part of trying hard.

Complex Modeling and Simulation.   Researchers sometimes collect a large number of data points for multiple variables and then test the relationships through models or simulations. According to Bailey (1989), a model is "a mathematical/physical system, obeying specific rules and conditions, whose behavior is used to understand a real (physical, biological, human-technical, etc.) system to which it is analogous in certain respects." Models range from simple mathematical equations to highly complex simulations (runnable models), but in all cases, they are more restricted and less "real" than the system they reflect.

Simple models may be conceptual or mathematical. Conceptual models specify a set of variables and their interrelationships without necessarily quantifying those relationships. Such conceptual models can be verified by collecting correlational data for the variables and submitting it to a model verification program such as LISREL (Joreskog & Sorbom, 1976). Such model testing directly tests the research hypotheses rather than testing the null or "no effect" hypothesis, as is done in traditional research.

Other simple models may be mathematical equations linking two or more variables. These are often used to describe relationships in a physical system, or the physiological relationships in the human body. Mathematical models of the human body have been used to create simulations that support workstation design. As an example, COMBIMAN is a simulation model that provides graphical displays of the human body in various workstation configurations (McDaniel & Hofmann, 1990). It is used to evaluate the physical accommodation of a pilot to existing or proposed crew station designs.

Mathematical models can be used to develop complex simulations (see Elkind, Card, Hochberg, & Huey, 1990). That is, key variables in some particular system and their interrelationships are mathematically modeled and coded into a runnable simulation program. Various scenarios are "run" and the model shows what would happen to the system. The predictions of a simulation can be validated against actual human performance. This gives future researchers a powerful tool for evaluating the effects of design changes. An example of this type of modeling is currently being carried out for human cognitive performance. For example, Woods, Roth, and Pople (1990) have developed an artificial intelligence program called Cognitive Environment Simulation (CES) that models human problem solving performance and errors for operators in a nuclear power plant. This allows human factors specialists to predict what circumstances will be most likely to lead to errors *and why*. Other simulation models focus on variables such as task sequences, operator workload, and related performance problems (e.g., Baron, 1988; Sarno & Wickens, 1995). One important advantage of using models for research is that they can replace evaluation using human subjects to assess the impact of harmful environmental conditions (Kantowitz, 1992; Moroney, 1994).

MEASURING VARIABLES

For both experimental and descriptive research, a key component is measurement of variables. As an example, in applied research we might be interested in evaluating how system design factors or environmental factors would impact a pilot's flying performance. The question then becomes: How do you measure flying performance? As Kantowitz states, "Measures are the gears and cogs that make empirical research efforts run. No empirical study can be better than its selected measures" (Kantowitz, 1992). Much of the advancement in human factors revolves around developing sound methods for measuring variables of interest. This problem is more difficult than it may appear on the surface.

As an example, consider the concept of "mental workload." Researchers have hypothesized that people will perform poorer on tasks and make more errors as they are confronted with "too much mental workload." For example, air traffic controllers may try to perform too many tasks at one time and experience an overload. What does it mean to say "high workload?" This question of measuring mental workload may seem easy, but it is not. For example, we might define *workload* as the number of tasks a person is doing at once. However, it turns out that sometimes numerous tasks can be performed concurrently with little deterioration in performance. How can we predict when combinations of tasks will increase mental workload beyond a person's ability? That is, what factors cause high workload? To study these questions, we must have some way to measure mental workload. Unfortunately, this is a hypothetical variable that cannot be directly measured. We therefore try to find indirect measures that reflect different levels of mental workload and that do not reflect other factors.

Researchers have tried measuring the elusive mental workload with a number of different techniques (Hancock & Meshkati, 1988; Lysaght et al. 1989; Wierwille & Eggemeier, 1993). The various workload measurement methods generally fall into three categories: (1) subjective procedures that consist of subjects' estimates of workload experienced under various tasks, (2) performance measures where lower performance is assumed to reflect greater workload, and (3) physiological measures such as brain wave activity and heart rate or heart rate variability (Wierwille & Eggemeier, 1993). None of these are *pure* measures of mental workload; each is contaminated in a different way. For example, Wilson and O'Donnell (1988) concluded that simple heart rate is an index of overall physiological arousal, while Hart and Wickens (1990) contend that heart rate provides an index of the overall effect of task demands plus the emotional response of the operator to them.

Because different measures of a variable are contaminated in different ways, it is often desirable to use more than one measure for a single concept or variable. For example, if we were assessing the effect of different displays on mental workload, a researcher might use measurement techniques from each of the subjective, performance, and physiological measurement categories. If the data for the different measures agree, it provides converging data for the conclusions. If only some of the measures are affected, the data can be used in a diagnostic fashion (some measures are sensitive measures of workload only under certain circumstances).

For most performance measures, researchers make educated guesses as to the best measures for a particular problem, and theory is often the most valuable tool in guiding the selection of measures. Kantowitz (1992) provides a good discussion and several examples of how theory is useful in identifying the most relevant and useful measures for a study, whether basic research or applied.

System Performance

The human factors specialist is frequently concerned with monitoring the functioning of an entire system that includes humans as one component. For example, we might be interested in monitoring the "safety" of a power plant; however, there are no clear measures that reflect overall system safety. Olson et al. (1988) attempted to identify a set of consistent and objective safety indicators for a nuclear power plant (see Table 2.2). It can be seen in Table 2.2 that "safety" was related to a variety of measures that cluster around different issues, including radiation, equipment maintenance, and so forth. All of the initial indicators were evaluated on dimensions such as data quality, availability, and directness of the relationship to safety. The researchers concluded that no single measure was an adequate indicator of plant safety, but rather the use of a cluster of multiple indicators was necessary.

Objective versus Subjective Measures

It has been a long tradition in science to believe that the best measures are those that are most objective and least subjective (e.g., Kosso, 1989), where subjective measures are those that rely on human experience, judgment, perception, or cognition. These factors are assumed to distort or unfavorably alter the reality being measured. For this reason, researchers may assume that in measuring human performance, any objective measure, such as number of keystrokes, is more desirable

TABLE 2.2 Nuclear Power Plant Safety Measures

Management/ administration	Turnover rate
	% vacancies
	Number of administrative licensee event reports (LERs)
	Number of repeat violations
	Number of repeat human errors and equipment failures
	Amount of overtime worked by functional area
	Ratio of contractor to plant personnel
	Supervisory ratio
Operations	Operator exam pass-fail rate
	Time in limiting condition of operation (also relevant to maintenance)
	Operator error events (LERs, forced outages, violations)
	Control room instrument inoperability
	% continuously alarming annunciators
	Number of temporary procedures
Maintenance	Equipment out of service (or degraded)
	Safety system rework
	Maintenance work request status (backlog)
	Maintenance-related events (LERs)
	Preventive maintenance requests completed on safety-related equipment
	Number of maintenance requests issued on safety-related equipment
	Realignment errors during maintenance
	Wrong unit–wrong train events
Training/experience	Operator exam pass/fail rate
	Number of personnel errors
	Average years of licensed operator experience
Quality programs	Corrective action request backlog
	Quality assurance audit deficiencies
Health physics/ radiation control	Number of skin contaminations
	Water chemistry out of specification
	Work areas (or % of work areas contaminated)
	Collective exposure (person rems per site)
	Ratio of individual doses greater than 1.5 rems to the total collective dose
Configuration management	Backlog of design change requests
	Backlog of drawing updates

Source: Olson et al., 1988. *Development of programmatic performance indicators.* Washington, DC: U.S. Nuclear Regulatory Commission.

than subjective measures. As an example, some researchers are generally more skeptical of subjective ratings as a measure of mental workload, as compared to "objective" measures such as heart rate. In addition, as more performance involves interaction with computers, it becomes easier and easier for researchers to simply program the computer to measure a host of objective measures. Imagine the number of objective measures that could be obtained on a flight simulator (speed, altitude, attitude, rate of ascent, etc.). The question is: What would the measures tell us about performance? It often becomes very easy to collect volumes of objective data with little way to make sense of it.

Several good papers have been published on the objective versus subjective measurement issue (e.g., Hennesy, 1990; Muckler, 1992). If we evaluate the literature, it is clear that both objective and subjective measures have their uses. For example, in a study of factors that lead to stress disorders in soldiers, Solomon, Mikulincer, and Hobfoll (1987) found that objective and subjective indicators of event stressfulness and social support were both predictive of combat stress reaction and later posttraumatic stress disorder and that "subjective parameters were the stronger predictors of the two" (p. 581). Other researchers have noted similar conditions where subjective measures are actually superior to objective measures. For example, Hennessy (1990) notes that human performance testing and evaluation is often conducted in complex real-world environments where tasks are performed in highly varying conditions. In such circumstances, subjective measures have several advantages over objective measures, including the fact that subjective data can usually be summarized more quickly and easily because it has already been condensed down in the process of determining what to score or rate. In contrast, collection of vast amounts of objective data will result in large amounts of coding and data reduction before the performance measures can be analyzed.

QUALITIES OF GOOD RESEARCH

The quality of a study is usually evaluated in terms of three categories: construct validity, internal validity, and external validity. These characteristics are important because without validity, the results of a study cannot be used to draw any conclusions.

Construct Validity

Construct validity refers to the degree to which the researchers *manipulated* what they wanted to and also the degree to which the researchers *measured* the dependent variables they wanted to. As an example, if researchers were looking at the independent variable of "fatigue," it would be important that the subjects experienced different levels of fatigue. If the researcher thinks that fatigue refers to the state caused by excessive physical effort, then the physical effort must be extensive enough that subjects are, in fact, fatigued. If the researcher never performs a manipulation check, it is possible that subjects actually experienced a very minimal amount of fatigue. Similarly, if a researcher is looking at risk-taking, it might not be appropriate to measure the number of times a subject performs a task.

A good experiment starts with appropriate ways of manipulating the independent variables and valid ways of measuring the dependent variable(s) of interest. Similarly, descriptive research uses valid techniques for measuring all of the variables of interest (since there are no experimental manipulations). Construct validity is arguably the most critical factor in determining the worth of either applied or basic research.

Internal Validity

A study with high internal validity is an experiment where the causal or independent variable(s), and no other extraneous variables, caused a change in the effects (dependent variables) being measured. Studies that have confounds (where an extraneous variable covaries along with the causal variable under study) have low internal validity. Such studies are often virtually worthless because no causal inferences can be made. Confounds and their resulting lack of internal validity are frequent characteristics of studies conducted by untrained researchers. Often the experimenters are not even aware that there are confounding extraneous variables that could be responsible for the results. This is one reason why, in submitting papers for publication, authors are required to describe their procedures in great detail. This gives reviewers a chance to evaluate the study for possible confounding variables. The importance of internal validity is the underlying reason for using the experimental method (with its associated random assignment to groups and other controls), even in very applied research in the field.

External Validity

A final measure of the worth of human factors research is its *external validity*. This refers to the degree to which we can generalize the results of a study to other people, tasks, and/or settings. In human factors, the issue of external validity is critical. A study that yields results that are too narrow to be applicable elsewhere has little value to the professional community. This can happen because basic research is performed using unrealistically simple tasks or settings, but it can also occur in field research because the study is performed using highly ideosyncratic equipment and tasks. In either case, it may be difficult for other professionals to apply the research results to their problem.

ETHICAL ISSUES

It is evident from discussions in this chapter that the majority of human factors research involves the use of people as participants in research. Many professional affiliations and government agencies have written specific guidelines for the proper way to involve participants in research. Federal agencies rely strongly on the guidelines found in the Code of Federal Regulations HHS, Title 45, Part 46; Protections of Human Subjects (Department of Health and Human Services, 1991). Anyone who conducts research using human participants should become familiar with the federal guidelines as well as APA published guidelines for ethical treatment of human subjects (American Psychological Association, 1992). These guidelines fundamentally advocate the following principles:

- Protection of participants from mental or physical harm
- The right of participants to privacy with respect to their behavior
- The assurance that participation in research is completely voluntary
- The right of participants to be informed beforehand about the nature of the experimental procedures

When people act as participants in an experiment, they are told the general nature of the study. Often they cannot be told the exact nature of the hypotheses because this will bias their behavior. Participants should be informed that all results will be kept anonymous and confidential. This is especially important in human factors because often they are employees who fear that their performance will be evaluated by management. Finally, participants are often asked to sign a document, termed an *informed consent* form, stating that they understand the nature and risks of the experiment, that their participation is voluntary, and that they understand they may withdraw at any time. In human factors field research, the experiment is considered to be reasonable in risk if the risks are no greater than those faced in the actual job environment.

As one last note, experimenters should always treat participants with respect. Participants are usually self-conscious because they feel their performance is being evaluated (which it is in some sense) and they fear that they are not doing well enough. It is the responsibility of the investigator to put participants at ease, assuring them that the system components are being evaluated and not the people themselves. This is one reason that the term *user testing* has been changed to *usability testing* (see next chapter) to refer to situations where people are asked to use various system configurations in order to evaluate overall ease-of-use and other factors.

REFERENCES

American Psychological Association (1992). Ethical principles of psychologists and code of conduct. *American Psychological Association.* Washington, DC: American Psychological Association.

Bailey, R.W. (1989). *Human performance engineering using human factors/ergonomics to achieve computer system usability* (2nd ed.). Englewood Cliffs, NJ: Prentice Hall.

Baron, S. (1988). Pilot control. In E. Wiener and D. Nagel (eds.), *Human factors in aviation.* San Diego, CA: Academic Press.

Chapanis, A. (1991). To communicate the human factors message, you have to know what the message is and how to communicate it. *Human Factors Society Bulletin, 34* (11), 1–4.

Cook, T.D., and Campbell, D.T. (1979). *Quasi-experimentation: Design and analysis for field settings.* Boston, MA: Houghton Mifflin.

Department of Health and Human Services (1991). *Code of Federal Regulations, Title 45, Part 46: Protection of human subjects.* Washington, DC: HHS.

Elkind, J.I., Card, S.K., Hochberg, J., and Huey, B.M. (eds.) (1990). *Human performance models for computer-aided engineering.* San Diego, CA: Academic Press.

Elmes, D.G., Kantowitz, B.H., and Roediger III, H.L. (1995). *Research methods in psychology.* St. Paul, MN: West Publishing Company.

Hancock, P.A., and Meshkati, N. (eds.) (1988). *Human mental workload.* Amsterdam: North-Holland.

Harris, D. (1991). The importance of the Type II error in aviation safety research. In E. Farmer (ed.), *Stress and error in aviation* (pp. 151–157). Brookfield, VT: Avebury Technical.

Hart, S.G., and Wickens, C.D. (1990). Workload assessment and prediction. In H.R. Booher (ed.), *MANPRINT: An approach to systems integration* (pp. 257–296). New York: Van Nostrand Reinhold.

Hennessy, R.T. (1990). Practical human performance testing and evaluation. In H.R. Booher (ed.), *MANPRINT: An approach to systems integration* (pp. 433–479). New York: Van Nostrand Reinhold.

Joreskog, K., and Sorbom, D. (1976). LISREL III—Estimation of linear structural equation systems by maximum likelihood methods: A. Fortran IV program. Chicago: International Educational Services.

Kantowitz, B.H. (1992). Selecting measures for human factors research. *Human Factors, 34*(4), 387–398.

Kantowitz, B.H. (1990). Can cognitive theory guide human factors measurement? *Proceedings of the Human Factors Society 34th Annual Meeting* (pp. 1258–1262). Santa Monica, CA: Human Factors Society.

Keppel, G. (1992). *Design and analysis: A researcher's handbook* (3rd ed.). Englewood Cliffs, NJ: Prentice Hall.

Kosso, P. (1989). Science and objectivity. *Journal of Philosophy, 86,* 245–257.

Lysaght, R.J., Hill, S.G., Dick, A.O., Plamondon, B.D., Wherry, R.J., Jr., Zaklad, A.L., and Bittner, A.C., Jr. (1989). *Operator workload: Comprehensive review and evaluation of operator workload methodologies* (ARI Technical Report 851). Alexandria, VA: U.S. Army Research Institute for the Behavioral and Social Sciences.

McDaniel, J.W., and Hofmann, M.A. (1990). Computer-aided ergonomic design tools. In H.R. Booher (ed.), *MANPRINT: An approach to systems integration.* New York: Van Nostrand Reinhold.

Mitchell, M., and Jolley, J. (1992). *Research design explained* (2nd ed.). Fort Worth, TX: Harcourt Brace Jovanovich.

Moroney, W.F. (1994). Ethical issues related to the use of humans in human factors and ergonomics. *Proceedings of the Human Factors and Ergonomics Society 38th Annual Meeting* (pp. 404–407). Santa Monica, CA: Human Factors and Ergonomics Society.

Muckler, F.A. (1992). Selecting performance measures: "Objective" versus "subjective" measurement. *Human Factors, 34*(4), 441–455.

Olson, J., Chockie, A.D., Geisendorfer, C.L., Vallario, R.W., and Mullen, M.F. (1988). *Development of programmatic performance indicators* (NUREG/CR-5241 PNL-6680, BHARC-700/88/022). Washington, DC: U.S. Nuclear Regulatory Commission.

Rosenthal, L.J., and Reynard, W. (Fall, 1991). Learning from incidents to avert accidents. *Aviation Safety Journal, 7–10.*

Sarno, K.J., and Wickens, C.D. (1995). The role of multiple resources in predicting time-sharing efficiency: An evaluation of three workload models in a multiple task setting. *International Journal of Aviation Psychology, 5(1),* 107–130.

Smith, T.J. (1993). The scientific basis of human factors—A behavioral cybernetic perspective. *Proceedings of the Human Factors and Ergonomics Society 37th Annual Meeting* (pp. 534–538). Santa Monica, CA: Human Factors and Ergonomics Society.

Solomon, Z., Mikulincer, M., and Hobfoll, S.E. (1987). Objective versus subjective measurement of stress and social support: Combat-related reactions. *Journal of Consulting and Clinical Psychology, 55,* 577–583.

Sommer, R., and Sommer, B.B. (1986). *A practical guide to behavioral research.* New York: Oxford University Press.

Wickens, C.D. (1995). Aerospace techniques. In J. Wiemer (ed.), *Research techniques in human engineering* (pp. 112–142). Englewood Cliffs, NJ: Prentice Hall.

Wierwille, W.W., and Eggemeier, F.T. (1993). Recommendations for mental workload measurement in a test and evaluation environment. *Human Factors, 35(2),* 263–281.

Williges, R.C. (1995). Review of experimental design. In J. Weimer (ed.), *Research techniques in human engineering.* Englewood Cliffs, NJ: Prentice Hall.

Wilson, G.F., and O'Donnell, R.D. (1988). Measurement of operator workload with the neurophysiological workload test battery. In P.A. Hancock and N. Meshkati (eds.), *Human mental workload* (pp. 63–100). Amsterdam: North-Holland.

Woods, D.D., Roth, E.M., and Pople, H.E., Jr. (1990). Modeling operator performance in emergencies. *Proceedings of the Human Factors Society 34th Annual Meeting* (pp. 1132–1135). Santa Monica, CA: Human Factors Society.

CHAPTER 3

Design and Evaluation Methods

The goals of a human factors specialist are generally to make tasks easier, more effective, more satisfying to perform, and safer. In addition to conducting basic and applied research to broaden our understanding, this is done primarily by applying human factors principles, methods, and data to the design of new products or systems. However, the concept of "design" can be very broad, including activities such as the following:

- Design or help design products or systems, especially their interface.
- Modify the design of existing products to address human factors problems.
- Design ergonomically sound environments, such as individual workstations, large environments with complex work modules and traffic patterns, home environments for the handicapped, gravity-free environments, and so forth.
- Perform safety-related activities, such as conduct hazard analyses, implement industrial safety programs, design warning labels, and give safety-related instructions.
- Develop training programs and other performance support materials such as checklists or instruction manuals.
- Develop methods for training and appraising work groups and teams.
- Apply ergonomic principles to organizational development and restructuring.

In this chapter, we will review some of the methods that human factors specialists use to support the first activity, designing products or systems. Human factors methods and principles are applied in virtually all product design phases: predesign analysis, conceptual and technical design, and final test and evaluation. While the material in this chapter provides an overview of the human factors *process,* later chapters will provide some of the basic *content* information necessary to carry out those processes. The remaining activities listed above will be covered in later chapters, which will provide both the content and specialized methods for each topic.

OVERVIEW OF DESIGN AND EVALUATION

Many if not most products and systems are still designed and manufactured without adequate consideration of human factors. Designers tend to focus primarily on the product and its functions without fully considering the use of the product from the human point of view. In a book that should probably be read by every engineer, Norman (1988) writes cogently:

> Why do we put up with the frustrations of everyday objects, with objects that we can't figure out how to use, with those neat plastic-wrapped packages that seem impossible to open, with doors that trap people, with washing machines and dryers that have become too confusing to use, with audio-stereo-television-video-cassette-recorders that claim in their advertisements to do everything, but that make it almost impossible to do anything?

Poor design is common, and as our products become more technologically sophisticated, they frequently become more difficult to use.

Even when designers attempt to consider human factors, they often complete the product design first and only then hand off the blueprint or prototype to a human factors expert. This expert is then placed in the unenviable position of having to come back with criticisms of a design that a person or design team has probably spent months and many thousands of dollars to develop. It is not hard to understand why engineers are less than thrilled to receive the results of a human factors analysis. They have invested in the design, clearly believe in the design, and are often reluctant to accept human factors recommendations. The process of bringing human factors analysis in at the end of the product design phase inherently places everyone involved at odds with one another. Because of this induced friction and the designer's resistance to change, the result is often a product that is not particularly successful in supporting human performance and safety.

As we noted in Chapter 1, human factors can ultimately save companies time and money. But to maximize the benefits achieved by applying human factors methods, the activities must be introduced relatively early in the system design cycle. We will shortly describe how this is done. However, first we describe some methods that a designer can use to demonstrate the value of performing human factors analysis. The best way to demonstrate the value of human factors to management is to perform a cost/benefit analysis.

Cost/Benefit Analysis

Human factors analysis is sometimes seen as an extra expense that does not reap a monetary reward equal to or greater than the cost of the analysis. A human factors expert may be asked to somehow justify his or her involvement in a project and explicitly demonstrate a need for the extra expense. In this case, a *cost/benefit analysis* can be performed to demonstrate the overall advantages of the effort (Alexander, 1995; Bias & Mayhew, 1994; Mayhew, 1990). In other words, the cost/benefit analysis is used to show management that human factors should be included as part of the design effort even if it does entail an extra expense, because in the long run, it will save the company money.

In a cost/benefit analysis, one calculates the expected costs of the human factors effort and estimates the potential benefits in monetary terms. Mayhew (1992) provides a simple example of such an analysis. Table 3.1 shows a hypothetical example of the costs of conducting a usability study for a software prototype.

In most instances, estimating the *costs* for a human factors effort is relatively easy because the designer tends to be familiar with the costs for personnel and materials. Estimating the *benefits* tends to be more difficult and must be based on assumptions (Bias & Mayhew, 1994). It is best if the designer errs on the conservative side in making these assumptions. Some types of benefits are more common for one type of manufacturer or customer than another. Mayhew (1992) lists the following benefits that might be applicable, and that can be estimated quantitatively:

1. Increased sales
2. Decreased cost of providing training
3. Decreased customer support costs
4. Decreased development costs
5. Decreased maintenance costs
6. Increased user productivity
7. Decreased user errors
8. Improved quality of service
9. Decreased training time
10. Decreased user turnover

TABLE 3.1 Hypothetical Costs for Conducting a Software Usability Study

Human Factors Task	*# Hours*
Determine Testing Issues:	24
Design Test and Materials:	24
Test 20 Users:	48
Analyze Data:	48
Prepare/Present Results:	16
TOTAL HF HOURS:	160
160 HF hours @ $45 =	$7,200
48 Assistant hours @ $20	960
48 Cameraman hours @ $30	1,440
Videotapes:	120
TOTAL COST:	$9,720

Source: D. J. Mayhew, 1992. *Principles and guidelines in software user interface design.* Englewood Cliffs, NJ: Prentice-Hall Inc. Adapted by permission of Prentice-Hall, Inc., Upper Saddle River, NJ.

Other quantifiable benefits are health or safety related (Alexander, 1995), such as:

1. Decreased sick leave or time off
2. Decreased number of accidents or acute injuries
3. Decreased number of chronic injuries (such as cumulative trauma disorders)
4. Decreased medical and rehabilitation expenses
5. Decreased number of citations or fines
6. Decreased number of lawsuits
7. Increased employee satisfaction (lower turnover)

The total benefit of the effort is determined by first estimating values for the relevant variables without human factors intervention. The same variables are then estimated, assuming that even a moderately successful human factors analysis is conducted. The estimated benefit is the total cost savings between the two.

For example, in a software usability testing effort, one might calculate the average time to perform certain tasks using a particular product and/or the average number of errors and the associated time lost. The same values are estimated for performance if a human factors effort is conducted. The difference is then calculated. These numbers are multiplied by the number of times the tasks are performed and by the number of people performing the task (e.g., over a year or five years time). Mayhew (1992) gives an example for a human factors software analysis that would be expected to decrease the throughput time for fill-in screens by three seconds per screen. Table 3.2 shows the estimated benefits. It is easy to see that even small cost savings per task can add up over the course of a year. In this case, the savings of $43,125 in one year easily outweighs the cost of the usability study, which was $9,720. Karat (1990) reports a case where human factors was performed for development of software used by 240,000 employees. She estimated after the fact that the design effort cost $6,800, and the time-on-task monetary savings added up to a total of $6,800,000 for the first year alone. Designers who must estimate performance differences for software screen changes can refer to the large body of literature that provides specific numbers based on actual cases (see Bias & Mayhew, 1994; Mayhew, 1990) for a review.

Manufacturing plants can likewise make gains by reducing costs associated with product assembly and maintenance (e.g., Marcotte, Marvin, & Lagemann,

TABLE 3.2   Hypothetical Estimated Benefit for a 3-Second Reduction in Screen Use

	250 users
×	60 screens per day
×	230 days per year
×	processing time reduced by 3 seconds per screen
×	Hourly rate of $15
=	$43,125 Savings PER YEAR

Source: D.J. Mayhew, 1992. *Principles and guidelines in software user interface design.* Englewood Cliffs, NJ: Prentice-Hall Inc. Adapted by permission of Prentice-Hall, Inc., Upper Saddle River, NJ.

1995), and for injury and health-related analyses, the benefits can be even greater. Readers are referred to Alexander (1995), Bias and Mayhew (1994), Mantei and Teorey (1988), and Mayhew (1992), for a more detailed description of cost/benefit analysis.

Human Factors in the Product Design Lifecycle

One major goal in human factors is to support the design of products in a cost-effective and timely fashion, such that the products support, extend, and transform user work (Wixon, Holtzblatt, & Knox, 1990). As noted earlier, in order to maximally benefit the final product, human factors must be involved as early as possible in the product (or system) design rather than being performed as a final evaluation *after* product design. The goal of this section is to provide an overview of the role of human factors activities in different product design stages. The activities will then be described in more detail.

There are numerous systematic design models, which specify the optimal sequence of steps for product analysis, design, and production (e.g., see Bailey, 1996; Blanchard & Fabrycky, 1990; Dix et al., 1993; Meister, 1987; Shneiderman, 1992). Product design models are all relatively similar and include stages reflecting predesign or front-end analysis activities, design of the product per se, production, and field test and evaluation. Product *lifecycle models* also add product implementation, utilization and maintenance, and dismantling or disposal. Table 3.3 shows a generic lifecycle model and lists some of the major activities performed by human factors specialists in each stage.

While many people think of human factors as a "product evaluation" step done predominantly at one point in the design process, it can be seen from Table 3.3 that human factors activities occur in many of the stages. Most of the human factors analyses are performed early, during the *front-end analysis* stage and during the two *design* stages. Although the human factors work involves different activities and products in different stages, most of it includes evaluation of some type. This evaluation provides feedback for modification of the various work products.

During the first *front-end analysis* stage, also called requirements specification or predesign, the human factors specialist conducts detailed analyses centering around the user and job or task activities; identifying who the users will be, what functions the human-machine system will serve, what activities the user will perform, and the environment in which they will perform them. This analysis culminates in a detailed specification of user or customer requirements. As the engineers or system designers write system specifications to guide the design process, the human factors specialist makes sure the system functions are consistent with user needs and makes sure that human factors criteria are included in the list of requirements. Examples of this process will be given below.

In the two stages involving actual product *design,* the human factors specialist provides input to the designer or design team. This often requires numerous analyses and studies, such as detailed functional analysis and allocation decisions, task analysis, interface design and prototyping, heuristic evaluation of alternative designs, workload analysis, and iterative usability testing (Dennison & Gawron, 1995). Many of these, such as safety or workload analyses, will be performed for

TABLE 3.3 System Development Life Cycle and Associated Human Factors Activities

Stages in Product Life Cycle	Human Factors Activities
Stage 1: Front-End Analysis	User analysis
	Function analysis
	Preliminary task analysis
	Environment analysis
	Identify user preferences and requirements
	Provide input for system specifications
	• Make sure objectives and functions match user requirements
	• Provide ergonomic criteria
Stage 2: Conceptual Design	Functional allocation
	Support the conceptual design process
Stage 3: Iterative Design and Testing	Task analysis
	Interface design
	Develop prototype(s)
	Heuristic evaluation (design review)
	Additional evaluative studies/analyses:
	Cost-benefit analysis for alternatives
	Trade-off analyses
	Workload analysis
	Simulations or modeling
	Safety analysis
	Usability testing
Stage 4: Design of Support Materials	Develop or provide input for support materials, such as manuals
Stage 5: System Production	
Stage 6: Implementation and Evaluation	Evaluate fielded system
Stage 7: System Operation and Maintenance	Monitor system performance over time
Stage 8: System Disposal	

some types of system but not others. For each human factors activity listed in Table 3.3, this chapter will provide a short description of each procedure and give references for further guidance.

Although the first four stages in the design model are shown as being sequential, in actuality, they often co-occur or are performed in an iterative looping fashion. The extent to which the processes are repeated depends to some extent on what is being designed. For large-scale system design, such as the development of an entire aircraft system, the human factors input tends to be more sequential—where the human factors specialist may get only one chance at providing input at each stage.

For smaller-scale projects, such as design of the interface for an ATM, the human factors design work is often more iterative, repeated many times to produce a successively more effective design. For example, a mock-up prototype of a design might be built very early and used to elicit customer preferences or requirements. The design is then changed and more feedback solicited. Or as another example, the results of a safety analysis may require designers to go back and make design modifications.

The most effective way to involve human factors in product design is to have multidisciplinary design team members working together from the beginning. This is consistent with industry's new emphasis on concurrent engineering (Chao, 1993), in which design teams are made up from members of different functional groups who work on the product from beginning to end. Team members often include personnel from marketing, engineers and designers, human factors specialists, production or manufacturing engineers, service providers, and one or more users or customers. For large-scale projects, multiple teams of experts are assembled.

User-Centered Design

All of the specific human factors methods and techniques that we will review shortly are ways to carry out the overriding methodological principle in the field of human factors. That principle is to center the design process around the user, thus making it "*user-centered design*" (Norman & Draper, 1986). Another phrase that denotes a similar meaning is "know the user" or "honor thy user." Obviously, all of these phrases are suggesting the same thing. For a human factors specialist, system or product design revolves around the central importance of the user. How do we put this principle into practice? Primarily by taking time to adequately determine user needs and by involving the user at all stages of the design process. This means the human factors specialist will study the user's job or task performance, elicit their needs and preferences, ask for their insights and design ideas, and request their response to design solutions. User-centered design does not mean that the user *designs* the product or has control of the design process. The goal of the human factors specialist is to find a system design that supports the user's needs rather than making a system to which users must adapt. User-centered design is also embodied in a subfield known as *usability engineering* (Gould & Lewis, 1985; Nielson, 1993). Usability engineering has been most rigorously developed for software design (e.g., Nielson, 1993) and involves four general approaches to design:

- *Early focus on the user* and tasks
- *Empirical measurement* using questionnaires, usability studies, and usage studies focusing on quantitative performance data
- *Iterative design* using prototypes, where rapid changes are made to the interface design
- *Participatory design* where users are directly involved as part of the design team.

Several books and articles have now been published that provide designers with specific methods for usability engineering (e.g., Nielson, 1993), lengthy case studies (Wiklund, 1994), and methods for usability testing (Rubin, 1994). Usability engineering for software design will be reviewed in Chapter 15.

Sources for Design Work

Human factors specialists usually rely on several sources of information to guide their involvement in the design process, including previous published research, data compendiums, human factors standards, and more general principles and guidelines.

Data Compendiums.   As the field of human factors has matured, many people have emphasized the need for sources of information to support human factors aspects of system design (e.g., Boff et al., 1991; Rogers & Armstrong, 1977; Rogers & Pegden, 1977). Such information is being developed in several forms. One form consists of condensed and categorized databases, with information such as tables and formulas of human capabilities. An example is the four-volume publication by Boff and Lincoln (1988), *Engineering Data Compendium: Human Perception and Performance,* which is also published on CD-ROM under the title "Computer-Aided Systems Human Engineering" (CASHE).

Human Factors Design Standards.   Another form of information to support design is engineering or human factors *design standards.* Standards are precise recommendations that relate to very specific areas or topics. One of the commonly used standards in human factors is the military standard MIL-STD-1472D (U.S. Department of Defense, 1989). This standard provides detailed requirements for areas such as controls, visual and audio displays, labeling, anthropometry, workspace design, environmental factors, and designing for maintenance, hazards, and safety. Other standards include the relatively recent ANSI/HFES-100 VDT standard, and the ANSI/HFES-200 design standard for software ergonomics (Reed & Billingsley, 1996). Both of these standards contain two types of specifications, requirements and recommendations.

Human Factors Principles and Guidelines.   There are many situations where answers to design problems cannot be found in the existing standards. For example, if a designer is trying to decide where to place the user controls on a camera, there will be no standard in current publications to answer these questions. The designer must look to more abstract principles and guidelines for this information. There are hundreds, perhaps thousands, of sources for human factors principles and guidelines. One symptom of the relative youth of the field is the lack of centrality and organization to these materials. Efforts are being made within the human factors design community to organize an electronic database to provide access to the existing principles and guidelines. However, this is a daunting task. Unfortunately, at this time, the human factors practitioner must become familiar with the sources through regular literature reviews and attendance of the major conferences.

Human factors principles and guidelines cover a very wide range of topics, some more general than others. On the very general end, Donald Norman gives principles for designing products that are easy to use (Norman, 1992), and Van

Cott and Kinkade provide general human factors guidelines for equipment design (Van Cott & Kinkade, 1972). Some guidelines pertain to the design of physical facilities (e.g., McVey, 1990), while others are specific to video display units (e.g., Gilmore, 1985) or to the design of software interfaces (e.g., Galitz, 1993; Gould, 1988; Helander, 1988; Mayhew, 1992; Mosier & Smith, 1986; Shneiderman, 1992; Smith & Mosier, 1986). Even the Association for the Advancement of Medical Instrumentation has issued a human factors guideline (AAMI, 1988).

Many of the human factors guidelines are specific to system interface design (e.g., controls and displays). An example of a specific interface guideline for computer displays would be: "Do not use yellow on white." However, many interface guidelines are much more general, such as "be consistent" from one screen to the next. It is important to point out that many guidelines are just that, guides rather than hard-and-fast rules. Most guidelines require careful consideration and application by designers, who must think through the implications of their design solutions (Woods, Johannesen, & Potter, 1992).

FRONT-END ANALYSIS ACTIVITIES

In this section, we describe the major activities performed during the front-end analysis stage. Not all of the activities will be carried out in detail for every project, but in general, the designer should be able to answer the following questions *before* design solutions are generated in the concept design stage:

1. Who are the product/system users? (This includes not only users in the traditional sense, but also the people who will dispense, maintain, monitor, repair, and dispose of the system.)
2. What are the major functions to be performed by the system, whether it be by person or machine? What tasks must be performed?
3. What are the environmental conditions under which the system/product will be used?
4. What are the user's preferences or requirements for the product? Do the functions identified match user preferences or requirements?
5. Are there any existing constraints with respect to design of the system?
6. What are the human factors criteria for design solutions?

These questions are answered by performing various analyses, the most common of which are described below.

User Analysis

Before any other analysis is conducted, potential system users are identified and characterized for each stage of the lifecycle. The most important user population is those people who will be regular users or "operators" of the product or system. For example, designers of a more accessible ATM than those currently in use might characterize the primary user population as people ranging from teenagers to senior citizens with an education ranging from junior high to Ph.D. and having at least a third-grade English reading level. In evaluating such an ATM system, Abedini (1991) assumed that users might be confined to wheelchairs, have poor hearing or eyesight, or have missing limbs. After identifying characteristics of the "operator" user population, designers should also specify the users who will be installing or maintaining the systems.

It is important to create a complete description of the potential user population. This usually includes characteristics such as age, gender, education level or reading ability, physical size, physical abilities (or disabilities), familiarity with the type of product, and task-relevant skills. For situations where products or systems already exist, one way that designers can determine the characteristics of primary users is simply to sample the existing population of users over a period of time. For example, the ATM designer might measure the types of people who currently use ATMs. Notice, however, that this will result in a description of users who are capable of using, and do use, the *existing* ATMs. This is not an appropriate analysis if the goal is to attract, or design for, a wider range of users.

Function and Task Analysis

Much of the front-end analysis activity is invested in performing detailed analysis of the functions to be accomplished by the human/machine/environment system and the tasks performed by the human to serve the functions.

Function Analysis.   Once the population of potential users has been identified, the human factors specialist performs an analysis of the basic functions performed by the "system" (which may be defined as human-machine, human-software, human-equipment-environment, etc.). The functional description will simply list the general categories of functions served by the system. Functions for an automatic teller system might simply be something like, get person's funds into bank account, get funds from bank account to person, and so forth.

Task Analysis.   Depending on the nature of the system being designed, the human factors specialist might need to perform a preliminary task analysis (Nielson, 1993), also sometimes called an *activity analysis* (Meister, 1971). The preliminary task analysis traditionally specifies the jobs, duties, tasks, and actions that a person will be doing. For example, in designing a chain saw, the designer writes a list of the tasks to be performed with the saw. The tasks should be specific enough to include the types of cuts, type of materials (trees, etc.) to be cut, and so forth.

As a simple example, the initial task analysis for design of an ATM might result in a relatively short list of tasks that users would like to perform, such as:

- Withdraw money from bank checking account
- Deposit money into bank checking account
- Determine balance of checking account
- Withdraw money from bank savings account
- Deposit money into bank savings account
- Determine balance of savings account
- Withdraw money from credit card account

Often it is difficult to discriminate the function list from the preliminary task analysis list. For example, a letter opener has the function of opening letters (and perhaps packages), and the task is also to open letters. The short list of a preliminary task analysis is often adequate for the front-end analysis stage; a more extensive task analysis is performed during actual product design.

In general, the more complex the system, such as air traffic control, the more detail in the preliminary function and task analysis. It is not unusual for ergonomists to spend several months performing this analysis for a product or system. The analysis would result in an information base that includes user goals, major tasks to achieve goals, information required, output, and so on. As an example, imagine performing the preliminary analysis for the design of a camera. There are many different types of users, even if we eliminate "professionals" from our user description. Camera users vary widely in relevant characteristics such as reading ability, physical characteristics (e.g., hand and finger size), and background knowledge. Add to that the wide variety of tasks performed; different types of photos regularly taken by people—group snapshots, portraits, landscapes, sport or action shots, and so forth. After we specify the general types of photos taken by people, we must add more specific tasks such as buying film and loading the camera, standing some distance from the subject, locating the camera person and subject with respect to the sun, using flash, and so on. The preliminary analysis would be complex, and we still would not specify the exact tasks performed by the user (such as buttons pressed to open the camera) until the camera is actually designed. Finally, the analysis should also include evaluation of any other activities or jobs that may be performed at the same time as the primary tasks being studied. For example, task analysis of a cellular phone for automobile use should include a description of other activities (e.g., driving) that will be performed concurrently.

How to Perform the Preliminary Task Analysis. The task analysis performed in the *predesign* stage will be shorter than the more rigorous task analysis performed later for product design. However, it uses similar methods, and the reader is referred to our later description of task analysis for detailed methods of collecting and describing the information. Here, we will just briefly describe the methods commonly used in the front-end analysis stage.

A preliminary task analysis is conducted by interacting extensively with multiple users (Diaper, 1989; Johnson, 1992; Nielson, 1993). Users are usually first *interviewed,* with the human factors specialist asking them to describe the general activities they perform with respect to the system. Notice that for our camera example, one would need to find users who represent the different types of people who would be using the camera. We would interview each of them to identify activities or general tasks performed with the camera.

Sometimes small groups of users are gathered together for the interviewing process, known as conducting a *focus group* (Caplan, 1990; Greenbaum, 1993). Focus groups are groups of between six and ten users led by a facilitator familiar with the task and system (Caplan, 1990; Nielson, 1993). The facilitator should be neutral with respect to the outcome of the discussion. Focus groups are advantageous because they are more cost effective than individual interviews (less time for the analyst), and discussion among users often draws out more information because the conversation reminds them of things they would not otherwise remember.

A third major method is to *observe* users performing activities with existing versions of the product or system, if such systems exist (Nielson, 1993; Wixon et al., 1990). System users are asked to perform the activities under a variety of typical scenarios, and the analyst observes the work, asking questions as needed. Sometimes the activities are videotaped for later analysis. As Wixon et al. (1990) note, the structure of users' work is often revealed in their thoughts, goals, intentions, and general orientation taken toward the activities.

It is necessary for the analyst to evaluate not only how the users go about the activities but also their preferences and strategies. Analysts also note points where users fail to achieve their goals, make errors, show lack of understanding, and seem to be frustrated or uncomfortable (Nielson, 1993). Thomas and McClelland (1994) point out that the entire design team should visit the site and observe workers. The understanding that results from such visits then ensures that the system is "developed to serve the users, rather than simply supplying sophisticated functionality."

During the preliminary task analysis, it is important to evaluate characteristics of the environment, and also of the product or system, that may be constraining the manner in which users perform activities (Vicente, 1990). Users should be queried to determine whether they would perform the activity differently if the constraints were lifted; that is, would they ideally rather do it in a different way? Finally, it is important to remember that the preliminary task analysis should be completed before product/system design begins. The only exception is the case where a new mock-up or prototype is used for analyzing user activities because they cannot be sufficiently performed on any existing system.

A fourth method is to obtain information through the use of *surveys* or *questionnaires.* Questionnaires are usually written and distributed after designers have obtained preliminary descriptions of activities or basic tasks. The questionnaires are used to affirm the accuracy of the information, determine the frequency with which various groups of users perform the tasks, and identify any user preferences or biases (see next section). This will later help designers prioritize different design functions or features.

As a last precaution, designers should remember that there are certain limitations if the task analysis is done in too much detail using existing products or systems. As Roth and Woods (1989) pointed out, overreliance on activity and task analysis using existing systems means that new controls, displays, or other performance aids may be designed to enhance the ability to carry out existing operator strategies that "merely cope with the surface demands created by the impoverished representation of the current work environment." This is why the analysis should focus only on the basic user goals and activities and not exactly on *how they are carried out* using the existing products. In design, it is better to do the more extensive task analysis using prototypes of the new design solutions.

Environment Analysis

In most cases, the activities or basic tasks that are identified in the preliminary task analysis should be described with respect to the specific *environment* in which the activities are performed (Whiteside, Bennett, & Holtzblatt, 1988; Wixon et al., 1990). For the example above, if ATMs are to be placed indoors, environmental analysis would include a somewhat limited set of factors, such as type of access (e.g., will the locations be wheelchair accessible?), weather conditions (e.g., will it exist in a lobby type of area with outdoor temperatures?), what type of clothing will people be wearing (i.e., will they be wearing gloves?), etc. The environment analysis can be performed concurrently along with the preliminary task analysis.

Identify User Preferences and Requirements

Identifying user preferences and requirements is a logical extension of the preliminary task analysis. Human factors analysts will attempt to determine key needs and preferences that correspond to each of the major user activities or goals already identified. Sometimes these preferences will include issues related to automation; that is, do users prefer to do a task themselves or would they rather the system do it automatically?

As an example, for designing a camera, we might ask users (via interview or questionnaire) for the following types of information:

- The extent to which water resistance is important to users.
- There are a number of features or functions that could be designed into a camera, but to what degree are each of these features important to users, and what is the cost users are willing to pay for such features?
- Is camera size (compactness) more important than picture quality?
- At what point does camera weight become unacceptable to users?
- The percentage of time that they would like the camera to determine aperture and shutter speed automatically.
- Whether there are even any conditions under which they would rather perform the task of determining aperture and shutter speed themselves (and what those conditions would be).
- How quickly the camera should be able to focus automatically to be acceptable to users.

It is easy to see that user preference and requirements analysis can be quite extensive. Much of this type of analysis is closely related to market analysis, and the marketing expert on the design team should be a partner in this phase. Sometimes focus groups are brought together for *brainstorming* activities. Byrne and Barlow (1993) suggest that a facilitator conduct such groups to (1) overcome resistance to creativity, (2) evaluate existing products, and (3) develop ideas for new or different products. Finally, if there are extensive needs or preferences for product characteristics, some attempt should be made to weight or prioritize them.

Providing Input for System Specifications

Once information has been gathered with respect to user characteristics, basic tasks or activities, the environment(s), and user requirements, the design team writes a set of system specifications. System specifications usually include (1) the overall *objectives* for the system, (2) system performance *requirements,* and (3) design *constraints.*

The system objectives are very global and are written in abstract terms to avoid premature design decisions. As an example, the objectives for a camera targeted at novice to intermediate photographers might include the following (partial) list:

- Take photos using the most common 35 mm films
- Have flash capability
- Take photos outdoors or indoors in a wide range of lighting conditions
- Accept a variety of lenses
- Have a tripod mount

The objectives do not specify any particular product configuration and should not state specifically how the user will accomplish goals or activities.

After the objectives are written, designers determine the means by which the product/system will accomplish the functions. These are termed *performance requirements.* Performance requirements state what the system will be able to do and under what conditions. Examples for the camera design might include items such as:

- Use 35 mm ISO films 100, 200, and 400
- Provide flash and fill-in flash for distances up to 15 feet

The system requirements list provides a design space in which the design team develops various solutions. Finally, in addition to the requirements, the specifications document lists various design *constraints,* such as weight, speed, cost, abilities of users, and so forth. The constraints provide limitations for the design alternatives.

What is the role of the human factors specialist as the system specifications are written? First, he or she compares the requirements and constraints with the originally identified user characteristics, activities, environmental conditions, and especially the users' preferences or requirements (Bailey, 1996; Dockery & Neuman, 1994). This ensures that the design specifications meet the needs of users and do not add a great number of technical features that people do not necessarily want. Human factors designers have developed a simple yet effective method for this process known as the QFD "house of quality" (Barnett et al., 1992; Byrne & Barlow, 1993; Hauser & Clausing, 1988). The method is a tool that uses a matrix to map user requirements against system specifications. The matrix allows designers to see the degree to which their work will satisfy customer needs. New matrices can be developed as the system is designed in more detail. The matrix also supports analysis of conflicts between system requirements.

The second role for the human factors specialist is adding human factors criteria to the list of system requirements. This is especially common for software usability engineering (Dix et al., 1993). Human factors criteria, also sometimes termed *usability requirements,* specify characteristics that the system should include that pertain directly to human performance and safety. For software usability engineering, human factors requirements might include items such as the following:

- Forward error recovery
- Backward error recovery
- Support user interaction pertaining to more than one task at a time

As another example, for an ergonomic keyboard design, McAlindon (1994) specified that the new keyboard must eliminate excessive wrist deviation, eliminate excessive key forces, and reduce finger movement. The design that resulted from these requirements was a "keybowl," drastically different from the traditional QWERTY keyboard currently in use, but a design that satisfied the ergonomic criteria.

CONCEPTUAL DESIGN ACTIVITIES

In the conceptual design stage, the human factors specialist takes a *systems design* approach, analyzing the entire human-machine system to determine the best configuration of characteristics. The focus should be neither too strongly on the product nor too strongly on the person, but evenly strong on the entire system as a unit. To do this, the specialist first evaluates the basic functions that must be performed by the human-machine system in order to support or accomplish the activities identified earlier (Kirwan & Ainsworth, 1992). He or she then determines whether each function is to be performed by the system (automatic), the person (manual), or some combination. This process is termed *functional allocation* and is an important, sometimes critical, step in human factors engineering (Price, 1990).

Functional Allocation

According to the Institute of Electrical and Electronic Engineers (1988):

> Functional allocation refers to the conscious design decisions which determine the extent to which a given job, task, function, or responsibility is to be automated or assigned to human performance. Such decisions should be based upon aspects such as relative capabilities and limitations of humans versus machines in terms of reliability, speed, accuracy, strength and flexibility of response, cost, and the importance of successful and timely task or function accomplishment to successful and safe operations.

An example of functional allocation can be given for our camera analysis. We may have determined from the predesign analysis that users prefer a camera that will always automatically determine the best aperture and shutter speed when the camera is held up and focused. Given that the technology exists and that there are no strong reasons against doing so, these functions would then be allocated to the camera. The functional analysis is usually done in conjunction with a cost analysis to determine whether the allocation is feasible.

However, functional allocation is sometimes not so simple. There are numerous complex reasons for allocating functions to either machine or person. In 1951, Paul Fitts provided a list of those functions performed more capably by humans and those performed more capably by machines (Fitts, 1951). Many such lists have been published since that time, and some researchers have suggested that allocation simply be made by assigning a function to the more "capable" system component. Given this traditional view, where function is simply allocated to the most capable system component (either human or machine), we might ultimately see a world where the functional allocation resembles that depicted in Figure 3.1.

This figure demonstrates the functional allocation strategy now known as the "leftover approach." As machines have become more capable, human factors specialists have come to realize that functional allocation is more complicated than simply assigning each function to the component (human or machine) that is most capable in some absolute sense. There are other important factors, including whether the human would simply *rather* perform the function. Several researchers have written guidelines for performing functional allocation (Clegg, Ravden, Corbett, & Johnson; 1989; Kantowitz & Sorkin, 1987; Meister, 1971; Price, 1985, 1990; Pulliam & Price, 1985; Williams, 1988), although it is still more art than science. Functional allocation is closely related to the question of automation and is covered in more depth in Chapter 16.

Supporting the Conceptual Design Process

Once the major functions of the product/system have been allocated, the design team begins developing conceptual design solutions. These start out as relatively vague and become more progressively specific. Design solutions are often based on

FIGURE 3.1

Ultimate functional allocation when using a "capability" criterion. (*Source:* Cheney, 1989. New Yorker Magazine, Inc.)

other previous products or systems. As the design team generates alternative solutions, the human factors specialist focuses on whether the design will meet system specifications for operator performance and safety.

ITERATIVE DESIGN AND TESTING

Once one or more conceptual designs have been generated, the designer or design team begins to characterize the product in more detail. The human factors specialist usually works with the designer and one or more users to support the human factors aspects of the design. These are all of the design features that will affect use and safety of the product/system. Much of this work revolves around analyzing the way in which users must perform the functions that have been allocated to the human. More specifically, the human factors specialist evaluates each function to make sure that they require physical and cognitive actions that fall within the human capability limits. In other words, can humans perform the functions safely and easily? This evaluation is performed by first conducting a detailed task analysis, followed by other activities such as heuristic design evaluation, trade-off studies, prototyping and usability testing, and so on. The evaluation studies provide feedback for making modifications to the design or prototype. This redesign and evaluation continues for *many iterations,* sometimes as many as ten or twenty.

Task Analysis

At this point, for each basic function or activity that will be performed by the user, the human factors specialist performs a *task analysis* that goes into much more detail than the preliminary analysis performed in the predesign stage. The purpose of this task analysis is to identify:

- Major user goals and their associated activities (or any that are new or have changed)
- The tasks and subtasks required to successfully achieve the goals
- The conditions under which the tasks are performed (when/where do you do them?)
- The results or outcome of performing the tasks and subtasks
- Information or knowledge needed to perform the tasks
- Communications with others for performing the task
- Equipment needed to perform the tasks

Depending on the specific product or system, designers may also identify certain secondary factors associated with each task, such as frequency, importance, difficulty, time spent on the task, severity of performing the task incorrectly, whether there are tasks that will be performed concurrently, and minimum expectations for task performance.

Tasks can be *physical tasks* such as setting the shutter speed on a camera, or they can be *cognitive tasks* such as deciding on what the shutter speed should be, given other factors. Because an increasing number of jobs have a large proportion of cognitive subtasks, the traditional task analysis is being increasingly augmented by what is termed *cognitive task analysis*. These analyses focus on the mental processes, skills, strategies, and use of information required for task performance (Gordon, 1995; Gordon & Gill, 1997; Ryder, Redding & Beckshi, 1987; Roth & Woods, 1989; Schlager, Means, & Roth, 1990; Seamster, Redding & Kaempf, 1997). While there are many methods currently being developed specifically for cognitive task analysis, we will treat these as extensions of standard task analyses. In this section we will not distinguish between the methods and refer to all as *task analysis*. However, if any of the following characteristics are present, designers should pay strong attention to the cognitive components in conducting the analysis (Gordon, 1994):

- Complex decision making, problem solving, diagnosis, reasoning, or inferencing from incomplete data
- Large amounts of conceptual knowledge that must be used to perform subtasks
- Large and complex rule structures that are highly dependent on situational characteristics

There is now a relatively large literature on task analysis methods. One of the best resources is Kirwan and Ainsworth (1992), *A Guidebook to Task Analysis,* a book that describes forty-one different methods for task analysis (with detailed examples). Cognitive task analyses are described in Seamster et al. (1997). Because of the complexity of these methods, we cannot begin to give task analysis adequate coverage here. Table 3.4 shows the wide range of methods currently in use, organized according to three taxonomies: general methods for collecting task analysis data, general methods for representing the task analysis results, and several specific task analysis methods. In this section, we will only review the most commonly used of the methods; for a lengthier review of the techniques shown in Table 3.4, see Gordon (1994).

Task analysis involves evaluating how tasks are to be accomplished. This can be done by a variety of methods including analyzing the use of existing systems, analytically determining how a user would have to perform tasks given the proposed system, or having users perform tasks using mock-ups or prototypes, just to name a few. As Dix et al. (1993) note, task analysis is not a simple and sequential process of "collect the data, organize the data, and analyze the results." Rather it tends to be iterative itself, where the specialist will go back to the starting point with new questions or insights. It tends to be characterized by periods of data collection, analysis, developing new questions, making design changes, and then collecting more data. The following methods can be used in any combination during this iterative process. It is common for designers to begin with relatively short unstructured interviews with users.

Unstructured and Structured Interviews. Unstructured interviews refer to situations where the specialist asks the user to describe their activities and tasks but does not have any particular method for structuring the conversation. Unstructured interviews are not particularly efficient for task analysis, but the advantage is that they do not take any specific skills or training on the part of

TABLE 3.4 Common Methods for Task Analysis and Cognitive Task Analysis

General Methods for Data Collection	Document and equipment analysis
	Unstructured interviews
	Structured interviews
	Group interviews and focus groups
	Sorting and rating
	Observation
	Verbal protocol analysis
	Task performance with questioning
	Questionnaires
General Methods for Data Representation	List and outlines
	Matrix (cross-tabulation tables)
	Structural networks
	Hierarchical networks
	Flow charts
	Time-line charts
Specific Task-Analysis Methods	Controls and displays analysis
	Hierarchical task analysis
	The GOMS model
	Critical incident technique
	Conceptual graph analysis
	Activity sampling
	Operational-sequence diagrams

the analyst. Unstructured interviews tend to revolve around questions/statements such as: Tell me about . . . ; What kinds of things do you do . . . ?; and, How do you . . . ?

Structuring interviews with particular types of questions or method makes the interview process more efficient and complete (Creasy, 1980; Fewins, Mitchell, & Williams, 1992; Gordon & Gill, 1992; Graesser, Lang, & Elofson, 1987). Gordon and Gill (1989, 1992) and Graesser et al. (1987) have suggested the use of question probes, where questions include items such as:

- *How* do you perform task/subtask *x?*
- *Why* do you perform task/subtask *x?*
- *Under what conditions* or in what situations do you perform task/subtask *x?*
- What do you do *before* you perform task/subtask *x?*
- What happens *after* you perform task/subtask *x?*
- What is the *result or consequence* of performing task/subtask *x?*
- What is the *result or consequence of NOT* performing task/subtask *x?*

Usually the specialist conducts several interviews with each user, preparing notes and questions beforehand, and tape-recording the questions and answers.

Hierarchical network notation systems (graphs) work especially well with interviews structured with this type of question (Gordon & Gill, 1992).

Observation. It is often difficult for users to imagine and describe how they would/do perform a given task or activity. One of the best ways for the analyst to gain a deep understanding of task performance is to spend time watching users perform different tasks under different scenarios. Sometimes such task performance is videotaped to allow time for adequate analysis at a later point. It is important to identify different methods for accomplishing a goal, rather than only identifying the one typically used by a person. Observation can be performed in the field where the person normally accomplishes the task, or it can be done in a simulated or laboratory situation. As an example, we could ask users to come into a lab to show us how they use a camera, but we would gather a richer set of data by accompanying them into the field where they normally perform the activities. This analysis might be done with existing products, or it might be done using design prototypes.

Think-Aloud Verbal Protocol. Many researchers and designers conduct task analyses by having the user think out loud as they perform various tasks. This yields insight into underlying goals, strategies, decisions, and other cognitive components. The verbalizations regarding task performance are termed *verbal protocols,* and analysis or evaluation of the protocols is termed *verbal protocol analysis.* Verbal protocols are usually one of three types: *concurrent* (obtained during task performance), *retrospective* (obtained after task performance via memory or videotape review), and *prospective* (where the users are given a hypothetical scenario and think aloud as they imagine performing the task). Concurrent protocols are sometimes difficult to obtain. If the task takes place quickly or requires concentration, the user may have difficulty verbalizing thoughts. Retrospective protocols can thus be easier on the user, and a comparative evaluation by Ohnemus and Biers (1993) showed that retrospective protocols actually yielded more useable information than did concurrent protocols. Bowers and Snyder (1990) noted that concurrent protocols tend to yield procedural information while retrospective protocols yield more by way of explanations.

Task Performance with Questioning. A variation on the collection of the verbal protocol is to ask users to perform the tasks while answering questions such as the question probes listed above. The advantage to this method over standard verbal protocols is that it may cue users to verbalize their underlying goals or strategies more frequently. The disadvantage to the method is that it can be disruptive. For this reason, retrospective analysis of videotapes is an effective method for task analysis. Users can be asked to provide think aloud verbalizations, and when they fail to provide the types of information being requested, the human factors specialist can pause the tape and ask the necessary questions. This functions like a structured interview with the added memory prompt of watching task performance.

Once task-related information has been gathered, it must be documented and organized in some form. There are several forms that are commonly used in conjunction with one another. These are (1) lists, outlines, or matrices; (2) hierarchies or networks; and (3) flow charts.

Representing Data with Lists, Outlines, and Matrices.   Task analysis usually starts with a set of lists such as those illustrated earlier in the chapter and then breaks the tasks down further into subtasks. An example is shown in Table 3.5. After the hierarchical outlines are relatively complete, the analyst might develop tables specifying related information for each task or subtask, such as information input, required actions, feedback, and so forth (e.g., Seamster et al., 1993).

Hierarchies and Networks.   The disadvantage of using outlines or tables is that tasks tend to have a hierarchical organization, and this is easiest to represent and analyze if the data is graphically depicted in a hierarchical form. This can be done by using either hierarchical charts or hierarchical networks. An example of a hierarchical chart is the frequently used method known as *Hierarchical Task Analysis* (HTA) (e.g., Kirwan & Ainsworth, 1992). This is a versatile graphical notation method that organizes tasks as sets of actions used to accomplish

TABLE 3.5   Part of Task Analysis for Using a Lawnmower, Shown in Outline Form

Step 1. Examine lawn
    a. Make sure grass is dry
    b. Look for any objects laying in the grass

Step 2. Inspect lawnmower
    a. Check components for tightness
        (1) Check to see that grass bag handle is securely fastened to the grass bag support
        (2) Make sure grass bag connector is securely fastened to bag adaptor
        (3) Make sure that deck cover is in place
        (4) Check for any loose parts (such as oil cap)
        (5) Check to make sure blade is attached securely
    b. Check engine oil level
        (1) Remove oil fill cap and dipstick
        (2) Wipe dipstick
        (3) Replace dipstick completely in lawnmower
        (4) Remove dipstick
        (5) Check to make sure oil is past mark on dipstick

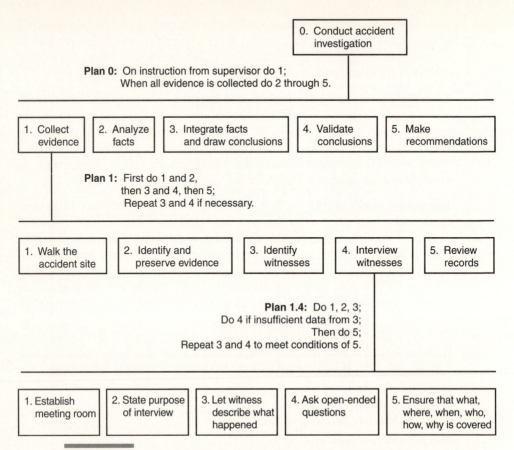

FIGURE 3.2

Hierarchical task analysis for conducting an industrial accident investigation. (*Source:* McCallister, D., unpublished task analysis, University of Idaho. Used with permission.)

higher level goals. As an illustration, consider the HTA shown in Figure 3.2 for conducting an accident investigation. The tasks are organized into plans, clusters of tasks that define the preferred order of tasks, and conditions which must be met to perform the tasks.

Another type of hierarchical graph is the representational format known as GOMS, short for goals, operators, methods, and selection rules (Card, Moran, & Newell, 1983; Kieras, 1988). The GOMS model is mostly used to analyze tasks performed when using a particular software interface (e.g., Gugerty et al., 1991; John, Vera, & Newell, 1994; Kieras, 1988) and is described in more detail in Chapter 15. Neither HTA nor GOMS represent detailed levels of cognitive information processing or decision making. For tasks that have a greater proportion of cognitive components, conceptual graphs or computer simulations are frequently used to represent information because they are more capable of depicting abstract concepts, rules, strategies, and other cognitive elements (Gordon & Gill, 1997).

Flow Charts.   Another graphical notation system frequently used for task analysis is a flow-chart format (Kirwan & Ainsworth, 1992). Flow charts capture the chronological sequence of subtasks as they are normally performed and depict the decision points for taking alternate pathways. One popular type of flow chart is the *operational sequence diagram* (Kirwan & Ainsworth, 1992). Operational sequence diagrams show the typical sequence of activity and also categorize the operations into various behavioral elements, such as decision, operation, receive, and transmit. They show the interacting among individuals and task equipment.

All of the methods described have advantages and disadvantages, and choosing the most appropriate method will depend on the type of activity being analyzed. If the tasks are basically linear and usually done in a particular order, such as changing a flat tire, it is appropriate to use an outline or flow-chart method. If there are more cognitive elements and many conditions for choosing among actions, hierarchical formats are more appropriate. There is one major disadvantage to flow charts that is often not readily apparent. There is evidence that people *mentally* represent goals and tasks in clusters and hierarchies. The design of controls and displays should map onto these clusters and hierarchies. However, when describing or performing a task, the actions will appear as a linear sequence. If the task analysis is represented in a flow-chart format, the cognitive groupings or "branches" are not evident. This makes it harder for the designer to match the interface with the mental model of the user.

Interface Design

As the design team progressively determines more detail for the design, the human factors specialist focuses on the interface—how the user interacts with the product or system. Frequently, more than one interface design solution is identified, or a solution has developed that has certain alternative design characteristics. There are several evaluative methods with which we might determine the best design alternative (discussed below).

In designing the interface, specialists rely on experience as well as a variety of published standards, principles, and guidelines. According to Nielson (1993), standards specify how the interface should appear to users, while guidelines give advice about usability characteristics. Extensive collections of general user interface guidelines include Brown (1988), Dumas (1988), Mayhew (1992), and Smith and Mosier (1986). Other authors, such as Norman (1992) and Nielson (1993), provide more *general* principles that designers must apply by analyzing the particular user-product interaction of the given situation. Design principles are also found in the remainder of this text as well as others.

As an example of the general type of human factors principles, consider the guidance offered by Don Norman (1992). The four principles offered by Norman are appropriate for any product or system for which ease of use is a prime consideration (which should be most, but not all, products). Norman (1992) proposes that products can be made easy to use by increasing the user's conceptual model of how they work and especially what we have to do to interact with them. This is done by applying the following four principles:

1. *Provide a good conceptual model.* If the product somehow conveys to us the basic structure and function of the system, we can imagine interacting with the product in our head. This means we have a good mental model and can correctly predict the results of our actions. As an example, if a person has a good, or at least adequate, conceptual model of their mountain bike, they will be able to imagine what would happen if they moved the right shift lever in a counterclockwise manner. Systems that do not convey an accurate conceptual model or do not convey *any* model tend to be more difficult to use. An interesting example is that of a standard household thermostat. The thermostat does not give users an accurate conceptual model of the household heating system. This is evidenced by the fact that when first turning up the heat in their house, many users turn the thermostat up too high in the belief that this will somehow make the temperature rise faster than it would otherwise (which is almost never the case).

2. *Make things visible.* Systems that have many functions and associated controls that are "hidden" tend to be difficult to use. An example provided by Norman (1992) is the modern-day telephone. Many phones have special features such as conference calls or call forwarding. However, it is not clear from the controls (alphanumeric push buttons) and displays (auditory beeps or buzzes) how to make use of these features. The structure, functions, and how to accomplish goals are all hidden. As a counterexample, Norman offers the automobile. The functions for driving a car are much more numerous. But if we evaluate the standard set of controls and displays, we see that most functions have individual and visible controls and displays. We control the speed by pressing on the accelerator and see the effects in the speedometer. While the functions of the car are more numerous than the functions of a phone, it is easier to use because the "interface" has more visible components. As a final example, consider the push-bar door. We often see people walk up to a door with a push-bar extending from one side to the other. The user has an adequate conceptual model of "how" the door works but cannot tell which side to push. The result is often an abrupt and embarrassing stop in front of the wrong side of the door. A simple "push here" sign on one side makes the required action visible.

3. *Use natural mappings.* To make things easy to use, designers should make use of natural mappings. Mapping refers to the relationship between input to or output from a system and the associated system state or event. For example, consider actions to control systems. To move an object up, it seems natural to push a control lever in the same direction. To turn the car to the right, we turn the steering wheel to the right, and to put the car window up, we press the lever up. These are natural mappings or correspondence between two variables. Figure 3.3a shows a stovetop that has a natural mapping. The drawing in Figure 3.3b represents an actual design of a glass cooktop sold by one of the most elite manufacturers in 1994. Informal observation and questioning of users revealed that people were unable to predict which control turned on the top left burner (it is the second from the top). This interface does not make use of natural mappings.

4. *Provide feedback.* Feedback is also important for ease of use. A product or system should be designed so that users know what action has been actually done and what the results have been within the system. Simple systems such as

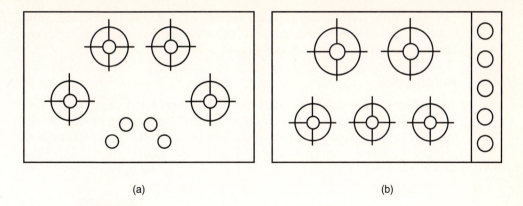

(a)   (b)

FIGURE 3.3

(a) Natural mapping from controls to burners on a cooktop. (b) Lack of a natural mapping from controls to burners on a cooktop.

scissors or lamps tend to have very straightforward feedback. It is easy to see the results of our actions. Other systems, such as computers, may have less adequate feedback. An example can be seen in older software systems where user input resulted in lag time in computer processing. The user did not know whether their input was "received" by the computer and so performed the action again. Designers finally realized that providing a signal, such as an hourglass, would provide users with feedback that their input had been received and that the computer was working.

Norman (1992) offers some particularly valuable guidelines that will be discussed in more detail in later chapters:

- Simplify the structure of tasks.
- Make things visible, including the conceptual model of the system, the alternative actions, and the results of the actions.
- Make it easy to determine what actions are possible at any moment.
- Make it easy to evaluate the current state of the system.
- Exploit the power of constraints (e.g., you can only do it one way—the right way).
- Design to allow for easy error recovery.
- When all else fails, standardize.

In Chapter 15 on human-computer interaction, we will review and summarize more specific guidelines to make systems more usable, as usability engineering has been developed the most rigorously in that field.

Even with relatively specific guidelines, it can be difficult to design a product that is easy to use, and the more complex the product, the more difficult the design becomes. Norman (1992) suggests that to keep a system easy to use, in general, a designer should match the number of controls to the number of functions and organize the control/display panels according to function. Finally, controls or displays not needed for the current task can be "hidden" to reduce the *appearance* of system complexity if that is a design goal.

Prototypes

To support interface design, usability testing, and other human factors activities, product *mock-ups* and *prototypes* are built very early in the design process. Mock-ups are very crude approximations of the final product, often being made out of foam or cardboard. Prototypes frequently have more of the look and feel of the final product but do not yet have full functionality. The use of prototypes during the design process has a number of advantages including:

- Support of the design team in making ideas concrete
- Support of the design team by providing a communication medium
- Support for heuristic evaluation
- Support for usability testing by giving users something to react to and use

In designing computer interfaces, specialists often use *rapid prototyping* tools that allow extremely quick changes in the interface so that many design iterations can be performed in a short period of time. Bailey (1993) studied the effectiveness of prototyping and iterative usability testing. He demonstrated that user performance improved 12 percent with each design iteration and that the average time to perform software-based tasks decreased 35 percent from the first to the final design iteration. Prototypes may potentially be used for any of the evaluations listed below.

Heuristic Evaluation

A heuristic evaluation of the design(s) means analytically considering the characteristics of a product or system design to determine whether they meet human factors criteria (Desurvire & Thomas, 1993). For usability engineering, heuristic evaluation means examining every aspect of the interface to make sure that it meets usability standards (Nielson, 1993; Nielson & Molich, 1990). However, there are important aspects of a system that are not directly related to usability, such as safety and comfort. Thus, in this section heuristic evaluation will refer to a systematic evaluation of the product design to judge compliance with human factors guidelines and criteria (see O'Hara, 1994, for a detailed description of one method). Heuristic evaluations are usually performed by comparing the system interface with the human factors criteria listed in the requirements specification and also with other human factors standards and guidelines. For simple products/systems, checklists may be used for this purpose. Heuristic evaluation can also be performed to determine which of several system characteristics, or design alternatives, would be preferable from a human factors perspective.

While an individual analyst can perform the heuristic evaluation, the odds are great that this person will miss most of the usability or other human factors problems. Nielson (1993) reports that, averaged over six projects, only 35 percent of the interface usability problems were found by single evaluators. Since different evaluators find different problems, the difficulty can be overcome by having multiple evaluators perform the heuristic evaluation. Nielson (1993) recommends using at least three evaluators, preferably five. Each evaluator should inspect the product design or prototype in isolation from the others. After each has finished the evaluation, they should be encouraged to communicate and aggregate their findings.

Once the heuristic evaluations have been completed, the results should be conveyed to the design team. Often this can be done in a group meeting, where the evaluators and design team members not only discuss the problems identified but also brainstorm to generate possible design solutions (Nielson, 1994a). Heuristic evaluation has been shown to be very cost effective. For example Nielson (1994b) reports a case study where the cost was $10,500 for the heuristic evaluation, and the expected benefits were estimated at $500,000 (a 48:1 ratio).

Additional Evaluative Studies and Analyses

After the design (or set of alternative designs) has received a preliminary review for human factors design flaws, the human factors specialist may perform several other types of analysis. This will depend on the complexity of the system, whether the tasks to be performed are difficult or performed under high workload conditions, and whether there are safety issues associated with the product/system. Analyses that may be performed at this point include:

- Cost/benefit analysis for design alternatives
- Trade-off analyses or studies (e.g., which display works best)
- Workload analysis
- Simulations and modeling
- Safety, human reliability, or hazard analyses

Cost/Benefit Analysis for Design Alternatives.   Cost/benefit analysis refers to the comparison of different design features and their implications. The cost can be defined monetarily or in other ways. For example, product weight might be greater for one design than another. The most common method for doing a quantitative cost/benefit analysis is to do a decision matrix. The features, or variables, on which the design alternative differ are listed on the left side of a matrix. Examples might be weight, manufacturing cost, range of users who would have access to the product, and so on. Each feature is given a weight representing how important the feature is in the overall picture. Then, each design alternative is assigned a number representing where it stands with respect to the feature. Finally, each design alternative is given a total score by multiplying individual scores by the feature weights and then adding the scores together.

Trade-Off Analyses.   Sometimes a design feature, such as a particular display, can be implemented in more than one way. The human factors analyst might not have data or guidelines to direct a decision between alternatives. Many times a small-scale study is conducted to determine which design alternative results in the best performance (e.g., fastest or most accurate). These studies are referred to as trade studies. Sometimes the analysis can be done by the designer without actually running studies, using methods such as modeling or using performance estimates. If multiple factors are considered, the design trade-offs might revolve around the design with the greatest number of advantages and the smallest number of disadvantages.

Workload Analysis.   The product or system being designed may be complex enough to evaluate whether it is going to place excessive mental workloads on the user, either alone or performed in conjunction with other tasks. When this is the case, the human factors specialist performs an analysis to predict the workloads that will be placed on the user during various points of task performance (Aldrich, Szabo, & Bierbaum, 1988; Fontenelle & Laughery, 1999; Hamilton & Bierbaum, 1990). Sometimes this can be done using just the results of the task analysis if the information is sufficiently detailed. Hamilton and Bierbaum (1990) describe a tool, TAWL, that can be used for estimating mental workload on the basis of a task analysis. It does this by evaluating the total attentional demand that will be placed on users as they perform the various tasks required for job activities.

Simulations or Modeling.   In evaluating the effects of the system on the user, designers frequently use models or simulations. The most well-developed of these have been designed to address ergonomic issues by modeling the human body in different workstation configurations (Dennison & Gawron, 1995). Newer modeling programs, such as HUMANCAD, are capable of depicting complex movement based on human biodynamics (Dennison & Gawron, 1995), and models such as the Air Force COMBIMAN include anthropometric data for arm and leg reach, visual fields, and strength for operating various controls (MATRIS, 1994). Other simulation programs such as MicroSAINT (Chubb, Laughery, & Pritsker, 1987) are able to simulate complex tasks in relationship to various combinations of controls and displays, a primary focus for many human factors practitioners (e.g., Eisenhut & Beaton, 1995). Finally, the Ergonomic Design using Graphic Evaluation (EDGE) provides advanced modeling of physiological factors such as metabolic expenditure, torso biomechanics, and NIOSH lifting limits (Evans, 1991). All of these modeling tools and simulations are used to test the human factors characteristics of design configurations in the abstract before they undergo the cost of manufacturing.

Similarly, more recent modeling and simulation efforts are geared toward evaluation of cognitive processing in complex problem-solving and decision-making environments (e.g; Amendola et al., 1987; Elkind et al., 1990; Woods, Roth, & Pople, 1990). Simulation tools such as CES, Cognitive Environment Simulation, can be used to predict human errors by estimating the mismatch between cognitive resources and demands of the particular problem-solving task (Woods, Roth, & Pople, 1990).

Safety Analysis.   Any time a product or system has implications for human safety, analyses should be conducted to identify potential hazards or the likelihood of human error. There are several standard methods for performing such analyses, such as Failure Modes and Effects Analysis, or Human Reliability Analysis. These analyses are specific to safety and will therefore be covered in Chapter 14.

Designers must assess hazards associated with the product during all stages of the system life cycle. As an example, old refrigerators have posed a safety hazard because children climb inside abandoned units and become locked inside.

Usability Testing

Designers conduct heuristic evaluations and other studies to narrow the possible design solutions for the product/system. They can determine whether it will cause excessive physical or psychological loads, and they analyze associated hazards. However, if the system involves controls and displays with which the user must interact, there is one task left. The system must be evaluated with respect to usability. *Usability* is primarily the degree to which the system is easy to use or "user friendly." This translates into a cluster of factors including the following five variables (from Nielson, 1993):

- *Learnability:* The system should be easy to learn so that the user can rapidly start getting some work done.
- *Efficiency:* The system should be efficient to use so that once the user has learned the system, a high level of productivity is possible.
- *Memorability:* The system should be easy to remember so that the causal user is able to return to the system after some period of not having used it, without having to learn everything all over again.
- *Errors:* The system should have a low error rate so that users make few errors during the use of the system, and so that if they do make errors, they can easily recover from them. Further, catastrophic errors must not occur.
- *Satisfaction:* The system should be pleasant to use so that users are subjectively satisfied when using it; they like it.

Designers determine whether a system is usable by submitting it to *usability testing* (a process that was originally called user testing, but the connotation was that the users were somehow being "tested"). Usability testing is the process of having users interact with the system to identify human factors design flaws overlooked by designers. Usability testing conducted early in the design cycle can consist of having a small number of users evaluate rough mock-ups. As the design evolves, a larger number of users are asked to use a more developed prototype to perform various tasks. If users exhibit long task times or a large number of errors, designers revise the design and continue with additional usability testing.

Because usability testing has evolved primarily in the field of human-computer interaction, the methods will be described in Chapter 15. However, it should be noted that those methods generalize to essentially any interaction when a system has control and display components.

Support Materials

Finally, as the product design becomes more complete, the human factors specialist is often involved in design of support materials, or what Bailey calls "facilitators" (Bailey, 1996). Products are often accompanied by manuals, assembly instructions, owner's manuals, training programs, and so forth. A large responsibility for the human factors member of the design team is to make sure that these materials are compatible with the characteristics and limitations of the human user. For example, the owners manual accompanying a table saw contains very important information on safety and correct procedures. This information is critical, and must be presented in a way that maximizes the likelihood that the user will read it, understand it, and comply with it. The development of support materials will be discussed in more depth in Chapter 14 and in Chapter 18.

FINAL TEST AND EVALUATION

We have seen that the human factors specialist performs a great deal of evaluation during the system design phases. Once the product has been fully developed, it should undergo final test and evaluation. In traditional engineering, system evaluation would determine whether the physical system is functioning correctly. For our example of a camera, testing would determine whether the product meets design specifications and operates as it should (evaluating factors such as mechanical functions, testing for water resistance, impact resistance, etc.). For human factors test and evaluation, designers are concerned with any aspects of the system that affect human performance, safety, or the performance of the entire human-machine system. For this reason, evaluation inherently means involving users. Data is collected for variables such as acceptability, usability, performance of the user or human-machine system, safety, and so on. In this section, we will briefly review the basics of final system evaluation. Most of the methods used for evaluation are the same experimental methods that are used for research. Therefore, the material presented in Chapter 2 is applicable. However, evaluation is a complex topic, and readers who will conducting evaluation studies should seek more detailed information from publications such as Weimer (1995) or Meister (1986) and an extensive treatment of testing and evaluation procedures by Carlow International (1990).

In conducting evaluation studies, the procedure is essentially the same as that described in Chapter 2. The human factors specialist should determine the design or type of study to be conducted. This includes deciding what independent variables will be evaluated, what dependent variables will be measured, who the participants will be, what tasks will be performed, and so forth. These considerations are briefly outlined below.

Evaluation Design

Usually the evaluation consists of a comparison between the new product and some other treatment "condition," such as the old product. For example, users might perform the same set of tasks using the old controls and display system and also using the new system. Performance is to demonstrate effectiveness of the new system with respect to variables such as increased accuracy, reduced task time, reduced error rate, increased user satisfaction, and so on. The two most common research design are:

- A between-subjects design where different groups of users perform tasks using the new product or system, the old product or system, or a different product or system

- A within-subjects design, where the same users perform tasks using the new product/system and also comparison systems.

Each of these options has certain advantages and disadvantages as discussed in Chapter 2. In most cases, comparison systems should be those which have the most external validity. That is, are they realistic alternative systems? For our camera example, we might decide on an evaluation design in which a group of users is asked to perform all of the critical tasks identified in the design task analysis using a variety of cameras. One would be our company's old design, one would be the new design, and others would be competitors' designs. We would have different groups of users operate the cameras in different orders to overcome order effects.

Test Participants.   In conducting evaluation studies, it is critical to obtain test participants who are representative of the final user population. Their subjective reactions and performance using the system will not be informative if designers cannot generalize the findings to the ultimate user population. Critical characteristics include age, physical characteristics, education level, knowledge and skills, job-related ability, and so forth.

Measures.   In Chapter 2 we discussed the importance of determining appropriate measures or dependent variables. In evaluation studies, the dependent variables fall into one of two categories, proximal measures and distal measures. *Proximal* measures are those that are directly associated with the person's performance or thought:

- User satisfaction
- Usability (as defined above)
- Task performance levels (accuracy, task time, etc.)
- Number of performance errors related to safety issues

After the product or system is fielded, designers may need to measure more *distal* measures, which capture the impact of the product on more global factors pertaining to the company or organization as a whole, including measures such as:

- Manufacturing costs, efficiency, waste, etc.
- Personnel costs
- Number of accidents and injuries
- Number of disability claims
- Sick leave and other health indices

In most cases, the variables being measured will fluctuate over time, reducing the reliability of the measure. Since reliability of a measure affects the statistical evaluation (and makes "significant results" harder to obtain), designers should take multiple measures of the factors being studied both before and after the new product/system is introduced. For example, a time-series study could be conducted for the number of accidents with respect to a certain piece of equipment for a period of time before and after a human factors redesign.

PROGRAMS OF CHANGE

Up until this point, we have mostly discussed the design and evaluation of a single product or system. Some of the work performed by ergonomists concerns more programmatic design and analysis. For example, a human factors specialist might go into an entire manufacturing plant and conduct an ergonomic analysis. This analysis would consider a wide range of factors including:

- Design of individual pieces of equipment from human factors perspective
- Hazards associated with equipment, workstations, environments, etc.
- Safety procedures and policies
- Design of workstations
- Efficiency of plant layout
- Efficiency of jobs and tasks
- Adequacy of employee training
- Organizational design, job structures
- Reward/incentive or policies
- Information exchange and communication

After evaluating these facets, the human factors specialist would develop a list of recommendations for the plant.

An example is given by Eckbreth (1993), who reports an ergonomic evaluation and improvement study for a telecommunications equipment manufacturer. This company had experienced a variety of employee injuries and illness among cable formers in its shops. A team evaluated the shop, with the team consisting of process engineer, supervisor, plant ergonomist, production associates, and maintenance personnel. The team assessed injury and accident records and employee complaints and reviewed task performance videotapes. An ergonomic analysis was carried out, and the team came up with recommendations and associated costs. The recommendations included:

Training: Thirty-six employees were taught basic ergonomic principles including the best working positions, how to use the adjustability of their workstations, and positions to avoid.

Changes to Existing Equipment: Repairs were made to a piece of equipment which changed the force required to rotate a component (from 58 pounds down to 16).

Equipment Redesign or Replacement: Some equipment, such as the board for forming cables, was redesigned and constructed to allow proper posture and task performance in accordance with ergonomic principles. Other equipment, such as scissors, was replaced with more ergonomically sound equipment.

Purchase of Step Stools: The purchase of step stools eliminated overhead reaching that had occurred with certain tasks.

Antifatigue Mats: Floor mats to reduce fatigue and cumulative trauma disorder were purchased.

Job Rotation: Job rotation was recommended but was not able to be implemented because it was the only Level 2 union job in the company.

It can be seen from this example that frequently a workstation or plant analysis will result in a wide variety of ergonomic recommendations. After the recommended changes have been instituted, the human factors specialist should evaluate the effects of the changes. This program evaluation is carried out using research methods as discussed earlier. Obviously, the most common research design for program evaluation is the pretest-posttest quasi-experiment. Because the design is not a true experiment, there are certain factors that can make the results uninterpretable. Ergonomists should design program evaluation studies carefully in order to avoid drawing conclusions that are unfounded (see Chapter 2 and other sources on experimental methods).

It is clear that human factors concerns more than just the characteristics or interface of a single product or piece of equipment. An increasing number of human factors specialists are realizing that often an entire re-engineering of the organization, including the beliefs and attitudes of employees, must be addressed for real long-term changes to occur. This global approach to system redesign, termed *macroergonomics,* is a new and growing subfield in human factors. We will briefly review some of the basic concepts of macroergonomics in Chapter 19, which deals with social factors.

REFERENCES

Abedini, K. (1991). Automated machines designed to interface with the extremely resistant population. *Proceedings of the Human Factors Society 35th Annual Meeting* (pp. 435–439). Santa Monica, CA: Human Factors Society.

Aldrich, T.B., Szabo, S.M., and Bierbaum, C.R. (1988). Development and application of models to predict operator workload during system design. In G.R. Macmillan, D. Beemis, E. Salas, M.H. Strub, Sutton, and L. van Breda (eds.), *Applications of human performance models to system design.* New York: Plenum Press.

Alexander, D.C. (1995). The economics of ergonomics: Part II. *Proceedings of the Human Factors and Ergonomics Society 39th Annual Meeting* (pp. 1025–1027). Santa Monica, CA: Human Factors and Ergonomics Society.

Amendola, A., Bersini, U., Cacciabue, P., and Mancini, G. (1987). Modelling operators in accident conditions: Advances and perspectives on a cognitive model. *International Journal of ManMachine Studies, 27,* 599–612.

Association for the Advancement of Medical Instrumentation (1988). *Human factors engineering guidelines and preferred practices for the design of medical devices* (AAMI HE-1988). Arlington, VA: AAMI.

Bailey, G.D. (1993). Iterative methodology and designer training in human-computer interface design. *Proceedings of InterCHI'93,* 198–205.

Bailey, R.W. (1996). *Human performance engineering* (3rd ed.). Englewood Cliffs, NJ: Prentice Hall.

Barnett, B.J., Arbak, C.J., Olson, J.L., and Walrath, L.C. (1992). A framework for design traceability. *Proceedings of the Human Factors Society 36th Annual Meeting* (pp. 2–6). Santa Monica, CA: Human Factors Society.

Bias, R.G., and Mayhew, D. (1994). *Cost-justifying usability.* New York: Academic Press.

Blanchard, B.S., and Fabrycky, W.J. (1990). *Systems engineering and analysis.* Englewood Cliff, NJ: Prentice Hall.

Boff, K., and Lincoln, J. (1988). *Engineering data compendium: Human perception and performance.* (4 Volumes). Wright-Patterson Air Force Base, OH: Armstrong Aerospace Medical Research Laboratory, AAMRL/NATO.

Boff, K.R., Monk, D.L., Swierenga, S.J., Brown, C.E., and Cody, W.J. (1991). Computer-aided human factors for systems designers. *Proceedings of the Human Factors Society 35th Annual Meeting* (pp. 332–336). Santa Monica, CA: Human Factors Society.

Bowers, V.A., and Snyder, H.L. (1990). Concurrent versus retrospective verbal protocol for comparing window usability. *Proceedings of the Human Factors Society 34th Annual Meeting* (pp. 1270–1274). Santa Monica, CA: Human Factors Society.

Brown, C.M. (1988). *Human-computer interface design guidelines.* Norwood, NJ: Ablex Publishing Co.

Byrne, J.G., and Barlow, T. (1993). Structured brainstorming: A method for collecting user requirements. *Proceedings of the Human Factors and Ergonomics Society 37th Annual Meeting* (pp. 427–431). Santa Monica, CA: Human Factors and Ergonomics Society.

Caplan, S. (1990). Using focus group methodology for ergonomic design. *Ergonomics, 33*(5), 527–533.

Card, S., Moran, T., and Newell, A. (1983). *The psychology of human-computer interaction.* Hillsdale, NJ: Lawrence Erlbaum Associates.

Carlow International (1990). *Human factors engineering: Part I. Test procedures; Part II: Human factors engineering data guide for evaluation (HEDGE).* Washington, DC: Army Test and Evaluation Command. ADA226480.

Chao, B.P. (1993). Managing user interface design using concurrent engineering. *Proceedings of the Human Factors and Ergonomics Society 37th Annual Meeting* (pp. 287–290). Santa Monica, CA: Human Factors and Ergonomics Society.

Chubb, G.P., Laughery, K.R. Jr., and Pritsker, A.B. (1987). Simulating manned systems. In G. Salvendy (ed.), *Handbook of human factors* (pp. 1298–1327). New York: Wiley.

Clegg, C., Ravden, S., Corbett, M., and Johnson, G. (1989). Allocating functions in computer integrated manufacturing: A review and new method. *Behavior and Information Technology, 8*(3), 175–190.

Creasy, R. (1980). Problem solving, the FAST way. *Proceedings of Society of Added-Value Engineers Conference* (pp. 173–175). Irving, TX: Society of Added-Value Engineers.

Dennison, T.W., and Gawron, V.J. (1995). Tools and methods for human factors test and evaluation: Mockups, physical and electronic human models, and simulation. *Proceedings of the Human Factors and Ergonomics Society 39th Annual Meeting* (pp. 1228–1232). Santa Monica, CA: Human Factors and Ergonomics Society.

Desurvire, H., and Thomas, J.C. (1993). Enhancing the performance of interface evaluators using non-empirical usability methods. *Proceedings of the Human Factors and Ergonomics Society 37th Annual Meeting* (pp. 1132–1136). Santa Monica, CA: Human Factors and Ergonomics Society.

Diaper, D. (1989). *Task analysis for human-computer interaction.* Chichester, UK: Ellis Horwood.

Dix, A., Finlay, J., Abowd, G., and Beale, R. (1993). *Human-computer interaction.* Englewood Cliffs, NJ: Prentice Hall.

Dockery, C.A., and Neuman, T. (1994). Ergonomics in product design solves manufacturing problems: Considering the users' needs at every stage of the product's life. *Proceedings of the Human Factors and Ergonomics Society 38th Annual Meeting* (pp. 691–695). Santa Monica, CA: Human Factors and Ergonomics Society.

Dumas, J.S. (1988). *Designing user interfaces for software.* Englewood Cliffs, NJ: Prentice-Hall.

Eckbreth, K.A. (1993). The ergonomic evaluation and improvement of a cable forming process: A case study. *Proceedings of the Human Factors and Ergonomics Society 37th Annual Meeting* (pp. 822–825). Santa Monica, CA: Human Factors and Ergonomics Society.

Eisenhut, S.M., and Beaton, R.J. (1995). Micro SAINT modeling of visual displays and controls consoles. *Proceedings of the Human Factors and Ergonomics Society 39th Annual Meeting* (pp. 16–19). Santa Monica, CA: Human Factors and Ergonomics Society.

Elkind, J., Card, S., Hochberg, J., and Huey, B. (eds.) (1990). *Human performance models for computer-aided engineering.* New York: Academic Press.

Evans, S.M. (1991). EDGE: A CAD tool for system design. In Boyle, Ianni, Easterly, Harper, and Korna (eds.), *Human-centered Technology for Maintainability: Workshop Proceedings* (AL-TP-1991-0010). Wright-Patterson Air Force Base, OH: Armstrong Laboratory.

Fewins, A., Mitchell, K., and Williams, J.C. (1992). Balancing automation and human action through task analysis. In B. Kirwan and L.K. Ainsworth (eds.), *A guide to task analysis* (pp. 241–251). London: Taylor & Francis.

Fitts, P.M. (ed.) (1951). *Human engineering for an effective air-navigation and traffic control system.* Washington, DC: NRC.

Fontenelle, G.A., and Laughery, K.R. (1988). A workload assessment aid for human engineering design. *Proceedings of the Human Factors Society 32nd Annual Meeting* (pp. 1122–1125). Santa Monica, CA: Human Factors Society.

Galitz, W.O. (1993). *User-interface screen design.* New York: Wiley.

Gilmore, W.E. (1985). *Human engineering guidelines for the evaluation and assessment of video display units* (NUTREG-CR-4227). Washington, DC: U.S. Nuclear Regulatory Commission.

Gordon, S.E. (1994). *Systematic training program design: Maximizing effectiveness and minimizing liability.* Englewood Cliffs, NJ: Prentice-Hall.

Gordon, S.E. (1995). Cognitive task analysis using complementary elicitation methods. *Proceedings of the Human Factors and Ergonomics Society 39th Annual Meeting* (pp. 525–529). Santa Monica, CA: Human Factors and Ergonomics Society.

Gordon, S.E., and Gill, R.T. (1989). Question probes: A structured method for eliciting declarative knowledge. *AI Applications in Natural Resource Management, 3,* 13–20.

Gordon, S.E., and Gill, R.T. (1992). Knowledge acquisition with question probes and conceptual graph structures. In T. Lauer, E. Peacock, and A. Graesser (eds.), *Questions and information systems* (pp. 29–46). Hillsdale, NJ: Lawrence Erlbaum Associates.

Gordon, S.E., and Gill, R.T. (1997). Cognitive task analysis. In C. Zsambok and G. Klein (eds.), *Naturalistic decision making.* (Hillsdale, NJ: Lawrence Erlbaum Associates.

Gould, J.D. (1988). How to design usable systems. In M. Helander, (ed.), *Handbook of human-computer interaction* (pp. 757–789). The Netherlands: Elsevier.

Gould, J.D., and Lewis, C. (1985). Designing for usability: Key principles and what designers think. *Communications of the ACM, 28*(3), 360–411.

Graesser, A.C., Lang, K.L., and Elofson, C.S. (1987). Some tools for redesigning system-operator interfaces. In D.E. Berger, K. Pezdek, and W.P. Banks (eds.), *Applications of cognitive psychology: Problem solving, education, and computing* (pp. 163–181). Hillsdale, NJ: Lawrence Erlbaum Associates.

Greenbaum, T.L. (1993). *The handbook of focus group research.* New York: Lexington Books.

Gugerty, L., Halgren, S., Gosbee, J., and Rudisill, M. (1991). Using GOMS models and hypertext to create representations of medical procedures for online display. *Proceedings of the Human Factors Society 35th Annual Meeting* (pp. 713–717). Santa Monica, CA: Human Factors and Ergonomics Society.

Hamilton, D.B., and Bierbaum, C.R. (1990). Task Analysis/Workload (TAWL): A methodology for predicting operator workload. *Proceedings of the Human Factors Society 34th Annual Meeting* (pp. 1117–1121). Santa Monica, CA: Human Factors and Ergonomics Society.

Hauser, J.R., and Clausing, D. (1988). The house of quality. *Harvard Business Review,* May–June, 63–73.

Helander, M. (ed.) (1988). *Handbook of human-computer interaction.* The Netherlands: Elsevier.

Institute of Electrical and Electronic Engineers (1988). *IEEE STD-1023, Guide for the application of human factors engineering to systems, equipment, and facilities of nuclear power generating stations.* New York: Institute of Electrical and Electronic Engineers.

John, B.E., Vera, A.H., and Newell, A. (1994). Towards real-time GOMS: A model of expert behavior in a highly interactive task. *Behavior and Information Technology, 13,* 255–267.

Johnson, P. (1992). *Human-computer interaction: Psychology, task analysis and software engineering.* London: McGraw-Hill.

Kantowitz, B.H., and Sorkin, R.D. (1987). Allocation of functions. In G. Salvendy (ed.), *Handbook of human factors* (pp. 355–369). New York: Wiley.

Karat, C. (1990). Cost-benefit analysis of usability engineering techniques. *Proceedings of the Human Factors Society 34th Annual Meeting* (pp. 839–843). Santa Monica, CA: Human Factors Society.

Kieras, D.E. (1988). Towards a practical GOMS model methodology for user interface design. In M. Helander (ed.), *Handbook of human-computer interaction.* Amsterdam: Elsevier Science Publishers.

Kirwan, B., and Ainsworth, L.K. (eds.) (1992). *A guide to task analysis.* London: Taylor & Francis.

Mantei, M., and Teorey, T.J. (1988). Cost/benefit for incorporating human factors in the software lifecycle. *Communications of the ACM, 31*(4), 428–439.

Marcotte, A.J., Marvin, S., and Lagemann, T. (1995). Ergonomics applied to product and process design achieves immediate, measurable cost savings. *Proceedings of the Human Factors and Ergonomics Society 39th Annual Meeting* (pp. 660–663). Santa Monica, CA: Human Factors and Ergonomics Society.

MATRIS Office (1994). *Directory of design support methods.* San Diego, CA: DTIC-AM.

Mayhew, D.J. (1990). Cost-justifying human factors support—A framework. *Proceedings of the Human Factors Society 34th Annual Meeting* (pp. 834–838). Santa Monica, CA: Human Factors and Ergonomics Society.

Mayhew, D.J. (1992). *Principles and guidelines in software user interface design.* Englewood Cliffs, NJ: Prentice-Hall.

McAlindon, P.J. (1994). The development and evaluation of the keybowl: A study on an ergonomically designed alphanumeric input device. *Proceedings of the Human Factors and Ergonomics Society 38th Annual Meeting* (pp. 320–324). Santa Monica, CA: Human Factors and Ergonomics Society.

McVey, G.F. (1990). The application of environmental design principles and human factors guidelines to the design of training and instructional facilities: Room size and viewing considerations. *Proceedings of the Human Factors Society 34th Annual Meeting* (pp. 552–556). Santa Monica, CA: Human Factors Society.

Meister, D. (1971). *Human factors: Theory and practice.* New York: Wiley.

Meister, D. (1986). *Human factors testing and evaluation.* New York: Elsevier.

Meister, D. (1987). System design, development, and testing. In G. Salvendy (ed.), *Handbook of human factors* (pp. 17–41). New York: Wiley.

Mosier, J.N., and Smith, S.L. (1986). Application guidelines for designing user interface software. *Behavior and Information Technology, 5,* 39–46.

Nielson, J. (1993). *Usability engineering.* Cambridge, MA: Academic Press Professional.

Nielson, J. (1994a). Heuristic evaluation. In J. Nielson and R.L. Mack (eds.), *Usability inspection methods.* New York: Wiley.

Nielson, J. (1994b). Guerilla HCI: Using discount usability engineering to penetrate the intimidation barrier. In R.G. Bias and D.J. Mayhew (eds.), *Cost-justifying usability* (pp. 245–272). Boston, MA: Academic Press.

Nielson, J., and Molich, R. (1990). Heuristic evaluation of user interfaces. *Proceedings of the ACM CHI '90 Conference* (pp. 249–256). Association for Computing Machinery.

Norman, D.A. (1988). *The design of everyday things.* New York: Doubleday-Currency.

Norman, D.A. (1992). *Turn signals are the facial expressions of automobiles.* Reading, MA: Addison-Wesley Publishing.

Norman, D. A., and Draper, S.W. (eds.) (1986). *User centered system design.* Hillsdale, NJ: Lawrence Erlbaum Associates.

O'Hara, J.M. (1994). Evaluation of complex human-machine systems using HFE guidelines. *Proceedings of the Human Factors and Ergonomics Society 38th Annual Meeting* (pp. 1008–1012). Santa Monica, CA: Human Factors and Ergonomics Society.

Ohnemus, K.R., and Biers, D.W. (1993). Retrospective versus concurrent thinking-out-loud in usability testing. *Proceedings of the Human Factors and Ergonomics Society 37th Annual Meeting* (pp. 1127–1131). Santa Monica, CA: Human Factors and Ergonomics Society.

Price, H.E. (1985). The allocation of functions in systems. *Human Factors, 27*(1), 33–45.

Price, H.E. (1990). Conceptual system design and the human role. In H.R. Booher (ed.), *Manprint: An approach to systems integration* (pp. 161–203). New York: Van Nostrand Reinhold.

Pulliam, R., and Price, H.E. (1985). *Automation and the allocation of functions between human and automatic control: General method* (AFAMRL-JTR-85-017). Wright Patterson Air Force Base, OH: Aerospace Medical Division, Air Force Aerospace Medical Research Laboratory.

Reed, P., and Billingsley, P. (1996). Software ergonomics comes of age: The ANSI/HFES-200 standard. *Proceedings of the Human Factors and Ergonomics Society 40th Annual Meeting* (pp. 323–327). Santa Monica, CA: Human Factors and Ergonomics Society.

Rogers, J.G., and Armstrong, R. (1977). Use of human engineering standards in design. *Human Factors, 19*(1), 15–23.

Rogers, J.G., and Pegden, C.D. (1977). Formatting and organizing of a human engineering standard. *Human Factors, 19*(1), 55–61.

Roth, E.M., and Woods, D.D. (1989). Cognitive task analysis: An approach to knowledge acquisition for intelligent system design. In G. Guida and C. Tasso (eds.), *Topics in expert system design.* The Netherlands: Elsevier.

Rubin, J. (1994). *Handbook of Usability Testing: How to plan, design and conduct effective tests.* New York: Wiley.

Ryder, J.M., Redding, R.E., and Beckshi, P.F. (1987). Training development for complex cognitive tasks. *Proceedings of the Human Factors Society 31st Annual Meeting* (pp. 1261–1265). Santa Monica, CA: Human Factors Society.

Schlager, M.S., Means, B., and Roth, C. (1990). Cognitive task analysis for the real (-time) world. *Proceedings of the Human Factors Society 34th Annual Meeting* (pp. 1309–1313). Santa Monica, CA: Human Factors Society.

Seamster, T.L., Redding, R.E., Cannon, J.R., Ryder, J.M., and Purcell, J.A. (1993). Cognitive task analysis of expertise in air traffic control. *The International Journal of Aviation Psychology, 3*(4), 257–283.

Seamster, T.L., Redding, R.R., and Kaempf, G.F. (1997). *Applied cognitive task analysis in aviation.* Brookfield, VT: Ashgate Publishing.

Shneiderman, B. (1992). *Designing the user interface: Strategies for effective human-computer interaction* (2nd ed.). Reading, MA: Addison-Wesley.

Smith, S.L., and Mosier, J.N. (1986). *Guidelines for designing user interface software* (Technical Report NTIS No A177 198). Hanscom Air Force Base, MA: USAF Electronic Systems Division.

Thomas, B., and McClelland, I. (1994). The development of a touch screen based communications terminal. *Proceedings of the Human Factors and Ergonomics Society 38th Annual Meeting* (pp. 175–179). Santa Monica, CA: Human Factors and Ergonomics Society.

Van Cott, H.P., and Kinkade, R.G. (eds.) (1972). *Human engineering guide to equipment design.* Washington, DC: U.S. Government Printing Office.

Vicente, K.J. (1990). A few implications of an ecological approach to human factors. *Human Factors Society Bulletin, 33*(11), 1–4.

U.S. Department of Defense (1989). *Human engineering design criteria for military systems, equipment, and facilities* (MIL-STD-1472D). Washington, DC: Department of Defense.

Weimer, J. (ed.) (1995). *Research techniques in human engineering.* Englewood Cliffs, NJ: Prentice-Hall.

Whiteside, J., Bennett, J., and Holtzblatt, K. (1988). Usability engineering our experience and evolution. In M. Helander (ed.), *Handbook of Human-Computer Interaction* (pp. 791–817). New York: North Holland.

Wiklund, M.E. (1994). *Usability in practice: How companies develop user-friendly products.* Cambridge, MA: Academic Press Professional.

Williams, J.C. (1988). Human factors analysis of automation requirements—A methodology for allocating functions. *10th Advances in Reliability Technology Symposium.* Warrington: U.K. Atomic Energy Authority.

Wixon, D., Holtzblatt, K., and Knox, S. (1990). Contextual design: An emergent view of system design. *CHI '90 Proceedings,* April, 329–336.

Woods, D.D., Johannesen, L., and Potter, S.S. (1992). The sophistry of guidelines: Revisiting recipes for color use in human-computer interface design. *Proceedings of the Human Factors Society 36th Annual Meeting* (pp. 418–422). Santa Monica, CA: Human Factors Society.

Woods, D.D., Roth, E.M., and Pople, H.E. (1990). Modeling operator performance in emergencies. *Proceedings of the Human Factors Society 34th Annual Meeting* (pp. 1132–1135). Santa Monica, CA: Human Factors and Ergonomics Society.

CHAPTER 4

Visual Sensory Systems

The 50-year-old traveler, completing his flight to an unfamiliar city on a dark rainy night, has proceeded to pick up the rental car. Dropping the traveler off in the parking lot, the rental agency bus driver points to "the red sedan over there" and drives off, but in the dim light of the parking lot, our traveler cannot easily tell which car is red and which is brown and for a moment finds himself climbing into the wrong car. Eventually correcting his mistake and settled at last in the correct vehicle, he now pulls out the city map to figure his way out of the airport. But in the dim illumination of the dome light, the printed street names on the map appear to be just a haze of black, with little form or shape. Giving up on the map, he remains confident that he will see the appropriate signage to Route 60 that will direct him toward his destination, and so he starts the motor to pull out of the lot. The rain streaming down forces him to search for the wiper switch, but the switch remains hard to find because the dark printed labels cannot be read against the gray color of the interior. A little fumbling, however, and the wipers are on, and he emerges from the lot onto the highway. The rapid traffic closing behind him and bright glare of the headlights in his rearview mirror force him to accelerate to an uncomfortably rapid speed. He cannot read the contents of the first sign to his right as it speeds by. Was that sign announcing Route 60 or Route 66? He drives on, assuming that when the turnoff arrives it will be announced again and so peers ahead to await its arrival. Suddenly there it is on the left side of the highway, not the right where he had expected it, and now it has passed him before he has had a chance to react. Frustrated, he turns on the dome light to glance at the map again, but in the fraction of a second his head is down, the sudden sound of gravel on the undercarriage signals that he has slid off the highway. As he drives along the berm, waiting to pull back on the road, he fails to see the huge pothole that unkindly brings his car to an abrupt halt.

Our unfortunate traveler is in a situation that is far from unique. Night driving in unfamiliar locations is one of the more hazardous endeavors that humans undertake (Evans, 1991), especially as they become older (see Chapter 17). The reasons the dangers are so great relate very much to the pronounced limits of the visual sensory system. As we discuss below, many of these limits reside within the very peripheral features of the eyeball itself and the neural pathways that send messages of visual information to the brain. Others relate more directly to brain processing and can be related to many of the perceptual processes we discuss in more detail in Chapter 6. In the present chapter we will first discuss the nature of the light stimulus and the eyeball anatomy as it processes this light. We shall then discuss several of the important characteristics of human visual performance as it is affected by this interaction between characteristics of the stimulus and the human perceiver.

THE STIMULUS: LIGHT

As shown in Figure 4.1a, essentially all visual stimuli that the human can perceive may be described as a wave of electromagnetic energy. The wave can be represented as a point along the visual *spectrum.* This point has a *wavelength,* typically expressed in nanometers, and an amplitude. The wavelength determines the *hue* of the stimulus that is perceived, and the amplitude determines its *brightness.* As the figure shows, the range of wavelengths that are typically visible to the eye runs from short wavelengths of around 400 nm (typically observed as blue-violet) to long wavelengths of around 700 nm (typically observed as red). In fact the eye rarely encounters "pure" wavelengths. On the one hand, mixtures of different wavelengths may act as stimuli. For example, the figure depicts a spectrum that is a mixture of red and blue, which would be perceived as purple. On the other hand, the "pure" wavelengths, characterizing a hue, like blue or yellow, may be "diluted" by mixture with varying amounts of *achromatic* light (like gray: light with no dominant hue and therefore not represented on the spectrum). Undiluted wavelengths, like a pure red, are said to be *saturated.* Diluted wavelengths, like a pink, are of course unsaturated. Hence, a given light stimulus can be characterized by its hue, saturation, and brightness.

The actual hue of a light is typically specified by the combination of the three primary colors—red, green, and blue—necessary to achieve it (Helander, 1997). This specification follows a procedure developed by the Commission Internationel de L'Elairage and hence is called the CIE color system.

As shown in Figure 4.1b, the CIE color space represents all colors in terms of two primaries of long and medium wavelengths specified by the *x* and *y* axes (Wyszecki, 1986). Those colors on the rim of the space are pure "saturated" colors. Monochrome is represented at the point C in the middle. The figure does not represent brightness, which can be conceived as a third dimension running above and below the color space of 4.1b. Use of this standard coordinate system allows common specification of colors across different users.

While we can measure or specify the hue of a stimulus reaching the eyeball by its wavelength, the measurement of brightness is more complex because of the several interpretations of light "intensity." In Figure 4.2, we see a source of light, like

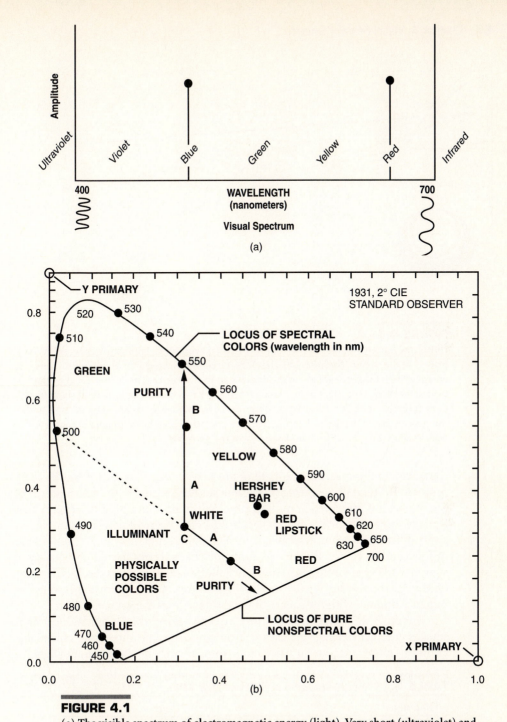

FIGURE 4.1

(a) The visible spectrum of electromagnetic energy (light). Very short (ultraviolet) and very long (infrared) wavelengths falling just outside of this spectrum are shown. Monochromatic (black, gray, white) hues are not shown because these are generated by the combinations of wavelengths. (b) The CIE color space, showing typical colors created by levels of *x* and *y* specifications. (*Source*: Helander, M., 1987. The design of visual displays. In *Handbook of Human Factors*. G. Salvendy, ed., New York: Wiley, Fig. 5.1.35, p. 535, Fig. 5.1.36, p. 539. Reprinted by permission of John Wiley & Sons, Inc.)

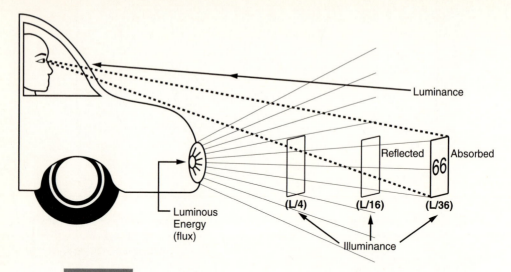

FIGURE 4.2

Illustrates concepts behind the perception of visual brightness. Luminance energy (flux) is present at the source (the headlight), but for a given illuminated area (illuminance), this energy declines with the square of the distance from the source. This is illustrated by the values under the three signs at increasing intervals of two units, four units, and six units away from the headlight. Some of the illuminance (solid rays) is absorbed by the sign, and the remainder is reflected back to the observer, characterizing the *luminance* of the viewed sign. Brightness is the subjective experience of the perceiver.

the sun or, in this case, the headlight of our driver's car. This source may be characterized by its *luminous intensity* or luminous flux, related to the actual energy of the source. It is measured in units of *candela*. But the amount of this energy that actually strikes the surface of an object to be seen—the road sign, for example—is a very different measure, described as the *illuminance* and measured in units of *lux* or foot candles. Hence, the term *illumination* characterizes the lighting quality of a given working environment. How much illuminance an object receives depends on the distance of the object from the light source. As the figure shows, the illuminance declines with the square of the distance from the source.

Although we may sometimes be concerned about the illumination of light sources in direct viewing (the glaring headlights from the oncoming vehicles, for example), more often our human factors concerns are with the amount of light *re-*

TABLE 4.1 Physical Quantities of Light and Their Units

Quantity	Units
Luminous flux	1 candela or 12.57 lumins
Illuminance	Foot candle or 10.76 LUX
Luminance	Candela/M^2 or foot lambert
Reflectance	A ratio
Brightness	

flected off of objects to be detected, discriminated, and recognized by the observer when these objects are not themselves the source of light. This may characterize, for example, the road sign in Figure 4.2. We refer to this measure as the *luminance* of a particular stimulus typically measured in foot lamberts (FL). Luminance is different from illuminance because of differences in the amount of light that the surface either reflects or absorbs. Black surfaces absorb most of the illuminance striking the surface, leaving little luminance. White surfaces reflect most. In fact, we can define the *reflectance* of a surface as the ratio:

$$\text{Reflectance (\%)} = \frac{\text{luminance (FL)}}{\text{illuminance (FC)}} \qquad (4.1)$$

(A useful hint is to think of the illuminance light, leaving some of itself [the "il"] on the surface, and sending back to the eye, only the luminance.) Naturally, the luminance will also decline with the square of the distance of the observer from the illuminated stimulus.

The *brightness* of a stimulus then is the actual experience of visual intensity, an intensity that often governs its visibility. From this discussion, one can see how the visibility or brightness of a given stimulus may be the same if it is a dark (poorly reflective) sign that is well illuminated or a white (highly reflective) sign that is poorly illuminated. Visibility is also affected by the *contrast* between the stimulus and its surround, but that is another story that we shall describe in a few pages.

Table 4.1 summarizes these various measures of light and shows the units by which they are typically measured. A photometer is the electronics device that can measure luminous intensity.

THE RECEPTOR SYSTEM: THE EYEBALL AND THE OPTIC NERVE

Light, electromagnetic energy, must be transformed to electrochemical neural energy, a process that is accomplished by the eye. Figure 4.3 presents a schematic view of the wonderful receptor system for vision, the eyeball. As we describe certain key features of its anatomy and how this anatomy affects characteristics of the light energy that passes through it, we will identify some of the distortions and distractions that disrupt our ability to see in many working environments and therefore should be the focus of concern for the human factors engineer.

The Lens

As we see in the figure, the light rays first pass through the cornea, which is a protective surface that will absorb some of the light energy (and does so progressively more as we age). Light rays then pass through the pupil, which dilates (in darkness) or constricts (in brightness) to try to admit adaptively more light when illumination is low, and less when illumination is high. The *lens* of the eye is then responsible for adjusting its shape, or *accommodating,* to bring the image to a precise focus

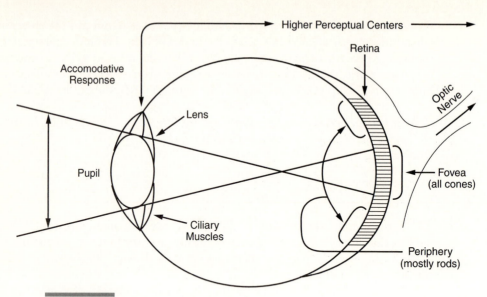

FIGURE 4.3

Key aspects of the anatomy of the eyeball.

on the back surface of the eyeball, a surface called the *retina.* This accommodation is accomplished by a set of ciliary muscles surrounding the lens, muscles that communicate with the higher perceptual centers of the brain. When we view images up close, the light rays emanating from the images converge as they approach the eye, and the muscles must accommodate by changing the lens to a rounder shape. When the image is far away and the light rays approach in essentially parallel fashion, the muscles accommodate by creating a flatter lens. Somewhere in between, there is a point where the lens comes to a natural "resting" point, at which the muscles are doing little work at all. This is referred to as the *resting state* of accommodation. The visual fatigue experienced during prolonged viewing of close images is based on the fatigue of the ciliary muscles.

As should be evident, the amount of accommodation can be described in terms of the distance of a focused object from the eye. Formally, the amount of accommodation required is measured in *diopters,* which equal 1/viewing distance (meters). Thus, 1 diopter is the accommodation required to view an object at 1 meter.

As our driver discovered when he struggled to read the fine print of the map, our eyeball does not always accommodate easily. It takes time to change its shape, and sometimes there are factors that limit the amount of shape change that is possible. *Myopia,* otherwise known as nearsightedness, results when the lens cannot flatten and hence distant objects cannot be brought into focus. *Presbyopia,* otherwise known as farsightedness, results when the lens cannot accommodate to very near stimuli. As we grow older, the lens becomes less flexible in general, but farsightedness in particular becomes more evident. Hence, we see that the older reader, when not using corrective lenses, must hold the map farther away from the eyes to try to gain focus, and it will take longer for that focus to be achieved.

While accommodation may be hindered by limits on flexibility of the lens, and compensated by corrective lenses, it is also greatly influenced by the amount of visibility of the image to be fixated, a visibility that is determined both by its brightness and by its contrast. We discuss these issues below.

The Visual Receptor System

An image, whether focused or not, eventually reaches the retina at the back of the eyeball. The image may be characterized by its intensity (luminance), its wave-lengths, and its size. The image size is typically expressed by its *visual angle*, which is depicted by the two-headed arrows in front of the eyes in Figure 4.3. The visual angle of an object of height H, viewed at distance D, is approximately equal to Arctan (H/D) (the angle whose Tangent = H/D). For visual angles less than around 10 degrees, the angle may be expressed in minutes of arc and approximated by the formula:

$$VA \; = \; \frac{3438H}{D} \tag{4.2}$$

Importantly, the image can also be characterized by *where* it falls on the back of the retina because this location determines the types of visual receptor cells that are responsible for transforming electromagnetic light energy into the electrical impulses of neural energy to be relayed up the optic nerve to the brain. There are two different types of receptor cells, the *rods* and the *cones,* each with six distinctly different properties. Collectively, these different properties have numerous implications for our visual sensory processing, and we consider each in some detail.

1. *Location.* The middle region of the retina, a region called the *fovea,* consisting of an area of around 2 degrees of visual angle, is inhabited exclusively by the cones (Fig. 4.3). Outside of the fovea, the *periphery* is inhabited by rods as well as cones, but the concentration of cones declines rapidly moving farther away from the fovea (i.e., with greater *eccentricity*).

2. *Acuity.* The amount of fine detail that can be resolved is far greater when the image falls on the closely spaced cones than on the more sparsely spaced rods. We refer to this ability to resolve detail as the *acuity,* often expressed as the inverse of the smallest visual angle (in minutes of arc) that can just be detected. Thus, an acuity of 1.0 means that the operator can just resolve a visual angle of 1 minute of arc (1/60 of 1 degree). Table 4.2 provides various ways of measuring visual acuity. Note that since acuity is higher with cones than rods, it is not surprising that our best ability to resolve detail is in the fovea, where the cone density is greatest. Hence, we "look at" objects that require high acuity, meaning that we orient the eyeball to bring the image into focus on the fovea. While visual acuity drops rapidly toward the periphery, the sensitivity to *motion* declines at a far less rapid rate. In fact, we often use the relatively high sensitivity to motion in the periphery as a cue for something important on which we later fixate.

3. *Sensitivity.* Although the cones have an advantage over the rods in acuity, the rods have an advantage in terms of sensitivity, characterizing the minimum amount

TABLE 4.2 Some Measures of Acuity

Minimum separable acuity	General measurement of smallest detail detectable
Vernier acuity	Are two parallel lines aligned?
Landolt ring	Is the gap in a ring detectable?
Snellen acuity	Measurement of detail resolved at 20 feet, relative to the distance at which a normal observer can resolve the same detail (e.g., 20/30)

of light that can just be detected or the *threshold*. Sensitivity and threshold are reciprocally related. Since there are no rods in the fovea, it is not surprising that our fovea is very poor at picking up dim illumination (i.e., it has a high threshold). To illustrate this, note that if you try to look directly at a faint star, it will appear to vanish. *Scotopic vision* refers to vision at night when only the rods are operating. *Photopic vision* refers to vision when the illumination is sufficient to activate both rods and cones (but when most of our visual experience is due to actions of the cone).

4. *Color sensitivity.* The rods cannot discriminate different wavelengths of light (unless they also differ in intensity). The rods are "color blind," and so the extent to which hues can be resolved declines both in peripheral vision (where fewer cones are present) and at night (when only the rods are operating). Hence, we can understand how our driver, trying to locate his car at night, was unable to discriminate the poorly illuminated red car from its surrounding neighbors.

5. *Adaptation.* When stimulated by light, the rods rapidly lose their sensitivity, and it will take a long time for them to regain it (up to a half-hour) once they are returned to the darkness that is characteristic of the rod's "optimal viewing environment." Environments in which operators may be periodically exposed to bright light but often need to use their scotopic vision will then be particularly disruptive. In contrast to the rods, the low sensitivity of the cones is little affected by light stimulation. However, the cones may become *hypersensitive,* when they have received little stimulation. This is the source of *glare* from bright lights at night. We discuss glare further in Chapter 13.

6. *Differential wavelength sensitivity.* Whereas the cones are generally sensitive to all wavelengths, the rods are particularly *insensitive* to long (i.e., red) wavelengths. Hence, red objects and surfaces look very black at night. More important, illuminating objects in red light, in an otherwise dark environment, will not destroy the rod's dark adaptation. For example, on the bridge of a ship, the navigator may use the red lamp to stimulate the cones to read the fine detail of the chart, but this will not destroy dark adaptation and disrupt the ability of personnel to scan the horizon for faint lights or dark forms.

Collectively, these pronounced differences between rods and cones are responsible for a wide range of visual phenomena, many of which are probably familiar to the reader. In the pages below, we consider some of the more complex implications of these phenomena to human factors issues related to three important aspects of our sensory processing: contrast sensitivity, night vision, and color vision.

SENSORY PROCESSING LIMITATIONS

⋇ Contrast Sensitivity

Our unfortunate driver could discern neither the wiper control label nor the map detail nor the pothole for a variety of reasons—all related to the vitally important human factors concept of *contrast sensitivity. Contrast sensitivity* may be defined as the reciprocal of the minimum contrast between a lighter and darker spatial area that can just be detected; that is, with a level of contrast below this minimum, the two areas appear homogeneous. Hence, the ability to detect contrast is essential to the ability to detect and recognize shapes, whether the discriminating shape of a letter or the blob of a pothole. The contrast of a given visual pattern is typically expressed as the ratio of the *difference* between the luminance of light and dark areas to the *sum* of the luminance values:

$$C = (L - D)/(L + D) \tag{4.3}$$

The higher contrast sensitivity (*CS*) that an observer possesses, the smaller is the minimum amount of contrast that can just be detected (C_M). Hence,

$$CS = 1/C_M$$

From this definition, we can see that the minimum separable acuity (the light separating two dark lines) represents one measure of contrast sensitivity because a gap that is smaller than this minimum will be perceived as a uniform line of homogeneous brightness.

Contrast sensitivity may often be measured by a *grating,* such as that shown along the *x* axis of Figure 4.4. If the grating appears to be a smooth bar like the grating on the far right of the figure (if it is held at a distance), the viewer is unable to discern the alternating patterns of dark and light, and the contrast is below the viewer's *CS* threshold.

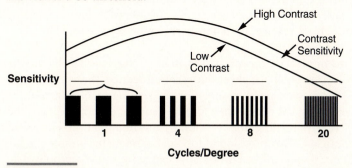

FIGURE 4.4

Illustrates spatial frequency gratings, used to measure contrast sensitivity. Remember that the particular values on the *x* axis will vary as a function of visual angle and therefore the distances at which the figure is held from the eyes. The bar above each grating will occupy 1 degree of visual angle when the book is viewed at a distance of 52cm. The two curves represent patterns of different contrast levels.

Expressed in this way, we can consider the first of several influences on *CS*, and that is the *spatial frequency* of the grating. As shown in Figure 4.4, spatial frequency may be expressed as the number of cycles of dark and lightness that occupy 1 degree of visual angle (cycles/degrees or *C/D*). If the reader holds this book approximately 1 foot away, then the spatial frequency of the left grating is *0.6 C/D,* of the next grating is *1.25 C/D,* and of the third grating is *2.0 C/D.* We can also see that the spatial frequency is inversely related to the width of the light or dark bar. It turns out that the human eye is most sensitive to spatial frequencies of around 3 cycles/degrees, as shown by the contrast sensitivity function drawn across the axis of Figure 4.4. Very fine lines (high spatial frequencies) blur together, whereas thicker lines (lower spatial frequencies), while easily visible at the high contrast shown here, tend to be less visible as the amount of contrast between light and dark decreases.

As we describe in more detail below, the high spatial frequencies on the right characterize our sensitivity to small visual angles and fine detail (and hence, reflect the standard measurement of visual acuity), such as that involved in reading fine print, or making fine adjustments on a vernier scale. Much lower spatial frequencies characterize the recognition of *shapes* of objects that may be seen under blurred or degraded conditions, like the road sign sought by our lost driver at the opening of the chapter or the unseen pothole that terminated his trip. Low contrasts at low spatial frequencies often characterize the viewing of images that are degraded by poor "sensor resolution," like those from infrared radar (Uttal, Baruch, & Allen, 1994).

A second important influence on contrast sensitivity is the *contrast* itself. As seen in Figure 4.4, lower contrast will be less easily discerned. Hence, we can understand the difficulty our driver has in trying to read the black printed "wiper" label against the gray dashboard. Had the label been printed against a white background, it would have been far easier to read. Many users of common household products like VCRs are frustrated by the "black on black" format of much of the raised printing instructions (Fig. 4.5). It should be noted that color contrast does not necessarily produce luminance good-contrast ratios. Thus, for example, slides that produce black text against a blue background may be very hard for a viewing audience to read.

A third influence on contrast sensitivity is the level of *illumination* of the stimulus. Not surprisingly, lower illumination reduces the sensitivity to contrast and appears to do so more severely for the sensing of high spatial frequencies (which depend on the cones) than for low frequencies. This explains the obvious difficulty we have reading fine print under low illumination. However, low illumination can also disrupt vision at low spatial frequencies: note the loss of visibility that our driver suffered for the low spatial frequency pothole.

Two final influences on contrast sensitivity are the resolution of the eye itself and the *dynamic* characteristics of the viewing conditions. Increasing age reduces the amount of light passing through the cornea and greatly reduces contrast sensitivity. This factor, coupled with the loss of visual accommodation ability at close viewing, produces a severe deficit for older readers in poor illumination. Contrast sensitivity declines also when the stimulus is moving relative to the viewer as our driver found when trying to read the highway sign.

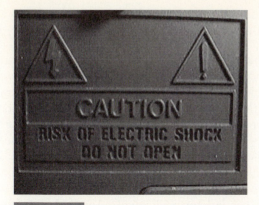

FIGURE 4.5
Difficult visibility of low-contrast raised-plastic printing. With small letters and black plastic, such information is often nearly illegible in poor illumination. (*Source:* Courtesy of Anthony D. Andre, Interface Analysis Associates, San Jose, CA.)

Collectively all of these factors, summarized in Table 4.3, are critical for predicting whether or not detail will be perceived and shapes will be recognized in a variety of degraded viewing conditions, and hence critical for indirectly informing the designer of certain standards of design that should be adhered to in order to guarantee viewability of certain critical symbols. Many of these standards may be found in handbooks like Boff and Lincoln (1989) or textbooks such as Sanders and McCormick (1993) or Salvendy (1997).

Human factors researchers are also trying to develop models to show how all the influences in Table 4.3 *interact* in a way that would, for example, allow one to specify the minimum text size for presenting instructions to be viewed by someone with 20/40 vision in certain illumination, or determine the probability of recognizing targets at night at a particular distance (Owens, Antonoff, & Francis, 1994). However, the accuracy of such models has not yet reached a point where they are readily applicable when several variables are involved. What can be done instead is to be explicit on the implications of these factors for trying to achieve the *best* design whenever print

TABLE 4.3 Some Variables That Affect Contrast and Visibility

Variable	Effect	Example
↓ Contrast	↓ Visibility	Black print on gray
↓ Illumination	↓ Contrast sensitivity	Reading map in poor light
Polarity	Black on white better than white on black	Designing viewgraphs
Spatial frequency	Optimum *CS* at 3 *C/D*	Ideal size of text font given viewing distance
Visual accommodation	*CS*	Map reading during night driving
Motion	↓ *CS*	Reading a road sign while moving

or symbols must be read under less than optimal circumstances. We describe below some of these guidelines as they pertain to the readability of the printed word.

Reading Print.   Most obviously, print should not be too fine in order to guarantee its readability. When space is not at a premium and viewing conditions may be less than optimal, one should seek to come as close to the 3 cycles/degrees value as possible (i.e., stroke width of 1/6 degree) to guarantee maximum readability. Fine print and very narrow stroke widths are dangerous choices. Similarly, one should maximize contrast by employing black letters on white background rather than, for example, using the "sexier" but less readably hued backgrounds (e.g., black on blue). Black on red is particularly dangerous with low illumination, since red is not seen by the cones. Because of certain asymmetries in the visual processing system, it turns out that dark text on lighter background ("negative contrast") also offers higher contrast sensitivity than light on dark ("positive contrast"). The disruptive tendency for white letters to spread out or "bleed" over a black background is called "irradiation."

The actual character font matters too. Fonts that adhere to "typical" letter shapes like the text of this book are better read because of their greater familiarity, than those that create block letters or other non standardized shapes. Another effect on readability is the *case* of the print. For single isolated words, UPPERcase appears to be as good as if not better than lowercase print, as for example, the label of an "on" switch. This advantage results in part because of the wider visual angle and lower spatial frequency presented. However, for multiword text, UPPERCASE PRINT IS MORE DIFFICULT TO READ than lowercase or mixed-case text. This is because lowercase text typically offers a greater variety of *word shapes.* This variety conveys sensory information at lower spatial frequencies that can be used to discern some aspects of word meaning in parallel with the high spatial frequency analysis of the individual letters (Broadbent & Broadbent, 1980; Allen, Wallace, & Weber, 1995). BLOCKED WORDS IN ALL CAPITALS will eliminate the contributions of this lower spatial frequency channel. Other guidelines for text size and font type may be found in Sanders and McCormick (1993) or Salvendy (1997).

Color Sensation

As you will recall, color vision is a facility employed in the well-illuminated environment. Our driver had trouble judging the color of his red sedan because of the poor illumination in the parking lot. A second characteristic that limits the effectiveness of color is the fact that approximately 7 percent of the male population is *color deficient;* that is, they are unable to discriminate certain hues from each other. Most prevalent here is so-called red-green "color blindness" *(protanopia),* in which the wavelengths of these two hues create identical sensations if they are of the same luminance intensity.

Because of these two important sensory limitations on color processing, a most important human factors guideline is to *design for monochrome first* (Shneiderman, 1987) and use color only as a redundant back up to signal important information. Thus for example the traffic signal uses the *location* of the illuminated lamp (top, middle, bottom) redundantly with its color to signal the important traffic command information.

There are two additional characteristics of the sensory processing of color that have some effect on its use. *Simultaneous contrast* refers the tendency of some hues to appear different when viewed adjacent to other hues (e.g., a green will look deeper when viewed next to a red than when viewed next to a neutral gray). This may affect the usability of multicolor-coded displays, like maps, as the number of colors grows large, an issue we treat further in our discussion of absolute judgment in Chapter 8. The *negative afterimage* is a similar phenomenon to simultaneous contrast but describes the greater intensity of certain colors when viewed *after* prolonged viewing of other colors.

Night Vision

It should be apparent from our discussion above how the loss of contrast sensitivity at all spatial frequencies can inhibit the perception of print as well as the detection and recognition of objects by their shape or color in poorly illuminated viewing conditions. Coupled with the loss of contrast sensitivity due to age, it is apparent that night driving for the older population is a hazardous undertaking, particularly in unfamiliar territory (Waller, 1991; Shinar & Schieber, 1991).

Added to these hazards of night vision are those associated with *glare,* which may be defined as irrelevant light of high intensity. Beyond its annoyance and distraction properties, glare has the effect of destroying the rod's sensitivity to low spatial frequencies. Hence, the glare-subjected driver will be less able to spot the dimly illuminated road hazard (the pothole or the darkly dressed pedestrian). Furthermore, given the nature of dark adaptation, we know that this destruction will be long lived, reducing sensitivity for up to a half an hour.

A second interesting phenomenon that is characteristic of night vision on the highway is the tendency for drivers to "overspeed"—to drive faster than the speed at which they can safely stop or swerve to avoid unexpected obstacles (Leibowitz, 1988). The reason for this dangerous phenomenon relates back to the differential sensitivity and location of rods and cones. As you will recall, the rods, which are used at night, provide fairly good peripheral perception of motion. Hence, the night driver may feel fairly comfortable about his or her visual capabilities, given the strong and accurate sense of motion perceived from the "streaming" of peripherally viewed roadside elements (guardrails, vegetation, side lines, etc.). However, it is a very different visual system, often using the foveal cones, that must be brought into play to detect and recognize the unexpected object that must be avoided in the roadway (Leibowitz & Dichgans, 1980). The driver has no sense of how visible this hazard will be until it actually appears, and by then it may be too late. In short, calibration of safe driving speed on the basis of continuous motion of the side elements will dangerously overestimate the distance at which objects in foveal vision can be seen. We consider more aspects of night driving safety in Chapter 17.

BOTTOM-UP VERSUS TOP-DOWN PROCESSING

Up to now, we have discussed primarily the factors of the human visual system that effect the *quality* of the sensory information that arrives at the brain in order to be perceived. As represented in Figure 4.6, we may represent these influences

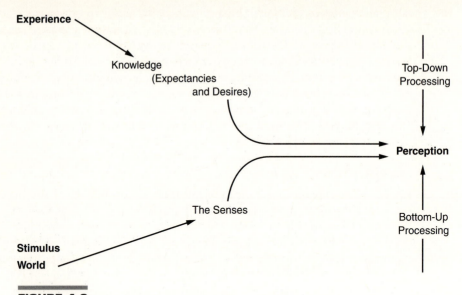

FIGURE 4.6

The relation between bottom-up and top-down processing.

as those that effect processing from the *bottom* (lower levels of stimulus processing) *upward* (toward the higher centers of the brain involved with perception and understanding). As examples, we may describe loss of acuity as a degradation in bottom-up processing or describe high-contrast sensitivity as an enhancement of that processing.

In contrast, an equally important influence on processing may be said to operate from the *top down*ward. This is perception based on our knowledge (and desire) of what *should be* there. Thus, if I read the instructions, "After the procedure is completed, turn the system off," I need not worry as much if the last word happens to be printed in very small letters or is visible with low contrast because I can pretty much guess what it will say. As we see below and in the following chapters, much of our processing of perceptual information depends on the delicate interplay between top-down processing, signaling what *should be* there, and bottom-up processing, signaling what *is* there. Deficiencies in one can often be compensated by the operation of the other. Our initial introduction into the interplay between these two modes of processing will be in a discussion of depth perception, and the two modes will be amplified further in our treatment of detection.

DEPTH PERCEPTION

Humans navigate and manipulate in a three-dimensional (3-D) world, and we usually do so quite accurately and automatically. Yet there are times when our ability to perceive where we and other things are in 3-D space breaks down. In our story at the beginning of the chapter, for example, the driver underestimated the speed with which he was moving *toward* the next intersection; that is, he underestimated his change in distance from the intersection over time. Airplane pilots flying without using their instruments are also very susceptible to dangerous illusions of where they are in 3-D space and how fast they are moving through that space (O'Hare & Roscoe, 1990; Hawkins, 1993; Leibowitz, 1988).

In order to judge our distance from objects (and the distance between objects) in 3-D space, we rely on a host of *depth cues* to inform us of how far away things are. The first three cues we will discuss—accommodation, binocular convergence, and binocular disparity—are all inherent in the physiological structuring and wiring of the visual sensory system. Hence, they may be said to operate on *bottom-up* processing.

Accommodation, as we have seen, refers to the changing shape of the lens to accommodate the focus on objects viewed at different distances. As shown in Figure 4.3, the ciliary muscles that accomplish this change send signals to the higher perceptual centers of the brain that inform those centers of how much accommodation was accomplished and hence the extent to which objects are close or far (within a range of about 3 m). (As we will discuss in Chapter 5, these signals from the muscles to the brain are referred to as *proprioceptive input.*)

Convergence is a corresponding cue based on the amount of inward rotation ("cross-eyedness") that the muscles in the eyeball must accomplish to bring an image to rest on corresponding parts of the retina on the two eyes. The closer the distance at which the image is viewed, the greater is the amount of proprioceptive "convergence signal" sent to the higher brain centers by the neurons that control these muscles.

Binocular Disparity, sometimes referred to as *stereopsis,* is a depth cue that results because the closer an object is to the observer, the greater the amount of disparity there is between the view of the object received by each eyeball. Hence, the brain can use this disparity measure, computed soon after the visual signals from the two eyes combine in the brain, to estimate how far away the object is.

All three of these bottom-up cues are only effective for judging distance, slant, and speed for objects that are within a few meters from the viewer (Cutting et al, 1995). (However, stereopsis can be created in stereoscopic displays to simulate depth information at much greater distances.) Judgment of depth and distance for more distant objects and surfaces depends on a host of what are sometimes called "pictorial" cues because they are the kinds of cues that artists will put into pictures to convey a sense of depth. Because pictorial cues are based on past experience, they are subject to top-down influences.

As shown in Figure 4.7, some of the important pictorial cues to depth are:

Linear perspective: The converging of parallel lines (i.e., the road) toward the more distant points.

Relative size: A cue based on the knowledge that if two objects are the same true size (the two trucks in the figure, e.g.), the object that occupies a smaller visual angle (the more distant vehicle in the figure) is farther away.

Interposition: Nearer objects will tend to obscure the contours of objects that are farther away (see the two buildings).

Light and shading: Three-dimensional objects will tend to both cast shadows, and reveal reflections and shadows on themselves from illuminating light. These shadows provide evidence as to their location and their 3-D form (Ramachandran, 1988).

Textural gradients: Any textured surface, viewed from an oblique angle, will show a gradient or change in texture density (spatial frequency) across the visual field (see the Illinois cornfield in the figure). The finer texture signals the more distant region, and the amount of texture change per unit visual angle, signals the angle of slant, relative to the line of sight.

Relative motion, or *motion parallax* describes the fact that objects that are more distant will show relatively smaller movement across the visual field as the observer moves. Thus, we often move our head back and forth to judge the relative distance of objects. Relative motion also accounts for the accelerating growth in the retinal image size of things as we approach them in space, a cue sometimes called *looming* (Regan et al., 1986).

Collectively, these cues provide us with a very rich sense of our position and motion in 3-D space as long as the world through which we move is well illuminated and contains rich visual texture. However, when cues are degraded, impoverished, or eliminated by darkness or other unusual viewing circumstances, depth perception can be distorted. This sometimes leads to dangerous circumstances. For example, the pilot flying at night or over an untextured snow cover has very poor visual cues to inform him or her of where he or she is relative to the ground

FIGURE 4.7
Some pictorial depth cues. (*Source:* Wickens, C.D., 1992. *Engineering psychology and human performance.* New York: HarperCollins. Reprinted by permission of Addison Wesley Educational Publishers, Inc.)

(O'Hare & Roscoe, 1990), and so assistance *must* be offered by (and accepted from) more precise flight instruments (see Chapter 8). Correspondingly, the implementation of both edge markers and high-angle lighting on highways greatly enriches the cues available for speed (changing position in depth) and for the judgments of distance of hazards and as a result allows for safer driving (see Chapter 17). In Chapter 8 we will discuss how this information is useful for the design of three-dimensional displays.

Just as we may predict poorer performance in tasks that demand depth judgments when the quality of depth cues is impoverished, so too we can also predict certain *distortions* of perception, resulting when features of the world violate our expectations and top-down processing takes over to give us an inappropriate perception. For example, Eberts and MacMillan (1985) established that the higher-than-average rate at which small cars are hit from behind results because of the cue of relative size. A small car is perceived as more distant from the observer approaching it from the rear than it really is. Hence, the small car will be approached faster (and braking will begin later) than is appropriate.

Of course, clever application of human factors can sometimes turn these distortions to advantage, as in the case of the redesign of a dangerous traffic circle in Scotland (Denton, 1980). Drivers were tending to overspeed when coming into the traffic circle with a high accident rate as a consequence. In suggesting a solution, Denton decided to "trick" the driver's perceptual system by drawing lines of diminishing separation across the roadway, as seen in Figure 4.8. Approaching the circle at a constant (and excessive) speed, the driver will experience the "flow" of texture past the vehicle as signaling increasing in speed (i.e., accelerating). Because of the near automatic way in which many aspects of perception are carried out, the driver should instinctively brake in response to the perceived acceleration, bringing the speed closer to the desired safe value. This is exactly the effect that was observed in relation to driving behavior after the marked pavement was introduced,

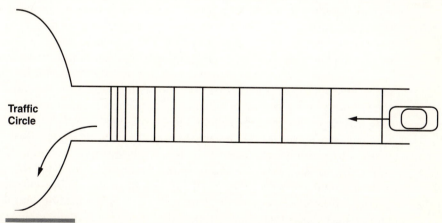

FIGURE 4.8

Technique used by Denton (1980) to slow down vehicles approaching the traffic circle (driving from right to left in the figure).

resulting in a substantial reduction in fatal accidents at the traffic circle, a result that has been sustained for several years (Godley, 1997).

VISUAL SEARCH AND DETECTION

A critical aspect of human performance in many systems concerns the closely linked processes of visual search and detection. Our driver at the beginning of the chapter was searching for several things: the appropriate control for the wipers, the needed road sign, and of course any number of possible hazards or obstacles that could appear on the road (the pothole was one that was missed). The goal of these searches was to *detect* the object or thing in question. These tasks are analogous to the kind of processes we go through when we search the phone book for the pizza delivery listing, search the index of this book for a needed topic, search a cluttered graph for a data point, or when the quality control inspector searches the product (say a circuit board) for a flaw. In all cases, the search may or may not successfully end in a detection.

Despite the close linking between search and detection, it is important to separate our treatment of these topics, both because different factors affect each and because human factors personnel are sometimes interested in detection when there is no search (e.g., the detection of a fire alarm). We consider below the process of search itself, but to understand visual search, we must first consider the nature of eye movements. Then we consider the process of detection.

Eye Movements

Eye movements are necessary to search the visual field (Monty & Senders, 1976; Hallett, 1986). Eye movements can generally be divided into two major classes. *Pursuit* movements are those of constant velocity that are designed to follow moving targets, for example, following the rapid flight of an aircraft across the sky. More related to visual search are *saccadic* eye movements, which are abrupt discrete movements from one location to the next. Each saccadic movement can be characterized by a set of critical features: an *initiation latency,* a *destination,* a *movement time (or speed),* a *dwell duration,* and a *useful field of view.* In continuous search, the initiation latency and the dwell duration cannot be distinguished.

The actual movement time is generally quite fast (typically less than 50 msec) and is not much greater for longer than shorter movements. Instead, the greatest time is spent during dwells and initiations. These limits are such that, even in rapid search, there are no more than about 3 to 4 dwells per second (Moray, 1986), and this frequency is usually lower because of variables that prolong the dwell. The destination of a scan is usually driven by top-down processes (i.e., expectancy), although on occasion a saccade may be drawn by salient bottom-up processes (e.g., a flashing light, see below). The dwell duration is governed jointly by two factors: (1) the *information content* of the item fixated (e.g., when reading, long words require longer dwells than short ones), and (2) the ease of *information extraction,* which is often influenced by stimulus quality (e.g., in target search, longer dwells on a degraded target). Finally, once the eyes have landed a saccade on a particular location, the useful field of view defines how large an area, surrounding the center of fixation, is available for information extraction (Sanders, 1970; Ball et al., 1988). The UFOV defines the diameter of the region within which a target might be detected, if it is present.

The useful field of view should be carefully distinguished from the area of *foveal vision,* defined earlier in the chapter. Foveal vision defines a specific area of approximately 2 degrees of visual angle surrounding the center of fixation, which provides high visual acuity and low sensitivity. The diameter of the useful field of view, in contrast, is task dependent. It may be quite small if the operator is searching for very subtle targets but may be much larger than the fovea if the targets are conspicuous and can be easily detected in peripheral vision.

Recent developments in technology have produced more efficient means of measuring eye movements with *oculometers.* These function by measuring the orientation of the eyeball relative to an image plane and can therefore be used to infer the precise destination of a saccade.

Visual Search

The Serial Search Model. In describing the operator searching any visual field for something, we distinguish between *targets* and *nontargets* (nontargets are sometimes called *distractors*). The latter may be thought of as "visual noise" that has to be inspected in order to determine that it is not in fact the desired target. Many searches are *serial,* in that each item is inspected in turn to determine whether it is or is not a target. If each inspection takes a relatively constant time and the expected location of the target is unknown beforehand, then it is possible to predict the average time it will take to find the target as:

$$T = (NXI)/2, \tag{4.4}$$

where I is the average inspection time for each item, and N is the total number of items in the search field (Neisser, Novick, & Lazar, 1964). Because, *on the average,* the target will be encountered after *half* of the targets have been inspected (sometimes earlier, sometimes later), the product (NXI) is divided by two. This serial search model has been applied to the prediction of performance in numerous environments in which people are searching through lists, such as phone books or computer menus (Lee & MacGregor, 1985).

If the visual search space is organized coherently, people tend to search from top to bottom and left to right. However, if the space does not benefit from such organization (e.g., searching a map for a target or searching the ground below the aircraft for a downed airplane [Stagar & Angus, 1978]), then people's searches tend to be considerably more random in structure and do not "exhaustively" examine all locations (Wickens, 1992; Stagar & Angus, 1978). If targets are not readily visible, this nonexhaustive characteristic leads to a search-time function that looks like that shown in Figure 4.9 (Drury, 1975). Note that the figure suggests that there are diminishing returns associated with giving people too long to search a given area if time is at a premium.

Search models can be extremely important in human factors (Brogan, 1993) for predicting search time in time-critical environments; for example, how long

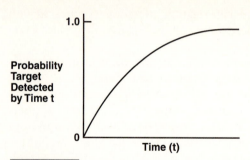

FIGURE 4.9
Predicted search success probability as a function of the time spent searching. (*Source:*
Adapted from Drury, C., 1975. Inspection of sheet metal: Models and data. Reprinted with
permission from *Human Factors, 17.* Copyright 1975 by the Human Factors and
Ergonomics Society.)

will a driver keep eyes off the highway to search for a road sign? Unfortunately,
however, there are two important circumstances that can render the strict serial
model inappropriate, one related to bottom-up processing and the other to top-
down processing. Both factors force models of visual search to become more
complex and less precise.

Conspicuity.   The bottom-up influence is the *conspicuity* of the target. Certain targets are so conspicuous that they may "pop out" no matter where they are in the
visual field, and so nontarget items need not be inspected (Yantis, 1993; Treisman,
1986). Psychologists describe the search for such targets as *parallel* because, in
essence, all items are examined at once, and in contrast to the equation 4.3, search
time does not increase with the total number of items. Such is normally the case
with "attention grabbers" as, for example, a flashing warning signal, a moving target, or a uniquely colored, highlighted item on a checklist.

Conspicuity is a desirable property if the task requires the target to be processed,
but an undesirable one if the conspicuous item is irrelevant to the task at hand. Thus,
if I am designing a checklist that highlights emergency items in red, this may help
the operator in responding to emergencies but will be a distraction if the operator
is using the list to guide normal operating instructions; that is, it will be more difficult to focus attention on the normal instructions. As a result of these dual consequences of conspicuity, the choice of highlighting (and the effectiveness of its
implementation) must be guided by a careful analysis of the likelihood that the user
will *need* the highlighted item as a target (Fisher & Tan, 1989). Table 4.4 lists some
key variables that can influence the conspicuity of targets and, therefore, the likelihood that the field in which they are embedded will be searched in parallel.

Expectancies.   The second influence on visual search that leads to departures from
the serial model has to do with the top-down implications of *searcher expectancies*
of where the target might be likely to lie. Our driver did not expect to see the road
sign on the left of the highway and, as a result, only found it after it was too late. As
another example, when searching a phone book we do not usually blanket the en-

TABLE 4.4 Target Properties Inducing Parallel Search

1. Discriminability from background elements.
    a. In color (particularly if nontarget items are uniformly colored)
    b. In size (particularly if the target is larger)
    c. In brightness (particularly if the target is brighter)
    d. In motion (particularly if background is stationary)

2. Simplicity: Can the target be defined only by one dimension (i.e., "red") and not several (i.e., "red and small")

3. Automaticity: a target that is highly familiar (e.g., one's own name)

Note that unique *shapes* (e.g., letters, numbers) do not generally support parallel search (Treisman, 1986).

tire page with fixations, but our *knowledge* of the alphabet allows us to start the search near or around the spelling of the target name that we want. Similarly, when searching an index, we often have a hypothesis about what the topic is likely to be called, which guides our starting point. In a very different domain, it has been found that radiologists, searching an x-ray plate for a tumor, will start their search in the region believed most likely to contain the tumor (Parasuraman, 1986).

It is important to realize that these expectancies only come with experience. Hence, we might predict that the skilled operator will have more top-down processes driving visual search than the unskilled one, and as a result will be more efficient, a conclusion born out by research (Parasuraman, 1986). These top-down influences also provide guidance for designers who develop search fields such as indexes and menu pages, to understand the subjective orderings and groupings of the items that users have. This topic will be addressed again in Chapter 15.

Conclusion.   In conclusion, research on visual search has four general implications, all of which are important in system design.

   1. Knowledge of conspicuity effects can lead the designer to try to enhance the visibility of target items (consider, for example, reflective jogging suits [Owens et al., 1994] or highlighting critical menu items).

   2. Knowledge of the serial aspects of many visual search processes should forewarn the designer about the costs of *cluttered* displays (or search environments). When too much information is present many maps present an extraordinary amount of clutter. For electronic displays, this fact should lead to consideration of *decluttering* options in which certain categories of information can be electronically either turned off or deintensified (Mykityshyn, Kuchar, & Hansman, 1994; Schultz, Nickols, & Curran, 1985; Stokes, Wickens, & Kite, 1990). However, careful use of color and intensity as discriminating cues between different classes of information can make decluttering unnecessary.

   3. Knowledge of the role of top-down processing in visual search should lead the designer to make the *structure* of the search field as apparent to the user as possible and consistent with the user's knowledge (i.e., past experience). For verbal information, this may involve an alphabetical organization or one based on the semantic similarity of items (Somberg, 1987). In positioning road signs, this will involve the use of *consistent* placement.

4. Knowledge of all of these influences can lead to the development of *models* of visual search that will predict how long it will take to find particular targets, such as the flaw in a piece of sheet metal (Drury, 1975), an item on a computer menu (Lee & MacGregor, 1985; Fisher & Tan, 1989), or a traffic sign by a highway (Theeuwes, 1994). For visual search, however, the major challenge of such models resides in the fact that search appears to be guided much more by top-down processes than by bottom-up ones (Theeuwes, 1994), and developing precise mathematical terms to characterize the level of expertise necessary to support top-down processing is a major challenge.

Detection

Once a possible target is located in visual search, it then becomes necessary to *confirm* that it really is the item of interest (i.e., *detect* it). This process may be trivial if the target is well known and reasonably visible (e.g., the name on a list), but it is far from trivial if the target is degraded, like a faint flaw in a piece of sheet metal, a small crack in an x-rayed bone, or the faint glimmer of the lighthouse on the horizon at sea. In these cases, we must describe the operator's ability to *detect signals*. Indeed signal detection is often critical even when there is no visual search at all. For example, the quality-control inspector may have only one place to look to examine the product for a defect. Similarly, the ability to detect a flashing warning light is far less influenced by where it is in the visual field than by other factors that we describe below.

Signal Detection Theory.   In any of a variety of tasks, the process of signal detection can be modeled by *signal detection theory* (SDT) (Swets, Tanner, & Birdsall, 1961; Green & Swets, 1988; Swets, 1996). SDT assumes that "the world" (as it is relevant to the operator's task) can be modeled as either one in which the "signal" to be detected is present or is absent (Fig. 4.10). Whether the signal is present or absent, the world is assumed to contain "noise." Thus, the luggage inspected by the airport security guard may contain a weapon (signal) in addition to a number of things that might look like weapons (i.e., the "noise" of hair blowers, calculators, carabiners, etc.), or it may contain the "noise" alone.

The goal of the operator in detecting signals is actually to *discriminate* signals from noise. Thus, we may describe the relevant behavior of the observer as that represented by the two rows of Figure 4.10—saying "yes (I see a signal)" or "no (there is only noise)." This combination of two states of the world and two responses yields four joint events shown as the four cells of the figure that are labeled *hits, false alarms, misses,* and *correct rejections*. As shown in the figure, two of these cells (hits and correct rejections) clearly represent "good" outcomes and *should* ideally characterize much of the performance, while two are "bad" (misses and false alarms) and, ideally should never occur.

If several encounters with the state of the world (signal detection trials) are aggregated, some involving signals and some involving noise alone, we may then

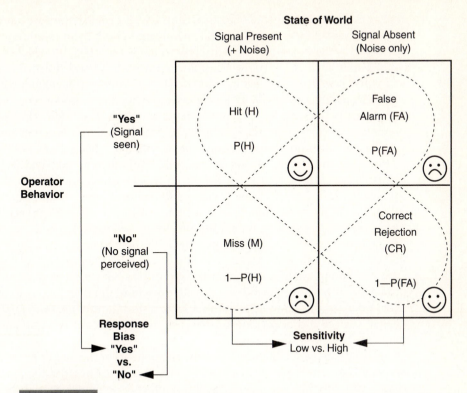

State of World

FIGURE 4.10

Representation of the outcomes in signal detection theory. The figure shows how changes in the four joint events within the matrix, influence the primary performance measures of response bias and sensitivity, shown at the bottom.

express the numbers within each cell as the *probability* of a hit [#hits/#signals = p(hit)]; the *probability* of a miss [$1 - p$(hit)]; the probability of a false alarm [#FA/#no-signal encounters]; and the probability of a correct rejection [$1 - p(FA)$]. In other words, if the values of p(hit) and $p(FA)$ are measured, the other two cells contain entirely redundant information.

Thus, the data from a signal detection environment (e.g., the performance of an airport security inspector) may easily be represented in the form of the matrix shown in Figure 4.10 if a large number of trials are observed so that the probabilities can be reliably estimated. However, SDT considers these same numbers in terms of two fundamentally different *influences* on human detection performance: *sensitivity* and *response bias*. Following the terminology introduced earlier in this chapter, we can think of these two as reflecting bottom-up and top-down processes, respectively.

Sensitivity and Response Bias.   As Figure 4.10 shows, the measure of sensitivity, often expressed by the measure d′ ("d prime") expresses how *good* an operator is at the signal detection task, reflecting essentially the number of "good" outcomes relative to the total number of outcomes. Sensitivity is higher, if there are more correct responses and fewer errors. It will be influenced both by the keenness of the senses and by the strength of the signal relative to the noise (i.e., the *signal-to-noise ratio*). For example, sensitivity will usually improve with experience on the job up to a point; it will be degraded by poor viewing conditions (including poor eyesight). An alert inspector will have a higher sensitivity than a drowsy one. The formal calculation of sensitivity will not be discussed in this book. However, Table 4.5 presents some values of d′ that might be observed from signal detection analysis.

The measure of response bias, or *response criterion*, reflects the *bias* of the operator to respond "yes, signal" versus "no, noise." Although formal signal detection theory characterizes response bias by the term *Beta*, which has a technical measurement (Green & Swets, 1988; Wickens, 1992), one can more simply express response bias as the probability that the operator will respond "yes" [p(yes)/(Total Responses)]. Response bias is typically affected by two variables, both characteristic of top-down processing. First, increases in the operator's *expectancy* that a signal will be seen will lead to corresponding increases in the probability of saying "yes." For example, if a quality-control inspector has knowledge that a "batch" of products may have been made on a defective machine and therefore may contain a lot of defects, this knowledge should lead to a shift in response criterion to say "signal" (defective product) more often. The consequences of this shift are both more hits *and* more false alarms.

Second, changes in the *values* or costs and benefits of the four different kinds of events shown in Figure 4.10 can also shift the criterion. The air traffic controller cannot afford to miss detecting a signal (a conflict between two aircraft) because of the potentially disastrous consequences of a midair collision (Bisseret, 1981). As a result the controller will set the response criterion at such a level that misses are very rare, but the consequences are that the less costly "false alarms" are more frequent. (In representing the air traffic controller as a signal detector, these false alarms are circumstances when the controller detects a potentially conflicting path and redirects one of the aircraft to change its flight course even if this was not necessary.)

TABLE 4.5   Some Values of d′

P (hit)	P (false alarm)					
	0.01	*0.02*	*0.05*	*0.10*	*0.20*	*0.30*
0.51	2.34	2.08	1.66	1.30	0.86	0.55
0.60	2.58	2.30	1.90	1.54	1.10	0.78
0.70	2.84	2.58	2.16	1.80	1.36	1.05
0.80	3.16	2.89	2.48	2.12	1.68	1.36
0.90	3.60	3.33	2.92	2.56	2.12	1.80
0.95	3.96	3.69	3.28	2.92	2.48	2.16
0.99	4.64	4.37	3.96	3.60	3.16	2.84

Source: Selected values from *Signal Detection and Recognition by Human Observers* (Appendix 1, Table 1) by J. A. Swets, 1969, New York: Wiley. Copyright 1969 by John Wiley & Sons, Inc. Reproduced by permission.

Interventions and Vigilance. The reason why the distinction between sensitivity and response criterion made by SDT is so important is because it allows the human factors practitioner to understand the consequences of different kinds of interventions that may be intended to improve detection performance in a variety of circumstances. For example, any instructions that "exhort" operators to "be more vigilant" and not miss signals will probably increase the hit rate but will also show a corresponding increase in false-alarm rate. This is because the instruction is a motivational one reflecting costs and values, which typically affects the setting of the response criterion. (Financially rewarding hits will have the same effect.) Correspondingly, it has been found that directing the radiologist's attention to a particular area of an x-ray plate where an abnormality is likely to be found will tend to shift the response criterion for detecting abnormalities at that location but will not increase the sensitivity (Swennsen, Hessel, & Herman, 1977). Hence, the value of such interventions must consider the relative costs of hits and false alarms.

However, there are certain things that *can* be done that do have a more desirable direct influence on increasing sensitivity. As we have noted, training the operator for what a signal looks like can improve sensitivity. So also can providing the inspector with a "visual template" of the potential signal that can be compared with each case that is examined (Kelly, 1955). Several other forms of interventions to influence signal detection and their effects on sensitivity or response bias are shown in Table 4.6. These are described in more detail in Wickens (1992). We will describe in Chapter 5 how signal detection theory is also important in the design of alarms.

Human factors personnel have been particularly interested in signal detection theory in *vigilance* tasks when the operator must sustain visual attention toward the source of the target for periods of 15 to 20 minutes or more. This interest is shown because inspectors appear to show a *decrement* in vigilance performance (a loss of hits) that builds up over the time on watch. This performance loss is referred to as the *vigilance decrement* (Parasuraman, Warm, & Dember, 1987). This

---

TABLE 4.6 Influences on Signal Detection Performance

Payoffs (typically influence response bias)

Introducing "false signals" to raise signal rate artificially [response bias: P (yes) increase]

Providing incentives and exhortations (response bias)

Providing knowledge of results (usually increases sensitivity, but may calibrate response bias if it provides observer with more accurate perception of probability of signal)

Slowing down the rate of signal presentation (slowing the assembly line) (increase sensitivity)

Differentially amplifying the signal (more than the noise) (increases sensitivity)

Making the signal dynamic (increases sensitivity)

Giving frequent rest breaks (increases sensitivity)

Providing a visual (or audible) template of the signal (increases sensitivity)

Providing experience seeing the signal (increases sensitivity)

Providing redundant representations of the signal (increases sensitivity)

decrement can be observed whether the signals are visual (e.g., a night security guard) or auditory (e.g., a sonar watch). For inspectors on an assembly line, the long-term decrement in performance may be substantial, sometimes leading to miss rates as high as 30–40 percent. The guidance offered in Table 4.6 suggests some of the ways in which these deficiencies might be addressed. To emphasize the point made above, however, it is important for the human factors practitioner to realize that any intervention that influences response criterion to increase hits will have a consequent increase in false alarms. Hence, it should be accepted that the costs of these false alarms are less severe than the costs of misses.

Special Topic: Midair Target Detection

In 1987, two planes collided in midair near San Diego, killing both occupants of the light Cessna and all passengers aboard the commercial aircraft. Both planes were flying in reasonably good weather, and at least one aircraft should have been able to see the other in the forward view. So why did they collide? It turns out that midair target search and detection is a task that imposes on several of the vulnerabilities of human visual processing that we have discussed above. Let us consider some of the reasons:

First the midair targets (another aircraft in space) are usually quite inconspicuous, occupying a small visual angle even as they may represent very real threat. (Two aircraft flying directly toward each other at cruising speed will can be over a mile apart as little as 5 seconds before they collide. Viewed from a mile away, an aircraft will occupy a very small visual angle.) Second, the most *dangerous* targets those on a collision course are those that will show no relative movement across the visual field. Hence, the added conspicuity of movement, which is particularly helpful in peripheral vision where acuity is low, will be missing when the targets represent the greatest danger. Third, the target may be camouflaged, as viewed either against the "noisy" background of clouds or the mottled earth below. Hence, a search for that target will be serial, with many distractors. Fourth, if visual attention has been recently directed into the cockpit, the pilot's state of visual accommodation will not be appropriate for resolving the high spatial frequency of the tiny distant target, thereby losing sensitivity. Finally, although all of the above have degrading effects on bottom-up signal quality, there are circumstances in which top-down processes of expectancy may inhibit detection; for example, when flying in an uncrowded airspace, where little other traffic is anticipated, the pilot will be likely to set a very "conservative" response criterion and will be unlikely to detect the signal.

Fortunately, help is available from three sources to protect the pilot from this extreme vulnerability. First, pilot training places tremendous importance on teaching a regular out-the-window scan pattern (although we have seen that such visual search fails to blanket exhaustively the region to be searched). Second, air traffic control often assumes responsibility for maintaining safe separation between other aircraft (see Chapter 16). Third, an *automated monitoring device* known as the *Traffic Alert and Collision Avoidance System* (TCAS) has been developed to replace, or at least augment, the pilot's eyes by assessing the air space for nearby traffic and representing this clearly on a display with salient warnings presented when a "neighbor" appears to be on a conflict path (Chappell, 1989, 1990). This example of automation, developed to address the vulnerabilities of human performance, is relevant to an issue we shall consider in much greater detail in Chapter 16, pointing out its potential weaknesses as well as its strengths. However, for now, TCAS appears to be a nice example of a well-researched human factors solution, designed to address key limits of human sensory performance.

DISCRIMINATION

Very often, issues in human visual sensory performance are based on the ability to *discriminate* between one of two signals rather than to *detect* the existence of a signal. Our driver was able to *see* the road sign (detect it) but, in the brief view with dim illumination, failed to discriminate whether the road number was "60" or "66" (or in another case perhaps, whether the exit arrow pointed left or right). He was also clearly confused over whether the car color was red or brown. Confusion, the failure to discriminate, results whenever stimuli are similar. Even fairly different stimuli, when viewed under degraded conditions, can produce confusion. As one example, it is believed that one cause of the crash of a commercial jet liner in Europe was the fact that the automated setting that controlled its flight path angle with the ground (3.3 degrees) looked so very similar to the automated setting that controlled its vertical speed (3,300 ft/sec) (Billings, 1966; see Fig. 4.11a). As a result, pilots could easily have confused the two, thinking that they had "dialed in" the 3.3-degree angle when in fact they had set the 3,300 ft/min vertical speed (which is a much more rapid decent rate than that given by the 3.3-degree angle). Gopher and Donchin (1986) have pointed out the dangers in medicine that results from the extreme visual similarity of very different prescription doses or different fluids delivered to a patient. The danger of confusing similar drug names is illustrated by the existence of drug pairs like capastat and cepastat, mesantoin and metinon, and Norflox and Norflex, each having different health implications for prescriptions, yet being quite similar in terms of visual appearance. Such possible confusions are likely to be amplified when the prescription is filtered through the physician's (often illegible) handwriting.

Thus, it is important for the designer of either controls that must be reached and manipulated or of displays that must be interpreted to consider the alternative controls (or displays) that *could* be activated. Can they be adequately discriminated? Are they far enough apart in space or distinguished by other features like color, shape, or other labels so that confusion will not occur? It is important to remember, however, that if only verbal labels are used to discriminate the displays or controls from each other, then attention *must* be given to the visibility and readability issues discussed above. We discuss the issue of discrimination and confusion further, as we address the issue of displays in Chapter 8.

ABSOLUTE JUDGMENT

As we have seen, discrimination refers to judgment of differences between two sources of information that are actually (or potentially) present, and generally people are very good at this task, as long as the differences are not small and the viewing conditions are favorable. In contrast, *absolute judgment* refers to the very limited human capability to *judge* the absolute value of a variable signaled by a coded stimulus. If I am asked to estimate the height of the bar graph in Figure 4.12

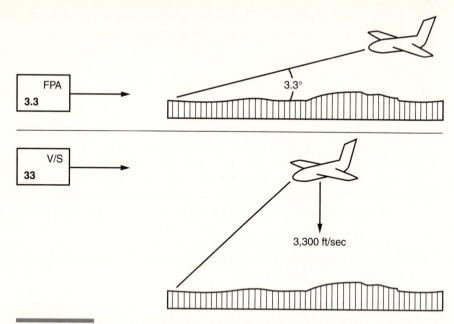

FPA
3.3

3.3°

V/S
33

3,300 ft/sec

FIGURE 4.11

Illustrates the confusion in the automated setting feedback believed to have contributed to the cause of a commercial airline crash. The pilots believed the top condition to exist, when in fact, the bottom existed. The display illustrating the two conditions was very similar, and hence the two were quite confusable.

to the nearest digit, I am performing an absolute judgment task with ten levels. Correspondingly, if I am asked to judge the color of a traffic signal (ignoring its spatial position), this is an absolute judgment task with only three levels of stimulus value. People are not generally very good at these absolute value judgments of attaching "labels to levels." (Wickens, 1992) It appears that they can only be guaranteed to do so accurately if fewer than around five different levels of any sensory continuum are used (Miller, 1956) and that people are even worse when making absolute value judgments in some sensory continua like pitch, sound loudness, or the saltiness of taste; that is, even with five levels they may be likely to make a mistake, such as confusing level three with level four.

The lessons of these absolute judgment limitations for the designer are that the number of levels that should be judged on the basis of some absolute coding scheme, like position on a line or color of a light, should be chosen conservatively. It is recommended, for example, that no more than seven colors be used if precise accuracy in judgment is required (and an adjacent color scale for comparison is not available); even this guideline should be made more stringent under potentially adverse viewing conditions (e.g., a map that is read in poor illumination). In designing the density of markings on a scale, one should not assume that the scale will be read more accurately than at half the distance between markers. For example, on the scale shown in Figure 4.12, one should not assume that the scale will be read more accurately than every five units.

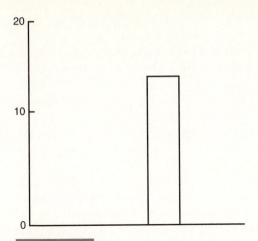

FIGURE 4.12

Absolute value task: Read the height of the bar graph to the nearest digit. The observer is asked to judge the absolute value of the bar graph top, along the unmarked scale between 10 and 20.

CONCLUSION

In conclusion, we have seen in this chapter how limits of the visual system influence the nature of the visual information that arrives at the brain for more elaborate perceptual interpretation. Indeed we have also begun to consider some aspects of this interpretation, as we consider top-down influences like expectancy, learning, and values. In the next chapter, we consider similar issues regarding the processing of auditory and other sensory information. Together, these chapters then describe the sensory processing of the "raw" ingredients for the more elaborative perceptual and cognitive aspects of understanding the world. Once we have addressed these issues in Chapter 6, we are then able to consider how all of this knowledge—of bottom-up sensory processing, perception, and understanding—can guide the design of *displays* that will support tasks confronting the human user. This will be the focus of Chapter 8.

REFERENCES

Allen, P.A., Wallace, B., and Weber, T.A., (1995). Influence of case type, word frequency, and exposure duration on visual word recognition. *Journal of Experimental Psychology: Human Perception and Performance, 21* (4) 914–934.

Ball, K.K., Beard, B.L., Roenker, D.L., Miller, R.L., and Griggs, D.S. (1988). Age and visual search: Expanding the useful field of view. *J. Opt. Soc. Am. A., 5*(12), 2210–2219.

Billings, C. (1966). *Toward a human centered approach to automation.* Englewood Cliffs, NJ: Lawrence Erlbaum.

Bisseret, A. (1981). Application of signal detection theory to decision making in supervisory control. *Ergonomics, 24,* 81–94.

Boff, K., and Lincoln, J. (1988). *Engineering data compendium.* Wright-Patterson AFB, OH: Harry Armstrong Aerospace Medical Res. Lab.

Broadbent, D., and Broadbent, M.H. (1980). Priming and the passive/active model of word recognition. In R. Nickerson (ed.), *Attention and performance, VIII.* New York: Academic Press.

Brogan, D., (ed.) (1993). *Visual search 2: Proceedings of the second international conference on visual search.* London: Taylor and Francis.

Chappell, S.L. (1989). Avoiding a maneuvering aircraft with TCAS. *Proceedings of the Fifth International Symposium on Aviation Psychology.* Columbus, OH: Dept. of Aviation, Ohio State University.

Chappell, S.L. (1990). Pilot performance research for TCAS. *Managing the Modern Cockpit: Third Human Error Avoidance Techniques Conference Proceedings* (pp. 51–68). Warrendale, PA: Society of Automotive Engineers.

Cutting, J.E., and Vishton, P.M. (1995). Perceiving layout and knowing distances: The integration, relative potency, and contextual use of different information about depth. In W. Epstein and S.J. Rogers, eds., *Handbook of Percepton and Cognition: Volume 5, Perception of Space and Motion.* New York: Academic Press.

Denton, G.G. (1980). The influence of visual pattern on perceived speed. *Perception, 9,* 393–402.

Drury, C. (1975). Inspection of sheet metal: Model and data. *Human Factors, 17,* 257–265.

Eberts, R.E., and MacMillan, A.G. (1985). Misperception of small cars. In R.E. Eberts and C.G. Eberts (eds.), *Trends in ergonomics/human factors II* (pp. 33–39). Amsterdam: Elsevier Sci. Pubs.

Evans, L. (1991) *Traffic safety and the driver.* New York: Van Nostrand.

Fisher, D.L., and Tan, K.C. (1989). Visual displays: The highlighting paradox. *Human Factors, 31*(1), 17–30.

Godley, S. (1997). Perceptual countermeasures for speeding: Theory, literature review and empirical research. In D. Harris (ed.), *Engineering psychology and cognitive ergonomics.* Brookfield, VT: Ashgate.

Gopher, D., and Donchin, D. (1986). Workload—An examination of the concept. In K.R. Boff, L. Kaufman, and J.P. Thomas (eds.), *Handbook of perception and human performance, Vol. II: Cognitive processes and performance* (pp. 41-1–41-49). New York: Wiley.

Green, D.M., and Swets, J.A. (1988). *Signal detection theory and psychophysics.* New York: Wiley.

Hallett, P.E. (1986). Eye movements. In K.R. Boff, L. Kaufman, and J.P. Thomas (eds.), *Handbook of perception and human performance, Vol. 1* (pp. 10-1–10-112). New York: Wiley.

Hawkins, F.H. (1993). *Human factors in flight.* Brookfield, VT: Ashgate.

Helander, M.G. (1987). Design of visual displays. In G. Salvendy (ed.), *Handbook of human factors* (pp. 507–548). New York: Wiley.

Kelly, M.L. (1955). A study of industrial inspection by the method of paired comparisons. *Psychological Monographs, 69,* (394), 1–16.

Lee, E., and MacGregor, J. (1985). Minimizing user search time in menu retrieval systems. *Human Factors, 27*(2), 157–162.

Leibowitz, H. (1988). The human senses in flight. In E. Wiener and D. Nagel (eds.), *Human factors in aviation* (pp. 83–110). San Diego: Academic Press.

Leibowitz, H.W., and Dichgans, J. (1980). The ambient visual system and spatial orientation. *NATO AGARD Conference Proceedings No. 287: Spatial disorientation in flight: Current problems* (pp. B4-1/B4-4). Neuilly-sur-Seine, France.

Miller, G.A. (1956). The magical number seven plus or minus two: Some limits on our capacity for processing information. *Psychological Review, 63,* 81–97.

Monty, R. A., and Senders, J. W. (1976). Eye movements and psychological processes. Hillsdale, NJ:Laurence Erlbaum.

Moray, N. (1986). Monitoring behavior and supervisory control. In K. Boff, L. Kaufman, and J. Thomas (eds.), *Handbook of perception and human performance,* Vol. II. New York: Wiley.

Mykityshyn, M.G., Kuchar, J.K., and Hansman, R.J. (1994). Experimental study of electronically based instrument approach plates. The *International Journal of Aviation Psychology, 4*(2), 141–166.

Neisser, U., Novick, R., and Lazar, R. (1964). Searching for novel targets. *Perceptual and Motor Skills, 19,* 427–432.

O'Hare, D., and Roscoe, S.N. (1990). *Flightdeck performance: The human factor.* Ames, IA: Iowa State University Press.

Owens, D.P., Antonoff, R.J., and Francis, E. (1994). Biological motion and nighttime pedestrian conspicuity. *Human Factors, 36,* 718–732.

Parasuraman, R., Warm, J.S., and Dember, W.N. (1987). Vigilance: Taxonomy and utility. In L.S. Mark, J.S. Warm, and R.L. Huston (eds.), *Ergonomics and human factors* (pp. 11–31). New York: Springer-Verlag.

Parasuraman, R. (1986). Vigilance, monitoring, and search. In K. Boff, L. Kaufman, and J. Thomas (eds.), *Handbook of perception and human performance, Vol. 2: Cognitive processes and performance* (pp. 43.1–43.39). New York: Wiley.

Regan, D.M., Kaufman, L., and Lincoln, J. (1986). Motion in depth and visual acceleration. In K. Boff, L. Kaufman, and J. Thomas (eds.), *Handbook of perception and human performance* (pp. 19-1–19-46). New York: Wiley.

Ramachandran, V.S. (1988). Perceiving shape from shading. *Scientific American, 259,* 76–83.

Salvendy, G. (Ed.). (1997). *The handbook of human factors and ergonomics* (2nd ed.). New York: Wiley.

Sanders, A.F., (1970). Some aspects of the selective process in the functional visual field. *Ergonomics, 13,* 101–117.

Sanders, M.S., and McCormick, E.J. (1993). *Human factors in engineering and design* (7th ed.). New York: McGraw Hill.

Schultz, E.E., Nickols, D.A., and Curran, P.S. (1985). Decluttering methods for high density computer generated displays. *Proceedings of the 29th Annual Meeting of the Human Factors Society.* Santa Monica, CA: Human Factors Society.

Shinar, D., and Schieber, F. (1991). Visual requirements for safety and mobility of older drivers. *Human Factors, 33*(5), 507–520.

Shneiderman, B. (1987). *Designing the user interface: Strategies for effective human-computer interaction.* Reading, MA: Addison-Wesley.

Somberg, B.L. (1987). A comparison of rule-based and positionally constant arrangements of computer menu items. *Proceedings of CHI and GI '87, Conference on Human Factors in Computing Systems.* New York: Association for Computing Machinery.

Stagar, P., and Angus, R. (1978). Locating crash sites in simulated air-to-ground visual search. *Human Factors, 20,* 453–466.

Stokes, A.F., Wickens, C.D., and Kite, K. (1990). *Display technology: Human factors concepts.* Warrendale, PA: Society of Automotive Engineers.

Swennsen, R.G., Hessel, S.J., and Herman, P.G. (1977). Omissions in radiology: Faulty search or stringent reporting criteria? *Radiology, 123,* 563–567.

Swets, J.A. (1996). *Signal detection theory and ROC analysis in psychology and diagnostics.* Mahwah, NJ: Lawrence Erlbaum Associates.

Swets, J.A., Tanner, W.P., and Birdsall, T.G. (1961). Decision processes in perception. *Psychological Review, 68,* 301–340.

Theeuwes, J. (1994). Visual attention and driving behavior. In C. Santos (ed.), *Human factors in road traffic* (pp. 103–123). Lisboa, Portugal: Escher.

Treisman, A. (1986). Properties, parts, and objects. In K.R. Boff, L. Kaufman, and J.P. Thomas (eds.), *Handbook of perception and human performance.* New York: Wiley.

Uttal, W.R., Baruch, T., and Allen, L. (1994). Psychophysical foundations of a model of amplified night vision in target detection tasks. *Human Factors, 36,* 488–502.

Waller, P. (1991). The older driver. *Human Factors, 33*(5), 499–505.

Wickens, C.D. (1992). *Engineering psychology and human performance* (2nd ed.). New York: HarperCollins.

Wyszecki, C. (1986). Color appearance. In K. Boff, L. Kaufman, and J. Thomas (eds.), *Handbook of perception and human performance,* Vol I. New York: Wiley.

Yantis, S. (1993). Stimulus-driven attentional capture. *Current Directions in Psychological Science, 2,* 156–161.

CHAPTER 5

Auditory, Tactile, and Vestibular System

The worker at the small manufacturing company was becoming increasingly frustrated by the noise level at her workplace. It was unpleasant and stressful, and she came home each day with a ringing in her ears and a headache. What concerned her in particular was an incident the day before when she could not hear the emergency alarm go off on her own equipment, a failure of hearing that nearly led to an injury. Asked by her husband why she did not wear earplugs to muffle the noise, she responded: "They're uncomfortable. I'd be even less likely to hear the alarm, and besides, it would be harder to converse with the worker on the next machine, and that's one of the few pleasures I have on the job." She was relieved to hear that an inspector from Occupational Safety and Health Administration (OSHA) would be visiting the plant in the next few days to evaluate her complaints.

The worker's concerns illustrate the effects of three different types of sounds: the undesirable *noise* of the workplace, the critical *tone* of the alarm, and the important communications through *speech*. Our ability to process these three sources of acoustic information, whether we want to (alarms and speech) or not (noise), and the influence of this processing on performance, health, and comfort will be the focus of the first part of this chapter. We will then conclude by discussing three other sensory channels in less detail—tactile, proprioceptive-kinesthetic, and vestibular—that have played a smaller but significant role in the design of human-machine systems.

Our discussion of sound and hearing will consider first the nature of the stimulus input and the peripheral hearing mechanism. We then address the auditory experience, the role of sound in alarms, the role of the voice in speech communications, and finally the role of noise. In Chapter 18, we will discuss many more aspects of voice communications between people as the *content* of that communication influences group performance.

SOUND: THE AUDITORY STIMULUS

As shown in Figure 5.1a, the stimulus for hearing is sound, a vibration (actually compression and rarefaction) of the air molecules. The acoustic stimulus can therefore be represented as a sine wave, with amplitude and frequency. This is analogous to the representation of spatial frequency discussed in Chapter 3; however, the frequency in sound is played out over time rather than space. Figure 5.1b shows three frequencies, each of different values and amplitudes. These are typically plotted on a spectrum as shown in Figure 5.1c. The position of each bar along the spectrum represents the actual frequency, expressed in cycles/second or *Hertz (Hz)*. The height of the bar reflects the amplitude of the wave and is typically plotted as the square of the amplitude or the *power*.

Any given sound stimulus can be presented as a single frequency, a small set of frequencies, as shown in Figure 5.1c, or a continuous *band* of frequencies, as shown in Figure 5.1d. As we will discuss in more detail below, the frequency of the stimulus more or less corresponds to its *pitch*, and the amplitude corresponds to

SPEECH PERCEPTION

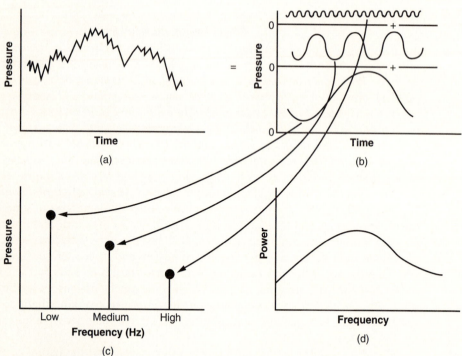

FIGURE 5.1

Different schematic representations of speech signal: (a) time domain; (b) three frequency components of (a); (c) the power spectrum of (b); (d) a continuous power spectrum of speech.

its *loudness*. When describing the effects on hearing, the amplitude is typically expressed as a *ratio* of sound pressure, *P*, measured in *decibels* (db). That is:

$$\text{Sound intensity (db)} = 20 \log (P1/P2).$$

As a ratio, the decibel scale can be used in either of two ways: first, as a measure of *absolute* intensity, the measure P2 is fixed at a value near the threshold of hearing (i.e., the faintest sound that can be heard under optimal conditions). This is a pure tone of 1,000 Hz at 20 micro Newtons/square meter. Table 5.1 provides some examples of the absolute intensity of different everyday sounds along the decibel scale. Second, because it is a ratio measure, the decibel scale can also be employed to characterize the *ratio* of two sounds; for example, the OSHA inspector at the plant may wish to determine how much *louder* the alarm is than the ambient background noise. Thus, we might say it is 15 db more intense, or we might characterize a set of earplugs as reducing the noise level by 20 db.

Sound intensity may be measured by the sound intensity meter. This meter has a series of different scales that can be selected, which will enable sound to be measured more specifically within particular frequency ranges. In particular, the A scale differentially weights sounds to reflect the characteristics of human hearing, providing greatest weighting at those frequencies where we are most sensitive. The C scale weights all frequencies nearly equally.

In addition to amplitude (intensity) and frequency (pitch), two other critical dimensions of the sound stimulus are its temporal characteristics, sometimes referred to as the *envelope* in which a sound occurs, and its location. The temporal characteristics are what may distinguish the wailing of the siren from the steady

---

TABLE 5.1 The Decibel Scale

Sound Pressure Level (db)	
140	Ear damage possible; jet at take-off
130	Painful sound
120	Propeller plane at take-off
110	Loud thunder
100	Subway train
90	Truck or bus
80	Average auto; loud radio
70	
60	Normal conversation
50	Quiet restaurant
40	Quiet office, household sounds
30	
20	Whisper
10	Normal breathing
0	Threshold of hearing

blast of the car horn, and the location (relative to the hearer) is, of course, what might distinguish the siren of the fire truck pulling up from behind from that about to cross the intersection in front (Caelli & Porter, 1980).

THE EAR: THE SENSORY TRANSDUCER

The ear has three primary components that are responsible for differences in our hearing experience. As shown in Figure 5.2, the *pinnea* serves to both collect sound and, because of its asymmetrical shape, provide some information regarding where the sound is coming from (i.e., from behind or in front). Mechanisms of the *outer and middle ear* (the ear drum or tympanic membrane, and the hammer, anvil, and stirrup bones) conduct and amplify the sound waves into the inner ear and are potential sources of breakdown or deafness (e.g., from a rupture of the eardrum or buildup of wax). The muscles of the inner ear are responsive to very loud noises and will reflexively contract to attenuate the amplitude of vibration before it is conveyed to the inner ear. This "aural reflex" thus offers some protection to the inner ear. The *inner ear,* consisting of the *cochlea,* within which lies the basilar membrane, is that portion where the physical movement of sound energy is transduced to electrical nerve energy that is then passed up the auditory nerve to the brain. This transduction is accomplished by displacement of tiny hair cells along the basilar membrane as the membrane moves differently to sounds of different frequency. Intense sound experience can lead to selective hearing loss at particular frequencies as a result of damage to the hair cells at particular locations along the basilar membrane. Finally, the neural signals are compared between the two ears to determine the delay and amplitude differences between them. These differences provide another cue for sound localization, because these features will only be identical if a sound is presented directly along the midplane of the listener.

THE AUDITORY EXPERIENCE

To amplify our previous discussion of the sound stimulus, the four dimensions of the raw stimulus all map onto psychological experience of sound: as noted, loudness maps to intensity, pitch maps to frequency, and perceived location maps to location. The quality of the sound is determined both by the set of frequencies in the stimulus and by the envelope. In particular, the *timbre* of a sound stimulus—what makes the trumpet sound different from the flute—is determined by the set of higher *harmonic* frequencies that lie above the *fundamental* frequency (which determines the pitch of the note). Various temporal characteristics, including the envelope and the rhythm of successive sounds, also determine the sound quality. As we shall see later, differences in the envelope are critically important in distinguishing speech sounds.

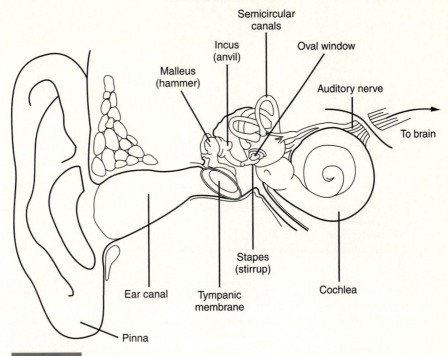

VESTIBULAR SYSTEM

FIGURE 5.2

Anatomy of the ear. (*Source:* Bernstein, D., Clark-Stewart, A., Roy, E., and Wickens, C.D., 1997. *Psychology,* 4th ed. Copyright © 1997 by Houghton-Mifflin. Reprinted with permission.)

Loudness and Pitch

Loudness is a psychological experience that correlates with, but is not identical to, the physical measurement of sound intensity. Two important reasons why loudness and intensity do not directly correspond are reflected in the psychophysical scale of loudness and the modifying effect of pitch. We discuss each of these in turn.

Psychophysical Scaling.   We note first that equal increases in sound intensity (on the db scale) do not create equal increases in loudness; that is, an 80 db sound does not sound twice as loud as a 40 db sound, and the increase from 40 to 50 db will not be judged as the same loudness increase as that from 70 to 80 db. Instead the *psychophysical scale* that related physical intensity to the psychological experience of loudness, expressed in units called *sones*, is that shown in Figure 5.3.

One sone is established arbitrarily as the loudness of a 40 db tone of 1,000 Hz. A tone twice as loud will be two sones. As an approximation, we can say that loudness doubles with each 10 db increase in sound intensity. It is important to distinguish two critical levels along the loudness scale. As noted, the *threshold* is the minimum intensity at which a sound can be detected. At some higher level, around

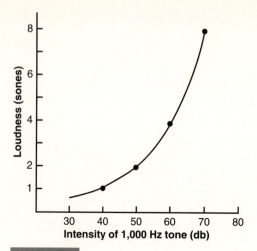

FIGURE 5.3

Relation between sound intensity and loudness.

85–90 db is a point at which potential danger to the ear occurs. Both of these levels, however, as well as the loudness of the intensity levels in between, are influenced by the frequency (pitch) of the sound, and so we must now consider that influence.

Frequency Influence.   Figure 5.4 plots a series of "equal loudness curves" shown by the various wavy lines. The equal loudness contours follow more or less parallel tracks. As shown in the figure, the frequency of a sound stimulus, plotted on the *x* axis influences all of the critical levels of the sound experience: threshold, loudness, and danger levels. As shown in the figure, the range of human hearing is limited between around 20 Hz and 20,000 Hz. Within this range, we appear to be most sensitive (lowest threshold) to sounds of around 4,000 Hz (although we shall see that this threshold is age-dependent); that is, for example, a 100 Hz tone of around 70 db would have the same perceived loudness as a 500 Hz tone of around 57 db. (In the figure, all equal loudness curves are described in units of *phons*. One phon = 1 db of loudness of a 1,000 Hz tone, the standard for calibration. Thus, all tones lying along the 40 phon line have the same loudness—1 sone—as a 1,000 Hz tone of 40 db.)

Masking.   As our worker at the beginning of the chapter discovered, sounds can be *masked* by other sounds. The nature of masking is actually quite complex (Handel, 1989; Yost, 1992), but a few of the most important principles for design are the following:

1. The minimum intensity difference necessary to ensure that a sound can be heard is around 15 db (above the mask), although this value may be larger if the pitch of the sound to be heard is unknown.
2. Sounds tend to be masked most by sounds in a critical frequency band surrounding the sound that is masked.

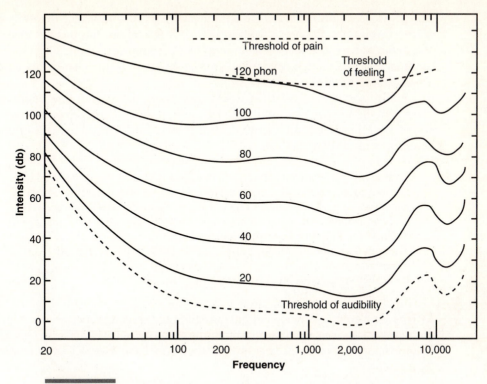

FIGURE 5.4

Equal loudness contours showing the intensity of different variables as a function of frequency. All points lying on a single curve are perceived as equally loud. (*Source:* Van Cott, H.P., and Kinkade, R.G., eds., 1972. *Human Engineering Guide to System Design.* Fig. 4-6. Washington, DC: U.S. Government Printing Office.)

3. Low-pitch sounds mask high-pitch sounds more than the converse. Thus, a woman's voice is more likely to be masked by other male voices than a man's voice would be masked by other female voices even if both voices are speaking at the same intensity level.

We will discuss the effects of masking in considerably more detail at later points in this chapter.

ALARMS

The design of effective alarms, the critical signal that was nearly missed by the worker in our opening story, depends very much on a good understanding of human auditory processing. Alarms tend to be a uniquely auditory design for one good reason: the auditory system is *omnidirectional;* that is, unlike visual signals, we can sense auditory signals no matter how we are oriented. Furthermore, it is much more difficult to "close our ears" than it is to close our eyes. For these and other reasons, auditory alarms induce a greater level of compliance than visual alarms (Wolgather, Kalsher, & Racicot, 1993). Task analysis thus dictates that if there is an alarm signal that *must be sensed* like a fire alarm, it should be given an auditory form (although redundancy in the visual or tactile channel may be worthwhile in certain circumstances).

While the choice of modality is straightforward, the issue of how auditory alarms should be designed is far from trivial. Consider the following quotation from a British pilot, taken from an incident report, which illustrates many of the problems with auditory alarms.

> I was flying in a jetstream at night when my peaceful revelry was shattered by the stall audio warning, the stick shaker and several warning lights. The effect was exactly what was *not* intended; I was frightened numb for several seconds and drawn off instruments trying to work out how to cancel the audio/visual assault, rather than taking what should be instinctive actions. The combined assault is so loud and bright that it is impossible to talk to the other crew member and action is invariably taken to cancel the cacophony before getting on with the actual problem. (Patterson, 1990)

Criteria for Alarms.   Patterson (1990) has discussed several properties of a good alarm system that can avoid the two opposing problems of detection, experienced by our factory worker at the beginning of the chapter and "overkill" experienced by the pilot.

1. Most critically, the alarm must be *heard* above the background ambient noise. This means that the noise spectrum must be carefully measured at the hearing location of all users who must respond to the alarm. Then the alarm should be tailored to be at least 15 db *above* the threshold of hearing above the noise level. This will typically require about a 30 db difference above the noise level in order to *guarantee* detection (see Fig. 5.5). As shown in the figure, it is also wise to include components of the alarm at several different frequencies well distributed across the spectrum, in case the particular malfunction that triggered the alarm creates its own noise (e.g., the whine of a malfunctioning engine), which exceeds the ambient level.

2. The alarm should not be above the danger level for hearing, whenever this condition can be avoided. (Obviously if the ambient noise level is close to the danger level, one has no choice but to make the alarm louder by criterion 1, which is most important.) This danger level is around 85–90 db. Careful selection of frequencies of the alarm can often be used to meet both of the above criteria. For example, if ambient noise is very intense (90 db), but only in the high frequency range, it would be counterproductive to try to impose a 120 db alarm in that same frequency range when several less-intense components in a lower frequency range could adequately be heard.

3. Ideally, the alarm should not be overly startling. This can be addressed by tuning the *rise time* of the alarm pulse, as we see below.

4. In contrast to the experience of the British pilot, the alarm should not disrupt the processing of other signals (e.g., other simultaneous alarms) or any back-

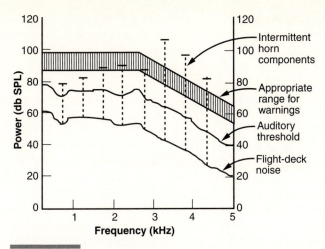

FIGURE 5.5

The range of appropriate levels for warning sound components on the flight deck of the Boeing 737 (vertical line shading). The minimum of the appropriate-level range is approximately 15 db above auditory threshold (broken line), which is calculated from the spectrum of the flight deck noise (solid line). The vertical dashed lines show the components of the intermittent warning horn, some of which are well above the maximum of the appropriate-level range. (*Source:* Patterson, R.D., 1990. *Auditory Warning Sounds in the Work Environment. Phil. Trans. R. Soc. London B.,* 327, p. 487, Fig. 1.).

ground speech communications that may be essential to deal with the alarm. This criterion in particular necessitates the performance of a careful *task analysis* of the conditions under which the alarm might sound and of the necessary communications tasks to be undertaken as a consequence.

  5. Last but not least, the alarm should be *informative,* signaling to the listener the nature of the emergency and, ideally, some indication of the appropriate action to take. The criticality of this informativeness criterion can be seen in one alarm system that was found in an intensive care unit of a hospital (an environment often in bad need of alarm remediation [Patterson, 1990]). The unit contained six patients, each monitored by a device with 10 different possible alarms: 60 potential signals which the staff may have to rapidly identify. Some aircraft have been known to contain at least 16 different auditory alerts, each of which, when heard, are supposed to trigger in the pilot's mind automatically and unambiguously the precise identification of the alarming condition. Such alarms are often found to be wanting in this regard. Hence, in addition to being informative, the alarm must not be *confusable* with others that may be heard in the same context. As you will recall from our discussion of vision in Chapter 4, this means that the alarm should not impose on the human's restrictive limits of *absolute judgment.* Just five or six different alarms may be the maximum allowable to meet this criterion.

Designing Alarms.   So, how should an alarm system be designed to avoid, or at least minimize, the potential costs described above?

First, as we have noted, *environmental and task analysis* must be undertaken to understand the quality and intensity of the other sounds (noise or communications) that might characterize the environment in which the alarm is presented to guarantee detectability and minimize disruption of other essential tasks.

Second, to guarantee informativeness *and* to minimize confusability, one should try to stay within the limits of absolute judgments. However within these limits, one can strive to make the parameters of the different alarm sounds as different from each other as possible by capitalizing on the various dimensions along which sounds differ. As shown in Figure 5.6, we may think of sounds lying at "points" along (at least) three dimensions: their pitch (fundamental pitch or frequency band), their envelope (e.g., rising, "woop woop," constant "beep beep"), and their rhythm (for example: synchronous "da da da" versus asynchronous "da *da* da *da*"). A fourth dimension that could be considered (but not easily represented graphically in the figure) is the timbre of the sound that may contrast, for example, a horn versus a flute. Two alarms will be maximally discriminable (and minimally confusable) if they are constructed at points on opposite ends of all three (or four) dimensions (see points A and B). Correspondingly, three alarms can be placed far apart in the multidimensional space, although the design problem becomes more complex with more possible alarms. However, the philosophy of maintaining wide separation (discriminability) along each of several dimensions can still be preserved.

A third step involves designing the specifics of the individual sound itself. Patterson (1990) recommends the procedure outlined in Figure 5.7, a procedure that itself has several embedded rationales. At the top of the figure, each individual "pulse" in the alarm is configured with a rise envelope that is not too abrupt (i.e., at least 20 msec) so that it will avoid the "startle" created by more abrupt rises. The *set* of pulses in the alarm sequence, shown in the middle of the figure, are config-

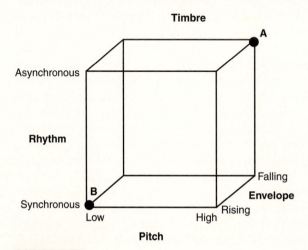

FIGURE 5.6

Making alarm sounds different by choosing levels far apart on the three dimensions shown here. A fourth dimension which is not represented but could be employed is the timbre.

ured with two goals in mind: (1) the unique set of pauses between each pulse can be used to create a unique rhythm which, we saw above, can be used to help avoid confusions; and (2) the increase then decrease in intensity gives the perception of an approaching then receding sound, which creates a psychological sense of urgency. Edworthy, Loxley, and Dennis (1991) have provided more elaborate guidelines on how to create the psychological perception of urgency from alarms.

Finally, the bottom row of Figure 5.7 shows the philosophy by which repeated presentations of the alarm sequence can be implemented. The first two presentations may be at high intensity to guarantee their initial detection (first sequence) and identification (first or second sequence). Under the assumption that the operator has probably been alerted, the third and fourth may be diminished in intensity to avoid "overkill" and possible masking *of* other sounds by the alarm (e.g., voice communications that may be initiated by the alarming condition). However,

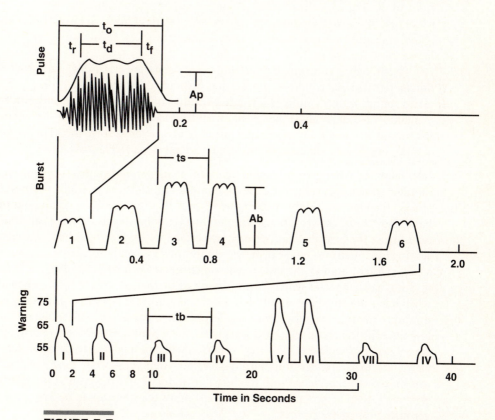

FIGURE 5.7

The modules of a prototype warning sound: the sound pulse at the top is an acoustic wave with rounded onsets and offsets and a distinctive spectrum; the burst shown in the middle row is a set of pulses with a distinctive rhythm and pitch contour; the complete warning sound sequence, shown at the bottom, is a set of bursts with varying intensity and urgency. (*Source:* Patterson, R.D., 1990. *Auditory Warning Sounds in the Work Environment. Phil Trans. R. Soc. London B.*, 327, p. 490, Fig. 3.)

an intelligent alarm system may infer, after a few sequences, that no action has been taken and hence repeat the sequence a couple of times at an even higher intensity.

Voice Alarms.   Alarms composed of synthetic voice provide one answer to the problems of discriminability and confusion. Unlike "symbolic" sounds, the hearer does not need to depend on an arbitrary learned connection to associate sound with meaning (Simpson et al., 1987). The loud sounds *"Engine fire!"* or *"Stall!"* in the cockpit mean exactly what they seem to mean. Indeed voice alarms are employed in several circumstances (the two aircraft warnings above are an example). But voice alarms themselves have limitations that must be considered. First, they will be likely to be more confusable with (and less discriminable from) a background of other voice communications, whether this is the ambient background at the time the alarm sounds or the task-related communications of dealing with the emergency. Second, unless care is taken, they may be more susceptible to frequency specific masking noise. Third, care must be taken if their meaning is to be interpreted by listeners who are less familiar with the language of the voice.

The preceding concerns with voice alarm suggest the advisability of using a *redundant* system that combines the alerting, distinctive features of the (nonspeech) alarm sound, with the more informative features of synthetic voice (Simpson & Williams, 1980). Echoing a theme that we introduced at the end of the last chapter, *redundancy gain* is a fundamental principle of human performance that can be usefully employed in alarm system design (Selcon et al., 1995).

False Alarms.   Alarms are, of course one form of *automation,* in that they typically monitor some process for the human operator and alert the operator whenever "they" (the logic within the alarm system) infer that the process is getting out of hand and requires some form of human intervention. Alarms then are little different from the human signal detector described in the previous chapter. When sensing low-intensity signals from the environment (a small increase in temperature, a wisp of smoke), the system will sometimes make mistakes, "inferring" that nothing has happened when it has (the miss) or that *something* has happened when it has not (the false alarm). Most alarm designers and users would chose to minimize the miss rate for obvious safety reasons. But as we learned, when the low-intensity signals on which the alarm decision is made are themselves noisy, the consequence of setting a "miss-free" criterion will be a higher than desirable false alarm rate: to paraphrase from the old fable, the system "cries wolf" too often. Such was indeed the experience with the initial introduction of the ground proximity warning system in aircraft, designed to alert pilots that they might be flying dangerously close to the ground.

From a human performance perspective, the obvious concern is that users may come to distrust the alarm system and perhaps ignore it even when it provides valid information (Hancock et al., 1996; Parasuraman, Hancock, and Olofinboba, 1997). More serious yet, users may attempt to disable the annoying alarms (Sorkin, 1989). Many of these concerns are related to the issue of *trust* in automation which we will discuss later in Chapter 16 (Muir, 1988; Lee & Moray, 1992).

Four logical steps may be taken to avoid the circumstances of "alarm false-alarms." First, it is possible that the alarm criterion itself has been set to such an extremely sensitive value that readjustment to allow fewer false alarms will still not appreciably increase the miss rate. Second, more sophisticated decision algorithms within the system may be developed to improve the *sensitivity* of the alarm system, a step that was taken to remediate the problems with the ground proximity warning system. Third, users can be trained about the inevitable tradeoff between misses and false alarms, and therefore can be taught to accept the false alarm rates as an inevitability of automated protection in a probabilistic world rather than as a system failure. (This acceptance will be more likely if care is taken to make the alarms noticeable by means other than shear loudness; Edworthy, Loxley, & Dennis, 1991.) Finally, a logical approach suggested by Sorkin, Kantowitz, and Kantowitz (1988) is to consider the use of *graded* or *likelihood alarm systems,* in which more than a single level of alert is provided. Hence, two (or more) levels can signal to the human the system's *own* confidence that the alarming conditions are present. That evidence in the fuzzy middle ground (e.g., the odor from the slightly burnt piece of toast), which previously might have signaled the full fire alarm, now triggers a signal of noticeable but reduced intensity. Sorkin et al. have found that such a system, when coupled with the human user, produces greater overall sensitivity than does the typical two-state (on or off) alarm.

THE SOUND TRANSMISSION PROBLEM

Our example at the beginning of the chapter illustrated the worker's concern with her ability to communicate with her neighbor at the workplace. A more tragic illustration of communications breakdowns is provided by the 1979 collision between two jumbo jets on the runway at Tenerife airport in the Canary Islands, in which over 500 lives were lost (Hawkins, 1993). One of the jets, a KLM 747, was poised at the end of the runway, engines primed, and the pilot was in a hurry to take off while it was still possible before the already poor visibility got worse and the airport closed operations. Meanwhile, the other jet, a Pan American airplane that had just landed, was still on the same runway, trying to find its way off. The air traffic controller instructed the pilot of the KLM: "Okay, stand by for takeoff and I will call." Unfortunately, because of a less than perfect radio channel, and because of the KLM pilot's extreme desire to proceed with the takeoff, he apparently *heard* just the words "Okay . . . take off." The takeoff proceeded until the aircraft collided with the Pan Am 747, which had still not steered itself clear from the runway.

In Chapter 4, we discussed the influences of both bottom-up (sensory quality) and top-down (expectations and desires) processing on perception. The Canary Island accident tragically illustrates the breakdown of both processes. The communications signal from ATC was degraded (loss of bottom-up quality), and the KLM pilot used his own expectations and desires to "hear what he wanted to hear" (inappropriate top-down processing) and to interpret the message as authorization to "take off." In this section we will consider in more detail the role of both of these processes in what is arguably the most important kind of auditory communications, the processing of human speech. (We have already discussed the communications of warning information. A third form of auditory communication, the use of synthetic natural sound—earcons—to symbolize certain events, will be addressed in the next chapter; Ballas & Mullins, 1991; Gaver, 1986). We will first describe the nature of the speech stimulus and then discuss how it may be distorted in its transmission by changes in signal quality and by noise. Finally, we consider possible ways of remediating breakdowns in the speech transmission process.

The Speech Signal

The Speech Spectrograph. The sound waves of a typical speech signal look something like the pattern shown in Figure 5.8a. As we have seen, such signals are more coherently presented by a spectral representation, as shown in Figure 5.8b. However, for speech, unlike noise or tones, many of the key properties are captured in the *time-dependent changes* in the spectrum; that is, in the *envelope* of the sound. To represent this information graphically, speech is typically described by the *speech spectrograph,* as shown in Figure 5.8c. One can think of each vertical slice of the spectrograph as the momentary spectrum, existing at the time labeled on the *x* axis. Where there is darkness (or thickness), there is power (and greater darkness represents more power). However, the spectral content of the signal changes as the time axis moves from left to right. Thus, the particular speech signal shown at the bottom of Figure 5.8c represents a very faint initial pitch that increases in its value and amplitude over the first few msec to reach a steady state at a higher frequency. Collectively, the two bars shown in the figure characterize the sound of the human voice saying the letter *d* (dee). Figure 5.8d shows the spectrum of more continuous speech.

Masking Effects of Noise. As we have learned, the potential of any auditory signal to be masked by other sounds depends on both the intensity (power) of that signal, and on its frequency. These two variables are influenced by the speaker's gender and by the nature of the speech sound. First, since the female voice typically has a higher base frequency than the male, it is not surprising that the female voice is more vulnerable to masking of noise. Second, as Figure 5.8c illustrates, the power or intensity of speech signals (represented by the thickness of the lines) is much greater in the vowel range *eee*, than in the initial consonant part *d.* This difference in salience is further magnified because the vowel sounds often stretch out over a longer period of time than the consonants. Finally, certain consonant sounds like *s* and *ch* have their distinguishing features at very high frequencies, and high frequencies, we saw, were more vulnerable to masking by low frequencies than the converse. Hence, it is not surprising that consonants are much more susceptible to masking and other disruptions than are vowels. This characteristic is particularly disconcerting because consonants typically transmit more information in speech than do vowels (i.e., there are more of them). One need only think of the likely possibility of confusing "fly to" with "fly through" in an aviation setting to realize the danger of such consonant confusion (Hawkins, 1993; Miller & Nicely, 1955).

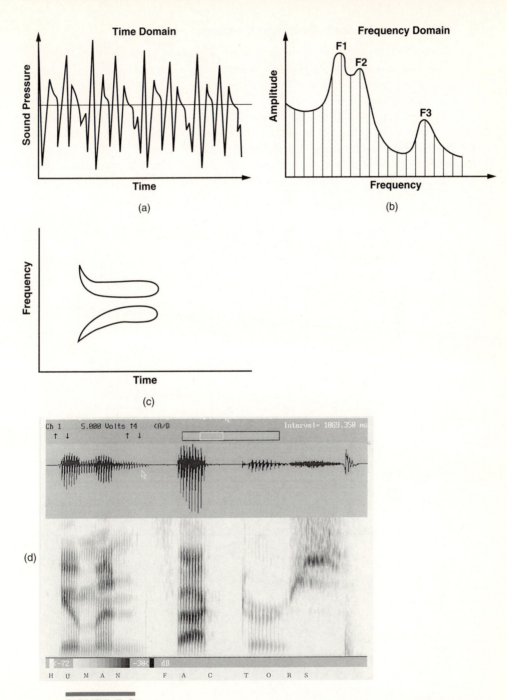

FIGURE 5.8

(a) Voice time signal; (b) Voice spectrum (*Source:* Yost, W.A., 1994 *Fundamentals of Hearing,*
3rd ed. San Diego: Academic Press.); (c) Schematic speech spectrograph (the sound *dee*); (d)
A real speech spectrograph of the words "human factors." (*Source:* Courtesy of Speech and
Hearing Department, University of Illinois.)

Measuring Speech Communications

Human factors engineers know that noise degrades communications, but they must often assess (or predict) precisely how much communications will be lost in certain degraded conditions. For this, we must consider the measurement of speech communications.

There are two different approaches to measuring speech communications, based on bottom-up and top-down processing, respectively. The *bottom-up* approach derives some objective measure of speech quality. It is most appropriate in measuring the potential degrading effects of noise. Thus the *articulation index,* computes the signal-to-noise ratio (db of speech sound minus db of background noise) across a range of the spectrum in which useful speech information is imparted (see Fig. 5.9). This measure can be weighted by the different frequency bands, providing greater weight to the ratios within bands that contribute relatively more heavily to the speech signal.

While the objective merits of the bottom-up approach are clear, its limits in predicting the understandability of speech should become apparent when one

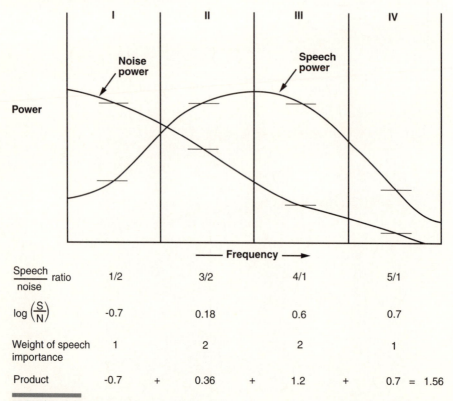

Speech/noise ratio	1/2		3/2		4/1		5/1	
$\log\left(\frac{S}{N}\right)$	-0.7		0.18		0.6		0.7	
Weight of speech importance	1		2		2		1	
Product	-0.7	+	0.36	+	1.2	+	0.7	= 1.56

FIGURE 5.9

Schematic representation of the calculation of an articulation index. The speech spectrum has been divided into four "bands" weighted in importance by the relative power that each contributes to the speech signal. (*Source:* Wickens, C.D. *Engineering Psychology and Human Performance,* 2nd ed. New York: HarperCollins, 1992. Reprinted by permission of Addison-Wesley Educational Publishers, Inc.)

considers the contributions of top-down processing to speech perception. For example, two letter strings, *abcdefghij*, and *wcignspexl*, might both be heard at intensities with the same Articulation Index. But it is clear that more letters of the first string would be correctly understood (Miller, Heise, & Lichten, 1951). Why? Because the listener's knowledge of the predictable *sequence* of letters in the alphabet allows perception to "fill in the gaps" and essentially guess the contents of a letter whose sensory clarity may be missing. This, of course, is the role of *top-down processing.*

A measure that takes top-down processing into account is the *speech intelligibility level* (SIL). This index measures the percentage of items correctly heard. Naturally, at any given bottom-up Articulation Index (AI) level, this percentage will vary as a function of the listener's expectation of and knowledge about the message communicated, a point illustrated in Figure 5.10.

Speech Distortions. While the AI can objectively characterize the damaging effect of noise on bottom-up processing of speech, it cannot do the same thing with regard to *distortions.* These distortions may result from a variety of causes, for example, clipping of the beginning and ends of words, reduced bandwidth of high-

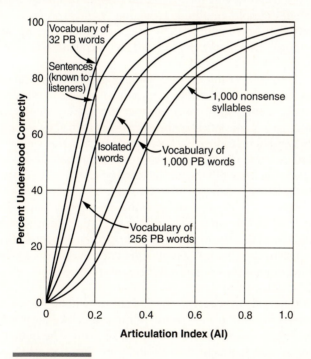

FIGURE 5.10

Relationship between the Articulation Index (AI) and the intelligibility of various types of speech test materials. Note that at any given AI, a greater percentage of items can be understood if the vocabulary is smaller or if the word strings form coherent sentences. (*Source:* Adapted from Kryter, K., 1972. Speech Communications. In *Human Engineering Guide to System Design,* H.P. Van Cott, and R.G. Kinkade, eds., Washington, DC: U.S. Government Printing Office.)

demand communications channels, echoes and reverberations, and even the low quality of some digitized synthetic speech signals (Pisoni, 1982).

While the bottom-up influences of these effects cannot be as accurately quantified as the effects of noise, there are nevertheless important human factors guidelines that can be employed to minimize their negative impact on voice recognition. One issue that has received particular attention from acoustic engineers is how to minimize the distortions resulting when the high information speech signal must be somehow "filtered" to be conveyed over a channel of lower bandwidth (e.g., through digitized speech).

For example, a raw speech waveform such as that shown in Figure 5.8b may contain over 59,000 bits of information per second (Kryter, 1972). Transmitting the raw waveform over a single communications channel might then overly restrict that channel, which perhaps must also be made available to share with several other signals at the same time. There are, however, a variety of ways of reducing the information content of a speech signal, as shown schematically in Figure 5.11. One may filter out the high frequencies, digitize the signal to discrete levels, clip out bits of the signal, or reduce the range of amplitudes by clipping out the middle range. Human factors studies have been able to inform the engineer which way works best by preserving the maximum amount of speech intelligibility (Kryter, 1972). For example, amplitude reduction (e and f) seems to preserve more speech quality and intelligibility than does frequency filtering, and frequency filtering is much better if only very low and high frequencies are eliminated (Kryter, 1972).

Of course, with the increasing availability of digital communications and voice synthesizers, the issue of transmitting voice quality with minimum bandwidth is lessened in its importance. Instead, one may simply transmit the symbolic contents of the message (e.g., the letters of the words) and then allow a speech synthesizer at the other end to reproduce the necessary sounds. (This will, of course, eliminate the uniquely human "nonverbal" aspects of communications—a result that may not be desirable when talking on the telephone.) Then the issue of importance becomes the level of fidelity of the voice synthesizer necessary to (1) produce recognizable speech, (2) produce recognizable speech that can be heard in noise, and (3) support "easy listening." The third issue is particularly important, as Pisoni (1982) has found that listening to synthetic speech takes more mental resources than does listening to natural speech and hence can produce greater interference with other ongoing tasks that must be accomplished concurrently with the listening task (see Chapter 6).

One final characteristic of speech communications will be visited again in Chapter 6. The voice, unlike the printed word, is transient. Once the word is spoken it is gone and cannot be referred back to, unlike print. The human information-processing system is designed to prolong the duration of the spoken word for a few seconds through what is called *echoic memory*. However, beyond this time, spoken information must be actively rehearsed, a demand that competes for resources with other tasks. Hence, when displayed messages are more than a few words, they should be delivered visually or at least backed up with a redundant visual signal.

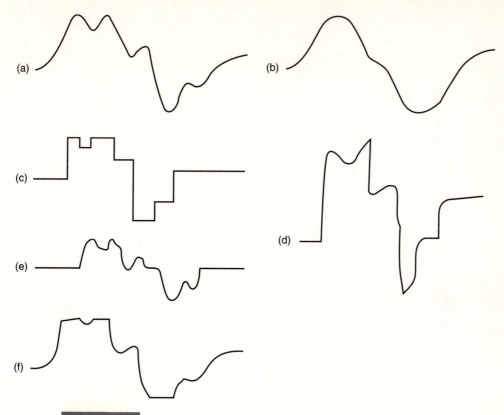

FIGURE 5.11

Illustrates different ways of reducing the bandwidth of the raw speech signal shown schematically in (a); (b) high frequency filtering; (c) digitizing; (d) time compression; (e) amplitude compression; (f) peak clipping.

Hearing Loss

In addition to noise and distortions, a final factor responsible for loss in voice transmission is the potential loss of hearing of the listener. As shown in Figure 5.12, simple age is responsible for a large portion of hearing loss, particularly in the high-frequency regions, a factor that should be considered in the design of alarm systems, particularly in nursing homes. On top of the age-related declines may be added certain occupation-specific losses, related to the hazards of a noisy workplace (Taylor et al., 1965). As we discuss below, these are the sorts of hazards that organizations like OSHA make efforts to eliminate.

NOISE REVISITED

We have already discussed noise as a factor disrupting the transmission of infor-mation. In this section we consider two other important human factors concerns with noise: its potential as a health hazard in the workplace and its potential as an

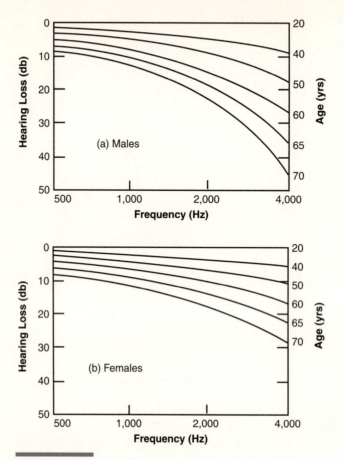

FIGURE 5.12

Idealized median (50th percentile) hearing loss at different frequencies for males and females as a function of age. (*Source:* Kryter, K., 1983. *Addendum: Presbycusis, Sociocusis and Nococusis. Journal of Acoustic Society of America,* 74, pp. 1907–1909. Reprinted with permission. Copyright Acoustic Society of America.)

irritant in the environment. In Chapter 13, we also consider noise as a stressor that has degrading effects on performance other than the communications masking effect we have discussed here. We conclude by offering various possible remediations to the degrading effects of noise in all three areas: communications, health, and environment.

The worker in our story at the beginning of the chapter was concerned about the impact of noise at her workplace on her ability to hear. When we examine these effects of noise, we can actually consider three components of the potential hearing loss. The first, masking, has already been discussed; this is a loss of sensitivity to a signal *while the noise is present.*

The second form of noise-induced hearing loss is the *temporary threshold shift.* If our worker steps away from the machine to a quieter place to answer the telephone, she may still have some difficulty hearing because of the "carry-over" effect of the previous noise exposure. This temporary threshold shift (TTS) is large immediately after the noise is terminated but declines over the following minutes as hearing is "recovered" (Fig. 5.13). The TTS is typically expressed as the loss in hearing (shift in threshold in db), that is present two minutes after the source of noise has terminated. The TTS will be increased by a longer prior noise exposure, and a greater prior level of that exposure. The TTS can actually be quite large. For example the TTS after being exposed to 100 db noise for 100 minutes is 60 db.

The third form of noise-induced hearing loss, and that with the most serious implications for worker health, is the *permanent threshold shift* (PTS). This measure describes the "occupational deafness" that may set in after workers have been exposed to months or years of high-intensity noise at the workplace. Like the TTS, the PTS will be greater with both louder and longer prior exposure to noise. Also, like the age-related hearing loss discussed above, the PTS tends to be more pronounced at higher frequencies.

During the last 20 years in the United States, the Occupational Safety and Health Administration has taken steps to try to ensure worker safety from the hazardous effects of prolonged noise in the workplace by establishing workplace standards that can be used to trigger remediating action (OSHA 1983). These standards are based on a *time weighted average* of noise experienced in the workplace. If the TWA is above 85 db, the so called *action level,* then employers are required to implement a hearing protection plan in which ear protection devices are made available, some instruction is given to workers regarding potential damages to hearing and steps that can be taken to avoid that damage, and regular hearing testing is to be implemented. If the TWA is above 90 db, a level referred to as the *permissible exposure level,* then the employer is *required* to takes steps toward noise reduction through procedures that we discuss below.

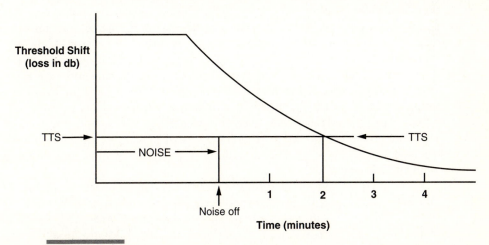

FIGURE 5.13

Temporary threshold shift (TTS) following the termination of noise. Note that sensitivity is recovered (the threshold shift is reduced over time). Its level at two minutes is arbitrarily defined as the TTS.

Of course many workers do not experience steady continuous noise of these levels but may be exposed to bursts of intense noise, followed by periods of greater quiet. The OSHA standards provide means of converting the varied time histories of noise exposures into the single equivalent standard of the TWA (Sanders & McCormick, 1993). It is also important to keep in mind that the "noise level" at a facility cannot be expressed by a single value but may vary from worker to worker, depending on their location. For this reason, TWAs must be computed on the basis of noise dose meters, or *dosemeters,* that can be worn by individual workers. These will collect the data necessary to compute the TWA over the course of the day.

NOISE REMEDIATION

The steps that should be taken to remediate the effects of noise might be very different, depending on the particular nature of the noise related problem and the level of the noise that exists before remediation. On the one hand, if noise problems relate to communications difficulties in situations when the noise level is below 85 db (e.g., a noisy phone line), then *signal enhancement* procedures may be appropriate. On the other hand, if noise is above the action levels (a characteristic of many industrial workplaces), then *noise reduction* procedures must be adopted because enhancing the signal intensity (e.g., louder alarms) will do little to alleviate the possible health and safety problems. Finally, if noise is a source of irritation and stress in the environment (e.g., residential noise from an airport or nearby freeway), then many of the sorts of solutions that might be appropriate in the workplace, like wearing earplugs, are obviously not applicable.

Signal Enhancement

Besides obvious solutions of "turning up the volume" (which may not work, if this amplifies the noise level as well and so does not change the signal/noise ratio) or talking louder, there may be other more effective solutions for enhancing the amplitude of speech or warning sound signals, relative to the background noise. First, careful consideration of the *spectral content* of the masking noise may allow one to use signal spectra that have less overlap with the noise content. For example, the spectral content of synthetic voice messages or alarms can be carefully chosen to lie in regions where noise levels are lower. Also, synthetic speech devices or earphones can often be used to bring the source of signal closer to the operator's ear than if the source is at a more centralized location where it must compete more with ambient noise.

There are also signal-enhancement techniques that emphasize more the *redundancy* associated with top-down processing. As one example, it has been shown that voice communications is far more effective in a face-to-face mode than it is when the listener cannot see the speaker (Sumby & Pollack, 1954). This is because of the contributions made by many of the redundant cues provided by the lips (Massaro & Cohen, 1995), cues of which we are normally unaware unless they are gone or distorted. (To illustrate the important and automatic way we typically in-

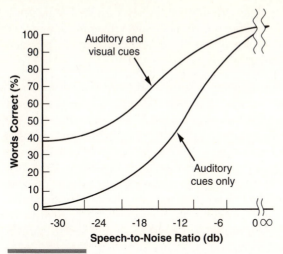

FIGURE 5.14

Intelligibility of words when perceived with and without visual cues from observing the speaker. (*Source:* Sumby, W., and Pollack, I., 1954. *Visual Contribution to Speech Intelligibility in Noise. Journal of Acoustical Society of America,* 26, pp. 212–215. Reprinted by permission.)

tegrate sound and lip reading, recall, if you can, the difficulty you may have had in understanding the speech of poorly dubbed foreign films when speech and lip movement do not coincide in a natural way.)

As we discussed above, in the context of communications measurement, another form of redundancy is achieved through the choice of vocabulary. Restricted vocabulary, common words, and standardization of communications procedures, such as that adopted in air traffic control (and further emphasized following the Tenerife disaster) will greatly restrict the number of *possible* utterances that could be heard at any given moment, and hence will better allow perception to "make an educated guess," as to the meaning of a sound if the noise level is high (Fig. 5.10).

Another form of redundancy is involved in the use of the phonetic alphabet ("alpha bravo charlie . . . charlie . . ."). In this case, more than a single sound is used to convey the content of each letter, so that if one sound is destroyed (e.g., the consonant *b*), other sounds can unambiguously "fill in the gap" (*ravo*).

Noise Reduction in the Workplace

We may choose to reduce noise in the workplace by focusing on the source, the path or environment, or the listener. The first is the most preferred method; the last is the least.

The Source: Equipment and Tool Selection.   Many times, effective reduction can be attained by the appropriate and careful choice of tools or sound producing equipment. Ventilation or fans, or hand tools, for example, vary in the sound they produce, and appropriate choices in purchasing these can be made. One should consider also the fact that the irritation of noise is considerably greater in the high frequency region (the shrill pierced whine) than in the mid- or low-frequency region (the low rumble). Hence, to some extent the choice of tool can reduce the irritating quality of its noise.

The Environment.   The *environment* or path from the sound source to the human can also be altered in several ways. Changing the environment near the source, for example, is illustrated in Figure 5.15, which shows the attenuation in noise achieved by surrounding a piece of equipment with a plexiglass shield. Sound absorbing walls, ceilings, and floors can also be very effective in reducing the noise coming from reverberations. Finally, there are many circumstances when repositioning workers relative to the source of noise can be effective. The effectiveness of such relocation will be considerably enhanced when the noise emanates from only a single source. This in turn will be more likely to be the case if the source is present in a more sound-absorbent environment (less reverberating).

The Listener: Ear Protection.   If noise cannot be reduced to acceptable levels at the source or path, then solutions can be applied to the listener. Ear protection devices of the type that must be made available when noise levels exceed the action level are of two generic types: Earplugs, which fit inside the ear; and ear muffs, which fit over the top of the ear. As commercially available products, each is provided with a certified *noise reduction ratio* (NRR), expressed in dB, and each may also

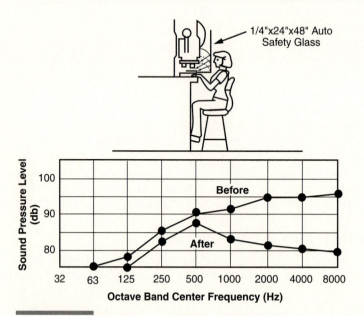

FIGURE 5.15

Use of a 1/4-in.- (6-mm-) thick safety glass barrier to reduce high-frequency noise from a punch press. (*Source:* American Industrial Hygiene Association, 1975, Fig. 11.73. Reprinted with permission by the American Industrial Hygiene Association.)

have very different spectral characteristics (i.e., different dB reduction across the spectrum). For both kinds of devices, it appears that the manufacturer's specified NRR is typically greater (more optimistic) than is the actual noise reduction experienced by users in the workplace (Casali, Lam, & Epps, 1987). This is because the manufacturer's NRR value is typically computed under ideal laboratory conditions, whereas users in the workplace may not always wear the device properly.

Of the two devices, earplugs can offer a greater overall protection, *if properly worn* (Sanders & McCormick, 1993). However, this qualification is extremely important because earplugs are more likely to be worn improperly than are ear muffs. Hence, without proper training (and adherence to that training), certain muffs may be more effective than plugs. A second advantage of muffs is that they can readily double as headphones through which critical signals can be delivered, hence simultaneously achieving signal enhancement and noise reduction.

Comfort is another feature that cannot be neglected in considering protector effectiveness in the workplace. It is likely that devices that are annoying and uncomfortable may be disregarded in spite of their safety effectiveness (see Chapter 14). Interestingly, however, concerns such as that voiced by the worker at the beginning of the chapter that hearing protection may not allow her to hear conversations are not always well grounded. After all, the ability to hear conversation is based on the signal-to-noise ratio. Depending on the precise spectral characteristics and amplitude of the noise and the signal *and* the noise-reduction function, the consequences of wearing such devices may actually be to *enhance* rather than reduce the s/n ratio, even as both signal and noise intensity are reduced. The benefit of earplugs to increasing the signal to noise ratio is greatest with louder noises, above about 80–85 dB. (Kryter, 1972).

Finally, it is important to note that the adaptive characteristics of the human speaker may themselves produce some unexpected consequences on speech comprehension. We automatically adjust our voice level, in part, on the basis of the intensity of sound that we hear, talking louder when we are in a noisy environment (or when we are listening to loud stereo music through headphones). Hence, it is not surprising that speakers in a noisy environment will talk about 2–4 db *softer* (and also somewhat faster) when they are wearing ear protectors than when they are not. This means that listening to such speech may be disrupted in environments in which all participants wear protective devices, unless speakers are trained to avoid this automatic reduction in the loudness of their voice.

Environmental Noise

As we discussed above, noise in residential or city environments, while presenting less of a health hazard than at the workplace, is still an important human factors concern, and even the health hazard is not entirely absent. Meecham (1983), for example, reported that the death rate from heart attacks of elderly residents near the Los Angeles Airport was significantly higher than the rate recorded in a demographically equivalent nearby area that did not receive the excessive noise of aircraft landings and takeoffs.

Measurement of the irritating qualities of environmental noise levels follows somewhat different procedures from the measurement of workplace dangers. In particular, in addition to the key component of intensity level, there are a number of other "irritant" factors that can drive the annoyance level upward. For example, high frequencies are more irritating than low frequencies. Nighttime noise is more irritating than daytime noise. Noise in the summer is more irritating than in the winter (when windows are likely to be closed). While these and other considerations cannot be precisely factored into an equation to predict "irritability," it is nevertheless possible to estimate their contributions in predicting the effects of environmental noise on resident complaints (Environmental Protection Agency, 1974).

Is All Noise Bad?

Before we leave our discussion of noise, it is important to identify certain circumstances in which softer noise may actually be helpful. For example, low levels of continuous noise (the hum of a fan) can mask the more disruptive and startling effects of discontinuous or distracting noise (the loud ticking of the clock at night or the conversation in the next room). Soft background music may accomplish the same objective. Under certain circumstances, noise can perform an alerting function that can maintain a higher level of vigilance (Parasuraman, Warm, & Dember, 1987; Broadbent, 1972; see Chapter 4). Furthermore, it is certainly the case that one person's noise may be another person's "signal" (as is often the case with conversation).

This last point brings us back to reemphasize one final issue that we have touched on repeatedly: the importance of *task analysis*. The full impact of adjusting sound frequency and intensity levels on human performance can never be adequately predicted without a clear understanding of what sounds will be present when, who will listen to them, who *must* listen to them, and what the costs will be to task performance, listener health, and listener comfort if hearing is degraded.

THE OTHER SENSES

Vision and hearing have held the stage during this chapter and the previous one for the important reason that the visual and auditory senses are of greatest importance and have the greatest implications for the design of human-machine systems. The "other" senses, critically important in human experience, have played considerably less of a role in system design. Hence, we will not discuss at all the senses of smell and taste, important as both of these are to the pleasures of eating (although smell can provide an important safety function as an advanced warning of fires and overheating engines). We will discuss briefly below, however, three other categories of sensory experience each of which have some direct relevance to design: the sense of touch and feel (the tactile/haptic sense), the sense of limb position and motion (proprioception and kinesthesis), and the sense of whole-body orientation and motion (the vestibular senses). All of these offer important channels of information that help coordinate human interaction with many physical systems.

Touch: Tactile and Haptic Senses

Lying just under the skin are sensory receptors that respond to pressure on the skin, and these relay their information to the brain regarding the subtle changes in force applied by the hands and fingers (or other parts of the body) as they interact with physical things in the environment. Along with the sensation of pressure, these senses, tightly coupled with the proprioceptive sense of finger position, also provide *haptic* information regarding the *shape* of manipulated objects and things (Loomis & Lederman, 1986; Kaczmarer & Bach-T-Rita, 1995). We see the importance of these sensory channels in the following examples:

1. A problem with the membrane keyboards sometimes found on calculators is that they do not offer the same "feel" (tactile feedback) when the fingers are positioned on the button, as do mechanical keys (see Chapter 9).

2. Gloves, to be worn in cold weather (or in other hazardous operations), must be designed with sensitivity to maintaining some tactile feedback if manipulation is required (Karis, 1987).

3. Early concern about the *confusion* that pilots experienced between two very different controls—the landing gear and the flaps—was addressed by redesigning the control handles to feel quite distinct (Fig. 5.16) (and, incidentally, to also feel and look somewhat like the system that they activate; see Chapter 9).

4. The tactile sense is well structured as an alternative channel to convey both spatial and symbolic information for the blind through the braille alphabet.

5. Designers of *virtual environments* (Durlach & Mavor, 1995; Kaczmarer & Bach-T-Rita, 1995), which we will discuss more in Chapter 15, attempt to provide artificial sensations of touch and feel via electrical stimulation to the fingers, as the hand manipulates "virtual objects."

Proprioception and Kinesthesis

We briefly introduced the *proprioceptive* channel in the previous section in the context of the brain's knowledge of finger position. In fact, a rich set of receptor systems, located within all of the joints of the body, convey to the brain an accurate representation of joint angles everywhere and, by extension, a representation of limb position in space. The proprioceptive channel is tightly coupled with the *kinesthetic* channel, which conveys a sense of the *motion* of the limbs as exercised by the muscles. Collectively, the two senses of kinesthesis and proprioception provide a rich feedback that is critical for our everyday interactions with things in the environment. One particular area of relevance for these senses is in the design of manipulator controls, such as the joystick or mouse with a computer system, the steering wheel on a car, the clutch on a machine tool, or the control on an aircraft (see Chapter 9). As a particular example, an *isometric* control is one that does not move but responds only to pressure applied upon it. Hence, the isometric control fails to offer any proprioceptive feedback regarding *how far* the control has been moved. Early efforts to introduce isometric side stick controllers in aircraft were,

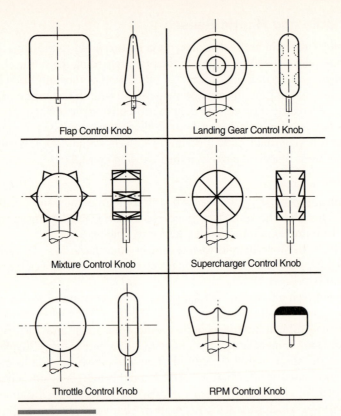

Flap Control Knob   Landing Gear Control Knob

Mixture Control Knob   Supercharger Control Knob

Throttle Control Knob   RPM Control Knob

FIGURE 5.16

Top row: Appearance of typical flaps and landing gear control on an aircraft. Note the haptic discriminability between them. The other rows depict the shape coding for other flight controls. (*Source:* O'Hare, D., and Roscoe, S.N., 1990. *Flight Deck Performance: The Human Factor.* Ames, IA: Iowa State University Press.)

in fact, resisted by pilots because of this elimination of the "feel" of control deflection. The pilots concern is backed up by research, showing that tracking can be performed better with moving controls, and so the current version of side stick controllers can now be displaced when a force is applied on them.

The Vestibular Senses

Located deep within the inner ear (and visible in Fig. 5.2) are two sets of receptors, located in the *semicircular canals* and in the *vestibular sacs*. These receptors convey information to the brain regarding the angular and linear *accelerations* of the body, respectively. Thus, when I turn my head with my eyes shut, I "know" that I am turning, not only because kinesthetic feedback from my neck tells me so but also because there is an angular acceleration, experienced by the semicircular canals. Because the head can rotate in three axes, there are three semicircular canals aligned to each axis. Correspondingly, the vestibular sacs (along with the tactile sense from the "seat of the pants") inform the passenger or driver of linear acceleration or braking in a car. These organs also provide the constant information about the accelerative force of gravity downward, and hence they are continuously used to maintain our sense of balance (knowing which way is up, and correcting for departures).

Not surprisingly, the vestibular senses are most important for human system interaction when the systems either move directly (as vehicles) or *simulate* motion (as vehicle simulators or virtual environments). The vestibular senses play two important (and potentially negative) roles here, related to *illusions* and to *motion sickness*.

Vestibular illusions of motion, discussed further in Chapter 17, occur because certain vehicles, particularly aircraft, place the passenger in situations of sustained acceleration and nonvertical orientation for which the human body was not naturally adapted. Hence, for example, when the pilot is flying "in the clouds" without sight of the ground or horizon, the vestibular senses may sometimes be "tricked" into thinking that up is in a different direction from where it really is. This illusion presents some real dangers of *spatial disorientation* and the possible loss of control of the aircraft that may result (O'Hare & Roscoe, 1990).

The vestibular senses also play a key role in motion sickness. Normally, our visual and vestibular senses convey compatible and redundant information to the brain regarding how we are oriented and how we are moving. However, there are certain circumstances in which these two channels become *decoupled* so that one sense tells the brain one thing and the other tells it something else. These are conditions that invite *motion sickness* (Reason & Brand, 1975; Crampton, 1990). One example of this decoupling results when the vestibular cues signal motion and the visual world does not. When riding in a vehicle with no view of the outside world (e.g., the toddler sitting low in the backseat of the car, the ship passenger below decks with the portholes closed, or the aircraft passenger flying in the clouds), the visual view forward, which is typically "framed" by a man-made rectangular structure, provides no visual evidence of movement (or evidence of where the "true" horizon is). In contrast, the continuous rocking, rolling, or swaying of the vehicle provides very direct stimulation of movement to the vestibular senses. When the two senses are in conflict like this, motion sickness often results (a phenomenon that was embarrassingly experienced by the first author at his first turn to general quarters with the portholes closed below ship in the Navy).

Conflict between the two senses can also result from the opposite pattern. The visual system can often experience a very compelling sense of motion in video games, driving or flight simulators, and virtual environments, even when there is no motion of the platform whatsoever. Here again there is conflict, and here again there is real danger of a loss of function (or wasted experience) when the brain is distracted by the unpleasant sensations of motion sickness. We return to this topic again in the chapter on stress (Chapter 13).

Concerns about motion sickness induced by vestibular-visual uncoupling have led researchers and practitioners to develop various remediations (Jackson, 1994).

CONCLUSION

Audition, when coupled with vision and the other senses, can offer the brain an overwhelming array of information. Each sensory modality appears to have particular strengths and weaknesses, and collectively the ensemble nicely compensates for the collective weaknesses of each sensory channel alone. Clever designers can capitalize on the strengths and avoid the weaknesses in rendering the sensory information available to the higher brain centers for perception, interpretation, decision making and further processing. In the following two chapters, we consider the characteristics of these higher level information-processing or *cognitive* operations before addressing, in Chapter 8, how sensory processing and information processing may be gracefully connected in human factors by the careful engineering design of displays.

REFERENCES

American Industrial Hygiene Association (1975). *Industrial noise manual* (3rd ed.). Akron, OH.

Ballas, J.A., and Mullins, R.T. (1991). Effects of context on the identification of everyday sounds. *Human Performance, 4,* 199–219.

Broadbent, D.E. (1972). *Decision and stress.* New York: Academic Press.

Caelli, T., and Porter, D. (1980). On difficulties in localizing ambulance sirens. *Human Factors, 22,* 719–724.

Casali, J., Lam, S., and Epps, B. (1987). Rating and ranking methods for hearing protector wearability. *Sound and Vibration, 21*(12), 10–18.

Crampton, G. (1990). *Motion and space sickness.* Boco Raton, FL: Chemical Rubber Company Press.

Durlach, N.I., and Mavor, A. (eds.). (1995). *Virtual reality: Scientific and technological challenges.* Washington, DC: National Academy Press.

Edworthy, J., Loxley, S., and Dennis, I. (1991). Improved auditory warning design: Relations between warning sound parameters and perceived urgency. *Human Factors, 33,* 205–231.

Environmental Protection Agency (1974). *Information on levels of environmental noise requisite to protect public health and welfare with an adequate margin of safety* (EPA 550/9-74-004). Washington, DC.

Gaver, W.W. (1986). Auditory icons: Using sound in computer interfaces. *Human-Computer Interaction, 2,* 167–177.

Hancock, P.A., Parasuraman, R., and Byrne, E.A. (1996). Driver-centered issues in advanced automation for motor vehicles. In R. Parasuraman and M. Mouloua (eds.), *Automation and human performance: Theory and applications* (pp. 337–364). Mahwah, NJ: Lawrence Erlbaum.

Handel, S. (1989). *Listening: An introduction to the perception of auditory events.* Cambridge, MA: MIT Press.

Hawkins, F.H. (1993). *Human factors in flights.* Brookfield, VT: Ashgate.

Jackson, J. (1994). A multimodal method for assessing and treating airsickness. *The International Journal of Aviation Psychology, 4*(1), 85–96.

Kaczmarer, K., and Bach-T-Rita, P. (1995). Haptic displays. In W. Barfield and T. Furness (eds.) *Virtual environments and advanced interface design.* New York: Oxford University Press.

Karis, D. (1987). Fine motor control with CBR protective gloves. *Proceedings of the 31st Annual Meeting of the Human Factors Society* (pp. 1206–1210). Santa Monica, CA: Human Factors Society.

Kryter, K.D. (1972). Speech communications. In H.P. Van Cott and R.G. Kinkade (eds.), *Human engineering guide to system design.* Washington, DC: U.S. Government Printing Office.

Kryter, K.D. (1983). Presbycusis, sociocusis and nosocusis. *Journal of the Acoustical Society of America, 73*(6), 1897–1917.

Lee, J., and Moray, N. (1992). Trust, control strategies and allocation of function in human-machine systems. *Ergonomics, 35,* 1243–1270.

Loomis, J.M., and Lederman, S.J. (1986). Tactual perception. In K. Boff, L. Kaufman, and J. Thomas (eds.), *Handbook of human perception and performance.* New York: Wiley.

Massaro, D.W., and Cohen, M.M. (1995). Perceiving talking faces. *Current Directions in Psychological Science, 4,* 104–109.

Meecham, W. (1983, May 10). Paper delivered at Acoustical Society of America Meeting, Cincinnati, Ohio, as reported in *Science News, 123,* p. 294.

Miller, G.A., Heise, G.A., and Lichten, W. (1951). The intelligibility of speech as a function of the text of the test materials. *Journal of Experimental Psychology, 41,* 329–335.

Miller, G.A., and Nicely, P.E. (1955). An analysis of some perceptual confusions among some English consonants. *J. Acoust. Soc. Amer. 27,* 338.

Muir, B.M. (1988). Trust between humans and machines, and the design of decision aids. In E. Hollnagel, G. Mancini, and D.D. Woods (eds.), *Cognitive engineering in complex dynamic worlds* (pp. 71–83). London: Academic Press.

O'Hare, D., and Roscoe, S.N. (1990). *Flightdeck performance: The human factor.* Ames, IA: Iowa State University Press.

Occupational Safety and Health Administration (1983). Occupational noise exposure: Hearing conservation amendment. *Federal Register, 48,* 9738–9783.

Parasuraman, R., Hancock, P., and Olofinboba, O. (1997). Alarm effectiveness in driver-centered collision warning systems. *Ergonomics 40,* 390–399.

Parasuraman, R., Warm, J.S., and Dember, W.N. (1987). Vigilance, taxonomy and utility. In L.S. Mark, J.S. Warm, and R.L. Huston (eds.), *Ergonomics and human factors* (pp. 11–31). New York: Springer-Verlag.

Patterson, R.D. (1990). Auditory warning sounds in the work environment. *Phil. Trans. R. Soc. Lond. B, 327,* 485–294.

Pisoni, D.B. (1982). Perception of speech: The human listener as a cognitive interface. *Speech Technology, 1,* 10–23.

Reason, J.T., and Brand, J. J. (1975). *Motion sickness.* New York: Academic Press.

Sanders, M.S., and McCormick, E.J. (1993). *Human factors in engineering and design* (7th ed.). New York: McGraw Hill.

Selcon, S.J., Taylor, R.M., and McKenna, F.P. (1995) Integrating multiple information sources: Using redundancy in the design of warnings. *Ergonomics, 38*(11), 2362–2370.

Simpson, C. (1987). Speech controls and displays. In G. Salvendy (ed.), *Handbook of human factors.* New York: Wiley.

Simpson, C., and Williams, D.H. (1980). Response time effects of alerting tone and semantic context for synthesized voice cockpit warnings. *Human Factors, 22,* 319–330.

Sorkin, R.D. (1989). Why are people turning off our alarms? *Human Factors Bulletin, 32*(4), 3–4.

Sorkin, R.D., Kantowitz, B.H., and Kantowitz, S.C. (1988). Likelihood alarm displays. *Human Factors, 30,* 445–460.

Sumby, W., and Pollack, I. (1954). Visual contribution to speech intelligibility in noise. *Journal of the Acoustical Society of America, 26,* 212–215.

Taylor, W., Pearson, J., Mair, A., and Burns, W. (1965). Study of noise and hearing in jute weavers. *Journal of the Acoustical Society of America, 38,* 113–120.

Wickens, C.D. (1992). *Engineering psychology and human performance* (2nd ed.). New York: HarperCollins.

Wolgather, M.S., Kalsher, M.J., and Racicot, B.M. (1993). Behavioral compliance with warnings: Effects of voice, context, and location. *Safety Science, 16,* 637–654.

Yost, W.A. (1994). *Fundamentals of hearing* (3rd ed.). San Diego, CA: Academic Press.

CHAPTER 6

Cognition

Imagine you drive to a downtown city mall for the day to do some Christmas shopping. Conveniently, the mall has its own ten-story parking structure adjacent to it. You spiral up until you find a parking space on one floor near the elevator. Locking your car, you proceed down the elevator and to one of the side entrances to the mall. Five hours later, you carry eight bags back to the elevator, congratulating yourself on the fine job you did of buying gifts for all your friends and relatives. Getting out on the sixth floor, you find that your car is nowhere in sight. After panicking for a brief moment, you carry the eight bags and wander to two other levels before finally locating your car.

Sue had been a casual photographer off and on for years; she usually took outdoor pictures of her family when they went on vacation. When pressed one day, Sue told her sister that she would be willing to take pictures at her sister's wedding reception. On the morning of this auspicious occasion, Sue went to the store and bought film. She wasn't quite sure what film speed to buy for indoor portraits and group shots, so she bought a "medium" 200 speed film, thinking it would be safe. She loaded the film into her 35 mm camera, and hurried to the reception (forgetting to change the setting from 100 to 200 speed film). To take her pictures, Sue knew she had to set the aperture and shutter speed correctly relative to each other because both combine to determine whether the film is exposed to the right amount of light. Sue also remembered that setting the aperture opening in a certain manner would result in the subject being in focus and the background being fuzzy, a feature desirable for portraits. Unfortunately, she couldn't remember whether the aperture should be large or small to get that effect. She inspected the camera control for setting the aperture. The aperture was set with "f stops," (not that she really understood what the "f" meant), and the numbers ranged from 2 to 11, with smaller numbers indicating a larger aperture opening (she didn't understand the reason for this either). Looking at the f stops didn't help her remember *what setting to use, and Sue didn't bring her owner's manual. She realized that while she had once before done this same type of thing, her memory and understanding of the camera were too vague for it to work this time. Finally, not knowing how to determine the settings, Sue gave up and decided to use her mother's instamatic camera—it wouldn't take the same quality of picture, but at least it was easy to use and would do a reliable job.*

During each day, we must process large amounts of information from our environment to accomplish various goals and to make our way successfully through the world. The previous illustrations are typical problems we experience because of a poor match between man-made equipment (or the environment) and the human information processing system. Sometimes these mismatches cause misperceptions, and sometimes people just experience memory failures. While the scenarios described above may seem rather trivial, there are dozens of other cases where difficulties result in injury or death (Casey, 1993; Danaher, 1980; Wickens, 1992). Some of these cases will be discussed later in Chapter 14 on safety. In this chapter, we will consider the basic mechanisms by which people perceive, think, and remember, generally known as *cognition*. As we learn about the various limitations of the human cognitive system, we will consider the implications of, and some solutions for, design problems.

When researchers study the human information processing system, they often cluster the steps into three or four stages. As an example, Kantowitz (1989) suggests three stages: (1) *perceptual stage* in which we bring information in through the senses (sensation) and compare it with knowledge from memory to give it meaning (perception); (2) *cognitive stage* which is a central processing or thought stage where we compare the new information with current goals and memories, transform the information, make inferences, solve problems, and consider responses; and (3) *action stage* in which the brain selects a response and then coordinates/sends motor signals for action. In the previous two chapters, we reviewed the various senses and how information is initially encoded. In this chapter, we briefly discuss some further perceptual processes and then consider the basic mechanisms that occur in the cognitive or *central processing* part of the sequence. In the next chapter, we describe more complex cognitive processes that form the basis of decision making, in Chapter 8, we discuss the implications of this information for display design, and in Chapter 9 we discuss the implications for control.

INFORMATION PROCESSING MODELS

The information processing approach assumes that we receive information from the environment, cognitively act on that information in various ways, and then emit some response back to the environment. The information processing approach is useful for organizing information about the human system and also for guiding human factors designs. There are many theories and models that fall under this category (Wickens & Carswell, 1997), but all portray human information processing as a flow of information between various information stores and transformational processes.

Most information processing models assume a linear progression of processing in stages similar to those depicted in Figure 6.1, which depicts a relatively generic model of human information processing. Recall from Chapters 4 and 5 that sensory information is received by various receptor cells for sight, hearing, smell, taste, and feeling. After the receptor cells have been activated, a sensory trace is stored in the sensory registers. While we have one or more distinct registers for each sensory modality, the entire system is often called the sensory register, or *sensory memory* (Best, 1995). Sensory memory holds a great deal of detailed information but only for a very short period of time (visual sensory memory is about 2–3 seconds). As we discussed in Chapter 4, any information receiving attention is processed further in the *perception* stage. Perception adds meaning to the information by comparing it with relatively permanent information brought from long-term memory. As a result, many stimuli are then assigned to a single perceptual category. As an example, if I look out the window, I might see an amorphous area of white and gray surrounded by blue, and the process of perception compares the lines, shadows, and colors to previous knowledge and recognizes the object as a cloud in a blue sky.

Once meaning is added to sensory information, we either immediately react to the perceptions with a response of some type, or we send the information on to working memory for further processing. *Working memory* is a term for both the short-term store of whatever information is currently active in central processing, and also for a kind of workbench of consciousness in which we compare, evaluate, and transform cognitive representations. Information in working memory decays quite rapidly unless it is rehearsed to keep it there. This activity is maintained

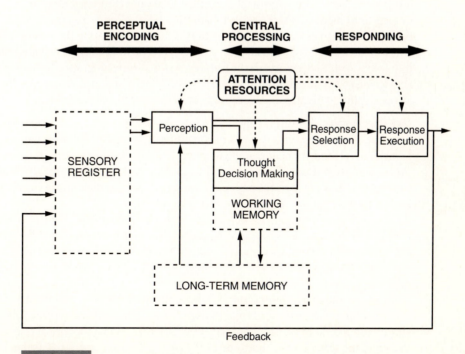

FIGURE 6.1

Generic model of human information processing with three memory systems.

until response selection and execution processes occur. Under certain circumstances, information is encoded into *long-term memory* for later use. These memory stores will be described in more detail at a later point. Finally, most cognitive processes require some allocation of *attentional resources* to proceed efficiently. The two exceptions are the sensory register (which is sometimes described as "preattentive") and the maintenance of material in long-term memory.

OBJECT AND PATTERN PERCEPTION

Perceptual recognition is a cognitive process that compares incoming stimulus information with stored knowledge to categorize the information. Thus, a set of sensory elements are transformed into a mental representation or code. These codes then become the concepts and images with which we work in central processing. Perception is a many-to-one mapping; as it gives meaning to sensory input, it efficiently reduces many simple information "bits" into fewer representations. For human factors design, there are at least two important characteristics of this process: (1) perception by feature analysis and (2) simultaneous top-down and bottom-up processing. In this section, we review these concepts with respect to the visual system. However, auditory perception relies on these same phenomena (Anderson, 1995).

Feature Analysis

Complex stimuli can be broken down into component parts or *features*. To give meaning to stimuli, the features are analyzed individually and compared to features stored in long-term memory (Neisser, 1964; Selfridge, 1959). *Feature analysis* involves recognizing the features that make up a pattern and then evaluating their combination (Anderson, 1995). It is essentially a three-stage process: we break the stimulus pattern into component features, match the features to stored patterns in long-term memory, and decide which stored pattern is the best match. The best match determines the object perception. This appears to occur for both text and object perception.

Text Perception. Feature analysis is relatively straightforward for text perception. For example, the visual stimulus for the letter *A* can be broken down into the features of /, \, and -. The top angle would count as a feature as well. When we see the letter *A*, we compare the features with stored knowledge specifying the features for a capital *A*. If the features match the memory features for *A* more closely than for any other letter, we recognize the letter as a capital *A*.

Feature analysis is performed quickly and, for familiar objects such as letters, without our direct awareness. As a demonstration of this process, consider the experiment performed by Pritchard in 1961. Using an elaborate system of mirrors attached to a contact lens worn by subjects, Pritchard stabilized simple images onto the subject's retina. Two of the images used are shown on the left side of Figure 6.2. In the experiment, subjects became blind within a matter of seconds because retinal receptors need time to refresh. However, subjects reported that the stimuli did not disappear immediately but rather faded in a piecemeal fashion, as shown in the series on the right side of Figure 6.2. It can be seen that as the image faded, the remaining stimuli corresponded to features that were still being processed automatically and recognized as meaningful letters or numbers.

FIGURE 6.2

Disintegration of image stabilized on retina. (*Source:* R. M. Pritchard, 1961. Stabilized images on the retina. *Scientific American, 204[6],* 72–78. Courtesy Eric Mose/Scientific American 1961. Copyright 1961 Eric Mose.)

The perception of print usually proceeds in a hierarchical manner. Features are combined into letters, letters into words, and words into sentences. There are, however, occasions where this process is bypassed. For example, words that we see extremely frequently begin to be processed holistically as a single word rather than as a set of letters or features. Thus, if we see the word *the* enough times, we begin to process it automatically as a global shape rather than as a set of features (Haber & Schindler, 1981; see also Chapter 4). This transformation from feature analysis into more global processing is called *unitization* (Wickens, 1992). In some environments, unitization is a distinct perceptual advantage because the features can be very degraded and the general shape of the word still recognized.

There are several implications of the various processes involved in feature analysis and unitization for the design of textual displays. Among others, these are:

1. *Feature compatibility.* Accuracy and speed of recognition will be greatest when the features in the display are in a format compatible with the features and units in memory. For example, the features for printed words stored in memory preserve diagonal lines, angles differing from 90 degrees, and curves. Text that is displayed on grids or with only horizontal and vertical lines will be less well perceived. This is especially critical when the display must be read in a short time frame or under degraded conditions, such as a long distance or poor lighting.

2. *Upper- and lowercase.* For isolated words, printed capital letters are recognized more easily than lowercase letters (Vartabedian, 1972). However, *in sentences,* a mixture of uppercase and lowercase print is most easily perceived (Tinker, 1955).

3. *Use print for text display.* Print is more easily recognized and read than cursive writing. This and #2 explain why the post office now wants mail addressed with printed words; even the computerized word recognition systems read this most easily.

4. *Minimize abbreviations.* In general, full words rather than abbreviations should be used for displays (e.g., Norman, 1981). When abbreviations must be used, it is best to employ a consistent rule, where the same transformation is always made to determine the abbreviation (Moses & Ehrenreich, 1981). Finally, the best abbreviation rule is truncation, in which only the first few letters of the word are used, such as "reinf" for reinforcement (Wickens, 1992).

5. *Space between words or character strings.* Gaps between words or even arbitrary strings of letters or digits are important for accurate perception

(Wickelgren, 1979). In addition, if random alphanumeric strings are being displayed, the most effective number of characters to "chunk" together between gaps is three to four (Klemmer, 1969). An example would be two small groups of letters or numbers on a vehicle license plate rather than six or seven items all clustered together. There are other advantages to such chunking that will be described when we discuss working memory later in this chapter.

Object Perception.   Feature analysis may be useful in explaining relatively simple patterns such as letters, but what about more complex objects such as buildings, cars, or people? There is evidence that the same type of feature analysis can account for object recognition (Anderson, 1995; Biederman, 1987; Biederman & Ju, 1988; Waltz, 1975). Biederman (1987) has suggested that everyday objects are recognized on the basis of combinations of subobjects. These subobjects are simple geometric shapes called *geons*. Figure 6.3 shows six of Biederman's proposed thirty geons. Geons are made up of defining features just like letters, and object recognition proceeds much like word recognition. We recognize an object by three steps: (1) break the object up into its component geons, (2) categorize each geon on the basis of feature match, and (3) identify the object on the basis of the component geons and their configuration.

An important feature of this type of object recognition is that only edges of the geons are critical for object recognition. Other characteristics such as color, pattern, or texture are not used. Of course, when discriminating between objects having the same geon, such as between an orange and a basketball, these characteristics would become important. The implication for design, especially for computer displays, is straightforward. For object displays, line drawings are often sufficient, but they should convey the edges of the object subcomponents or

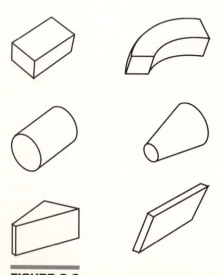

FIGURE 6.3
Sample of geometrical subobjects or "geons."

geons. Line drawings may be superior to photo renderings that have poorly articulated edges, or lower contrast between objects and background (Spencer, 1988;
Schmidt & Kysor, 1987). Color and detail will only be necessary if the subobject
shapes are similar for two or more objects, and the objects therefore cannot be discriminated on the basis of component shape.

Top-Down and Bottom-Up Processing

Up until now, object recognition has been described as being *bottom-up* or data
driven, where the entire process is guided by sensory features. However, one sensory pattern may be recognized as different objects under different environmental conditions. For example, a round object may be recognized as a basketball in
one situation and as a beachball in another. The context surrounding an object
provides information that is used in the recognition process. Figure 6.4 illustrates
a case where the same ambiguous sensory features are recognized as two different
objects; the middle item in the string 48627 is recognized as a digit (6), whereas
the same physical stimulus in the word *table* is recognized as a letter (b). How we
perceive something is determined by what is around it. The process of using context to recognize information is termed *top-down processing* or conceptually driven processing because high-level concepts and information is used to process
"low-level" perceptual features. In fact we have already considered top-down processing in describing the influences of expectancy on visual search and signal detection in Chapter 4 and the influence of sentence context of speech recognition
in Chapter 5.

The use of top-down processing occurs simultaneously and automatically
along with bottom-up processing. It occurs with text, visual stimuli such as drawings, icons, or photographs, and with auditory stimuli. The context effects of top-
down processing are especially critical when stimuli are unclear or incomplete. To
get a feeling for this process, imagine the pharmacist or nurse reading a hand-
scrawled prescription from a doctor. Many of the letters may be completely
unidentifiable individually but may be easy to read in the context of the entire
word or sentence describing the disease for which the medication is prescribed.
This example illustrates the principle of *redundancy.* When we read a word, there
is a great deal of redundant information because, in context, we do not need to
read all of the letters in a word to recognize it. Anderson (1995) gives an example

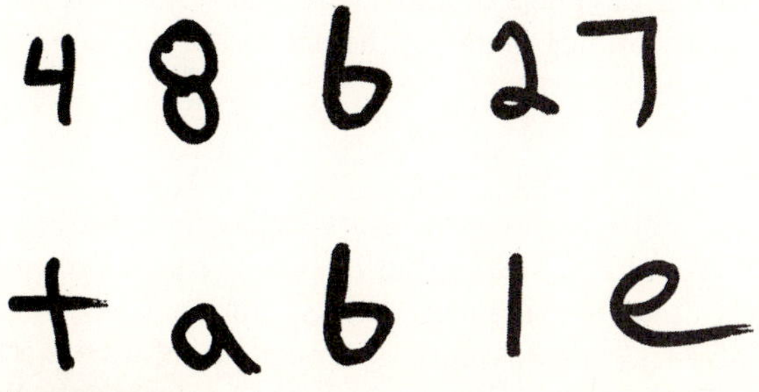

FIGURE 6.4
Context effects where the same stimulus is perceived as the number 6 or the letter *b*.

of this principle with the following sentence: I cxn rxplxce xvexy txirx lextex of x sextexce xitx an x, anx yox stxll xan xanxge xo rxad xt—ix wixh sxme xifxicxltx. Even when the stimulus is degraded, we can still recognize the letters and therefore the word. Because of top-down processing, sentence context or other surrounding information (such as the general topic) can facilitate recognition of words or other objects.

While the printed word endures in front of us, the voice image is fleeting. Therefore top-down processing is even more critical for speech recognition than reading; the verbal context around critical spoken words greatly facilitates their recognition. For example, in an experiment by Simpson (1976), pilots listened to synthesized speech warnings presented against background noise. The warnings were either the critical words only, such as "fuel low," or the warnings in a sentence context, such as "Your fuel is low." Recognition for the warnings was much more accurate in the sentence context condition.

Top-down and bottom-up processing often trade off against one another. When the stimulus quality is high, bottom-up processing will predominate. As stimulus quality degrades, increases in context and redundancy will be necessary so that more top-down processing can keep recognition levels high. The relative effects of top-down and bottom-up processing are important for design of text displays, icons, or other stimuli. The following guidelines should be employed:

1. *Optimize bottom-up processing* for text and objects by optimizing critical factors such as size, contrast, etc. (see Chapters 4 and 8).

2. *Optimize top-down processing* for text and objects by methods such as using actual words rather than random text strings, using more rather than fewer words. Second, restrict the total overall message vocabulary; if there are fewer possible words to be recognized, top-down processing becomes more efficient. Third, provide as much context information as possible to aid in recognition and comprehension of information.

3. *Evaluate tradeoffs.* Given a limited space for displaying text or objects, evaluate total environment for degraded viewing conditions and availability of context effects to determine the appropriate trade-off between bottom-up and top-down processing.

4. *Usability Testing.* When performing usability testing, we often evaluate the recognition (and comprehension) of icons. Given that real-world recognition involves top-down processing, designers should *not* do usability testing for icons in a laboratory without the surrounding environmental and/or task context.

Pictures and Icons

It is becoming more common to use icons for short displays rather than words, especially for computer applications such as buttons on a screen. Designers often have to decide whether it is better to use text or icons. Unfortunately, there are not clearcut answers on this issue, but we can consider certain information that will provide guidelines. A more detailed discussion of display elements will be provided in Chapter 8.

Previous research has shown that familiar objects in pictures can be understood at least as rapidly as words (e.g., Potter & Faulconer, 1975). In addition, familiar objects are recognized and stored in memory as both an analog spatial image as well as a semantic or symbolic (idea) encoding (Wickens, 1992). If we combine this fact with the consideration that pictures are universal and not language dependent, they seem to be the ideal element for displays. For this reason, we see an increasing use of pictorial icons for applications such as highway signs, building signs, and computer displays.

Pictures and icons should be used with caution for two reasons (Wickens, 1992). The first is an issue of *legibility*. As we saw, objects are discriminated on the basis of general shape or shape of components. If icons are perceived under suboptimal viewing conditions, they may be difficult to discriminate. As described in Chapter 8, symbols and pictorial messages should be designed to share a minimal number of features.

The second issue is one of comprehensive or *interpretation* (although this can also be a problem with words). Interpretation of a symbol or icon can be broken into two steps: determining what object is being represented and determining what that object means. Even if a symbol is recognized, its meaning may not be interpreted correctly. For example, an arrow on a computer screen could be perceived as an arrow. However, it might be interpreted as pointing to a particular area, commanding an action in a particular direction, showing a button allowing movement to the next page, and so forth. Even within the context of the task, it may be unclear what symbols and icons mean. In the chapter on safety, we will see that the design of warning symbols and labels can be difficult. Often the difficulties center around the ability of people to interpret correctly the meaning of short or abstract warning signs and symbols.

The implications for the design of symbols and icons are clear. Icons should be designed so that they are easily discriminated from one another, and so that their meaning is apparent. Unfortunately, this is often more difficult that it sounds. To help with this situation, symbols are becoming *standardized* so that over time, all users know what certain symbols stand for. This is especially common in public use circumstances such as roadways and public buildings. Several organizations, such as American National Standards Institute (ANSI) and International Organisation for Standardization (ISO) are standardizing international symbols. In addition, most experts suggest that when possible, words should be used along with symbols (Norman, 1981; Wickens, 1992). This redundancy helps reduce uncertainty in viewers.

Finally, any time a new set of symbols or icons is being designed, the set should be usability tested to make sure operators will interpret their meaning correctly. When possible, this usability testing should be performed in the operating environment and within the context of task performance.

TRANSFER TO WORKING MEMORY

Information, once recognized, either leads directly to a response (as in an automatic stimulus-response association) or goes to *working memory* for further processing.

A DESIGN EXAMPLE

In research conducted in 1988, Aurelio found that only part of the symbols used for cameras conveyed the intended meaning and that "there was a significant amount of confusion" among the symbols. Crist and Aurelio (1990) determined to develop and test a set of symbols that would be interpreted correctly by camera operators. They first developed a set of messages or statements in verbal form and then translated these into symbols. After considering the full range of manual to automatic cameras, the researchers had developed a set of 81 verbal statements. These included messages such as Rewind release, Film speed setting, Rewind start, Soft focus select, Regular lens, Zoom in, Wait for flash, and so on.

The designers evaluated the importance and frequency of use for the various messages and then narrowed the set down to fifteen concepts or statements. Symbols were developed for almost all of the statements. The authors noted that some symbols were easier to design than others. For example, symbols having to do with concrete objects, such as the battery or film, were relatively easy to design by incorporating figures of the objects as part of the icon. Others were more difficult because the message did not involve a concrete object. For example, the message "wait for flash" resulted in no acceptable symbol at all. Some symbols had already been standardized by ANSI (ANSI, 1988); for example, the symbol for wide-angle lens is shown on the left side of Figure 6.5. Note that a person must first recognize that the symbol represents three trees and then must realize that it denotes the type of lens one would use for trees (a wide-angle lens). It can be seen that even though a symbol is standardized, it does not mean that it will be readily interpreted by the novice user. Other symbols were developed specifically for the study, such as the middle and right symbols in Figure 6.5. For example, the flash-fill symbol is "lightning bolt plus sun" because the lightning bolt is the standardized symbol for flash. However, this does not mean that the average camera operator will know that a symbol combining a lightning bolt and the sun means fill-flash. To determine whether users can interpret symbols, de-

FIGURE 6.5

Symbol used to represent regular lens (as opposed to telephoto), zoom, and fill-flash, respectively. (*Source:* Crist, B., and Aurelio, D. N., 1990. Development of camera symbols for consumers. *Proceedings of the Human Factors Society 34th Annual Meeting* [pp. 489–493]. Santa Monica, CA: Human Factors Society. Reprinted with permission. Copyright 1990 by the Human Factors and Ergonomics Society. All rights reserved.)

signers must use systematic methods to generate alternative symbols and then test them using a representative set of users in the context of the task. As an example, Figure 6.6 shows five alternative symbol designs for fill-flash (Crist & Aurelio, 1990).

FIGURE 6.6
Alternative symbols to represent fill-flash. (*Source:* Crist, B., and Aurelio, D.N., 1990. Development of camera symbols for consumers. *Proceedings of the Human Factors Society 34th Annual Meeting* [pp. 489–493]. Santa Monica, CA: Human Factors Society. Reprinted with permission. Copyright 1990 by the Human Factors and Ergonomics Society. All rights reserved.)

Working memory is the temporary "workbench" of the mind, where information is transformed and acted on. One of the things that has been firmly established in cognitive psychology is that only a very limited amount of information can be brought from the sensory register to working memory (Anderson, 1995; Best, 1995). This can be thought of as the first major bottleneck in the information processing system, one that is often overlooked in system design.

The sensory register only holds visual information for about 1 second, and auditory information for 3–5 seconds. During that time, attention may be focused on a subset of the information and brought into working memory for further processing. This attentional process is called *selective attention* and refers to the process of focusing on some pieces of information but not others. An analogy is that of a *spotlight,* which can be moved around a field and narrowed in on certain objects or information. In Chapter 4, we saw this spotlight operating in serial visual search tasks. The information in the spotlight is highly detailed, while other "surrounding" information is perceived and processed in only a very rough or general way. As an example, in the auditory domain, if you are in a room with five conversations going on around you, you are able to focus attention on one message and bring it into working memory for processing. You will only be dimly aware of the other messages including certain basic physical characteristics such as gender. These other messages are not processed at a detailed level (unless you switch attention back and forth). Thus, we say that people can only attend to one auditory channel at a time. The spotlight of selective attention can also be directed inwardly to purely mental activity, such as rehearsal and problem solving.

The implications of these cognitive limitations for the design of displays are strong. If people can attend to only a part of the information they receive at any given time, designers cannot assume that just because information is presented, it will be processed. The limitations can be broken down into two factors: how much information is presented to the operator and in what way the information is presented. First, designers must be careful not to present a large quantity of information and expect people to be able to process it in a short time. It is estimated that in the Three-Mile Island incident, at one point operators had to attend to *several hundred* messages, signals, or displays at one time (Wickens, 1992). However, as we will discuss in Chapter 8, sometimes designers can *configure* multiple displays to appear more as a single unified whole and thus processed as one by the spotlight, much as two voices can be selected for attention at once if they are both singing harmonious parts of the same song.

Second, designers should realize that for displays with numerous components, only a small amount of information will be attended to at a time. This means that the information most critical to task performance must be provided in a way that will catch the person's attention. Visually, this is accomplished by putting it directly in front of the operator, making it noticeable or *salient*. Sometimes automation can temporarily highlight information that will be most relevant at one particular time (see Chapter 16). These factors are considered more fully in the chapter on display design.

WORKING MEMORY

Failures of memory occur for everyone, and relatively frequently. Sometimes the failures are trivial, such as forgetting to let the cat back in the house (unless it is −30° outside, then the problem is not so trivial). Other times memory failures are more critical. For example, in 1915, a railroad switchman at a station in Scotland forgot that he had moved a train to an active track. As a result, two oncoming trains used the same track and the ensuing crash killed over 200 people (Rolt, 1978).

In the next few sections, we will be focusing on the part of cognition that involves human memory systems. There is substantial evidence that there are two very different types of memory storage. The first, *working memory* (sometimes termed *short-term memory*), is relatively transient and limited to holding a small amount of information that may be either rehearsed or "worked on" by other cognitive transformations. It is the temporary store that keeps information *active* while we are using it or until we use it. Some examples are: looking up a phone number and then holding it in working memory until we have completed dialing the number; a nurse rehearsing the instructions given by the physician until they can be executed; or the use of working memory to "hold" the subsums while we multiply two two-digit numbers together. We will see that working memory holds two different types of information, verbal and spatial.

The other memory store, *long-term memory,* involves the storage of information after it is no longer active in working memory and then the retrieval of the information at a later point in time. Conceptually, working memory is the temporary holding of information that is active, while long-term memory is the *reactivation* of information. When we are performing central information processing in working memory, we bring information from the sensory register and also from long-term memory into working memory. The limitations of working memory hold major implications for system design. Consider the problem confronted by the user of a computer system who must look up error instructions in two separate pages of a manual and hold each of these in working memory, while also examining the computer screen. Working memory must be able to accommodate these demands while still supporting active problem-solving operations.

A Model of Working Memory

Imagine you have just looked up a phone number in the book and are about to dial the number. A friend begins talking to you and asks a question. You answer, but then realize you have forgotten the phone number. It has been "bumped out" of the limited-capacity working memory system.

Working memory can be understood in the context of a model proposed by Baddeley (1986, 1990). Working memory consists of three components, as shown in Figure 6.7. In this model, a central executive component acts as an attentional control system that coordinates information from the two "storage" systems. The visuospatial sketch pad holds information in an analog spatial form (e.g., visual imagery) while it is being used. These images consist of encoded information that has been brought from the visual-sensory register or from long-term memory. Thus the air traffic controller will use the visual-spatial sketchpad to retain information regarding where planes are located in the airspace. This representation will be essential if the display is momentarily lost from view. The phonological loop represents verbal information in an acoustical form (Baddeley, 1990). It is kept active, or "rehearsed," by articulating words or sounds, either vocally or subvocally. Thus, when we are trying to remember a phone number, we subvocally sound out the numbers until we no longer need them.

Whether material is verbal (in the phonetic loop) or spatial (in the visuospatial sketchpad), our ability to maintain information in working memory is limited in two respects: how *much* information can be kept active and how *long* it can be kept active; that is, capacity and time.

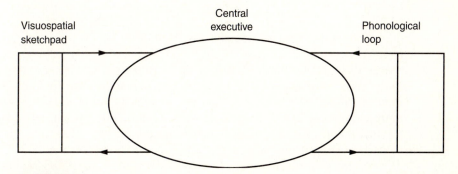

FIGURE 6.7

Baddeley's model of working memory with two storage subsystems serving a central executive coordinating system. (*Source:* Baddeley, A. D., 1986. *Working memory.* New York: Oxford University Press. Copyright © 1986. Reprinted by permission of Oxford University Press.)

Capacity.   Researchers have defined the upper limit of the *capacity* of working memory to be around 7 ± 2 *chunks* of information (Miller, 1956). A chunk is the unit of working memory space. A chunk in working memory is defined jointly by the physical and cognitive properties that *bind* items together. Thus the sequence: 8 4 7 9 consists of four chunks. The sequence: 28 36 45 89 also consists of four physical chunks, even though there are twice as many digits. In each case, there is greater physical spacing between the units than within. While the concept of chunks is useful, it is still the case that working memory capacity will be smaller as chunks become larger. Thus, while we may be able to retain seven single digits, our capacity for the two-digit numbers will be somewhat less.

Sometimes cognitive binding can replace (or augment) the physical binding. Thus, for example, the string USAFBICIA represents only three chunks of information to the American reader familiar with government organizations, even though there is no physical spacing between the elements. However, there are *cognitive rules* stored in long-term memory, as a result of our experience, that bind the letters in USA, FBI, and CIA together in such a way that this string only occupies three and not nine spaces in working memory. As this example illustrates, chunking is not an all-or-none thing. The extent to which units are grouped as cognitive chunks depends on the degree of user familiarity with those groupings.

Chunking benefits the operations in working memory in several ways. First, and most directly, it reduces the number of items in working memory and therefore increases the capacity of working memory storage. Second, ideally, cognitive chunking makes use of meaningful associations in long-term memory, and this will aid in retention of the information. Third, because of the reduced number of items in working memory, material can be more easily rehearsed and is more likely to be transferred to long-term memory (which then reduces load on working memory).

Time.   The capacity limits of working memory are closely related to the second limitation of working memory, the limit of *how long* information may remain. The strength of information in working memory decays over time unless it is periodically *reactivated,* a process referred to as *maintenance rehearsal.* Maintenance rehearsal for acoustic items is essentially a serial process of subvocally articulating each item. Thus, for a string of items, the interval for reactivating any particular item depends on the length of time to proceed through the whole string. For a seven-digit phone number, we can serially reactivate all items in a relatively short time, short enough to keep all items active (i.e., so that the first digit in the phone number will still be active by the time we have cycled through the last item). The more chunks contained in working memory, the longer it will take to cycle through the items in maintenance rehearsal, and the more likely it will be that items have decayed beyond the point where they can be reactivated. To help predict working memory decay for differing numbers of chunks, Card, Moran, and Newell (1986) combined the data from several studies to determine the "half life" of items in working memory (the delay after which recall is reduced by one-half). The half-life was estimated to be approximately 7 seconds for a memory store of three chunks and 70 seconds for one chunk. The visuospatial sketchpad shows an analogous decay of the accuracy with which position can be remembered (Moray, 1986).

There are two additional variables that influence the rate of working memory loss: attention and similarity. For example, if instead of rehearsing the phone number we are trying to retain, we divert our attention to a verbal message, there will be a greater decay of the numbers before they can be reactivated, and it will be more likely to be lost from working memory. The decay may cause items to be lost completely, or it may cause critical acoustic features, such as the phoneme that discriminates *b* from *d,* to be lost. Hence, decay and time are more critical for similar-sounding material.

Human Factors Implications of Working Memory Limits

1. *Minimize working memory load.* An overall rule of thumb is that both the time and the number of alphanumeric items that human operators have to retain in working memory during task performance should be kept to a minimum (Loftus, Dark, & Williams, 1979). Hence, any technique that can off-load more information in working memory sooner will be of value. As an example, an advantage of the touch tone phone over the old rotary dial system was the greater speed of number entry with the touch tone and therefore a shorter time that the phone number needed to be stored in the phone user's vulnerable working memory.

2. *Provide visual echoes.* Wherever synthetic voice is used to convey verbal messages, these messages can, and ideally should, be coupled with a redundant visual (print) readout of the information so that the human's use of the material is not vulnerable to working memory failures. For example, since automated telephone assistance can now "speak" phone numbers with a synthetic voice, a small visual panel attached to the phone could display the same number as a "visual echo."

3. *Exploit chunking.* We have seen how chunking can increase the amount of material held in working memory and increase its transfer to long-term memory. Thus, any way in which we can take advantage of chunking will be beneficial. There are several ways in which this can be done:

- *Physical chunk size.* For presenting arbitrary strings of letters, numbers, or both, the optimal chunk size is three to four numbers or letters per chunk (Bailey, 1989; Wickelgren, 1964).
- *Meaningful sequences.* The best procedure for creating cognitive chunks is to find or create meaningful sequences within the total string of characters. A meaningful sequence should already have an integral representation in long-term memory. This means that the sequence is retained as a single item rather than a set of the individual characters. Meaningful sequences include things such as 555, JUNE, or 4321.
- *Superiority of letters over numbers.* In general, letters induce better chunking than numbers because of their greater potential for meaningfulness. Advertisers on TV have capitalized on this principle by moving from numbers such as "1-800-663-5900," which has eight chunks, to letter-based chunking such as "1-800-GET HELP," which has three chunks ("1-800" is a sufficiently familiar string that it is just one chunk).

Grouping letters into one word, and thus one chunk, can greatly increase working memory capabilities.

■ *Keeping numbers separate from letters.* If displays must contain a mixture of numbers and letters, it is better to keep them separated (Preczewski & Fisher, 1990). For example, a license plate containing one numeric and one alphabetic chunk, such as "458 GST," will be more easily kept in working memory than a combination such as "4G58ST" or "4G58 ST."

4. *Minimize confusability.* The principle of confusability applies to working memory just as it does to visual and auditory perception (Chapters 4, 5, and 8). Thus, the items in working memory will be more difficult to recall in their correct order if they sound similar. The sequence DPZETG is more difficult to remember in its correct order than is the sequence JTFWRU. Similar arguments can be made with regard to the visuo-spatial sketchpad: It will be more difficult for the air traffic controller to remember the relative locations of three similar-looking aircraft than of three distinct ones.

Confusability in working memory can be reduced by building physical distinctions into material to be retained. We have already noted that making words and letters sound more different will reduce the likelihood that they will be confused during rehearsal. Hess, Detweiler, and Ellis (1994) have examined similar effects in "keeping track" tasks, in which the operator must keep track of the state of several items that change over time (e.g., the vehicle dispatcher who monitors the state of readiness, use, and location of several vehicles). They find a great advantage to working memory for item states if each item is represented in a separate spatial location on a display rather than when all are consigned to be viewed within a single window. Here spatial location represents a salient cue to reduce item confusibility.

5. *Exploit different working-memory codes.* We have seen that working memory processes and retains two qualitatively different types of information, visual-spatial and verbal-phonetic. These two subsystems in Baddeley's model are sometimes referred to as working memory *codes.* Each of these systems seems to process information somewhat independently, and each has its own resources. This means that if one code is being used in working memory, it will be interrupted more by processing that *same type* of information than by processing information in the alternative code. There is a large body of evidence for this assumption (see Wickens, 1992). For example, when people perform tasks that rely on visual imagery (visuo-spatial code), they can add a *concurrent* task involving verbal or phonetic material with much greater success than adding a secondary task involving visual information (e.g., Brooks, 1968; Wickens & Liu, 1988). In summary, visual-spatial information suffers from greater interference if additional information or tasks involve visual rather than verbal-phonetic information. And verbal information is interfered with more if the additional information is verbal material, regardless of whether it is spoken or print. (This principle was apparently not known when one of our daughters brought in a piece of paper with a question written on it, assuming that this would interfere less with the process of book writing than if the question was asked orally.)

6. *Ordering of text and instructions.* Text can be written that places greater or lesser loads on working memory. For example, comprehension will be made more difficult by any text that requires retention of words whose meaning are not immediately apparent until a later portion of the sentence is read. A related issue concerns the use of *congruent* versus *incongruent* instructions (Wickens, 1992). With congruent instructions, the order of words (or commands) in the instructions corresponds with the actual order in which they are to be carried out ("Do A, then do B, then do C"); whereas with incongruent instructions, this matching of order is missing ("Prior to doing C, do B, and before B is done, do A"). More details on text and instructional design will be given in Chapter 18.

LONG-TERM MEMORY

We constantly maintain information in working memory for its immediate use, but we also need a mechanism for storing information and retrieving it at later times. This mechanism is termed *long-term memory,* or long-term store. *Learning* is the processing of storing information in long-term memory, and when specific procedures are designed to facilitate learning, we refer to this as instruction or *training,* an issue we will treat in depth in Chapter 18.

Long-term memory can be distinguished by whether it involves memory for general knowledge, which we refer to as *semantic memory,* or specific events, which we refer to as *event memory.* Psychologists distinguish between two types of event memory, pertaining to the past, and to the future. *Episodic memory* is memory for an episode that has occurred in the past, like an accident or incident at the workplace. *Prospective memory* represents the requirement to *remember to do something* in the future, like bringing a particular book to the office or meeting someone at a place and time.

The ability to remember key information from long-term memory is important for many tasks in daily life. We saw at the beginning of this chapter that failure to recall even simple types of information can cause annoying problems, such as forgetting where we parked, forgetting where we put the keys, forgetting to call a person, and so forth. In many jobs, forgetting to perform even one part of a job sequence can have catastrophic consequences. In this section, we will review the basic mechanisms that underlie storage and retrieval of information from long-term memory and how to design around the limitations of the long-term memory system.

Basic Mechanisms

Most tasks require us to think about task-relevant information—interpret displays, choose responses, and so forth. Thinking involves activation of the task-relevant material in working memory. This activation may be triggered by perception, such as when we see a warning signal that triggers understanding of the appropriate action to take. Alternatively, it may be triggered directly from long-term memory, such as when we recall an action that needs to be taken, or it may recall the steps for logging onto a computer without reference to a manual.

The availability of information to be reactivated from long-term memory is influenced by two major factors: the *strength* of the pattern itself and how strongly it is *associated* with other items in memory.

Item Strength.   Let us consider an example of the first factor, item strength. If a person uses his or her social security number every day, it is activated frequently. The more often it is activated, the stronger the memory trace, and the easier it is to activate it in the future. In addition, the more recently it has been activated, the easier its retrieval will be because the trace has not decayed appreciably. So for the first factor, we can say that the ability to retrieve or reactivate information depends on its strength, which in turn depends on the *frequency* and the *recency* of its activation.

On the one hand, if a job sequence is carried out by someone every day, we can assume that at some point the frequency and recency will cause the items to have a strong representation, and they will be able to retrieve the sequence at will without difficulty (this does not imply they will never make errors). On the other hand, if a person does the task infrequently (i.e., an unusual emergency procedure) or is a "casual user," remembering the information will be more difficult. This is why institutions such as the armed services must constantly train its personnel—so that necessary knowledge and skills stay accessible. It is also why task analysis should include evaluation of the frequency with which tasks are performed. Infrequently accessed knowledge needs a different type of design support than knowledge and skills that are used relatively frequently. Some systems, such as computer software or cameras, must be designed for both frequent and casual users.

Associations.   The second factor, *association* with other items, is related to how the information is initially processed. If we process two pieces of information in working memory at the same time, they become associated in memory. These associations can form the basis for later reactivation. For example, in learning a new technical job, trainees may need to learn to associate names—often abbreviations or acronyms—with specific pieces of equipment. Seeing the equipment may then cause the abbreviation to become active. This *associative memory* process can be experienced if you try to recall what you ate for dinner yesterday. It is likely that you imagine the place and the people you were with and gradually reconstruct the multitude of experiences that eventually cause you to think of the food. Associations between items have a strength of their own, just as individual items do. As time passes, if associations are not repeated, they become weaker. At some later point, the worker might see the equipment but be unable to remember its name.

Information in long-term memory will become more available as a function of the richness or *number* of associations that can be made. Like strings tied to an underwater object, the more strings there are, the greater likelihood that any one (or several) can be found and pulled to retrieve the object. Thus, thinking about the material you learn in class in many different contexts, with different illustrative examples, will improve your ability to later remember that material.

Forming meaningful associations between items and storing them in long-term memory results in the formation of *chunks,* which is valuable in reducing the load on working memory. Sometimes however, when rehearsing items through simple repetition, our memories may be based solely on frequency and recency, which is essentially "rote memory." When children memorize mathematical facts, they must rely on rote memory because there are few associations to help with retrieval. This is a second reason that advertisers have moved from solely digit-based phone numbers to items such as 1-800-GET-HELP. Such phone numbers have fewer items and more associative meaning.

Forgetting.   The decay of item strength and association strength occurs in the form of an exponential curve, where people experience a very rapid decline in memory within the first few days. This is why evaluating the effects of training immediately after an instructional unit is finished does not accurately indicate the degree of one's eventual memory.

Even when material is rehearsed to avoid forgetting, if there are many associations that must be acquired within a short period of time, they can interfere with each other or become confused, particularly if the associations pertain to similar material. New trainees may well recall the equipment they have seen and the names they have learned but they confuse which piece of equipment is called which name, as the newer associations interfere with the older ones.

Thus, memory retrieval often fails because of (1) weak strength due to low frequency or recency, (2) weak or few associations with other information, and (3) interfering associations. To increase the likelihood that information will be remembered at a later time, it should be processed in working memory frequently and in conjunction with other information in a meaningful way.

Organization of Information in Long-Term Memory

It is apparent from the description of working memory that we do not put isolated pieces of information in long-term memory the way we would put papers in a filing cabinet. Instead, we store items in connection with related information. The information in long-term memory is stored in associative networks, where each piece of information (or image or sound) is associated with other related information. Much of our knowledge that we use for daily activities is *semantic* knowledge, that is, the basic meaning of things. Cognitive psychologists have performed research showing that our knowledge seems to be organized into *semantic networks,* where sections of the network contain related pieces of information. Thus, you probably have a section of your semantic network that relates all of your knowledge about college professors, both general information and specific instances based on previous experience. These semantic networks are then linked to other associated information such as images, sounds, and so on.

Since long-term memory is largely based on semantic networks, retrieval of information is based largely on semantic associations. That is, to retrieve an item, people must first activate something with which it has a semantic association. We often reactivate a memory by simultaneously thinking of several semantically related concepts. This initiates *parallel processing* where activation spreads to associated concepts, hopefully providing enough activation at the right place to trigger recall of the desired information.

Consider our initial example of parking in a parkade and then shopping for the day. Knowing that you parked on the sixth level is a relatively isolated piece of information. Even if the garage has color-coded levels, knowing that you parked on the "red" floor is still an isolated piece of information that may be difficult to reactivate later. To make the information easier to retrieve, it must be associated with something meaningful and memorable. As an example, you might think that red is the color for anger and that you were angry at your dog for chewing up a chair. Later when you try to remember to color of the floor you parked on, you will think to yourself . . . color of parking floor, story about dog, dog chewed chair, angry at dog, red is color of anger. Unfortunately developing such a memory aid is a process that most people do not indulge in, so a well-designed parkade would instead be better off designed with a machine to stamp your parking ticket with the floor color.

Schemas.   The information we have in long-term memory tends to be organized around central concepts or topics. The entire knowledge structure about a particular topic is often termed a *schema*. People have schemas about all aspects of their world, including equipment and systems that they use. Examples of common schemas are semantic networks associated with "college courses," "cups," or "vacations." Schemas that describe a typical *sequence* of activities, like going on a date, getting up in the morning, or dealing with a crisis at work, are called *scripts* (Schank & Abelson, 1977).

Mental Models.   People also have schemas about equipment or systems. The fact that systems are typically dynamic in nature makes them unique, and schemas of them are often referred to as *mental models* (Gentner & Stevens, 1983; Norman, 1988; Rouse & Morris, 1986; Wilson & Rutherford, 1989). Mental models typically include our understanding of system components, how the system works, and how to use it. In particular, mental models generate a set of *expectancies* about how the equipment or system will behave.

Mental models may vary on their degree of *completeness* and *correctness*. For example, a correct mental model of aerodynamics posits that an aircraft stays aloft because of the vacuum created over the wings. An incorrect model assumes that it stays aloft by virtue of the speed through the airspace. Mental models may also differ in terms of whether they are personal (possessed by a single individual), or are similar across large groups of people. In the latter case the mental model defines a *population stereotype*. Designs that are consistent with the population stereotype are said to be *compatible* with the stereotype (such as turning a knob clockwise should move a radio dial to the right). Later chapters on displays, controls, and computer-supported decision making will illustrate the importance of knowing the user's mental model.

Sometimes people have a related *set* of mental models that vary for different pieces of equipment because of lack of standardization. For example, when a computer printer runs out of paper, one model might continue printing if the user presses "reset," while another might resume printing immediately after paper is loaded. The need for a different mental model for every different brand or model of a given type of equipment greatly increases the memory load for operators.

Implications for Design

Designers frequently fail to realize or predict the difficulty people will experience in using their system. One reason is that they are extremely familiar with the system and have a very detailed and complete mental model (Norman, 1988). They know how the system works, when it will do various things, and how to control the system to do what the user wishes. They fail to realize that the average user does not have this mental model and will probably never interact with the system enough to develop one. When people have to do even simple tasks on an infrequent basis, they will forget things. Manufacturers write owner's manuals as if they will be read thoroughly, and all of the information will be remembered for the life of the equipment. Neither is necessarily the case. Even if we have very clear and explicit instructions for operating our programmable VCR (which is unlikely), or our 35 mm camera (which is also unlikely), what average owner wants to get the instructions out every time he or she must perform a task?

What are some ways that we can design the environment and systems within it so that people do not have problems, errors, accidents, and inconveniences due to poor retrieval from long-term memory?

1. *Encourage regular use of information* to increase frequency and recency.

2. *Standardize.* One way that we can decrease the load on long-term memory is to standardize environments and equipment, including controls, displays, symbols, and operating procedures. Knowing how to perform basic operations with one microwave oven should be retrievable and applicable to all other microwave ovens. An example from the automotive industry where a control is being standardized is the shift pattern, and where a control has still not been standardized is the location and operation of electronic windows and lighting. Standardization results in development of strong yet simple schemas that are applicable to a wide variety of circumstances. Computer software designers are beginning to realize the benefits of standardization, with Microsoft Windows being a good example.

3. *Use memory aids.* When a task will be performed infrequently, or when correct task performance is critical, designers should provide computer-based or hardcopy memory aids. These consist of information critical for task performance and can be as simple as a list of procedures. In an office near one of us, a fax machine is endowed with a particularly poor interface. People who used it infrequently had trouble remembering the correct sequence of procedures. Someone wrote a simple yet effective memory aid and posted it on the wall, part of which was:

> *FOR LONG-DISTANCE FAX*
> - Press blue TEL/DIAL button
> - Press 9
> - Press PAUSE/REDIAL button
> - Enter 1-area code-number

This sequence was difficult to remember because there was no inherent meaning to the sequence, and it was therefore difficult to reconstruct. Norman (1988) characterizes memory aids as putting "knowledge in the world" so that the operator does not have to rely on "knowledge in the head." Chapter 15 demonstrates that, for human-computer interaction, computer menus provide printed options that represent knowledge in the world, whereas memorized commands require knowledge in the head.

4. *Carefully design information to be remembered.* Information that must be remembered and later retrieved unaided should have characteristics such as the following:

- Be meaningful to the individual and semantically associated with other information
- Concrete rather than abstract words when possible
- Distinctive concepts and information (to reduce interference)
- Well-organized sets of information (grouped or otherwise associated)
- An item should be able to be guessed based on other information
- A diverse set of modalities
- Little technical jargon
- Adequate context and background knowledge

5. *Encourage active verbalization or production of information that is to be recalled.* For example, taking notes in class, or requiring active recitation or "readback" of heard instructions will increase the likelihood that the information will not be forgotten.

6. *Design information to be consistent with existing mental models and population stereotypes.* This guideline emphasizes the point made in Chapter 3 on design: Know Thy User.

7. *Design to support development of mental models.* One way to do this is to apply the concept of visibility, as suggested by Norman (1988). This guideline suggests that a device has visibility if one can immediately and easily determine the state of the device and the alternatives for action. For example, switches that have different positions when activated have visibility, whereas push/toggle switches do not. The concept of visibility also relates to the ability of a system to show variables intervening between an operator's action and the ultimate system response. An example would be an oven display showing that an input has been read, the heat system is warming up, and the temperature has not reached the target temperature. Mental model development can also be encouraged by the appropriate wording of instructional manuals that describe *why* a particular action is required, as well as what the action is.

Declarative and Procedural Knowledge

In a previous section, we talked about information in long-term memory and how it is stored in the form of semantic networks. However, as we noted at the outset, the distinction between declarative and procedural knowledge is important. To elaborate, *declarative knowledge,* or knowledge about things that we can verbalize (Anderson, 1995), is what we store in semantic networks, and it

DESIGNING FOR LONG-TERM MEMORY: A CASE STUDY

In the beginning of this chapter, we described a female who is a casual photographer and uses her camera on an intermittent basis. Like many other amateurs, she is dissatisfied with a totally automatic or "instamatic" camera because it is very limited and only takes standard snapshots. What other choice does she have? Manufacturers originally offered amateur photographers a choice of 35 mm cameras on two ends of a continuum: completely automatic or a completely manual single lens reflex (SLR). The SLR allowed the use of different lenses, different filters, flash attachments, and a host of other options. However, it also required that the operator perform many tasks including: select film speed, set the aperture, set the shutter speed, focus, choose appropriate lighting combinations, choose the appropriate lens/filter combination, and other tasks that are complex and difficult for many people. To address this complexity, manufacturers are beginning to offer equipment that can be thought of as manual cameras that have part of the settings automated (and many also have one optional setting that makes *everything* automatic). Given what we know about long-term memory, how successful are these cameras likely to be?

In order to evaluate some features of camera design from the perspective of support for long-term memory, we must first evaluate certain aspects of the basic system itself. Consider the variables involved in taking a picture, which for a manual 35 mm camera must be considered and "set" by the operator. In all cases, the operator must consider the needs of the current shot(s), and make choices for all of the variables listed in Table 6.1. For any given type of shot that the operator wants to achieve (such as a portrait shot, off-center, in bright sunlight, with the background out of focus), there is a certain combination of choices for these eight variables that will best produce the desired result. If we evaluate the variables in light of what we know about long-term memory, we can immediately see several problems. First, for some of the variables, the settings are not meaningful. For a novice, the fact that aperture is set by "f stop" increments makes no sense. To remember that a smaller number means a bigger aperture is equally meaningless because we do not know why. In setting shutter speed, the operator must recall the different speeds that are required to capture different types of actions, such as walking, running, cycling, driving, and so forth. In sum, the relevant knowledge about most of the tasks will be difficult to reactivate at a later time because to a novice it is arbitrary and not meaningful.

Second, different types of shots require different *combinations* of the eight variables. Even if an operator remembers the meaning of all eight variables and their settings, they may not remember the particular combination of settings that would be appropriate for the shot desired.

TABLE 6.1 Tasks Required for Taking Pictures with Manual SLR Camera

1. Choose film (which means choice of film speed)	Film is categorized as having a "speed," which means how sensitive it is to light. Fast film is more sensitive and therefore doesn't need to be exposed as long. Film speed is described in numbers such as 50, 100, 200, 400 and 1,000 with larger numbers meaning a faster film.
2. Choose lens, and if zoom	Lenses are described in metrics, such as 50 mm, 70 mm, or zooms such as 75–200 mm. There are also specialized lenses such as a fisheye lens.
3. Choose filter	Filters can block certain types of light, make the picture fuzzy around the edge, etc.
4. Choose distance from subject	
5. Choose aperture settings	Aperture is the size of the opening between the outside picture and the film. Aperture settings are described in "f stops" with numbers such as f/2, f/2.8, f/4, f/5.6, f/8, and f/11. Smaller numbers represent a larger aperture opening. The larger the aperture, the less time the shutter needs to be open to expose the film. Also, the larger the aperture, the less will be in focus other than the subject.
6. Choose shutter speed	Shutter speed is the amount of time the shutter is open exposing the film to the light waves (picture) coming into the camera. Shutter speed is measured in fractions of a second, such as 1/125 sec or 1/250 sec. It must be combined correctly with aperture setting.
7. Focus camera lens	
8. Use sunlight, flash, or combination	

Third, many of the variables *interact* with each other in ways that are difficult to remember. For example, depth of field (how much is in focus) is determined by a combination of distance from the subject, type of lens, and aperture setting. A minimum depth of field (much of the picture out of focus) would be obtained by taking a picture close up, using a telephoto lens and a wide aperture. In summary, the *mental model* required to combine and remember all eight variables correctly for a specific desired shot is beyond the capabilities of the average human, at least without extensive training and practice.

It is for these reasons that manufacturers are trying to automate some of the functions associated with setting variables such as aperture. For example, if people want to take a portrait shot, they can simply set a dial to "portrait setting." This tells the camera the basic goal of the operator (shoot a portrait), and the camera then automatically focuses on the center object, measures the amount of light at that point, and sets the aperture and shutter speed so that the object where the camera is focused will be crisp and objects significantly in front or in back will be out of focus. Thus, this partial automation should be successful in helping operators reach their goal. It is only partial automation because the user still specifies the type of shot they think is best for their particular goals.

Other ways to help long-term memory limitations of users revolve around standardization and the appropriate use of icons and letter codes. As an example, consider the symbols shown in Figure 6.8 to represent settings on a dial to select different modes of operation for two different cameras. In general, the symbols and icons used for camera A will be easier for the casual user to remember because they map more directly onto the underlying meaning (P for *program mode,* which is a "standardized" photography term to represent fully automatic). After reading the owner's manual once, the settings for camera A are more likely to be interpreted correctly.

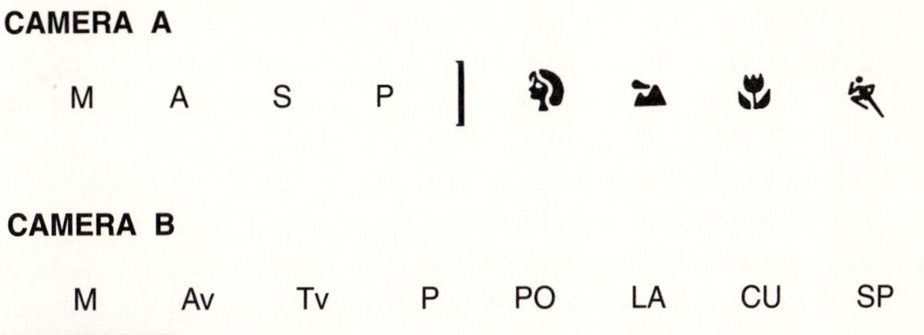

CAMERA A

CAMERA B

M   Av   Tv   P   PO   LA   CU   SP

FIGURE 6.8

Symbols for eight settings on SLR camera dial. For both cameras, the settings represent: manual mode, aperture priority (you set the aperture and the camera autoselects the shutter speed), shutter priority (you set the shutter speed and the camera autoselects the aperture), program mode (completely automatic), portrait shot, landscape shot, close-up shot, and sport shot.

In summary, cameras can be redesigned to support long-term memory in several ways. First, they can be partially automated to reduce the load on both long-term and working memory. Second, symbols used for controls and displays can be meaningfully associated with the underlying variables, such as aperture setting or "portrait." Unfortunately, there are likely to be remaining problems, largely because some suboptimal standards have already been set by the industry (such as using "f stops" for aperture settings and the negative relationship between f stop numbers and aperture size).

is the retrieval of declarative knowledge that has been the focus of our discussions thus far. Declarative knowledge includes what we know about concepts, facts, principles, rules, procedures, steps for doing various tasks, schemas, mental models, and so on.

However, there is a second type of knowledge or information that can be learned and retrieved. This type of knowledge, *procedural knowledge,* is implicit and skill-based (Anderson, 1995). It is knowledge that results in our ability to do tasks, but it is difficult to verbalize directly. One example is our ability to speak a language. We can do it but cannot articulate how we do it or the rules we use to combine words into sentences. Another example would be a math instructor who can work a problem on the board but cannot verbalize how or why he or she did it in that particular way.

There is a growing body of research indicating that we learn in both declarative and procedural modes simultaneously (e.g., Sanderson, 1989). However, declarative knowledge is gained quickly and used when we are relatively novice at a task, while procedural knowledge is acquired much more slowly and is characteristic of experts (see Gordon, 1992). Many perceptual and psychomotor tasks, such as riding a bike or flying a plane, are particularly likely to give rise to procedural knowledge. Although we acquire declarative knowledge more quickly, it also decays more quickly. Procedural knowledge takes time to acquire but appears to have a slower decay function (possibly because of the repetition factor).

There are implications of this distinction for a number of human factors design decisions, many of which will be addressed in later chapters. However, as an example, if we are developing displays for nuclear power plant operators, novices may need qualitatively different types of information than experts, who are more likely to operate at a highly skilled (procedural) level of knowledge (Rasmussen, 1986). This points out the frequent problem of designing displays for a combination of operators ranging from novice to expert. The two will not have equivalent information needs (see Chapter 7 for a more detailed discussion).

There are also implications for training program design that will be discussed more fully in Chapter 18. Designers must spend some effort in the task-analysis stage to determine whether subtasks will be performed using declarative knowledge. When they are, it is appropriate to provide information in that same form during training. If tasks will be performed using procedural knowledge, training is more appropriately conducted using actual task performance. As a simple example, a man recounted his training for what to do if an earthquake hits in the middle of the night. He learned that one should keep shoes by the bed and put them on to leave the room if an earthquake occurs (because of the hazards of broken glass). He experienced an earthquake one night, and while his shoes were by the bed, he walked out barefoot. He knew the information in declarative form but had never practiced it. He had failed to develop the direct associations between waking up during an earthquake and putting on shoes by the bed. This situation is relatively common, where trainees may exhibit declarative knowledge on a paper-and-pencil test, but that does not mean they will *exhibit* the necessary behavior based on procedural learning because it must be gained through practice (Gordon, 1994).

Event Memory: Episodic and Prospective

Episodic Memory.   In contrast to both procedural and declarative knowledge, often embodied in schemas, scripts, or skills and acquired from multiple experiences, the personal knowledge or memory of a specific event or *episode* is, almost by definition, acquired from a single experience. This may be the first encounter with an employer or co-worker, a particular incident or accident at the home or workplace, or the eyewitness view of a crime or accident. Such memories are very much based on visual imagery, but the memories themselves are not always faithful "video replays" of the events, having a number of biases (Loftus et al., 1979).

The biases observed in episodic memory are not unlike the top-down biases of perception. Just as perception is affected by *expectancies* of how the perceptual world is usually constructed, so episodic memories may be biased by *plausible scenarios* (or scripts) of how the episode in question might have been expected to unfold. Thus, for example, the eyewitness to a plane crash might report seeing a ball of flame or smoke shoot from the aircraft or hearing an explosion even if there was none because these are plausible associations to make with a plane crash.

Such biases toward the "typical" may become more pronounced as time passes (Bartlett, 1932) and may also be influenced by suggestion during the period of time after the episode in question. In criminal proceedings, lawyers or investigators may make suggestions that can influence the way a witness believes he or she actually experienced the crime scene (Buckhout, 1974). Unfortunately people do not tend to be aware of these biases. Indeed the confidence with which they assert the accuracy of their episodic recall appears to be only poorly related to the actual accuracy of that recall (Wells, Lindsay, & Ferguson, 1979). So caution must be taken by accident and incident investigators about automatically placing firm trust in the testimony of witnesses, even if the witnesses assert their recollections with certainty. For those who witness a serious episode about which they might be later queried, it is good advice to attempt to write down everything about it as soon as the episode has occurred and at that time to think clearly about and indicate their degree of certainty or uncertainty about the events at the time.

Prospective Memory.   Whereas failures of episodic memory refers to inaccurate recollection of things that happened in the past, failures of *prospective memory* represent the forgetting to do something in the future. (Harris & Wilkins, 1982).

In 1991, an air traffic controller positioned a commuter aircraft at the end of a runway and later forgot to move the aircraft to a different location. The unfortunate aircraft was still positioned there as a large transport aircraft was cleared to land on the same runway. Several lives were lost in the resulting collision (NTSB, 1992).

Failures of prospective memory may sometimes be referred to as "absent-mindedness." Several system and task design procedures are incorporated in systems to support prospective memory. Strategies can be adopted to implement *reminders*. These may be things like tying a string around one's finger, setting a clock to go off at a future time, taping the note for an errand to the steering wheel of your car, or putting the package you need to remember to mail in front of the door so that you will be sure to notice it (if not trip on it!) on the way out. In systems with multiple operators, sharing the knowledge of what one or the other is to do will decrease the likelihood that both will forget that it is to be done. Also, loss of prospective memory will be reduced by verbally stating or physically taking some action (e.g., writing down or typing in) regarding the required future activity the moment it is scheduled. Checklists are aids for prospective memory.

ATTENTION AND MENTAL RESOURCES

Most of the processing operations shown in Figure 6.1 require a certain amount of cognitive capacity or "resources." If we devote our resources to one activity, others are likely to suffer. Many jobs require large amounts of information processing in relatively short amounts of time. It is a key role for the human factors analyst to determine when cognitive capabilities will be overloaded and how to design tasks to minimize such overload. We begin with a reconsideration of the concept of attention.

Attention and Time-Sharing

Recall that attention can act much like a spotlight in focusing on only part of all the information held in sensory memory. This *selective* attention allows us to process important information, and *focused* attention allows us to filter out unwanted information. However, although it is useful to be able to focus on only the information relevant to the task at hand, there are many occasions where we want to *divide* our attention and do several things at once.

For example, if we are driving a car, we want to be able to watch the road, steer the car, give the correct amount of gas, and talk to a passenger. This process of doing all of the various tasks at once is termed *time-sharing*. Time-sharing is the ability to perform more than one cognitive task by attending to both at once or by rapidly switching attention back and forth between them. Some researchers have found that this shifting of attention is an ability that deteriorates for older drivers, especially those with certain types of neurological disorders (Brouwer et al., 1991; Parasuraman & Nestor, 1991; Ponds, Brouwer, & van Wolffelaar, 1988).

Because our cognitive resources for attention are relatively limited, time-sharing between two tasks frequently results in a drop in performance for one or both tasks, relative to their single task baselines, a drop which we can refer to as a *time-sharing decrement*. However, when time sharing two tasks, people are also able to *modulate* the resources given to one or the other, sometimes emphasizing one task at the expense of the other, and sometimes emphasizing the other at the expense of the first (Norman & Bobrow, 1975). In addressing the issues related to how well people can divide their attention between tasks, the issue of time-sharing efficiency, there are several underlying questions important to human factors, including:

- How can we design tasks, environments, or systems to minimize the time-sharing decrement and therefore maximize our time-sharing efficiency?
- How can we measure/predict the amount of attention or processing required by a particular task?
- How can we measure/predict a person's ability to perform multiple tasks?

There are at least four major factors that play a role in determining the extent to which two or more tasks can be time-shared: the degree to which one or more of the tasks are trained to automaticity, the skill in resource allocation, the degree of shared resources, and the degree to which task elements can become confused.

Automaticity: Controlled versus Automatic Processing

There are documented phenomena where two tasks that would be considered relatively difficult to most of us can be time-shared perfectly. An example is a study by Allport, Antonis, and Reynolds (1972) that showed that skilled pianists could sight-read music and engage in a verbal shadowing task (mimic a verbal message) with no disruption to either task. Shaffer (1975) similarly showed an ability of skilled typists to simultaneously shadow a verbal message with no decrement to either task. One explanation for this apparent paradox is that, because of the highly skilled operators involved, one of the tasks is automated to such an extent that it does not interfere with the other.

Walter Schneider and Richard Shiffrin proposed a model of attention and cognitive processing in which people use either controlled or automatic processing (Schneider & Shiffrin, 1977; Shiffrin & Schneider, 1977). *Controlled processing* refers to "effortful cognitive processes that seem to require attention to initiate and sustain them" (Best, 1995). Controlled processing is used when we must process relatively unfamiliar or complex information. With extensive practice, the consistent associations between input and response, between input and long-term memory activation, or between response components become so automatic that they no longer require attention to be executed.

Automatic processing refers to processes that can be initiated and run without any cognitive demand on attentional resources. Processes do not become automatic without being performed hundreds or even thousands of times. In order for a task to become automatic, it must exhibit *consistent* mapping between its elements. In driving an automobile, stopping at a red stoplight becomes automatic after we emit the same response to a red light hundreds of times. In recognizing our own name spoken when our attention is directed elsewhere, we have consistently oriented to the spoken phonemes of our name thousands of times; and in automatically going through either the keypresses to log into a computer or the motions to sign our name, we have consistently linked the separate motor elements. At some level of practice, we no longer have to allocate much or any attention to these processes. When tasks are combined, there will be less cross-interference in time-sharing to the extent that one or both tasks are automated (Hunt & Lansman, 1981; Schneider & Fisk, 1982; Schneider & Shiffrin, 1977). In summary, a key feature in accounting for the efficiency of time-sharing is the level of automaticity of at least one task, a quantity inversely related to the degree of resource demand.

Time-Sharing Skill

Practice at a single task will help to produce automaticity, particularly if the task contains consistencies. Such automaticity will make time-sharing more efficient when another task must be performed concurrently. However, practice with two tasks concurrently can also help to develop a *time-sharing skill* that is unrelated to automaticity (Gopher, Weil, & Baraket, 1994; Gopher, 1993; Damos & Wickens, 1980). It appears that a major component of this skill is learning the *strategy* of how to allocate resources differentially to the two tasks in the most optimal fashion, and how to schedule sequential activities so that different tasks are performed at the best time.

For example, the pilot may learn when to sample the instruments and when to scan the outside in a way that contributes best to both the task of stabilizing the aircraft (which depends on instrument scanning) and monitoring for traffic (which depends on outside scanning). If you are trying to complete a homework assignment for one class while listening to the lecture for another, you may learn to efficiently choose the moments when it is important to pay attention to what the professor is saying, and then turn your attention to concentrating on the homework assignment for the rest of the time. We also can learn that certain tasks are more automated than others, and hence, we learn not to "waste" too many resources on an automated task (which does not need them) when those resources can be more productively allocated to a demanding task requiring controlled processing.

Multiple Resources

Differences in time-sharing efficiency may occur, not because of differences in the resource demands of one or the other of the tasks, but because the two tasks use different physical or cognitive structures. On the one hand, clearly one cannot read a book and watch television at the same time. Both require access to foveal vision and are separated by a much larger visual angle than that of the fovea. On the other hand, one can more easily listen to a spoken version of the book text while watching TV. Psychologists have suggested that this is because visual and auditory processing require separate resources. In fact, there appear to be several (multiple) kinds of resources in the human information-processing system that allow time sharing to be more successful (Navon & Gopher, 1979).

Research has identified at least three different dichotomies in the information-processing system that account for differences in time-sharing efficiency and thereby seem to suggest that one level of each dichotomy uses different resources from the other (Wickens, 1984; 1992). When tasks are combined, their time-sharing will be improved to the extent that they use different resources. Figure 6.9 shows (a) the three dichotomous dimensions and (b) examples of tasks or task components that illustrate each kind of resource.

1. Stages: Early versus Late Processing. Research evidence indicates that the processing resources used for perceptual processing and central processing or cognitive activity are largely separate from resources used for response selection and execution (e.g., Isreal, Wickens, Chesney, & Donchin, 1980). This implies that adding the task of "responding" will not significantly interfere with perception of input or processing in working memory. We can easily scan the roadside (early processing) while we steer (late processing), but our steering performance will be more disrupted if we are concurrently fiddling with another manual control task (late processing, e.g., pushing buttons).

2. Input Modalities: Visual versus Auditory. We are generally better at dividing our attention between one visual and one auditory input (cross-modal time-sharing) than between two visual or two auditory channels (intramodal time-sharing).

1. **Processing Modalities**
   (Auditory versus visual)

2. **Processing Codes**
   (Spatial versus verbal)
   (Spatially guided responses versus vocal responses)

3. **Processing Stages**
   (Perceptual/cognitive processes versus response)

(a)

Perceptual / Cognitive		Response
Perceiving	**Central Processing**	**Response**
VERBAL		
• Print	• Logical problem solving	• Voice
• Speech	• Rehearsal: digits/words	
	• Mental arithmetic	
SPATIAL		
• Analog quantities	• Mental rotation	• Manually
• Flow field		guided response
• Spatial patterns	• Imagining	

(b)

FIGURE 6.9

(a) The three dimensions of multiple resources. (b) Example of tasks defined by codes and stages.

For example, Parkes and Coleman (1990) found that subjects were better able to drive a simulated vehicle when route guidance was presented auditorily than when it was presented visually. As another example, Violanti and Marshall (1996) found that use of a cellular phone while driving results in five times as many accidents as the rate for driving without use of a cellular phone, a rate that is roughly equal to that reported for drunk driving.

There is some question as to whether the advantages of cross-modal time-sharing really come from structural differences in resources or from other factors such as demands due to visual scanning (e.g., Wickens & Liu, 1988). However, as a general design guideline, we can say that dual-task interference is generally reduced by spreading input across visual and auditory modalities. There is also recent interest in whether other sensory modalities (such as touch or pressure) can further increase our time-sharing abilities for input processing.

3. Processing Codes: Spatial versus Verbal in Early Processing and Manual versus Vocal in Responding.   We have already reviewed the distinction between spatial and verbal processing in perception and working memory. Research evidence suggests that spatial and verbal processing, or codes, whether occurring in perception, central processing, or responding, depend on distinct resources (Polson & Friedman, 1988). Note that this distinction can explain the results described earlier obtained by Allport et al. (1972); that is, an expert pianist can also perform a verbal shadowing task because the piano playing is performed in the visual/manual code, while the verbal shadowing task is performed in the verbal/vocal mode. It also explains why it is easier to "voice dial" a cellular phone while driving than it is to input the phone number by key presses. We discuss voice control in Chapter 9.

In summary, to the extent that any two tasks draw on separate rather than common resources, time-sharing will generally be more efficient, and increasing the difficulty of one task will be less likely to impact performance of the concurrent task. As an example, consider the design of instructions (see Chapter 18). Capitalizing on the importance of redundancy, we might choose to present instructions on a *pair* of channels, selected from voice, print, or pictures. The principle of multiple resource separation would suggest using voice and pictures, since these can be processed in parallel, using different modalities and codes. Indeed research suggests that this is the most effective combination (Nugent, 1987).

Confusion

Even when the same resources are used for two tasks, the amount of interference between them will be increased or decreased by differences in the *similarity* of the information that is processed. We saw, both in our discussion of sensation and of working memory, that similarity induces confusion. You will have a harder time rehearsing a phone number if someone is trying to tell you the score of a basketball game at the same time (similar, numerical information) than if someone is telling you what is for dinner (different, verbal information). When two tasks get confused, this sometimes produces *crosstalk* in which outputs intended for one task inadvertently get delivered to the other (Fracker & Wickens, 1989; Navon &

Miller, 1987). Thus in the previous example, you might dial the basketball score (or at least a few digits of it) rather than the intended phone number.

General Implications for Design

Considering the previous information on divided attention, controlled versus automatic processing, and multiple resources for time-sharing, we can identify several design guidelines for maximizing performance for concurrent tasks:

1. Input modes, response devices, and tasks should be combined such that they are as dissimilar as possible in terms of processing stages, input modalities, and processing codes.
2. The greater the automation of any particular task, the better the time-sharing capability.
3. Information should be provided so that the person knows the importance of each task and therefore how to allocate resources between the tasks.

The ability to share resources and perform concurrent tasks is critical for many jobs. This ability is strongly related to the workload imposed by various tasks: if we are performing a primary task that imposes a heavy *mental workload,* we are unlikely to add a secondary task successfully. In Chapter 13, we discuss the concept of mental workload within the overall framework of stress.

REFERENCES

Allport, D.A., Antonis, B., and Reynolds, P. (1972). On the division of attention: A disproof of the single channel hypothesis. *Quarterly Journal of Experimental Psychology, 24,* 255–265.

Anderson, J.R. (1995). *Cognitive psychology* (4th ed.). New York: W.H. Freeman.

ANSI (1988). American National Standard for photography (equipment)—graphic symbols for controls and features. ANSI PH3.624. American National Standards Institute.

Aurelio, D.N. (1988). *Evaluation of camera symbols.* Internal report, PPG Human Factors, Eastman Kodak Company, Rochester, New York.

Baddeley, A.D. (1986). *Working memory.* New York: Oxford University Press.

Baddeley, A.D. (1990). *Human memory: Theory and practice.* Boston, MA: Allyn and Bacon.

Bailey, R.W. (1989). *Human performance engineering using human factors/ergonomics to achieve computer system usability* (2nd ed.). Englewood Cliffs, NJ: Prentice Hall.

Bartlett, F.C. (1932). *Remembering: A study in experimental and social psychology.* New York and London: Cambridge University Press.

Best, J.B. (1995). *Cognitive psychology* (4th ed.). St. Paul, MN: West Publishing.

Biederman, I. (1987). Recognition-by-components: A theory of human image understanding. *Psychology Review, 94*(2), 115–147.

Biederman, I., and Ju, G. (1988). Surface vs. edge-based determinants of visual recognition. *Cognitive Psychology, 20,* 38–64.

Brooks, L.R. (1968). Spatial and verbal components in the act of recall. *Canadian Journal of Psychology, 22,* 349–368.

Brouwer, W.H., Waterink, W., van Wolffelaar, P.C., and Rothengatter, T. (1991). Divided attention in experienced young and older drivers: Lane tracking and visual analysis in a dynamic driving simulator. *Human Factors, 33,* 573–582.

Buckout, R. (1974). Eyewitness testimony. *Scientific American, 231*(6), 307–310.

Card, S., Moran, T., and Newell, A. (1986). The model human processor. In K. Boff, L. Kaufman, and J. Thomas (eds), *Handbook of perception and human performance* (vol. 2). New York: Wiley.

Casey, S. (1993). *Set phasers on stun and other true tales of design, technology, and human error.* Santa Barbara, CA: Aegean Publishing.

Crist, B., and Aurelio, D.N. (1990). Development of camera symbols for consumers. *Proceedings of the Human Factors Society 34th Annual Meeting* (pp. 489–493). Santa Monica, CA: The Human Factors Society.

Damos, D., and Wickens, C.D. (1980). The acquisition and transfer of time-sharing skills. *Acta Psychologica, 6,* 569–577.

Danaher, J.W. (1980). Human error in ATC system. *Human Factors, 22,* 535–546.

Fracker, M.L., and Wickens, C.D. (1989). Resources, confusions, and compatibility in dual axis tracking: Display, controls, and dynamics. *Journal of Experimental Psychology: Human Perception and Performance, 15,* 80–96.

Gentner, D., and Stevens, A.L. (1983). *Mental models.* Hillsdale, NJ: Erlbaum.

Gopher, D. (1993). The skill of attention control: Acquisition and execution of attention strategies. In D.E. Meyer and S. Kornblum (eds.), *Attention and performance XIV.* Cambridge, MA: MIT Press.

Gopher, D., Weil, M., and Baraket, T. (1994). Transfer of skill from a computer game trainer to flight. *Human Factors, 36,* 387–405.

Gordon, S.E. (1992). Implications of cognitive theory for knowledge acquisition. In R. Hoffman (ed.), *The cognition of experts: Psychological theory and empirical AI* (pp. 99–120). New York: Springer-Verlag.

Gordon, S.E. (1994). *Systematic training program design: Maximizing effectiveness and minimizing liability.* Englewood Cliffs, NJ: Prentice Hall.

Haber, R.N., and Schindler, R.M. (1981). Error in proofreading: Evidence of syntactic control of letter processing? *Journal of Experimental Psychology: Human Perception and Performance, 7,* 573–579.

Harris, J.E., and Wilkins, A.J. (1982). Remembering to do things: A theoretical framework and illustrative experiment. *Human Learning, 1,* 123–136.

Hess, S.V., Detweiler, M.C., and Ellis, R.D. (1994). The effects of display layout on monitoring and updating system states. *Proceedings of the Human Factors and Ergonomics Society 38th Annual Meeting* (pp. 1336–1341). Santa Monica, CA: Human Factors and Ergonomics Society.

Hunt, E., and Lansman, M. (1981). Individual differences in attention. In R. Sternberg (ed.), *Advances in the psychology of intelligence* (vol. 1). Hillsdale, NJ: Erlbaum.

Isreal, J., Wickens, C.D., Chesney, G., and Donchin, E. (1980). The event-related brain potential as a selective index of display monitoring load. *Human Factors, 22,* 211–224.

Kantowitz, B.H. (1989). The role of human information processing models in system development. *Proceedings of the Human Factors Society 33rd Annual Meeting* (pp. 1059–1063). Santa Monica, CA: Human Factors Society.

Klemmer, E.T. (1969). Grouping of printed digits for manual entry. *Human Factors, 11,* 397–400.

Loftus, G.R., Dark, V.J., and Williams, D. (1979). Short-term memory factors in ground controller/pilot communication. *Human Factors, 21,* 169–181.

Miller, G.A. (1956). The magical number seven plus or minus two: Some limits on our capacity for processing information. *Psychological Review, 63,* 81–97.

Moray, N. (1986). Monitoring behavior and supervising control. In K.R. Boff, L. Kaufman, and J.P. Thomas (eds.), *Handbook of perception and human performance.* New York: Wiley.

Moses, F.L., and Ehrenreich, S.L. (1981). Abbreviations for automated systems. *Proceedings of the 25th Annual Meeting of the Human Factors Society.* Santa Monica, CA: Human Factors Society.

National Transportation Safety Board (1992). *Aircraft accident report. Runway collision of USAIR FLIGHT 1493 and Skywest Flight 5569.* NTSB/AAR-91/08. Washington, DC: National Transportation Safety Board.

Navon, D., and Gopher, D. (1979). On the economy of the human processing system. *Psychological Review, 86,* 254–255.

Navon, D., and Miller, J. (1987). The role of outcome conflict in dual-task interference. *Journal of Experimental Psychology: Human Perception and Performance, 13,* 435–448.

Neisser, U. (1964). Visual search. *Scientific American, 210*(6), 94–102.

Norman, D.A. (1981). The trouble with UNIX. *Datamation, 27*(12), 139–150.

Norman, D.A. (1988). *The psychology of everyday things.* New York: Harper & Row.

Norman, D., and Bobrow, D. (1975). On data-limited and resource-limited processing. *Journal of Cognitive Psychology, 7,* 44–60.

Nugent, W.A. (1987). A comparative assessment of computer-based media for presenting job task instructions. *Proceedings of the Human Factors Society 31st Annual Meeting* (pp. 696–700). Santa Monica, CA: Human Factors Society.

Parasuraman, R., and Nestor, P.G. (1991). Attention and driving skills in aging and Alzheimer's disease. *Human Factors, 33,* 539–557.

Parkes, A.M., and Coleman, N. (1990). Route guidance systems: A comparison of methods of presenting directional information to the driver. In E.J. Lovesey (ed.), *Contemporary ergonomics 1990* (pp. 480–485). London: Taylor & Francis.

Polson, M.C., and Friedman, A. (1988). Task-sharing within and between hemispheres: A multiple-resource approach. *Human Factors, 30,* 633–643.

Ponds, R.W.H.N., Brouwer, W.B., and van Wolffelaar, P.C. (1988). Age differences in divided attention in a simulated driving task. *Journal of Gerontology, 43,* 151–156.

Potter, M.C., and Faulconer, B.A. (1975). Time to understand pictures and words. *Nature, 253,* 437–438.

Preczewski, S.C., and Fisher, D.L. (1990). The selection of alphanumeric code sequences. *Proceedings of the Human Factors Society 34th Annual Meeting* (pp. 224–228). Santa Monica, CA: Human Factors Society.

Pritchard, R.M. (1961). Stabilized images on the retina. *Scientific American, 204*(6), 72–78.

Rasmussen, J. (1986). *Information processing and human-machine interaction: An approach to cognitive engineering.* New York: Elsevier.

Rolt, L.T.C. (1978). *Red for danger.* London: Pan Books.

Rouse, W.B., and Morris, N.M. (1986). On looking into the black box: Prospects and limits in the search for mental models. *Psychological Bulletin, 100,* 349–363.

Sanderson, P.M. (1989). Verbalizable knowledge and skilled task performance: Association, dissociation, and mental models. *Journal of Experimental Psychology: Learning, Memory, and Cognition, 15,* 729–747.

Schank, R.C., and Abelson, R. (1977). *Scripts, plans, goals, and understanding.* Hillsdale, NJ: Lawrence Erlbaum Associates.

Schmidt, J.K., and Kysor, K.P. (1987). Designing airline passenger safety cards. *Proceedings of the Human Factor Society 31st Annual Meeting* (pp. 51–55). Santa Monica, CA: Human Factors Society.

Schneider, W., and Fisk, A.D. (1982). Concurrent automatic and controlled visual search: Can processing occur without cost? *Journal of Experimental Psychology: Learning, Memory, and Cognition, 8,* 261–278.

Schneider, W., and Shiffrin, R.M. (1977). Controlled and automatic human information processing: I. Detection, search, and attention. *Psychological Review, 84,* 1–66.

Selfridge, O. (1959). Pandemonium: A paradigm for learning. In *Symposium on the mechanization of thought processes.* London: HM Stationary Office.

Shaffer, L.H. (1975). Multiple attention in continuous verbal tasks. In S. Dornic (ed.), *Attention and performance V.* New York: Academic Press.

Shiffrin, R.M., and Schneider, W. (1977). Controlled and automatic human information processing: II. Perception, learning, automatic attending and a general theory. *Psychological Review, 84,* 127–190.

Simpson, C. (1976, May). Effects of linguistic redundancy on pilot's comprehension of synthesized speech. *Proceedings of the 12th Annual Conference on Manual Control* (NASA TM-X-73, 170). Washington, DC: U.S. Government Printing Office.

Spencer, K. (1988). *The psychology of educational technology and instructional media.* London: Routledge.

Tinker, M.A. (1955). Prolonged reading tasks in visual research. *Journal of Applied Psychology, 39,* 444–446.

Vartabedian, A.G. (1972). The effects of letter size, case, and generation method on CRT display search time. *Human Factors, 14,* 511–519.

Violanti, J.M., and Marshall, J. R. (1996). Cellular phones and traffic accidents: An epidemiological approach. *Accident Analysis and Prevention, 28*(2), 265–270.

Waltz, D. (1975). Understanding line drawings of scenes with shadows. In P. Winston (ed.), *The psychology of computer vision* (pp. 19–92). New York: McGraw-Hill.

Wells, G.L., Lindsay, R.C., and Ferguson, T.I. (1979). Accuracy, confidence, and juror perceptions in eyewitness testimony. *Journal of Applied Psychology, 64,* 440–448.

Wickelgren, W.A. (1964). Size of rehearsal group in short-term memory. *Journal of Experimental Psychology, 68,* 413–419.

Wickelgren, W.A. (1979). *Cognitive psychology.* Englewood Cliffs, NJ: Prentice Hall.

Wickens, C.D. (1984). Processing resources in attention. In R. Parasuraman and R. Davies (eds.), *Varieties of attention* (pp. 63–101). New York: Academic Press.

Wickens, C.D. (1992). *Engineering psychology and human performance* (2nd ed.). New York: HarperCollins.

Wickens, C.D., and Carswell, C.M. (1997). Information processing. In G. Salvendy (ed.), *Handbook of human factors and ergonomics* (2nd ed.). New York: Wiley.

Wickens, C.D., and Liu, Y. (1988). Codes and modalities in multiple resources: A success and a qualification. *Human Factors, 30,* 599–616.

Wilson, J.R., and Rutherford, A. (1989). Mental models: Theory and application in human factors. *Human Factors, 31*(6), 617–634.

CHAPTER 7

Decision Making

An anesthesiology team in a large hospital consisted of four physicians, three of whom were residents in training. The group was asked to assist with four procedures in one building (an in vitro fertilization, a perforated viscus, reconstruction of a leg artery, and an appendectomy) and an exploratory laparotomy in another building. All procedures were urgent and could not be delayed for regular operating-room scheduling. There were several delays in preoperative preparation, and several surgeons and nurses were pressuring the team to get the procedures finished. The situation was complicated by the fact that the staff was only able to run two operating rooms simultaneously, and the best use of resources was to overlap procedures so that one case was started as another was finishing. The anesthesiologist in charge had to decide how to allocate the four members of the anesthesiology team to the five needed procedures. Also, there was always the possibility that a large emergency case would come into the hospital's trauma center, in which case the anesthesiologist in charge was expected to be immediately available. The decision was a relatively simple one: Should she allocate only the other three anesthesiologists to the five procedures, or should she help out also, leaving no one available should a major emergency come in unexpectedly? (Adapted from Cook & Woods, 1994.)*

While this scenario happens to occur in the domain of medical decision making, everyone spends a great deal of their "average" daily cognitive processing on decision-making activity—considering multiple pieces of information, determining what the information represents or really "means," and selecting the best course of action. The information we process may be simple or complex, clear or distorted, and complete or filled with gaps. Because of this variability in information complexity and completeness, we often just interpret it to the best of our ability and make "educated guesses" about what to do.

In many cases, the increasing complexity of the systems with which we interact is causing decision making and problem solving to become more difficult and prone to error. This makes decision making a central concern to the human factors specialist. It is important to understand how people make decisions, the limitations they typically experience in decision making, how time pressures and attentional limitations affect the process, and how we can design systems to support and enhance decision making.

In Chapter 6, we discussed basic cognitive mechanisms such as perception, working memory, attention, and retrieval of information from long-term memory. Each of these functions plays a critical role in cognition, and each has certain limitations that impact the overall information-processing system. In this chapter, we will expand on those concepts because human decision making and problem solving are *high-level* cognitive processes that make use of the simpler processes.

In this chapter, we first consider the question "What is decision making?" We will see that even this simple question has no one answer. What used to be considered decision making is now viewed as overly simplistic and narrow. Researchers are looking at decision making as part of the larger task of problem solving in often complex, dynamic environments. Thus, we see the line between *decision making* and *problem solving* growing blurred. For example, medical treatment, process control, fault diagnosis, resource management, air traffic control, and many other jobs involve elements of both decision making and problem solving. Because more researchers appear to be using the term *decision making* for these cognitive tasks, we will use that term here. Toward the end of the chapter, we will briefly discuss a few topics that seem to relate more specifically to true problem solving than to decision making.

Our goals of the chapter are to review the basic processes used in decision making, present the types of difficulties and biases people exhibit in the various stages of decision making, and describe how decision support systems might be used to counteract those difficulties. Later, in Chapter 14, we will reconsider some of the decision-making topics specifically as they relate to risk taking and human error.

DEFINITION OF DECISION MAKING

What does it mean to say something is a decision-making task? Most researchers assume it is a task where (a) a person must select one choice from a number of choices, (b) there is some amount of information available with respect to the choices, (c) the time frame is relatively long (longer than a second), and (d) the choice is associated with uncertainty; that is, it is not clear which is the best choice. By definition, decision making involves risk, and a good decision maker will effectively assess risks associated with each choice (Medin & Ross, 1992). Examples of decision making that are frequently studied in human factors include medical diagnosis and the associated choice of treatment, pilot flight judgments, jury decision making, human and/or equipment resource allocation, process control, fault diagnosis in a mechanical or electrical system, consumer behavior, and risk-taking or other safety-related behavior such as the decision to wear protective gear. While these examples are all different with respect to the *domain* of task performance, they appear to be similar in the types of basic cognitive activities used to perform them (Cook & Woods, 1994; Wickens, 1992).

Now consider a different example of decision making. A driver is speeding down the road at night and sees something in the crosswalk. He decides it is a dog and slams on the brakes. Was this actually a decision or merely a perceptual process depending on simultaneous bottom-up and top-down processing? We will see that there seems to be a distinction between quick and automatic "perception-action" decisions and more controlled, effortful, and analytical "decision making." Some researchers call both of these processes decision making but use different descriptive terms. Decisions that are quick and relatively automatic are often termed *intuitive decision making,* whereas decisions that are more slow, deliberate, and controlled are referred to as *analytical decision making* (e.g., Taggart, 1986; Hammond 1993). This distinction is useful in understanding decision making under different types of circumstances, and we will return to it later in the chapter.

CLASSICAL DECISION THEORY

Most of the original research on decision making focused on the study of optimal, *rational* decision making (Fischhoff, 1988). The assumption was that if researchers could specify the values (costs or benefits) associated with different choices, mathematical models could be applied to those values, yielding the optimal choice. Early decision theory was thus a set of formal models that prescribed what people should do when faced with a set of decision choices, and it was also a yardstick by which to judge people's deviations from the optimal decision (Coombs, Dawes, & Tversky, 1970; Edwards, 1954, 1961; Pitz & Sachs, 1984; Slovic, Fischhoff, & Lichtenstein, 1977). Rational models of decision making are also sometimes called *normative models,* because they specify what people ideally *should* do; they do not necessarily describe how people actually perform decision-making tasks. Normative models were extremely popular and set the background for decision research for many years. They are important to understand because they form the basis for many computer-based decision aids (Edwards, 1987). Later researchers became interested in describing actual human decision-making behavior and developed a number of *descriptive models.*

Normative Decision Models

Normative decision models revolved around the central concept of *utility,* the overall value of a choice, or how much each outcome or product is "worth" to the decision maker. One example of an early normative model is *expected value theory.* This theory applies to any decision that involves a "gamble" type of decision, where each choice has one or more outcomes with an associated worth and probability. For example, a person might be offered a choice between:

1. Winning $50 with a probability of .20, or
2. Winning $20 with a probability of .60.

Expected value theory assumes that the overall value of a choice is the sum of the worth of each outcome multiplied by its probability:

$$E(v) = \sum_{i=1}^{n} p(i)v(i)$$

where $E(v)$ is the expected value of the choice, $p(i)$ is the probability of the ith outcome, and $v(i)$ is the value of the ith outcome. The expected value of the first choice for the example given above is $50 \times .20$ or $10, meaning that if the choice were selected many times, one would expect an average gain of $10. The expected value of the second choice is $20 \times .60$ or $12, which is a higher overall value. In a variety of decision tasks, researchers compared results of the normative model to actual human decision making and found that people often vary from the "optimal" choice.

Expected value theory was relatively limited in scope and had other problems as well. For example, it quickly becomes clear that many choices in life have different values to different people. For example, one person might value fuel efficiency in an automobile, while another does not. This facet of human decision making led to the development of *subjective expected utility theory (SEU)*. Subjective expected utility theory still relies on the concepts of expected probability times worth or "value" for each possible outcome. However, the worth component is subjective, determined individually for each person; that is, instead of an objective (e.g., monetary) worth, an outcome has some value or "utility" to each individual. Thus, each choice a person can make is associated with one or more outcomes, and each outcome has an associated probability and some subjective utility.

As an example, consider our first scenario at the beginning of the chapter. The anesthesiologist must allocate either three or all four team members (which would include herself) to five procedures. For the sake of simplicity, we will describe the decision as a choice between allocating the three residents to the five procedures and herself remaining free for a trauma or allocating all four team members and assuming a trauma case would not come in. Each possible action has two (or more) possible outcomes: (1) She begins one of the procedures and no emergency enters the trauma center, (2) she begins a procedure and an emergency comes in, (3) she does not begin the procedure and no emergency comes in, and (4) she does not begin the procedure and an emergency comes in (see Table 7.1). The physician must estimate the likelihood of each outcome, which of course depends on the likelihood of a trauma case coming in at that particular hour of the day. She must also place a value, or *subjective utility,* on each of the four alternatives listed above by considering the values of assisting with the current surgery versus the value of helping with a trauma case. The model assumes that to determine the optimal action, we would first multiply the estimated probability times the subjective expected utility for each of the four possible outcomes. Then the numbers would be summed for the outcomes associated with beginning the procedure (1 and 2) and also for waiting (3 and 4). Whichever choice had the highest numerical value would be the best choice for the physician. Table 7.1 illustrates this process with *hypothetical* numerical values. Note that with these values, the model suggests

TABLE 7.1 Hypothetical Values in a Subjective Expected Utility Model for Two Possible Outcomes

Alternative/ Outcomes	Probability	Utility (−10 to +10)	P × u	Alternative Expected Utility
Use three anesthesiologists				
No emergency: Use only three for the existing surgeries	.80	−4	−3.2	
Emergency: Have one person available to assist trauma	.20	+10	2.0	___
				−1.2
Use four anesthesiologists				
No emergency: Have all four people available for surgeries	.80	+6	4.8	
Emergency: Have no one available to assist trauma	.20	−10	−2.0	___
				2.8

that the best choice is to use all four anesthesiologists, which, according to Cook and Woods (1994), is the common practice.

The subjective expected utility model assumes that the person will (or at least should) select the action with the highest overall subjective expected utility value. By knowing the probability and utility of the consequences associated with decision choices, researchers could use the model to predict "rational" or internally consistent choices. Thus the models can be used for a number of goals: studying conditions under which humans make rational decisions, developing training for more rational decision making, and developing aids (such as decision tables) to help people make more rational decisions (Edwards, 1987).

Descriptive Decision Models

Numerous researchers have evaluated the extent to which humans follow normative decision models of consequential choice, especially subjective expected utility theory. The conclusion, based on several years of experimentation, was that human decision making frequently violates key assumptions of the normative models. For example, Tversky and Kahneman (1981) found changes in decision making depending on how the decision problem was presented. People make different decisions based on slight factors, such as whether the problem is worded in terms of lives lost or lives saved (even when the problems are formally identical). Such changes in decisions that are caused by differences in presentation form are known as *framing effects*. As an example, McNeil, Pauker, Cox, and Tversky (1982) found that both physicians and patients varied their decisions based on whether the problem was "framed" in terms of the probability of living versus the probability of dying. Other research found that engineers and managers made project decisions differently depending on whether information was framed in terms of previous team successes or team failures (Duchon, Dunegan, & Barton, 1989). Finally, there also appear to be circumstances where people make decisions without explicitly evaluating the alternative outcomes at all (Lipshitz, 1993).

Because actual decision making commonly showed violations of normative model assumptions, researchers began to search for more descriptive models, models that would capture how humans actually make decisions. These researchers believed that rational consideration of all factors associated with all possible choices, as well as their outcomes, is frequently just too difficult. They suggested models of decision making where people rely on simpler and less-complete means of selecting among choices. Because they represent simplified shortcuts, descriptive models are sometimes referred to as "heuristics." One well-known example of an early descriptive model is Simon's *satisficing*.

Simon (1957) argued that people do not usually follow a goal of making the absolutely best or optimal decision. Instead, they opt for a choice that is "good enough" for their purposes, something satisfactory. This shortcut method of decision making is termed *satisficing*. In satisficing, the decision maker generates and considers choices until one is found that is acceptable. Going beyond this choice to identify something that is better simply has too little advantage to make it worth the effort. Consider a typical example. George Smith has decided to have a house built. After finding a design and blueprint, he must find a general contractor. George could identify every possible contractor in town and find out dozens of characteristics relevant to each. He could then evaluate all of the characteristics and finally choose the best candidate. However, he is more likely to look into a few and choose the first one that seems satisfactory.

In satisficing, sampling procedures are critical because not all possible choices are likely to be considered. Notice that the use of this type of decision making for hiring employees is explicitly forbidden in many companies because it is considered to be unfair to the applicants. Satisficing is a very reasonable approach given that people have limited cognitive capacities and limited time. Often the decision simply does not merit the time and difficulties of using a more thorough analysis.

In summary, if the amount of information is relatively small and time is unconstrained, careful analysis of the choices and their "utilities" is desirable and possible. To the extent that the amount of information exceeds cognitive-processing limitations, that time is limited, or both, people will shift to simplifying heuristics. Research has demonstrated that people are, in fact, able to adapt to different decision circumstances by moving from analytical modes to appropriate heuristics such as satisficing (Hammond, 1993; Payne, 1982; Payne, Bettman, & Johnson, 1988).

Other factors such as time stress and attentional resource limitations also necessitate the use of decision making *simplifications* (Janis, 1982). This is commonly found in complex and dynamic operational control environments, such as hospitals, power or manufacturing plant control rooms, air traffic control towers, and aircraft cockpits. In the next section, we will consider a number of simplifying heuristics that occur at specific points in the decision-making process.

HEURISTICS AND BIASES

Cognitive *heuristics* represent easy ways of thinking about things that are usually very powerful and efficient but that do not always guarantee the best solution. Unfortunately, because they represent simplifications, heuristics sometimes lead to biases or misperceptions. For that reason, and because they represent deviations from a rational or normative model, they are also sometimes referred to as *biases*.

In this section, we consider some of the major heuristics that have been identified in judgment and decision-making processes. Most of the heuristics are simplifying methods that occur for a particular type of decision or at a particular point in the decision process. To provide some structure for understanding these heuristics, we will first describe decision making in terms of a basic information-processing model.

An Information-Processing Framework

One way to think about decision making is within the framework of a relatively simple information-processing model, such as that shown in Figure 7.1 (from Wickens, 1992). This model features the cognitive components critical to con-

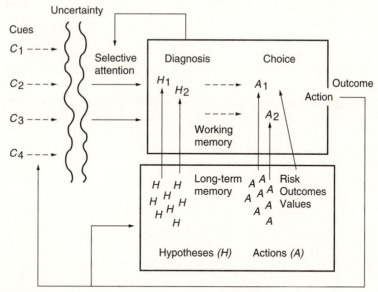

FIGURE 7.1

Information-processing model of decision making. Cues are selectively sampled (on the left); hypotheses are generated through retrieval from long-term memory; possible actions are retrieved from long-term memory, and an action is selected on the basis of risks and the values of their outcomes. (*Source:* Wickens, C.D., 1992. *Engineering Psychology and Human Performance* [2nd ed.]. New York: HarperCollins Publishers. Reprinted by permission of Addison-Wesley Educational Publishers, Inc.)

scious, effortful, decision making: selective attention, activities performed within working memory, and information retrieval from long-term memory. According to this model, the following activities occur in working memory:

1. *Cue Reception and Integration.* A number of *cues,* or pieces of information, are received from the environment and go into working memory. For example, a physician sees a patient who exhibits multiple symptoms including cough, wheezing, fatigue, and feelings of chest tightness, or a fighter pilot sees data about an unknown aircraft on his or her radar scope. The cues must be interpreted and somehow integrated with respect to one another. The cues may also be incomplete, fuzzy, or erroneous; that is, they may be associated with some amount of *uncertainty.*

2. *Hypothesis Generation.* The cues instigate generation of one or more *hypotheses,* guesses as to what the cues mean. This is accomplished by retrieving information from long-term memory. For example, a physician hypothesizes that the set of symptoms described above is caused by asthma. Many of the decision tasks studied in human factors require such *inferential diagnosis,* which is the process of inferring the underlying or "true" state of a system. Examples of inferential diagnosis include *medical diagnosis, fault diagnosis* of a mechanical or electrical system, *inference of weather conditions* based on measurement values or displays, and so on.

3. *Hypothesis Evaluation and Selection.* The hypotheses brought into working memory are *evaluated* with respect to how likely they are to be correct. This is accomplished by gathering additional cues from the environment to either confirm or disconfirm each hypothesis. In addition, hypotheses may need to be revised, or a new one may need to be generated. When a hypothesis is found to be adequately supported by the information, that hypothesis is chosen as the basis for a course of action. This process can be seen in the following scenario. A resident surgeon is assigned to see a female patient brought into the emergency room. She complains of nausea and severe abdominal pain, which had lasted several hours. Because these symptoms could represent a large number of problems, the surgeon orders a standard battery of blood and urine tests. The woman's blood pressure is within normal limits, and her blood tests come back showing an elevated white blood count. The physician suspects that the woman is suffering from appendicitis. Consistent with this hypothesis, she seems particularly reactive to pressure on the right lower side of her abdomen. He has several possible courses of action: he could wait, operate, or do additional tests. He tells the patient he thinks it is best to operate; if they wait, the appendix could burst and that would create an extremely serious condition. In the operating room, the surgeon finds her appendix to be normal, but he also finds that she has gastric cancer.

In this example, the emergency room surgeon decided that the most likely diagnosis was acute appendicitis. He obtained additional confirming evidence (reactive pain in lower-right abdomen) for his diagnosis, and at that point felt certain enough to move on to selecting a course of action.

4. *Generating and Selecting Actions.* One or more alternative actions are generated by retrieving possibilities from memory. For example, after diagnosing acute appendicitis, the surgeon in our scenario generated several alternative actions, including: waiting, conducting additional tests, and performing surgery. Depending on the decision time available, one or more of the alternatives are generated and considered.

To select an action, the decision maker might evaluate information such as possible outcomes of each action (where there may be multiple possible outcomes for each action), the likelihood of each outcome, and the negative and positive factors associated with each outcome. For example, the surgeon who hypothesized that his patient had acute appendicitis briefly considered waiting, conducting more tests, and performing surgery. Each action is associated with multiple possible outcomes, some of which are more likely than others. In addition, these outcomes may vary from mildly to extremely positive (i.e., one outcome from surgery is that the appendix is removed without complication), or from mildly to extremely negative (i.e., he could wait, the appendix bursts, she dies, and he is sued for malpractice).

In many real-world decisions, a person may iterate through the steps we have described a number of times. Finally, some decisions include only selecting a course of action, where hypothesis generation and selection is unnecessary.

If we consider the activities depicted in Figure 7.1, it is apparent that there are a variety of factors and cognitive limitations that will strongly influence decision-making processes. These include the following factors, some of which are from Cook and Woods (1994) and Reason (1990):

- *The amount or quality of cue information brought into working memory.* This can be due to environmental constraints or cognitive factors, such as mental workload and attentional demands.
- *The amount of time available for each decision-making activity.* For example, in a medical emergency or in a physical system failure, the person or team may have very little time to make a decision.
- *Attentional resources* that may limit the person's ability to perform the activity in an optimal fashion.
- The *amount and quality of knowledge* the person holds in long-term memory that is relevant to a particular activity (possible hypotheses, courses of action, likely outcomes, etc.).
- The person's *ability to retrieve relevant information, hypotheses, or actions* from long-term memory. People often have knowledge that is relevant to the decision at hand but fail to retrieve it under the particular circumstance. This is sometimes referred to as a problem of *inert knowledge* (Perkins & Martin, 1986; Woods & Roth, 1988a).
- *Working Memory capacity limitations* that result in a very limited ability to consider all possible hypotheses simultaneously, associated cues, costs and benefits of outcomes, and so forth.

These limitations will potentially affect each activity in the decision process, and often cause the use of simplifying heuristics. Some may even cause subprocesses to be omitted entirely. For example, under time stress or high-attentional workloads, a person might only generate one hypothesis and not attempt to evaluate it further (e.g., Hendry & Burke, 1995).

This list of influencing factors and cognitive limitations gives us some amount of insight into the conditions that will lead to suboptimal decision making. People will have the most difficulty with decisions made with too little or erroneous information, extreme time stress, high cognitive workload, changing dynamic informational cues, conflicting goals imposed on the decision maker, and a novel or unusual circumstance that will lead to either a lack of correct knowledge or retrieval failure (Cook & Woods, 1994). Many high-risk environments have all or most of these elements, and it is therefore important to design control and display systems to support individual and team decision making maximally (discussed in more detail at a later point).

The Use of Heuristics

Heuristics can be categorized in a number of ways. Looking at Figure 7.1, we see that the decision process is divided into several activities that *might* apply to a given circumstance depending on factors such as amount of time available, knowledge level of the decision maker, and complexity of the task. These activities include obtaining and integrating cues, hypothesis generation, hypothesis evaluation or updating by considering additional cues, generating alternative actions, and selecting a choice of action by evaluating trade-offs. In the following sections, we consider a variety of heuristics and biases that occur in these subprocesses. Familiarity with the heuristics can help designers develop information displays and cognitive support systems that counteract the biases inherent in human information processing (examples are described later in this chapter and also in Chapter 8).

Heuristics in Obtaining and Using Cues

Decision making or problem solving usually begins with obtaining some information from the environment. The information might be presented all at once, it might appear over time (as in consecutive medical tests), or it might *change* over time. There are a number of simplifying heuristics or biases that often occur in this stage:

1. *Attention to a limited number of cues.* Due to working memory limitations, people can only use a relatively small number of cues to develop a picture of the world or system. This is one reason why configural displays that visually integrate several variables or factors into one display are useful (see Chapter 8 for a description).

2. *Cue primacy.* In decisions where people receive cues over a period of time, there are certain trends or biases in the use of that information. First, the first few cues receive greater than average weight or importance. This is a *primacy* effect, found in many information-processing tasks, where preliminary information tends to carry more weight than subsequent information (e.g., Adelman et al., 1996). Some researchers have suggested that the order of information has an effect not because of the weight given to it per se but because people use the information to construct plausible stories or "mental models" of the world or system. These models will differ depending on which information was used first (Pennington & Hastie, 1988). The key point is that, for whatever reason, information processed early is often most influential, and this will ultimately affect decision making.

3. *Inattention to later cues.* Separate from underweighting, cues occurring later in time or cues that change over time are often likely to be totally ignored, which may be attributable to attentional factors. In medical diagnosis, this would mean that presenting symptoms, or cues, would be more likely to be brought into working memory and remain dominant.

4. *Cue salience.* Another bias has an insidious interaction with the primacy and attentional factors just described; that is, the finding that *perceptually salient cues* are more likely to receive attention, and are given more weight (Endsley, 1995; Wickens, 1992). As you would expect, salient cues in displays are things such as information at the top of a display, the loudest alarm, the largest display, and so forth. Unfortunately, the most salient display cue is not necessarily the most diagnostic.

5. *Overweighting of unreliable cues.* Finally, people often simplify the processing and integration of cues by treating all cues *as if* they are equal (Wickens, 1992). Although some cues may actually be more valid or reliable than others, people tend to cognitively process them as if they are all equally valid and reliable. The result is that people tend to overweight unreliable information relative to reliable information (Johnson, Cavanagh, Spooner, & Samet, 1973; Schum, 1975).

Heuristics in Hypothesis Generation

After a limited set of cues is processed in working memory, the decision maker generates hypotheses by retrieving one or more from long-term memory. There are a number of heuristics and biases that affect this process:

1. *A limited number of hypotheses are generated.* First, due to working memory limitations, people can only consider a few hypotheses at a time (Lusted, 1976; Mehle, 1982; Rasmussen, 1981). Thus, people will bring in somewhere between one and four hypotheses for evaluation. People consider a *small subset* of possible hypotheses at one time and often never consider all relevant hypotheses at all (Elstein, Schulman, & Sprafka, 1978; Wickens, 1992). Recent research in real-world decision making under time stress has indicated that in these circumstances, decision makers often only consider a single hypothesis (Flin, Slaven & Stewart, 1996; Hendry & Burke, 1995; Klein, 1993).

This problem is exacerbated by the manner in which long-term memory is accessed. As we mentioned earlier, researchers have shown that much of our knowledge remains *inert;* that is, we have the relevant knowledge but fail to retrieve it because it is not associated with the necessary "triggering cues" (Cook & Woods, 1994; Glaser, 1984; Perkins & Martin, 1986; Woods & Roth, 1988b). As a result, while people strive to retrieve hypotheses that are most likely to be correct for the specific set of cues being considered, this goal may not be achieved, especially if they do not make an adequate effort to consider alternative hypotheses. As an example, consider police detectives who are expected to consider (hypothesize) all possible suspects for a case. While they explicitly claim to the public that "no one has been ruled out," indicating that the number of hypotheses is large, the truth is that they only search out evidence bearing on a small number of hypotheses at one time.

2. *Availability heuristic.* Memory research suggests that people will retrieve hypotheses most easily that have been considered *recently* or that have been considered *frequently* (Anderson, 1990). Unusual illnesses are simply not the first things that come to mind to a physician. This is related to another heuristic, termed the *availability heuristic* (Kahneman, Slovic, & Tversky, 1982; Tversky & Kahneman, 1974). This heuristic assumes that people make certain types of judgment, for example, estimates of frequency, by cognitively assessing how easily the state or event is brought to mind. The implication here is that although people try to generate "rationally" the most likely hypotheses, the reality is that if something comes to mind relatively easily, they will assume it is common and therefore a good hypothesis. As an example, if a physician readily thinks of a hypothesis, such as acute appendicitis, he or she will assume it is relatively common, leading to the judgment that it is a likely cause of the current set of symptoms. In actuality, availability may not be a reliable basis for estimating frequency.

3. *Representativeness heuristic.* Finally, another kind of heuristic that also biases hypothesis generation is the *representativeness heuristic* (Kahneman, Slovic, & Tversky, 1982; Tversky & Kahneman, 1974). The representativeness heuristic refers to "a tendency to judge an event as likely if it "represents" the typical features of (or is similar in its essential properties to) its category (Medin & Ross, 1992). As a consequence of applying this heuristic, people will assume that if a given set of actual cues highly resembles the cue set for a particular hypothesis, they will generate that hypothesis as a likely candidate. Usually this is a very effective strategy. However, in unusual cases, it is misleading. Consider the scenario described earlier within this chapter. An emergency room physician sees a set of symptoms that is prototypical of acute appendicitis. The surgeon takes this as his primary hypothesis, and does not do enough information gathering to rule out other medical problems. In the majority of cases, the strategy will lead to correct decision making. But sometimes it does not, and in these cases, the surgeon will fail to acquire enough information to identify the correct diagnosis.

4. *Overconfidence.* Finally, people are often biased in their confidence with respect to the hypotheses they have brought into working memory (Mehle, 1982), believing that they are correct more often than they actually are.

Heuristics in Hypothesis Evaluation and Selection

Once the hypotheses have been brought into working memory, additional cues are potentially sought in order to evaluate them. The process of considering additional cue information is affected by cognitive limitations, just as the other subprocesses are:

1. *Cognitive fixation.* Once a hypothesis has been generated or chosen, people tend to underutilize subsequent cues. We remain stuck on our initial hypothesis, a process known as *cognitive fixation* (Botney et al., 1993; Cook & Woods, 1994; Dekeyser & Woods, 1990). Examples of cognitive fixation abound in the literature (e.g., Xiao, Mackenzie, & LOTAS Group, 1995). Consider one example, where process control room operators develop a hypothesis and begin a sequence of actions. Research has shown that even though the system and its indicators may *change* unexpectedly, the operators often fail to notice this and blindly continue with the initially selected course of action, causing errors and further system malfunctioning (Woods, O'Brien, & Hanes, 1987). There is evidence that for some domains, such as medical diagnosis, cognitive fixation lessens with practice and experience (Arocha & Patel, 1995).

Cognitive fixation can also be problematic because it can cause people to stick with hypotheses that were generated through biased methods (and are therefore incorrect). Such biases can be very serious and often lead to human performance errors; physicians stay fixated on incorrect diagnoses, or process control operators stay fixated on an incorrect hypothesis about what has caused a disturbance. Notice that this is a different effect than the cue primacy effect when the decision maker is first generating hypotheses.

2. *Confirmational bias.* There are other equally problematic biases when people consider additional cues to evaluate working hypotheses. First, they tend to seek out only *confirming* information and not disconfirming information, even when the disconfirming evidence can be more diagnostic (Einhorn & Hogarth, 1978; Mynatt, Doherty, & Tweney, 1977; Schustack & Sternberg, 1981). It is hard to imagine a physician doing tests for various physical conditions that he thinks the patient *does not* have (an exception to this general bias would be when police detectives ask their suspects if they have an alibi). In a similar vein, people tend to underweight, or fail to remember, disconfirming evidence (Arkes & Harkness, 1980; Wickens, 1992) and fail to use the *absence* of important cues as diagnostic information (Balla, 1980; Rouse, 1981). This type of cognitive *tunnel vision* is exaggerated under conditions of high stress and mental workload (Cook & Woods, 1994; Janis, 1982; Sheridan, 1981; Wright, 1974).

Heuristics and Biases in Action Selection

Choice of action is also subject to a variety of heuristics or biases. Some are based on basic memory processes that we have already discussed.

1. *Retrieve a small number of actions.* Long-term memory provides possible action plans. People are limited in the number they can retrieve and keep in working memory.

2. *Availability heuristic for actions.* In retrieving possible courses of action from long-term memory, people will retrieve the most "available" actions. In general, the availability of items from memory are a function of recency, frequency, and how strongly they are associated with the "hypothesis" or situational assessment that has been selected.

3. *Availability of possible outcomes.* Other types of availability effects will occur, including the generation/retrieval of associated outcomes. As discussed above, when more than one possible action is retrieved, the decision maker must select one based on how well the action will yield desirable outcomes. Each action has associated consequences, which are probabilistic. As an example, a surgeon might consider surgery versus chemotherapy for a cancer diagnosis. Each has some probability of eliminating the cancer. Each also has other possible outcomes that may range from likely to unlikely and mild to severe. The physician's estimate of these likelihoods will not be objective based on statistics. They are more likely to be based on the "availability" of instances in memory; that is, if they have heard of many instances of chemotherapy leading to acute nausea and weight loss, they are likely to think the probability is high, even if statistically the probability is low. Thus, the "availability heuristic" will bias retrieval of some outcomes and not others. This process is evident when people make decisions and fail to foresee outcomes that are readily apparent with hindsight.

The decision maker is extremely unlikely to retrieve all of the *possible* outcomes for an action. Thus, selection of action suffers from the same cognitive limitations as other decision activities we have discussed (retrieval biases and working-memory limitations). Because of these cognitive limitations, selection of action tends to follow a "satisficing" model; if an alternative action passes certain criteria, it is selected. If the action does not work, another is considered. It is worth repeating that system designers should be familiar with these various biases.

NATURALISTIC DECISION MAKING

One recent trend in human factors research has been toward the study of cognition and decision making as it occurs in real-world, dynamic and complex environments (e.g., Zsambok & Klein, 1997). As Orasanu and Connolly (1993) note, ". . . in everyday decisions, decisions are embedded in larger tasks that the decision maker is trying to accomplish. . . . Decisions are embedded in task cycles that consist of defining what the problem is, understanding what a reasonable solution would look like, taking action to reach that goal, and evaluating the effects of that action." In other words, "decision events" are important, but are often only one component in a bigger picture, a picture that resembles, and is sometimes referred to as, complex problem solving (Xiao, Milgram, & Doyle, 1997). Examples include: figure out how to bring a forest fire under control effectively but safely, determine how to anesthetize a patient with hypertension, identify and resolve a fault in a power plant, fly a plane into a busy airport, or figure out what to do when your parachute does not open.

Naturalistic decision making has been defined as "the way people use their experience to make decisions in field settings" (Zsambok, 1997). Researchers studying it (e.g., Cannon-Bowers, Salas, & Pruitt; 1996; Cook, Woods, & McDonald, 1991; Gaba, Howard, & Small, 1995; Orasanu & Connolly, 1993) have emphasized that decision-making tasks performed in a real-world environment tend to have the following characteristics:

- Ill-structured problems
- Uncertain, dynamic environments

- Information-rich environments where situational cues may change rapidly
- Cognitive processing that proceeds in iterative action/feedback loops
- Multiple shifting and/or competing individual and organizational goals
- Time constraints or time stress
- High risk
- Multiple persons somehow involved in the decision

To see how some of these characteristics combine, consider the scenario at the beginning of the chapter. An anesthesiologist was required to make a decision concerning whether to be conservative and keep herself available for an incoming major trauma, or to help with ongoing procedures because there were not enough other anesthesiologists available. There was incomplete, complex, and dynamically changing information; time stress; high risk; and a large set of outcomes, costs, and benefits. Another problem in making this decision is that she had multiple and conflicting goals imposed from the outside: making the surgeons happy, helping the patients needing immediate surgery, keeping hospital costs low, avoiding lawsuits, maintaining good relationships with staff, and maintaining resources available for a possible major emergency.

The multitude of factors affecting everyday decisions underscores the *cognitive complexity* of decision making in the real world. Dozens of factors all affect the decision-making process, including safety-related factors such as risk perception and tendency to take risk-taking behavior (e.g., see Chapter 14). Researchers are only beginning to get a handle on how people cognitively deal with such complexity.

On occasion, researchers focusing on naturalistic decision making have claimed that the traditional decision research was so narrow that it does not generalize to real-world complex decisions (Klein & Calderwood, 1991; Orasanu & Connolly, 1993). However, others have tested the generality of many of the heuristics and biases described above, and have obtained findings in the real world that paralleled those found in original decision-making laboratory research (e.g., Botney et al., 1993; DeKeyser & Woods, 1990; Elstein et al., 1978; Fontenelle, 1983; Gaba et al., 1995). We therefore view the traditional work on decision making and the more recent naturalistic approach to be complementary rather than mutually exclusive.

Research on real-world decision making in complex environments has yielded a number of descriptive models (Klein et al., 1993; Zsambok & Klein, 1997). We will describe a few of these models, focusing especially on Rasmussen's *SRK* model of task performance, which has received increasing attention in the field of human factors (Goodstein, Andersen, & Olsen, 1988; Reason, 1988). It is consistent with accepted and empirically supported models of cognitive information-processing, such as the three-stage model of expertise proposed by Fitts (1964) and Anderson (1983) and has also been used in popular accounts of human error (Reason, 1988, 1990; see also discussions of human error in Chapter 14). After we review some of these new viewpoints, we integrate them into a single information-processing model and evaluate how computer-based aiding systems could provide cognitive support for the subprocesses in the model.

Skill-, Rule-, and Knowledge-Based Task Performance

Rasmussen's *SRK model* (skill, rule, knowledge) describes three different levels of cognitive control that might potentially be used by a person during task performance (Rasmussen, 1983, 1986, 1993). People operate at one of the levels, depending on the nature of the task and their degree of experience with the particular situation (Hammond, 1993; Rasmussen, 1993). Figure 7.2 illustrates the three levels of cognitive control: skill-based behavior, rule-based behavior, and knowledge-based behavior. Information enters the system at the lower left, as a function of attentional processes. The information then results in cognitive processing at either the skill-based level, the rule-based level, or the knowledge-based level, depending on the operator's degree of experience with the particular circumstance.

If people are extremely experienced with the task, they will process the information at the *skill-based* level of performance, reacting to the raw perceptual elements at an automatic, subconscious level. They do not have to interpret and integrate the cues or think of possible actions. Performance is governed by pure stimulus-response associations developed at a neurological level. Because the behavior is automatic, attentional resources are minimally needed. Errors at the skill-based level are usually caused by either (a) misdirected attention, where the person intends to deviate from the normal course of action and then momentarily pays attention to something else and performs the automatic habit, or (b) paying attention to the task, which then interrupts an automated sequence of behavior.

When people are familiar with the task but do not have extensive experience, they will process the information and perform at the *rule-based* level. The cues are recognized as meaning certain things, termed *signs,* and these signs then trigger rules accumulated from past experience. The rules are *If-Then* associations between cue sets and the appropriate actions. Errors made in decision making at this level tend to result from a misclassification of the situation with an application of the wrong rule.

When the situation is novel, decision makers will not have any rules stored from previous experience to call on. They will therefore have to operate at the *knowledge-based* level, which is essentially analytical processing using conceptual information. After the person assigns meaning to the cues and integrates them into an identification of what is happening, they begin to process this information with respect to goals in working memory. Effortful analysis and memory retrieval support problem solving and planning activities. Mental models are often used to run cognitive simulations in evaluating an action plan. In fact, some authors describe knowledge-based behavior as problem solving rather than decision making, because of the need for problem definition, solution generation, and trying to determine which course of action might be successful or best (Bainbridge, 1988). Errors made at the knowledge-based level are a result of factors associated with analytical thinking, such as limited working memory, biases in generating hypotheses or actions, cognitive fixation, and so forth (Reason, 1988). According to the SRK model, a person might operate at the knowledge, rule, or skill-based level and will switch between them depending on task familiarity.

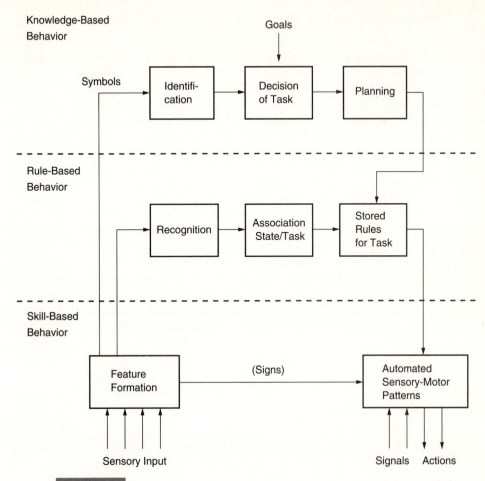

FIGURE 7.2

Rasmussen's skill-based, rule-based, and knowledge-based levels of cognitive control. (*Source:* Goodstein, L.P., Andersen, H.B., and Olsen, S.E., 1988. *Tasks, Errors, and Mental Models.* London: Taylor & Francis. Reprinted by permission of Taylor & Francis.)

The levels can also be used to characterize people with differing degrees of experience. A novice can work only at the analytical knowledge-based level. At an intermediate point of learning, people will have a qualitatively different knowledge base, and also some rules in their repertoire from training or experience. They work predominantly at the rule-based level but must move to knowledge-based processing when the situation is a new one. The expert has yet a different knowledge base, a greatly expanded rule base, and a skill base as well. Thus, the expert moves between the three levels depending on the task. When a novel situation arises, such as a system disturbance not previously experienced, lack of familiarity with the situation moves even the expert back to the analytical knowledge-based level.

Additional Views of Naturalistic Decision Making

Some models or descriptions of naturalistic decision making focus on strategies used under more specific types of circumstances, for example, when decision makers must make very rapid decision. Other researchers study a small portion of the decision-making process, such as the use of mental models. We briefly review some of these efforts, but due to space limitations, readers are referred to Klein et al. (1993) and Zsambok and Klein (1997) for more in-depth treatments.

Cognitive Continuum Theory.   A number of researchers have suggested that decision-making processes will occur somewhere along a cognitive continuum ranging from *intuition* to *analysis* (e.g., Hamm, 1988a; Hammond 1980, 1993; Hammond et al., 1987). In fact, processing might oscillate relatively rapidly between intuition and analysis (Hamm, 1988b). Intuitive processes are characterized by low control and low conscious awareness, rapid processing, and high confidence in the answer (Hammond, 1993). Analytical processes are characterized by higher levels of cognitive control, slow processing, and lower confidence in the answer. Analytical processing could be considered similar to Rasmussen's knowledge-based processing. Hammond suggests that the use of intuitive versus analytical processing is determined by two factors: (1) certain tasks induce either intuitive or analytical processing, and (2) failure in the use of one type causes switching to the other. Tasks that induce intuitive processing have relatively large numbers of cues, provide simultaneous and brief display of cues, large relationships among the cues, and a relatively short period for decision making. Analytical processing will occur with fewer cues, high confidence in the task, and long sequential availability of cues.

Situation Awareness.   Researchers studying a variety of decision-making and problem-solving tasks have realized that the first critical step for successful task performance is to evaluate the "situation" adequately. People receive cues from the environment and must use them to make sense of the current state of the world, a process termed either *situation assessment* or *situation awareness* (Endsley, 1997; Noble, 1993; Orasanu, Dismukes, & Fischer, 1993; Roth, 1997; Waag & Bell, 1997). Endsley (1988) defines situation awareness (SA) as "the perception of the elements in the environment within a volume of time and space, the comprehension of their meaning and the projection of their status in the near future." She also notes that there are different "levels" of SA, which vary in cognitive complexity: Level 1 SA is *perceiving* the status, attributes, and dynamics of relevant elements in the environment; Level 2 SA is *comprehending* the relevant cues in light of one's goals (includes activities such as diagnosis or fault identification); and Level 3 SA is *projecting* the future activity of the elements in the environment (Endsley, 1997). Not everyone needs to, or is able to, achieve all three levels during problem solving.

The cognitive processing required for situation awareness includes the integration of cues into sometimes complex mental representations of a system, accomplished by using pre-existing knowledge to interpret and give meaning to the cues. This may be as simple as reading a thermometer and determining that the person has a fever or as complex as evaluating dozens of displays to identify the fault in a process control plant. Situation assessment may also require evaluation of important factors such as risk level and time available for the decision (Orasanu &

Fischer, 1997). One reason that situation awareness has become an important topic is that in times of high mental workload and stress, people seem to "lose" situation awareness; that is, they fail to keep in mind the current state of the world (e.g., Gugerty & Tirre, 1996; Waag & Bell, 1997). For jet pilots, this might mean a spatial disorientation or loss of knowledge about relative aircraft positions. Unfortunately, SA has proven difficult to directly measure without being contaminated by the actual decision making and performance tasks (Garland et al., 1996).

Recognition-Primed Decision Making.   Some researchers have focused their study on experts making decisions under time stress. For example, in his theory of recognition-primed decision making (RPD), Klein (1989) suggested that in most instances, experts simply recognize a pattern of cues and recall a single course of action, which is then implemented (Klein, 1989; Klein & Calderwood, 1991; Klein, Calderwood, & Clinton-Cirocco, 1986). Simon describes this type of decision process as "intuition" derived from a capability for rapid recognition linked to a large store of knowledge (Simon, 1987). Thus, people do not seem to use *analytical* processes in which alternative actions are retrieved or constructed and then systematically compared for relative utility.

There are three critical assumptions of the RPD model: first, people use their experience to generate a plausible option the first time around; second, if the decision makers are experts, time pressure should not cripple performance because they use rapid pattern matching, which has been shown to be resistant to time pressure; and finally, experienced decision makers can "adopt a course of action without comparing and contrasting possible courses of action" (Klein, 1997). Research over the last 10 years has supported the idea that expert decision making in the real world often follows this pattern.

In spite of the prevalence of rapid pattern-recognition decisions, most researchers assume that there are cases where decision makers will use analytical methods. More specifically, if uncertainty exists and time is adequate, additional analyses are performed to evaluate the current situation assessment, modify the retrieved action plan, or generate alternative actions (Flin, Slaven, & Stewart, 1996; Klein, 1997; Orasanu & Fischer, 1997). The extent of this switch to analytical processing varies greatly across tasks. For example, Klein and associates reported that, in a study of decision making in Navy antiair warfare, 78 percent of the decisions adopted the first course of action without any deliberation, 18 percent relied on evaluation using mental simulation, and 4 percent involved comparison of strengths and weaknesses of alternative actions (Kaempf, Wolf, Thordsen, & Klein, 1992). However, Orasanu and Fischer reported in a study of pilot decision making that 40 percent of the decisions appeared to be based on condition-action rules, where another 54 percent were analytical knowledge-based decisions (Orasanu & Fischer, 1997).

Schemas, Stories, and Mental Models.   When analytical processing is performed in the course of decision making, it starts with the situation assessment. In Endsley's (1997) Level 2 situation awareness, information from the environment is used to construct a "mental representation" of some type. Depending on the domain, this representation is variously termed a story, mental model, or some more abstract type of causal model (e.g., Cohen, Freeman, & Wolf, 1996; Klein &

Crandall, 1995; Lipshitz & Ben Shaul, 1997; Pennington & Hastie, 1993; Roth, 1997). There have been a number of people suggesting one or more of these ideas, but all seem to be saying that people use previous knowledge, or *schemas,* to comprehend and integrate the situational cues into a dynamic model of the situation they are trying to evaluate or diagnose. The mental models or conceptual representations include important causal relationships, like those developed for problem solving (Greeno, 1973). Once constructed, the mental models can be "run" to support further evaluation processes. The use of mental models is supported by research in both problem solving and decision making. For example, Passaro and colleagues found that inadequate mental models were responsible for decision errors leading to critical mine gas explosions (Passaro, Cole, & Wala, 1994), and Lehner & Zirk (1987) found that use of poor mental models can cause a drop in decision performance of anywhere between 30 percent and 60 percent.

As one example of this view, Pennington and Hastie developed a model of *explanation-based decision making* by analyzing jury member think-aloud protocols (Pennington & Hastie, 1988, 1993). According to their model, decision making consists of three activities: (1) people receive information and construct a *causal story* that can account for the information (a sort of "diagnosis"), (2) a possible set of actions is generated, and (3) a matching process is performed to find one action that best fits the causal story. A decision is made when "the causal model of the evidence is successfully matched to an alternative in the choice set" (Pennington & Hastie, 1993). The focus of the model is predominantly on the first activity; that is, construction of the causal explanation is pivotal in determining the action chosen. In support of this idea, others have analyzed decision-making protocols, and found that causal stories are frequently used to evaluate hypotheses (e.g., Adelman et al., 1996; Cohen et al., 1996). This view is important because it suggests the need for computer-based support that would help a person build and use a coherent causal story.

In a similar vein, a number of people have suggested that we perform situation assessment by constructing a *mental model* of the relevant system or environment, and then using it to run simulations throughout the remainder of the decision-making process (e.g., see Zsambok & Klein, 1997; and discussion of mental models in Chapter 6). The simulation is used to generate expectations for other cues not previously considered or to guide observation of changes in system variables (Roth, 1997). The decision maker critiques and modifies the mental model until it fits the environmental information, performing an *active* search for an explanation of diverse cues. Mental models are then used to evaluate goals, actions, and plans and also to make predictions useful in monitoring actions and their consequences in the system or environment (e.g., Klein, 1997; Roth, 1997).

AN INTEGRATED MODEL OF REAL-WORLD DECISION MAKING

While each model or view of naturalistic decision making provides a unique perspective, it is also possible to synthesize them roughly into one generic information-processing model that organizes the potential decision-making processes

(Gordon, 1997). The framework for such a generic model begins with Rasmussen's work on levels of control (Rasmussen, 1986, 1993). The SRK model is expanded into an information-processing model that accommodates many of the processes observed or postulated by others. Such a synthesis of ideas from naturalistic decision making models is shown in Figure 7.3 (from Gordon, 1997).

The flowchart in Figure 7.3 illustrates processes that occur in working memory, with information coming from the environment (lower left) and from long-term memory (bottom of figure). In this model, information enters the system and then is processed at one of three levels: *automatic* skill-based processing, *intuitive* rule-based processing, and *analytical* knowledge-based processing. Automatic processing is a function of which environmental cues are sensed (affected by selective attention), but beyond that, there is no demand on cognitive resources. Raw cue elements directly trigger an action response, and the decision maker often will

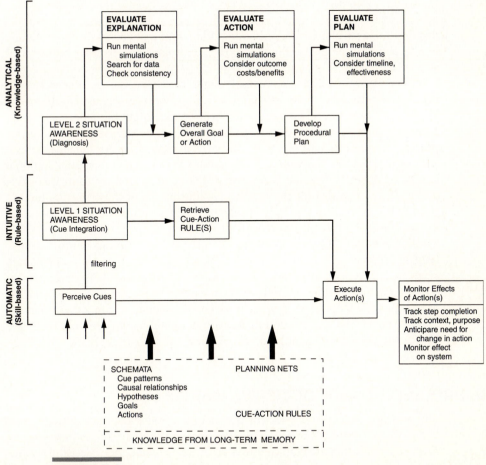

FIGURE 7.3

A generic information-processing model integrating views of naturalistic decision making.

not even know which of the entire set of cue elements actually triggered the response. In a sense, this is not even really decision making or problem solving.

For intuitive rule-based processing, there is more active cognitive processing required, as the person must consider a variety of cues. This corresponds to Endsley's (1997) Level 1 SA. The cues trigger retrieval of appropriate cue-action rules from memory, and these specify the desired goal and action sequence that is to be executed. We would expect that people making their decision at the intuitive level would often not be able to explain "how" they made their decision because it was based on stored memory associations rather than reasoning per se (Gordon, 1992).

When rule-based intuitive processes do not provide a satisfactory solution or decision and time is available, the decision process will move upward in the model shown; that is, uncertainty coupled with available time will allow a person to use a more careful analytical process. This can occur at several different points, indicated in the figure by dashed arrows. Knowledge-based analysis begins with level 2 SA—development of an integrated understanding of the state of the world, including construction of causal stories, mental models, and/or tentative diagnoses. Under some circumstances, even with analytical processing, a decision maker will generate only one explanation or hypothesis, generate one overall action to be taken (the "decision"), and plan the necessary sequence of steps to carry out the action.

If the situation is difficult or complex and time allows, the decision maker will utilize one or more of the most complex *evaluative* processes noted at the top of Figure 7.3. The evaluation process relies heavily on mental simulation to help assess the hypothesis, action, or plan under consideration (Orasanu, 1993). In this process, the decision maker searches the environment for further data (as in medical diagnosis). The use of cognitive simulations to generate ideas about additional cues to be obtained would explain why people tend to look for confirming evidence. This is because only the generation and running of "false" mental models would yield disconfirming cues to search for. This seems unlikely to occur in many situations, especially those with a time urgency.

If the working hypothesis, action, or plan fails to meet minimum criteria (which are heavily affected by time constraints), the decision maker may generate a new hypothesis, action, or plan. When a plan is finally selected, it is executed and the person monitors the environment to update their situation assessment and to determine whether changes in procedures must be made. Note that this model reflects Hamm's (1988b) assertion that expert decision making will often vacillate between levels at a *molecular* level, that is, within one single decision.

IMPROVING HUMAN DECISION MAKING

The previous sections have shown that people often experience difficulties at many different processing points during decision making. In fact, analyses of "human error" often focus on cognitive errors (e.g., made a poor decision) rather than behavioral errors (e.g., hand slipped off the control). Types of cognitive errors will be discussed more fully in Chapter 14. In this section, we will briefly discuss some possibilities for improving human decision making, with the alternatives falling into the categories of *redesign for performance support, training,* and *decision aids.*

Redesign for Performance Support

We often jump to the conclusion that poor performance in decision making means that we need to do something "to the person" to make him or her a better decision maker. However, sometimes a change in the information provided by the external environment will automatically support better decision making, eliminating the need to change the person him- or herself. As an example, consider the following scenario. A parachutist has a chute that fails to open properly. He looks up and, as trained, tries to untangle the cords so that the chute opens properly. He does not realize that he is spinning rapidly to the ground and should deploy the reserve chute. He finally deploys the reserve chute within 200 feet of the ground, which is too late. It would be easy to come to the conclusion that the person needed better training. However, a close analysis of the event might show that the person did have adequate training. The problem was that he could not tell by looking up at the plain white chute what was occurring with respect to the cloth and lines. In addition, he was paying attention to the fault and did not realize when it was critical to open the reserve (lack of adequate situation awareness). Redesign could reduce both of these problems. For example, the parachute cloth could have a multicolored design intended to maximize problem diagnosis when viewed from the underside.[1] In addition, an altitude sensor and auditory warning device could be used to notify the parachutist when he or she must begin to deploy a reserve. Notice that in terms of Figure 7.3, the chute design supports diagnosis generation and selection, and the warning device supports situation awareness as well as notification that problem-solving time is up. The operator would still need training with respect to the best actions to perform depending on the different possible chute malfunctions, but the chances of an accident would be reduced.

Training

Training can address decision making at each of the three levels of control shown in Figure 7.3. First, one method for improving analytical decision making has been to train people to overcome the heuristics/biases described earlier. Some of these efforts focused on teaching the analytical, normative attribute utility methods for decision making (e.g., Zakay & Wooler, 1984). Although people can learn the methods, the training efforts were largely unsuccessful simply because people find the methods cumbersome and not worth the cognitive effort. Other training efforts have focused on counteracting specific types of bias, such as the confirmation bias

---

[1]Design enhancement suggested by Curt Braun in personal communication.

(e.g., Tolcott, Marvin, & Bresnick, 1989). This type of training has sometimes reduced decision biases, but many studies show little to no effect (Means et al., 1993). A more effective approach might be to allow the natural use of varying strategies, but to teach people when to use them and the shortcomings of each.

As another approach, Cohen, Freeman, and Thompson (1997) suggest training people to do a better job at metacognition. This would include teaching people how to: (1) consider appropriate and adequate cues to develop situation awareness, (2) check situation assessments or explanations for completeness and consistency with cues, (3) analyze data that conflict with the situation assessment, and (4) recognize when too much conflict exists between the explanation or assessment and the cues. Others suggest training skills such as development of mental models and management of uncertainty and time pressure (Klein, 1997). A look at the literature on teaching problem solving suggests that people are better at learning to problem solve or make decisions in a particular area rather than simply learning to do it in general (Frederiksen, 1984). This means that training should focus on knowledge and procedures relevant to the job, as described in Chapter 18.

At the intuitive rule-based level, operators can be provided with training to enhance their perceptual and pattern-recognition skills. Flin et al. (1996) and Orasanu (1995) suggest focusing on situation assessment, where trainees learn to recognize critical situational cues and to improve the accuracy of their time availability and risk judgments. This can be achieved by having learners either explicitly memorize the cue-action rules or practice a broad variety of trials to implicitly acquire the rules. For example, Kirlik et al. (1996) enhanced perceptual learning and pattern recognition by either (a) having trainees memorize rules or (b) alternating trainee-practice scenarios with "modeling" scenarios where the critical situational cues and correct actions were highlighted. Both of these training methods were effective. As we will see in Chapter 18, to teach pattern recognition effectively, training must encompass a broad variety of examples and "nonexamples" with relatively extensive practice (Gordon, 1994).

Finally, to support better processing at the automatic level, training would have to focus on the relevant cues in *raw data form.* Work on automaticity suggests that training skill-based processing takes hundreds of repetition for the associations to become strong enough for automatic processing (e.g., Schneider, 1985). In addition, this approach only works for situations where a cue set *consistently* maps onto a particular action. For both rule-based and skill-based training, simulation is often a better medium for extensive practice because it can allow more varied scenarios, and often in less time, than the real life context (Means et al., 1993). Finally, for any of the training approaches described, the decision maker should receive feedback, preferably for each cognitive step rather than the decision as a whole (Gordon, 1994). Additional suggestions for training decision making in complex environments can be found in Means et al. (1993).

One of the problems in using a training approach is that it does not really overcome problems associated with memory limitations. These limitations have the greatest impact in knowledge-based analytical processing (Rasmussen, 1993). For example, one could teach people a large store of knowledge to use for decision making, but much of it might still remain *inert* and unretrieved. As a second example, if working memory can only accommodate a certain amount of information, training will not expand that significantly. Designers are accepting the fact that training can only do so much, and other methods of cognitive support must be considered.

Decision Aids

Explicit help for decision makers can take many forms, ranging from simple tables to elaborate expert systems. One method that is popular for business managers is the decision table. Decision tables are used to list the possible outcomes, probabilities, and utilities of the action alternatives. The decision maker enters estimated probabilities and values into the table. Calculated average expected utilities for each alternative show the decision maker the rational choice. Use of a decision table is helpful because it deflects the load placed on working memory. A similar type of analysis tool is the decision tree.

Decision trees are useful for representing decisions that involve a sequence of decisions and possible consequences (Edwards, 1987). With this method, a branching point is used to represent the decision alternatives; this is followed by branching points for possible consequences and their associated probabilities. This sequence is repeated as far as necessary for decision making. This allows the user to see the overall probability for each entire action-consequence sequence.

Expert Systems.   Other decision aids make extensive use of the computational power of new technologies. One example of such a computer-based decision aid is the expert system. *Expert systems* are computer programs designed to capture one or more experts' knowledge and provide answers in a consulting type of role (Grabinger, Jonassen, & Wilson, 1992). The programs typically use concepts, principles, rules of thumb, and other knowledge about a given field, combined with methods of applying the knowledge or rules, to make inferences. Expert systems have been developed to help with an extremely wide variety of tasks such as speech understanding, image analysis, medical diagnosis, military planning, weather forecasting, computer debugging, system fault diagnosis, and business management (see Garg-Janardan et al., 1987; and White, 1990, for reviews).

In most cases, expert systems take situational cues as input and provide either a diagnosis and/or suggested action as an output. As an example, a medical expert system might have symptoms as input and a diagnosis as the output (e.g., MYCIN, Shortliffe, 1976). Expert system programs are typically built either on a rule base that associates cues with actions or sometimes on a "system model" that allows deep reasoning to be used for fault diagnosis (Gordon, 1991). Sometimes, expert systems also explain their underlying reasoning, but these attempts have been only partially successful.

Overall, traditional expert systems have not been particularly successful in many complex decision environments. It has been suggested that one reason for this lack of success and user enthusiasm is that having a computer system doing the *whole* task and the human playing a subordinate role by gathering information is not subjectively appealing to people (Gordon, 1988); that is, a person goes through the various activities of decision making and then uses a computer that displays its choice. The person has no basis for knowing whether his or her decision is any better or worse than that of the expert system. To make matters worse, there is usually no way to communicate or collaborate the way one might with a human expert. (Interestingly, Alty and Coombs [1980] showed that similar types of consultations with highly controlling human advisers were also judged unsatisfactory by "users.")

An additional problem is that even though computers are usually better at identifying solutions than the users, research has shown that expert systems tend to be mistrusted relative to the person's own ability (Kleinmuntz, 1990). And finally, the use of expert systems with the user in a subordinate role leads to *joint cognitive breakdowns* when novel problems arise (Roth, Bennett, & Woods, 1987; Woods & Roth, 1988b). The use of expert systems is strongly related to the issue of automation, a topic covered in detail in Chapter 16.

Cognitive Support. A much more successful approach that is becoming increasingly popular is the use of computers to help overcome biases or information-processing limitations for one or more of the cognitive subprocesses, acting as tools or instruments for cognitive support (Woods & Roth, 1988a). Many of these decision aids fall in the category of *decision support systems.* According to Zachary (1988), a decision support system is "any interactive system that is specifically designed to improve decision making of its user by extending the user's cognitive-decision-making abilities." Because this often requires information display, it can be difficult to distinguish between a "decision support system" and a technologically advanced information display. Also, many researchers consider expert systems to be one type of decision support system (e.g., Zachary, 1988).

Some decision aids utilize computers to support working memory and perform calculations. One widely used approach has been designed to support the traditional "decision analysis" cognitive process of weighing alternative actions (see top of Fig. 7.3). Computers are programmed to calculate and display the utilities for each possible choice (Edwards, 1987; White, 1990). Many of the these traditional decision aids are of limited value since they rely on strategies that may seem foreign to people. However, for those tasks where choices involve high risk and widely varying probabilities, such as types of treatment for cancer, it can be worth training users to be more comfortable with this type of aid.

Theoretically, decision support systems could be developed to support each of the processes shown in Figure 7.3. It would also be possible to design a system that would support all of these processes, adapting to the cognitive level at which the person is currently working (Rasmussen, 1986). In other words, a person would be supported through displays that made the critical situational cues most salient or through a monitoring system that tracks actions performed and changes in the system (e.g., Rouse, Rouse, & Hammer, 1982). One could view this type of support as simply good display design rather than a decision support system per se. For any cognitive support method, it is important to perform an appropriate analysis of the task in order to determine what information should be provided or what calculations or modeling needs to be performed.

Research on specific methods for providing cognitive support, especially at the analytical level, is relatively new, and for that reason, we can only review the relatively abstract suggestions that have been provided up to this point. However, we also refer you to Chapter 8, because much of the technology for supporting decision making is inherently part of good display design.

INFORMATION ACQUISITION AND MONITORING
1. Display and call attention to important cues.
2. Use intelligent systems to monitor relevant variables or cues and notify operator when the variables move out of acceptable limits (Eberts et al., 1984). Such a system can be made flexible so that each operator is able to specify variables and limits for different circumstances (Guerlain & Bullemer, 1996).
3. Design displays to provide the information specifically required for decision making rather than all possible system cues.
4. Present, in a readily comprehensible format, the reliability, certainty, or *value* of each cue.

SITUATION AWARENESS
1. Use cue filtering, integration, or other methods to support situational assessment (Bennett & Flach, 1992; McDaniel & Rankin, 1991; Roth, 1994; Wisudha, 1985).
2. Augment normal cues with more abstract but directly useful cues (examples include configural displays and rankine cycle displays as described in Chapter 8). As an example, Kirlik and colleagues (Kirlik et al., 1996) have had success in *augmenting* displays used for decision making. By performing ecological task analysis, they determined the types of information *directly* needed for the decision task (which may be more abstract than individual cues reflecting system variables). For example, in a military setting, a map might contain information regarding terrain and the location of a threat vehicle. But an analysis of the terrain combined with vehicle type would yield information about where the vehicle would be capable of moving. The map used for decision making could include a color-coded transparent overlay indicating the areas where the vehicle can and cannot locomote (Kirlik et al., 1996). Thus, displays can contain the original "raw" cues plus more abstract augmenting information. Such displays are especially successful when decision makers must operate under time stress (Kirlik et al., 1996).
3. Use spatial techniques to organize data for processing evidence-state relationships (Woods, 1988). See Chapter 8 for examples.
4. As described above, some newer systems make use of temporary, situation-specific, and operator-defined computer-based monitoring to detect and notify of system state changes. During prolonged problem solving, this system can be used to "warn" the operator that important variables have changed, resulting in a heightened situation awareness without the need for frequent checking (Guerlain & Bullemer, 1996).

INTUITIVE, RULE-BASED PROCESSING:
1. Many researchers have suggested presentation of rules, including conditions and actions, and any discrepancies from a match (e.g., deGreef & Neerincx, 1995; Neerincx & Griffioen, 1996).

2. A slightly different approach is *case-based reasoning,* where *cases* or entire descriptions of situations are stored in computer memory over time (Kolodner, 1993; Mitchell et al., 1997; Weiner, Thurman, & Mitchell, 1996). These are used as an information database to support processing of new situations. The operator might browse the database or a computerized intelligent agent could perform the search. In this case, cues corresponding to the current situation are used to find the most closely matching previous cases, and these cases or "explanations" are presented to the operator. The cases may have a broad range of information, including critical cues, goals, constraints, action plans, and so on. The cases are then used by the operator or modified as necessary.

ANALYTICAL, KNOWLEDGE-BASED PROCESSING

1. Provide an external memory aid for the diagnosis process (e.g., diagram mark-ups-evaluated by Toms & Patrick, 1989).
2. Generate hypotheses and show the probability of a match between the cue set and each hypothesis.
3. Provide a visual or topographical display of system functioning via mimic diagrams (Edlund & Lewis, 1994; Moore & Corbridge, 1996; Reising & Sanderson, 1996), animated mimic diagrams (e.g., Bennett, 1994), or other techniques (see Chapter 8). Mimic diagrams are schematic displays that closely resemble the system they are representing. In an industrial setting, a mimic diagram might show a network of pipes and valves. Other mimic diagrams might also include more abstract or "invisible" parameters that are more directly used in problem solving (e.g., Edlund & Lewis, 1994; Reising & Sanderson, 1996).
4. Provide dynamic simulations based on the person's current working hypothesis. This can support hypothesis confirmation, goal evaluation, and planning. Provide a display of current system functioning that maps well onto users' mental models, and providing a display of the discrepancy between normal and current systems (e.g., Yoon & Hammer, 1988).
5. Suggest additional testing of the hypothesis or explanation, or suggest cues to be obtained.
6. Generate possible goal(s) and action(s) (Eberts et al, 1984).
7. Provide calculational power and displays for "what-if" scenarios (Roth, 1994; Smith, McCoy, & Layton, 1993; Yoon & Hammer, 1988).
8. Display confirming evidence, disconfirming evidence, and assumptions for various hypotheses (e.g., Morrison, Kelly, & Hutchins, 1996).
9. Show a qualitative display of relative outcome probabilities, costs, and benefits, integrating them so that the best choice emerges.
10. Provide information to help predict future states and events. For example, Schraagen describes a support system for decisions related to naval firefighting (Schraagen, 1997). Novices had difficulty predicting (or even considering) the compartments to which fires were most likely to spread. A support system could determine and display a list of compartments most likely to be affected and could also make action recommendations regarding the actions needed to mitigate the effects.

11. Show information related to alternative actions such as relevance, resource requirements, assumptions, physical configuration, and so on. (Roth, 1997; Rouse & Valusek, 1993).
12. Provide planning aids (e.g., Descotte & Latombe, 1981; Lembersky & Chi, 1993).

This partial list suggests the many ways that the human cognitive activities could be supported or augmented through computer support. One important issue is the question of what processes or strategies are most likely to need support; that is, which of these strategies are people most likely to use? It has become apparent that the answer to this question depends on the specific domain or job, level of expertise, amount of time, amount of uncertainty, and so forth. We do not currently have the knowledge and methods to be able to predict what strategies a person will use given a particular circumstance. In fact, Miller and Woods (1997) point out that even the system and its displays will affect the type of decision strategies selected by operators.

Another consideration is whether designers should deliberately try to alter rather than fit the strategy of the moment. For example, Pierce (1996) found that people overrely on rapid, intuitive decisions rather than perform the more difficult deliberate analyses. This suggests that decision aids might support human decision making by somehow counteracting this "shortcut" or satisficing tendency—at least when it is important and there is ample time for analytical processing (e.g., life-threatening decisions).

Current work shows that, like other aspects of interface design, adequate usability testing is critical for advanced features such as decision support. To illustrate, Cook and Woods (1996) evaluated the implementation of a new physiological monitoring system for use in cardiac anesthesia. The system had several advanced features, including automation of certain functions and calculational aids. Users tried, then usually abandoned, use of the computational aids because they were too difficult to be worth while.

Finally, additional considerations follow from a view of decision aids as a human-machine system where the human has supervisory control and the computer is a semiautonomous but subordinate cognitive system (Rasmussen, 1986; Woods & Roth, 1988b). The concerns are the same as those that come with any automation technology. As Woods and Roth (1988b) point out, a decision support system will be successful if the user can control and/or redirect the subsystem, and the user and subsystem have common or shared representations of the state of the world and problem status. Chapter 16 addresses these and other important issues.

PROBLEM SOLVING

We have already seen that task performance in complex environments relies on a variety of cognitive activities. These activities are sometimes more of a decision choice and sometimes more like "problem solving." Often the generation of an alternative action is a problem in itself. For example, how can a ship captain avoid an obstacle that suddenly presents itself? How can a pilot land his plane when a malfunction has occurred? Much of the task depends on creative problem solving that will yield an action sequence to meet the goals of the situation. In this section, we consider activities that have the traditional characteristics of a *problem:* one or more goals, a set of conditions or "givens," a variety of means or methods by which to change the conditions and reach the goals, and obstacles—resulting in no immediately available knowledge of a solution.

Characteristics of Problem Solving

Some of the problem solving typically studied in human factors revolves around use of a mechanical system to achieve some goal. For example, a person might want to program a VCR to record a particular channel, on a particular day, at a particular time. However, it is a "problem" because the person does not have the method to do this task directly stored in memory. What often makes this type of problem solving difficult is that (1) the person does not have the working memory capacity to solve the problem (Larkin et al., 1980), (2) the person does not have enough system knowledge to solve the problem, and/or (3) the person has the system knowledge, but it is disconnected and unorganized, and the person does not access it from long-term memory (Gordon & Gill, 1989).

It is not entirely clear in real-world tasks how decision making and problem solving fit together. Some researchers believe that decision making fits into the overall problem solving task (Means et al., 1993). Another view is that problem solving is that set of activities seen at the top of the decision-making model in Figure 7.3. In other words, knowledge-based decision making and problem solving share many similar basic cognitive processes. It is likely that problem solving differs mostly in that generating a solution (the action sequence) is much more difficult than it is in most decision tasks. In problems, the solution path is usually a set of "subroutines" or steps that are combined to solve the current problem. Looking at Figure 7.3, problem solving would rely extensively on the two activities of "generating actions" and "planning." Some of the implications are that successful problem solving requires large amounts of relevant knowledge, good strategies for generating potential solutions, and effective mental models for running cognitive simulations. Effective problem solving would be hindered by working memory limitations, lack of knowledge in long-term memory, and lack of good memory-retrieval strategies.

Errors and Biases in Problem Solving

After reviewing the difficulties and biases made in decision making, it is relatively easy to predict problem solving difficulties. The first type of difficulty is caused by the representation that people build of the problem (similar to situation assessment for decision making). If the representation is overly constrained, omits constraints, or only allows one view of things, a solution will be less likely to be generated. Simon points out that "the relative ease of solving a problem will depend on how successful the solver has been in representing critical features of the task environment in his problem space" (Simon, 1987, p. 276).

Another common problem is a failure to generate the correct solution plan, even when the problem representation is clear. Sometimes this is due to fixation on previous plans that worked in the past. It is often difficult to search long-term memory for alternative solutions because memory activation tends to not spread to "distant" or weakly associated concepts. People are also prone to showing "functional fixedness," looking at the functionality of objects only in terms of their normal use. The movie *Apollo 13* demonstrated the ability of people to move beyond this type of functional fixedness. Recall that the astronauts were stranded without an adequate air purifier system. To solve this problem, the ground control crew assembled all of the "usable" objects known to be on board the spacecraft (tubes, articles of clothing, etc.). Then they did free brainstorming with the objects in various configurations until they had assembled a system that worked. Finally, they walked the astronauts through the assembly procedure.

Many failures to develop a solution plan are caused by limitations of working memory; that is, often a long sequence of action "packets" must be composed into a "plan." Then a cognitive simulation must be carried out to evaluate the plan. This process frequently involves too many bits of information to be handled in working memory. As a simple example, imagine playing chess and trying to simulate three moves into the future—including the possible choices the opponent might make. The number of alternative combinations simply overwhelms the player's capabilities.

It is apparent that limitations in problem solving have much in common with limitations and biases in decision making, especially those due to memory retrieval and working-memory limitations. Computer-based problem-solving support can overcome many of these difficulties by using the support mechanisms previously identified for intuitive and analytical decision making. However, designers should be cautious; initial research has shown that insufficiently developed decision and problem-solving aids can lead humans to make more errors than they would when left to perform the task unaided (e.g., Smith, et al., 1993). In addition, no one has yet identified a way for computer aids to help generate creative solutions to new problems. Perhaps the closest system that has been developed is the retrieval of previous problems and solutions for the operator to use in generating appropriate solutions for the current problem, that is, *cased-based reasoning*.

REFERENCES

Adelman, L., Bresnick, T., Black, P.K., Marvin, F.F., and Sak, S.G. (1996). Research with patriot air defense officers: Examining information order effects. *Human Factors, 38*(2) 250–261.

Alty, J.L., and Coombs, M.J. (1980). Face-to-face guidance of university computer users—I: A study of advisory services. *International Journal of Man-Machine Studies, 12,* 390–406.

Anderson, J.R. (1983). *The architecture of cognition.* Cambridge, MA: Harvard University Press.

Anderson, J.R. (1990). *Cognitive psychology and its implications* (3rd ed.). San Francisco: W.H. Freeman.

Arkes, H., and Harkness, R.R. (1980). The effect of making a diagnosis on subsequent recognition of symptoms. *Journal of Experimental Psychology: Human Learning and Memory, 6,* 568–575.

Arocha, J.F., and Patel, V.L. (1995). Novice diagnostic reasoning in medicine: Accounting for evidence. *The Journal of the Learning Sciences, 4*(4), 355–384.

Bainbridge, L. (1988). Types of representation. In L.P. Goodstein, H.B. Andersen, and S.E. Olsen (eds.), *Tasks, errors, and mental models* (pp. 70–91). London: Taylor & Francis.

Balla, J. (1980). Logical thinking and the diagnostic process. *Methodology and Information in Medicine, 19,* 88–92.

Bennett, K.B. (1994). Animated mimic displays. *Proceedings of the Human Factors and Ergonomics Society 38th Annual Meeting* (pp. 1341–1345). Santa Monica, CA: Human Factors and Ergonomics Society.

Bennett, K.B., and Flach, J.M. (1992). Graphical displays: Implications for divided attention, focused attention, and problem solving. *Human Factors, 34*(5), 513–533.

Botney, R., Gaba, D., Howard, S., and Jump, B. (1993). The role of fixation error in preventing the detection and correction of a simulated volatile anesthetic overdose (Abstract). *Anesthesiology, 79,* A1115.

Cannon-Bowers, J.A., Salas, E., and Pruitt, J.S. (1996). Establishing the boundaries of a paradigm for decision-making research. *Human Factors, 38*(2), 193–205.

Cohen, M.S., Freeman, J.T., and Wolf, S. (1996). Metarecognition in time-stressed decision making: Recognizing, critiquing, and correcting. *Human Factors, 38*(2), 206–219.

Cohen, M.S., Freeman, J.T., and Thompson, B.B. (1997). Training the naturalistic decision maker. In C.E. Zsambok and G. Klein (eds.), *Naturalistic decision making* (pp. 257–268). Mahwah, NJ: Erlbaum.

Cook, R.I., and Woods, D.D. (1994). Operating at the sharp end: The complexity of human error. In M.S. Bogner (ed.), *Human error in medicine* (pp. 255–301). Hillsdale, NJ: Erlbaum.

Cook, R.I., and Woods, D.D. (1996). Adapting to new technology in the operating room. *Human Factors, 38*(4), 593–613.

Cook, R., Woods, D., and McDonald, J. (1991). *Human performance in anesthesia: A corpus of cases* (Technical Report CSEL91.003). Columbus: Ohio State University, Cognitive Systems Engineering Laboratory.

Coombs, C.H., Dawes, R.M., and Tversky, A. (1970). *Mathematical psychology.* Englewood Cliffs, NJ: Prentice Hall.

deGreef, H.P., and Neerincx, M.A. (1995). Cognitive support: Designing aiding to supplement human knowledge. *International Journal of Human-Computer Studies, 42,* 531–571.

DeKeyser, V., and Woods, D. (1990). Fixation errors: Failures to revise situational assessment in dynamic and risky systems. In A. Colombo and A. Bustamante (eds.), *Systems reliability assessment* (pp. 231–251). Dordrecht, Holland: Kluwer Academic.

Descotte, Y., and Latombe, J. (1981). GARI: A problem solver that plans how to machine mechanical parts. *Proceedings of IJCAI-81,* pp. 766–772.

Duchon, D., Dunegan, K.J., and Barton, S.L. (1989). *IEEE Transactions on Engineering Management, 36*(1), 25–27.

Eberts, R.E., Nof, S.Y., Zimolong, B., and Salvendy, G. (1984). Dynamic process control: Cognitive requirements and expert systems. In G. Salvendy (ed.), *Human-computer interaction* (pp. 215–228). Amsterdam: Elsevier Science Publishers.

Edlund, C., and Lewis, M. (1994). Comparing ecologically constrained and conventional displays in control of a simple steam plant. *Proceedings of the Human Factors and Ergonomics Society 38th Annual Meeting* (pp. 486–490). Santa Monica, CA: Human Factors and Ergonomics Society.

Edwards, W. (1954). The theory of decision making. *Psychological Bulletin, 51,* 380–417.

Edwards, W. (1961). Behavioral decision theory. *Annual Review of Psychology, 12,* 473–498.

Edwards, W. (1987). Decision making. In G. Salvendy (ed.), *Handbook of human factors* (pp. 1061–1104). New York: Wiley.

Einhorn, H.J., and Hogarth, R.M. (1978). Confidence in judgment: Persistence of the illusion of validity. *Psychological Review, 85,* 395–416.

Elstein, A.S., Schulman, L.S., and Sprafka, S.A. (1978). *Medical problem solving: An analysis of clinical reasoning.* Cambridge, MA: Harvard University Press.

Endsley, M. (1988). Design and evaluation for situation awareness enhancement. In *Proceedings of the Human Factors Society 32nd Annual Meeting* (pp. 97–101). Santa Monica, CA: Human Factors Society.

Endsley, M. (1995). Toward a theory of situation awareness in dynamic systems. *Human Factors, 37*(1), 32–64.

Endsley, M. (1997). The role of situation awareness in naturalistic decision making. In C.E. Zsambok and G. Klein (eds.), *Naturalistic decision making* (pp. 269–283). Mahwah, NJ: Erlbaum.

Fischhoff, B. (1988). Judgment and decision making. In R.J. Sternberg and E.E. Smith (eds.), *The psychology of human thought* (pp. 153–187). Cambridge, NY: Cambridge University Press.

Fitts, P.M. (1964). Perceptual-motor learning skill. In A.W. Melton, (ed.), *Categories of human learning* (pp. 243–285). New York: Academic Press.

Flin, R., Slaven, G., and Stewart, K. (1996). Emergency decision making in the offshore oil and gas industry. *Human Factors, 38*(2), 262–277.

Fontenelle, G.A. (1983). *The effect of task characteristics on the availability heuristic for judgments of uncertainty* (Report No. 83-1). Office of Naval Research, Rice University.

Frederiksen, N. (1984). Implications of cognitive theory for instruction in problem solving. *Review of Educational Research, 54*(3), 363–407.

Gaba, D.M., Howard, S.K., and Small, S.D. (1995). Situation awareness in anesthesiology. *Human Factors, 37*(1), 20–31.

Garg-Janardan, C., Eberts, R.E., Zimolong, B., Nof, S.Y., and Salvendy, G. (1987). Expert systems. In G. Salvendy (ed.), *Handbook of human factors* (pp. 1130–1176). New York: Wiley.

Garland, D.J., Endsley, M.R., Andre, A.D., Hancock, P.A., Selcon, S.J., and Vidulich, M.A. (1996). Assessment and measurement of situation awareness. *Proceedings of the Human Factors and Ergonomics Society 40th Annual Meeting* (pp. 1170–1173). Santa Monica, CA: Human Factors and Ergonomics Society.

Glaser, R. (1984). Education and knowledge: The role of thinking. *American Psychologist, 39,* 93–104.

Goodstein, L.P., Andersen, H.B., and Olsen, S.E. (eds.) (1988). *Tasks, errors, and mental models.* London: Taylor & Francis.

Gordon, S.E. (1988). Focusing on the human factor in future expert systems. In M.C. Majumdar, D. Majumdar, and J. Sackett (eds.), *Artificial intelligence and other innovative computer applications in the nuclear industry* (pp. 345–352). New York: Plenum Press.

Gordon, S.E. (1991). Front-end analysis for expert system design. *Proceedings of the Human Factors Society 35th Annual Meeting* (pp. 278–282). Santa Monica, CA: Human Factors Society.

Gordon, S. E. (1992). Implications of cognitive theory for knowledge acquisition. In R. Hoffman (Ed.), *The Psychology of Expertise: Cognitive Research and Empirical AI* (pp. 99–120). New York: Springer-Verlag.

Gordon, S.E. (1994). *Systematic training program design: Maximizing effectiveness and minimizing liability.* Englewood Cliffs, NJ: Prentice Hall.

Gordon, S.E. (1997). *An Information-Processing Model of Naturalistic Decision Making.* Presentation at Annual Meeting of the Idaho Psychological Association, Sun Valley, Idaho.

Gordon, S.E., and Gill, R.T. (1989). *The formation and use of conceptual structures in problem-solving domains.* Technical Report for the Air Force Office of Scientific Research, grant #AFOSR-88-0063.

Grabinger, R., Jonassen, D., and Wilson, B.G. (1992). The use of expert systems. In H.D. Stolovitch and E.J. Keeps (eds.), *Handbook of human performance technology* (pp. 365–380). San Francisco, CA: Jossey-Bass.

Greeno, J.G. (1973). The structure of memory and the process of solving problems. In R. Solso (ed.), *Contemporary issues in cognitive psychology: The Loyola Symposium.* Washington, DC: Winston.

Guerlain, S., and Bullemer, P. (1996). User-initiated notification: A concept for aiding the monitoring activities of process control operators. *Proceedings of the Human Factors and Ergonomics Society 40th Annual Meeting* (pp. 283–287). Santa Monica, CA: Human Factors and Ergonomics Society.

Gugerty, L.J., and Tirre, W.C. (1996). Situation awareness: A validation study and investigation of individual differences. *Proceedings of the Human Factors and Ergonomics Society 40th Annual Meeting* (pp. 564–568). Santa Monica, CA: Human Factors and Ergonomics Society.

Hamm, R.M. (1988a). Clinical intuition and clinical analysis: Expertise and the cognitive continuum. In J. Dowie and A. Elstein (eds.), *Professional judgment: A reader in clinical decision making* (pp. 78–105). Cambridge, UK: Cambridge University Press.

Hamm, R.M. (1988b). Moment-by-moment variation in experts' analytic and intuitive cognitive activity. *IEEE Transactions on Systems, Man, and Cybernetics, 18*(5), 757–776.

Hammond, K.R. (1980). Introduction to Brunswikian theory and methods. In K.R. Hammond and N.E. Wascoe (eds.), *Realizations of Brunswik's experimental design.* San Francisco, CA: Jossey-Bass.

Hammond, K.R. (1993). Naturalistic decision making from a Brunswikian viewpoint: Its past, present, future. In G.A. Klein, J. Orasanu, R. Calderwood, and C. Zsambok (eds.), *Decision making in action: Models and methods* (pp. 205–227). Norwood, NJ: Ablex Publishing.

Hammond, K.R., Hamm, R.M., Grassia, J., and Pearson, T. (1987). Direct comparison of the efficacy of intuitive and analytical cognition in expert judgment. *IEEE Transactions on Systems, Man, and Cybernetics, SMC-17*(5), 753–770.

Hendry, C., and Burke, E. (1995, July). *Decision making on the London incident ground.* Presented at the Fourth European Congress of Psychology, Athens, Greece.

Janis, I.L. (1982). Decision making under stress. In L. Goldberger and S. Breznitz (eds.), *Handbook of stress: Theoretical and clinical aspects* (pp. 69–87). New York: Free Press.

Johnson, E.M., Cavanagh, R.C., Spooner, R.L., and Samet, M.G. (1973). Utilization of reliability measurements in Bayesian inference: Models and human performance. *IEEE Transactions on Reliability, 22,* 176–183.

Kaempf, G.L., Wolf, S., Thordsen, M.L., and Klein, G. (1992). *Decision making in the AEGIS combat information center.* Fairborn, OH: Klein Associates. (Prepared under contract N66001-90-C-6023 for the Naval Command, Control and Ocean Surveillance Center, San Diego, CA.)

Kahneman, D., Slovic, P., and Tversky, A. (eds.) (1982). *Judgment under uncertainty: Heuristics and biases.* New York: Cambridge University Press.

Kirlik, A., Walker, N., Fisk, A.D., and Nagel, K. (1996). Supporting perception in the service of dynamic decision making. *Human Factors, 38*(2), 288–299.

Klein, G. (1989). Recognition-primed decisions. *Advances in Man-Machine Systems Research, 5,* 47–92.

Klein, G. (1993). A recognition-primed decision (RPD) model of rapid decision making. In G. Klein, J. Orasanu, R. Calderwood, and C.E. Zsambok (eds.), *Decision making in action: Models and methods* (pp. 138–147). Norwood, NJ: Ablex.

Klein, G. (1997). The recognition-primed decision (RPD) model: Looking back, looking forward. In C.E. Zsambok and G. Klein (eds.), *Naturalistic decision making* (pp. 285–292). Mahwah, NJ: Erlbaum.

Klein, G., and Calderwood, R. (1991). Decision models: Some lessons from the field. *IEEE Transactions on Systems, Man and Cybernetics, 21,* 1018–1026.

Klein, G., Calderwood, R., and Clinton-Cirocco, A. (1986). Rapid decision making on the fire ground. *Proceedings of the Human Factors Society 30th Annual Meeting, 1,* 576–580.

Klein, G., and Crandall, B.W. (1995). The role of mental simulation in problem solving and decision making. In P. Hancock, J. Flach, J. Caird, and K. Vicente (eds.), *Local applications of the ecological approach to human-machine systems* (Vol. 2, pp. 324–358). Hillsdale, NJ: Erlbaum.

Klein, G., Orasanu, J., Calderwood, R., and Zsambok, C.E. (eds.) (1993). *Decision making in action: Models and methods.* Norwood, NJ: Ablex.

Kleinmuntz, B. (1990). Why we still use our heads instead of formulas: Toward an integrative approach. *Psychological Bulletin, 107*(3), 296–310.

Kolodner, J.L. (1993). *Case-based reasoning.* San Mateo, CA: Morgan Kaufmann.

Larkin, J., McDermott, J., Simon, D.P., and Simon, H.A. (1980). Expert and novice performance in problem solving physics problems, *Science, 209,* 1335–1342.

Lehner, P., and Zirk, D.A. (1987). Cognitive factors in user/expert-system interaction. *Human Factors, 29*(1), 97–109.

Lembersky, M., and Chi, U. (1984). Decision simulators speed implementation and improve operations. *Interfaces, 14*(4), 1–15.

Lipshitz, R. (1993). Converging themes in the study of decision making in realistic settings. In G. Klein, J. Orasanu, R. Calderwood, and C.E. Zsambok (eds.), *Decision making in action: Models and methods* (pp. 103–137). Norwood, NJ: Ablex.

Lipshitz, R., and Ben Shaul, O. (1997). Schemata and mental models in recognition-primed decision making. In C.E. Zsambok and G. Klein (eds.), *Naturalistic decision making* (pp. 293–303). Mahwah, NJ: Erlbaum.

Lusted, L.B. (1976). Clinical decision making. In D. Dombal and J. Grevy (eds.), *Decision making and medical care.* Amsterdam: North Holland.

McDaniel, W.C., and Rankin, W.C. (1991). Determining flight task proficiency of students: A mathematical decision aid. *Human Factors, 33*(3) 293–308.

McNeil, B.J., Pauker, S.G., Cox, H.C., Jr., and Tversky, A. (1982). On the elicitation of preferences for alternative therapies. *New England Journal of Medicine, 306,* 1259–1262.

Means, B., Salas, E., Crandall, B., and Jacobs, T.O. (1993). Training decision makers for the real world. In G. Klein, J. Orasanu, R. Calderwood, and C.E. Zsambok (eds.), *Decision making in action: Models and methods* (pp. 306–326). Norwood, NJ: Ablex.

Medin, D.L., and Ross, B.H. (1992). *Cognitive psychology.* Orlando, FL: Harcourt Brace Jovanovich.

Mehle, T. (1982). Hypothesis generation in an automobile malfunction inference task. *Acta Psychologica, 52,* 87–116.

Miller, T.E., and Woods, D.D. (1997). Key issues for naturalistic decision making researchers in system design. In C.E. Zsambok and G. Klein (eds.), *Naturalistic decision making* (pp. 141–150). Mahwah, NJ: Erlbaum.

Mitchell, C.M., Morris, J.G., Ockerman, J.J., and Potter, W.J. (1997). Recognition-primed decision making as a technique to support reuse in software design. In C.E. Zsambok and G. Klein (eds.), *Naturalistic decision making* (pp. 305–318). Mahwah, NJ: Erlbaum.

Moore, P., and Corbridge, C. (1996). Designing mimic diagrams: Moving from art to science. *Proceedings of the Human Factors and Ergonomics Society 40th Annual Meeting* (pp. 328–332). Santa Monica, CA: Human Factors and Ergonomics Society.

Morrison, J.G., Kelly, R.T., and Hutchins, S.G. (1996). Impact of naturalistic decision support on tactical situation awareness. *Proceedings of the Human Factors and Ergonomics Society 40th Annual Meeting* (pp. 199–203). Santa Monica, CA: Human Factors and Ergonomics Society.

Mynatt, C.R., Doherty, M.E., and Tweney, R.D. (1977). Confirmation bias in a simulated research environment: An experimental study of scientific inference. *Quarterly Journal of Experimental Psychology, 29,* 85–95.

Neerincx, M.A., and Griffioen, E. (1996). Cognitive task analysis: harmonizing tasks to human capacities. *Ergonomics, 39*(4), 543–561.

Noble, D. (1993). A model to support development of situation assessment aids. In G. Klein, J. Orasanu, R. Calderwood, and C.E. Zsambok (eds.), *Decision making in action: Models and methods* (pp. 287–305). Norwood, NJ: Ablex.

Orasanu, J. (1993). Decision-making in the cockpit. In E.L. Weiner, B.G. Kanki, and R.L. Helmreich (eds.), *Cockpit resource management* (pp. 137–168). San Diego, CA: Academic Press.

Orasanu, J. (1995). Training for aviation decision making: The naturalistic decision making perspective. *Proceedings of the Human Factors and Ergonomics Society*

39th Annual Meeting (pp. 1258–1262). Santa Monica, CA: Human Factors and Ergonomics Society.

Orasanu, J., and Connolly, T. (1993). The reinvention of decision making. In G. Klein, J. Orasanu, R. Calderwood, and C.E. Zsambok (eds.), *Decision making in action: Models and methods* (pp. 3–20). Norwood, NJ: Ablex.

Orasanu, J., Dismukes, R.K., and Fischer, U. (1993) Decision errors in the cockpit. *Proceedings of the Human Factors and Ergonomics Society 37th Annual Meeting* (pp. 363–367). Santa Monica, CA: Human Factors and Ergonomics Society.

Orasanu, J., and Fischer, U. (1997). Finding decisions in natural environments: The view from the cockpit. In C.E. Zsambok and G. Klein (eds.), *Naturalistic decision making* (pp. 343–357). Mahwah, NJ: Erlbaum.

Passaro, P.D., Cole, H.P., and Wala, A.M. (1994). Flow distribution changes in complex circuits: Implications for mine explosions. *Human Factors, 36*(4), 745–756.

Payne, J.W. (1982). Contingent decision behavior. *Psychological Bulletin, 92*, 382–402.

Payne, J.W., Bettman, J.R., and Johnson, E.J. (1988). Adaptive strategy selection in decision making. *Journal of Experimental Psychology: Learning, Memory, and Cognition, 14*, 534–552.

Pennington, N., and Hastie, R. (1988). Explanation-based decision making: Effects of memory structure on judgment. *Journal of Experimental Psychology: Learning, Memory, and Cognition, 14*(3), 521–533.

Pennington, N., and Hastie, R. (1993). A theory of explanation-based decision making. In G. Klein, J. Orasanu, R. Calderwood, and C.E. Zsambok (eds.), *Decision making in action: Models and methods* (pp. 188–201). Norwood, NJ: Ablex.

Perkins, D., and Martin, F. (1986). Fragile knowledge and neglected strategies in novice programmers. In E. Soloway and S. Iyengar (eds.), *Empirical studies of programmers.* Norwood, NJ: Ablex.

Pierce, P.F. (1996). When the patient chooses: Describing unaided decisions in health care. *Human Factors, 38*(2), 278–287.

Pitz, G.F., and Sachs, N.J. (1984). Judgment and decision: Theory and application. *Annual Review of Psychology, 35*, 139–163.

Rasmussen, J. (1981). Models of mental strategies in process plant diagnosis. In J. Rasmussen and W.B. Rouse (eds.), *Human detection and diagnosis of system failures.* New York: Plenum Press.

Rasmussen, J. (1983). Skills, rules, knowledge: Signals, signs, and symbols and other distinctions in human performance models. *IEEE Transactions on Systems, Man, and Cybernetics, 13*(3), 257–267.

Rasmussen, J. (1986). *Information processing and human-machine interaction: An approach to cognitive engineering.* New York: Elsevier.

Rasmussen, J. (1993). Deciding and doing: Decision making in natural contexts. In G. Klein, J. Orasanu, R. Calderwood, and C.E. Zsambok (eds.), *Decision making in action: Models and methods* (pp. 158–171). Norwood, NJ: Ablex.

Reason, J. (1988). Framework models of human performance and error: A consumer guide. In L. P. Goodstein, H.B. Andersen, and S.E. Olsen (eds.), *Tasks, errors, and mental models* (pp. 35–49). London: Taylor & Francis.

Reason, J. (1990). *Human error.* New York: Cambridge University Press.

Reising, D.V., and Sanderson, P.M. (1996). Work domain analysis of a pasteurization plant: Using abstraction hierarchies to analyze sensor needs. *Proceedings of the Human Factors and Ergonomics Society 40th Annual Meeting* (pp. 293–297). Santa Monica, CA: Human Factors and Ergonomics Society.

Roth, E.M. (1994). Operator performance in cognitive complex simulated emergencies: Implications for computer-based support systems. *Proceedings of the Human Factors and Ergonomics Society 38th Annual Meeting* (pp. 200–204). Santa Monica, CA: Human Factors and Ergonomics Society.

Roth, E.M. (1997). Analysis of decision making in nuclear power plant emergencies: An investigation of aided decision making. In C.E. Zsambok and G. Klein (eds.), *Naturalistic decision making* (pp. 175–182). Mahwah, NJ: Erlbaum.

Roth, E., Bennett, K., and Woods, D.D. (1987). Human interaction with an "intelligent" machine. *International Journal of Man-Machine Studies, 27,* 479–525.

Rouse, W.B. (1981). Experimental studies and mathematical models of human problem solving performance in fault diagnosis tasks. In J. Rasmussen and W. Rouse (eds.), *Human detection and diagnosis of system failures.* New York: Plenum Press.

Rouse, S.H., Rouse, W.B., and Hammer, J.M. (1982). Design and evaluation of an on-board computer-based information system for aircraft. *IEEE Transactions on Systems, Man, and Cybernetics, 12,* 451–463.

Rouse W.B. and Valusek, J. (1993). Evolutionary design of systems to support decision making. In G. Klein, J. Orasanu, R. Calderwood, and C.E. Zsambok (eds.), *Decision making in action: Models and methods* (pp. 270–286). Norwood, NJ: Ablex.

Schneider, W. (1985). Training high-performance skills: Fallacies and guidelines. *Human Factors, 27,* 285–300.

Schraagen, J.M. (1997). Discovering requirements for a naval damage control decision support system. In C.E. Zsambok and G. Klein (eds), *Naturalistic decision making* (pp. 269–283). Mahwah, NJ: Erlbaum.

Schum, D. (1975). The weighing of testimony of judicial proceedings from sources having reduced credibility. *Human Factors, 17,* 172–203.

Schustack, M.W., and Sternberg, R.J. (1981). Evaluation of evidence in causal inference. *Journal of Experimental Psychology: General, 110,* 101–120.

Sheridan, T. (1981). Understanding human error and aiding human diagnostic behavior in nuclear power plants. In J. Rasmussen and W. Rouse (eds.), *Human detection and diagnosis of system failures.* New York: Plenum Press.

Shortliffe, E.H. (1976). *Computer-based medical consultations: MYCIN.* New York: Elsevier.

Simon, H.A. (1957). *Models of man.* New York: Wiley.

Simon, H.A. (1987). Decision making and problem solving. *Interfaces, 17,* 11–31.

Slovic, P., Fischhoff, B., and Lichtenstein, S. (1977). Behavioral decision theory. *Annual Review of Psychology, 28,* 1–39.

Smith, P.J., McCoy, E., and Layton, C. (1993). Design-induced error in flight planning. *Proceedings of the Human Factors and Ergonomics Society 37th Annual Meeting* (pp. 1091–1095). Santa Monica, CA: Human Factors and Ergonomics Society.

Taggart, W. (1986). An information processing model of the managerial mind: Some MIS implications. *Proceedings of the Symposium on Human Factors in Management Information Systems.* College Station, TX: Texas A&M University.

Tolcott, M.A., Marvin, F.F., and Bresnick, T.A. (1989). *The confirmation bias in military situation assessment.* Reston, VA: Decision Science Consortium.

Toms, M., and Patrick, J. (1989). Components of fault-finding: Symptom interpretation. *Human Factors, 31*(4), 465–483.

Tversky, A., and Kahneman, D. (1974). Judgment under uncertainty: Heuristics and biases. *Science, 185,* 1124–1131.

Tversky, A., and Kahneman, D. (1981). The framing of decisions and the psychology of choice, *Science, 211,* 453–458.

Waag, W.L., and Bell, H.H. (1997). Situation assessment and decision making in skilled fighter pilots. In C.E. Zsambok and G. Klein (eds.), *Naturalistic decision making* (pp. 247–254). Mahwah, NJ: Erlbaum.

Weiner, A.J., Thurman, D.A., and Mitchell, C.M. (1996). FIXIT: An architecture to support recognition-primed decision making in complex system fault management activities. *Proceedings of the Human Factors and Ergonomics Society 40th Annual Meeting* (pp. 209–213). Santa Monica, CA: Human Factors and Ergonomics Society.

White, C.C. (1990). A survey on the integration of decision analysis and expert systems for decision support. *EEE Transactions on Systems, Man, and Cybernetics, 20*(2), 358–364.

Wickens, C.D. (1992). *Engineering psychology and human performance* (2nd ed.). New York: HarperCollins Publishers.

Wisudha, A.D. (1985). Design of decision-aiding system. In G. Wright (ed.), *Behavioral decision making* (pp. 235–256). New York: Plenum.

Woods, D.D. (1988). Coping with complexity: The psychology of human behavior in complex systems. In L.P. Goodstein, H.B. Andersen, and S.E. Olsen (eds.), *Tasks, errors, and mental models* (pp. 128–148). Bristol, PA: Taylor & Francis.

Woods, D.D., and Roth, E.M. (1988a). Cognitive engineering: Human problem solving with tools. *Human Factors, 30*(4), 415–430.

Woods, D.D., and Roth, E.M. (1988b). Cognitive systems engineering. In M. Helander (ed.), *Handbook of human-computer interaction* (pp. 3–43). New York: North Holland.

Woods, D.D., O'Brien, J.F., and Hanes, L.F., (1987). Human factors challenges in process control: The case of nuclear power plants. In G. Salvendy (ed.), *Handbook of human factors* (pp. 1724–1770). New York: Wiley.

Wright, P. (1974). The harassed decision maker: Time pressures, distractions, and the use of evidence. *Journal of Applied Psychology, 59,* 555–561.

Xiao, Y., Mackenzie, C.F., and the LOTAS Group (1995). Decision making in dynamic environments: Fixation errors and their causes. *Proceedings of the Human Factors and Ergonomics Society 39th Annual Meeting* (pp. 469–473). Santa Monica, CA: Human Factors and Ergonomics Society.

Xiao, Y., Milgram, P., and Doyle, D. J. (1997). Capturing and modeling planning expertise in anesthesiology: Results of a field study. In C.E. Zsambok and G. Klein (eds.), *Naturalistic decision making* (pp. 197–205). Mahwah, NJ: Erlbaum.

Yoon, W.C., and Hammer, J.M. (1988). Deep-reasoning fault diagnosis: An aid and a model. *IEEE Transactions on Systems, Man, and Cybernetics, 18*(4), 659–675.

Zachary, W.W. (1988). Decision support systems: Designing to extend the cognitive limits. In M. Helander (ed.), *Handbook of human-computer interaction* (pp. 997–1030). Amsterdam: North Holland.

Zakay, D., and Wooler, S. (1984). Time pressure, training, and decision effectiveness. *Ergonomics, 27,* 273–284.

Zsambok, C.E. (1997). Naturalistic decision making: Where are we now? In C.E. Zsambok and G. Klein (eds.), *Naturalistic decision making* (pp. 3–16). Mahwah, NJ: Erlbaum.

Zsambok, C.E., and Klein, G. (1997). *Naturalistic decision making.* Mahwah, NJ: Erlbaum.

CHAPTER 8

Displays

The operator of an energy-generating plant is *peacefully monitoring its operation when suddenly an alarm sounds to indicate that a failure has occurred. Looking up at the top panel of display warning indicators, he sees a flashing of several of the warning "tiles," some in red, some in amber. Making little sense out of this "Christmas Tree" pattern, he looks below at the jumbled array of steam gauges and strip charts that present the continuously changing plant variables. Some of the indicators appear to be out of range, but they present no coherent pattern, and it is not easy to see which ones are associated with the warning tiles, arrayed in the separate display region above. He then turns to the operating manual, which contains a well-laid-out flow diagram of the plant on the early pages. However, he must search through to a page at the back to find information on the emergency warning indicators and locate still a different page describing the procedures to take. Trying to scan rapidly between these five disconnected sources of information in an effort to attain a coherent understanding of what is happening within the plant, he finally despairs and shuts down the plant entirely, causing a large loss in profit for the company.*

Our unfortunate operator could easily sense the changes in display indicators and read the individual text and diagrams in the manual. He could perceive individual elements. But his ability to perceive the overall meaning of the information was hindered by the poor integration of the displays.

In Chapters 4 and 5 we described how the various sensory systems (primarily the eyes and ears) process the raw sensory information and use this information as the bottom-up basis of *perception,* that is, an interpretation of the *meaning* of that information, with the assistance of expectancies and knowledge driving top-down processing. In Chapters 6 and 7 we described the manner in which perceived information was processed further and was stored temporarily in working memory, or more permanently in long-term memory, and used for diagnosis and decision making. The present chapter now focuses on *displays,* which are typically human-made artifacts designed to support the perception of relevant system variables and facilitate the further processing of that information (Fig. 8.1). The speedometer on the car; the warning tone in the aircraft, the message on the phone-based menu system, the instruction panel on the automatic teller, the steam gauge in the industrial plant, or the fine print on the application form are all examples of displays, in various modalities, conveying various forms of information used in various tasks. In this chapter we will first describe 13 key human factors principles in the design of displays. Then the bulk of the chapter will focus on describing different categories of tasks for which displays are intended, illustrating as we go various application of the 13 principles.

WAYS OF CLASSIFYING DISPLAYS

It is possible to classify displays along at least three different dimensions. First, there are differences in the *physical implementation* of the display device. One may think of these as the *physical tools* that the designer has to work with in creating a display. For example, a display may use color or monochrome; it may use the visual or auditory modality; a 3-D display may use stereo, and so on. Several of these tools are listed in Table 8.1.

All of these tools will be mentioned at various points in the chapter. However, before fabricating a display the designer must first ascertain the nature of the *task* that display is intended to support: Is it navigating, controlling, decision making, learning, and so forth? Our chapter will, in fact, be organized around displays to support these various tasks, as we see how different display tools may be optimally

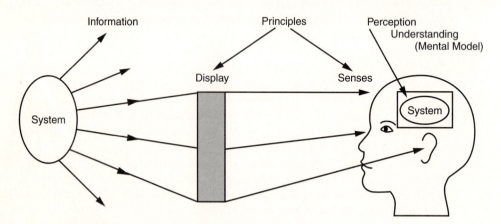

FIGURE 8.1

The figure illustrates key components in display design. A system generates information, some of which must be processed by the operator to perform a task. That necessary information (but *only* that information) is presented on a display and formatted according to principles in such a way that it will support perception and understanding. Often this understanding is facilitated by an accurate mental model of the displayed process.

TABLE 8.1 Physical Tools and Variables That the Display Designer May Manipulate

- Location
    - in XY space
    - superimposed (the head-up display)
- Color (color versus monochrome)
- Dimensionality
    - planar versus perspective
    - mono versus stereo
- Motion
    - what moves
    - how it moves
- Intensity: what is bright, what is dim
- Coding
    - what physical dimensions (i.e., color, size, shape) are assigned to variables
    - analog versus digital coding
    - analog and pictures versus text
- Modality: vision versus audition
- What to display: information analysis

suited for different tasks. However, we note here that defining the task is only a first step. Once the task and its goals are identified (e.g., designing a map to help a driver navigate from point A to point B), one must carry out a detailed *information analysis* that will identify what the operator needs to know to carry out the task. Where such knowledge does not already exist "in the head of the user" in the form of skill, it is a likely candidate for the display.

Finally, and most important, the reason no single display tool is best suited for all tasks is because of characteristics of the human user who must perform those tasks. For example, a digital display may be appropriate if the task requires precise reading of the exact value of an indicator, but because of the way our visual system works, the same display is not good for assessing at a quick glance the approximate rate of change and value of the indicator. As Figure 8.1 shows, the key mediating factor that determines the best mapping between the physical form of the display and the task requirements is a series of *principles* of human perception and information processing. These principles are grounded in the strengths and weaknesses of human perception and performance (Wickens, 1992; Boff, Kaufman, & Thomas, 1986), and it is through the careful application of these principles to the output of the information analysis that the best displays will emerge. We turn now to an overview of the principles.

THIRTEEN PRINCIPLES OF DISPLAY DESIGN

One of the basic tenants of human factors is that lists of longer than five or six items are not easily retained, unless they are provided with some organizational structure. To help retention of the otherwise daunting list of 13 principles of display design presented below, we may then associate them into four distinct categories: (1) those that directly reflect *perceptual* operations, (2) those that can be traced to the concept of the *mental model*, (3) those that relate to *human attention*, and (4) those that relate to *human memory*. Some of these principles have been presented in previous chapters, (4, 5 and 6) and others will be discussed more fully later in this chapter.

Perceptual Principles

These are illustrated in Figure 8.2.

    1. Avoid *absolute judgment limits.* As we noted in Chapter 4 and again in Chapter 5 when discussing alarm sounds, do not require the operator to judge the level of a represented variable on the basis of a single sensory variable like color, size, or loudness, which contains more than five to seven possible levels. To require greater precision as in a color-coded map with nine hues will be to invite errors of judgment.

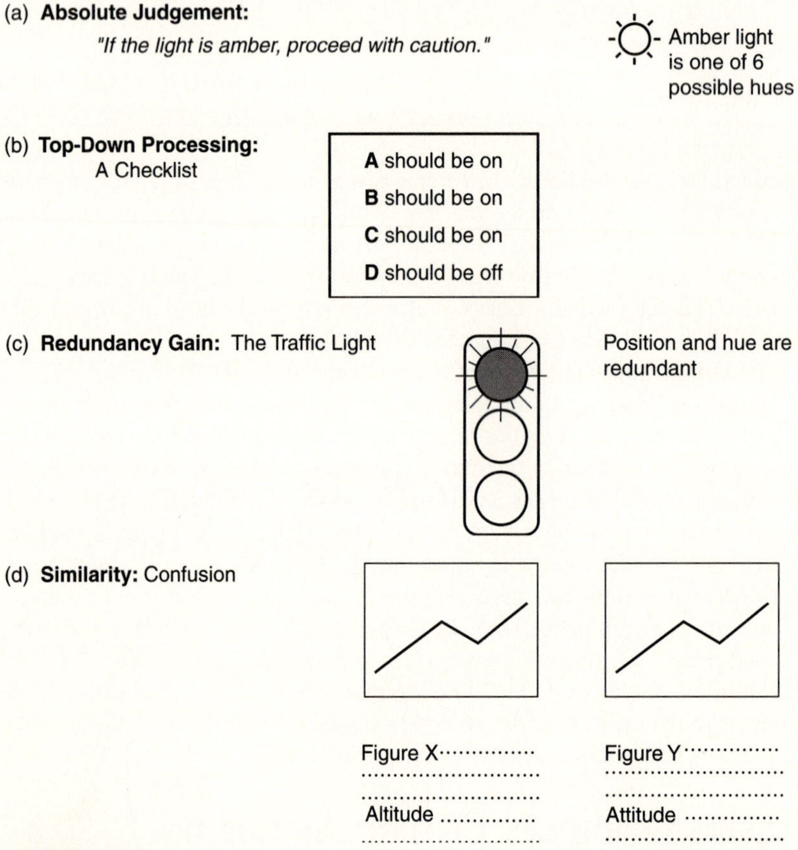

(a) **Absolute Judgement:**
    "If the light is amber, proceed with caution."
    Amber light is one of 6 possible hues

(b) **Top-Down Processing:**
    A Checklist
    A should be on
    B should be on
    C should be on
    D should be off

(c) **Redundancy Gain:** The Traffic Light
    Position and hue are redundant

(d) **Similarity:** Confusion
    Figure X ⋯⋯⋯
    Altitude ⋯⋯⋯
    Figure Y ⋯⋯⋯
    Attitude ⋯⋯⋯

FIGURE 8.2

Some examples of four *perceptual* principles of display design, described in the text. (a) Absolute judgment; (b) Top-down processing (a tendency to perceive as "D should be on"); (c) Redundancy gain; and (d) Similarity → confusion.

2. *Top-down processing.* People will perceive and interpret signals in accordance with what they *expect* to perceive on the basis of their past experience. If a signal is presented that is contrary to expectations, like the warning or alarm for an unlikely event, then *more physical evidence* of that signal must be presented to guarantee that it will be interpreted correctly.

3. *Redundancy gain.* When the same message is expressed more than once, it will be more likely to be interpreted correctly. This will be particularly true if the same message is presented in *alternative* physical forms (e.g., tone and voice, voice and print, print and pictures, color and shape); that is, redundancy is not simply the same as repetition. When alternative physical forms are used, there is a greater chance that the factors that might degrade one form (e.g., noise degrading an auditory message) will not degrade the other (e.g. printed text).

4. *Discriminability: Similarity causes confusion.* Similar appearing signals will be likely to be confused, either at the time they are perceived or after some delay if the signals must be retained in working memory before action is taken. What causes two signals to be similar is the *ratio* of similar features to dissimilar ones (Tversky, 1977). Thus, AJB648 is more similar to AJB658 than is 48 similar to 58, even though in both cases only a single digit is different. Where confusion could be serious, the designer should delete unnecessary similar features and highlight *dis*similar (different) ones in order to create distinctiveness. Note, for example, the high degree of confusability of the two captions in Figure 8.2d. In Figure 4.11 we illustrated another examples of the danger of similarity and confusion in visual information.

Mental Model Principles

When operators perceive a display, they often interpret what the display looks like and how it moves in terms of their expectations or *mental model* of the system being displayed, a concept that was discussed in Chapter 6 (Norman, 1988; Johnson-Laird, 1983; Gentner & Stevens, 1983). The information presented to our system monitor in the opening story was not consistent with the mental model of the operator. Hence, it is appropriate for the format of the display to capture aspects of that mental model, based on user's experience of the system whose information is being displayed. Principles 5, 6, and 7 illustrate how this can be achieved.

5. *Principle of pictorial realism* (Roscoe, 1968). A display should *look like* (i.e., be a picture of) the variable that it represents. Thus if we think of temperature as having a high and low value, a thermometer should be oriented vertically. If the display contains multiple elements, then these elements can be *configured* in a manner that looks like how they are configured in the environment that is represented (or how the operator conceptualizes that environment). In this instance we can define a variant of the principle of pictorial realism as the *principle of configural displays* (Sanderson et al., 1989).

6. *Principle of the moving part* (Roscoe, 1968). The moving element(s) of any display of dynamic information should move in a spatial pattern and direction that is compatible with the user's mental model of how the represented element moves. Thus, if a pilot thinks that the aircraft moves upward when altitude is gained, the moving element on an altimeter should also move upward with increasing altitude.

7. *Ecological interface design.* Collectively, adherence to the principle of pictorial realism and the principle of the moving part can create displays that have a close correspondence with the environment that is being displayed. Because of this adherence to the *ecology* of the displayed world, these types of displays have been recently referred to as *Ecological Interfaces* (Vicente & Rasmussen, 1992; Bennett, Toms, & Woods, 1993; Rasmussen, Pejtersen, & Goodstein, 1995).

Principles Based on Attention

Complex multielement displays require three components of attention to process (Parasuraman, Davies, & Beatty, 1984). *Selective attention* may be necessary to choose the displayed information sources necessary for a given task. *Focused attention* allows those sources to be perceived without *distraction* from neighboring sources, and *divided attention* may allow parallel processing of two (or more) sources of information if a task requires it. All four of the attentional principles described below characterize ways of capitalizing on attentional strengths or minimizing their weaknesses.

8. *Minimizing information access cost.* There is typically a cost in time or effort to "move" selective attention from one display location to another to access information. Our display monitor in the opening story wasted valuable time going from one page to the next in the book and visually scanning from there to the instrument panel. The information access cost may also include the time to key through a computer menu structure to find the correct "page." Thus, good designs will be those that can minimize the net cost by keeping frequently accessed sources in such a location that the cost of traveling between them is small. This principle was not supported in the maintenance manual in the episode at the beginning of the chapter. We discuss it again in Chapter 10.

9. *Proximity compatibility principle* (Wickens & Carswell, 1995). Sometimes two or more sources of information are related to the same task and must be *mentally integrated* to complete the task (e.g., a graph line and its legend or the plant layout and the warning indicator meanings in our opening story); that is, divided attention between the two sources for the one task is desirable. These information sources are said to have close "mental proximity." As described in principle 8, good display design should then provide them with close "display proximity" by displaying them close together so that their information access cost will be low (Wickens & Carswell, 1995). However, close display proximity can also be obtained by displaying them in a common color by linking them together with lines, or by "configuring" them in a pattern, as discussed in principles 5 and 7 above (Fig. 8.3a). But, as Figure 8.3b shows, too much close display proximity is not always good, particularly if one of the elements must be the subject of focused attention. In this case of focused attention, close proximity may be harmful, and it is better for the sources to be more separated. The "low mental proximity" of the focused attention task is

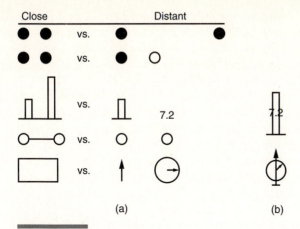

Close   Distant

FIGURE 8.3

The proximity compatibility principle. (a) Five examples of "close" display proximity (on the left) that will be helpful for tasks requiring integration of information in the two sources shown. (b) Two examples of close proximity that will hurt the ability to focus on one indicator and ignore the other.

then best served by the "low display proximity" of separation. Thus, the two types of proximity, display and mental, are "compatibly related."

10. *Principle of multiple resources.* As we noted in Chapter 6, sometimes processing of a lot of information can be facilitated by dividing that information across resources—presenting visual and auditory information concurrently, for example—rather than presenting all information visually or all auditorily.

Memory Principles

As we learned in Chapter 6, human memory is vulnerable. Working memory is vulnerable because of its limited capacity: We can only keep a small number of "mental balls" in the air at one time and so, for example, may easily forget the phone number before we have had a chance to dial it or write it down. Our operator in the opening story had a hard time remembering information on one page of the manual while he was accessing or reading the other. Our long-term memory is vulnerable because we forget certain things or, sometimes, because we remember other things *too well* and persist in doing them when we should not. The final three principles address different aspects of these memory processes.

11. *Principle of predictive aiding.* Humans are not very good at predicting the future. In large part this limitation results because prediction is a difficult cognitive task, depending heavily on working memory. We need to think about current conditions, possible future conditions, and the rules by which the former may generate the latter. When our mental resources are consumed with other tasks, prediction falls apart, and we become *reactive,* responding to what has already happened, rather than *proactive,* responding in anticipation of the future. Since

proactive behavior is usually more effective than reactive, it stands to reason that displays that can explicitly predict what will (or is likely to) happen will generally be quite effective in human performance. A predictive display removes a resource demanding cognitive task, and replaces it with a simpler perceptual one. Figure 8.4 shows some examples of effective predictor displays.

12. *Principle of knowledge in the world.* D. Norman (1988) has written eloquently about two kinds of knowledge that support people's interactions with systems. Knowledge in the head, on the one hand, is what we typically think of when we think of knowledge. It is remembering what needs to be done when, which is a pretty good memory system for routine tasks but not so good for tasks that are complex, recently learned, or poorly explained. *Knowledge in the world,* on the other hand, involves placing explicit visible reminders or statements of what is to be done at the time and place that will trigger the appropriate action. A pilot's checklist is a good example of knowledge in the world (Degani & Wiener, 1990). So too would be a computer menu that, at each step, provides the user with a complete list of all the possible options so that the appropriate action can be easily recognized. Clearly, when knowledge is put in the world, it will not be forgotten, whereas when it must be accessed only in the head, forgetting is possible.

Of course sometimes too much knowledge in the world can lead to clutter problems, and systems designed to rely on knowledge in the head are not necessarily bad. For example in using computer systems, experts might like to be able to retrieve information by direct commands (knowledge in the head) rather than stepping through a menu (knowledge in the world) (see Chapter 15). Good design must balance the two kinds of knowledge.

13. *Principle of consistency.* When our memory works *too* well, it may continue to trigger actions that are no longer appropriate, and this is a pretty instinctive and automatic human tendency. Old habits die hard. Because there is no way of avoiding this, good designs should try to accept it and "go with the flow" by designing displays in a manner that is consistent with other displays that the user may be perceiving concurrently (e.g., a user alternating between two computer systems) or may have perceived in the recent past. Hence, the old habits from those other displays will transfer positively to support processing of the new displays. Thus, color coding should be consistent across a set of displays so that, for example, red always means the same thing. As another example, a set of different display panels should be consistently organized, thus, through learning, reducing information access cost each time a new set is encountered.

Conclusion

In concluding our discussion of principles, it should be immediately apparent that principles sometimes conflict or "collide." Making all displays consistent, for example, may sometimes cause certain displays to be less compatible than others, just as making all displays optimally compatible may make them inconsistent. Correspondingly, putting too much knowledge in the world or incorporating too much redundancy can create very cluttered displays, thereby making focused attention more difficult. Alas, there is no easy solution to say what principles are

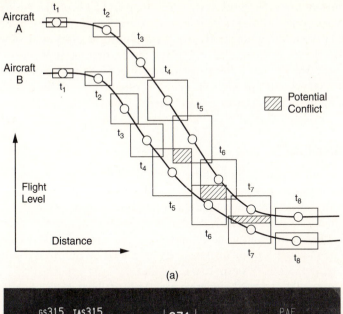

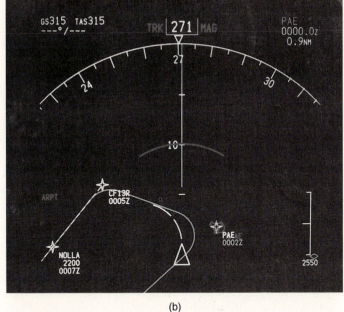

FIGURE 8.4

Some effective predictive displays. (a) A proposed air traffic control predictive conflict display that shows where two aircraft will come in potential conflict if each continues its present descent profile. (*Source:* Whitfield, D.A., Ball, R.G., and Ord, G., 1980. Some human factor aspects of computer-aided contents for air traffic controllers. *Human Factors,* 22, pp. 569–580. ©[British] Crown Copyright, 1997/Defence Evaluation and Research Agency. Reproduced with the permission of the Controller, Her [Britannic] Majesty's Stationery Office.); (b) an aircraft flight predictor, shown by the curved, dashed line extending from the triangular symbol at the bottom. (*Source:* Courtesy of the Boeing Corporation.)

more important than others when two or more principles collide. But clever and creative design can sometimes enable certain principles to be more effectively served, without violating others. We will see this in some cases as we now turn to a discussion of various categories of displays, illustrating, as we go, the manner in which certain principles have been applied to achieve better human factors. As we encounter each principle in application in the following pages, we will place a reminder of the principle number in parentheses, for example, (P12).

ALERTING DISPLAYS

We discussed alerting displays to some extent already in Chapter 5 in the context of auditory warnings. If it is critical to *alert* the operator to a particular condition, then the "omnidirectional" auditory channel is best. However, there may well be several different levels of seriousness of the condition to be alerted, and not all of these need or should be announced auditorily. For example, if my car passes a mileage level in which a particular service is needed, I do not need the time-critical and intrusive auditory alarm to tell me that.

Conventionally, system designers have classified three levels of alerts: warnings, cautions, and advisories, which can be defined in terms of the severity of consequences of failing to heed their indication. Warnings, the most critical category, should be signaled by salient auditory alerts; cautions may be signaled by auditory alerts that are less salient (e.g., softer voice signals); advisories need not be auditory at all, but can be purely visual. Both warnings and cautions can clearly be augmented by redundant visual signals as well (P3). In order to avoid possible confusion of alerting severity, the aviation community has also established explicit guidelines for *color coding,* such that warning information will always be red; caution information will be yellow or amber; advisory information can be other colors (e.g., white), clearly discriminable from red and amber (P4).

Note that the concept of defining three levels of condition severity is consistent with the guidelines for "likelihood alarms" discussed in Chapter 5 (Sorkin, Kantowitz, & Kantowitz, 1988).

LABELS

Labels may also be thought of as "displays," although they are generally static and unchanging features for the user. Their purpose is to unambiguously signal the identity or function of an entity, such as a control, display, piece of equipment, entry on a form, or other system component; that is, they present "knowledge in the world" (P12) of what something is. Labels are usually presented as print but may sometimes take the form of icons (Fig. 8.5). The four-key design criteria for labels are visibility, discriminability, meaningfulness, and location.

1. *Visibility/legibility.* This criterion relates directly back to issues of contrast sensitivity discussed in Chapter 4. Stroke width of lines (in text or icons) and contrast from background must be sufficient so that the shapes can be discerned

FIGURE 8.5
Some typical icons.

under the poorest expected viewing conditions. This entails some concern for the low spatial frequency shape of icons.

2. *Discriminability* (P4). This criterion dictates that any feature that is necessary to discriminate a given label from an alternative *that may be inferred by the user to exist in that context* is clearly and prominently highlighted. We noted above that confusability increases with the ratio of shared to distinct features between potential labels. So two figure legends that show a large amount of identical (and perhaps redundant) text will be more confusable than two in which this redundancy is deleted (Fig. 8.2). Figure 4.11 in Chapter 4 illustrated some particularly dangerous examples of confusability in medical drug labeling (Bogner, 1994). When these similar appearing names get passed through the filter of a physician's handwriting, the dangerous consequences are clear.

A special "asymmetrical" case of confusion is the tendency to confuse negative labels ("No entry") with positive ones ("Entry"). Unless the negative "No," "Do Not," "Don't," etc. is clearly and saliently displayed, it is very easy for people to miss it and assume the positive version, particularly when viewing the label (or hearing the instructions) under degraded sensory conditions. We illustrated the disastrous consequences of such a misinterpretation when we discussed the pilot's mishearing of the communication to "hold for take off," in the context of the Canary Islands aircraft disaster in Chapter 5. Note finally that even when the negative is initially perceived correctly, if the instruction is not carried out immediately, the negative may be *forgotten* during the delay, and what is remembered will only be the positive version.

3. *Meaningfulness.* Even if a word or icon is legible and unique, this is no guarantee that it "triggers" the appropriate meaning in the mind of the viewer when it is perceived. What, for example, do all the icons in Figure 8.5 mean? Or, for the English viewer of the sign along the German Autobahn, what does the word *anfang* mean? Unfortunately, too often icons, words, or acronyms that are highly meaningful in the mind of the designer, who has certain expectations of the mindset that the user *should* have when the label is encountered, are next to meaningless in the mind of some proportion of the actual users.

Because this unfortunate situation is far more likely to occur with the use of abbreviations and icons than with words, we argue here that labels based *only* on icons or abbreviations should be avoided where possible (Norman, 1981). Icons may well be advantageous where the word labels may be read by those who are not fluent in the language (e.g., international highway symbols) and sometimes under degraded viewing conditions (Long & Kearns, 1996); thus, the *redundancy gain*

(P3) that such icons provide is usually of value. But the use of icons *alone* appears to carry an unnecessary risk when comprehension of the label is important.

4. *Location.* One final obvious but sometimes overlooked feature of labels: They should be physically close to and unambiguously associated with the entity that they label, thereby adhering to the proximity compatibility principle (P9).

More recently, computer designers are applying the concept of icons to sound, in the generation of "earcons," synthetic sounds that have a direct meaningful association with the thing they represent (Blattner, Sumikawn, & Greenberg, 1989). Thus, for example, a "cut" activity in editing text might be expressed by the synthetic sound of scissors.

MONITORING

Displays for monitoring are those that support the viewing of potentially changing quantities, usually represented on some analog or ordered value scale, such as a channel frequency, a speed, temperature, noise level, or changing job status. A variety of tasks may need to be performed on the basis of such displays. A monitored display may need to be *set,* as when an appropriate frequency is "dialed in" to a radio channel. It may simply need to be *watched* until it reaches a value at which some discrete action is taken as characterizing the operator in our story at the beginning of the chapter; or it may need to be *tracked,* in which case another variable must be manipulated to follow the changing value of the monitored variable. (Tracking is discussed in considerably more detail in Chapter 9.) Whatever the action to be taken on the basis of the monitored variable—discrete or continuous, immediate or delayed—there is a series of guidelines that can be used to optimize the monitoring display.

1. *Legibility.* Display legibility is of course the familiar criterion we revisited in the previous section, and it relates back to the issues of contrast sensitivity discussed in Chapter 4. If monitoring displays are digital, the issues of print and character resolution must be addressed. If the displays are analog dials or pointers, then the visual angle and contrast of the pointer become critical, as well as the legibility of the scale against which the pointer moves. A series of guidelines may be found in Sanders and McCormick (1993) and Helander (1997) to assure such legibility. But designers must be aware of the possible degraded viewing conditions (e.g., low illumination) under which such scales may need to be read and must design to accommodate such conditions.

2. *Analog Versus Digital.* Most variables to be monitored are continuously changing quantities. Furthermore, users often form a "picture" or mental model of the changing quantity. Hence, adhering to the principle of pictorial realism (P5, Roscoe, 1968) would suggest the advantage of an analog (rather than digital) representation of the continuously changing quantity, and indeed the data appear to support this guideline (Boff & Lincoln, 1988). In comparison to digital displays (Fig. 8.6a), analog displays like the moving pointer in Figure 8.6b can be more easily read at a glance; the value of an analog display can be more easily estimated *when* the display is changing, and it is easier to estimate the rate and direction of that change. At the same time, digital displays *do* have an advantage if very precise "check reading" or setting of the exact value is required. But unless these are the *only* tasks required of a monitoring display and the value changes slowly, then any digital display should be redundantly provided with its analog counterpart (P3), like the altitude display shown in Figure 8.6c, which we discuss below.

3. *Analog Form and Direction.* If an analog format is chosen for display, then the *principle of pictorial realism* (P5; Roscoe, 1968) would state that the orientation of the display scale should be in a form and direction that is congruent with the operator's mental model of the displayed quantity. Cyclical or circular variables (like compass direction or a 24-hour clock) share an appropriate circular form for a round dial or "steam gauge" display, whereas linear quantities, with clearly defined "high" and "low" points, should ideally be reflected by linear scales. These scales ideally should be vertically arrayed so that "high" is up and "low" is down. This feature is easy to realize when employing the fixed-scale moving pointer displays (Figure 8.6b) or the moving scale fixed-pointer display in Figure 8.6c.

However, many displays are fairly dynamic, showing substantial movement while the operator is watching (or setting) them. The *principle of the moving part* (P6) suggests that displays should move in a direction consistent with the user's mental model: An increase in speed (or any other quantity) should be signaled by a movement *upward* on the moving element of the display (rightward and clockwise are also acceptable, but less powerful movement stereotypes for increase). While the moving pointer display in Figure 8.6b clearly adheres to this stereotype, the moving scale display in Figure 8.6c does not. Upward display movement will signal a decrease in the quantity. The moving scale version in Figure 8.6d with the scale inverted can restore the principle of the moving part, but only at the expense of a violation of the principle of pictorial realism (P5) because the scale is now inverted. We note also that *both* moving scale displays suffer from a difficulty of reading the scale value while the quantity is changing rapidly.

Despite its many advantages, there is one cost with a linear moving pointer display (Figure 8.6b). It cannot present a wide range of scales values within a small range of physical space. If the range of scale over which the variable travels

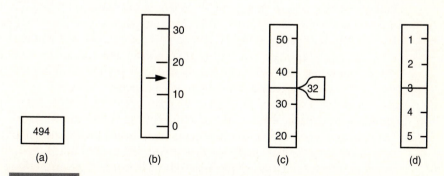

FIGURE 8.6
Digital display; (b) Moving pointer analog display; (c) Moving scale analog display with redundant digital presentation adheres to principle of pictorial realism; (d) Inverted moving scale display adheres to principle of the moving part.

is large and the required reading precision is also high (a pilot's altimeter, for example), this can present a problem. One answer is to revert to the moving scale display, which can present high numbers at the top, if the variable does not change rapidly (i.e., little motion means that the principle of the moving part has less relevance). A second option is to use circular moving pointer displays that are more economical of space. While these options may destroy some adherence to the principle of pictorial realism (if displaying linear quantities), they still possess a reasonable stereotype of increase → clockwise. A third possibility is to employ a "frequency separated" concept of a hybrid scale, in which high-frequency changes drive a moving pointer against a stable scale, while sustained low-frequency changes can gradually shift the scale quantities to the new (and appropriate) range of values as needed (maintaining high numbers at the top).

Clearly, as in any design solution, there is no "magic layout" that will be cost-free for all circumstances. As always, task analysis regarding the rate of change of the variable, its needed level of precision, and its range of possible values should be undertaken before a display format is chosen.

One final factor influencing the choice of display concerns the nature of *control* that may be required to set or to track the displayed variable. Fortunately for designers, many of the same laws of display expectations and mental models apply to control; that is, just as the user expects (P2) that an upward (or clockwise) movement of the display signals an increasing quantity, so the user also expects that an upward (or clockwise) movement of the control will be required to *increase* the displayed quantity. We revisit this issue in more detail in Chapter 9 when we address issues of display-control compatibility.

4. *Prediction and Sluggishness.* Many monitored variables are "sluggish" in that they change relatively slowly. But as a consequence of the dynamic properties of the system that they represent, the slow change means that their future state can be known with some degree of certainty. Such is the case of the supertanker, for example: Where the tanker is now in the channel and how it is moving will quite accurately predict where it will be several minutes into the future. Another characteristic of such systems is that efforts to "control them," executed now, will also not have an influence on their state till much later. Thus, the shift in the supertanker's rudder will not change the ship's course until later; and the adjustment of the heat delivered to a chemical process will not change the process temperature until much later (Chapter 16). Hence, control should be based on the operator's prediction of *future* state, not present conditions. But as we saw, prediction is not something we do very well, particularly under stress; hence, good predictor displays (P11) can be a great aid to human performance (Fig. 8.4).

Predictive displays of physical systems are typically "driven" by a computer model of the dynamics of the system under control and by knowledge of the current inputs (forces) acting on the system. Because, like the crystal ball of the fortune-teller, these displays really are making inferences about the future, they may not always be correct and will be less likely to be correct the further into the future is being predicted. Hence, the designer should be wary of predicting forward further than is reasonable and might consider depicting limits on the degree of certainty of the predicted variable.

MULTIPLE DISPLAYS

Many real-world systems are complex. The typical nuclear reactor may have at least 35 variables that are considered critical for its operation, while the aircraft is assumed to have at least seven that are important for monitoring in even the most routine operations. Hence, an important issue in designing multiple displays is to decide where they go; that is, what should be the *layout* of the multiple displays (Wickens, Vincow, & Schopper, 1997). In the following section we discuss several principles of display layout, and while these are introduced in the context of monitoring displays, the reader should realize that the principles apply to nearly any type of display. We then address issues related to head-up displays and to configural displays.

Display Layout

In many work environments, the designer may be able to define a *primary visual area* (PVA) (see Chapter 10). For the seated user, this may be the region of forward view as the head and eyes look straightforward. For the vehicle operator, it may be the view of the highway (or runway in an aircraft approach). Defining this region (or point in space) of the PVA is critical because the first of six principles of display layout, (1) *frequency of use,* dictates that frequently used displays should be adjacent to the PVA. This makes sense because their frequent access dictates a need to "minimize the travel time" between them and the PVA (P8). Note that sometimes a very frequently used display can itself define the PVA. With the conventional aircraft display suite shown in Figure 8.7, this principle is satisfied by positioning the most frequently used instrument, the attitude directional indicator or ADI, at the top and center, closest to the view out the windshield on which the pilot must fixate to land the aircraft and check for other traffic.

The principle of (2) *display relatedness* or *sequence of use* dictates that "related displays" and those pairs that are often used in sequence should be close together. (Indeed these two criteria are often correlated. Displays are often consulted sequentially *because* they are related—like the desired setting and actual setting of an indicator.) We see this principle as capturing the key feature of the proximity compatibility principle (P9) (Wickens & Carswell, 1995). We saw the manner in which it was violated for the operator in our opening story. As a positive example, in Figure 8.7, the vertical velocity indicator and the altimeter, in close spatial proximity on the right side, are also related to each other since both signal information about the vertical position of the aircraft. As another example, as we saw (and will see again when we discuss graphs), graph labels should be close to the lines that they depict.

The principle of (3) *consistency* is related to both memory and attention. If displays are always consistently laid out with the same item positioned in the same spatial location, then our memory of where things are serves us well and memory can easily and automatically guide selective attention to find the items we need (P8, P13). Thus, for example, the Federal Aviation Administration has provided strong guidelines that, even as new technology can revolutionize the design of flight instruments, the basic form of the four most important instruments in the panel in Figure 8.7—those forming a *T*—should always be preserved (FAA, 1987).

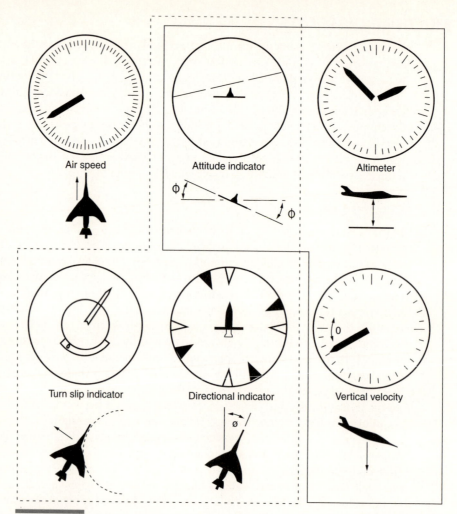

FIGURE 8.7

Conventional aircraft instrument panel. The attitude directional indicator is in the top center. The outlines surround displays that are related in the control of the vertical (solid box) and lateral (dashed box) position of the aircraft. Note that each outline surrounds physically proximate displays.

Unfortunately, there are many instances in which the principle of consistency conflicts with those of frequency-of-use and relatedness. These instances define *phase-related* operations, when the variables that are important (or related and used in sequence) during one phase of operation may be very different from those during another phase. In nuclear power plant monitoring, what is important in start-up and shut-down is different from what is important during routine operations. In flying, the information needed during cruise is quite different from that needed during landing, and in many systems, information needed during emergency is very different from that needed during routine operations. Under such circumstances, totally consistent layouts may be unsatisfactory and current "soft" computer-driven displays allow flexible formats to be created in a phase-dependent layout. However, if such flexibility is imposed, then three key design guidelines must be kept in mind: (1) it should be made very clear to the user by *salient visible* signals which configuration is in effect (P4, P12); (2) where possible some consistency (P13) across all formats should be sought; (3) the designer should resist the temptation to create excessive flexibility (Andre & Wickens, 1992). Remember that as long as a display design *is* consistent, the user's memory will help guide attention to find the needed information rapidly, even if that information may not be in the very best location for a particular phase.

The principle of (4) *organizational grouping* is one that can be used to contrast the display array in Figure 8.8a with that in Figure 8.8b. An organized "clustered" display such as that seen in 8.8a will provide an aid that can easily guide visual attention to particular groups as needed (P8) as long as all displays within a group are functionally related and their relatedness is clearly known and identified to the user. If these guidelines are *not* followed, however, and unrelated items belong to a common spatial cluster, then such organization may actually be counterproductive (P9).

Two final principles of display layout are (5) the principle of *stimulus-response compatibility*, which dictates that displays should be close to their associated controls, and (6) *clutter avoidance*, which dictates that there should ideally be a minimum visual angle between all pairs of displays. We discuss S-R compatibility in Chapter 9 and clutter avoidance in the following sections.

Head-Up Displays

We have already seen that one important display layout guideline involves moving important information sources close to the primary visual area or PVA. The ultimate example of this approach is to actually *superimpose* the displayed information on top of the PVA, creating what is known as the *head-up display* (HUD)

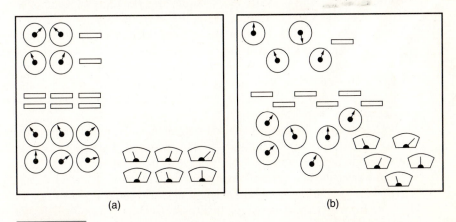

(a)   (b)

FIGURE 8.8

Differences in display organization: (a) high; (b) low. All displays within each physical grouping must be somehow related in order for the display layout on the left to be effective.

(Weintraub & Ensing, 1992; Newman, 1995). These are often proposed (and used) for vehicle control but may have other uses as well when the PVA can be clearly specified. For example, a HUD might be used to superimpose a computer graphics designer's palate information over the design work space (Harrison & Vicente, 1996). Two examples of head-up displays, one for aircraft and one for automobiles, are shown in Figure 8.9.

The proposed advantages of HUDs are threefold. First, assuming that the driver or pilot should spend most of the time with the eyes directed outward, then overlapping the HUD imagery should allow both the "far domain" environment and the "near domain" instrumentation to be monitored in parallel. Second, particularly with aircraft HUDs, it is possible to present imagery that has a direct spatial counterpart in the far domain. Such imagery, like a schematic runway or horizon line that overlays its counterpart is said to be "conformal." By positioning this imagery in the HUD, divided attention between the two domains is supported (P9). Third, many HUDs are projected via *collimated imagery,* which essentially reorients the light rays from the imagery in a parallel fashion, thereby making the imagery to appear to the eyes to be at an accommodative distance of "optical infinity." The advantage of this is that the lens of the eyeball accommodates to more distant viewing than the nearby windshield and so does not have to reaccommodate to shift between focus on instruments and far domain viewing (see Chapter 4).

Against these advantages must be considered one very apparent cost. Moving imagery too close together (i.e., superimposed) violates the sixth principle of display layout: creation of excessive *clutter.* Hence, it is possible that the imagery may be difficult to read against the background of varied texture and that the imagery itself may obscure the view of critical visual events in the far domain (Neisser & Becklen, 1975).

Evaluation of HUDs indeed suggests that the overall benefits tend to outweigh the costs. In aircraft, flight control performance is generally better when critical flight instruments are presented head-up (and particularly so if they are conformal; Wickens & Long, 1995). In driving, the digital speedometer instrument is sampled for a shorter time in the head-up location (Kiefer, 1991), although in both driving or flying, speed control is not substantially better with a head-up display than a head-down display (Kiefer, 1991; Sojourner & Antins, 1990; Wickens & Long, 1995). There is also evidence that relatively expected discrete events are better detected when the display is in the head-up location (Sojourner & Antins, 1990; Weintraub, Haines, & Randle, 1984, 1985; Larish & Wickens, 1991).

Nevertheless, the designer should be aware that there are potential costs from the head-up display of overlapping imagery. In particular, these clutter costs have been observed in the detection of unexpected events in the far domain such as, for example, the detection of an aircraft taxiing out onto the runway toward which the pilot is making an approach (Wickens & Long, 1995; Fischer, Haines, & Price, 1980).

In summary, the data suggest that there may be some real benefits for HUDs, as long as the information presented there is both *critical* and *minimal* and particularly if the information (and its imagery) is *conformal.* Decisions to shift too much nonconformal information to the head-up location will create the danger-

(a)

(b)

FIGURE 8.9

Head-up displays: (a) for automobile (*Source:* Kaptein, N. A. Benefits of In-car Head-up Displays. Report TNO-TM 1994 B-20. Soesterberg, TNO Human Factors Research Institute.); (b) for aircraft. (*Source:* Courtesy of *Flight Dynamics.*)

ous clutter situation that may neutralize any advantages and possibly harm detection of the unexpected event. The reader should consult Weintraub and Ensing (1992) and Newman (1995) for many of the details required to implement HUDs appropriately.

Head-Mounted Displays

A close cousin to the HUD is the head-mounted or helmet-mounted display, in which a display is rigidly mounted to the head so that it can be viewed no matter which way the head and body are oriented (Kocian & Task, 1995). Such a display has the advantage of allowing the user to view superimposed imagery across a much wider range of the far domain than is possible with the HUD. In an aircraft, the head-mounted displays (HMDs) can allow the pilot to retain a view of HMD flight instruments while scanning the full range of the outside world for threatening traffic. The use of a head-orientation sensor with conformal imagery can also present information on the HMD specifying the direction of particular locations in space, for example, the location of traffic, the direction of an airport, or due north. For other mobile operators, the HMD can be used to minimize information access costs. For example, consider a maintenance worker, operating in an awkward environment in which the head and upper torso must be thrust into a tight space to perform a test on some equipment. Such a worker would greatly benefit by being able to consult information on how to carry out the test, displayed on an HMD, rather than needing to pull his head out of the space every time the test manual needs to be consulted.

HMDs can be either monocular (presented to a single eye), biocular (presented as a single image to both eyes), or binocular (presented as a separate image to each eye); furthermore monocular HMDs can be either opaque (allowing only the other eye to view the far domain) or transparent (superimposing the monocular image on the far domain). Each version has its benefits and costs (National Research Council, 1995). We have noted above the issues of clutter in viewing the outside world. The clutter costs may be mitigated somewhat by using a monocular HMD, which gives one eye unrestricted view of the far domain. However, presenting different images to the two eyes can sometimes create problems of *binocular rivalry* or *binocular suppression,* in which the two eyes compete to present their own image to the brain (Arditi, 1986).

To a greater extent than with HUDs, efforts to place conformal imagery on HMDs can be problematic because of potential delays in image updating. When conformal displays are used to depict spatial positions in the outside world, then they must be updated each time the display moves relative to that world. Aircraft and even ground vehicles rotate relatively slowly compared to the speed of body or head rotation. Hence, conformal image updating on the HMD must be fast enough to keep up with potentially rapid head rotation. If it is not, then the image can become disorienting and lead to motion sickness (Durlach & Mavor, 1995); alternatively, it can lead users to adopt an unnatural strategy of reducing their head movements (Seagull & Gopher, 1995).

Configural Displays

Sometimes multiple displays of "raw data" can be arrayed in both space and format so that certain properties that are relevant to the monitoring task will "emerge" from the combination of values on the individual raw variables. Figure 8.10a shows an example, a patient respiration monitoring display developed by Cole (1986). In each rectangle the height indicates the volume or depth of breathing and the width indicates the rate. Therefore, the total area of the rectangle indicates the total *amount* of oxygen respired by the patient (right) and imposed by the respirator (left). This relationship holds because the amount = rate × depth and the rectangle area = height × width. Thus, the display has been *configured* in such a way to produce what is called an *emergent feature* (Pomerantz & Pristach, 1989; Sanderson et al., 1989); that is, a property of the configuration of raw variables (in this case depth and rate) "emerges" on the display to signal a significant task-relevant, integrated variable (the rectangle area or amount of oxygen (P9). Note also in the figure that a second emergent feature may be perceived as the *shape* of the rectangle; the ratio of height to width that signals either shallow rapid breathing or slow deep breathing (i.e., different "styles" of breathing).

Another example, shown in Figure 8.10b, is the safety parameter monitoring display developed by Woods, Wise, and Hanes (1981) for a nuclear power control room. Here the eight critical safety parameters are configured in an octagon such that when all are within their safe range, the easily perceivable emergent feature of *symmetry* will be observed. Furthermore, if a parameter departs from its normal value, as the result of a failure, then the distorted *shape* of the polygon can uniquely signal the nature of the underlying fault, a feature that was sadly lacking for our operator in the story at the beginning of the chapter.

In the case of the two displays in Figure 8.10, configuring the to-be-integrated variables as dimensions of a single object creates a sort of attentional "glue" that fuses them together, thus adhering to the proximity compatibility principle (P9). But configural displays do not have to come from a single object. In Figure 8.11, the four bar graphs, representing perhaps the speed or power of each of four engines, will "configure" to define an imagined straight line across the top to signal the key state that all four are running with equal efficiency. This indeed was a primary reason why certain designers have chosen to configure instruments on four engine aircraft as bar graphs rather than as round dial meters (Fadden et al., 1994).

Indeed configural displays can reach a level of complexity that considerably exceeds that of the engine instruments, safety parameter monitors, or respiration monitor (Vicente, 1995). Figure 8.12 provides an example of a configural display that have been designed to support the monitoring of complex energy conversion processes. The display designed by Bennett, Toms, and Woods (1993) contains a number of emergent features to signal that the energy conversion process is functioning normally and to make directly visible the nature of failures that might occur.

One alternative to designing a configural display is to design one in which the raw data are presented and additional indicators directly present the key integrated task-relevant variables. In the example of Cole's patient respirator display, shown

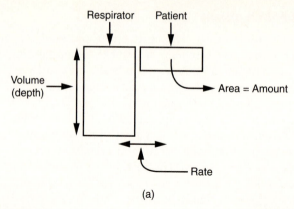

(a)

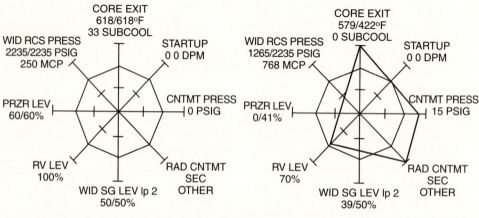

(b)

FIGURE 8.10

(a) Configural respiration monitoring display (*Source:* developed by Cole, W. 1986. *Medical Cognitive Graphics. Proceedings of CHI. Human Factors in Computing Systems.* New York: Association for Computing Machinery); (b) Integrated spoke or polar display for monitoring critical safety parameters in nuclear power. Left: normal operation; Right: wide-range iconic display during lost-of-coolant accident. (*Source:* Woods, D.D., Wise, J., and Hanes, L. *An Evaluation of Nuclear Power Plant Safety Parameter Display Systems. Proceedings of the 25th Annual Meeting of the Human Factors Society,* 1981, p. 111. Santa Monica, CA: Human Factors Society. Copyright 1981 by the Human Factors Society, Inc. Reproduced by permission.)

in Figure 8.10a, for example, the rate and depth indicators could be supplemented by a third display that indicates total *amount* of oxygen. This possibility seems feasible in some circumstances. If explicit presentation of the integrated variable were redundantly presented with its graphical representation in the emergent feature, then the only possible cost is the clutter of an added display. However, if presentation of this integrated variable *replaces* the graphical configural representation that includes the raw data, then something important may be lost: a direct and clear *per-

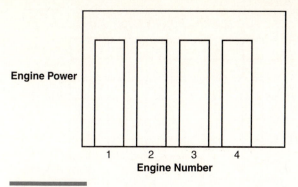

FIGURE 8.11
Engine instrument monitoring display such as that found on some four engine aircraft.

ceptual representation of how the higher level integrated variable (created by the emergent feature) is influenced by changes in the raw data.

NAVIGATION DISPLAYS AND MAPS

A navigational display (the most familiar of which is the map) should serve four fundamentally different classes of tasks: (1) provide guidance about how to get to a destination, (2) facilitate planning, (3) help recovery if the traveler becomes lost (i.e., "Where am I now?"), and (4) maintain situation awareness regarding the location of a broad range of objects (Garland & Endsley, 1995). (For example, a pilot map might depict other air traffic or weather in the surrounding region.) The display itself may be paper or electronic. Environments in which these tasks should be supported range from cities and countrysides to buildings and malls. Recently these environments have also included spatially defined "electronic environments" such as databases, hypertext, or large menu systems (see Chapter 15 HCI). We also note that navigational support may sometimes need to be provided in multitask conditions, while the traveler is engaged in other tasks, like driving the vehicle.

Route Lists and Command Displays

The simplest form of navigational display is the route list or "command display." This display typically provides the traveler with a series of "commands" (turn left, go straight, etc.) to reach a desired location. In its electronic version, it may provide markers or pointers of where to turn at particular intersections. The command display is easy to use. Furthermore, most navigational commands can be expressed in words and if commands are issued verbally, they can be easily processed while the navigator's visual attention is focused "on the road" (Streeter, Vitello, & Wonsiewicz, 1985), following the attention principle of multiple resources (P10) described in Chapter 6.

Still, to be effective, command displays must possess an accurate knowledge of where the traveler is as each command is issued. Thus, for example, a paper-route list is vulnerable if the traveler strays off the intended route, and any sort of

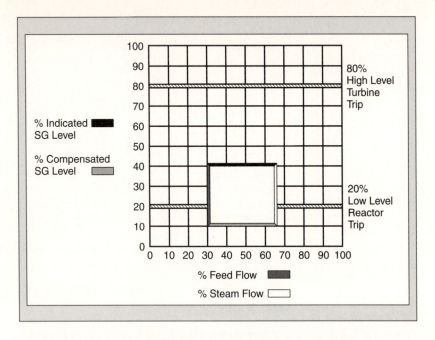

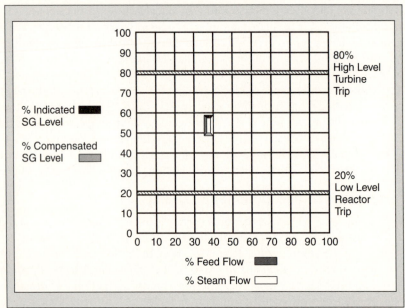

FIGURE 8.12

Configural display for process control monitoring (*Source:* Bennett, K.B., Toms, M.L., and Woods, D.D., 1993. Emergent features and graphical elements: Designing more effective configural displays. *Human Factors,* 35 [1]. Reprinted with permission. Copyright 1993 by the Human Factors and Ergonomics Society. All rights reserved.).

electronically mediated command display will suffer if navigational choice points (i.e., intersections) appear in the environment that were not in the data base (our unfortunate traveler turns left into the unmarked alley). Thus, command displays are not effective for depicting where one is (allowing recovery if lost), and they are not very useful for planning and maintaining situation awareness. In contrast, spatially configured maps do a better job of providing these other kinds of services (planning and situation awareness). There are a large number of different possible design features within such maps, and we consider them in turn.

Maps

Legibility. To revisit a recurring theme, maps must be legible to be useful. For paper maps, care must be taken to provide necessary contrast between labels and background, and adequate visual angle of text size. If color-coded maps are used, then use of low-saturation coding of background areas will enable text to be more visible (Reynolds, 1994). In designing such features, attention should also be given to the conditions in which the maps may need to be read (e.g., poor illumination as discussed in Chapter 4). Unfortunately, legibility may sometimes be forced to suffer because of the need for detail (a lot of information). With electronic maps, detail can be achieved without sacrificing legibility if *zooming* capabilities are incorporated.

Clutter. Another feature of detailed maps is their tendency to become cluttered. Clutter has two negative consequences: it will slow down the time to access information (i.e., to search for and find an item, as we discussed in Chapter 4), and it will slow the time to read the items, as a consequence of masking by nearby items (the focused attention disruption resulting from close proximity, P9). Besides the obvious solution of creating "minimalist maps," three possible solutions avail themselves. First, effective color coding can present different classes of information in different colors. Hence, the human selective attention mechanism is more readily able to focus on features of one color (e.g., roads), while "filtering out" the temporarily unneeded items of different colors (e.g., text symbols, rivers, terrain). Care should be taken to avoid an extensive number of colors (if absolute judgment is required, P1) and to avoid highly saturated colors (Reynolds, 1994). Second, with electronic maps it is possible for the user to be able to highlight (intensify) needed classes of information selectively while leaving others in the background. The enhanced intensity of target information can be a more effective filter for selective and focused attention than will be the different color. Third, carrying the concept of highlighting to its extreme, *decluttering* will allow the user to simply turn off unwanted categories of information altogether (Stokes, Wickens, & Kite, 1990; Mykityshyn, Kuchar, & Hansman, 1994). One problem with both highlighting and decluttering is that the more flexible the options are, the greater is the degree of choice imposed on the user that may impose unnecessary decision load. Furthermore, decluttering has the disadvantage of possibly eliminating information from view that should be consulted for a particular navigational decision. If that information is not visible because it had been temporarily "erased" by the decluttering option, its existence may not be remembered by the user ("out of sight, out of mind"), and hence the quality of the decision may suffer.

Position Representation. Users will benefit in navigational tasks if they are presented with a direct depiction of where they are on the map. This feature can be helpful in normal travel, as it relieves the traveler of the mental demands of inferring the direction and rate of travel. In particular, however, this feature is extremely critical in aiding recovery from getting lost. This, of course, is the general purpose of "you are here" maps in malls, buildings, and other medium-scale environments (Levine, 1982).

Map Orientation. A key feature of good maps is their ability to support the navigator's rapid and easy cross-checking between features of the environment (the forward view) and the map (Schreiber et al., 1996). This can be done most easily if the map is oriented in the direction of travel so that "up" on the map is forward and, in particular, left on the map corresponds to left in the forward view. Otherwise, time-consuming and error prone mental rotation is required (Aretz, 1991; Aretz & Wickens, 1992; Warren, Rossano, & Wear, 1990). To address this problem, electronic maps can be designed to rotate so that "up" on the map is in the direction of travel (Wickens et al., 1996), and "you are here" maps can be mounted such that the top of the map corresponds to the direction of orientation as the viewer stands observing the map (Levine, 1982; Fig. 8.13).

Despite the advantages of map rotation for navigation however, there are some costs associated. For paper maps, the text will be upsidedown if the traveler is headed south. For electronic maps containing a lot of detail, considerable graphics computer power will be needed. Furthermore, for some aspects of planning and communications with others, the stability and universal orientation of a fixed

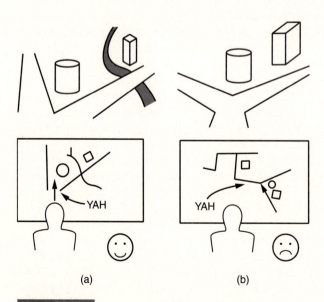

(a)   (b)

FIGURE 8.13
Good (a) and poor (b) mounting of "you are here" map.

north-up map can be quite useful (Baty, Wempe, & Huff, 1974; Aretz, 1991). Thus, electronic maps should be designed with a fixed-map option available.

Scale.   In general, we can assume that the level of detail, scale or availability with which information needs to be presented becomes less in direct proportion to the distance away from the traveler and falls off more rapidly in directions behind the traveler than in front (because the front is more likely to be in the future course of travel). It is for this reason that electronic maps often position the navigator near the bottom of the screen (see Figure 8.4b). The map scale should be user-adjustable if possible, not only because of the issue of clutter discussed above, but because the nature of the traveler's needs can vary, from planning, in which the location of a route to very distant destinations may need to be visualized (large scale), to guidance, in which only detailed information regarding the next choice point is required (small scale).

One possible solution to addressing the issue of scale is in the creation of dual maps in which local information regarding one's momentary position and orientation is presented alongside more global large-scale information regarding the full environment. The former can be ego-referenced and correspond to the direction of travel, and the latter can be world-referenced. Figure 8.14 shows some examples. Such a "dual map" creation will be particularly valuable if the user's momentary position and/or orientation is highlighted on the wide-scale, world-referenced map (Aretz, 1991; Olmos et al., 1997), thereby capturing the principle of *visual momentum* in linking the two cognitively related views (P9) (Woods, 1984). Both maps in figure 8.14 indicate the position of the local view within the global one.

Three-Dimensional Maps.   Increasing graphics capabilities have enabled the creation of effective and accurate 3-D or perspective maps that depict terrain and landmarks. If it is a rotating map, then such a map will nicely adhere to the principle of

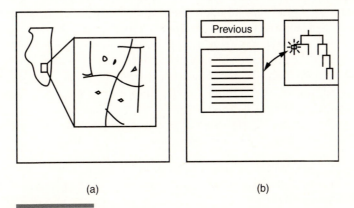

(a)   (b)

FIGURE 8.14

Examples of global and local map presentation: (a) from typical state quadrangle map; (b) "map" of a hierarchical data base. Note that the region depicted by the local map is also depicted in the global map.

pictorial realism (P5 Roscoe, 1968). But are 3-D maps helpful? The answer depends on the extent to which the vertical information, or the visual identity of 3-D landmark objects, is necessary for navigation. For the pilot flying high over the ground, or for the driver navigating a "gridlike" road structure, vertical information is likely to play little role in navigation. But for the hiker or helicopter pilot in mountainous terrain, for the pilot flying low to the ground, or the vehicle driver trying to navigate by recognizing landmark objects in the forward-field-of-view, the advantages of vertical depiction became far more apparent (Wickens, 1997). This is particularly true given the difficulties that unskilled users have reading 2-D contour maps. More guidance on the use of 3-D displays is offered in the following section.

Planning Maps and Data Visualization. Up to now, our discussion of maps has assumed the importance of a *traveler* at a particular location and orientation in the map-depicted data base. But there are several circumstances in which this is not the case; the user does not "reside" within the database. Here we consider examples such as air traffic control displays, vehicle dispatch displays, command and control status displays, construction plans, wiring diagrams, and the display of three-dimensional scientific data spaces. Here the user is more typically a "planner" who is using the display to understand the spatial relations between its elements.

Many of the features we have described above apply to these "maps for the nontraveler" as well (e.g., legibility and clutter issues, flexibility of scale). But since there typically is no "direction of travel," map rotation is not an issue, and "north-up" is typically the fixed orientation of choice (although for maps like the wiring diagram, this orientation is often more arbitrary).

The costs or benefits of 3-D displays for such maps tend to be more task specific. For maps to support a good deal of 3-D visualization (like an architect's plan), 3-D map capabilities can be quite useful (Wickens, Merwin, & Lin, 1994). In tasks such as air traffic control, where very precise separation along lateral and vertical dimensions must be judged, however, 3-D displays may impose costs because of the ambiguity with which they present this information (see Chapter 4). Perhaps the most appropriate guidance that should be given is to stress the need for careful task and information analysis before choosing to implement 3-D maps: (1) How important *is* vertical information in making decisions? (2) Does that information need to be processed at a very precise level (in which case "perspective" representations of the vertical dimensions are not good; May et al., 1996), or can it be processed just to provide some "global" information regarding "above" or "below," in which case the 3-D displays can be more effective?

If a 3-D (perspective) map is chosen, then three important design guidelines can be offered (Wickens, Todd, & Seidler, 1989).

1. As noted in Chapter 4, the greater number of natural depth cues that can be rendered in a synthetic display, the more compelling will be the sense of depth or three dimensionality.

2. Given the graphics cost of implementing a full array of depth cues, particularly for dynamic displays, it is important to realize that some cues are stronger than others, and every effort should be maintained to preserve those. Particularly strong cues appear to be interposition (nearer objects hiding the contours of farther ones) and *either* motion parallax *or* stereo (Wickens, Todd, & Seidler, 1989; Sollenberger & Milgram, 1993). The latter distinction is important. If the user has the ability to "rotate" or change the viewpoint of the display, thereby creating motion parallax, then stereo becomes less of a requirement to create a compelling sense of depth. However, for static noninteractive displays, stereo can be very helpful.

3. If display viewpoint rotation is an option, it is worthwhile to have a "2-D viewpoint" (i.e., overhead lookdown) available as a default option.

QUANTITATIVE INFORMATION DISPLAYS: TABLES AND GRAPHS

Some displays are designed to present a range of numbers and values. These may be as varied as tables depicting the nutrition and cost of different products for the consumer, the range of desired values for different maintenance testing outcomes, a spreadsheet, or a set of economic or scientific data. An initial choice can be made between representation of such values via tables or graphs. As with our discussion of dynamic displays, when the comparison was between digital and analog representation, one key consideration is the *precision* with which a value must be read. If high precision is required, the table may be a wise choice. Furthermore, unlike dynamic digital displays, tables do not suffer the problems of reading digital information while it is changing. However, as shown in Figure 8.15, tables do not support a very good perception of change over space; that is, the increasing or decreasing trend of values across the table is not very discernible, compared to the same data presented in line-graph form in Figure 8.15. Tables are even less supportive of perception of the *rate* of trend and less so still for trends that exist over two dimensions of space (i.e., an interaction between variables), which can be easily seen by the divergence of the two lines in the right side of the graph of Figure 8.15.

Thus, if absolute precision is not required and the detection or perception of trend information is important, the graph represents the display of choice. If so, then the question remains: What kind of graph? Bar or line? Pie? 2-D or 3-D?, and so on. While the reader is referred to Kosslyn (1994), Gillan and Lewis, (1994) or Lhose, (1993) for good treatments of human factors of graphic presentation, a number of fairly straightforward guidelines can be offered as follows.

Legibility. The issues of contrast sensitivity are again relevant. However, in addition to making lines and labels of large enough visual angle to be readable, a second critical point relates to *discriminability* (P4). Too often lines that have very different meanings are distinguished only by points that are highly confusable (Fig. 8.16a). Here is where attention to incorporating salient and *redundant* coding (P3) of differences (Figure 8.16b) can be quite helpful.

Clutter. Graphs can easily become cluttered by presenting a lot more lines and marks than the actual information they convey. As we know, excessive clutter can sometimes be counterproductive (Lhose, 1993), and this has led some to argue that the *data-ink ratio* should always be maximized (Tufte, 1983, 1990); that is, the

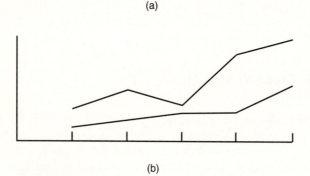

| 22 | 25 | 26 | 24 | 28 |
| 26 | 32 | 29 | 38 | 42 |

(a)

(b)

FIGURE 8.15

(a) Tabular representation of trend variables; (b) Graphical representation of the same trend variables as (a). Note how much easier it is to see the trend in (a).

greatest amount of data should be presented with the smallest amount of *ink*. While adhering to this guideline is a valuable safeguard against the excessive ink of "boutique graphs" (Fig. 8.17a), the guideline can be counterproductive if carried too far (Carswell, 1992). Thus, for example, the "minimalist" graph in Figure 8.17b, which maximizes data-ink ratio, gains little in its "decluttering" and loses a lot in its representation of the trend, compared to the line graph of Figure 8.17c. The dot graph of 8.17b is, of course, much more vulnerable to the conditions of poor viewing (or the misinterpretation caused by the dead bug on the page!).

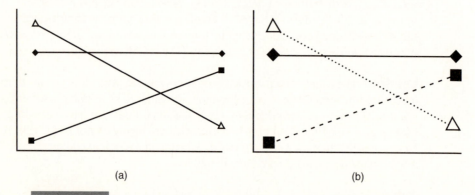

(a)   (b)

FIGURE 8.16

(a) Confusable lines on a graph; (b) Discriminable lines created in part by use of redundancy. (*Source:* Wickens, C.D., 1992b. The human factors of graphs at HFS annual meetings. *Human Factors Bulletin,* 35 [7], 1–3.)

FIGURE 8.17

(a) Example of a "Boutique" graph with a very low data ink ratio. The graph contains the unnecessary and totally noninformative representation of the depth dimension; (b) "Minimalist" graph with very high data ink ratio; (c) Line graph with intermediate data ink ratio. Note the redundant trend information added by the line.

Proximity.   Visual attention must sometimes do a lot of "work," traveling from place to place on the graph (P8), and if this visual search effort is excessive, it can hinder graph interpretation, competing for resources with the cognitive processes required to understand what the graph means. Hence, it is important to construct graphs so things that need to be compared (or integrated) are either close together in space or can be easily "linked" perceptually by a common visual code. This, of course, is a feature for the *proximity compatibility principle* (P9) and might apply to keeping legends close to the lines that they identify (Fig. 8.18a) rather than in remote captions or boxes (Fig. 8.18b), and keeping two lines that need to be compared on the same panel of a graph (Fig. 8.18c) rather than on separate panels (8.18d).

Format.   While there are a wide range of possible formats for presenting information, line graphs and bar graphs represent the typical choices (Gillan & Lewis, 1994). One advantage of line graphs is that they require fewer marks to create the same spatial information and hence can appear less cluttered as the number of data points grow large (i.e., more levels of one variable or more different variables). A second advantage, present primarily when there are trends observable across the data (Fig. 8.15), is that the slope of the line provides a perceptual *emergent feature* that reflects this trend. Ordinarily, however, categorical data, in which the different entries along the x axis have no intrinsic order, may be served just as well if not better by bar graphs, since these graphs can support more precise reading of absolute values.

Finally, we note that as the number of data points in graphs grows quite large, the display is no longer described as a graph but rather as one of "data visualization," some of whose features were described in the previous section on maps. Others will be discussed in Chapter 15.

CONCLUSION

In this chapter we have presented a wide range of display principles, designed to facilitate the transmission of information from the senses, discussed in Chapters 4 and

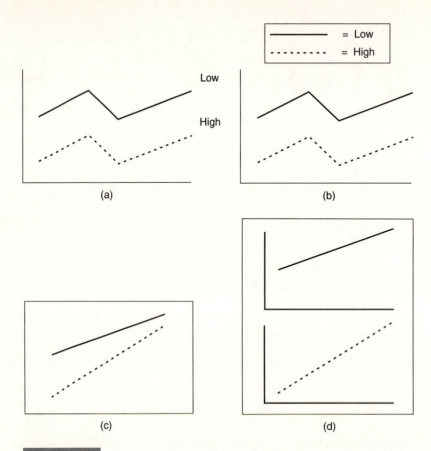

FIGURE 8.18

Graphs and proximity: (a) Close proximity of label to line; (b) Low proximity of label to line; (c) Close proximity of lines to be compared; (d) Low proximity of lines to be compared.

5, to cognition, understanding, and decision making, discussed in Chapters 6 and 7. Much of this information eventually leads to *action*—to an effort to *control* either some aspect of a system or the environment. In the next chapter, we discuss some of the ways in which the human factors engineer can assist with that control process.

REFERENCES

Andre, A., and Wickens, C.D. (1992). Compatibility and consistency in display-control systems: Implications for aircraft decision aid design. *Human Factors, 34*(6), 639–653.

Arditi, A. (1986). Binocular vision. In K. Boff, L. Kaufman, and J. Thomas (eds.), *Handbook of perception and human performance, Vol. 1.* New York: Wiley.

Aretz, A.J. (1991). The desing of electronic map displays. *Human Factors, 33*(1), 85–101.

Aretz, A.J., and Wickens, C.D. (1992). The mental rotation of map displays. *Human Performance, 5,* 303–328.

Baty, D.L., Wempe, T.E., and Huff, E.M. (1974). A study of aircraft map display location and orientation. *IEEE Transaction on Systems, Man, and Cybernetics, SMC-4,* 560–568.

Bennett, K.B., Toms, M.L., and Woods, D.D. (1993). Emergent features and graphical elements: Designing more effective configural displays. *Human Factors, 35*(1), 71–98.

Blattner, M., Sumikawn, D., and Greenberg, R. (1989). Earcons and icons: Their structure and commanding principles. *Human Computer Interaction 4,* 11–44.

Boff, K.R., Kaufman, L., and Thomas, J.P. (eds.). (1986). *Handbook of perception and human performance.* New York: Wiley.

Boff, K.R., and Lincoln, J. (1988). Engineering data compendium: Human perception and performance (4 Volumes). Wright-Patterson Air Force Base, OH: Armstrong Aerospace Medical Research Laboratory, AAMRL/NATO.

Bogner, M.S. (1994). *Human error in medicine.* Hillsdale, NJ: Lawrence Erlbaum.

Carswell, C.M. (1992). Reading graphs: Interactions of processing requirements and stimulus structure. In B. Burns (ed.), *Percepts, concepts, and categories* (pp. 605–647). Amsterdam: Elsevier Science Publications.

Cole, W.G. (1986). Medical cognitive graphs. *Proceedings of the ACM-SIGCHI: Human Factors in Computing Systems* (pp. 91–95). New York: Association for Computing Machinery.

Degani, A., and Wiener, E.L. (1990). *Human factors of flight-deck checklists: The normal checklist* (NASA Contractor Report 177549). Moffett Field, CA: NASA Ames Research Center.

Durlach, N.I., and Mavor, A. (1995). *Virtual reality: Scientific and technological challenges.* Washington, DC: National Academy Press.

Fadden, D.M., Braune, R., and Wiedemann, J. (1991). Spatial displays as a means to increase pilot situational awareness. In S.R. Ellis, M.K. Kaiser, and A.J. Grunwald (eds.), *Pictorial communication in virtual and real environments* (pp. 173–181). London: Taylor and Francis.

Federal Aviation Administration (1987). U.S. Federal Aviation Administration Advisory Circular #25-11. *Transport Category Airplane Electronic Display Systems.* Washington, DC: U.S. Department of Transportation.

Fischer, E., Haines, R.F., and Price, T.A. (1980). *Cognitive issues in head-up displays* (NASA Technical Paper 1711). Moffett Field, CA: NASA Ames Research Center.

Garland, D., and Endsley, M. (1995). *Proceedings International Congress on Experimental Analysis of Situation Awareness.* Daytona Beach FL: Embrey Riddle.

Gentner, D., and Stevens, A.L. (1983). *Mental Models.* Hillsdale, NJ: Erlbaum.

Gillan, D.J., and Lewis, R. (1994). A componential model of human interaction with graphs. I. Linear regression modeling. *Human Factors, 36*(3), 419–440.

Harrison, B.L., and Vicente, K.J. (1996). A case study of transparent user interfaces in a commerical 3D modeling and paint application. *Proceedings of the 40th Annual Meeting of the Human Factors and Ergonomics Society.* Santa Monica, CA: Human Factors and Ergonomics Society.

Helander, M.G. (1987). Design of visual displays. In G. Salvendy (ed.), *Handbook of human factors* (pp. 507–548). New York: Wiley.

Johnson-Laird, P.N. (1983). *Mental models.* Cambridge, MA: Harvard University Press.

Kiefer, R.J. (1991). *Effect of a head-up versus head-down digital speedometer on visual sampling behavior and speed control performance during daytime automobile dri-*

ving (SAE Technical Paper Series 910111). Warrendale, PA: Society of Automotive Engineers.

Kocian, D.F., and Task, H.L. (1995). Visually coupled systems hardware and the human interface. In. W. Barfield and T. Furness (eds.), *Virtual environments and advanced interface design.* New York: Oxford University Press.

Kosslyn, S.M. (1994). *Elements of graph design.* New York: W.H. Freeman and Co.

Larish, I., and Wickens, C.D. (1991). *Divided attention with superimposed and separated imagery: Implications for head-up displays.* University of Illinois Institute of Aviation Technical Report (ARL-91-4/NASA HUD-91-1). Savoy, IL: Aviation Research Laboratory.

Levine, M. (1982). You-are-here maps: Psychological considerations. *Environment and Behavior, 14,* 221–237.

Lhose, J. (1993). A cognitive model for perception and understanding. In S.P. Rebertson et al. (eds.) Human Factors in Computing Systems. CHI 1991 Conference Proceedings, pp. 137–144. NY: Association for Computing Machinery.

Long, G.M., and Kearns, D.F. (1996). Visibility of text and icon highway signs under dynamic viewing conditions. *Human Factors, 38*(4), 690–701.

May, P.A., Campbell, M., and Wickens, C.D. (1996). Perspective displays for air traffic control: Display of terrain and weather. *Air Traffic Control Quarterly, 3*(10), 1–17.

Mykityshyn, M.G., Kuchar, J.K., and Hansman, R.J. (1994). Experimental study of electronically based instrument approach plates. *The International Journal of Aviation Psychology, 4*(2), 141–166.

National Research Council (1995). *Human factors in the design of tactical displays for the individual soldier: Phase 1 report.* Washington, DC: National Academy Press.

Neisser, U., and Becklen, R. (1975). Selective looking: Attention to visually specified events. *Cognitive Psychology, 7,* 480–494.

Newman, R.L. (1995). *Head-up displays: Designing the way ahead.* Brookfield, VT: Avebury.

Norman, D.A. (1981). The trouble with UNIX. *Datamotion 27,* 139–150.

Norman, D.A. (1988). *The psychology of everyday things.* New York: Harper & Row.

Olmos, O., Liang, C.C., and Wickens, C.D. (1997). Electronic map evaluation in simulated visual meteorological conditions. *International Journal of Aviation Psychology, 7*(1), 37–66.

Parasuraman, R., Davies, D.R., and Beatty, J. (1984). *Varieties of attention.* New York: Academic Press.

Pomerantz, J.R., and Pristach, E.A. (1989). Emergent features, attention, and perceptual glue in visual form perception. *Journal of Experimental Psychology: Human Perception and Performance, 15,* 635–649.

Rasmussen, J., Pejtersen, A., and Goodstein, L. (1995). Cognitive engineering: Concepts and applications. New York: Wiley.

Reynolds, L. (1994). Colour for air traffic control displays. *Displays, 15,* 215–225.

Roscoe, S.N. (1968). *Airborne displays for flight and navigation. Human Factors, 10,* 321–332.

Sanders, M.S., and McCormick, E.J. (1993). *Human factors in engineering and design.* New York: McGraw Hill.

Sanderson, P.M., Flach, J.M., Buttigieg, M.A., and Casey, E.J. (1989). Object displays do not always support better integrated task performance. *Human Factors, 31,* 183–189.

Schreiber, B., Wickens, C.D., Renner, G., and Alton, J. (1996). Navigational checking: Implications for electronic map design. *Proceedings of the 40th Annual Meeting of the Human Factors and Ergonomics Society.* Santa Monica, CA: Human Factors and Ergonomics Society.

Seagull, J., and Gopher, D. (1995). Training head movement in visual scanning: An embedded approach to the development of piloting skills with helmet-mounted displays. In *Proceedings 39th Annual Meeting of the Human Factors Society.* Santa Monica, CA: Human Factors.

Sollenberger, R.L. and Milgram, P. (1993). Effects of stereoscopic and rotational displays in a 3D path-tracing task. *Human Factors, 35*(3), 483–499.

Sojourner, R., and Antins, S. (1990). The effects of a simulated headup display speedometer on perceptual task performance. *Human Factors, 32,* 329–340.

Sorkin, R.D., Kantowitz, B.H., and Kantowitz, S.C. (1988). Likelihood alarm displays. *Human Factors, 30,* 445–460.

Stokes, A.F., Wickens, C.D., and Kite, K. (1990). *Display technology: Human factors concepts.* Warrendale, PA: Society of Automotive Engineers.

Streeter, L.A., Vitello, D., and Wonsiewicz, S.A. (1985). How to tell people where to go: Comparing navigational aids. *International Journal on Man-Machine Studies, 22,* 549–562.

Tufte, E.R. (1983). *The visual display of quantitative information.* Cheshire, CT: Graphics Press.

Tufte, E.R. (1990). *Envisioning information.* Cheshire, CT: Graphics Press.

Tversky, A. (1977). Features of similarity. *Psychological Review, 84,* 327–352.

Vicente, K.J. (1995). Supporting operator problem solving through ecological interface desin. *IEEE Transactions on Systems, Man, and Cybernetics, 25*(4), 529–545.

Vicente, K.J., Moray, N., Lee, J.D., Rasmussen, J., Jones, B.G., Brock, R., and Toufsk, D. (1996). Evaluation of a Rankine cycle display for nuclear power plant monitoring and diagnosis. *Human Factors, 38,* 506–522.

Vicente, K.J., and Rasmussen, J. (1992). Ecological interface design: Theoretical foundations. *IEEE Transactions on Systems, Man, and Cybernetics, 22*(4), 589–606.

Warren, D.H., Rossano, M.J., and Wear, T.D. (1990). Perception of map-environment correspondence: The roles of features and alignment. *Ecological Psychology, 2,* 131–150.

Weintraub, D.J., and Ensing, M.J. (1992). *Human factors issues in head-up display design: The book of HUD* (SOAR CSERIAC State of the Art Report 92-2). Crew System Ergonomics Information Analysis Center, Wright-Patterson AFB, Dayton, OH.

Weintraub, D.J., Haines, R.F., and Randle, R.J. (1984). The utility of head-up displays: Eye-focus versus decision time. *Proceedings of the 28th Annual Meeting of the Human Factors Society* (pp. 529–533). Santa Monica, CA: Human Factors Society.

Weintraub, D.J., Haines, R.F., and Randle, R.J. (1985). Head-up display (HUD) utility, II: Runway to HUD transitions monitoring eye focus and decision times. *Proceedings of the 29th Annual Meeting of the Human Factors Society* (pp. 615–619). Santa Monica, CA: Human Factors Society.

Wickens, C.D. (1992a). *Engineering psychology and human performance* (2nd ed.). New York: HarperCollins.

Wickens, C.D. (1992b). The human factors of graphs at HFS annual meetings. *Human Factors Bulletin, 35*(7), 1–3.

Wickens, C.D. (1997). Frame of reference for navigation. In D. Gopher and A. Koriat (eds.), *Attention and performance,* Vol. 16. Orlando, FL: Academic Press.

Wickens, C.D., and Carswell, C.M. (1995). The proximity compatibility principle: Its psychological foundation and its relevance to display design. *Human Factors, 37*(3), 473–494.

Wickens, C.D., Liang, C-C, Prevett, T., and Olmos, O. (1996). Electronic maps for terminal area navigation: Effects of frame of reference on dimensionality. *International Journal of Aviation Psychology, 6*(3), 241–271.

Wickens, C.D., and Long, J. (1995). Object- vs. space-based models of visual attention: Implications for the design of head-up displays. *Journal of Experimental Psychology: Applied, 1*(3), 179–194.

Wickens, C.D., Merwin, D.H., and Lin, E. (1994). Implications of graphics enhancements for the visualization of scientific data: Dimensional integrality, stereopsis, motion, and mesh. *Human Factors, 36*(1), 44–61.

Wickens, C.D., Todd, S., and Seidler, K.S. (1989). *Three-dimensional displays: Perception, implementation, and applications* (CSERIAC SOAR 89-001). Crew System Ergonomics Information Analysis Center, Wright-Patterson AFB, OH.

Wickens, C.D., Vincolo, M.A., Schopper, A.W., and Lincoln, S.E. (1997). Computational models of human performance in the design and layout of controls and displays. Wright-Patterson AFB, OH: CSERIAC.

Woods, D.D. (1984). Visual momentum: A concept to improve the cognitive coupling of person and computer. *International Journal of Man-Machine Studies, 21,* 229–244.

Woods, D., Wise, J., and Hanes, L. (1981). An evaluation of nuclear power plant safety parameter display systems. *Proceedings of the 25th Annual Meeting of the Human Factors Society* (pp. 110–114). Santa Monica, CA: Human Factors Society.

CHAPTER 9

Control

The rental car was new, and as he pulled onto the freeway entrance ramp at dusk, he started to reach for what he thought was the headlight control. Suddenly, however, his vision was obscured by a gush of washer fluid across the windshield. As he reached to try to correct his mistake his other hand twisted the very sensitive steering wheel and the car started to veer off the ramp. Quickly he brought the wheel back but overcorrected, and then for a few terrifying moments the car seesawed back and forth along the ramp until he brought it to a stop, his heart pounding. He cursed himself for failing to learn the location of controls before starting his trip. Reaching once more for the headlight switch, he now activated the flashing hazard light—fortunately, this time, a very appropriate error.

Our hapless driver experienced several difficulties in control. One way to briefly paraphrase the human information-processing model discussed in Chapter 6 is: knowing the state of affairs, knowing what to do, and then doing it. Control is the "doing it" part of this description. It is both a noun (a control) and an action verb (to control). Referring to the model of information processing presented in Chapter 6, we see that "control" primarily involves the selection and execution of responses—that is, the last two stages of the model—along with the feedback loop that allows the human to determine that the control response has been executed in the manner that was intended. In the current chapter, we first describe some important principles concerning the selection of responses. Then we discuss various aspects of response execution that are dictated by the nature of the control device, which is closely intertwined with the task to be performed. Our sections address discrete activation of controls or switches, controls used as setting or pointing devices, controls used for verbal or symbolic input (e.g., typing), and continuous control used in tracking and traveling.

PRINCIPLES OF RESPONSE SELECTION

The difficulty and speed of selecting a response or an action is influenced by several variables (Fitts & Posner, 1967; Wickens, 1992), of which five are particularly critical for system design: decision complexity, expectancy, compatibility, the speed-accuracy tradeoff, and feedback.

Decision Complexity

The speed with which an action can be selected is strongly influenced by the number of possible alternative actions that could be selected in that context. We refer to this as the complexity of the decision of what action to select. Thus, each action of the Morse code operator, in which only one of two alternatives is chosen ("dit" or "dah") follows a much simpler choice than each action of the typist, who must choose between one of 26 letters. Hence, the Morse code operator can generate a greater number of key strokes per minute. Correspondingly, users will be able to select an action more rapidly from a computer menu with two options than from the more complex menu with eight options. Engineering psychologists have characterized this dependency of response selection time on decision complexity by the *Hick-Hyman Law* of reaction time, shown in Figure 9.1 (Hick 1952; Hyman, 1953).

The Hick-Hyman law does not, however, imply that systems designed for users to make simpler decisions are superior. In fact, if a given amount of *information* needs to be transmitted by the user, it is generally more efficient to do so by a smaller number of complex decisions than a larger number of simple decisions. This is referred to as the *decision complexity advantage* (Wickens, 1992). For example, a typist can convey the same message more rapidly than can the Morse code operator; although key strokes are made more slowly, there are

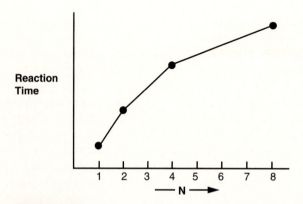

FIGURE 9.1

The Hick-Hyman Law of reaction time. The figure shows the logarithmic increase in RT as the number of possible stimulus-response alternatives (*N*) increases. This can sometimes be expressed by the formula: $RT = a + b\log_2 N$.

many fewer of them. Correspondingly, as we learn in Chapter 15, "shallow" menus with many items (i.e., eight in the example above) are better than "deep" menus with few items.

Response Expectancy

In Chapters 4, 6, and 8, we learned that we perceive rapidly (and accurately) that information that we *expect.* In a corresponding manner, we select more rapidly and accurately those actions we expect to carry out than those that are surprising to us. We do not, for example, expect the car in front of us to come to an abrupt halt on a freeway. Not only are we slow in perceiving its sudden expansion in the visual field, but we are much slower in applying the brake than we would be when the light turns yellow at an intersection that we are approaching.

Compatibility

In Chapter 8 we discussed the concept of display compatibility between the orientation and movement of a display and the operator's expectancy of movement, or *mental model* of the displayed system. *Stimulus-response compatibility* (or display control compatibility) describes the expected relationship between the location of a control or movement of a control response and the location or movement of the stimulus or display to which the control is related (Fitts & Seeger, 1953).

Two subprinciples characterize a compatible (and hence, good) mapping between display and control (or stimulus and response): (1) *Location compatibility:* The control location should be close to (and, in fact, closest to) the entity being controlled, or the display of that entity. Figure 3.3 showed how location compatibility is applied to good and bad stove burner design, (2) *movement compatibility:* The direction of movement of a control should be congruent with the direction both of movement of the feedback indicator and of the system movement itself. A violation of movement compatibility would occur if the operator needed to move a lever to the left to move a display indicator to the right.

The Speed-Accuracy Tradeoff

For the preceding three principles, the designer can assume that factors that make the selection of a response longer (complex decisions, unexpected actions, or incompatible responses) will also make errors more likely. Hence, there is a *positive correlation* between response time and error rate or, in other terms, a positive correlation between speed and accuracy. These variables do not trade off. However, there are some circumstances in which the two measures do trade off: For example, if we try to execute actions very rapidly (carrying out procedures under a severe time deadline), we are more likely to make errors. If we must be very cautious because the consequences of errors are critical, we will be slow. Hence, there is in these two examples a *negative correlation,* or *tradeoff* between speed and accuracy. Here the tradeoff was caused by user strategies. As we will see below, sometimes control devices differ in the speed-accuracy tradeoff because one induces faster but less precise behavior and the other more careful but slower behavior.

Feedback

Most controls and actions that we take are associated with some form of visual feedback that indicates the *system* response to the control input. For example, in a car the speedometer offers visual feedback from the control of the accelerator. However, good control design must also be concerned with more direct feedback of the control state itself. As we learned in Chapter 5, this feedback may be kinesthetic/tactile (e.g., the "feel" of a button as it is depressed to make contact or the resistance on a stick as it is moved). It may be auditory (the "click" of the switch or the beep of the phone tone), or it may be visual (a light next to a switch to show it is "on" or even the clear and distinct visual view that a push button has been depressed).

Through whatever channel, we can state with some certainty that more feedback of both the current control state (through vision) and the change in control state is good as long as the feedback is nearly instantaneous. However, feedback that is delayed by as little as 100 msec can be harmful if rapid sequences of control actions are required. Such delays are particularly harmful if the operator is less skilled (and therefore depends more on the feedback) or if the feedback is auditory so that it cannot be filtered out by selective attention mechanisms (Wickens, 1992).

DISCRETE CONTROL ACTIVATION

Our driver in the opening story was troubled, in part, because he simply did not know, or could not find, the right controls to *activate* the wipers. Many such controls in systems are designed primarily for the purpose of activating or changing the discrete state of some system. In addition to making the controls easily visible (Norman, 1988), there are several other design features that make the activation of such controls less susceptible to errors and delays.

Physical Feel

As we have noted, feedback is a critical positive feature of discrete controls. Some controls offer more feedback channels than others. The toggle switch is very good in this regard. It will change its state in an obvious *visual* fashion and will provide an auditory "click" and a tactile "snap" (a sudden loss of resistance) as it moves into its new position. The auditory and tactile feedback provide the operator with instant knowledge of the toggle's change in state, while the visual feedback provides continuous information regarding its new state. A push button that remains depressed when "on" has similar features, but the visual feedback may be less obvious, particularly if the spatial separation between the button at the two positions is small.

Care should be taken in the design of other types of discrete controls that the feedback (indicating that the system has received the state change) is obvious. Touch screens do not do this so well; neither do push button phones that lack an auditory "beep" following each keypress. Many computer-based control devices may replace the auditory and tactile state-change feedback with artificial visual feedback (e.g., a light that turns on when the switch is depressed). If such visual feedback is meant to be the only cue to indicate state change (rather than a redundant one), then there will be problems that are associated both with an increase in the *distance* between the light and the relevant control (this distance should be kept as short as possible) and with the possible electronic failure of the light. Hence, feedback lights ideally should be redundant with some other indication of state change; of course, any visual feedback should be immediate.

Size. The size of keys or control buttons typically represents a tradeoff between two competing factors. Closer spacing will allow more rapid movement between keys if key size is not reduced accordingly. However, when keys are so closely packed that they must be made small, for example, because of constraints on control panel or keyboard size, then no gain in performance can be expected, and there will be a possible cost associated with "blunder" errors when the wrong key (or two keys) are inadvertently pressed.

Confusion and Labeling. Keypress or control activation errors also occur if the identity of a key is not well specified to the novice or casual user (i.e., one who does not "know" the location by touch). This happened to our driver at the beginning of the chapter. These confusions are more likely to occur (a) when large sets of identically appearing controls are unlabeled or poorly labeled (see Chapters 5, 6, and 8) and (b) when labels are physically displaced from their associated controls, hence violating the proximity compatibility principle.

POSITIONING CONTROL DEVICES

A common task in much of human-machine interaction is the need to *position* some entity in space. This may involve moving a cursor to a point on a screen, reaching with a robot arm to contact an object, or moving the "setting" on a radio dial to a new frequency. Generically, we refer to these spatial tasks as those involving positioning or *pointing* (Baber, 1997). A wide range of control *devices,* such as the mouse or joystick, are available to accomplish such tasks. Before we compare the properties of such devices, however, we consider the important nature of the human performance skill underlying the pointing task: movement of a controlled entity, which we call a *cursor,* to a destination, which we call a *target.* We consider a model that accounts for the time to make such movements.

Movement Time

Controls typically require movement of two different sorts: (1) movement is often required for the hands or fingers to *reach* the control (not unlike the movement of attention to access information, discussed in Chapter 8), and (2) the control may then be moved in some direction. Even in the best of circumstances, in which control location and destination are well learned, these movements take time. Fortunately for designers, such times can be relatively well predicted by a model known as *Fitts' Law* (Fitts, 1954; Jagacinski, 1989), which states that:

$$MT = a + b \, \log_2(2A/W)$$

where A = amplitude of the movement and W = width or desired precision of the target. In words, this means that movement time is linearly related to the logarithm of the term ($2A/W$), a term that is referred to as the *Index of Difficulty* of the movement. Hence, referring to Figure 9.2, each time the distance to the key doubles, movement time will increase by a constant amount. Correspondingly, each time the required precision of the movement is doubled (the target width or allowable precision is halved, the movement time will also increase by a constant amount unless the distance is correspondingly halved (Fig. 9.2b). As we saw in the previous section, moving keys proportionately closer together will not decrease movement time if their size (w) decreases by the same proportion. Alternatively, if we require a movement of a given amplitude (A) to be made within a certain time constraint (MT), then the precision of that movement (W) will decrease in a manner predicted by Fitts' Law. This characterizes a speed-accuracy tradeoff in pointing movements. The value of W in this case can be thought of as characterizing the distribution of endpoints of the movement.

The mechanisms underlying Fitts' Law are based heavily on the visual feedback aspects of controlled aiming, and hence the law is equally applicable to the actual physical movement of the hand to a target (i.e, reaching for a key) as to the movement of a displayed cursor to a screen target achieved by manipulation of some control device (e.g., using a mouse to bring a cursor to a particular item in a computer menu; Card et al., 1978). It is also applicable to movements as coarse as a foot reaching for a pedal (Drury, 1975), and as fine as assembly and manipulation under a microscope (Langolf et al., 1976). This generality gives the law great value in allowing designers to predict the costs of different keyboard layouts and target sizes in a wide variety of circumstances (Card et al., 1983).

Device Characteristics

The various categories of control devices that can be used to accomplish these pointing or position tasks may be grouped into four distinct categories. In the first category are *direct position controls* (light pen and touch screen), in which the position of the human hand (or finger) directly corresponds with the desired location of the cursor. The second category contains *indirect position controls*—the mouse, touch pad, and tablet—in which changes in the position of the limb directly correspond to changes in the position of the cursor, but the limb is moved on a surface different from the display cursor surface.

The third category contains *indirect velocity controls,* such as the joystick and the cursor keys. Here, typically an activation of control in a given direction yields a velocity of cursor movement in that direction. For cursor keys, this may involve either repeated presses or holding it down for a long period. For joystick movements, the magnitude of deflection typically creates a proportional velocity. Joysticks may be of three sorts: *isotonic,* in which case they can be moved freely and will rest wherever they are positioned; *isometric* (see Chapter 5), in which case they are rigid but produce movement proportional to the force applied; or *spring-loaded,* in which case they offer resistance proportional to force applied but are also displaced, springing back to the neutral position when pressure is released. The spring-loaded stick, offering both proprioceptive and kinesthetic feedback of movement extent is typically the most preferred. (While joysticks can be config-

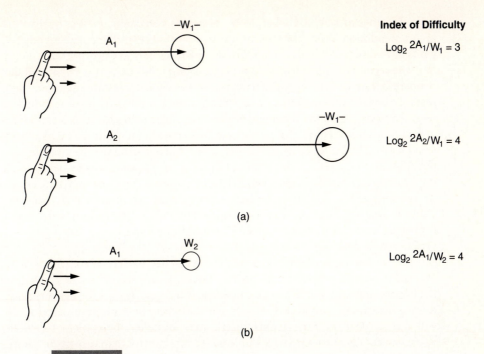

Index of Difficulty

$Log_2\ 2A_1/W_1 = 3$

$Log_2\ 2A_2/W_1 = 4$

(a)

$Log_2\ 2A_1/W_2 = 4$

(b)

FIGURE 9.2

Illustrates Fitts' Law of movement time. (a) Shows the doubling of movement amplitude from $A_1 \rightarrow A_2$; (b) Shows halving of target width $W_1 \rightarrow W_2$ (or doubling target precision). Next to each movement is shown the calculation of the *index of difficulty* of the movement. Movement time will be directly proportional to this index of difficulty.

ured as position controls, these are not generally used, for reasons discussed below.) The final category is that of voice control.

Across all display types, there are two important variables that affect usability of controls for pointing (and they are equally relevant for controls for tracking as discussed later in this chapter). First, as noted in section 2, *feedback* of the current state of the cursor should be salient, visible, and immediate. System lags will greatly disrupt pointing activity, particularly if this activity is at all repetitive. Second, performance will be affected in a more complex way by the system *gain*. Gain may be described by the ratio:

$$G = (change\ of\ cursor)/(change\ of\ control\ position).$$

Thus, a high-gain device is one in which a small displacement of the control produces a large movement of the cursor, or a fast movement in the case of a velocity control device. (It should be noted that this variable is sometimes expressed as the reciprocal of gain or the "control/display ratio.") The gain of direct position controls, such as the touch screen and light pen, will obviously be 1.0. There is some evidence that the ideal gain for other control devices should be in the range of 1.0–3.0 (Baber, 1997). However, two characteristics qualify this recommendation. First, humans appear to adapt successfully to a wide range of gains in their control behavior (Wickens, 1986; Jellinek & Card, 1990).

The second qualification is that the ideal gain tends to be somewhat task dependent because of the very differing properties of low-gain and high-gain systems. Low-gain systems tend to be *effortful,* since a lot of control response is required to produce a small movement; however, high-gain systems tend to be *imprecise,* since it is very easy to "overcorrect" when trying to position a cursor on a small target. Hence, for example, to the extent that a task requires a lot of repetitive and lengthy movements to large targets, a higher gain will be better. This might characterize the actions required in the initial stages of a system layout using a computer-aided design tool. In contrast, to the extent that small, high-precision movements are required, a low-gain system will be more suitable. These properties would characterize text editing or uniquely specifying data points in a very dense cluster.

A large number of factors can influence the effectiveness of control devices. The *task* is perhaps the most important influence. In this section we are discussing the positioning task, but it will be evident that the best devices for discrete positioning may not be best for other tasks, like data entry or continuous control. We will also see that the *performance* metric may influence the choice of devices. Some devices may provide faster but less accurate control than others, for example. A third influence on effectiveness concerns the *work space* within which the device is or must be used. This includes both properties of the *display* on which cursor and target are represented and the physical space available to position the control device. Finally, we will see that the *environment* within which the device is used can influence the effectiveness of different devices. We consider these various influences below.

Task Performance Dependence

For the most critical tasks involved in pointing (designating targets and "dragging" them to other locations), there is some emerging evidence that the best overall devices are the two direct position controls (touch screen and light pen) and the mouse (Fig. 9.3; Baber, 1997; Epps, 1987; Card et al., 1978). Analysis by Card et al. (1978), using Fitts' Law to characterize the range of movement distances and precisions, suggested that the mouse is superior to the direct pointing devices. However, Figure 9.3 also reveals the existence of a speed-accuracy trade-off between the direct position controls, which tend to be very rapid but less accurate, and the mouse, which tends to be slower, but generally more precise. Problems in accuracy with the direct positioning devices arise from possible parallax errors, instability of the hand or fingers (particularly on nonhorizontal screens), and, in the case of touch screens, the imprecision of the finger area in specifying small targets. In addition to greater accuracy, another clear advantage of the indirect over the direct positioning devices is that the gain may be adjustable, depending on the required position accuracy (or effort) of the task.

When pointing and positioning is required for more complex spatial activities, like drawing or handwriting, the advantages for the indirect positioning devices disappear in favor of the most natural feedback offered by the direct positioning devices.

Cursor keys, not represented in the table, are adequate for some tasks. But they do not produce long movements well and generally are constrained by "city block" movement, such as that involved in text editing. As we will discuss below, voice control may be feasible in designating targets by nonspatial means (e.g., calling out the target *identity* rather than its location). But this will only be feasible if targets have direct, visible, and unambiguous symbolic labels.

Tables 9.1 and 9.2 (Baber, 1997) provide further distinctions between control devices in terms of usability and workload.

The Work Space

One property of the broader work space within which the device is used is the display, which presents target and cursor information. As we have noted, display size (or the physical separation between display elements) will influence the extent of device-movement effort necessary to access targets. Greater dispersion will place a greater value on "efficient" high-gain devices. In contrast, smaller, more precise targets (or smaller displays) will place greater value on precise manipulation. Targets whose identity cannot be uniquely verbalized will impose a greater cost on voice recognition devices.

The physical characteristics of the display also influence usability. Vertically mounted displays or those that are distant from the body impose greater costs on direct positioning devices. Frequent interaction with keyboard editing will foster a greater benefit of devices that are physically integrated with the keyboard (i.e., cursor keys rather than the mouse) or can be used in parallel with it (i.e., voice

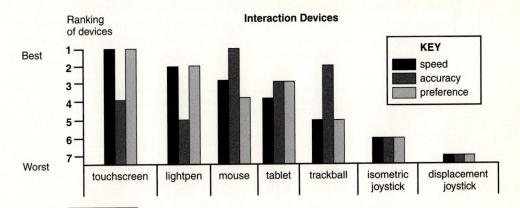

FIGURE 9.3

A comparison of performance of different control devices, based on speed, accuracy and user preference. (*Source:* Baber, C., 1997. *Beyond the Desktop.* San Diego, CA: Academic Press.)

TABLE 9.1 **Interaction Devices Classified in Terms of Usability**

Usability issues	Interaction Devices					
	Touchscreen	Lightpen	Tablet	Mouse	Joystick	Trackball
Learnability	+	0	0	0	0	0
Effectiveness (speed)	+	+	0	0	−	−
Effectiveness (accuracy)	−	0	+	+	−	0
Attitude	+	+	0	0	−	−
Flexibility	−	−	0	0	+	+

KEY: + better than average; 0 average; − worse than average. *Source:* Baber, C., 1997. *Beyond the Desktop.* San Diego, CA: Academic Press.

control). Finally, the available work space *size* may constrain the ability to use certain devices (Table 9.3). In particular, devices like joysticks or cursor keys that are less effective in desktop workstations will become relatively more advantageous for control in mobile environments, like the vehicle cab or small airplane cockpit, in which there is little room for a mouse pad.

The Environment

Finally, the environment itself can have a major impact on usability. For example, direct position control devices will suffer greatly in the vibrating environment such as a vehicle cab. Voice control will be more difficult in a noisy environment. Table 9.4 provides some evidence of the presence or absence of degrading effects of different environments on operations of different control devices (Baber, 1997).

In summary, the preceding discussion should make clear that it is difficult to specify in advance what the best device will be for a particular combination of task, work space, and environment. It should, however, be possible to eliminate certain devices from contention in some circumstances and at the same time to use the factors discussed above to understand why users may encounter difficulties with early prototype testing. The designer is referred to Baber (1997), regarding more detailed treatment of the human factors of control device differences.

TABLE 9.2 **Interaction Devices Classified in Terms of Workload**

Interaction Device	Cognitive Load	Perceptual Load	Motor Load	Fatigue
Light pen	Low	Low	Medium	Medium
Touch panel	Low	Low	Low	Low
Tablet (stylus)	High	Medium	Medium	High
Alphanumeric keyboard	High	High	High	High
Function keyboard	Low	Medium	Low	Low
Mouse	Low	Medium	Medium	Medium
Trackball	Low	Medium	Medium	Medium

Source: Baber, C., 1997. *Beyond the Desktop.* San Diego, CA: Academic Press.

TABLE 9.3 Interaction Devices Classified in Terms of Desk Space Requirements (measurements in millimeters)

Device	230 mm screen (200 × 110)	300 mm screen (270 × 150)
Keyboard	415 × 200	415 × 200
Mouse (1:1)	200 × 110	270 × 150
Mouse (1:2)	100 × 55	135 × 75
Tablet (1:1)	200 × 110	270 × 150
Touchscreen	0	0
Lightpen	0	0
Trackball	50 × 75	50 × 75

Source: Baber, C. 1977. *Beyond the Desktop.* San Diego, CA: Academic Press.

VERBAL AND SYMBOLIC INPUT DEVICES

Spatial positioning devices do not generally offer a compatible means of inputting or specifying much of the symbolic, numerical, or verbal information that is involved in system interaction (Wickens, Sandry, & Vidulich, 1983). For this sort of information, keyboards or voice control have generally been the interfaces of choice.

Numerical Data Entry

For numerical data entry, numerical keypads (Fig. 9.4) or voice remain the most viable alternatives. While voice control is most compatible and natural, it is hampered by certain technological problems discussed in the following section, which slow the rate of possible input. Numeric keypads, shown in Figure 9.4, are typically represented on one of three forms. The linear array, shown in Figure 9.4a, is generally not preferred because of the extensive movement time required to move from key to key. The two square arrays shown in 9.4b (the "calculator" or "789" layout) and 9.4c (the "telephone" or "123" layout), both minimize movement distance (and therefore time). General design guidelines suggest that the "123" layout is preferable (Baber, 1997), although the advantage is probably not great enough to warrant redesign of the many existing "7-8-9" keyboards.

TABLE 9.4 Interaction Devices and Environmental Factors

Device	Noise	Vibration	Acceleration	Heat	Mud/snow
Keyboard	?	?	?	—	—
Pen	?	?	?	?	—
Speech	—	—	—	?	0
Mouse	?	—	?	?	—
Trackball	?	—	?	?	—
Joystick	—	—	?	?	—

Source: Baber, C., 1997. *Beyond the Desktop.* San Diego, CA: Academic Press.

Linguistic Data Entry

For data entry of linguistic material, the typewriter or computer keyboard has traditionally been the device of choice. At the current time, difficulties with machine handwriting recognition leave direct writing input devices as at severe disadvantage. The layout of the traditional letter keyboard has long been a subject of debate (Norman, 1988). While the design of the standard QWERTY layout over 100 years ago was based in part on ergonomic considerations, many other considerations were based on mechanical constraints designed to prevent physical "key jamming," factors that are now quite irrelevant in the era of electronic data input. Still, the more recently designed Dvorak keyboard, which was developed with more consideration given to the nature and constraints of human finger movement, has not been found to give a sufficient increase in performance (only 5–10% increase in typing speed) to be accepted by the vast majority of touch typists, who are well familiar now with the QWERTY keyboard (Norman & Fisher, 1982). In this regard we should remember that consistency (with previous design) is another key to good human factors.

An alternative to dedicated keys that require digit movement is the *chording keyboard* in which individual items of information are entered by the simultaneous depression of combinations of keys, on which the fingers may remain (Fig. 9.5; Seibel, 1964; Gopher & Raij, 1988). Chording works effectively in part by allowing a single complex action to convey a large amount of information and hence benefit from the decision complexity advantage, discussed earlier in this chapter. A single press with a ten-key keyboard can, for example, designate any of $2^{10} - 1$ (or 1023) possible actions/meanings.

Such a system has three distinct advantages. First, since the hand (or hands) never needs to leave the chord board, there is no requirement for visual feedback to monitor the correct placement of a digit. Consider, for example, how useful this

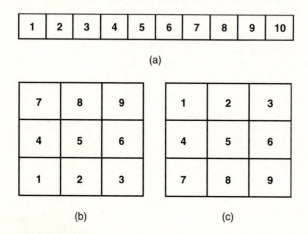

(a)

(b)   (c)

FIGURE 9.4

(a) Linear number pad; (b) Calculator or "7-8-9" number pad; (c) Telephone or "1-2-3" number pad.

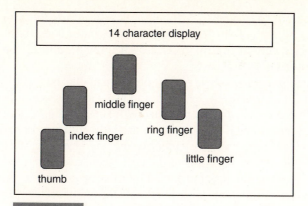

FIGURE 9.5

Example of a chording keyboard. (*Source:* Baber, C., 1997. *Beyond the Desktop.* San Diego, CA: Academic Press.)

would be for entering data in the high-visual-workload environment characteristic of helicopter flight, or in a continuous visual inspection task. Second, because of the absence of a lot of required movement, the chording board is less susceptible to repetitive stress injury or "carpal tunnel syndrome" (Chapter 10). Finally, after extensive practice, chording keyboards have been found to support more rapid word transcription processing than the standard typewriter keyboard, an advantage due to the absence of movement-time requirements (Seibel, 1964; Barton, 1986; see Wickens, 1992).

The primary cost of the chording keyboard is in the extensive learning required to associate the finger combinations with their meaning (Richardson et al., 1987). In contrast, typewriter keyboards provide "knowledge in the world" regarding the appropriate key since each key is labeled on the top (Norman, 1988). For the chord board there is only "knowledge in the head," which is more difficult to acquire and may be easier to lose through forgetting. Still, however, various chording systems have found their way into productive use; examples are both in postal mail sorting (Barton, 1986) and in court stenotyping (Seibel, 1964).

VOICE INPUT

Within the last few years, increasingly sophisticated voice recognition technology has made this a viable means of control, although such technology has both costs and benefits.

Benefits of Voice Control

While chording is efficient because a single action can select one of several hundred items, an even more efficient linguistic control capability can be obtained by voice, where a single utterance can represent any of several thousand possible meanings. Furthermore, as we know, voice communications is usually a very "natural" communications channel for symbolic linguistic information, for which we have had nearly a lifetime's worth of experience. This naturalness may be (and has been) exploited in certain control interfaces when the benefits of voice control outweigh their technological costs.

Particular benefits of voice control may be observed in dual task situations. As discussed more in Chapter 6, when the hands and eyes are busy with other tasks like driving (which prevents dedicated manual control on a keyboard, and the visual feedback necessary to see if the fingers are properly positioned), designs in which the operator can "time-share" by talking to the interface using separate resources are of considerable value. Some of the greatest successes have been realized, for example, in using the voice to enter radio-frequency data in the heavy visual-manual load environment of the helicopter. "Dialing" of cellular phones by voice command while driving is considered a useful application of voice recognition technology as also would be the use of this technology in assisting baggage handlers to code the destination of a bag. There are also many circumstances in which the *combination* of voice and manual input for the same task can be beneficial (Baber, 1997). Such a combination, for example, would allow manual interaction to select objects, (a Spatial Task) and voice to convey symbolic information to the system about the selected object (Martin, 1989).

Costs of Voice Control

Against these benefits may be arrayed four distinct costs that limit the applicability of voice control or at least highlight precautions that should be taken in its implementation. These costs are related closely to the sophistication of the technology necessary for computers to translate the complex four-dimensional analog signal that is voice (see Chapter 5) into a categorical vocabulary, which is programmed within the computer-based voice recognition system (McMillan et al., 1997).

Confusion and Limited Vocabulary Size. Because of the demands on computers to resolve differences in sounds that are often subtle (even to the human ear), and because of the high degree of variability (from speaker to speaker and occasion to occasion) in the physical way a given phrase is uttered, voice recognition systems are prone to make confusions in classifying similar-sounding utterances (e.g., "cleared to" versus "cleared through"). How such confusions may be dealt with can vary (McMillan et al., 1997). The recognizing computer may simply take its "best guess" and pass it on as a system input (this is what a computer keyboard would do if you hit the wrong letter). Alternatively, the system may provide feedback if it was uncertain about a particular classification (or if an utterance was not even close to anything in the computer's vocabulary). The problem here is that if the recognition capabilities of the computer are not great, the repeated occurrences of this feedback will greatly disrupt the smooth flow of voice communications if this feedback is offered in the auditory channel. If the feedback is offered visually, then it may well neutralize the dual task benefit described above (i.e., keeping the "eyes free"). These costs of confusion and misrecognition can only be addressed by reducing the vocabulary size and constructing the vocabulary in such a way that acoustically similar items are avoided.

Constraints on Speed. Most voice recognition systems do not easily handle the continuous speech of natural conversation. This is because the natural flow of our speech does not necessarily place physical pauses between different words (see Chapter 5; Fig. 5.8d). Hence, the computer does not easily know when to stop "counting syllables" and demarcate the end of a word to look for an association of the sound with a given item in the vocabulary. To guard against these limitations, the speaker may need to speak unnaturally slowly, pausing between each word.

A related point concerns the slowing required to "train" many voice systems to understand the individual speaker's voice, prior to the system's use in operation. This training is required because there are so many *physical* differences between the way people of different gender, age, and dialect may speak the same word. Hence, the computer can be far more efficient if it can "learn" the pattern of a particular individual (speaker-dependent system) than it can if it must master the dialect and voice quality of all potential users (speaker-independent system). For this reason, it is usually the case that speaker-dependent systems can handle a larger vocabulary.

Acoustic Quality and Noise and Stress. Two characteristics can greatly degrade the acoustic quality of the voice and hence challenge the computer's ability to recognize it. First, a noisy environment will be disruptive, particularly if there is a high degree of spectral overlap between the signal and noise (e.g., recognizing the speaker's message against the chatter of other background conversation). Second, under conditions of stress, one's voice can change substantially in its physical characteristics, sometimes as much as doubling the fundamental frequency (the high-pitched "Help, emergency!"; Sulc, 1995). As we note in Chapter 13, stress appears to occur often under emergency conditions, and hence great caution should be given before designing systems in which voice control must be used as part of emergency procedures.

Compatibility. Finally, we have noted that voice control is less suitable or compatible for controlling continuous movement than are most of the available manual devices (Wickens, et al., 1985; Wickens, Vidulich, & Sandry-Garza, 1984). Consider, for example, the greater difficulties of trying to steer a car along a curvy road by saying "a little left, now a little more left," and so on.

Conclusion. Clearly all of these factors—the costs, the benefits, and the design cautions (like restricting vocabulary)—play off against each other in a way that makes it hard to say precisely when voice control will be better or worse than manual control. The picture is further complicated because of the development of sophisticated computer algorithms that are beginning to address the two major limitations of many current systems (continuous speech recognition and speaker dependence). However, even if such systems do successfully address these problems, they are likely to be expensive, and for many applications, the cheaper, simpler systems can be useful within the constraints described above.

CONTINUOUS CONTROL AND TRACKING

Our discussion of the positioning task focused on guiding a cursor to a fixed target, either through fairly direct hand movement (the touch screen or light pen) or as mediated by a control device (the trackball, joystick, or mouse). However, much of the world of both work and daily life is characterized by making a cursor or some corresponding system (e.g., vehicle) output follow or "track" a *continuously moving dynamic* target. This may involve tasks as mundane as bringing the fly swatter down on the moving pest or riding the bicycle around the curve, or as complex as guiding an aircraft through a curved flight path in the sky, guiding your viewpoint through a "virtual environment" or bringing the temperature of a nuclear reactor up to a target value through a carefully controlled trajectory. These cases, and many more are described by the generic task of *tracking* (Poulton, 1974; Wickens, 1986), that is, the task of making a system output correspond in time and space to a time-varying target input.

The Tracking Loop: Basic Elements

Figure 9.6 presents the basic elements of a tracking task. Each element receives a time-varying input and produces a corresponding time-varying output. These elements can be described within the context of automobile driving (Chapter 17), although it is important to think about how they may generalize to any number of different tracking tasks.

When driving an automobile, the *human operator* perceives a discrepancy or *error* between the desired state of the vehicle and its actual state. The car may have deviated from the center of the lane or may be pointing in a direction away from the road. The driver wishes to reduce this error function of time, $e(t)$. To do so, a force (actually a torque), $f(t)$, is applied to the steering wheel, or *control* device. This force in turn produces a rotation, $u(t)$, of the steering wheel itself, a rotation that we call the *control output*. (Note that our frame of reference here is the human. Hence, we use the term *output* from the human rather than *input* to the system.)

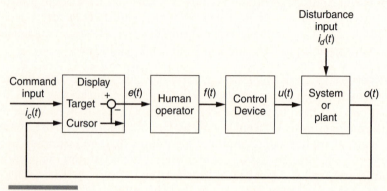

FIGURE 9.6
The tracking loop.

The relationship between the force applied and the steering-wheel-control output is defined as the *control dynamics,* and these dynamics are responsible for the proprioceptive feedback that the operator receives.

Movement of the wheel or control according to a given time function, $u(t)$, then causes the vehicle's actual position to move laterally on the highway. This movement is referred to as the *system output, o(t)*. As we have noted earlier in this chapter, when presented on a display, the representation of this output position is called the *cursor.* The relationship between control output, $u(t)$, and system response, $o(t)$, is defined as the *plant dynamics* or *system dynamics.* In discussing positioning control devices, we saw the difference between position and velocity system dynamics. If the driver is successful in the correction applied to the steering wheel, then the discrepancy between vehicle position on the highway, $o(t)$, and the desired, or "commanded," position at the center of the lane, $i_c(t)$, will be reduced. That is, the error, $e(t)$, will be reduced to 0. On a display, the symbol representing the input is called the *target.* The difference between the output and input signals is the error, $e(t)$, the starting point of our discussion. The good driver will respond in such a way as to keep $o(t) = i(t)$ or $e(t) = 0$. The system represented in Figure 9.6 is called a closed loop feedback control system (Powers, 1973)

Because errors in tracking stimulate the need for corrective responses, the operator need never respond at all as long as there is no error. This might happen while driving on a straight smooth highway on a windless day. However, errors typically arise from one of two sources. *Command inputs, $i_c(t)$,* are changes in the *target* that must be tracked. For example, if the road curves, it will generate an error for a vehicle traveling in a straight line and so will require a corrective response. *Disturbance inputs, $i_d(t)$,* are those applied directly to the system, for which the operator must compensate. For example, a wind gust that blows the car off the center of the lane is a disturbance input. So is an accidental movement of the steering wheel by the driver, as happened in the story at the beginning of the chapter.

The source of all information necessary to implement the corrective response is the *display* (see Chapter 7). For the automobile driver, the display is simply the field of view seen through the windshield, but for the aircraft pilot making an instrument landing, the display is represented by the instruments depicting pitch, roll, altitude, and course information. An important distinction may be drawn between *pursuit* and *compensatory* tracking displays (Fig. 9.7). A pursuit display presents an independent representation of movement of both the target and the cursor. Thus, the driver of a vehicle sees a pursuit display since movement of the automobile can be distinguished and viewed independently from the curvature of the road (the command input; Fig. 9.7a). A compensatory display presents only movement of the error relative to a fixed reference on the display. The display provides no indication of whether this error arose from a change in system output or command input (Roscoe, Corl, & Jensen, 1981). Flight navigation instruments are typically compensatory displays (Fig. 9.7b).

As we noted in Chapter 8, displays may contain *predictive* information regarding the future state of the system, a valuable feature if the system dynamics are sluggish. The automobile display is a kind of predictor because the current direction of

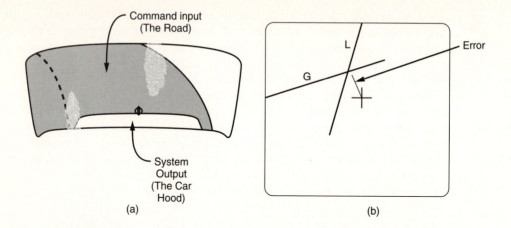

FIGURE 9.7

(a) A pursuit display (the automobile); (b) A compensatory display (the aircraft instrument landing system).

heading, relative to the vanishing point of the road, provides a prediction of the future lateral deviation.

Finally, tracking performance is typically measured in terms of *error*. It is calculated at each point in time as the absolute deviation and then is cumulated and averaged (divided by the number of sample points) over the duration of the tracking trial. Kelley (1968) discussed different methods of calculating tracking performance.

Now that we have seen the elements of the tracking task, which characterizes the human's efforts to make the system output match the command target input, we can ask what characteristics of the human-system interaction make tracking difficult (increased error or increased workload). With this knowledge in mind, it is then possible for the designer to intervene to try to improve tracking systems. As we will see, some of the problems lie in the tracking system itself, some lie within the human operator's processing limits, and some involve the interaction between the two.

The Input

Drawing a straight line on a piece of paper or driving the car down a straight stretch of road on a windless day are both examples of tracking tasks. There is a command target input and a system output (the pencil point or the vehicle position). But the input does not vary; hence, the task is easy. After you get the original course set, there is nothing to do but move forward, and you can drive fast (or draw fast) about as easily as you can drive (or draw) slowly. However, if the target line follows a wavy course, or if the road is curvy, there are corrections you have to make and uncertainty to process, and as a result both error and workload can increase if you try to move faster. This happens because the frequency of corrections you must make will increase with faster movement and the human's ability to generate a series of rapid responses to uncertain or unpredictable stimuli (wiggles in the line or highway) is limited. Hence, driving too fast on the curvy road, you will begin to deviate more from the center of the lane and your workload will be higher if you attempt to stay in the center. We refer to the properties of the input, which determine the frequency with which corrections must be issued as the *bandwidth* of the input. While the frequency of "wiggles" in a command input is one source of bandwidth, so too is the frequency of disturbances from a disturbance input like wind gusts (or drawing a straight line on the paper in a bouncing car).

In tracking tasks, we typically express the bandwidth in terms of the cycles per second (Hz) of the highest input frequency present in the command or disturbance input. It is very hard for people to perform tracking tasks with random-appearing input having a bandwidth above about 1 Hz.

High bandwidth inputs keep an operator very busy with visual sampling and motor control, but they do not involve very much cognitive complexity. The latter however is contributed by the *order* of a control system, to which we now turn.

Control Order

Position Control.   We have been introduced to the concept of control order in our discussion of positioning controls, when position and velocity control systems were contrasted (e.g., the mouse and the joystick, respectively). Thus, the *order* of a control system refers to whether a change in the position of the control device (by the human operator) leads to a change in the *position* (0-order), *velocity* (first-order), or *acceleration* (second-order) of the system output. Consider moving a pen across the paper or a pointer across the blackboard, twisting an old analog dial on your radio tuner to bring the station to a new frequency setting, or moving the computer mouse to position a cursor on the screen. In each case a new *position* of the control device leads to a new *position* of the system output. If you hold the control still, the system output will also be still. This is 0-order control (see Figure 9.8a).

Velocity Control.   Now consider the "scanner" on a typical digital car radio. Depressing the button (a new position) creates a constant rate of change or *velocity* of the frequency setting. In some controls, depressing the button harder or longer will lead to a proportionately greater velocity. This is a first-order control. As noted earlier in the chapter, most pointing device joysticks use velocity control. An analogous first-order control relation is between the *position* of your steering wheel (input) and the *rate of change* (velocity) of heading of your car (output). As shown in Figure 9.8b, a new steering wheel angle (position) brings about a constant rate of change of heading. A greater steering wheel angle leads to a tighter turn (greater rate of change of heading). In terms of integral calculus, the order of control corresponds to the number of time integrals between the input and output; that is, for first-order control:

$$O(t) = \int i(t)dt$$

Both 0 (position) and first- (velocity) order controls are important in designing manual control devices. Each has its costs and its benefits. To some extent the "which

$$O(t) = \int i(t)dt$$

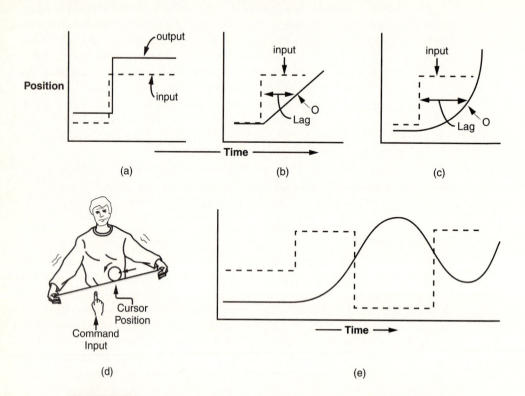

FIGURE 9.8

(a) Response of a 0-order system; (b) Response of a first-order system. Note the "lag;"
(c) Response of a second-order system. Note the greater lag; (d) A second-order system:
Tilt the board so the pop can lines up with the "command input" finger; (e) Overcorrection
and oscillations typical of control of second-order systems.

is best" question has an "it depends" answer. In part, this depends on the goals. If, on
the one hand, accurate positioning is very important (like positioning a cursor at a
point on a screen), then position control has its advantages, as we saw in Figure 9.3.
On the other hand, if following a moving target or traveling (moving forward) on a
path is the goal (matching velocity), then one can see the advantages of first-order velocity control. An important difference is that 0-order control often requires a lot of
physical effort to achieve repeated actions. Velocity control can be more economical
of effort because you just have to set the system to the appropriate velocity in the correct direction and let it go on till system output reaches the desired target.

Any control device that uses first-order dynamics should have a clearly defined
and easily reachable neutral point, at which no velocity is commanded to the cursor.
This is because stopping is a very frequent default state. This is the advantage of
spring-loaded joysticks for velocity control because the natural resting point is set to

give 0 velocity. It represents a problem when the mouse is configured as a first-order control system, since there is no natural 0 point on the mouse tablet. While first-order systems are effort conserving, as shown in Figure 9.8b, first-order systems tend to have a little more lag or delay between when the human commands an output to the device (applies a force) and when the system reaches its desired target position.

Acceleration Control.   Consider the astronaut who must maneuver a spacecraft into a precise position by firing thrust rockets. Because of the inertia of the craft, each rocket thrust will produce an *acceleration* of the craft for as long as the rocket is firing. The time course will look similar to that shown in Figure 9.8c. This, in general, is a *second-order* acceleration control system, described in the equation $o(t) = \int\int i(t)\, dt$. To give yourself an intuitive "feel" for second-order control, try rolling a pop can to a new position or command input, *i,* on a board (Figure 9.8d). Second-order systems are generally very difficult to control because they are both *sluggish* and *unstable.* The sluggishness can be seen in the greater lag in Figure 9.8c. As we will see, both of these properties require the operator to *anticipate* and *predict* (control based on the future, not the present), and, as we learned in Chapter 8, this is a cognitively demanding source of workload for the human operator.

Because second-order control systems are hard to control, they are rarely if ever intentionally designed into systems. However, a lot of systems that humans are asked to control have a sluggish accelerationlike response to a position input because of the mass and inertia of controlled elements in the physical world. As we saw, applying a new position to the thrust control on a spacecraft will cause it to accelerate (endlessly). Applying a new position to the elevators of an aircraft will (more or less) cause its altitude to accelerate upward or downward. Applying a new position to the steering wheel (a fixed lateral rotation) will cause the car's position, with regard to the center of a straight lane, to accelerate (at least initially). In some chemical or energy conversion processes discussed in Chapter 16, application of the input (e.g., added heat) yields a second-order response to the controlled variable. Hence, second-order systems are important for human factors practitioners to understand because of the things that designers or trainers can do to address their harmful effects (increased tracking error and workload) when humans must control them.

Recall that these harmful effects result because the second-order system is both sluggish and unstable. Its sluggishness means that the system does not move much when it is initially controlled (and the operator may not even see any initial feedback from the control movement; see Figure 9.8e). Operators then have to *anticipate* where and how fast the system output is going, and they may not do this well or at all (see Chapter 8). Thus, by the time the system output has "built up steam," it may be too late to "put on the brakes" or reverse the control input and stop it at the target. An overshoot will result, and when the operator tries to apply a reverse correction and unstable oscillations around the target will result (see Fig. 9.8e). When second-order control systems produce these sorts of responses in aviation, they are sometimes called *pilot-induced oscillations* (PIO), resulting because the pilot does not have a well enough formed mental model of the system dynamics, or cannot use the mental model fast enough, to judge and correct for the anticipated path of the vehicle.

There are three forms of solutions to the problems created by second-order systems, or for that matter any system that contains high lags. One solution, which should be recalled from Chapter 8, is the implementation of *predictive* displays, whose value in numerous sluggish vehicle control tasks (submarines, ships, heavy aircraft) has been well demonstrated, as well as in tasks involving the control of sluggish thermodynamic systems (e.g., nuclear power and process control plants; see Chapter 16).

Of course to be useful, predictive displays of where the system *will be x* seconds into the future should be accompanied by a *preview* of where the system *should be x* seconds into the future. This is the same as preview of the command input. Preview is like the visibility of the roadway ahead of the driver on a clear day in contrast to the lack of visibility in thick fog (preview absent). An aircraft display with both prediction and preview is shown in Figure 9.9 (Haskell & Wickens, 1995).

A second solution is to teach the tracker *strategies* of anticipation; in essence, teach where to look in order to predict the future. One of the best cues about where things *will be* in the future is to perceive *trend* information of where they *are going* right now; that is, attend to the current rate of change. For example, in driving, one of the best clues to where the vehicle will be (with regard to the center of the lane)

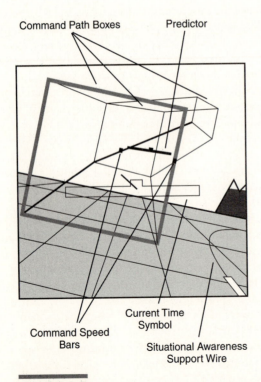

Command Path Boxes   Predictor

Command Speed
Bars

Current Time
Symbol

Situational Awareness
Support Wire

FIGURE 9.9

A predictor display for flight path control. (*Source:* Haskell, I. D., and Wickens, C. D., 1993. Two- and three-dimensional displays for aviation: A theoretical and empirical comparison. *International Journal of Aviation Psychology,* 3 [2].)

is where and how fast it is heading *now.* This latter information can be better gained by looking down the roadway to see if the direction of heading corresponds with the direction of the road than it can be by looking at the deviation immediately in front of the car. This is why expert drivers tend to scan farther down the road than novices (Mourant & Rockwell, 1972). They have learned that that is where they need to look in order to predict the car's trajectory farther ahead on the highway.

A third solution to the problem of these difficult higher order control task is to *automate,* and try to develop computer controls that will handle many of the higher order tracking tasks. This is what is going on in more advanced commercial and military aircraft, in which designers are trying to "reduce" the pilot's order of control down to first-order (and sometimes from third- down to second-order). We shall cover these issues of automation in Chapter 16, focusing on the costs as well as the benefits of automation.

Time Delays and Transport Lags

In the previous paragraphs we saw how higher order systems (and particularly second-order ones) had a lag (see Figs. 9.8b and c). Lags may sometimes occur in systems of lower order as well. For example, if one controls a 0-order system that has a "dead space," then any movement of the control device will not instantaneously produce a system output change. If one is controlling a vehicle on the moon from a workstation on Earth, then one's steering inputs will not be seen on the display until a few seconds later (the time to relay the commands to the vehicle and the vehicle camera to send the updated position back to Earth). When navigating through electronic spaces or "virtual environments" that must be rendered with time-consuming computer graphic routines, there is often a delay between moving the control device and updating the position or viewpoint of the displays (see Chapter 15). These time delays or "transport lags" produce the same problems of anticipation that we saw with higher order systems: lags require anticipation, which is a source of human workload and system error.

Gain

As we noted in discussing input devices, system gain describes how much output the system provides from a given amount of input. Hence, gain may be formally defined as the ratio $\Delta O/\Delta I,$ where Δ is a given change or difference in the relevant quantity. In a high-gain system, a lot of output is produced by a small change of input. A sports car is typically high gain because a small correction on the steering wheel produces a large change in output (change in heading). In contrast, the old sluggish station wagon typically has a pretty low gain.

Just as we noted in our discussion of the pointing task, whether high, low, or medium gain is "best" is somewhat task dependent. When system output must travel a long distance (or change by a large amount), high-gain systems are preferable because the large change can be achieved with little control effort (for a position control system) or in a rapid time (for a velocity control system). However, as we noted, when precise positioning is required, high-gain systems present problems of overshooting and undershooting or, as we see below, *instability.* Hence, low gain is preferable. As might be expected, gains in the midrange of values are generally best since they address both issues (reduce effort and maintain stability) to some degree (Wickens, 1986).

Stability

Now that we have introduced concepts of lag (due to higher system order or transport delay), gain, and bandwidth, we can discuss briefly one concept that is extremely important in the human factors of control systems—the notion of *stability*. When we discussed second-order systems, we gave the example of pilot induced oscillations resulting when the pilot first overshoots and then overcorrects in trying to reach the target altitude. This is an example of unstable behavior known as *closed-loop instability*. In fact, instability of this sort results from a particular combination of three factors:

1. There is a lag (somewhere in the total control loop in Figure 9.6 either from the system lag or from the Human Operator's response time).

2. The gain is too high (this high gain can either represent the system's gain—too much change for a given steering wheel deflection—or the human's gain—a tendency to "overcorrect" if there is an error).

3. The human is trying to correct too fast and is not waiting until the system output stabilizes before applying another corrective input. Technically this third factor results when the input bandwidth is high relative to the system lag, and the operator chooses to respond with corrections to all of the "wiggles" (i.e., does not "filter out" the high-frequency inputs).

Exactly how much of each of these quantities (bandwidth, gain, lag) are responsible for producing the unstable behavior is beyond the scope of this chapter, but there are good *models* of both the machine and the human that have been used to predict the conditions under which this unstable behavior will occur (McRuer, 1980; Wickens, 1986, 1992). This is, of course, a critical situation for a model to be able to predict.

Human factors engineers can offer five solutions that can be implemented to reduce closed-loop instability: (1) Lower the gain. (2) Reduce the lags (if possible). This might be done for example, by reducing the required complexity of graphics in a virtual reality system (Pausch, 1991). (3) Caution the operator to change strategy in such a way that he or she does not try to correct every input but filters the high-frequency ones, thereby reducing the bandwidth. (4) Change strategy to seek input that can anticipate and predict (like looking farther down the road when driving, and attending to heading). (5) Change strategy to go "open loop." This is the final tracking concept we shall discuss.

Open- Versus Closed-Loop Systems

In all of the examples we have described, we have implicitly assumed that the operator is perceiving an error and trying to correct it; that is, the "loop" depicted in Figure 9.6 is "closed." Suppose, however, that the operator did not try to correct the error but just "knew" where the system output needed to be and responded with just enough correction to the control device to produce it. Since the operator does not then need to perceive the error and therefore will not be looking at the system output, this is a situation akin to the "loop" in Figure 9.6 being broken (i.e., "opening the loop"). In open-loop behavior the operator is not, therefore, trying to correct for outputs that may be visible only after system lags. As a result, the operator will not fall prey to the evils of closed-loop instability. Of course open-loop behavior depends on the operator's knowledge of where the target will be and of how the system output will respond to his or her control input, that is, a well-developed mental model of the system dynamics (Chapter 6). Hence, open-loop behavior is typical only of trackers who are highly skilled in their domain.

Open-loop tracking might typify the process control operator (Chapter 16) who knows exactly how much the heat needs to be raised in a process to reach a new temperature, tweaks the control by precisely that amount, and walks away. It must characterize the skilled baseball hitter, who takes one quick sample of the fast ball's initial trajectory and knows exactly how to swing the bat to connect (in this case there is no time for closed-loop feedback to operate in such a way as to guide the response); it also characterizes the skilled computer user who does not need to wait for screen readout, prior to depressing each key in a complex sequence of commands. Of course such users still receive feedback *after* the skill is performed, feedback that will be valuable in learning or "fine tuning" the mental model (Chapter 18).

REMOTE MANIPULATION OR TELEROBOTICS

There are many circumstances in which continuous and direct human control is desirable but not feasible. Two examples are *remote manipulation,* such as when operators control an undersea or planetary explorer, and *hazardous manipulation,* as for example is involved in the manipulation of highly radioactive material. This task, which is sometimes known as *telerobotics* (Sheridan, 1997), possesses several distinct challenges, resulting because of the absence of direct viewing. The goal of the designer of such systems is to create a sense of "telepresence," that is, a sense that the operator is actually immersed within the environment and is directly controlling the manipulation as an extension of his or her arms and hands. Similar goals of creating a sense of presence have been sought by the designers of virtual reality systems (Durlach & Mavor, 1995; Barfield & Furness, 1995). Yet there are several control features of the situation that prevent this goal from being easily achieved in either telerobotics or virtual reality (Stassen & Smets, 1995).

Time Delay

Systems often encounter time delays between the manipulation of the control and the availability of visual feedback. In some cases these may be *transmission delays.* For example, as we have noted, the "round trip" delay between Earth and the moon is 5 seconds, for an operator on Earth carrying out remote manipulation on the moon. Sometimes the delays might simply result from the inherent sluggishness of high inertial systems that are being controlled. In still other cases the delays might result from the time it takes for a computer system to construct and update elaborate graphics imagery as the viewpoint is translated through or rotated within the environment. In all cases, as we have seen such delays present challenges to effective control.

Depth Perception and Image Quality

Teleoperation normally involves tracking or manipulating in three dimensions. Yet as we have seen in Chapter 4, human depth perception in 3-D displays is often less than adequate for precise judgment along the viewing axis of the display. One solution that has proven quite useful is the implementation of stereo (Chapter 8). The problem with stereo, however, lies in the fact that two cameras must be mounted and two separate dynamic images must be transmitted over what may be a very limited bandwidth channel, for example, a "tethered" cable connecting the robot on the ocean floor to the operator workstation in the vessel above. Similar constraints on the bandwidth may affect the quality or fuzziness of even a monoscopic image, a fact that could severely hamper the operator's ability to do fine coordinated movement. It is apparent that the tradeoff between image quality and image updating grows more severe as the behavior of the controlled robot becomes more dynamic.

Proprioceptive Feedback

While visual feedback is absolutely critical to such tasks, there are many circumstances in which proprioceptive or tactile feedback is of great importance (Durlach & Mavor, 1995). This is true because the remote manipulators are often designed so that they can produce extremely great forces, necessary, for example, to move heavy objects or rotate rusted parts. As a consequence, they are capable of doing great damage, unless they are very carefully controlled when they come in contact with or apply force to the object of manipulation. Consider, for example, the severe consequences that might result if a remote manipulator accidently punctured a container of radioactive material by squeezing too hard or stripped the threads while trying to unscrew a bolt. To prevent these sorts of accidents, designers would like to present the same tactile and proprioceptive sensations of touch, feel, pressure, and resistance that we experience as our hands grasp and manipulate objects. Yet it is extremely challenging to present such feedback effectively and intuitively, particularly when there are substantial "loop delays." Visual feedback of the forces applied must often be used to replace or augment the more natural tactile feedback.

The Solutions

Perhaps the most severe problem in many teleoperator systems is the time delay. As we have seen, the most effective solution here is to reduce the delay. When the delay is imposed by graphics complexity, it may be feasible to sacrifice some complexity. While this may lower the reality and "sense of presence," it is a move that can improve usability (Pausch, 1991).

A second effective solution is to develop predictive displays that are able to anticipate the future motion and position of the manipulator on the basis of its present state and the operator's current control actions and future intentions (see Chapter 8). While such prediction tools have proven to be quite useful (Bos, Stassen, & van Lunteren, 1995), they are only as effective as the quality of the control laws of system dynamics that they embody. Furthermore, the system will not allow effective prediction (i.e., preview) of a randomly moving target, and without reliable preview, many of the advantages of prediction are gone.

A third solution is to avoid the delayed feedback problem altogether by implementing a computer model of the system dynamics (without the delay) allowing the operator to implement the required manipulation in "fast time" off line, relying on the now instant feedback from the computer model (Sheridan, 1997). When the operator is then satisfied that he or she has created the maneuver effectively, this stored trajectory can be passed on to the real system. This solution has the problem that it places fairly intensive demands on computer power and, of course, will not be effective if the target environment itself happened to change before the planning manipulation was implemented.

Clearly, as we consider designs in which the human plans an action but the computer is then assigned responsibility for carrying those actions out, we are crossing the boundary from manual control to automated control, an issue we will discuss in depth in Chapter 16. We also note two other important aspects of control that will be covered in other chapters: process control because of its high levels of automation, and its many facets that have little to do with actual control (e.g., monitoring and diagnosis) will be covered in Chapter 16; and air traffic control, which also has many human factors aspects that go beyond the control features discussed here, will be covered in the chapter on transportation (Chapter 17). Finally, as we have noted, many characteristics of telerobotics are similar to those being addressed in the implementation of *virtual reality* systems, which will be discussed again in Chapter 15.

REFERENCES

Baber, C. (1997). *Beyond the desktop.* San Diego, CA: Academic Press.

Barfield, W., and Furness, T.A. III (eds.) (1995). *Virtual environments and advanced interface design.* New York: Oxford University Press.

Barton, P.H. (1986). The development of a new keyboard for outward sorting foreign mail. *IMechE,* 57–63.

Bos, J.F.T., Stassen, H.G., and van Lunteren, A. (1995). Aiding the operator in the manual control of a space manipulator. *Control Eng. Practice, 3*(2), 223–230.

Card, S.K., English, W.K., and Burr, B.J. (1978). Evaluation of mouse, rate-controlled isometric joystick, step keys, and task keys for text selection on a CRT. *Ergonomics, 21*(8), 601–613.

Card, S., Moran, T.P., and Newell, A. (1983). *The psychology of human-computer interactions.* Hillsdale, NJ: Erlbaum.

Drury, C. (1975). Application to Fitts' Law to foot pedal design. *Human Factors, 17,* 368–373.

Durlach, N.I., and Mavor, A. (eds.) (1995). *Virtual reality: Scientific and technological challenges.* Washington, DC: National Academy Press.

Epps, B.W. (1987). A comparison of cursor control devices on a graphic editing task. *Proceedings of the 31st Annual Meeting of the Human Factors Society* (pp. 442–446). Santa Monica, CA: Human Factors Society.

Fitts, P.M. (1954). The information capacity of the human motor system in controlling the amplitude of movement. *Journal of Experimental Psychology, 47,* 381–391.

Fitts, P.M. and Posner, M.I. (1967). *Human Performance.* Belmont, CA: Brooks/Cole.

Fitts, P.M., and Seeger, C.M. (1953). S-R compatibility: Spatial characteristics of stimulus and response codes. *Journal of Experimental Psychology, 46,* 199–210.

Gopher, D., and Raij, D. (1988). Typing with a two hand chord keyboard—Will the QWERTY become obsolete? *IEEE Trans. in System, Man, and Cybernetics, 18,* 601–609.

Haskell, I.D., and Wickens, C.D. (1993). Two- and three-dimensional displays for aviation: A theoretical and empirical comparison. *International Journal of Aviation Psychology, 3*(2), 87–109.

Hick, W.E. (1952). On the rate of gain of information. *Quarterly Journal of Experimental Psychology, 4,* 11–26.

Hyman, R. (1953). Stimulus information as a determinant of reaction time. *Journal of Experimental Psychology, 45,* 423–432.

Jagacinski, R.J. (1989). Target acquisition: Performance measures, process models, and design implications. In G.R. McMillan, D. Beevis, E. Salas, M.H. Strub, R. Sutton, and L. Van Breda (eds.), *Applications of human performance models to system design* (pp. 135–150). New York: Plenum Press.

Jellinek, H.D., and Card, S.K. (1990). Powermice and user performance (pp. 213–220). *CHI'90.* New York: Association for Computing Machinery.

Kelley, C.R. (1968). *Manual and automatic control.* New York: Wiley.

Langolf, C.D., Chaffin, D.B., and Foulke, S.A. (1976). An investigation of Fitts' law using a wide range of movement amplitudes. *Journal of Motor Behavior, 8,* 113–128.

Martin, G. (1989). The utility of speech input in user-computer interfaces. *International Journal of Man-Machine System Study, 18,* 355–376.

McMillan, G., Eggleston, R.G., and Anderson, T.R. (1997). Nonconventional Controls. In G. Salvendy (ed.) *Handbook of Human Factors and Ergonomics.* New York: Wiley.

McRuer, D. (1980). Human dynamics in man-machine systems. *Automatica, 16,* 237–253.

Mourant, R.R., and Rockwell, T.H. (1972). Strategies of visual search by novice and expert drivers. *Human Factors, 14,* 325–336.

Norman, D. (1988). *The psychology of everyday things.* New York: Basic Books.

Norman, D., & Fisher, D. (1982). Why alphabetic keyboards are not easy to use. *Human Factors, 24,* 509–520.

Pausch, R. (1991). Virtual reality on five dollars a day. *Computer Human Interaction (CHI) Proceedings* (pp. 265–269). New York: American Society for Computer Machinery.

Poulton, E.C. (1974). *Tracking skill and manual control.* New York: Academic Press.

Powers, W.T. (1973). *Behavior: The Control of Perception.* New York: Aldine de Gruyter.

Richardson, R.M.M., Telson, R.U., Koch, C.G., and Chrysler, S.T. (1987). Evaluations of conventional, serial, and chord keyboard options for mail encoding. *Proceedings of the 31st Annual Meeting of the Human Factors Society* (pp. 911–915). Santa Monica, CA: Human Factors Society.

Roscoe, S.N., Corl, L., and Jensen, R.S. (1981). Flight display dynamics revisited. *Human Factors, 23*, 341–353.

Seibel, R. (1964). Data entry through chord, parallel entry devices. *Human Factors, 6*, 189–192.

Sheridan, T. (1997). Supervisory control. In G. Salvendy (ed.), *Handbook of human factors.* New York: Wiley.

Stassen, H.G., and Smets, G.J.F. (1995). Telemanipulation and telepresence.

Sulc, S. (1996). Speech characteristics in the course of coping with in-flight emergencies. In *Situation Awareness: Limitations and Enhancements in the Aviation Environment.* NATD AGARD CP-575 Neuilly-Sur-Seine, France: AGARD.

Wickens, C.D. (1986) The effects of control dynamics on performance. In K.R. Boff, L. Kaufman, and J.P. Thomas (eds.), *Handbook of Perception and Performance, Vol. II* (pp. 39-1–39-60). New York. Wiley.

Wickens, C.D. (1992). *Engineering psychology and human performance* (2nd ed.). New York: HarperCollins.

Wickens, C.D., Sandry, D., and Vidulich, M. (1983). Compatibility and resource competition between modalities of input, central processing, and output: Testing a model of complex task performance. *Human Factors, 25*, 227–248.

Wickens, C.D., Vidulich, M., and Sandry-Garza, D. (1984). principles of S-C-R compatibility with spatial and verbal tasks: The role of display-control location and voice-interactive display-control interfacing. *Human Factors, 26*, 533–543.

Wickens, C.D., Zenyuh, J., Culp, V., and Marshak, W. (1985). Voice and manual control in dual task situations. *Proceedings of the 29th Annual Meeting of the Human Factors Society.* Santa Monica, CA: Human Factors Society.

CHAPTER 10

Engineering Anthropometry and Work-Space Design

We do not like to wear clothes that do not fit our body. We cannot walk steadily if our shoes are of wrong size. We look awkward and feel terrible when we sit on a chair that is either too wide or too narrow. We cannot reach and grasp an object if it is too high on a wall or too far on a table.

These descriptions seem to offer no new insight to any of us because they all seem to be common sense. We all seem to know that the physical dimensions of a product or workplace should fit the body dimensions of the user. However, some of us may be surprised to learn that inadequate dimensions are one of the most common causes of error, fatigue, and discomfort because designers often ignore or forget this requirement or do not know how to put it into design.

In some power plants and chemical processing plants, displays are located so high that operators must stand on stools or ladders in order to read the displayed values. In the cockpits of some U.S. Navy jet aircrafts, 10 percent of the controls could not be reached even by the tallest aviators, and almost 70 percent of the emergency controls were beyond the reach of the shortest aviators. To find some examples around us, one simply needs to look around and pay attention to the desks, chairs, and other furnishings in a classroom or a home. Are they well designed from the human factors point of view? Try to answer this question now, and then answer it again after finishing studying this chapter.

In this chapter we introduce the basic concepts of a scientific discipline called anthropometry, which provides the fundamental basis and quantitative data for matching the physical dimensions of workplaces and products with the body dimensions of intended users. We also describe some general principles and useful rules-of-thumb for applying anthropometric information in design.

Anthropometry is the study and measurement of human body dimensions. The word *anthropometry* is derived from two Greek words: *anthropos* ("man") and *metron* ("measure"). The size and the proportions of the human body have been the subject of study for artists, anatomists, doctors, and land measurers for a long time. The ancient Egyptians used the distance from elbow to tip of the longest finger as a standard unit of length called the royal cubit (around 52 cm), which was used to calculate sculpture and relief dimensions as well as land areas. Adolphe Quetelet, a Belgian statistician, first applied statistics to anthropological data in the middle of the nineteenth century, and this was regarded as the beginning of modern anthropometry.

In designing workplaces, equipments, and various products for human use, engineers have gradually realized the importance of anthropometric information. The measurement and use of anthropometric data in engineering design is the primary concern of engineering anthropometry. Currently, anthropometric data are extensively used by design engineers and human factors professionals to specify the physical dimensions of products, tools, and workplaces to maximize the match between the physical dimensions of the designed products and workplaces and the body dimensions of the users.

Anthropometric data are used to develop design guidelines for heights, clearances, grips, and reaches of workplaces and equipments for the purpose of accommodating the body dimensions of the potential work force. Examples include the dimensions of workstations for standing or seated work, production machinery, supermarket checkout counters, and aisles and corridors. The work force includes men and women who are tall or short, large or small, strong or weak, as well as those who are physically handicapped or have health conditions that limit their physical capacity.

Anthropometric data are also applied in the design of consumer products such as clothes, automobiles, bicycles, furniture, hand tools, and so on. Because products are designed for various types of consumers, an important design requirement is to select and use the most appropriate anthropometric data base in design. Grieve and Pheasant (1982) notes that "as a rule of thumb, if we take the smallest female and the tallest male in a population, the male will be 30–40 percent taller, 100 percent heavier, and 500 percent stronger." Clearly, products designed on the basis of male anthropometric data would not be appropriate for many female consumers. Similarly, the design of clothes and bicycles for children should not be based on the anthropometric measurements of adults or elderly. When designing for an international market, applying the data collected from one country to other regions with significant size differences will be inappropriate.

In ergonomics, another use of anthropometric information is found in occupational biomechanics, the subject of discussion of the next chapter. Anthropometric data are used in biomechanical models in conjunction with information about external loads to assess the stress imposed on worker's joints and muscles during the performance of work.

Because of the importance of considering human variability in design, this chapter starts with a discussion of the major sources of human variability and how statistics can help designers analyze human variability and use this information in design. We then describe briefly some of the devices and methods used for anthropometric measurements and the major types of anthropometric data. Some general procedures of applying anthropometric data in design are then introduced, followed by a discussion of the general principles for work-space design. Design of standing and seated work areas is discussed in the last section.

HUMAN VARIABILITY AND STATISTICS
Human Variability

Human body dimensions vary considerably with age, health condition, sex, race or ethnic group, occupation, and so on. Clearly, the natural variations of human physical characteristics have important implications for the way products, devices, and workplaces are designed. In this section we describe some of the major sources of variability.

Age Variability. Many body dimensions change as a function of age. Everyone knows that the stature of a person changes quickly from childhood to adolescence. In fact, a number of studies have compared the stature of people at each year of age. The data indicate stature increases to about age 20 to 25 (Roche & Davila, 1972; VanCott & Kinkade, 1972) and starts to decrease after about age 35 to 40, and women show more shrinkage than men (Trotter & Gleser, 1951; VanCott & Kinkade, 1972). Unlike stature, some other body dimensions such as weight and chest circumference may increase through age 60 before declining.

Sex Variability. Adult men are, on the average, taller and larger than adult women. However, twelve-year-old girls are, on the average, taller and heavier than their male counterparts because girls see their maximum growth rate from ages 10 to 12 (about 2.5 in./year), whereas boys see theirs around ages 13 to 15 (about 2.7 in./year). Girls continue to show noticeable growth each year until about age 17, whereas the growth rate for boys tapers off gradually until about age 20 (Stout, Damon, McFarland, & Roberts, 1960). On the average, adult female dimensions are about 92 percent of the corresponding adult male values (Annis, 1978). However, significant differences exist in the magnitude of the differences between males and females on the various dimensions. Although adult men are, on the average, larger than adult women on most dimensions, some dimensions such as hip and thigh measurements do not show major differences between men and women, and women exceed men on a number of dimensions such as skinfold thickness.

Racial and Ethnic Group Variability. Body size and proportions vary greatly between different racial and ethnic groups and populations and nationalities. The tallest people in the world are the Northern Nilotes of southern Sudan in Africa, who average about 6 feet tall. The shortest people are the pygmy people of central Africa with an average stature of about 4.5 feet (Roberts, 1975). Anthropometric surveys of black and white males in the U.S. Air Force show that their average height was identical, but blacks tended to have longer arms and legs and shorter torsos than whites (Long & Churchill, 1965; NASA, 1978). Comparisons of the U.S. Air Force data with the Japanese Air Force data (Yokohori, 1972) found that the Japanese were shorter in stature, but their average sitting height did not differ much from the American data. Similar differences were also found between the

American, the French, and the Italian anthropometric data. On the basis of these differences, Ashby (1979) states that if a piece of equipment was designed to fit 90 percent of the male U.S. population, it would fit roughly 90 percent of Germans, 80 percent of Frenchmen, 65 percent of Italians, 45 percent of Japanese, 25 percent of Thai, and 10 percent of Vietnamese.

Occupational Variability. Differences in body size and dimensions can be easily observed between people working in different occupational groups. Professional basketball players are much taller than most American males. Ballet dancers tend to be thinner than average. Existing data show that truck drivers tend to be taller and heavier than average (Sanders, 1977), and coal miners appear to have larger torso and arm circumferences (Ayoub et al., 1982). Occupational variability can result from a number of factors including the type and amount of physical activity involved in the job, the special physical requirements of certain occupations, and the self-evaluation and self-selection of individuals in making career choices.

Generational or Secular Variability. Annis (1978) graphed the trend of change in stature of the American population since 1840 and noted that there has been a growth in stature of about 1 cm per decade since the early 1920s. Improved nutrition and living conditions are offered as some of the possible reasons for this growth. However, it appears that this trend toward increasing stature and size is leveling off (Hamil et al., 1976). Griener and Gordon (1990) examined the secular trends in 22 body dimensions of male U.S. Army soldiers and found that some dimensions still show a clear trend of growth (e.g., body weight and shoulder breath), while others are not changing considerably (e.g., leg length).

Transient Diurnal Variability. Kroemer (1987) notes that person's body weight varies by up to 1 kg per day because of changes in body water content. The stature of a person may be reduced by up to 5 cm at the end of the day, mostly because of the effects of gravitational force on a person's posture and the thickness of spinal disks. Measuring posture in different positions also may yield different results. For example, leaning erect against a wall may increase stature by up to 2 cm as opposed to free standing. Chest circumference changes with the cycle of breathing. Clothes can also change body dimensions.

Statistical Analysis

In order to deal with these variabilities in engineering design, an anthropometric dimension is analyzed as a statistical distribution, rather than a single value. Normal distribution (also called Gaussian distribution in some science and engineering disciplines) is the most commonly used statistical distribution because it approximates most anthropometric data quite closely.

Normal Distribution. The normal distribution can be visualized as the normal curve, shown in Figure 10.1 as a symmetric, bell-shaped curve. The mean and the standard deviation are two key parameters of the normal distribution. The mean is a measure of central tendency that tells us about the concentration of a group of scores on a scale of measurement. The mean (most often referred to as the average in our everyday conversations) is calculated as the sum of all the individual measurements divided by the sample size (the number of people measured). To put it in a formula form, we have,

$$M = \Sigma(X_i)/N,$$

where

M is the mean of the sample,
X_i represents the ith measurement,
N is the sample size.

The standard deviation is a measure of the degree of dispersion or scatter in a group of measured scores. The standard deviation, s, is calculated with the following formula:

$$s = \sqrt{\frac{\Sigma (X_i - M)^2}{N - 1}}$$

In Figure 10.1, the value of the mean determines the position of the normal curve along the horizontal axis, and the value of the standard deviation determines whether the normal curve has a more peaked or flat shape. A normal curve with a smaller mean is always located to the left of a normal curve with a larger mean. A small value of the standard deviation produces a "peaked" normal curve, indicating that most of the measurements are close to the mean value. Conversely, a large value of the standard deviation suggests that the measured data are more scattered from the mean.

Percentiles. In engineering design, anthropometric data are most often used in percentiles. A percentile value of an anthropometric dimension represents the percentage of the population with a body dimension of a certain size or smaller. This information is particularly important in design because it helps us estimate the percentage of a user population that will be accommodated by a specific design. For example, if the width of a seat surface is designed using the 50th percentile value of the hip breadth of U.S. males, then we can estimate that about 50 percent of U.S. males (those with narrower hips) can expect to have their hips fully supported by this type of seat surface, whereas the other 50 percent (those with wider hips) cannot.

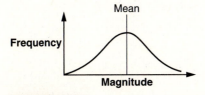

FIGURE 10.1
A graphical representation of the normal distribution.

For normal distributions, the 50th-percentile value is equivalent to the mean of the distribution. If a distribution is not normally distributed, the 50th-percentile value may not be identical to the mean. However, for practical design purposes, we often assume that the two values are identical or approximately the same, just as we assume that most anthropometric dimensions are normally distributed, though they may not be so in reality.

For normal distributions, percentiles can be easily calculated by using Table 10.1 and the following formula together:

$$X = M + F \times s,$$

where

X is the percentile-value being calculated,
M is the mean (the 50th percentile value) of the distribution,
s is the standard deviation,
F is the multiplication factor corresponding to the required percentile, which is the number of standard deviations to be subtracted from or added to the mean. F can be found in Table 10.1.

ANTHROPOMETRIC DATA

Measurement Devices and Methods

Many of the body dimensions can be measured with simple devices. Tapes can be used to measure circumferences, contours, and curvature, as well as straight lines. An anthropometer, which is a straight graduated rod with one sliding and one fixed arm, can be used to measure the distance between two clearly identifiable body landmarks. The spreading caliper has two curved branches joined in a hinge. The distance between the tips of the two branches is read on a scale attached on the caliper. A small sliding caliper can be used for measuring short distances, such

TABLE 10.1 Multiplication Factors for Percentile Calculation

Percentile	F
1th	−2.326
5th	−1.645
10th	−1.282
25th	−0.674
50th	−0
75th	+0.674
90th	+1.282
95th	+1.645
99th	+2.326

as hand length and hand breadth. Boards with holes of varying diameters drilled
on it can be used to measure finger and limb diameters. Figure 10.2 contains a set
of basic anthropometric instruments.

Use of anthropometric data collected by different measurers at different locations and in different time periods requires standardization of measuring methods. Body dimension must follow standard definitions and must be measured with
standardized procedures. Clearly identifiable body landmarks and fixed points in
space are usually used to define the various measurements. For example, *stature*
is defined as the distance between the standing surface (often the floor) and the top
of the head, whereas *hand length* is the distance from the tip of the middle finger
of the right hand to the base of the thumb.

The person being measured (often called the subject) is required to adopt a
standard posture specified by a measurer, who applies simple devices on the body
of the subject to obtain the measurements. For most measurements, the subject is
asked to adopt an upright straight posture, with body segments either in parallel
with each other or at 90° to each other. For example, the subject may be asked to

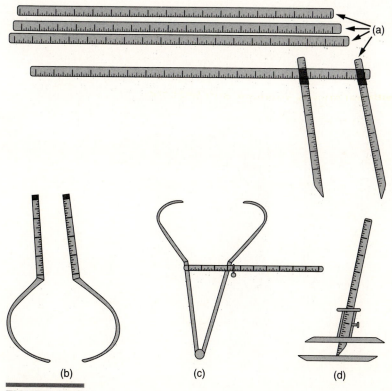

FIGURE 10.2

A basic set of anthropometric measuring instruments. (a) anthropometer with straight
branches, (b) curved branches for anthropometer, (c) Spreading calipers, (d) and sliding
compass.

"stand erect, heels together; butt, shoulder blades, and back of head touching a wall . . ." (Kroemer, 1987). The subject usually does not wear clothes and shoes. For seated measurements, the subject is asked to sit in a way that the thighs are horizontal, the lower legs vertical, and the feet flat on their horizontal support.

The Morant technique is a commonly used conventional measurement technique. This technique uses a set of grids that are usually attached on two vertical surfaces meeting at right angles. (Fig. 10.3). The subject is placed in front of the surfaces, and the body landmarks are projected onto the grids for anthropometric measurements.

Photographic methods, filming and videotaping techniques, use of multiple cameras and mirrors, holography and laser techniques are some of the major measurement techniques that have appeared in the past few decades. They continue to be used and improved for various design and research purposes.

To avoid potential ambiguity in interpretation, the following terms are defined and used in anthropometry (Kroemer, 1987):

Height: A straight-line, point-to-point vertical measurement.
Breadth: A straight-line, point-to-point horizontal measurement running across the body or segment.
Depth: A straight-line, point-to-point horizontal measurement running fore-aft the body.

FIGURE 10.3
Grid system used in anthropometric measurement.

Distance: A straight-line, point-to-point measurement between body landmarks.
Circumference: A closed measurement following a body contour, usually not
   circular.
Curvature: A point-to-point measurement following a body contour, usually
   neither circular nor closed.

Civilian and Military Data

Large-scale anthropometric surveys are time-consuming, labor-intensive, and expensive to carry out. Not surprisingly, significant gaps exist in the world anthropometric database. Most anthropometric surveys were carried out with special
populations such as pilots or military personnel. Civilian data either do not exist
for some populations or are very limited in scope. Much of the civilian data from
the U.S. and some other countries were collected many years ago and thus may not
be representative of the current user population.

Several large-scale surveys of civilian populations were carried out a few
decades ago. O'Brien and Sheldon (1941) conducted a survey of about ten thousand civilian women for garment sizing purposes. The National Center for Health
Statistics conducted two large-scale surveys of civilian men and women, the first
of which was conducted from 1960 to 1962 and measured 3,091 men and 3,581
women, and the second was from 1971 to 1974 and measured 13,645 civilians. Two
relatively small-scale surveys were carried out recently, one of which was the
Eastman Kodak Company's (1983) survey of about 100 men and 100 women and
the other was the Marras and Kim's (1993) survey of 384 males and 125 female of
industrial workers.

Clearly, these surveys of civilian populations were either rather outdated or
very limited in scope. Although measurements of body dimensions of military
personnel are most extensive and up-to-date, there may exist significant differences between the military and civilian populations. For example, Marras and Kim
(1993) found that significant differences exist in weight and abdominal dimensions between the industrial and military data. An industrial worker of 95th-per-
centile weight is much heavier than the 95th-percentile U.S. Army soldier.
However, 5th-percentile female industrial workers are slightly lighter than U.S.
Army women at the same percentile value.

Due to the lack of reliable anthropometric information on civilian populations in the United States and worldwide, the current practice in ergonomic design is to use military data as estimates of the body dimensions of the civilian
population. However, the documented differences between civilian and military
anthropometric data suggest that designers need to be cautious of any potential
undesirable consequences of using these estimates and be ready to make necessary
adjustments accordingly in design. Table 10.2 contains a sample of the anthropometric data obtained largely on U.S. Air Force and Army men and women (Clauser
et al., 1972; NASA, 1978; White & Churchill, 1971). The dimensions in Table 10.2
are depicted in Figure 10.4 and Figure 10.5.

TABLE 10.2 Anthropometric Data (unit: inches)

Measurement	Males 50th percentile	±1S.D.	Females 50th percentile	±1S.D.	Population Percentiles, 50/50 Males/Females 5th	50th	95th
Standing							
1. Forward Functional Reach							
a. includes body depth							
at shoulder	32.5	1.9	29.2	1.5	27.2	30.7	35.0
	(31.2)	(2.2)	(28.1)	(1.7)	(25.7)	(29.5)	(34.1)
b. Acromial Process to							
Function Pinch	26.9	1.7	24.6	1.3	22.6	25.6	29.3
c. Abdominal Extension to							
Functional Pinch	(24.4)	(3.5)	(23.8)	(2.6)	(19.1)	(24.1)	(29.3)
2. Abdominal Extension Depth	9.1	0.8	8.2	0.8	7.1	8.7	10.2
3. Waist Height	41.9	2.1	40.0	2.0	37.4	40.9	44.7
	(41.3)	(2.1)	(38.8)	(2.2)	(35.8)	(39.9)	(44.5)
4. Tibial Height	17.9	1.1	16.5	0.9	15.3	17.2	19.4
5. Knuckle Height	29.7	1.6	28.0	1.6	25.9	28.8	31.9
6. Elbow Height	43.5	1.8	40.4	1.4	38.0	42.0	45.8
	(45.1)	(2.5)	(42.2)	(2.7)	(38.5)	(43.6)	(48.6)
7. Shoulder Height	56.6	2.4	51.9	2.7	48.4	54.4	59.7
	(57.6)	(3.1)	(56.3)	(2.6)	(49.8)	(55.3)	(61.6)
8. Eye Height	64.7	2.4	59.6	2.2	56.8	62.1	67.8
9. Stature	68.7	2.6	63.8	2.4	60.8	66.2	72.0
	(69.9)	(2.6)	(64.8)	(2.8)	(61.1)	(67.1)	(74.3)
10. Functional Overhead Reach	82.5	3.3	78.4	3.4	74.0	80.5	86.9
Seated							
11. Thigh Clearance Height	5.8	0.6	4.9	0.5	4.3	5.3	6.5
12. Elbow Rest Height	9.5	1.3	9.1	1.2	7.3	9.3	11.4
13. Midshoulder Height	24.5	1.2	22.8	1.0	21.4	23.6	26.1
14. Eye Height	31.0	1.4	29.0	1.2	27.4	29.9	32.8
15. Sitting Height, Normal	34.1	1.5	32.2	1.6	32.0	34.6	37.4
16. Functional Overhead Reach	50.6	3.3	47.2	2.6	43.6	48.7	54.8
17. Knee Height	21.3	1.1	20.1	1.0	18.7	20.7	22.7
18. Popliteal Height	17.2	1.0	16.2	0.7	15.1	16.6	18.4
19. Leg Length	41.4	1.9	39.6	1.7	37.3	40.5	43.9
20. Upper-Leg Length	23.4	1.1	22.6	1.0	21.1	23.0	24.9
21. Buttocks-to-Popliteal Length	19.2	1.0	18.9	1.2	17.2	19.1	20.9
22. Elbow-to-Fist Length	14.2	0.9	12.7	1.1	12.6	14.5	16.2
	(14.6)	(1.2)	(13.0)	(1.2)	(11.4)	(13.8)	(16.2)
23. Upper-Arm Length	14.5	0.7	13.4	0.4	12.9	13.8	15.5
	(14.6)	(1.0)	(13.3)	(0.8)	(12.1)	(13.8)	(16.0)
24. Shoulder Breadth	17.9	0.8	15.4	0.8	14.3	16.7	18.8
25. Hp Breadth	14.0	0.9	15.0	1.0	12.8	14.5	16.3

TABLE 10.2 (continued)

Measurement	Males		Females		Population Percentiles, 50/50 Males/Females		
	50th percentile	±1S.D.	50th percentile	±1S.D.	5th	50th	95th
Foot							
26. Foot Length	10.5	0.5	9.5	0.4	8.9	10.0	11.2
27. Foot Breadth	3.9	0.2	3.5	0.2	3.2	3.7	4.2
Hand							
28. Hand Thickness, Metacarpal III	1.3	0.1	1.1	0.1	1.0	1.2	1.4
29. Hand Length	7.5	0.4	7.2	0.4	6.7	7.4	8.0
30. Digit Two Length	3.0	0.3	2.7	0.3	2.3	2.8	3.3
31. Hand Breadth	3.4	0.2	3.0	0.2	2.8	3.2	3.6
32. Digit One Length	5.0	0.4	4.4	0.4	3.8	4.7	5.6
33. Breadth of Digit One Interphalangeal Joint	0.9	0.05	0.8	0.05	0.7	0.8	1.0
34. Breadth of Digit Three Interphalangeal Joint	0.7	0.05	0.6	0.04	0.6	0.7	0.8
35. Grip Breadth, Inside Diameter	1.9	0.2	1.7	0.1	1.5	1.8	2.2
36. Hand Spread, Digit One to to Two, 1st Phalangeal Joint	4.9	0.9	3.9	0.7	3.0	4.3	6.1
37. Hand Spread, Digit One to Two, 2nd Phalangeal Joint	4.1	0.7	3.2	0.7	2.3	3.6	5.0
Head							
38. Head Breadth	6.0	0.2	5.7	0.2	5.4	5.9	6.3
39. Interpupillary Breadth	2.4	0.2	2.3	0.2	2.1	2.4	2.6
40. Biocular Breadth	3.6	0.2	3.6	0.2	3.3	3.6	3.9
Other Measurements							
41. Flexion-Extension, Range of Motion of Wrist, Degrees	134	19	141	15	108	138	166
42. Ulnar-Radial Range of Motion of Wrist, Degrees	60	13	67	14	41	63	87
43. Weight, in pounds	183.4	33.2	146.3	30.7	105.3	164.1	226.8

Source: Eastman Kodak Company, 1983.

Structural and Functional Data

Depending on how they are collected, anthropometric data can be classified into two types: Structural data and functional data. Structural data are also called static data; functional data are also called dynamic data. The two types of data serve different purposes in engineering design.

Structural anthropometric data are measurements of the body dimensions taken with the body in standard and still (static) positions. Examples include the

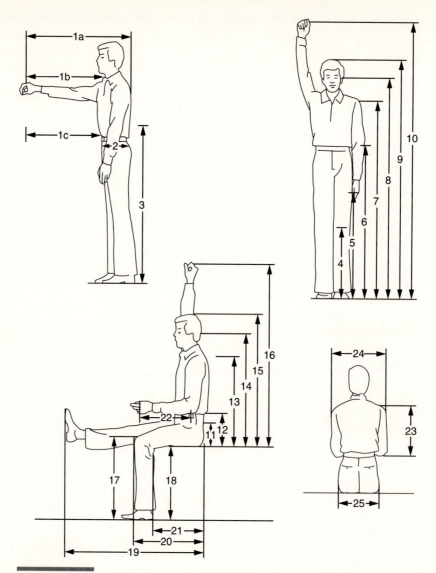

FIGURE 10.4

Anthropometric measures: standing and sitting. (*Source:* Eastman Kodak Company, 1986. *Ergonomic Design for People at Work,* Vol. 1. New York: Van Nostrand Reinhold.)

stature (the height of person), the shoulder breadth, the waist circumference, the length of the forearm, and the width of the hand.

Functional anthropometric data are obtained when the body adopts various working postures (i.e., when the body segments move with respect to standard reference points in space). For example, the area that can be reached by the right hand of a standing person defines a "standing reach envelope" of the right hand, which provides critical information for work-space design for right-handed standing workers.

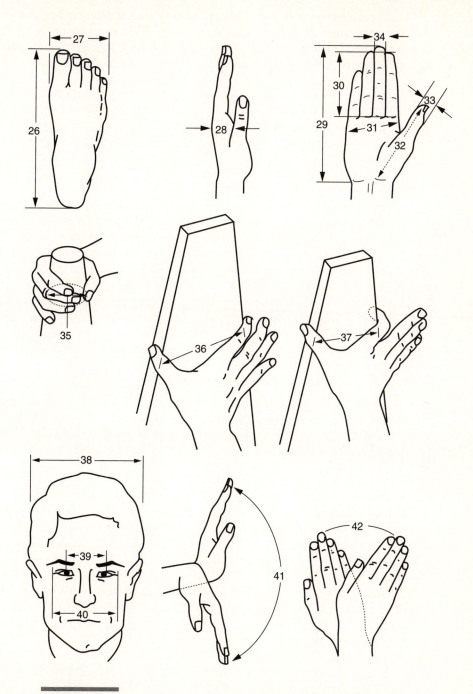

FIGURE 10.5

Anthropometric measures: hand, face, and foot. (*Source:* Eastman Kodak Company, 1986. *Ergonomic Design for People at Work,* Vol. 1. New York: Van Nostrand Reinhold.)

Most anthropometric data are static, although work activities can be more accurately represented by dynamic data. Because standard methods do not exist that allow one to convert static into dynamic data, the following procedure suggested by Kroemer (1983) may be useful for designers to make estimates:

1. Heights (stature, eye, shoulder, hip) should be reduced by 3 percent.
2. Elbow height requires no change or an increase of up to 5 percent if elbow needs to be elevated for the work.
3. Forward and lateral reach distances should be decreased by 30 percent if easy reach is desirable, and they can be increased by 20 percent if shoulder and trunk motions are allowed.

It should be noted here that some anthropometric dimensions are highly correlated with each other. For example, a tall person is likely to have long legs and be heavier than a short person. But some dimensions are not highly correlated. It appears, for example, that a person's stature says little about the breadth of that person's head. Detailed information about the correlation among various body dimensions can be found in Roebuck, Kroemer, and Thomson (1975).

Another issue that needs to be emphasized here is that it is very unlikely that one can find an "average person" in a given population who is average (50th-percentile value) on all body dimensions. A person with average stature may have a long or short hand, large or small shoulder breath, or wide or narrow feet.

Use of Anthropometric Data in Design

Data contained in anthropometric tables provide critical information with which designers can design workplaces and products. Use of the data, however, requires a thorough analysis on the designers' part of the design problem. The following procedure provides a systematic approach for the use of anthropometric data in design:

1. Determine the user population (the intended users). The key question to ask is: Who will use the product or workplace? As discussed earlier in this chapter, people of different age groups have different physical characteristics and requirements. Other factors that must also be considered include gender, race, and ethnic groups; military or civilian populations.

2. Determine the relevant body dimensions. The key question here is: Which body dimensions are most important for the design problem? For example, the design of a doorway must consider the stature and the shoulder width of the intended users. The width of a seat surface must accommodate the hip breadth of the users.

3. Determine the percentage of the population to be accommodated. Although a simple answer to this problem is that we should accommodate 100 percent of the population, this answer is not practical or undesirable in many design situations because of various financial, economical, and design constraints. For example, there may be limits on how far a seat can be adjusted in a vehicle to accomodate the smallest and largest 1 percent of drivers because to do so would force changes in the overall structrure of the design—at a tremendous expense. For most design problems, designers try to accommodate as large a proportion of the intended user population as possible within these constraints. There are three main approaches to this problem.

The first approach is called design for extremes, which means that for the design of certain physical dimensions of the workplace or living environment, designers should use the anthropometric data from extreme individuals, sometimes at one end and sometimes at both ends of the anthropometric scale in question. One example would be the strength of supporting devices. Designers need to use the body weight of the heaviest users in designing the devices to ensure that the devices are strong enough to support all potential users of the devices.

The second approach, called design for adjustable range, suggests that designers should design certain dimensions of equipment or facilities in a way that they can be adjusted to the individual users. Common examples include seats and steering wheels of automobiles and office chairs and desks.

According to the third approach, design for the average, designers may use average anthropometric values in the design of certain dimensions if it is impractical or not feasible to design for extremes or for adjustability because of various design constraints. Many checkout counters in department stores and supermarkets, for example, are designed for customers of average height. Although they are not ideal for every customer, they are more convenient to use for most customers than those checkout counters that are either too low or too high. Clearly, it is impractical to adjust the height of a counter for each customer. It should be noted, however, that design for the average should be used only as a last resort after having seriously considered the other two design approaches.

4. Determine the percentile value of the selected anthropometric dimension. The key design questions are: Which percentile value of the relevant dimension should be used: 5th, 95th, or some other value? Should the percentile value be selected from the male data or the female data? The percentage of the population to be accommodated determines the percentile value of the relevant anthropometric dimension to be used in design. However, one should realize that a design decision to accommodate 95 percent of the population does not always mean that the 95th-percentile value should be selected. Designers need to be clear whether they are designing a lower or an upper limit for the physical dimensions of the system or device.

For the design of lower-limit physical dimensions, designers set a lower limit as the minimum value for the dimension so that a certain percentage of a population can be accommodated. Here it should be emphasized that *lower-limit* refers to the physical size of the system, not the human user; that is, lower-limit means that the system cannot be smaller, or else it will be unusable by the largest users. Therefore, designers must use a high percentile for the design of lower-limit physical dimensions. For example, if a stool should be strong enough to support a very heavy person, then the 95th or 99th percentile of male body weight should be used as its minimum strength requirement. The logic is simple: If the heaviest (or tallest, largest, widest, etc.) people have no problem with this dimension, then almost everyone can use it. Another example of lower-limit dimensions is the width of a seat used in public places. The seat should be wide enough to accommodate the widest individuals. As discussed in detail in the next section, the dimensions of clearance spaces should be designed this way.

In contrast to the lower-limit dimensions, an upper-limit dimension requires the designers to set a maximum value (the upper limit) for the dimension so that a certain percentage of a population can be accommodated. Here, upper limit means that the physical size of the system cannot be bigger than this limit, or else it will not be usable by smallest users. Thus designers should use a low percentile for the design of upper-limit dimensions. In other words, in order to accommodate 95 percent of the population, the fifth percentile (most often from the female data) should be used in design. The logic is simple: If the shortest (or smallest, lightest, etc.) people have no problem with this dimension, then most people can use it. For example, the size and weight of a tray to be carried by workers should be small enough so that the smallest workers can carry it without any problem. Other examples of upper-limit dimensions include the height of steps in a stairway and the depth of seats. As discussed in detail in the next section, the reach distance of control devices should also be designed this way.

5. Make necessary design modifications to the data from the anthropometric tables. Most anthropometric measures are taken with nude or nearly nude persons, a method that helps standardize measurements but does not reflect real life situations. As discussed earlier, clothing can change body size considerably. A light shirt for the summer is very different from a heavy coat for winter outdoor activities. Therefore, necessary adjustments must be made in workplace design to accommodate these changes. Allowance for shoes, gloves, and headwear must also be provided if the workers are expected to wear them at work.

Another important reason for data adjustment is that most anthropometric data are obtained with persons standing erect or sitting erect. Most of us do not assume these types of body postures for long. In order to reflect the characteristics of a person's "natural" posture, necessary adjustments must be made. For example, the "natural standing (slump-posture)" eye height is about 2 cm lower than the erect standing eye height, and the "natural sitting" eye height is about **4**.5 cm lower than the erect sitting eye height (Hertzberg, 1972). As discussed later in this chapter, these considerations are critical for designing workplaces that have high viewing requirements.

The use of anthropometric tables to develop and evaluate various possible layouts is often a slow and cumbersome process when several physical dimensions are involved (e.g., a vehicle cab, which involves visibility seating adjustments and several different kinds of reach). The advent of advanced computer graphics is beginning to offer the use of more interactive anthropometric models, like Jack or Combiman, in which dynamic renderings of a human body can be created with varying percentile dimensions and then moved through the various dimensions of a computer-simulated work space, in order to assess the adequacy of design (Badler, Barsky, & Zeltzer, 1990; Karwowski, Genaidy, & Asfour, 1990).

6. Use mock-ups or simulators to test the design. Very often designers need to evaluate whether the design meets the requirements by building mock-ups or simulators with representative users carrying out simulated tasks. This step is im-

portant because various body dimensions are measured separately in a standard-ized anthropometric survey, but there may exist complicated interactions between the various body dimensions in performing a job. Mock-ups or simulators can help reveal some of the potential interactions and help designers make necessary corrections to their preliminary design. A limitation of mock-ups is often en-countered because the available human users for evaluation may not span the anthropometric range of potential users. This limitation points again to the po-tential advantages of anthropometric models, where such users can be simulated.

GENERAL PRINCIPLES FOR WORK-SPACE DESIGN

As discussed in the introduction chapter, the goal of human factors is to design systems that reduce human error, increase productivity, and enhance safety and comfort. Work-space design is one of the major areas in which human factors pro-fessionals can help improve the fit between humans and machines and environ-ments. This section summarizes some general principles of work-space design. Although we describe work-space design only from the human factors perspective, it should be emphasized that these human factors concerns should be considered in the context of other critical design factors such as cost, aesthetics, durability, and architectural characteristics. Design is an art, as well as a science. There are no for-mulas to ensure success. But the general guidelines described here may help re-mind the workplace designers of some of the basic requirements of a workplace and prevent them from designing workplaces that are clearly nonoptimal.

Clearance Requirement of the Largest Users

Clearance problems are among the most often encountered and most important issues in work-space design. The space between and around equipments, the height and width of passageways, the dimensions provided for the knees, the legs, the elbows, the feet, and the head are some examples of clearance design problems. Some workers may not be able to access certain work areas if there is not enough clearance provided. Inadequate clearance may also force some workers to adopt an awkward posture, thus causing discomfort and reducing productivity.

As mentioned earlier, clearance dimensions are lower-limit dimensions and should be adequate for the largest users who are planning to use the workplace. For most design applications, designers may start with the 95th-percentile value for the relevant anthropometric dimension. As discussed earlier, adjustments to this value are often needed to provide additional space for clothing and mobility require-ments. Because heavy clothing requires additional space, raw data from an an-thropometric table need to be adjusted upward to reflect the increased space needs of a person with heavy clothes.

While design for lower-limit dimensions such as clearance spaces always means that high percentiles are used in design, it does not always mean that male data should be used all the time. Clearly, for female-only workplaces, data from the female population should be used. What is not so obvious is that female data should also be used sometimes for mixed-sex workplaces. For example, the body width of a pregnant woman may need to be used to set the lower limit for some design dimensions.

Reach Requirements of the Smallest Users

Workers in a workplace often need to extend their arms to reach and operate a hand-operated device or to use their feet to activate a foot pedal. Similar to the clearance problems, inadequate-reach dimensions can reduce workers' comfort and productivity. In contrast to the clearance problem, which sets the design limits at the largest users, reach dimensions should be determined on the basis of the reach capabilities of the smallest users. For most design applications, designers may consider using the fifth-percentile value for the relevant dimension and make necessary adjustments to deal with the potential effects of other factors such as clothing. Because heavy clothing reduces a person's reach capability, raw data from an anthropometric table need to be adjusted downward to reflect the reduced reach capacity of a person with heavy clothes.

An important concept here is the concept of reach envelope (also called reach area), which is the three-dimensional space in front of a person that can be reached without leaning forward or stretching. Reach envelope represents the reach capability of a person. The seated reach envelope for a fifth-percentile female is shown in Figure 10.6, which is different from the standing reach envelope, shown in Figure 10.7. Both figures only show the right arm's reach area. For practical purposes, the left arm's reach can be approximated as the mirror image of the right arm's.

Clearly, objects that need to be reached frequently should be located within the reach area and as close to the body as possible. If these objects have different sizes and weights, large and heavy ones should be placed closer to the front of the worker. A worker may be allowed to lean forward occasionally to reach something outside the work area, but such activities should not become a frequent and regular part of jobs with short work cycles.

In considering the issues of object location, manipulation, and reach, it is clear that issues of strength and fatigue must also be addressed. The same physical layout for two workers of the same physical proportions will have very different long-term health and safety implications if the workers differ substantially in their strength, or if, for example, the parts to be lifted and moved from one point in the work space to another differ substantially in their weight. The role of these critical issues will be addressed in the next chapter.

Special Requirements of Maintenance People

A well-designed workplace should not only consider the regular functions of the workplace and the workers who work there everyday, but also the maintenance needs and the special requirements of maintenance personnel. Because maintenance people often need to access areas that do not have to be accessed by regular workers, designers need to analyze the special requirements of the maintenance

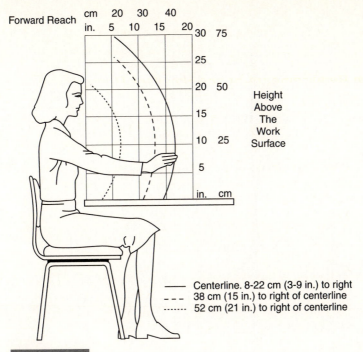

FIGURE 10.6
The seated forward reach of a small female's right hand. (*Source:* Eastman Kodak Company, 1986. *Ergonomic Design for People at Work,* Vol. 1. New York: Van Nostrand Reinhold; developed from data in Faulkner and Day, 1970.)

people and design the workplace accordingly. Because regular workers and maintenance people often have different needs, an adjustable workplace becomes particularly desirable, as discussed below.

Adjustability Requirements

As discussed earlier in this chapter, people vary in many anthropometric dimensions and their own measurements may change as a function of a number of factors such as the clothes they wear on a particular day. Because of the conflicting needs of different people, it is often impossible to have "one size fits all." A small person, on the one hand, would not feel comfortable sitting on a wide and deep seat. A large person, on the other hand, would not be able to squeeze into a small and narrow seat. Therefore, it is desirable to make every effort to make the workplace adjustable if it is feasible while considering other design requirements and constraints.

Designers should also make sure that the adjustment mechanisms are easy to use; otherwise, users are often intimidated by the complexity of the adjustment methods and refuse to use them. For example, the ease of adjusting automobile seating parameters can be greatly influenced both by placing those controls in a location where they themselves can be easily reached and by paying attention to

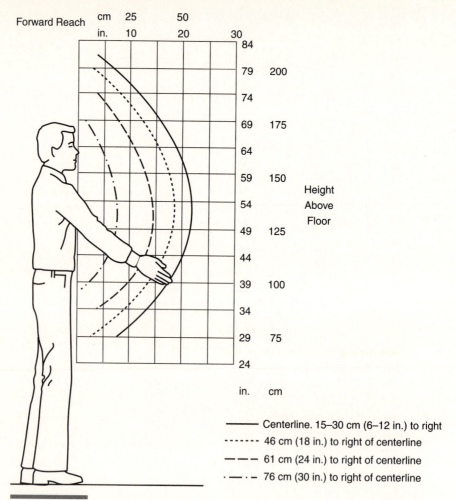

FIGURE 10.7

The standing forward reach area of a small male's right hand. (*Source:* Eastman Kodak Company, 1986. *Ergonomic Design for People at Work,* Vol. 1. New York: Van Nostrand Reinhold.)

issues of movement compatibility (discussed in Chapter 9) so that the direction in which a control should be moved to ajust the seat in a particular direction is obvious.

There are many ways in which a workplace can be adjusted. The following is a summary of four general approaches to workplace adjustment that should be considered in workplace design (Eastman Kodak Company, 1983).

1. *Adjusting the workplace.* The shape, the location, and the orientation of the workplace may be adjusted to achieve a good fit between the worker and the task. For example, front surface cutouts can be used to allow the worker to move closer to the reach point so that reach requirement can be minimized. Reach distance may also be reduced by height and orientation adjustments relative to the worker and other equipments involved in the same task.

2. *Adjusting the worker position relative to the workplace.* When workplace adjustments are not feasible because they are in conflict with the requirements of other vital equipments or services or because they exceed budget constraints, designers may consider various ways of adjusting the worker position relative to the workplace. Change in seat height and use of platforms or step-up stools are some of the means of achieving vertical adjustability. A swing chair may be used to change the orientation of the worker relative to the equipments.

3. *Adjusting the workpiece.* Lift tables or forklift trucks can be used to adjust the height of a workpiece. Jigs, clamps, and other types of fixtures can be used to hold a workpiece in a position and orientation for easy viewing and operation. Parts bins can help organize different types of bins for easier access.

4. *Adjusting the tool.* An adjustable-length hand tool can allow people with different arm lengths to reach objects at different distances. In an assembly plant, such tools can allow a worker to access an otherwise inaccessible workpiece. Similarly, in a lecture hall, a changeable-length pointing stick allows a speaker to point to items displayed on varying locations of a projection screen, without much change in his or her standing position and posture.

Visibility and Normal Line of Sight

Designers should ensure that the visual displays in a workplace can be easily seen and read by the workers. This requires that the eyes are at proper positions with respect to viewing requirements. In this regard, the important concept of "normal" line of sight is of particular relevance.

The "normal" line of sight is the "preferred" direction of gaze when the eyes are at a resting condition. It is considered by most researchers to be about 10–15° below the horizontal plane (Fig. 10.8). Grandjean, Hunting, and Pidermann (1983) reported the results of a recent study that showed that the normal line of sight is also the preferred line of sight of computer users watching a screen. Bhatnager, Drury, and Schiro (1985) studied how the height of a screen affected the performance, discomfort, and posture of the users. They found that the best performance and physical comfort were observed for the screen height closest to the normal line of sight. Therefore, visual displays should be placed within ± 15° in radius around the normal line of sight. When multiple visual displays are used in a workplace, primary displays should be given high priority in space assignment and should be placed in the optimal location.

Of course, presenting visual material within 15° around the normal line of sight is not sufficient to ensure that it will be processed. As we learned in Chapter 4, the visual angle and the contrast of the material must also be adequate for resolving whatever information is presented there, a prediction that also must take into account the viewing distance of the information, as well as the visual characteristics of the user.

Visibility analysis may also need to address issues of whether critical signals will be seen if they are away from the normal line of sight. Can flashing lights in

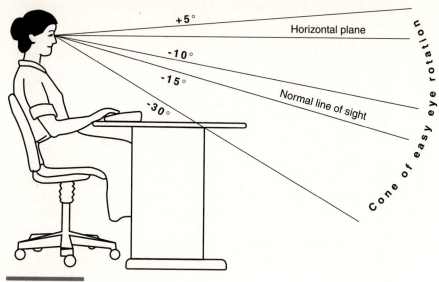

FIGURE 10.8

The normal line of sight and the range of easy eye rotation. (*Source:* Grandjean, E., 1988. *Fitting the Task to the Man* (4th Edition). London: Taylor and Francis. Reprinted by permission of Taylor and Francis.)

the periphery be seen? Might other critical warning signals be blocked by obstructions? Does the design of vehicle cabs include posts or obstructions that can obscure critical hazards or information signs in the outside world?

Component Arrangement

Part of a workplace designer's task is to arrange the displays and controls, equipments and tools, and other parts and devices within some physical space. Depending on the characteristics of the user and the tasks in question, optimum arrangements can help a user access and use these components easily and smoothly, whereas a careless arrangement can confuse the user and make the jobs harder. The general issue is to increase overall movement efficiency and reduce total movement distance, whether this is movement of the hands, of the feet, or of the total body through locomotion.

Principles of display layout discussed in Chapter 8 can be extended to the more general design problem of component arrangements. These principles may be even more critical when applied to components than to displays, since movment of the hands and body to reach those components requires greater effort than movement of the eyes (or attention) to see the displays. In our discussion here, the components include displays, controls, equipment and tools, parts and supplies, and any device that a worker needs to use to accomplish his or her tasks.

1. *Frequency of use principle.* Those components that are used most frequently should be placed in most convenient locations. Frequently used displays should be positioned in the primary viewing area, shown in Figure 10.8; frequently used hand tools should be close to the dominant hand, and frequently used foot pedals should be close to the right foot.

2. *Importance principle.* Those components that are more crucial to the achievement of system goals should be located in the convenient locations. Depending on their levels of importance for a specific application, displays and controls can be prioritized as primary and secondary. Primary displays should be located close to the primary viewing area, which is the space in front of an operator and 10–15° within the normal line of sight. Secondary displays can be located at the more peripheral locations. One suggested method of arranging controls according to their priority is shown in Figure 10.9 (Aeronautical Systems Division, 1980).

3. *Sequence of use principle.* Components which are used in sequence should be located next to each other, and their layout should reflect the sequence of operation. If an electronic assembly worker is expected to install an electronic part on a device immediately after picking the part up from a parts bin, then the parts bin should be close to the device if possible.

4. *Consistency principle.* Components should be laid out with the same component located in the same spatial locations to minimize memory and search requirements. Consistency should be maintained both within the same workplace and across workplaces designed for similar functions. For example, a person would find it much easier to find a copy machine in a university library if copy machines are located at similar locations (e.g., by the elevator) in all the libraries on a campus.

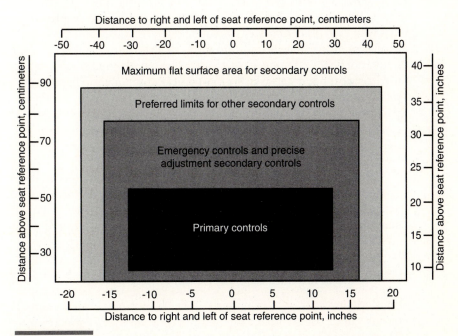

FIGURE 10.9

Preferred vertical surface areas for different classes of control devices. (*Source:* Sanders, M.S., and McCormick, E.J., 1993. *Human Factors in Engineering and Design* (7th Edition). New York: McGraw-Hill. Adapted from Aeronautical Systems Division, 1980.)

Standardization plays an important role in ensuring that consistency can be maintained across the borders of institutions, companies, and countries. Because arrangements of automobile components are rather standardized within the United States, we can drive cars made by different companies without much problem.

5. *Control-display compatibility principle of colocation.* This is a specific form of stimulus-response compatibility discussed in earlier chapters. In the context of component arrangement, this principle states that control devices should be close to their associated displays and in the case of multiple controls and displays, the layout of controls should reflect the layout of displays to make visible the control-display relationship.

6. *Clutter-avoidance principle.* We have discussed the importance of avoiding display clutter in the chapter on displays. Here we note that clutter avoidance is equally important in the arrangement of controls. Adequate space must be provided between adjacent controls such as buttons, knobs, or pedals to minimize the risk of accidental activation.

7. *Functional grouping principle.* Components with closely related functions should be placed close to each other. Displays and controls associated with power supply, for example, should be grouped together, whereas those responsible for communications should be close to each other. Various groups of related components should be easily and clearly identifiable. Colors, shapes, sizes, and separation borders are some of the means to distinguish the groups.

Ideally, we would like to see all the seven principles are satisfied in a design solution. Unfortunately, it is often the case that some of the principles will be in conflict with each other and thus cannot be satisfied at the same time. For example, a warning display may be most important for the safe operation of a system, but it may not be the component that is most frequently used. Similarly, a frequently used device is not necessarily the most crucial component. This type of situations calls for careful trade-off analysis on the designer's part to decide the relative importance of each principle in the particular situation. Some data appears to suggest that functional grouping and sequence of use principles are more critical than the importance principle in positioning controls and displays (Fowler, Williams, Fowler, & Young, 1968; Wickens, Vincow, & Schopper, 1997).

Applications of these principles require subjective judgments. For example, expert judgments are needed to evaluate the relative importance of each component and to group various components into functionally related groups. However, quantitative methods such as link analysis and optimization techniques are available that can be used in conjunction with these subjective approaches.

Link analysis is a quantitative and objective method for examining the relationships between components, which can be used as the database for optimizing component arrangements. A link between a pair of components represents a relationship between the two components. The strength of the relationship is reflected by link values. For example, a link value of three for the A-B link (connecting A to B) means that component B has been used three times immediately following the use of A. This type of link is called a sequential link. It may be applied to movement of the eyes across displays in visual scanning, to movement of the hands in a manual task, or to movement of the whole body within a workspace.

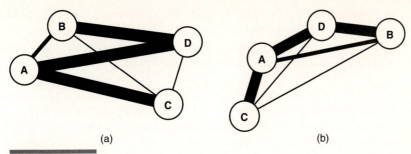

FIGURE 10.10

An example of applying link analysis in system design. Here the width of a link represents the travel times (or the strength of connection) between two components. The purpose of the design in to minimize the total travel time across all components. (a) Before reposition of components. Note that thick lines are long. (b) After reposition. Note that the thick lines are shorter.

Clearly, data about sequential links are useful for the application of sequence of use principle in workplace design. Link analysis will also yield a measure of the number of times that each component is used per unit of time. This measure is called functional links in the literature. If these component-use data are known for a particular application, then these values can be used to apply the frequency of use principle (McCormick, 1976).

One goal of link analysis is to support a design that minimizes the total travel time across all components; that is, to make the most traveled links the shortest. Figure 10.10 illustrates this process with a simple four-component system. Here the width of a link represents its strength. The system on the left shows the analysis before redesign, and that on the right shows the analysis after.

With simple systems that have a small number of components, such as that shown in Figure 10.10, designers may adopt a simple trial-and-error procedure in using link data to arrange components. Designers can develop a number of design alternatives and see how the link values change when the arrangements change and finally adopt the design option that best meet the needs of the design. With complex systems that have many components, however, designers may use mathematical methods to help them attack the problem. For example, designers may treat component layout as an optimization problem and use well-developed operations research methods such as linear programming to arrange the components in a way that optimizes some design criterion. The design criterion could be defined as some operational cost, which is expressed as a mathematical function of variables that define the spatial layout of the components.

DESIGN OF STANDING AND SEATED WORK AREAS

Choice Between Standing and Seated Work Areas

In most job environments, workers either stand or sit during work. Standing workplaces are usually used where the workers need to make frequent movements in a large work area, handle heavy or large objects, or exert large forces with their hands. Long-duration standing duty is also observed in the service industry, such as the jobs of the airline or hotel reservation clerks and bank tellers. Because prolonged standing is a strainful posture that puts excessive load on the body and may lead to body fluid accumulation in the legs, a worker should not be required to stand for a long time without taking a break. Use of floor mats and shoes with cushioned soles may also help increase a standing worker's comfort.

Whenever possible, a seated workplace should be used for long-duration jobs, because a seated posture is much easier to maintain and much less of a strain to the body. It also allows for better controlled arm movements, provides a stronger sense of balance and safety, and improves blood circulation. Workplace designers must make sure, however, that leg rooms or leg and knee clearance is provided for the seated worker. Furthermore, as will be discussed in the biomechanics chapter, prolonged sitting can be harmful to the lower back. Seated workplaces should also be provided with adjustable chairs and footrests, and workers should be allowed to stand up and walk around after a period of seated work.

A sit-stand workplace is sometimes used as a compromise or tradeoff between the standing and sitting requirements of a job. This type of workplace may be used when some of the job components are best done standing and others are best done sitting. Designers need to analyze the job components involved and decide which type of workplace is best for each.

Work Surface Height

The nature of the tasks being performed should determine the correct work surface height for a standing or seated work. In this respect, there is a simple but very useful rule of thumb to determine the work surface height. The rule of thumb is to design standing working heights at 5–10 cm (2–4 in.) below elbow level and to design seated working heights at elbow level, unless the job requires precise manipulation or great force application (Ayoub, 1973; Grandjean, 1988; Eastman Kodak Company, 1986).

Whether seated or standing, precise manipulation calls for working heights above the elbow level; the work surface must be raised to a level at which the worker can see clearly without bending his or her back forward. Great force application or coarse work involving much movement requires working heights lower than that specified by the rule of thumb but should not be so low that there is not enough knee or leg room left under the work surface. Figure 10.11 provides a schematic illustration of this rule of thumb for determining the surface height for standing work.

If feasible, working surface height should be adjustable to suit the workers of varying sizes. If it is impossible to do so for financial or various other practical reasons, then working heights should be set according to the anthropometric values of the tallest workers. Shorter workers should be provided with something to stand on.

Work Surface Depth

An important concept here is the concept of normal and maximum work areas. These areas were first proposed by Farley (1955) and Barnes (1963). The areas defined by Barnes are shown in Figure 10.12, in which the normal work area in horizontal plane is the area covered by a sweep of the forearm without extending the upper arm, and the maximum work area is the area defined by a sweep of the arm by extending the

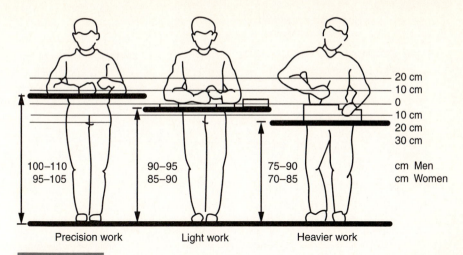

FIGURE 10.11

Recommended work surface height for standing work. The reference line (0 cm) is the height of the elbows above the floor. (*Source:* Grandjean, 1988. *Fitting the Task to the Man* [4th Edition]. London: Taylor and Francis.)

arm from the shoulder. In defining the normal work area, Barnes assumes that the elbow stays at a fixed point. The normal work area defined by Squires (1956) is also shown in Figure 10.12, which does not make this fixed-elbow assumption.

Clearly, normal and maximum work areas must be taken into account in determining work surface depth. Items that need to be reached immediately or frequently should be located within the normal work area and as close to the body as possible, while other items can be located within the maximum work area. It may be permissible to have a worker occasionally lean forward to reach an item outside the maximum work area, but such reaches should not occur regularly and frequently.

Work Surface Inclination

Most work surfaces are designed as horizontal surfaces. However, a number of studies have shown that slightly slanted surfaces (about 15°) should be used for reading. Eastman and Kamon (1976) and Bridger (1988) found that slant surfaces improve body posture, involve less trunk movement, require less bending of the neck, and produce less worker fatigue and discomfort. However, for other types of visual tasks such as extensive writing, a slanted surface may not be the best choice. Bendix and Hagberg (1984) found that users preferred horizontal desks for writing, although the same users preferred the slanted desks for reading.

CONCLUSION

Matching the physical layout of the workspace to the physical dimensions and constraints of the user is a necessary but not sufficient task to create a well-human-factored workspace. As we have noted before, just because a worker can reach a

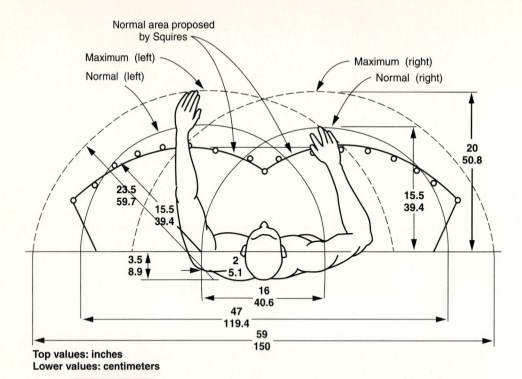

Top values: inches
Lower values: centimeters

FIGURE 10.12

Normal and maximum working areas (in inches and centimeters) proposed by Barnes and normal work area proposed by Squires. (*Source*: Sanders, M.S., and McCormick, E.J., 1993. *Human Factors in Engineering and Design* [7th Edition]. New York: McGraw-Hill. Copyright © 1993. Reprinted by permission of the McGraw-Hill Companies.)

component it does not mean that he or she can easily manipulate it or lift it without doing damage to the lower back. To address this second dynamic aspect of workspace design, we must consider the biomechanics of the human body, the issue to which we now turn in the next chapter.

REFERENCES

Annis, J.F. (1978). Variability in human body size, In *Anthropometric source book*, Vol. 1, Chap. 2. NASA Reference Publication 1025, NASA Scientific and Technical Office. Houston, TX: NASA.

Ashby, P. (1979). *Ergonomics Handbook 1: Body Size and Strength*. Pretoria: SA Design Institute.

Ayoub, M.M. (1973). Work place design and posture, *Human Factors, 15* (3), pp. 265–268.

Ayoub, M.M., Bethea, N., Bobo, M., Burford, C., Caddel, D., Intaranont, K., Morrissey, S., and Salan, J. (1982). *Mining in low coal, vol. 2: Anthropometry*. (OFR 162(2)-83). Pittsburgh: Bureau of Mines.

Badler, N.I., Barsky, B.A., and Zelter, D. (eds.) (1990). *Making Them Move: Mechanics, Control, and Animation of Articulated Figures.* Palo Alto, CA: Morgan-Kaufmann.

Barnes, R. M. (1963). *Motion and time study* (5th edition). New York: Wiley.

Bendix, T., and Hagberg, M. (1984). Trunk posture and load on the trapezius muscle whilst sitting at sloping desks. *Ergonomics, 27,* 873–882.

Bhatnager, V., Drury, C.G., and Schiro, S.G. (1985). Posture, postural discomfort and performance. *Human Factors, 27,* 189–199.

Bridger, R. (1988). Postural adaptations to a sloping chair and work surface. *Human Factors, 30* (2), 237–247.

Clauser, C.E., Tucker, P.E., McConville, J.T., Churchill, E., Laubach, L.L., and Reardon, J.A. (1972). *Anthropometry of Air Force women* (pp. 1-1157). AMRL-TR-70-5. Wright-Patterson Air Force Base, OH: Aerospace Medical Research Labs.

Eastman Kodak Company, Ergonomics Group (1986). *Ergonomic design for people at work,* Vol. 1. New York: Van Nostrand Reinhold.

Eastman, M.C., and Kamon, E. (1976). Posture and subjective evaluation at flat and slanted desks. *Human Factors, 18* (1), 15–26.

Farley, R.R. (1955). "Some principles of methods and motion study as used in development work." *General Motors Engineering Journal,* 2 (6), 20–25.

Fowler, R.L., Williams, W.E., Fowler, M.G., and Young, D.D. (1968). *An investigation of the relationship between operator performance and operator panel layout for continuous tasks.* Technical Report Number 68-170. Wright Patterson Air Force Base, Ohio.

Grandjean, E. (1988). *Fitting the task to the man* (4th ed.). London: Taylor and Francis.

Grandjean, E., Hunting, W., and Pidermann, M. (1983). VDT workstation design: preferred settings and their effects. *Human Factors, 25,* 161–175.

Griener T.M., and Gordon, C.C. (1990). *An assessment of long-term changes in anthropometric dimensions: Secular trends of U.S. Army males* (Natick/TR-91/006). Natick, MA: U.S. Army Natick Research, Development and Engineering Center.

Grieve, D., and Pheasant, S. (1982). Biomechanics. In W.T. Singleton (ed.), *The body at work.* Cambridge, England: Cambridge University Press.

Hamil, P., Drizo, T., Johnson, C., Reed, R., and Roche, A. (1976). *NCHS growth charts,* Monthly Vital Statistics Report, Health Examination Survey Data, HRA 76-1120, vol. 25, no. 3. National Center for Health Statistics.

Hertzberg, H.T.E. (1972). Engineering anthropometry. In H.P. Van Cott and R.G. Kinkade (eds.), *Human engineering guide to equipment design.* Washington, DC: U.S. Government Printing Office.

Karwowski, W., Genaidy, A., and Asfour, S. (eds.) (1990). *Computer-aided ergonomics.* London: Taylor and Francis.

Kroemer, K.H.E. (1987). Biomechanics of the human body. In G. Salvendy (ed.), *Handbook of human factors* (pp. 169–181). New York: Wiley.

Long, L., and Churchill, E. (1965). Anthropometry of USAF basic trainees contrasts of several subgroups. Paper presented to the 1968 meeting of the American Association of Physical Anthropometrists.

Marras, W.S., and Kim, J. Y. (1993). Anthropometry of industrial populations, *Ergonomics, 36* (4), 371–378.

McCormick, E.J. (1976). *Human factors in engineering and design.* New York: McGraw-Hill.

National Aeronautics and Space Administration (NASA). (1978). *Anthropometric source book, vol. 1: Anthropometry for designers; vol. 2: A handbook of anthropometric data; vol. 3: Annotated bibliography* (NASA Reference Publication 1024). Houston, TX: NASA.

O'Brien, R., and Sheldon, W.C. (1941). *Women's measurements for garment and pattern construction,* U.S. Department of Agriculture, Misc. Pub. No. 454. Washington, DC: U.S. Government Printing Office.

Robert, D. F. (1975). Population differences in dimensions, their genetic basis and their relevance to practical problems of design. In A. Chapanis (ed.), *Ethnic variables in human factors engineering* (pp. 11–29) Baltimore: Johns Hopkins University Press.

Roche, A.F., and Davila, G.H. (1972). Late adolescent growth in stature. *Pediatrics, 50,* 874–880.

Roebuck, J. A., Kroemer, K. H. E., and Thomson, W. G. (1975). *Engineering anthropometry methods.* New York: Wiley.

Sanders, M.S. (1977). *Anthropometric survey of truck and bus drivers: Anthropometry, control reach and control force.* Westlake Village, CA: Canyon Research Group.

Sanders, M.S., and McCormick, E.J. (1993). *Human factors in engineering and design* (7th ed.). New York: McGraw-Hill.

Squires, P. C. (1956). *The shape of the normal work area.* Report No. 275. New London, CT: Navy Department, Bureau of Medicine and Surgery, Medical Research Laboratory.

Stout, H.M., Damon, A., McFarland, R.A., and Roberts, J. (1960). Heights and weights of white Americans. *Human Biology, 32,* 331.

Trotter, M., and Gleser, G. (1951). The effect of aging upon stature. *American Journal of Physical Anthropology, 9,* 311–324.

Van Cott, H.P., and Kinkade, R. G. (1972). *Human engineering guide to equipment design.* Washington, DC: U.S. Government Printing Office.

White, R.M., and Churchill, E. (1971). *The body size of soldiers, U.S. Army anthropometry–1966* (pp. 1–329). Tech. Report 72-51-CE. Natick, MA: U.S. Army Natick Labs.

Wickens, C.D., Vincow, M., and Schopper, R. (1997). Computational Models of human performance in the layout of displays. CSERIAC state of the art report. Crew Systems Ergonomics Information Analysis Center, Wright Patterson Air Force Base: Ohio.

Yokohori, E. (1972). *Anthropometry of JASDF personnel and its implications for human engineering.* Tokyo: Aeromedical Laboratory, Japanese Air Self Defense Force, Tachikawa Air Force Base.

CHAPTER 11

Biomechanics
of Work

In the previous chapter, we discussed the importance of ensuring the fit between the physical dimensions of products and workplaces and the body dimensions of the users. Products and workplaces that are not designed according to the anthropometric characteristics of the users will either prevent the worker from using them or force them to adopt awkward postures that are hard to maintain and stressful to the body.

Awkward postures are not the only factor that can cause physical stress to the body. In this chapter, we bring another important factor into our discussion about ergonomic design of workplaces and devices. This factor is concerned with the mechanical forces exerted by a worker in performing a task such as lifting a load or using a hand tool. In fact, awkward postures and heavy exertion forces are two major causes of musculoskeletal problems, whose prevalence and severity can be illustrated with the following statistics.

According to a report of the National Institute for Occupational Safety and Health (NIOSH, 1981), about half a million workers in the United States suffer some kind of overexertion injury each year. The two most prevalent musculoskeletal problems are low back pain and upper extremity (fingers, hands, wrists, arms, and shoulders) cumulative trauma disorders. About 60 percent of the overexertion injuries reported each year involves lifting and back pain. The National Council on Compensation Insurance estimates that low-back-pain-related worker compensation payments and indirect costs total about $U.S. 27 to 56 billion in the United States (Pope, Andersson, Frymoyer, & Chaffin, 1991). Armstrong and Silverstein (1987) found that in industries where the work requires repetitive hand and arm exertions, more than one in 10 workers annually reported upper-extremity cumulative trauma disorders (UECTDs).

In this chapter we introduce the scientific discipline of occupational biomechanics, which plays a major role in studying and analyzing human performance and musculoskeletal problems in manual material handling and provides the fundamental scientific basis for ergonomic analysis of physical work. As defined by Chaffin and Andersson (1991, p. viii), occupational biomechanics is "a science concerned with the mechanical behavior of the musculoskeletal system and component tissues when physical work is performed. As such, it seeks to provide an understanding of the physics of manual activities in industry."

Occupational biomechanics is an interdisciplinary science that integrates knowledge and techniques from diverse physical, biological, and engineering disciplines. In essence, biomechanics analyzes the human musculoskeletal system as a mechanical system that obeys laws of physics. Thus, the most basic concepts of occupational biomechanics are those concerning the structure and properties of the musculoskeletal system and the laws and concepts of physics. These two aspects of biomechanics are covered first in this chapter. We then discuss low back pain and upper-extremity cumulative trauma disorders in two sections in detail because they are the two types of musculoskeletal problems that occur most often in work environments and incur greatest danger and cost.

THE MUSCULOSKELETAL SYSTEM

The musculoskeletal system is composed of the bones, muscles, and connective tissues, which include ligaments, tendons, fascia, and cartilage. Bone can also be considered as a connective tissue. The main functions of the musculoskeletal system are to support and protect the body and body parts, to maintain posture and produce body movement, and to generate heat and maintain body temperature.

Bones and Connective Tissues

There are 206 bones in a human body, and they form the rigid skeletal structure, which plays the major supportive and protective roles in the body. The skeleton establishes the body framework that holds all other body parts together. Some bones protect internal organs, such as the skull, which covers and protects the brain, and the rib cage, which shields the lungs and the heart from the outside. Some bones such as the long bones of the upper- and lower-extremities work with the attached muscles to support body movement and activities.

Each of the other four types of connective tissues has its own special functions. Tendons are dense fibrous connective tissues that attach muscles to bones and transmit the forces exerted by the muscles to the attached bones. Ligaments are also dense fibrous tissues, but their function is to connect the articular extremities of bones and help stabilize the articulations of bones at joints. Cartilage is a translucent elastic tissue that can be found on some articular bony surfaces and in some organs such as the nose and the ear. Fascia covers body structures and separates them from each other.

Two or more bones are linked with each other at joints, which can be classified into three types. Most joints are synovial joints, where no tissue exists between the highly lubricated joint surfaces. The other two types of joints are fibrous joints, such as those connecting the bones of the skull through fibrous tissues, and cartilaginous joints, such as those bridging vertebral bones as intervertebral discs. Depending on the type of movement allowed, joints can also be classified as no-mobility joints, hinge joints, pivot joints, and ball-and-socket joints. No-mobility joints do not support movement, such as the seams in the skull of an adult. A hinge joint such as the elbow joint permits motion in only one plane. A pivot joint allows two degrees of freedom in movement, an example of which is the wrist joint. A ball-and-socket joint has three degrees of freedom, such as the hip and shoulder joints.

Bones change their structure, size, and shape over time as a result of the mechanical loads placed on them. Wolff (1892) suggests that bones are deposited where needed and resorbed where not needed. It should be noted, however, the precise relationships between bone changes and mechanical loads remain unknown. More important, it should be realized that bones can fracture when they are exposed to excess or repetitive loading in the form of bending forces, torsional forces, or combined forces. The amount of load, the number of repetitions, and the frequency of loading are three most important factors that can cause bone fracture. Further, bone is capable of repairing small fractures if adequate recovery time is given. Thus, the repetition rate of manual exertions or the recovery period after exertions can become significant factors (Chaffin & Andersson, 1991).

Muscles

The musculoskeletal system has about 400 muscles, which make up about 40–50 percent of the body weight. Muscles consume almost half of the body's metabolism, which not only supplies the energy for maintaining body posture and producing body motion but is also used to generate heat and maintain body temperature. The energy metabolism of muscles will be discussed in the next chapter on work physiology. Here we describe the basic structures and mechanical properties of muscles.

Muscles are composed of bundles of muscle fibers, connective tissue, and nerves. Muscle fibers are long cylindrical cells, consisting largely of contractile elements called myofibrils. Muscles with larger cross-sections are able to exert larger forces. The connective tissue of muscle provides a channel through which nerves and blood vessels enter and leave the muscle. Muscles contain sensory and motor nerve fibers. Information about the length and tension of the muscle is transmitted through sensory nerve fibers to the central nervous system. Muscle activities are regulated by motor nerve fibers, which transmit impulses from the central nervous system to the muscles. Each motor nerve fiber regulates a group of related muscle fibers through its branches. The group of muscle fibers regulated by the branches of the same motor nerve is called *a motor unit,* which is the basic functional unit of the muscle. All the muscle fibers in the same motor unit function in an "all-or-none" fashion; that is, they respond to an impulse from the motor fiber on an on-off basis almost simultaneously.

In contrast to bones, which cannot be contracted or stretched, muscles can contract concentrically, eccentrically, and isometrically in response to motor nerve impulses. A concentric contraction is also called an isotonic contraction, in which the muscle shortens while contracting and producing a constant internal muscle force. An eccentric contraction is one in which the muscle lengthens while contracting, which occurs when the external force is greater than the internal muscle force. In an isometric contraction, the muscle length remains unchanged during the contraction process. Concentric contractions can be observed in the arm flexor muscles when an object is lifted upward. Eccentric contractions can be seen when a person picks up a heavy object and is unable to hold it in the desired position, and the muscles are forcibly lengthened (Eastman Kodak Company, 1986). Isometric contractions occur when a person pauses during lifting and holds the object in a static position. Muscle contraction produces muscle force or tension, which is transmitted to bones through tendons and is used to maintain body posture and perform physical work.

Currently no measuring device exists that can measure the tensions within the muscle directly. Hence, muscle "strength" is inferred from the amount of force or torque it exerts. Torque, also called moment, is the product of force and the perpendicular distance from its line of action to the axis of rotation. The movement of an arm is an example of a torque; the axis of rotation is at the center of the joint at the elbow or the shoulder. The torque generated by arm movement transforms arm muscle contraction into physical work such as pulling or pushing an object. Similarly, torques generated by movements of other body parts allow one to accomplish a variety of physical tasks.

Muscle strength is the amount and direction of force or torque measured by a measuring device under standardized measuring procedures (Chaffin and Andersson, 1991; Kroemer et al., 1994). Depending on whether the muscle exertion is static or dynamic, muscle strength can be classified as static strength and dynamic strength. Static strength is also called isometric strength, which is defined as the maximal voluntary isometric muscle exertion level. More specifically, static strength is measured when a group of static exertions is performed. Each lasts about 4–6 sec, with 30–120 sec rests provided between exertions. The mean exertion levels of the first 3 sec of the steady exertions are used as the measured strength level.

Dynamic muscle strength is more difficult to measure than static strength, because body acceleration have significant effects on the muscle force measured. Therefore, dynamic strength data can vary considerably depending on the dynamics of the task and the way in which the subjects perform it. Several methods have been developed to help standardize the measurement of dynamic strength. One method uses specially designed isokinetic equipments to ensure fixed-speed body motion by providing a variable resistance to the motion.

Another method, a psychophysical method, requires the subjects to adjust the load upward or downward after each trial in a simulated task situation until they believe the load has reached their maximum capacity. Clearly, a number of factors such as a person's motivation and cooperation may affect the measurement of a person's dynamic strength using the psychophysical method. However, until more comprehensive methods are developed, psychophysical method based on simulations of task situations may be the most accurate method of estimating a person's acceptable strength limit (Chaffin & Andersson, 1991).

Muscle strength data have been collected for some muscle groups. For example, Kamon and Goldfuss (1978) found that the average male worker has a forearm flexion and extension strength of about 276 Newtons when one arm is used, and the average female worker has a forearm strength of about 160 Newtons. Asmussen and Heebol-Nielsen (1961) found that the torque-generating capability of an average male is about 14.1 Newton-meters when turning a handle and about 4.1 Newton-meters when turning a key. The corresponding strength data for an average female are 8.6 Newton-meters and 3.2 Newton-meters, respectively (Eastman Kodak Company, 1986).

In performing a physical work, excessive loading can cause musculoskeletal problems such as bone fracture and muscle fatigue. To determine whether a load is excessive for a body segment, we need to quantify the magnitude of physical stress imposed on the body segment in performing the task. How do we obtain these quantitative estimates? Biomechanical modeling discussed in the next section provides an important method for answering this question.

BIOMECHANICAL MODELS

Biomechanical models are mathematical models of the mechanical properties of the human body. In biomechanical modeling, the musculoskeletal system is analyzed as a system of mechanical links, and the bones and muscles act as a series of levers. Biomechanical models allow one to predict the stress levels on specific musculoskeletal components quantitatively with established methods of physics and mechanical engineering and thus can serve as an analytical tool to help job designers identify and avoid hazardous job situations.

The fundamental basis of biomechanical modeling is the set of three Newton's laws. They are:

1. A mass remains in uniform motion or at rest until acted on by an unbalanced external force.
2. Force is proportional to the acceleration of a mass.
3. Any action is opposed by reaction of equal magnitude.

When a body or a body segment is not in motion, it is described as in static equilibrium. For an object to be in static equilibrium, two conditions must be met. The first condition states that the sum of all external forces acting on an object in static equilibrium must be equal to zero. The second condition for equilibrium states that the sum of all external moments acting on the object must be equal to zero. These two conditions play an essential role in biomechanical modeling and are further illustrated below.

The following is a description of two planar, static models of isolated body segments based on Chaffin and Andersson (1991). Planar models (also called two-dimensional models) are often used to analyze symmetric body postures with forces acting in a single plane. Static models assume that a person is in a static position with no movement of the body or body segments. Although these models are elementary, they serve the purpose of illustrating the methods of biomechanical modeling. Complex three-dimensional, whole-body models can be developed as expansions of these elementary models.

Single-Segment Planar, Static Model

A single-segment model analyzes an isolated body segment with the laws of mechanics to identify the physical stress on the joints and muscles involved. As an illustration, suppose a person is holding a load of 20-kg mass with both hands in front of his body and his forearms are horizontal. The distance between the load and elbow is 36 cm, as shown in the schematic diagram in Figure 11.1. The load is equally balanced between the two hands.

The forces and rotational moments acting on the person's elbow can be determined using the laws of mechanics. First, load weight can be calculated with the equation

$$W = mg$$

where

W is the weight of object measured in Newtons (N),
m is the mass of object measured in kilograms (kg),
g is the gravitational acceleration (a constant of 9.8 m/s^2).

For the current problem, we have

$$W = 20 \text{ kg} \times 9.8 \ m/s^2 = 196 \text{ N.}$$

When the center of mass of the load is located exactly between the two hands and the weight is equally balanced between both hands as in the current case, each hand supports half of the total weight. We have

$$W_{\text{on-each-hand}} = 98 \text{ N.}$$

Furthermore, for a typical adult worker, we assume that the weight of the forearm-hand segment is 16 N, and the distance between the center of mass of the forearm-hand segment and the elbow is 18 cm, as shown in Figure 11.1.

The elbow reactive force R_{elbow} can be calculated using the first condition of equilibrium described above. For the current problem, it means that R_{elbow} must be in the upward direction and large enough to resist the downward weight forces of the load and the forearm-hand segment. That is,

$$
\begin{aligned}
\Sigma \text{ (Forces at the elbow)} &= 0 \\
-16 \text{ N} - 98 \text{ N} + R_{\text{elbow}} &= 0 \\
R_{\text{elbow}} &= 114 \text{ N}
\end{aligned}
$$

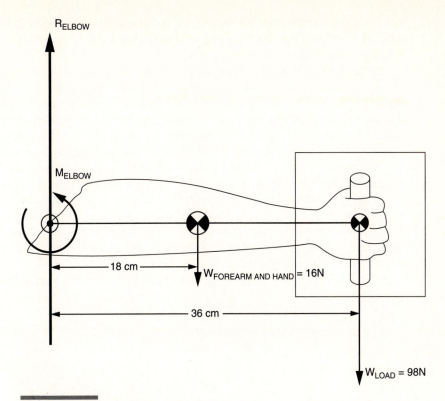

FIGURE 11.1

A single segment biomechanical model of a forearm and a hand holding a load in the horizontal position. (*Source:* Adapted from Chaffin, D.B., and Andersson, G.B.J., 1991. *Occupational Biomechanics* [2nd Edition]. New York: Wiley. Copyright © 1991. Reprinted by permission of John Wiley & Sons, Inc.)

The elbow moment M_{elbow} can be calculated using the second condition of equilibrium. More specifically, the clockwise moments created by the weight forces of the load and the forearm-hand segment must be counteracted by an equal-magnitude, counterclockwise M_{elbow}. That is,

$$\sum (\text{Moments at the elbow}) = 0$$
$$(-16 \text{ N})(0.18 \, m) + (-98 \text{ N})(0.36 \text{ m}) + M_{elbow} = 0$$
$$M_{elbow} = 38.16 \text{ N–}m$$

Two-Segment Planar, Static Model

The single-segment model is used above to determine the forces and moments at the elbow caused by external loads. In order to determine the physical stress at the body joints that are more distant from the external load such as the shoulders and the low back, the body segments involved in handling the load can be treated as a chain of links. Starting from the body segment that is in direct contact with the external load, one can work back one segment at a time toward the more distant segments until the segment in question is reached.

As an example, Figure 11.2 shows a two-segment model, which is an extension of the single-segment model in Figure 11.1. Here we are interested in determining the forces and moments at the shoulder joint for the same person and external load discussed in the single segment model. Assume that the distance between the elbow and the shoulder is 34 cm, and the weight of the upper arm is 20 N, as shown in Figure 11.2. Assume that the upper and lower arms are in a horizontal position.

R_{elbow} was determined earlier as 114 N (upward) and M_{elbow} was 38.16 N–m (counterclockwise). With respect to the upper arm, the elbow force (shown as R'_{elbow}) acts downward but has the same magnitude as R_{elbow}. Similarly, the elbow moment (shown as M'_{elbow}) acts clockwise but is the same as M_{elbow} in magnitude. After having "transferred" the elbow force and moment from the lower-arm to the upper arm in this way, we can now focus on the upper arm and calculate the forces and moments at the shoulder.

The shoulder reactive force $R_{shoulder}$ can be determined on the basis of the first condition of equilibrium. We have

$$\Sigma \text{ (Forces at the shoulder)} = 0$$
$$- R'_{elbow} - W_{upper\text{-}arm} + R_{shoulder} = 0$$
$$R_{shoulder} = R'_{elbow} + W_{upper\text{-}arm}$$
$$= 114 \text{ N} + 20 \text{ N}$$
$$= 134 \text{ N}$$

The shoulder reactive moment $M_{shoulder}$ can be determined by considering the second condition of equilibrium. That is,

$$\Sigma \text{ (moments at the shoulder)} = 0$$
$$- 38.16 \text{ N–}m + (- 114 \text{ N}) (0.34 \, m)$$
$$+ (- 20 \text{ N}) (0.14 \, m) + M_{shoulder} = 0$$
$$M_{shoulder} = 79.72 \text{ N–}m \text{ (counterclockwise)}$$

Comparing the solution for the two-segment model with that of the single-segment model, we can see clearly that $M_{shoulder}$ is more than twice as large as M_{elbow} when handling the same external load of 20 kg. This is because the shoulder joint is more distant from the load, and the weights of the upper and the lower arms add additional stress on the shoulder.

In general, because moment is the product of force and the perpendicular distance from its line of action to the point of rotation, the same load will create a much greater moment at a distant joint than at a joint close to the load. Because low back is more distant from a load handled by the hands than the shoulder and elbow, low back is often exposed to significant stress in material handling, as discussed in the following section.

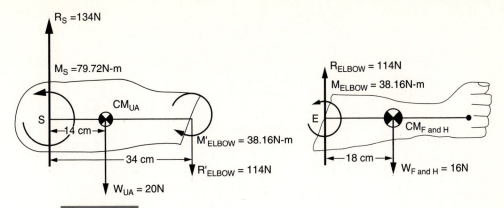

FIGURE 11.2

A two-segment biomechanical model of upper-arm and forearm-hand segments held in horizontal position. (*Source:* Adapted from Chaffin, D.B., and Andersson, G.B.J., 1991. *Occupational Biomechanics* [2nd Edition]. New York: Wiley. Copyright © 1991. Reprinted by permission of John Wiley & Sons, Inc.)

LOW-BACK PROBLEMS

As mentioned earlier, low-back pain is perhaps the most costly and prevalent work-related musculoskeletal disorder in industry. According to the estimates of the National Council on Compensation Insurance, low back pain cases account for approximately one-third of all workers' compensation payments. When indirect costs are included, the total costs estimates range from about $27 to $56 billion in the United States (Pope et al., 1991). About 60 percent overexertion injury reported each year in the United States are related to lifting (NIOSH, 1981). Further, it is estimated that low back pain may affect as high as 50–70 percent of the general population due to occupational and other unknown factors (Andersson, 1981; Waters et al., 1993).

Manual material handling involving lifting, bending, and twisting motions of the torso are a major cause of work-related low-back pain and disorders, both in the occurrence rate and the degree of severity. However, low back problems are not restricted to these situations. Low back pain is also common in sedentary work environments requiring a prolonged static sitting posture. Thus, manual handling and seated work become two of the primary job situations in which the biomechanics of the back should be analyzed. We discuss these two situations in this section.

Low-Back Biomechanics of Lifting

Low back is perhaps the most vulnerable link of the musculoskeletal system in material handling because the low back is most distant from the load handled by the hands, as shown in Figure 11.3. Both the load and the weight of the upper torso create significant stress on the body structures at the low back, especially at the disc between the fifth lumbar and the first sacral vertebrae (called the L5/S1 lumbosacral disc).

A more accurate determination of the reactive forces and moments at the L5/S1 disk requires the use of a multisegment model, as illustrated earlier when we estimated forces and moments at the shoulder. It also requires the consideration of abdominal pressure, created by the diaphragm and abdominal wall muscles (Morris, Lucas, & Bressler, 1961). However, a simplified single-segment model discussed here can be used to obtain a quick estimate of the stress at the low back (Chaffin & Andersson, 1991).

When a person with an upper-body weight of W_{torso} lifts a load with a weight of W_{load}, the load and the upper torso create a combined clockwise rotational moment that can be calculated as,

$$M_{load\text{-}and\text{-}torso} = W_{load} \times h + W_{torso} \times b$$

where

h is the horizontal distance from the load to the L5/S1 disc, and
b is the horizontal distance from the center of mass of the torso to the L5/S1 disc.

This clockwise rotational moment must be counteracted by a counterclockwise rotational moment, which is produced by the back muscles with a moment arm of about 5 cm. That is,

$$M_{back\text{-}muscle} = F_{back\text{-}muscle} \times 5 \text{ (N–cm)}.$$

According to the second condition of static equilibrium, we have,

$$\Sigma \text{ (moments at the L5/S1 disc)} = 0.$$

That is,

$$F_{muscle} \times 5 = W_{load} \times h + W_{torso} \times b$$
$$F_{muscle} = W_{load} \times h/5 + W_{torso} \times b/5.$$

Because h and b are always much larger than 5 cm, F_{muscle} is always much greater than the sum of the weights of the load and torso. For example, if we assume that $h = 40$ cm and $b = 20$ cm for a typical lifting situation, we have

$$F_{muscle} = W_{load} \times 40/5 + W_{torso} \times 20/5$$
$$= 8 \times W_{load} + 4 \times W_{torso}$$

This equation indicates that for a lifting situation discussed here, which is typical of many lifting tasks, the back muscle force is eight times the load weight and four times the torso weight combined. Suppose a person has a torso weight of 350 N and is lifting a load of 300 N (about 30 kg). The above equation tells us that the back muscle force would be 3,800 N. Which may exceed the capacity of some people. Suppose the same person lifts a load of 450 N, the above equation indicates that the muscle force would reach 5,000 N, which is at the upper limit of most people's muscle capability. Farfan (1973) estimates that the normal range of strength capability of the erector spinal muscle at the low back is 2,200–5,500 N.

In addition to the muscle strength considerations, one must also consider the compression force on the L5/S1 disc, which can be estimated with the following equation, on the basis of the first condition of equilibrium:

$$\Sigma \text{ (forces at the L5/S1 disc)} = 0.$$

As a simple approximation, we can ignore the abdominal force, f_a, shown in Figure 11.3, and we have

$$F_{\text{compression}} = W_{\text{load}} \times \cos \alpha + W_{\text{torso}} \times \cos \alpha + F_{\text{muscle}},$$

where α is shown in Figure 11.3 as the angle between the horizontal plane and the sacral cutting plane, which is perpendicular to the disc compression force.

This equation suggests that disc compression force can be even greater than the muscle force. For example, suppose $\alpha = 55°$. When a person with a torso weight of 350 N lifts a load of 450 N, we have

$$F_{\text{compression}} = 450 \times \cos 55° + 350 \times \cos 55° + 5000$$
$$= 258 + 200 + 5000 = 5458 \text{ N}$$

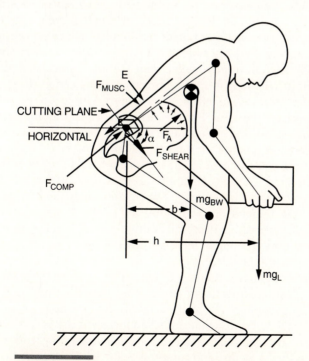

FIGURE 11.3

A low-back biomechanical model of static coplanar lifting. (*Source:* Chaffin, D.B., and Andersson, G.B.J., 1991. *Occupational Biomechanics* [2nd Edition]. New York: Wiley. Copyright © 1991. Reprinted by permission of John Wiley & Sons, Inc.)

As discussed in the following section, disc compression at this level can be hazardous to many workers.

In carrying out a lifting task, several factors influence the load stress placed on the spine. The analysis above considers explicitly two of the factors—the weight and the position of the load relative to the center of the spine. A number of other factors are also important in determining the load on the spine, including the degree of twisting of the torso, the size and shape of the object, and the distance the load is moved. Developing a comprehensive and accurate biomechanical model of the low back that includes all these factors is beyond the scope of this book. For practical ergonomics analysis purposes, the lifting guide developed by the National Institute for Occupational Safety and Health is of great value (described in detail in the next section).

NIOSH LIFTING GUIDE

The National Institute for Occupational Safety and Health (NIOSH) developed an equation in 1981 to assist ergonomists and occupational safety and health practitioners analyze lifting demands on low back (NIOSH, 1981). The purpose is to help prevent or reduce the occurrence of lifting-related low-back pain and injuries. The equation, known as the NIOSH lifting equation, provides a method for determining two weight limits that are associated with two levels of back injury risk. More specifically, the first limit is called an action limit (AL), which represents a weight limit above which a small portion of the population may experience increased risk of injury if they are not trained to perform the lifting task. The second limit, called the maximum permissible limit (MPL), is calculated as three times the action limit. This weight limit represents a lifting condition at which most people would experience a high risk of back injury. Lifting jobs must be redesigned if they are above the MPL. The NIOSH lifting equation can be used to identify high-risk lifting jobs and evaluate alternative job designs and has received wide acceptance among ergonomics and safety practitioners.

The 1981 equation could only be applied to symmetrical lifting tasks that do not involve torso twisting. The 1981 equation was revised and expanded in 1991 to apply to a greater variety of lifting tasks. The equation allows one to compute an index called the recommended weight limit (RWL), which represents a load value for a specific lifting task that nearly all healthy workers could perform for a substantial period of time without an increased risk of developing lifting-related low-back pain (Waters et al., 1993).

The lifting equation is based on three criteria established on the basis of research results and expert judgments from the perspectives of biomechanics, psychophysics, and work physiology. The biomechanical criterion selects 3.4 kN as the compressive force at the L5/S1 disc that defines an increased risk of low-back injury. In setting the biomechanical criterion, it is realized that lifting tend to incur the greatest stress at the L5/S1 disc and compressive force is likely to be the critical stress vector responsible for disc injuries such as disc herniation, vertebral end-plate fracture, and nerve root irritation. Although shear force and torsional force are also transmitted to the L5/S1 disc during lifting, their effects on back tissues remain unclear in the current state of knowledge and thus are not considered in designing the NIOSH lifting equation.

The 3.4 kN limit was established on the basis of epidemiological data and cadaver data. Epidemiological data from industrial studies provide quantitative evidence linking lifting-related low-back pain and injury incidence with estimated disc compressive force on the L5/S1 disc. For example, Herrin et al. (1986) traced the medical reports of 6,912 incumbent workers employed in 55 industrial jobs involving 2,934 potentially stressful manual material handling tasks. They found that the rate of reported back problems for jobs with predicted compressive force between 4.5 kN and 6.8 kN was more than 1.5 times greater than that for jobs with compressive force below 4.5 kN. Cadaver data have also been used to evaluate the compressive strength of the spine. For example, Jager and Luttman (1989) found a mean value of 4.4 kN with a standard deviation of 1.88 kN. In general, the studies show that spine specimens are more likely to show damage as the compressive force increases.

Physiological and psychophysical criteria were also used in developing the lifting equation. The physiological criterion was selected to limit loads for repetitive lifting. Activities such as walking, load carrying, and repeated load lifting use more muscle groups than infrequent lifting tasks. These kinds of activities require large energy expenditures, which should not exceed the energy producing capacity of a worker. The physiological criterion sets the limit of maximum energy expenditure for a lifting task at 2.2 to 4.7 kcal/min. The meaning and the importance of these terms will be discussed in the next chapter on work physiology.

The psychophysical criterion is developed on the basis of measurements of the maximum-acceptable-weight-of-lift, which is the amount of weight a person chooses to lift for a given task situation. The maximum-acceptable-weight-of-lift is obtained in experiments in which workers are asked to "work as hard as you can without straining yourself, or without becoming unusually tired, weakened, overheated, or out of breath" (Snook & Ciriello, 1991; Waters et al., 1993). Studies have shown that low-back pain and injuries are less likely to occur for lifting tasks that are judged acceptable by workers than those that are not. The psychophysical criterion of the NIOSH lifting equation was selected to ensure that the lifting demands would not exceed the acceptable lifting capacity of about 99 percent of male workers and 75 percent of female workers, which include about 90 percent of a 50-50 mixed-sex working population.

Based on these three criteria, the following lifting equation was developed for calculating the recommended weight limit (Waters et al., 1993):

$$RWL = LC \times HM \times VM \times DM \times AM \times FM \times CM$$

where

RWL is the recommended weight limit.

LC is called the load constant. It defines the maximum recommended weight for lifting under optimal conditions, which refers to lifting tasks satisfying the following conditions: symmetric lifting position with no torso twisting, occasional lifting, good coupling, $\leq$ 25 cm vertical distance of lifting.

HM is the horizontal multiplier, which reflects the fact that disc compression force increases as the horizontal distance between the load and the spine increases, and thus the maximum acceptable weight limit should be decreased from *LC* as the horizontal distance increases.

VM is the vertical multiplier. Lifting from near the floor is more stressful than lifting from greater heights. Thus, the allowable weights for lifts should be a function of the originating height of the load. *VM* is used to accommodate this consideration.

DM is the distance multiplier. *DM* was established on the basis of results of empirical studies that suggest physical stress increases as the vertical distance of lifting increases.

AM is the asymmetric multiplier. Asymmetric lifting involving torso twisting is more harmful to back spine than symmetric lifting. Therefore, the allowable weight of lift should be reduced when lifting tasks involve asymmetric body twists. *AM* incorporates this consideration into the lifting equation.

CM is the coupling multiplier, which takes on different values depending on whether the loads are equipped with appropriate handles or couplings to help grab and lift the loads.

FM is the frequency multiplier, which is used to reflect the effects of lifting frequency on acceptable lift weights.

The values of the first five components can be determined with the formulas in the Table 11.1. The values of *FM* and *CM* can be found in Tables 11.2 and 11.3, respectively. In Table 11.1,

H is the horizontal distance between the hands lifting the load and the midpoint between the ankles.

V is the vertical distance of the hands from the floor.

D is the vertical travel distance between the origin and the destination of the lift.

A is the angle of asymmetry (measured in degrees), which is the angle of torso twisting involved in lifting a load that is not directly in front of the person.

F is the average frequency of lifting measured in lifts/min (see Table 11.2).

TABLE 11.1 **Definition of Components of NIOSH Lifting Equation (1991)**

Component	Metric System	U.S. System
LC (load constant)	23 kg	51 lb
HM (horizontal multiplier)	(25/H)	(10/H)
VM (vertical multiplier)	$(1-0.003|V-75|)$	$(1-0.0075|V-30|)$
DM (distance multiplier)	(0.82+4.5/D)	(0.82+1.8/D)
AM (asymmetric multiplier)	$(1-0.0032A)$	$(1-0.0032A)$
FM (frequency multiplier)	from Table 10.2	from Table 10.2
CM (coupling multiplier)	from Table 10.3	from Table 10.3

TABLE 11.2 Frequency Multiplier (FM)

Frequency lifts/min	Work duration					
	≤1h		≤2h		≤8h	
	V<75	V≥75	V<75	V≥75	V<75	V≥75
0.2	1.00	1.00	0.95	0.95	0.85	0.85
0.5	0.97	0.97	0.92	0.92	0.81	0.81
1	0.94	0.94	0.88	0.88	0.75	0.75
2	0.91	0.91	0.84	0.84	0.65	0.65
3	0.88	0.88	0.79	0.79	0.55	0.55
4	0.84	0.84	0.72	0.72	0.45	0.45
5	0.80	0.80	0.60	0.60	0.35	0.35
6	0.75	0.75	0.50	0.50	0.27	0.27
7	0.70	0.70	0.42	0.42	0.22	0.22
8	0.60	0.60	0.35	0.35	0.18	0.18
9	0.52	0.52	0.30	0.30	0.00	0.15
10	0.45	0.45	0.26	0.26	0.00	0.13
11	0.41	0.41	0.00	0.23	0.00	0.00
12	0.37	0.37	0.00	0.21	0.00	0.00
13	0.00	0.34	0.00	0.00	0.00	0.00
14	0.00	0.31	0.00	0.00	0.00	0.00
15	0.00	0.28	0.00	0.00	0.00	0.00
>15	0.00	0.00	0.00	0.00	0.00	0.00

Source: Waters, T.R., Putz-Anderson, V., Garg, A., and Fine, L. (1993). Revised NIOSH equation for the design and evaluation of manual lifting tasks, *Ergonomics, 36,* 7, 749–776. Copyright © 1993. Reprinted by permission of Taylor & Francis.

The NIOSH lifting equation allows one to calculate the *RWL* for specific task situations as an index of the baseline capacity of workers. Clearly, the risk of back injury increases as the load lifted exceeds this baseline. To quantify the degree to which a lifting task approaches or exceeds the *RWL*, a lifting index (*LI*) was proposed for the 1991 NIOSH lifting equation, which is defined as the ratio of the load lifted to the *RWL*. The *LI* can be used to estimate the risk of specific lifting tasks in developing low-back disorders and to compare the lifting demands associated with different lifting tasks for the purpose of evaluating and redesigning them (Waters et al., 1993). The current belief is that lifting tasks with a *LI* > 1 are likely to pose an increased risk for some of the workers. When *LI* > 3, however, many or most workers are at a high risk of developing low-back pain and injury.

TABLE 11.3 Coupling Multiplier

Couplings	V < 75 cm (30 in.)	V ≥75 cm (30 in.)
	Coupling multipliers	
Good	1.00	1.00
Fair	0.95	1.00
Poor	0.90	0.90

An example of a lifting job that can be analyzed with the NIOSH lifting equation is illustrated in Figure 11.4. The job requires the worker to move tote boxes from an incoming flat conveyor to an outgoing J-hook conveyor at a rate of about three boxes per minute. Each tote box weighs 15 lbs, and the worker performs this job for 8 hours each day. The worker can grasp the tote box quite comfortably. The physical dimensions of the workplace that are relevant for using the NIOSH lifting equation are shown in Figure 11.4. More specifically, the horizontal distance between the hands and the midpoint between the ankles is 16 inches. It is assumed that this horizontal distance is kept relatively constant during lifting. The vertical distance of the hands from the floor at the starting position of lifting is 44 inches. The vertical distance of the hands from the floor at the destination is 62 inches, and thus the distance lifted is 18 inches ($62 - 44 = 18$). Although it is not shown in the figure, it is estimated that the worker needs to twist his or her torso about $80°$ while transferring a tote box from the incoming to the outgoing conveyor. These parameters can be summarized as follows:

$H = 16''$
$V = 44''$
$D = 18''$
$A = 80°$
$F = 3$ lifts/minute
C: Good coupling
Job duration: 8 hours per day
Weight lifted: 15 lbs

The six multipliers can be calculated as follows:

$HM = 10/H = 10/16 = 0.625$
$VM = 1 - 0.0075 \times |V - 30| = 1 - 0.0075 \times |44 - 30| = 0.895$
$DM = 0.82 + 1.8/D = 0.82 + 1.8/18 = 0.92$
$AM = 1 - 0.0032 \times A = 1 - 0.0032 \times 80 = 0.744$
$FM = 0.55$ (from Table 11.2, 3 lifts/min, 8 hours, $V < 75''$)
$CM = 1.0$ (from Table 11.3, good coupling)

So we have

$$RWL = 51 \times HM \times VM \times DM \times AM \times FM \times CM$$
$$= 51 \times 0.625 \times 0.895 \times 0.92 \times 0.744 \times 0.55 \times 1.0$$
$$= 10.74 \text{ (lbs)}$$
$$LI = \text{Weight of tote}/RWL = 15/10.74 = 1.40$$

The result of this analysis suggests that some workers would experience an increased risk of back injury while performing this lifting task because the lifting

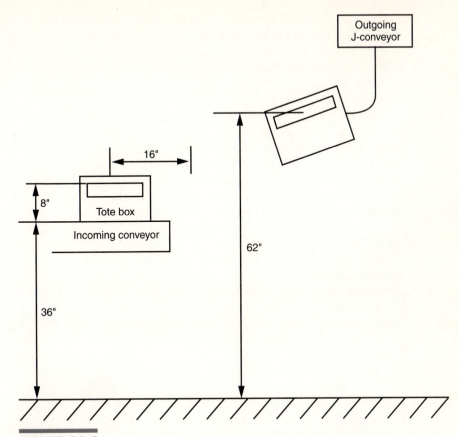

FIGURE 11.4
A schematic representation of the workplace for tote box transfer.

index (*LI*) of 1.4 associated with this job is slightly higher than 1.0. Necessary precautions must be taken to minimize the risk of injury, and the job may need to be redesigned to lower the *LI*.

Manual Materials Handling

The NIOSH lifting equation discussed above not only provides a job analysis tool for evaluating lifting demands, it also suggests a list of seven major design parameters that job designers should try to optimize in designing workplaces and devices for material handling.

The horizontal and the vertical multipliers in the NIOSH equation reminds job designers that loads or material handling devices (MHDs) should be kept close to the body and located at about thigh or waist height if possible. Large packages located on or near the floor are particularly hazardous because they cannot be easily kept close to the body and a person must lean the torso forward, resulting in a significant increase in low-back disc compression force as illustrated in the low-back biomechanical model discussed earlier. Thus, large packages should not be presented to a worker at a height lower than about midthigh (or about 30 in. above the floor) (Chaffin, 1997). For example, adjustable lift tables can be used to assist the workers when handling large or heavy objects, as illustrated in Figure 11.5. Use of lift tables can also help reduce the vertical travel distance that an object needs to be lifted, which is suggested by the distance multiplier.

The asymmetric multiplier reminds the designers that torso twisting should be minimized in materials handling. Figure 11.6 shows that a simple and careful redesign of workplace layout can help eliminate unnecessary torso twisting movements and significantly reduce the risk of worker discomfort and injury. To minimize torso twisting, a lifting task should be designed in a way that requires the use of both hands in front of the body and balances the load between the hands. Extra caution should be exercised in lifting bags of powdered materials because the contents of the bag may shift during lifting. This type of lifting should be avoided if possible.

The NIOSH lifting equation also reminds the job designers that the frequency of lifting should be minimized by adopting adequate lifting and work-rest schedules. Much of the frequent and heavy lifting in a workplace should be done with the assistance of MHDs. Furthermore, the loads or MHDs should be easy to grasp and handle. Every effort should be made to minimize the weight of the load by selecting lightweight materials if possible.

(a)   (b)

FIGURE 11.5

Use of adjustable lift tables to avoid stooped lifting of heavy materials: (a) A lift and tilt table, (b) a pallet lift table. (*Source:* Adapted from the United Auto Workers-Ford Job Improvement Guide, 1988.)

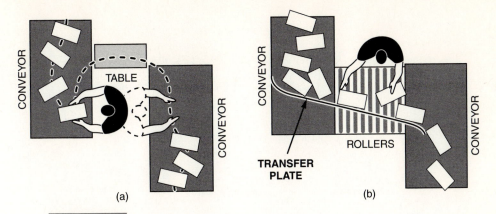

FIGURE 11.6

An example of workplace redesign: (a) Old workplace design requiring lifting and torso twisting; (b) redesigned workplace minimizing these requirements (*Source:* Adapted from the United Auto Workers-Ford Job Improvement Guide, 1988.)

Clearly, these design parameters do not constitute a complete list of the causes of musculoskeletal problems in manual materials handling. Other factors such as whole body vibration, psychosocial factors, age, health, physical fitness, and nutrition conditions of a person are also important in determining the incidence rate and severity of low back pain in material handling. Furthermore, lifting-related low-back pain comprise only a portion of all cases of low-back pain in the workplaces (Frymoyer et al., 1980; National Safety Council, 1990). The following discussion of seated work illustrates another common cause of low-back problems.

Seated Work and Chair Design

In Chapter 10 we mentioned that, whenever possible, a seated workplace should be used for long-duration jobs because a seated posture is much easier to maintain and less strainful to the body. It also allows for better-controlled arm movements, provides a stronger sense of balance and safety, and improves blood circulation. However, the sitting posture has its own cost: it is particularly vulnerable to low-back problems. In fact, low-back pain is common in seated work environments where no lifting or manual handling activities occur.

Low-back disorders in seated work are largely due to a loss of lordotic curvature in the spine and a corresponding increase in disc pressure for the sitting posture. The lumbar (low-back) spine of an adult human when standing erect is curved forward—a spinal posture called *lordosis,* while the thoracic spine is curve backward, known as *kyphosis.* When a person sits down, the pelvis rotates backward and the lumbar lordosis is changed into a kyphosis, particularly when a person sits with a slumped posture, as shown in Figure 11.7. Without proper body support, most people adopt a slumped sitting posture soon after sitting down, in which the front part of the intervertebral discs is compressed and the back part stretched. These forces cause the discs to protrude backward, pressurizing the

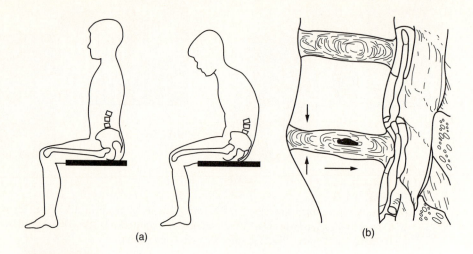

(a)   (b)

FIGURE 11.7
Low-back problems in prolonged sitting. (a) Most people do not maintain an erect posture for long but soon adopt a slumped posture. (b) The slumped sitting position produces anterior wedging of the intervertebral disk at the low back, which may pressurize the soft tissues between the anterior and posterior elements of the spine, causing low-back pain and disorders. (*Source:* Bridger, R.S., 1995. *Introduction to Ergonomics.* New York: McGraw-Hill. Copyright © 1995. Reprinted by permission of the McGraw-Hill Companies.)

spinal soft tissues and possibly the nerve roots, which may result in back pain (Bridger, 1995; Keegan, 1953).

Furthermore, loss of lumbar lordosis in a sitting posture increases the load within the discs because the trunk load moment increases when the pelvis rotates backward and the lumbar spine and torso rotate forward. A number of studies have shown that the disc pressures for upright standing postures were at least 35–40% lower than those for sitting (Nachemson & Morris, 1964; Chaffin & Andersson, 1991). In different unsupported sitting postures, the lowest pressure was found when sitting with the back straight. As shown in Figure 11.8, disc pressure is much lower in an erect sitting posture than in slumped sitting. Further, disc pressure varies considerably depending on the sitting posture.

To reduce the incidence rate and severity of low back pain in seated work, workplace designers need to pay special attention to the design of seats. A properly designed seat can support a person to adopt a less strainful posture and reduce the loads placed on the spine. In this regard, there are several seat-design parameters that are effective in achieving this purpose, including the backrest inclination angle, lumbar support, and arm rest.

Backrest is effective in reducing low-back stress. The most important parameter of back rest design is its inclination angle, which is the angle between the backrest and the seat surface. A 90° back-inclination angle (a seat with a straight back) is inappropriate because it forces a person to adopt a slumped posture. An

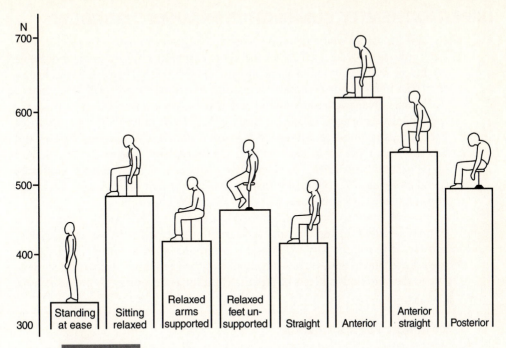

FIGURE 11.8

Disc pressure measurements in standing and unsupported sitting. (*Source:* Andersson, G.B.J., 1974. Biomechanical aspects of sitting: An application to VDT terminals. *Behavior and Information Technology* 6 (3) 257–269. Copyright © 1974. Reprinted by permission of Taylor & Francis.)

increase in backrest inclination results in an increase in the transfer of body weight to the backrest and a reduced disc pressure. The optimal inclination angle should be between 110° and 120° (Hosea et al., 1986; Andersson et al., 1974).

The backrest should also be provided with a pad in the lumbar region (called a lumbar support) which can greatly reduce the low-back stress because it helps a seated person maintain lordosis. Lumbar support is particularly important when the back inclination angle is small. There is also evidence that a lumbar support is as effective as a full back support (Chaffin and Andersson, 1991). The thickness of lumbar support should be about 5 cm. It is desirable, however, that the lumbar support is adjustable in height and size to maximize the comfort for people of different sizes.

Arm rests can help support part of the body weight of a seated person and thus reduce the load on the spine. A tiltable seat surface is also desirable in that it allows variations in posture, although there is no clear evidence that tiltable seat surface can change the spinal load significantly (Bendix et al., 1985). Properly adjusted seat height, use of cushioned seat surfaces, and adequate leg space can all help reduce back stress. Further, it should be emphasized that no matter how well seats are designed, a person should not adopt a static sitting posture for long. Sedentary workers should have regular breaks in which they should stand up and walk around.

UPPER-EXTREMITY CUMULATIVE TRAUMA DISORDERS

In some industries where repetitive hand and arm exertions are prevalent, cumulative trauma disorders (CTDs) of the upper extremities are common and can be even more costly than low-back problems. Since the early 1980s, there has been a sharp rise in reported CTD cases. Armstrong and Silverstein (1987) found that in workplaces involving frequent hand and arm exertions, more than 1 in 10 workers annually reported CTDs. According to CTD News (1995), the U.S. Bureau of Labor Statistics' most recent report shows that 302,000 CTD-related injuries and illnesses were reported in 1993, which is up more than 7 percent from 1992 and up 63 percent from 1990. CTD News (1995) estimates that American employers spend more than $7.4 billion a year in workers compensation costs and untold billions on medical treatment and other costs such as litigation.

Several other terms have been used to describe upper-extremity cumulative trauma disorders, including *cumulative effect trauma, repetitive motion disorders,* and *repetitive strain injury (RSI). RSI* is commonly used in Europe, and CTD is used in the United States. These terms all emphasize that the disorders are largely due to the cumulative effects of repetitive, prolonged exposure to physical strain and stress.

Common Forms of CTD

CTDs are disorders of the soft tissues in the upper extremities, including the fingers, the hand and wrist, the upper and lower arms, the elbow, and the shoulder. The following is a description of some of the commonly observed CTDs.

Tendon-Related CTD. As described earlier, tendons attach muscles to bones and transfer muscle forces to bones. When an increased blood supply is needed in repetitive work, the muscles may "steal" blood from tendons, particularly in static work in which there is an increased tension in tendons. These conditions may cause *tendon pain.* Excessive and repetitive use of tendons can cause inflammation of tendons, which is a common CTD known as *tendonitis.* The sheaths surrounding tendons provide the necessary nutrition and lubrication to the tendons. When the sheaths also show inflammation and secret excess synovial fluid, the condition is called *tenosynovitis.*

Neuritis. As described earlier, sensory and motor nerves enter and leave the muscles and connect the muscles to the central nervous system. Repeated use of the upper extremities in awkward posture can stretch the nerves or rub the nerves against bones and cause nerve damage, leading to neuritis. This ailment is accompanied by tingling and numbness in the affected areas of the body.

Ischemia. The sensations of tingling and numbness can also occur when there is a localized tissue anemia due to an obstruction of blood flow. Repeated exposures of the palm to pressure forces from the handle of a hand tool, for example, can cause obstructions of blood flow to fingers, leading to ischemia at the fingers.

Bursitis. Bursitis is the inflammation of a bursa, which is a sac containing synovia or viscous fluid. Bursae can be found near the joints, and they protect tendons from rubbing against bones and help reduce friction between tissues where friction would otherwise likely to occur. Bursitis is usually accompanied by a dull pain in the affected part of the body.

CTDs can also be classified according to specific body parts affected, that is, the fingers, hand and wrist, elbow, and shoulder.

CTDs of the Fingers. Repeated and prolonged use of vibrating hand tools may cause numbness, tingling, or pain when the hands are exposed to cold, which is an ailment known as *"vibration-induced white fingers"* or *Raynaud's phenomenon.* Excessive use of digit fingers against resistance or sharp edges and repeated use of index finger with pistol type of hand tools may cause a condition called *"trigger finger,"* in which the affected finger can not straighten itself once flexed. Forceful extensions of the thumb may cause impaired thumb movement, a condition called *"gamekeeper's thumb."*

CTDs of the Hand and Wrist. Carpal tunnel syndrome (CTS) is a common CTD affecting the wrist and hand. Several types of soft tissues pass through a narrow channel in the wrist known as the carpal tunnel. Finger movements are controlled by the muscles in the forearm, which are connected to the fingers by the long tendons passing through the carpal tunnel. Nerves and blood vessels also pass through this channel between the hand and the forearm.

CTS can have many occupational causes, including rapid and repetitive finger movements, repeated exertions with a bent wrist, static exertion for a long time, pressure at the base of the palm, and repeated exposure to hand vibration. CTS has been reported by typists and users of conventional computer keyboards, whose jobs require rapid finger movements and bent wrists (Hedge, McCrobie, Morimoto, Rodriguez, & Land, 1996). Use of conventional keyboards bend the wrists outward; it may also bend the wrist upward if a wrist-rest is not provided because the surfaces of the keys and the desk are at different heights. As shown in Figure 11.9, bending the wrist causes the finger tendons to rub against adjacent structures of the carpal tunnel and produces large intrawrist forces. Large forces and pressure in the carpal tunnel can cause tendon inflammation and swelling. Carpal tunnel syndrome develops if the median nerve in the carpal tunnel is affected, resulting in tingling and numbness in the palm and fingers.

CTDs at the Elbow. Many of the muscles of the forearm starts from the elbow; thus, wrist activities may affect the elbow. Repeated forceful wrist activities such as frequent use of a hammer can cause overexertion of the extensor muscles on the outside of the elbow and leads to tendon irritation, an ailment known as *"tennis elbow"* or *lateral epicondylitis.* When the flexor muscles and their tendons on the inside of the elbow are affected, the ailment is called *"golfer's elbow"* or *medial epicondylitis.* Another well-known CTD at the elbow is called *"telephone operator's elbow,"* which is often found in workplaces where workers rest their elbows on a sharp edge of a desk or a container. The constant pressure from the sharp edge may irritate the nerve and cause tingling and numbness in the vicinity of the little finger.

CTDs at the Shoulder. Working with fast or repetitive arm movements or with static elevated arms may cause shoulder pain and injuries, particularly when the

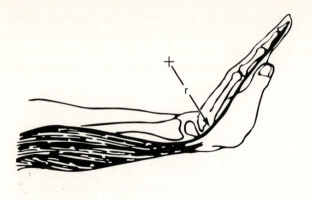

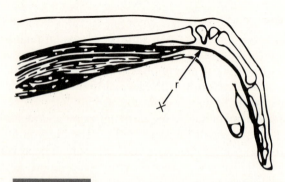

FIGURE 11.9

Bending the wrist causes the finger flexor tendons to rub on adjacent nerves and other tissues of the carpal tunnel. (*Source:* Armstrong, T.J., 1983. *An ergonomics guide to carpal tunnel syndrome.* Akron, OH: American Industrial Hygiene Association. Copyright © 1983. Reprinted by permission of Industrial Hygiene Association, Fairfax, VA.)

hands are raised above the shoulder height. These types of activities may cause cumulative trauma disorders at the shoulder such as tenosynovitis and bursitis, often known as impingement syndrome, "*rotator cuff irritation,*" "*swimmer's shoulder,*" or "*pitcher's arm.*"

Causes and Prevention of CTDs

From the discussion above, it is clear that CTDs can have many work-related causes, including repetitive motion, excessive force application, unnatural posture, prolonged static exertion, fast movement, vibration, cold environment, and pressure of tools or sharp edges on soft tissues.

Rapid, repetitive movements of hand or fingers can irritate the tendons and cause the sheaths surrounding tendons to produce excess synovial fluid, leading to tenosynovitis and tendonitis. These problems are more likely to occur when forceful exertions are involved because of the increased tensions in muscles and tendons. Unnatural joint postures such as bent wrists, elevated elbows, or raised shoulders preload and stretch the soft tissues and may press the tendons against the bones and increase their frictions with each other. Using a short tool handle against the base of the palm, grasping sharp objects in the hand, or resting the arm on a sharp edge can cause obstructions of blood flow and possibly irritate the nerves, which may also occur in vibrational or cold environments. These factors often combine in a job situation and increase the risk of CTDs.

A number of nonoccupational factors have also been identified as potential causes for CTDs. These factors include health condition, wrist size, pregnancy, use of oral contraceptives, sex, age, and psychosocial factors (Armstrong, 1983; Armstrong et al., 1993; Barton et al., 1992; Posch & Marcotte, 1976). People with preexisting health conditions such as arthritis, diabetes, and peripheral circulatory impairments are particularly vulnerable to the development of CTDs, which also appear to be more common among individuals with a small hand or wrist. Pregnancy, menopause, and use of oral contraceptives are also linked to the development of CTDs, which partially explains why women may be more prone to them. Elderly people have a greater risk of developing CTDs, particularly those with poor general health conditions. Further, psychosocial factors such as job satisfaction, self-esteem, and tolerance of discomfort are important factors in determining a person's vulnerability to developing CTDs.

The existence of the various occupational and nonoccupational causes calls for a comprehensive approach to the prevention of CTDs in workplaces through administrative and engineering methods. Administrative methods include worker education and training and the provision of appropriate work-rest schedules. Engineering methods refer to the use of engineering techniques to redesign the workplace and tools.

Human factors professionals and ergonomists need to work with the management and related worker organizations to establish continuing education programs to increase the workers' awareness and knowledge of the risks, causes, and preventive methods of CTDs. Attention to worker health conditions, establishment of regular exercise programs and facilities, and creation of a desirable social environment are some of the approaches that the management can adopt to minimize the risk of work-related CTDs.

Job schedules should be carefully evaluated and designed to reduce time and pace pressure and provide great flexibility. Warm-up exercises before the start of the work and the adoption of adequate work-rest cycles are effective ways of conditioning and relaxing the body in a work environment. Task rotation can increase task variety and help minimize the repetitive components of a job.

As discussed in the previous chapter, workers are forced to adopt an awkward posture when the workplace is not designed according to the anthropometric characteristics of workers. Elevated elbows and raised arms are required when using a high work surface. Static postures are unavoidable when the work space is too small to allow any movement. Neck and shoulder pain are likely to develop when the visual displays are located either too high or too low. Therefore, anthropometric design of workplaces is an important method for preventing work-related CTDs.

Use of automated equipments, provision of supporting devices, and careful design of work tools can also help reduce CTD risks. For example, highly repetitive tasks or tasks requiring forceful exertions should be done by automated equipments if possible. Provision of arm rests to support the weight of the arms can help reduce the load on the elbow and shoulder. Design of a work tool should be based on a careful analysis of the joint postures required in using the tool, and every effort should be made to avoid unnatural postures such as bent, twisted, or overextended joint positions. For computer keyboard users, provision of wrist rests with a proper surface contour and soft cloth material can help the wrists maintain a more natural posture and minimize the wrist contact with a potentially cold and sharp edge of the table. Because hand tools are used often in workplaces and everyday life, we discuss the design of hand tools in more detail in the following section.

Hand-Tool Design

Hand tools can be seen in everywhere. Screwdrivers, handsaws, hammers, pliers, scissors, forks, knives, and chopsticks constitute only a small sample of the hand tools used by millions of people every day. Hand tools extend the capabilities of the human hands to accomplish tasks that are otherwise impossible or dangerous. However, poorly designed hand tools may not only jeopardize task performance and productivity but become a major cause of CTDs. The following is a summary of four of the guidelines that have been developed for the design of hand tools to reduce the risk of developing CTDs (Armstrong, 1983; Chaffin & Andersson, 1991; Greenberg & Chaffin, 1976; Pheasant, 1986; Tichauer, 1978).

1. *Do not bend the wrist.* As discussed earlier, unnatural postures are harmful to the musculoskeletal structures involved. When using a hand tool, the wrist should remain straight, rather than bent or twisted. In other words, the hand, wrist, and forearm should remain in alignment when using a hand tool.

Straight-handled hand tools often require a bent-wrist posture for certain task situations, while a bent handle may help the worker maintain a straight wrist. As shown in Figure 11.10, the proper shape of the handle should be determined by a careful analysis of the task situation, some of which favor a bent handle and others favor straight ones. Figure 11.10 shows that pistol grip handles are desirable for powered drivers when working with a vertical surface at elbow height or a horizontal surface below waist height, whereas straight handles are better when working with a horizontal surface at elbow height.

2. *Shape tool handles to assist grip.* The center of the palm is vulnerable to force applications because the median nerve, the arteries, and the synovium for the finger flexor tendons are located in the area. Tool handles should be padded, be sufficiently long, and have a small curvature to help distribute the forces on either side of the palm and the fingers.

3. *Provide adequate grip span.* As shown in Figure 11.11, grip strength is a function of grip span, which is the distance between the two points where the hand contacts the two open handles of a hand tool. The grip strength of men is about twice as much as that of women, and both men and women achieve the maximum grip strength when the grip span is about 7–8 cm (Greenberg & Chaffin, 1976).

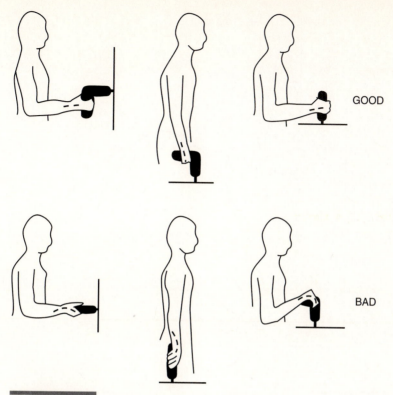

FIGURE 11.10

Wrist posture is determined by the height and orientation of the work surface and the shape of the hand tool. The three "good designs" illustrated in the figure allow the worker to maintain a good posture, that is, a straight wrist. The "bent wrist" shown in the three "bad designs" indicate bad postures which should be avoided in hand tool and workplace design. (*Source:* Adapted from Armstrong, T.J. 1983. *An ergonomics guide to carpal tunnel syndrome.* Akron, OH: AIHA Ergonomics Guide Series, American Industrial Hygiene Association. Copyright © 1983. Reprinted by permission of American Industrial Hygiene Association, Fairfax, VA.)

For round tool handles such as those for screwdrivers, the grip span is defined as the diameter of the handles. Ayoub and Lo Presti (1971) found that the maximum grip strength was observed when the grip span was about 4 cm. In general, the handle diameter should not be greater than 4–5 cm and should allow slight overlap of the thumb and fingers of the user (Pheasant & O'Neill, 1975; Bridger, 1995)

4. *Provide finger and gloves clearances.* Adequate finger clearance must be provided to ensure a full grip of an object and to minimize the risk of squeezing and crushing the fingers. Similarly, sufficient clearance for gloves should be provided if the workers are expected to wear them, such as in cold workplaces or when handling hazardous materials. Because gloves reduces both the sensory and the motor capabilities of the hands, extra caution must be exercised in tool and job design to avoid tool slippage or accidental activation of neighboring devices.

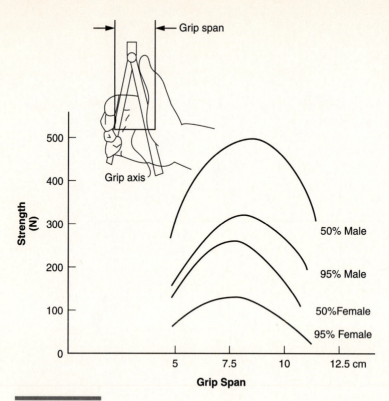

FIGURE 11.11

Maximum grip strength as a function of the width of a handle opening (grip span). (*Source: Chaffin, D.B., and Andersson, G.B.J., 1991. Occupational Biomechanics. New York: Wiley. Copyright © 1991. Reprinted by permission of John Wiley & Sons, Inc.*)

REFERENCES

Andersson, G.B.J. (1981). Epidemiological aspects on low-back pain in industry, *Spine, 6*(1), 53–60.

Andersson, G.B.J., Ortengren, A., Nachemson, A., and Elfstrom, G. (1974). Lumbar disc pressure and myoelectric back muscle activity during sitting. I. Studies on an experimental chair. *Scandinavian Journal of Rehabilitation Medicine, 3*, 104–114.

Armstrong, T.J. (1983). *An ergonomics guide to carpal tunnel syndrome.* AIHA Ergonomics Guide Series, American Industrial Hygiene Association, Akron, Ohio.

Armstrong, T.J., and Silverstein, B.A. (1987). Upper-extremity pain in the workplace—role of usage in causality. In N. Hadler (ed.), Clinical concepts in regional musculoskeletal illness (pp. 333–354). Orlando, Florida. Grune and Stratton.

Armstrong, T.J., Buckle, P.D., Fine, L.J., Hagberg, M., Jonsson, B., Kilbom, A., Kuorinka, I., Silverstein, B.A., Sjogaard, G., Viikari-Juntura, E.R.A. (1993). A conceptual model for work-related neck and upper limb musculoskeletal disorders. *Scandinavian Journal of Work, Environment and Health, 19*, 73–84.

Asmussen, E., and Heebol-Nielsen, K. (1961). Isometric muscle strength of adult men and women. *Communications from the Testing and Observation Institute of the Danish National Association for Infantile Paralysis,* NR-11, 1–41.

Ayoub, M.M., and Lo Presti, P. (1971). The determination of an optimum size cylindrical handle by use of electromyography. *Ergonomics, 4*(4), 503–518.

Barton, N.J., Hooper, G., Noble, J., and Steel, W. M. (1992). Occupational causes of disorders in the upper limb. *British Medical Journal, 304,* 309–311.

Bendix, T., Winkel, J., and Jersen, F. (1985). Comparison of office chairs with fixed forwards and backwards inclining, or tiltable seats. *European Journal of Applied Physiology, 54,* 378–385.

Bridger, R.S. (1995). *Introduction to ergonomics.* New York: McGraw-Hill.

Chaffin, D.B. (1997). Biomechanical aspects of workplace design. In G. Salvendy (ed.), *Handbook of human factors and ergonomics,* (2nd ed.). New York: Wiley.

Chaffin, D.B., and Andersson, G.B.J. (1991). *Occupational biomechanics.* New York: Wiley.

CTD News (1995). CTDs taking bigger bite of corporate bottom line. *CTD News,* vol. 4, no. 6, p. 1.

Farfan, H. (1973). *Mechanical disorders of the low back.* Philadelphia: Lea & Febiger.

Frymoyer, J.W., Pope, M.H., Constanza, M., Rosen, J., Goggin, J., and Wilder, D. (1980). Epidemiological studies of low back pain. *Spine, 5,* 419–423.

Greenberg, L., and Chaffin, D.B. (1976). *Workers and their tools.* Midland, MI: Pendell.

Hedge, A., McCrobie, D., Morimoto, S., Rodriguez, S., and Land, B. (1996). Toward pain-free computing. *Ergonomics in Design, 4*(1), 4–10.

Herrin, G.D., Jaraiedi, M., and Anderson, C.K. (1986). Prediction of overexertion injuries using biomechanical and psychophysical models. *American Industrial Hygiene Association Journal, 47*(6), 322–330.

Hosea, T.M., Simon, S.R., Delatizky, J., Wong, M.A., and Hsieh, C.C. (1986). Myoelectric analysis of the paraspinal musculature in relation to automobile driving. *Spine, 11,* 928–936.

Jager, M., and Luttman, A. (1989). Biomechanical analysis and assessment of lumbar stress during load lifting using a dynamic 19-segment human model. *Ergonomics, 32,* 93–112.

Kamon, E., and Goldfuss, A. (1978) In-plant evaluation of the muscle strength of workers. *American Industrial Hygiene Association Journal, 39,* 801–807.

Keegan, J.J. (1953). Alternations of the lumbar curve related to posture and seating. *Journal of Bone and Joint Surgery, 35A,* 589–603.

Kroemer, K.H.E., Kroemer, H.B., and Kroemer-Elbert, K.E. (1994). *Ergonomics: How to design for ease and efficiency.* Englewood Cliffs, NJ: Prentice-Hall.

Morris, N.M., Lucas, D.B., and Bressler, M.S. (1961). Role of the trunk in the stability of the spine. *Journal of Bone and Joint Surgery, 43A,* 327–351.

Nachemson, A., and Morris, J.M. (1964). In vivo measurements of intradiscal pressure. *Journal of Bone and Joint Surgery, 46A,* 1077.

National Safety Council (1990). *Accident facts.* Chicago: National Safety Council.

National Institute for Occupational Safety and Health (NIOSH) (1981). *Work practices guide for the design of manual handling tasks.* NIOSH.

Pheasant, S.T. (1986). *Bodyspace.* London: Taylor and Francis.

Pheasant, S.T., and O'Neill, D. (1975). Performance in gripping and turning: A study in hand/handle effectiveness. *Applied Ergonomics, 6,* 205–208.

Pope, M.H., Andersson, G.B.J., Frymoyer, J.W., and Chaffin, D.B. (eds.) (1991). *Occupational low back pain.* St. Louis: Mosby Year Book.

Posch, J.L., and Marcotte, D.R. (1976). Carpal tunnel syndrome, an analysis of 1201 cases. *Orthopedic Review, 5,* 25–35.

Snook, S.H., and Ciriello, V.M. (1991). The design of manual handling tasks: Revised tables of maximum acceptable weights and forces. *Ergonomics, 34,* 1197–1213.

Tichauer, E.R. (1978). *The Biomechanical basis of ergonomics.* New York: Wiley.

Waters, T.R., Putz-Anderson, V., Garg, A., and Fine, L. (1993). Revised NIOSH equation for the design and evaluation of manual lifting tasks, *Ergonomics, 36,* 7, 749–776.

Wolff, J. (1892). *Das Gesetz der Transformation der Knochen.* Berlin: Hirschwald.

CHAPTER 12

Work Physiology

The human body is able to maintain the body posture, walk and run, and lift and carry other objects because it has a musculoskeletal system of bones, muscles, and connective tissues, as we have described in the last chapter. In that chapter we focused on the mechanical aspects of physical work and described how awkward postures and heavy exertion forces can lead to severe musculoskeletal problems such as low-back pain and upper-extremity disorders. We also described how biomechanical methods can be applied to analyze the mechanical behavior of the musculoskeletal system.

In this chapter we shift the focus of discussion from the mechanical to the physiological aspects of muscular work. Physical work is possible only when there is enough energy to support muscular contractions. A central topic of this chapter is about how various physiological systems work together to meet the energy-expenditure requirements of work and how these requirements can be measured quantitatively and considered in the analysis of physical work.

This chapter starts with a description of the physiological structure of muscles and how energy is generated and made available for use by the muscles. We then describe how the raw materials for energy production are supplied and its waste products removed by the circulatory and respiratory systems. Energy expenditure requirements of various types of activities are then described, together with a discussion about how the levels of energy expenditure can be measured quantitatively. Clearly, there are upper limits of energy production and muscular work for each individual. The implications of these work capacity limits for ergonomic job design are discussed in the last section of the chapter.

MUSCLE STRUCTURE AND METABOLISM

Muscle Structure

The primary function of muscle is to generate force and produce movement. Three types of muscle cells (also known as muscle fibers) can be identified in the body: smooth muscle, cardiac muscle, and skeletal muscle. *Smooth muscle* is found in the stomach and the intestines, blood vessels, the urinary bladder, and uterus. Smooth muscle is involved in the digestion of food and the regulation of the internal environment of the body. The contraction of smooth muscle is not normally under conscious control. *Cardiac muscle,* as the name implies, is the muscle of the heart and, like smooth muscle, is not normally under direct conscious control. This chapter is primarily concerned with the third type of muscle, skeletal muscle, which is directly responsible for physical work.

Skeletal muscle can be regarded as the largest tissue in the body, accounting for about 40 percent of the body weight. Skeletal muscle is attached to the bones of the skeleton, and its contraction enables bones to act like levers. The contraction of most skeletal muscles is under direct conscious control, and the movements produced by skeletal muscle make physical work possible.

Each skeletal muscle is made up of thousands of cylindrical, elongated muscle fibers (muscle cells). The individual fibers are surrounded by a network of connective tissues through which blood vessels and nerve fibers pass to the muscle fibers. Each fiber actually consists of many cylindrical elements that are arranged in parallel to one another. These elements are called *myofibrils,* each of which is further divided longitudinally into a number of *sarcomeres* that are arranged in series and form a repeating pattern along the length of the myofibril. The sarcomeres are regarded as the contractile unit of skeletal muscle.

The sarcomere is comprised of two types of protein filaments—a thick filament called *myosin* and a thin one called *actin.* The two types of filaments are layered over each other in alternate dark and light bands, as shown in Figure 12.1. The layers of thick filaments are found in the central region of the sarcomere, forming the dark bands, known as the A bands. The layers of thin filaments are connected to either end of the sarcomere to a structure called the Z line. Two successive Z lines defined the two ends of one sarcomere.

An interesting discovery in muscle physiology is that when muscle shortens, the layers of thin filaments slide inward into the layers of thick filaments, but the lengths of the individual thin and thick filaments remain constant. This discovery led to *the sliding filament theory of muscle contraction.* According to this theory, muscle shortening during contraction is predominantly the result of the relative sliding movement of the thin filaments over the thick filaments and there is no change in the lengths of the two types of filaments (Needham, 1971; A.F. Huxley, 1974; Grinnell & Brazier, 1981).

Aerobic and Anaerobic Metabolism

Physical work is possible only when there is energy to support muscular contraction. The energy required for muscular contraction (and for many other physiological functions of the body) comes in the form of high-energy phosphate

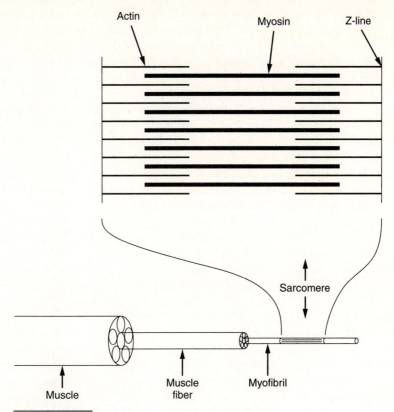

FIGURE 12.1

The structure of muscle.

compounds known as ATP (adenosine triphosphate) and CP (creatine phosphate). These compounds are derived from metabolism of nutrients either in the presence of oxygen *(aerobic metabolism)* or without oxygen *(anaerobic metabolism)*, and the process of creating high-energy phosphate compounds is called *phosphorylation.*

The ATP and CP compounds are energy carriers and are found in all body cells, where they are formed and used to fuel activities of the body and to sustain life. When energy is required for a reaction such as muscle contraction and relaxation, ATP is converted to ADP (adenosine diphosphate) by splitting off one of the phosphate bonds, and energy is made available for use in this process. In this respect, ATP behaves like a rechargeable battery, which provides a short-term storage of directly available energy (Astrand & Rodahl, 1986).

The body has a very limit capacity for ATP storage. For example, a 75-kg (165-lb) person has about 1 kilocalorie of ATP-stored energy available at any one time. Thus, if a muscle had to rely on its ATP storage for contraction, it would run out of this energy supply in a few seconds. To maintain the contractile activity of a muscle, ATP compounds must be continuously synthesized and replenished at the same rate as they are broken down. As described below, there are three sources for supplying this ATP: creatine phosphate (CP), oxidative phosphorylation (aerobic metabolism), and anaerobic glycolysis (anaerobic metabolism).

The molecules of CP contain energy that can be transferred to the molecules of ADP to "recharge" the ADP back to ATP. In this regard, the CP system acts like a backup storage for ATP and it provides the most rapid means of replenishing ATP in the muscle cell. However, although the CP system has an energy storage capacity that is about four times that of the ATP system, it is still of very limited capacity. The total energy supply from the ATP and CP systems can only support either heavy work for about ten seconds or moderately heavy work for about one minute.

If muscle activities are to be sustained for a longer period of time, the muscle cells must be able to form ATP from sources other than CP. When enough oxygen is available and muscle activity is at moderate levels (moderate rates of ATP breakdown), most of the required ATP can be supplied by the process of oxidative phosphorylation. In this process, nutrients (carbohydrates and fatty acids derived from fat) are burned in the presence of oxygen and energy is released to form ATP for muscle work. The nutrients are obtained from the food we eat, and oxygen is obtained from the air we breathe. The nutrients and oxygen are transported to the muscle cells by the blood through the circulatory system, as described later in this chapter. The nutrients can also be obtained from storage in the cells. The liver and muscle cells store the carbohydrates in the form of glycogen, which is derived from glucose in the blood stream. The muscle protein known as myoglobin allows the muscle to store a very small amount of oxygen, which can be used in short intense muscle contractions. This oxidative phosphorylation process releases energy for use by the muscles but also produces carbon dioxide as a waste byproduct, which must be removed from the tissues by the circulatory system.

Because it usually requires about one to three minutes for the circulatory system to respond to increased metabolic demands in performing physical tasks, skeletal muscles often do not have enough oxygen to carry out aerobic metabolism (oxidative phosphorylation) at the beginning of physical work. During this period of time, part of the energy is supplied through anaerobic glycolysis, which refers to the generation of energy through the breakdown of glucose to lactic acid in the absence of oxygen.

Although anaerobic glycolysis can produce ATP very rapidly without the presence of oxygen, it has the disadvantage of producing lactic acid as the waste product of this process. Lactic acid causes the acidity of the muscle tissue to increase and is believed to be a major cause of muscle pain and fatigue. The removal of lactic acid requires oxygen, and when oxygen is not available, lactic acid will diffuse out the muscle cells and accumulate in the blood. Under these situations it is said that anaerobic metabolism has caused an "oxygen debt," which must be paid back when the muscle activity ceases. In other words, to remove these waste products, the muscle needs to continue to consume oxygen at a high rate after it has stopped contraction so that its original state can be restored. Another disadvantage of anaerobic glycolysis is that it is not efficient in its use of glucose to produce energy. It requires much larger quantities of glucose to produce the same amount of ATP as compared to aerobic metabolism.

When enough oxygen is available, aerobic metabolism can supply all the energy required for light or moderate muscular work. Under these circumstances, the body is considered to be in the "steady state." For very heavy work, however, even when adequate oxygen is available, aerobic metabolism may not be able to produce ATP quickly enough to keep pace with the rapid rate of ATP breakdown. Thus, for very heavy work, anaerobic glycolysis serves as an additional source for producing ATP, and fatigue can develop rapidly as lactic acid accumulates in the muscle cells and in the blood.

It should be noted that, the overall efficiency with which muscle converts chemical energy to muscular work is only about 20 percent. Metabolic heat accounts for the remaining 80 percent of the energy released in metabolism (Edholm, 1967). The heavier the work, the greater is the amount of heat produced. This increased heat production may severely affect the body's ability to maintain a constant body temperature, especially in hot environments. Implications of metabolic heat production for job design are discussed later in this chapter.

THE CIRCULATORY AND RESPIRATORY SYSTEMS

As discussed earlier, muscular work can be sustained only when adequate amounts of nutrients and oxygen are continuously supplied to the muscle cells and when the waste products of metabolism such as carbon dioxide can be quickly removed from the body. It is the duty of the circulatory and respiratory systems to perform these functions and to meet these requirements. On the one hand, the circulatory system serves as the transportation system of the body and performs the function of delivering oxygen and nutrients to the tissues and removing carbon dioxide and waste products from the tissues. The respiratory system, on the other hand, performs the function of exchanging oxygen and carbon dioxide with the external environment.

The Circulatory System

The circulatory system is composed of the blood and the cardiovascular system, which is the apparatus that transports the blood to the various parts of the body.

The Blood. Blood consists of three types of blood cells and plasma. The red blood cells transport oxygen to the tissues and help remove carbon dioxide from them. The white blood cells fight invading germs and defend the body against infections. The platelets help stop bleeding. Plasma, in which the blood cells are suspended, contains 90 percent water and 10 percent nutrient and salt solutes.

Of the three types of specialized blood cells, the red blood cells are of most interest to work physiology because of their oxygen-carrying property. The red blood cells are formed in bone marrow and carry a special type of molecule known as the hemoglobin molecule (Hb). A hemoglobin molecule can combine with four molecules of oxygen to form oxyhemoglobin, allowing it to carry oxygen in the blood efficiently.

The total blood weight of an average adult is about 8 percent of his or her body weight. Because one kilogram of blood has a volume of about 1 liter (L), the total blood volume of an average adult, as measured in liters, is about 8 percent of his or her body weight, as measured in kilograms. Therefore, a 65-kg adult would have a total blood volume of about 5.2 liters (0.08 × 65 = 5.2), of which about 2.85 liters consist of plasma and 2.35 liters of blood cells.

Clearly, the ability of the blood to deliver oxygen and nutrients to the tissues and remove carbon dioxide from them will be reduced if an individual has a low blood volume or a low red-cell count. This ability will also be reduced if an individual works in a polluted or poorly ventilated environment or at high altitudes where the air has a low oxygen content. Working in these environments increases the stress on the circulatory system because it has to work harder to compensate for the reduced ability of the blood to perform its functions.

The Structure of the Cardiovascular System.   The cardiovascular system is composed of blood vessels, through which blood flows, and the heart, which is the pump that generates this flow.

The heart is a four-chambered muscular pump located in the chest cavity. It is divided into right and left halves, each consisting of two chambers, an *atrium* and a *ventricle* (Fig. 12.2). Between the two chambers on each side of the heart are the atrioventricular valves (AV valves), which forces one-directional blood flow from atrium to ventricle but not from ventricle to atrium. Furthermore, the right chambers do not send blood to the left chambers, and vice versa.

The cardiovascular system actually consists of two circuits of blood circulation, both originating and ending in the heart. In both circuits, the vessels carrying blood away from the heart are called *arteries,* and the vessels bringing blood back to the heart are called *veins.*

In the first circulation, known as *the systemic circulation,* fresh blood rich in nutrients and oxygen is pumped out of the left ventricle via a large artery called the aorta. From the aorta a series of ever-branching arteries conduct blood to the tissues and organs of the body. These arteries split into progressively smaller branches, and within each organ or tissue, the arteries branch into the next series of vessels called the *arterioles.* The arterioles further splits into a network of tiny, thin blood vessels called *capillaries* that permeates the tissues and organs. It is through this network of capillaries that the fresh blood delivers oxygen and nutrients to the tissues. It is also through this network of capillaries that blood collects carbon dioxide and waste products from the tissues and carries them away on its way back to the heart.

On its way back to the heart, the blood in the capillaries first merges into larger vessels called *venules,* and then the venules are further combined into still larger vessels, veins. Ultimately, the veins from the upper half of the body are joined into a large vein called the superior vena cava, and the veins from the lower half of the body are combined into another large vein called the inferior vena cava. Via these two veins blood is returned to the right atrium of the heart, completing a cycle of the systemic circulation.

In the second circulation, known as *the pulmonary circulation,* blood rich in carbon dioxide is pumped out of the right ventricle via the pulmonary artery, which splits into two arteries, one for each lung. Similar to the systemic circula-

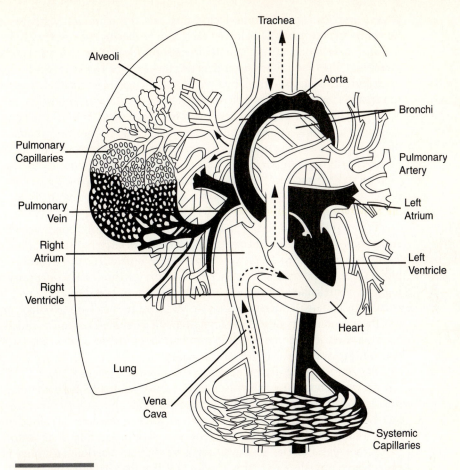

Trachea

Alveoli

Aorta

Bronchi

Pulmonary
Capillaries

Pulmonary
Artery

Left
Atrium

Pulmonary
Vein

Right
Atrium

Left
Ventricle

Right
Ventricle

Heart

Lung

Vena
Cava

Systemic
Capillaries

FIGURE 12.2

The anatomy of the circulatory and respiratory systems. The figure shows the major elements of the two systems and the two circuits of blood circulation: systemic (or general body) circulation and the pulmonary (or lung) circulation. (*Source:* Comroe, J.H., Jr., 1966. The lung. *Scientific American, 220,* 56–68. Copyright February 1966 by Scientific American. All rights reserved.)

tion, the arteries branch into arterioles, which then split into capillaries. Through the bed of capillaries in the lungs, blood expels carbon dioxide and absorbs oxygen (a process called *oxygenation*). On its way back to the heart, the oxygenated blood in the capillaries first merges into venules and then into progressively larger veins. Finally, via the largest of these veins, the pulmonary veins, the oxygenated blood leaves the lungs and returns to the left atrium of the heart, completing a cycle of the pulmonary circulation.

Blood Flow and Distribution. The heart generates the pressure to move blood along the arteries, arterioles, capillaries, venules, and veins. The heart pumps blood through its rhythmic actions of contraction and relaxation and at a rate that is adjusted to physical workload as well as other factors such as heat and humidity. Here we describe how although the heart plays the critical role in producing the sustained blood flow, the role of the blood vessels is much more sophisticated than that of simple inert plumbing. The blood flow encounters resistance in the blood vessels between the heart and the tissues, and the blood vessels can change their resistance to blood flow significantly to match the oxygen demands of various organs and tissues.

The resistance to flow is a function of the blood vessel's radius and length. The lengths of the blood vessels are normally considered as constants, whereas the radius of blood vessels can be changed significantly. Furthermore, very small changes in vessel radius produces large changes in blood flow. Therefore, the radius of blood vessels is the critical factor in determining resistance to blood flow. Increased blood flow to the working muscles is accomplished by dilating the blood vessels in the working muscles.

Each type of blood vessels makes its own unique contribution to achieving adequate blood distribution. Because the arteries have large radii, they offer little resistance to blood flow. Their role is to serve as a pressure tank to help move the blood through the tissues. The arteries show the maximum arterial pressure during peak ventricular contraction and the minimum pressure at the end of ventricular relaxation. The maximum arterial pressure is called *the systolic pressure,* and the minimum pressure is called *the diastolic pressure.* They are recorded as systolic/diastolic, for example, 135/70 mm Hg. The difference between systolic and diastolic pressure is called *the pulse pressure.*

In contrast to the negligible resistance offered by arteries, the radii of arterioles are small enough to provide significant resistance to blood flow. Furthermore, the radii of arterioles can be changed precisely under physiological control mechanisms. Therefore, arterioles are the major source of resistance to blood flow and are considered to be the primary site of control of blood-flow distribution.

Although capillaries have even smaller radii than arterioles, the huge number of capillaries provide such a large area for flow that the total resistance of all the capillaries is much less than that of the arterioles. Capillaries are thus not considered to be the main source of flow resistance. However, there does exist in the capillary network another mechanism for controlling blood flow distribution—*thoroughfare channels.* The thoroughfare channels are small blood vessels that provide direct links or shortcuts between arterioles and venules. These shortcuts allow the blood in the arterioles to reach the venules directly without going through the capillaries and are used to move blood away from resting muscles quickly when other tissues are in more urgent need of blood supply.

The veins also contribute to the overall function of blood flow. They contain one-way valves, which allow the blood in the veins to flow only in the direction of moving toward the heart. Furthermore, the rhythmic pumping actions of dynamic muscle activities can massage the veins and serve as a "muscle pump" (also called "secondary pump") to facilitate the blood to flow along the veins back to the heart.

The amount of blood pumped out of the left ventricle per minute is called *the cardiac output* (Q). It is influenced by physiological, environmental, psychological, and individual factors. The physiological demands of muscular work changes cardiac output greatly. At rest the cardiac output is about 5 liters per minute

(L/min). In moderate work the cardiac output is about 15 L/min. During heavy work it may increase as much as fivefold to 25 L/min. Work in hot and humid environments will also increase cardiac output when the body needs to supply more blood to the skin to help dissipate excess body heat. Cardiac output may also increase when an individual is excited or under emotional stress. Age, gender, health, and fitness conditions may also influence the cardiac output of an individual under various job situations.

The heart has two ways to increase its cardiac output: increase the number of beats per minute (called heart rate, or HR) or increase the amount of blood per beat (called stroke volume, or SV). In fact, cardiac output is the product of heart rate and stroke volume, as shown in the following formula:

$$Q \text{ (L/min)} = HR \text{ (beats/min)} \times SV \text{ (L/beat)}$$

In a resting adult stroke volume is about 0.05 to 0.06 L/beat. For moderate work stroke volume can increase to about 0.10 L/min. For heavy work, increased cardiac output is accomplished largely through heart rate increases. As discussed later in this chapter, heart rate is one of the primary measurements of physical workload at all workload levels.

Each tissue or organ receives a portion of the cardiac output. The blood-flow distribution for a resting adult is given in the left column of Table 12.1. At rest, the digestive system, the brain, the kidneys, and the muscles each receive about 15 to 20 percent of the total cardiac output. In moderate work, about 45 percent of cardiac output goes to the working muscles to meet their metabolic requirements. During very heavy work this percentage increases to about 70 to 75 percent. In hot environments more blood is distributed to the skin to dissipate the excess body heat. The fraction of blood that goes to the digestive system and the kidneys falls sharply with increased workload. An interesting aspect of blood-flow distribution is the remarkable stability of brain blood flow. The brain receives the same amount of blood under all situations, although it represents a smaller fraction of the total cardiac output in heavy work than at rest. As mentioned above, blood-flow distribution is made possible primarily by dilating and constricting arterioles in different organs and tissues on a selective basis.

TABLE 12.1 Blood Flow Distribution in Different Resting and Working Conditions

	Blood Flow Distribution		
Organs	*Resting*	*Moderate Work (38°C)*	*Heavy Work (21°C)*
Muscles	15–20	45	70–75
Skin	5	40	10
Digestive system	20–25	6–7	3–5
Kidney	20	6–7	2–4
Brain	15	4–5	3–4
Heart	4–5	4–5	4–5

Source: Adapted from Astrand and Rodahl, 1986; Brouha, 1967; Eastman Kodak, 1986.

The Respiratory System

The respiratory system is the gas-exchanger of the body. It obtains oxygen from and dispels carbon dioxide to the environment.

The Structure of the Respiratory System.   The respiratory system is composed of the nose, pharynx, larynx, trachea, bronchi, lungs, the muscles of the chest wall, and the diaphragm, which separates the chest cavity from the abdomen. The nose and the airway from the nose to the lungs not only conduct the air to the lungs but also filter it and help prevent dusts and harmful substances from reaching the lungs. They also moisturize the inspired air and adjust its temperature before it reaches the lungs.

The lungs consist of a huge number of *alveoli* (between 200 million and 600 million of them), which provide a large surface for the gas exchange to take place in the lungs. Blood flowing through the pulmonary capillaries absorbs oxygen from the alveoli and dispels carbon dioxide. The amount of gas exchanged per minute in the alveoli is called *the alveolar ventilation*. The respiratory system adjusts the alveolar ventilation according to the level of physical workload and demands of metabolism.

Air is breathed into the lungs when the muscles of the chest wall work with the abdominal muscles to expand the chest and lower the diaphragm. These muscle actions increase the chest volume and makes the lung pressure smaller than the atmospheric pressure, so air is brought into the lungs. Similarly, when the chest muscles relax and the diaphragm moves up, air is breathed out of the lungs.

Lung Capacity.   Not all the air in the lungs are breathed out even after a person tries his or her best to breathe out all the air in his or her lungs (called a maximum expiration). The amount of air that remains in the lungs after a maximum expiration is called *the residual volume*. The amount of air that can be breathed in after a maximum inspiration is called the *vital capacity*. The total lung capacity is the sum of the two volumes, as illustrated in Figure 12.3.

Maximum inspiration or maximum expiration rarely occurs in life. The amount of air breathed in per breath (called *tidal volume*) is less than the vital capacity, leaving an inspiratory reserve volume (IRV) and an expiratory reserve volume (ERV). A resting adult has a tidal volume of about 0.5 L, which can increase to about 2 L for heavy muscular work. The increase in tidal volume is realized by using portions of the inspiratory and expiratory reserve volumes.

The respiratory system adjusts the amount of air breathed per minute (called the *minute ventilation* or *minute volume*) by adjusting the tidal volume and the frequency of breathing. In fact, minute ventilation is calculated as the product of tidal volume and breathing frequency. The body carefully controls the two parameters to maximize the efficiency of breathing in meeting the needs of alveolar ventilation. A resting adult breathes about ten to fifteen times per minute. The tidal volume increases for light work, but the breathing frequency does not. This is because there is a constant anatomical space in the air pathways between the nose and the lungs that is ventilated on each breath and the air in that space does not reach the alveoli. The deeper the breath (the larger the tidal volume), the larger is the percentage of air that reaches the alveoli. Therefore, increasing the tidal volume is

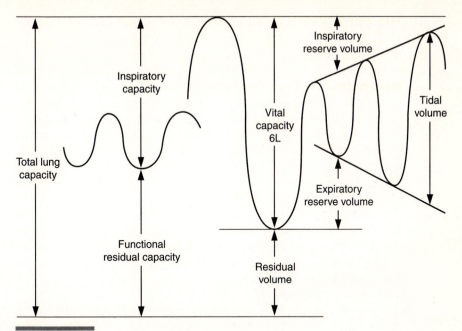

FIGURE 12.3

Respiratory capacities and volumes. (*Source:* Kroemer, K., Kroemer, H., and Kroemer-Elbert, K., 1990. *Engineering Physiology: Bases of Human Factors/Ergonomics,* 2nd ed. New York: Van Nostrand Reinhold. Copyright © 1990. Reprinted by permission of Van Nostrand Reinhold.)

more efficient than increasing the breathing frequency. As workload further increases, however, increasing tidal volume alone is not sufficient to meet the ventilation needs, and thus the frequency of breathing also increases rapidly with increasing workload. For heavy work, the respiratory frequency can increase three-fold over its resting level to about forty-five breaths per minute.

The environmental air we breathe is normally composed of 21 percent oxygen, 0.03 percent carbon dioxide, the remaining being mostly nitrogen. Clearly, if the working environment has poor ventilation or is polluted with smoke or other chemical substances, then the respiratory and the circulatory systems must work harder to compensate for the reduced oxygen supply. The respiratory and the circulatory systems are also under increased stress when working at high altitudes above sea level because of the lower oxygen content in the air and the reduced difference between the atmospheric pressure and the lung pressure.

ENERGY COST OF WORK AND WORKLOAD ASSESSMENT

Energy Cost of Work

The human body must consume energy to maintain the basic life functions even if no activities are performed at all. The lowest level of energy expenditure that is needed to maintain life is called the *basal metabolism*. The basal metabolic rate is measured in a quiet and temperature controlled environment for a resting person after he or she has been under dietary restrictions for several days and had no food intake for twelve hours. There are individual differences in their basal metabolic rate. Gender, age, and body weight are some of the main factors that influence a person's basal metabolic rate. Human energy expenditure is measured in kilocalories. The average basal metabolic rate for adults is commonly considered to be about 1,600 to 1,800 kcal per twenty-four hours (Schottelius & Schottelius, 1978) or about 1 kcal per kilogram of body weight per hour (Kroemer et al., 1994).

The basal metabolism is the minimal amount of energy needed to maintain life and is thus measured under highly restrictive conditions that are not representative of everyday life. Even for low-intensity sedentary or leisure activities, the human body needs more energy than that supplied at the basal metabolic level. Various estimates have been made about the energy costs of maintaining a sedentary nonworking life. For example, it is estimated that *the resting metabolism* measured before the start of a working day for a resting person is about 10 to 15 percent higher than basal metabolism (Kroemer et al., 1994). Luehmann (1958) and Schottelius and Schottelius (1978) estimate that the energy requirement is about 2,400 kcal per day for basal metabolism and leisure and low-intensity everyday nonworking activities.

With the onset of physical work, energy demand of the body rises above that of the resting level. The body increases its level of metabolism to meet this increased energy demand. The term *working metabolism,* or *metabolic cost of work,* refers to this increase in metabolism from the resting to the working level. The metabolic or energy expenditure rate during physical work is the sum of the basal metabolic rate and the working metabolic rate. Estimates of energy expenditure rates for some daily activities and certain types of work have been made and they range from 1.6 to 16 kcal/min. For example, Edholm (1967) reports that the energy expenditure rates for sitting and standing are 1.6 kcal/min and 2.25 kcal/min, respectively. Durnin and Passmore (1967) report that the work of a male carpenter has an energy requirement of about 2.9 to 5.0 kcal/min, and a female worker doing laundry work has an energy cost of about 3.0 to 4.0 kcal/min. Table 12.2 provides a sample list of energy expenditure rates for various activities.

As shown in Figure 12.4, it usually takes some time for the body to increase its rate of metabolism and meet the energy requirements of work. In fact, it usually takes about one to three minutes for the circulatory and respiratory systems to adjust to the increased metabolic demands and reach the level at which the energy requirements of work are met. During this initial warm-up period at the start of physical work, the amount of oxygen supplied to the tissues is less than the amount of oxygen needed, creating an "oxygen deficit." During this period, due to this oxygen deficit or the inadequate oxygen supply, anaerobic metabolism is a main source of energy. If the physical work is not too heavy, a *"steady state"* can be reached in which oxidative metabolism produces sufficient energy to meet all energy requirements. The oxygen deficit incurred at the start of work must be repaid at some time, either during work if the work is light or during the recovery period immediately after a work ceases if the work is moderate or heavy. This is why the respiratory and circulatory systems often do not return to their normal activity levels immediately on completion of a moderate or heavy work.

TABLE 12.2 **Estimates of Energy Expenditure Rates for Various Activities**

Activity	Estimates of Energy Expenditure Rates (kcal/min)
Sleeping	1.3
Sitting	1.6
Standing	2.3
Walking (3 km/hr)	2.8
Walking (6 km/hr)	5.2
Carpenter-assembling	3.9
Woodwork-packaging	4.1
Stock-room work	4.2
Welding	3.4
Sawing wood	6.8
Chopping wood	8.0
Athletic activities	10.0

Source: Based on Durnin and Passmore, 1967; Edholm, 1967; Passmore and Durnin, 1955; Vos, 1973; and Woodson, 1981.

The physical demands of work can be classified as light, moderate, heavy, very heavy, and extremely heavy according to their energy expenditure requirements (Astrand & Rodahl, 1986; Kroemer et al., 1994). In *light work,* the energy expenditure rate is fairly small (smaller than 2.5 kcal/min) and the energy demands can be met easily by oxidative metabolism of the body. *Moderate work* has energy requirements of about 2.5 to 5.0 kcal/min, which are still largely met through oxidative metabolic mechanisms. *Heavy work* requires energy at energy expenditure rates between 5.0 and 7.5 kcal/min. Only physically fit workers are able to carry out this type of work for a relatively long period of time with energy supplied through oxidative metabolism. The oxygen deficit incurred at the start of work cannot be repaid until the end of work. In *very heavy work* (with energy expenditure rates between 7.5 and 10.0 kcal/min) and *extremely heavy work* (greater than 10.0 kcal/min), even physically fit workers cannot reach a steady-state condition during the period of work. The oxygen deficit and the lactic acid accumulation continue to increase as the work continues and make it necessary for the worker to take frequent breaks or even to quit the work completely.

Measurement of Workload

Physiological and subjective methods have been developed to measure the physical demands of work in terms of energy requirements and physical effort.

The results of extensive research on work physiology have shown that energy expenditure rate of a work is linearly related to the amount of oxygen consumed by the body and to heart rate. Therefore, oxygen consumption rate and heart rate are often used to quantify the workload of physical work. In this section we describe the two measurements, along with blood pressure and minute ventilation, which are two less commonly used but sometimes useful physiological measures

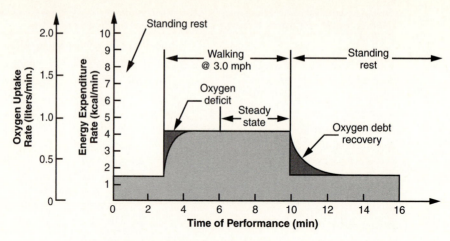

*Assumes 5 kcal of energy expended
per liter of oxygen used

FIGURE 12.4

The change in total energy expenditure rate as activity level changes. (*Source:* Garg, A.,
Herrin, G., and Chaffin, D., 1978. Prediction of metabolic rates from manual materials
handling jobs. *American Industrial Hygiene Association Journal, 39*[8], 661–674.)

of physical workload. We also describe subjective measures of workload which,
when used in conjunction with physiological measures, often provide the job analysts with a more comprehensive understanding of the working condition than
do physiological measures alone.

Oxygen Consumption.   As described earlier, aerobic (oxidative) metabolism is the
source of energy for sustained muscular work when the body is in a steady state.
Extensive research has shown that there is a linear relationship between oxygen
consumption and energy expenditure: For every liter of oxygen consumed, an average of about 4.8 kcal of energy is released. Thus, the amount of aerobic metabolism or energy expenditure of a work can be determined by measuring the
amount of oxygen a worker consumes while performing the work. More specifically, energy expenditure rate of a physical task (kcal/min) can be determined by
multiplying the oxygen consumption rate (l/min) by 4.8 (kcal/l).

The amount of oxygen consumed can be determined by measuring the
amount of air expired per unit of time and the difference between the fraction of
oxygen in the expired air and that in the inspired air. For most workplaces, except
those at high altitudes or in polluted work environments, the fraction of oxygen
in the inspired air can be assumed to be about 21 percent.

To collect the expired air in a workplace, the worker is asked to wear a face
mask or a mouthpiece, through which the air is inhaled and exhaled. The expired
air either is collected in a large bag (called the Douglas bag) and analyzed later for
its oxygen content or passes through an instrument directly where its oxygen content is analyzed (Astrand & Rodahl, 1986; Harrison et al., 1982). A flow meter installed in the face mask or mouthpiece can be used to determine the volume of

inspired or expired air. For the Douglas bag method, the volume of expired air can be determined by measuring the volume of air in the filled bag. Portable devices are available commercially for measuring expired air flow rates and oxygen consumption. An important requirement for these devices is that their usage should cause minimal interference with the worker's job performance. The equipment should not be too bulky for use in the field, and its airway (mask, tube, valves, etc.) should not cause great resistance to breathing during heavy physical work. Continuous efforts are made to improve the instruments and meet these requirements as closely as possible.

It should be noted here that measuring the amount of oxygen consumed during work can only help determine the amount of aerobic metabolism involved. To estimate the amount of anaerobic (nonoxidative) metabolism used in a work, one needs to measure the additional amount of oxygen consumed during the recovery period over that of the resting state. As described earlier, oxygen consumption rate does not return to its resting value immediately upon cessation of work. It remains elevated for a period of time and gradually falls back to the resting level. The excess oxygen used during this recovery period recharges the depleted stores of ATP and CP and repays the oxygen debt incurred at the start and during the period of work. The greater the amount of anaerobic metabolism involved in a work, the greater is the amount of excess oxygen needed to pay back the oxygen debt during the recovery period. Therefore, measurement of oxygen consumption during the recovery period provides an estimate of the amount of anaerobic metabolism of a job.

Another important issue that must be noted is that oxygen consumption can only be used to estimate the energy demands of "dynamic" work such as walking, running, and dynamic lifting, in which muscle contractions alternate with relaxation periods. It is not a good measure of the workload of "static" work, such as holding a heavy object at a fixed position for long. This is because static work usually recruits a small number of localized muscle groups and keeps them in a contracted state continuously. Sustained muscle contraction disrupts blood flow to these muscles because of their continued compression of the blood vessels. Energy supply to the contracted muscles is restricted due to inadequate blood flow. Therefore, although static work is very demanding and leads to fatigue quickly, static work effort is not well reflected in measures of oxygen consumption. Methods of evaluating static work are described in the last section of this chapter.

Heart Rate.   Heart rate, the number of heart beats per minute, is another commonly used physiological measure of physical workload. Heart rate usually increases as workload and energy demands increase. It reflects the increased demand for the cardiovascular system to transport more oxygen to the working muscles and remove more waste products from them. Extensive research has shown that for moderate work heart rate is linearly related to oxygen consumption (Astrand & Rodahl, 1986). Because heart rate is easier to measure than oxygen consumption, it is often used in industrial applications as an indirect measure of energy expenditure.

It should be emphasized that heart rate is not as reliable as oxygen consumption as a measure of energy expenditure. It is influenced by many factors and the linear relationship between heart rate and oxygen consumption can be violated by these factors. A partial list of these factors would include emotional stress, drinking coffee or tea, working with a static and awkward posture, or working in hot environments. Any of these circumstances can lead to disproportionately high heart rates without an equally significant increase in oxygen consumption. Furthermore, the relationship between heart rate and oxygen consumption varies from individual to individual. Different individuals can show different heart rates when they have the same level of oxygen consumption.

Despite these complicating factors, because of the convenience of measuring heart rate and its relative accuracy in reflecting workload, heart rate is considered to be a very useful index in physical work evaluation. The following is a description of the methods of measuring and interpreting heart rate in job evaluation.

Portable telemetry devices are available commercially that allows monitoring and recording the heart rate of a worker unobtrusively and at a distance from the worker. To measure the heart rate, the worker wears a set of electrodes on his or her chest that detects the signals from the heart. The signals are then transmitted to a receiver for recording and analysis. A simple but somewhat intrusive method to measure heart rate is to use the fingers to count the pulse of the radial artery located at the thumb side of the wrist. Heart rate can also be collected by counting the pulse of the carotid artery on the neck near the angle of the jaw.

Because the relationship between heart rate and oxygen consumption varies for different individuals, this relationship must be established for each worker before heart rate is used alone as an estimate of workload. This process requires the measurement of heart rate and oxygen consumption in controlled laboratory conditions in which several levels of workloads are varied systematically. After the relationship between the two variables are established for a worker, the same worker's energy expenditure rate in the workplace can then be estimated by collecting his or her heart rate and converting it to oxygen consumption and energy expenditure data. Studies have shown that heart-rate data offer valid estimates of energy expenditure rate when the heart rate-oxygen consumption relationship is calibrated for each worker (Bridger, 1995; Spurr et al., 1988).

In general, the change of heart rate before, during, and after physical work follows the same pattern as that of oxygen consumption or energy expenditure shown in Figure 12.4. A resting adult has a typical heart rate of about 60 to 80 beats/min, although large differences exist among different individuals. During physical work, the heart rate first rises and then levels off at the steady state, and it does not return to its resting value immediately on cessation of work. The amount of increase in heart rate from the resting to the steady state is a measure of physical workload, and so also is the heart rate recovery time. The heavier the physical work, the greater is the increase in heart rate, and the longer is the heart-rate recovery time.

There is a maximum heart rate for each individual, which is affected by many factors such as age, gender, and health and fitness level. The primary factor determining the maximum heart rate is age, and the decline of the maximum heart rate as a function of age can be estimated by the following linear equation (Astrand & Rodahl, 1986):

$$\text{maximum heart rate} = 206 - (0.62 \times \text{age}).$$

Another commonly used formula to estimate the maximum heart rate is (Astrand & Christensen, 1964; Cooper et al., 1975):

$$\text{maximum heart rate} = 220 - \text{age}.$$

As described later in this chapter, maximum heart rate directly determines the maximum work capacity or the maximum energy expenditure rate of an individual.

Blood Pressure and Minute Ventilation.   The term *blood pressure* refers to the pressure in the large arteries. As described earlier in this chapter, the arteries offer little resistance to blood flow and serve as a pressure tank to help move the blood through the tissues. The arteries show the maximum arterial pressure during peak ventricular contraction and the minimum pressure at the end of ventricular relaxation. The maximum arterial pressure is called systolic pressure, and the minimum pressure is called diastolic pressure. The two blood pressures can be measured with a blood pressure gauge (sphygmomanometer) and cuff and stethoscope and are recorded as systolic/diastolic, for example, 135/70 mm Hg.

Because blood pressure measurements require the workers to stop their work and thus interfere with or alter the regular job process, they are not used as often as oxygen consumption and heart-rate measurements. However, studies have shown that for work involving awkward static postures, blood pressure may be a more accurate index of workload than the other two measurements (Lind & McNichol, 1967).

Another physiological measurement that is sometimes used in job evaluation is minute ventilation or minute volume, which refers to the amount of air breathed out per minute. It is often measured in conjunction with oxygen consumption, and used as an index of emotional stress. When workers are under emotional stress as in emergency situation or under time pressure, they may show a change in their respiration pattern and an increase in their minute ventilation. However, there is usually not a corresponding increase in the measurement of oxygen consumption, because little additional oxygen is consumed by the body under these situations.

Subjective Measurement of Workload.   Subjective rating scales of physical workload have been developed as simple and easy-to-use measures of workload. A widely used subjective rating scale is the Borg RPE (Ratings of Perceived Exertion) Scale (Borg, 1985), which requires the workers to rate their perceived level of physical effort on a scale of 6 to 20. The two ends of the scale represent the minimum and maximum heart rate of 60 and 200 beats/min, respectively. Subjective scales are cheaper and easier to implement than physiological measures, and they often provide valid and reliable quantification of physical efforts involved in a job. However, subjective measures may be influenced by other factors such as worker's satisfaction of a workplace, motivation, and other emotional factors. Therefore, caution should be exercised in the use and analysis of subjective measures, and it is often desirable to use subjective ratings in conjunction with physiological measures to achieve a more comprehensive understanding of the work demands.

PHYSICAL WORK CAPACITY AND WHOLE-BODY FATIGUE

Short-Term and Long-Term Work Capacity

Physical work capacity refers to a person's maximum rate of energy production during physical work, and it varies as a function of the duration of the work. The maximum energy expenditure rate that can be achieved by an individual for a few minutes is called *the short-term maximum physical work capacity (MPWC)* or *aerobic capacity.* Figure 12.5 shows the linear relationship between energy expenditure rate and heart rate for a healthy individual with a maximum heart rate of 190 beats/min and a MPWC of about 16 kcal/min for dynamic work. It also shows that the MPWC is significantly reduced for static muscular work in which anaerobic metabolism takes place due to restricted blood flow to the muscles (Garg, Herrin, & Chaffin, 1978).

The short-term maximum physical work capacity (MPWC) or aerobic capacity is also referred to as "VO_{2max}" in the literature to describe a person's capacity to utilize oxygen. It is believed that the maximum physical work capacity is determined by the maximum capacity of the heart and the lungs to deliver oxygen to the working muscles. During physical work, heart rate and oxygen consumption both increase as workload increases. However, they cannot increase indefinitely. As workload further increases, a limit will be reached where the heart cannot beat faster and the cardiovascular system cannot supply oxygen at a faster rate to meet the increasing energy demands of the work. At this point, it is said that the person has reached his or her aerobic capacity or VO_{2max}.

There are great individual differences in their aerobic capacity. Age, gender, health and fitness level, training, and genetic factors all influence an individual's aerobic capacity. According to the data published by NIOSH (1981), the aerobic capacity for average healthy males and females are approximately 15 kcal/min and 10.5 kcal/min, respectively.

Physical work capacity drops sharply as the duration of work increases. The decline of *long-term maximum physical work capacity* from the level of short-term maximum work capacity is shown in Figure 12.6 (Bink, 1964). For job design purposes, NIOSH (1981) states that workers should not work continuously over an eight-hour shift at a rate over 33 percent of their short-term maximum work capacity. This means that for continuous dynamic work, healthy male workers should not work at a rate over 5 kcal/min, and healthy female workers should not work at a rate over 3.5 kcal/min. For dynamic jobs performed occasionally (1 hour or less during an 8-hour shift), NIOSH states that the recommended energy expenditure limit should be 9 kcal/min and 6.5 kcal/min for healthy males and females, respectively. Clearly, older and less-fit workers have lower levels of maximum work capacity than young and fit workers and will require reduced 8-hour work capacity limits.

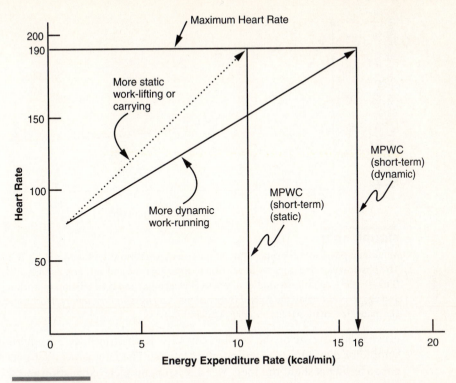

FIGURE 12.5

The relationship between heart rate and energy expenditure rate for static and dynamic work. The figure illustrates that at the same maximum heart rate, the maximum physical work capacity is larger for dynamic than for static work. (*Source*: Garg, A., Herrin, G., and Chaffin, D., 1978. Prediction of metabolic rates from manual materials handling jobs. *American Industrial Hygiene Association Journal*, 39[8], 661–674.)

In ergonomic job evaluation, the energy cost of different jobs can be measured and compared with the NIOSH recommendations mentioned above to determine whether a job can be performed by the work force and whether it needs to be redesigned to lower the required energy expenditure rate to make it acceptable to the intended work force. For example, if a job is identified to require an energy expenditure rate of about 5 kcal/min, then we know that only healthy male workers can perform this job continuously over an eight-hour shift. To make this job acceptable to a wider range of workers, we need to either redesign the job (e.g., use of automated material handling devices) or adopt an appropriate work-rest schedule, as discussed in the following section.

Causes and Control of Whole-Body Fatigue

A worker will be likely to experience whole-body fatigue during or at the end of an eight-hour shift if the energy demands of work exceeds 30 to 40 percent of his or her maximum aerobic capacity and will certainly feel fatigued if the energy cost

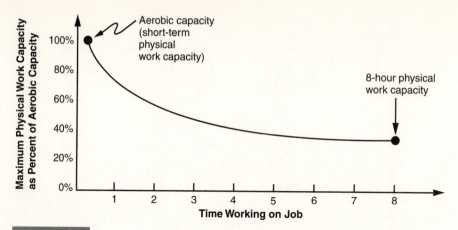

FIGURE 12.6

Maximum physical work capacity as a function of work duration (*Source:* Bink, B. 1962. The physical working capacity in relation to working time and age. *Ergonomics,* 5[1], 25–28; Bink, B., 1964. Additional studies of physical working capacity in relation to working time and age. *Proceedings of the Second International Congress on Ergonomics,* Dortmund, Germany: International Ergonomics Association.)

exceeds 50 percent of the aerobic capacity. Both subjective and physiological symptoms may appear as indicators of fatigue. The fatigued worker may experience a feeling of slight tiredness, weariness, or complete exhaustion and show impaired muscular performance or difficulties in keeping awake. There may also be an increase in blood lactic acid accumulation and a drop in blood glucose. Prolonged whole-body fatigue may lead to low job satisfaction and even increased risk of health problems such as heart attacks.

One explanation of the cause of whole-body fatigue is that when the energy expenditure rate exceeds 40 to 50 percent of the aerobic capacity, the body cannot reach the "steady state" in which aerobic metabolism supplies enough oxygen to meet all the energy needs. Consequently, anaerobic metabolism contributes an increasing proportion of the energy supplied and produces an increasing amount of waste products such as lactic acid during the process.

It should be noted, however, that the exact nature and causes of fatigue is still largely unknown (Astrand & Rodahl, 1986; Simonson, 1971; Kroemer et al., 1994). For example, although increased accumulation of lactic acid in the blood is often observed in prolonged heavy work, it is not usually associated with prolonged moderate work, which may also cause fatigue (Astrand & Rodahl, 1986). Depletion of ATP and CP has traditionally been regarded as a main cause for fatigue; however, this view is currently being challenged as well (Kahn & Monod, 1989; Kroemer et al., 1994). Fatigue may also be a symptom of disease or poor health condition. Furthermore, the development of fatigue is influenced by a worker's motivation, interest in the job, and other psychological factors. The same worker may develop fatigue more quickly in one job than in another, although the two jobs may have comparable energy requirements. Similarly, two workers of the same health and fitness condition may develop fatigue at different rates for the same job. However, regardless of the causes, complaints of job-related fatigue in a workplace should be treated as important warning signals and dealt with seriously so that related job hazards can be identified and removed.

Engineering and administrative methods can be used to reduce the risk of whole-body fatigue in industrial workplaces. Engineering methods refer to the use of engineering techniques to redesign the job and provide job aids. For example, use of conveyer belts or automated material handling devices can help reduce the need for load carrying. A better layout of the workplace designed according to the frequency and sequence of use of various workplace components can help reduce the distance of lifting, pushing, or pulling heavy objects and thus greatly reduce the energy expenditure requirements of work.

When an existing heavy job cannot be redesigned with engineering techniques due to various constraints, work-rest scheduling is the most commonly adopted administrative method to keep the work at acceptable energy expenditure levels.

When environmental heat load is not present, a work-rest schedule can be determined with the following formula:

Rest period as a fraction of total work time

$$= (PWC - E_{job})/(E_{rest} - E_{job})$$

where

PWC is the physical work capacity for workers of concern,

E_{job} is the energy expenditure rate required to perform the job, and

E_{rest} is the energy expenditure rate at rest. A value of 1.5 kcal/min is often used to represent the energy expenditure rate for seated rest.

As an illustrative example, suppose the energy expenditure rate of a physical work is 6.5 kcal/min and the work is performed by healthy male and female workers on an eight-hour shift basis. Recall that the NIOSH-recommended eight-hour work capacity limits are 5 kcal/min and 3.5 kcal/min for healthy males and females, respectively. It is clear that this job cannot be performed continuously for eight hours by either group of workers. If this job cannot be redesigned with engineering techniques, then a proper work-rest schedule must be implemented to reduce the risk of whole-body fatigue. Furthermore, the rest schedule should be determined separately for the two groups of workers because of the difference in their physical work capacities.

Use the formula presented above, we have, for male workers,

rest period as a fraction of total work time
$$= (5 - 6.5)/(1.5 - 6.5) = 1.5/5 = 0.30$$
For female workers, we have
rest period as a fraction of total work time
$$= (3.5 - 6.5)/(1.5 - 6.5) = 3/5 = 0.60$$

Therefore, during an 8-hour shift, male workers should have a total rest period of 2.4 hours ($0.30 \times 8 = 2.4$), and female workers should have a total rest period of 4.8 hours ($0.60 \times 8 = 4.8$) because of the heavy physical demands of the job. The total rest time should be divided into many short breaks and distributed throughout the 8-hour work shift rather than taken as few long breaks.

When environmental heat stress is present in a workplace, such as working in a hot climate or near heat sources, workers may need to take frequent rests even when the energy expenditure rate required for performing the physical task is not high. As discussed earlier, about 80 percent of metabolic energy is released in the form of metabolic heat (Edholm, 1967), which must be dissipated from the body so that the body can maintain a constant normal temperature of 98.6° F. Dissipation of metabolic heat can be difficult in a working environment in which large radiant heat or high humidity exist or there is a lack of adequate air flow. For these work situations workers need to take breaks in a cool area to avoid heat-related health risks.

Figure 12.7 contains a set of recommended work-rest schedules for various workloads at different levels of environmental heat conditions. A comprehensive index of the environmental heat load called wet bulb globe temperature (WBGT) must first be determined with the following equations (NIOSH, 1972) before using these guidelines:

When the level of radiant heat is low in a working environment, the WBGT is:

$$\text{WBGT} = 0.7 \text{ (natural wet bulb temperature)} + 0.3 \text{ (globe temperature)}.$$

When the level of radiant heat is high (e.g., working in sunlight or near a radiant heat source), WBGT is

$$\text{WBGT} = 0.7 \text{ (natural wet bulb temperature)} + 0.2 \text{ (globe temperature)} + 0.1 \text{ (dry bulb temperature)}$$

where,

NWBT is the natural wet bulb temperature, which is the temperature of a wet wick measured with actual air flow present. NWBT is the same as wet bulb temperature (WBT) when the air velocity is greater than 2.5 m/sec (8 ft/sec). NWBT = 0.9 WBT + 0.1 (dry bulb temperature) for slower air velocities.

Devices are available to measure and calculate these temperature indexes.

It is clear from Figure 12.7 that when working in a hot or humid workplace, frequent rests in a cool place are often necessary even when the energy cost of performing the physical task is not high. For example, although a light work of 3.4 kcal/min (204 kcal/h) can be performed continuously by most workers when heat stress is not present, the same physical task would require the workers to spend 50 percent of the time resting in a cool environment when the working environment has a WBGT of 88.5 degrees F.

Two cautionary notes must be made with regard to the use of Figure 12.7. First, although significant differences exist between males and females in their physical work capacities, Figure 12.7 does not take into account this difference. Second, the term *continuous work* used in Figure 12.7 does not necessarily mean that a work can be performed continuously for eight hours. For example, although a light work (< 200 kcal/min or 3.4 kcal/min) can be performed contin-

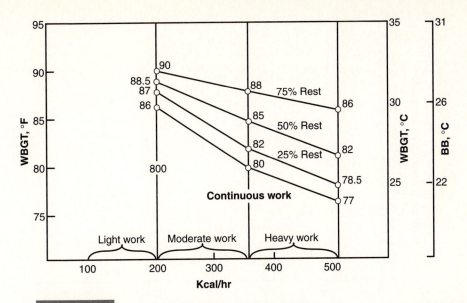

FIGURE 12.7

Recommended WBGT limits for various workload levels and work-rest schedules. (*Source: American Society of Heating, Refrigerating, and Air-Conditioning Engineers. ASHRAE Handbook, 1985 Fundamentals. New York: ASHRAE.*)

uously for 8 hours in a workplace with a 75° F WBGT by both male and female workers, a heavy work of 390 kcal/min (6.5 kcal/min) cannot be sustained by many healthy male workers, as we calculated earlier. Most workers cannot perform a very heavy work of 480 kcal/min (8 kcal/min) for long, even when there is no environmental heat stress.

Static Work and Local Muscle Fatigue

While whole-body fatigue is often associated with prolonged dynamic whole-body activities that exceed an individual's physical work capacity (aerobic capacity), local muscle fatigue is often observed in jobs requiring static muscle contractions. As described earlier, dynamic muscle activities provide a "muscle pump" that massages the blood vessels and assists blood flow through the muscle's rhythmic actions. Static muscle contractions, in contrast, impede or even occlude blood flow to the working muscles because the sustained physical pressure on the blood vessels prevents them from dilating as long as the contraction continues. The lack of adequate oxygen supply forces anaerobic metabolism, which can produce local muscle fatigue quickly due to the rapid accumulation of waste products and depletion of nutrients near the working muscles.

The maximum length of time a static muscle contraction can be sustained (muscle endurance time) is a function of the exerted force expressed as a percentage of the muscle's *maximum voluntary contraction (MVC)*, which is the maximal force that the muscle can develop. This relationship is shown in Figure 12.8,

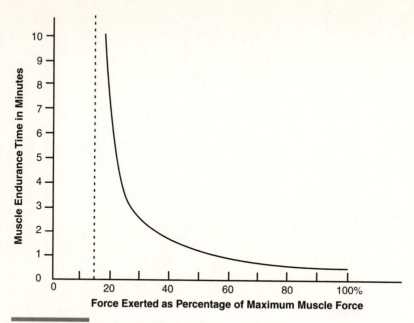

FIGURE 12.8

Relationship between static muscle endurance time and muscle exertion level. (*Source:* Rohmert, W., 1965. Physiologische Grundlagen der Erholungszeitbestimmung, *Zeitblatt der Arbeitswissenschaft,* 19, p. 1. Cited in Simonson, E., ed., 1971. *Physiology of Work Capacity and Fatigue,* Springfield, IL: Charles C. Thomas Publishers, p. 246.)

which is often called *the Rohmert curve* (Rohmert, 1965). It is clear from Figure 12.8 that the maximal force can be sustained for only a few seconds. A 50 percent force can be sustained for about one minute, but the static contraction can be maintained for minutes and even up to hours if the exerted muscle force is below 15 percent of the MVC (Simonson & Lind, 1971). Some studies suggest that static contractions can be held almost indefinitely only if the exerted force is less than 10 percent of the MVC (Bjorksten & Jonsson, 1977).

Muscle endurance time drops sharply at levels above 15 percent of the MVC, and muscle fatigue will develop quickly (in seconds) if the static work requires more than 40 percent of the MVC. The symptoms of local muscle fatigue include the feeling of muscle pain or discomfort, reduced coordination of muscle actions, and increased muscle tremor. Reduced motor control may lead to occupational injuries and accidents. Prolonged muscle fatigue may lead to disorders of the adjoining ligaments and tendons.

Two methods are commonly used to measure local muscle fatigue: electromyography (EMG) and subjective rating (psychophysical) scales. *Electromyography* is a technique for measuring the electrical activities of muscles from electrodes taped on the skin over the muscles. Extensive research has found that the EMG signals often shift to lower frequencies and show higher amplitudes as muscle fatigue develops (Hagberg, 1981; Lindstrom et al., 1977; Petrofsky & Lind, 1980). These changes in

EMG are often used as objective indicators of the development of local muscle fatigue.

As in the measurement of whole-body fatigue and work capacity, *subjective rating scales* can be used to measure muscle fatigue. The workers are asked to rate the level of fatigue experienced in a job on a set of rating scales, each of which represents a local muscle group (e.g., left shoulder, right shoulder, left wrist, right wrist). Each scale is marked with numerical markers such as 1 through 7, and the two ends of each scale represent very low and very high levels of muscle fatigue, respectively. In ergonomic job analysis of static work and muscle fatigue, it is often desirable to use subjective ratings in conjunction with EMG measurements.

As in the cases of whole-body fatigue, engineering and administrative methods can be used to reduce the risk of local muscle fatigue in industrial workplaces. Engineering methods focus on redesigning the job to eliminate static postures and reduce loads on various joints. This is often accomplished by improving workplace layouts and providing arm rests, body supports, and job aids. The biomechanical methods of job analysis described in Chapter 11 can be applied in this process to help identify stressful loads and evaluate alternative workplace layouts and work methods.

The most commonly adopted administrative method of reducing the risk of local muscle fatigue is to adopt job procedures that provide adequate muscle rests between exertions and during prolonged static work. The job procedure should allow the workers to change their postures periodically and use different muscle groups from time to time during the work. For example, periodic leg activities during prolonged seated work can greatly reduce swelling and discomfort at the lower legs and ankles, compared to continuous sitting during an eight-hour shift (Winkel & Jorgensen, 1985).

REFERENCES

Astrand, P. O., and Christensen, E. H. (1964). Aerobic work capacity. In F. Dickens and E. Neil (eds.), *Oxygen in the animal organism* (pp. 295–314). New York: Pergamon Press.

Astrand, P. O., and Rodahl, L. (1986). *Textbook of work physiology* (3rd ed.). New York: McGraw-Hill.

Bink, B. (1962). The physical working capacity in relation to working time and age. *Ergonomics, 5*(1), 25–28.

Bjorksten, M., and Jonsson, B. (1977). Endurance limit of force in long-term intermittent static contractions. *Scandinavian Journal of Work, Environment, and Health, 3,* 23–28.

Borg, G. (1985). *An introduction to Borg's RPE-Scale.* Ithaca, NY: Movement Publications.

Bridger, R. S. (1995). *Introduction to ergonomics.* New York: McGraw-Hill.

Brouha, L. (1967). *Physiology in Industry.* 2nd Edition. New York: Pergamon Press.

Cooper, K. H., Pollock, M. L., Martin, R. P., White, S. R., Linnerud, A. C., and Jackson, A. (1975). Physical fitness levels versus selected coronary risk factors. *Journal of the American Medical Association, 236*(2), 166–169.

Durnin, J.V.G.A., and Passmore, R. (1967). *Energy, work, and leisure.* London, UK: Heinemann.

Eastman Kodak Company (1986). *Ergonomic Design for People at Work.* Vol 2, New York: Van Nostrand Reinhold.

Edholm, O. G. (1967). *The biology of work.* McGraw-Hill, New York.

Garg, A., Herrin, G., and Chaffin, D. (1978). Prediction of metabolic rates form manual materials handing jobs. *Americal Industrial Hygiene Association Journal, 39*(8), 661–674.

Grinnell A. D., and Brazier, M. A. B. (eds.) (1981). *The regulation of muscle contraction: Excitation-contraction coupling.* New York: Academic Press.

Hagberg, M. (1981). Muscular endurance and surface electromyogram in isometric and dynamic exercise. *Journal of Applied Physiology: Respiration, Environment, and Exercise Physiology, 51,* 1.

Harrison, M. H., Brown, G. A., and Belyavin, A. J. (1982). The "Oxylog": An evaluation, *Ergonomics, 25,* 809.

Huxley, A. F. (1974). Muscular contraction. *Journal of Physiology, 243,* 1.

Kahn J. F., and Monod, H. (1989). Fatigue induced by static work, *Ergonomics, 32,* 839–846.

Kroemer, K., Kroemer, H., and Kroemer-Elbert, K. (1994). *Ergonomics.* Englewood Cliffs, NJ: Prentice-Hall.

Lind, A. R., and McNichol, G. W. (1967). Circulatory responses to sustained handgrip contractions performed during exercise, both rhythmic and static. *Journal of Physiology, 192,* 595–607.

Lindstrom, L., Kadefors, R., and Petersen, I. (1977). An electromyographic index for localized muscle fatigue. *Journal of Applied Physiology: Respiration, Environment, and Exercise Physiology, 43:* 750.

Luehmann, G. (1958). Physiological measurements as a basis of work organization in industry. *Ergonomics, 1,* 328–344.

Needham, D. M. (1971). *Machina carnis: The biochemistry of muscular contraction in its historical development.* Cambridge: Cambridge University Press.

NIOSH (1981). *Work practices guide for the design of manual handling tasks.* NIOSH.

Passmore, R., and Durnin, J. V. G. A. (1955). Human energy expenditure, *Physiological Review, 35,* 83–89.

Petrofsky, J. S., and Lind, A. R. (1980). The influence of temperature on the amplitude and frequency components of the EMG during brief and sustained isometric contractions, *European Journal of Applied Physiology, 44,* 189.

Rohmert, W. (1965). Physiologische Grundlagen der Erholungszeitbestimmung, *Zeitblatt der Arbeitswissenschaft,* 19, p. 1. Cited in E. Simonson, 1971, p. 246.

Schottelius, B. A., and Schottelius, D. D. (1978). *Textbook of physiology* (18th ed.). St. Louis: Mosby.

Simonson, E. (ed.) (1971). *Physiology of work and capacity and fatigue.* Springfield, IL: Charles Thomas Publisher.

Simonson E., and Lind, A. R. (1971). Fatigue in static work. In E. Simonson (ed.), *Physiology of work capacity and fatigue.* Springfield, IL: Charles Thomas Publisher.

Spurr G. B., Prentice, A. M., Murgatroyd, P. R., Goldberg, G. R., Reina, J. C., and Christman, N. T. (1988). Energy expenditure from minute-by-minute heart-rate recording: A comparison with indirect calorimetry. *American Journal of Clinical Nutrition, 48,* 552–559.

Vos, H. W. (1973). Physical workload in different body postures, while working near to or below ground level. *Ergonomics, 16,* 817–828.

Winkel, J., and Jorgensen, K. (1986). Evaluation of foot swelling and lower-limb temperatures in relation to leg activity during long-term seated office work. *Ergonomics, 29*(2), 313–328.

Woodson, W. (1981). *Human factors design handbook.* New York: McGraw-Hill.

CHAPTER 13

Stress and Workload

The proposal must be postmarked no later than 5 P.M., but as the copying is frantically pursued an hour before, the machine ceases to function, displaying a series of confusing error messages on its computer-driven display. With the panic of the approaching deadline gripping an unfortunate victim, he finds himself unable to decipher the complex and confusing instructions. In another building on campus, the job candidate, giving a talk, has fielded a few difficult (some might say nasty) questions and now turns to the video demo that should help answer the questions. Nervous and already upset, she now finds that the video player machine will not function, and while she fiddles with the various buttons, no one lifts a hand to assist her; instead, the audience waits impatiently for the show to go on.

Meanwhile, on the other side of the state, the climber has been concentrating on a difficult rock pitch when she suddenly realizes that the clouds have closed in around her. A sudden clap of thunder follows the tingle of electricity on her skin, and the patter of sleet on the now slippery rocks makes the once-challenging climb a truly life-threatening experience. To make matters worse, the cold has crept into her fingers, and as she fumbles with the rope through her protection on the rock, it takes all the concentration she can muster to deal with securing the protective rope. Inexplicably, rather than calling a retreat in the dangerous circumstances, she decided to continue to lead her team upward.

These three anecdotes all illustrate some of the varying effects of stress on performance—the stress of time pressure, the stress of threat and anxiety, and the stress imposed by factors in the environment, such as the cold on the rock. The concept of stress is most easily understood in the context of Figure 13.1. On the left of the figure is a set of *stressors,* influences on information availability and processing that are not inherent in the content of that information itself. Stressors may include such influences as noise, vibration, heat, and dim lighting, as well as such

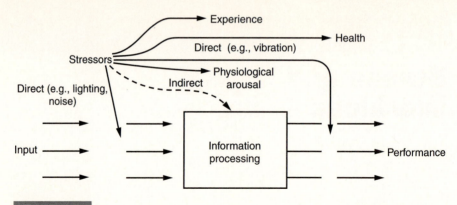

FIGURE 13.1

A representation of stress effects.

psychological factors as anxiety, fatigue, frustration, and anger. Such forces typically have four effects: (1) They produce a psychological *experience*. For example,
we are usually (but not always) able to report a feeling of frustration or arousal as
a consequence of a stressor. (2) Closely linked, a change in physiology is often observable. This might be a short-term change—such as the increase in heart rate associated with taking the controls of an aircraft or the stress of air traffic controllers
in high-load situations—or it might be a more sustained effect—such as the
change in the output of catecholamines, measured in the urine after periods of flying combat maneuvers or actual battlefield events (Bourne, 1971). The psychological experience and physiological characteristics are often, but not invariantly,
linked. (3) Stressors affect the efficiency of information processing, usually, but not
always by degrading performance (Driskell & Salas, 1996). (4) The stressors may
have long-term negative consequences for health.

As the figure shows, these effects may be either *direct* or *indirect*. Direct effects
influence the quality of information received by the receptors or the precision of
the response. For example, vibration will reduce the quality of visual input and
motor output, and noise will do the same for auditory input (Poulton, 1976). Time
stress may simply curtail the amount of information that can be perceived in a way
that will quite naturally degrade performance. Hence many of the negative influences of direct effect stressors on performance can be easily predicted.

Some of these stressors, however—like noise or vibration—as well as others
for which no direct effect can be observed—like anxiety or fear—appear to show
more indirect effects by influencing the efficiency of information processing
through mechanisms that have not yet been described. Many of the effects are mediated by *arousal*.

In this chapter, we consider first those *environmental* stressors that typically
have clearly defined direct effects (although they may have indirect effects as well).
We shall then consider internal "psychological" stressors of threat and anxiety,
those stressors associated with job and home, and finally conclude by considering

the interrelated effects of stress imposed by work overload, underload, and sleep disruption. As we discuss each stressor, we consider both the nature of negative stress effects on performance and the possible system remediations that can be used to reduce those effects.

ENVIRONMENTAL STRESSORS

We have already had an introduction to two of the most important environmental stressors in the form of *lighting* (in Chapter 4) and *noise* (in Chapter 5). Our discussion of both is instructive in setting the stage here for the stressors we discuss in this chapter; in both cases, the particular *level* of the variable involved determines whether a degradation of performance occurs, with intermediate levels often producing better performance than levels that are too low or too high. (This is particularly true with lighting, where both low illumination and glare can exert direct detrimental effects on performance.) Furthermore, in both cases, but particularly in the case of noise, the detrimental effects can be partitioned into those that disrupt performance of a task concurrent with the stressor (e.g., the noise masks the conversation) and those that have delayed effects that are more likely to endanger health (e.g., deafness in the case of noise). It is reasonable to argue that any stressor that produces delayed effects should trigger steps to reduce its magnitude, whether or not it also induces effects on concurrent performance. In contrast, those stressors that induce only direct effects may be tolerated as long as the level of performance loss sacrifices neither safety nor product quality.

Motion

Stress effects of motion can result from either high frequency motion, *vibration,* or from motion at much lower frequencies, inducing motion sickness (the effects of sustained motion on motion sickness are discussed along with our treatment of the vestibular system in Chapter 5).

Vibration. Vibration may be distinguished in terms of whether it is specific to a particular limb, such as the vibration produced by a hand-held power saw, or whether it influences the whole body, such as that from a helicopter or ground vehicle. The aversive long-term health consequences of the former type are well documented in terms of what is called the *vibrating white finger,* or VWF syndrome, an enduring loss in sensation to the fingers of a hand exposed to excessive continuous levels of high-frequency vibration from sources such as power tools (Chapter 10). As a consequence of this danger, standard "dosage" allowances for exposure to different levels of vibration have been established (Wasserman, 1987), not unlike the noise dosages discussed in Chapter 5. It is also obvious that hand vibration from a hand-held tool will disrupt the *precision* of the hand and arm in operating that tool (i.e., a direct effect) in such a manner as possibly to endanger the worker.

In addition to the remediations of limiting dose exposures, efforts can be made to select tools whose vibrations are reduced through design of the engine itself or incorporation of vibration-absorbing material.

In contrast to the well-documented vibrating white finger, the health consequences of full-body vibration are somewhat less well documented, although effects on both body posture and oxygen consumption have been observed (Wasserman, 1987). However, such vibration has clear and noticeable effects on many aspects of human performance (Griffin, 1997). Its presence in a vehicle can, for example, make touch screens extremely unreliable as control input devices and lead instead to the choice of dedicated keypads (see Chapter 9). Vibration may disrupt the performance of any eye-hand coordination task unless the hand itself is stabilized by an external source. Finally, vibration can disrupt the performance of purely visual tasks through the apparent blurring of the images to be perceived, whether these are words to be read or images to be detected (Griffin, 1997). As might be expected from our discussion in Chapter 4, the effect of any given high-frequency vibration amplitude can be predicted on the basis of the *spatial frequency resolution* necessary for the task at hand; the smaller the line or dot that needs to be resolved (the higher the spatial frequency), the greater will be the disruptive effect of a given vibration amplitude. Similar predictions can be made on the basis of the spatial precision of movement. Hence one remediation to vibration is to ensure that text fonts are larger than the minimum specified for stable environments and that target sizes for control tasks are larger. Naturally efforts to insulate both user and interface from the source of vibration using cushioning will also be helpful.

Motion Sickness.   As we discussed in Chapter 5, motion effects at a much lower frequency, such as the regular sea swell on a ship or the slightly faster rocking of the light airplane in flight, can lead to motion sickness. We discussed there the contributing factors of a *decoupling* between the visual and vestibular inputs (in such a way that motion sickness can be induced even where there is no true motion, as in full-screen visual displays). When considered as a stressor, the primary effects of motion sickness seem to be those of a *distractor*. Quite simply, the discomfort of the sickness is sufficiently intrusive that it is hard to concentrate on anything else, including the task at hand.

Thermal Stress

Both excessive heat and excessive cold can produce both performance degradation and health problems. A good context for understanding their joint effects can be appreciated by the representation of a "comfort zone," which defines a region in the space of temperature and humidity and is one in which most work appears to be most productive (Fanger, 1977). Regions above produce heat stress; those below produce cold stress. The temperature range is 73°F to 79°F in the summer, and 68°F to 75°F in the winter. The zone is skewed such that less humidity is allowed (60 percent) at the upper temperature limit of 79°F than at the lower limit of 68°F (85 percent humidity allowed).

The stress of excessive heat, either from the sun or from nearby equipment such as furnaces or boilers, produces well-documented decrements in performance (Konz, 1997), particularly on perceptual motor tasks like tracking and reaction time (Bowers, Weaver, & Morgan, 1996). Unlike the effects of vibration, those of heat are primarily *indirect,* affecting the efficiency of information processing, rather than the quality of information available in visual input or the motor stability of hand movement. The long-term consequences of heat exposure to health are not well-documented unless the exposure is one that leads to dehydration, heat stroke, or heat exhaustion.

In predicting the effects of certain levels of ambient heat (and humidity), it is important to realize the influence of three key moderating variables. First, the actual *body temperature* will be moderated by the clothing worn; protective clothing can reduce heat exposure, while clothing that cannot dissipate heat such as a rubber jacket may enhance it (Bensel & Santee, 1997). Second, the amount of *air movement,* induced by natural breezes or fans, has a substantial effect, diminishing the experienced heat. Third, the degree of *physical work* carried out by the operator, affecting the *metabolic activity* (see Chapter 12), can greatly increase the experience of heat. The joint influence of these latter two factors on the maximum degree of temperature recommended for exposure is presented in Table 13.1.

Implicit in the discussion of moderating factors above are the recommendations for certain kinds of remediations when heat in the workplace is excessive. For example, the choice of clothing can make a difference, the job may be redesigned to reduce the metabolic activity, and fans can be employed appropriately. Furthermore, ample amounts of liquids (and opportunities to consume them) should be provided.

The effects of cold stress are somewhat different from those of heat. Long-term cold exposure can obviously lead to frostbite, hypothermia, and health endangerment. Generally, cold effects on information processing (indirect effects) do not appear to be documented, other than through distraction of discomfort and trying to keep warm. As experienced by the mountain climber at the beginning of the chapter, the most critical performance aspects of cold stress are the direct effects related to the disruption of coordinated motor performance caused by that part of the body that appears to be most vulnerable, the hands and fingers. This disruption results from the joint effects of cold and wind. The remediations for cold stress are, obviously, the wearing of appropriate clothing to trap the body heat. Such clothing varies considerably in its effectiveness in this regard (Bensel & Santee, 1997), and, of course, there are many circumstances in which the protective value of some clothing, such as gloves and mittens, must be traded off against the loss in dexterity that results from their use.

TABLE 13.1   Threshold WBGT Temperatures (°C) as a Function of Air Velocity and Metabolic (Basal + Activity) Rate*

Metabolic Rate (W)	Low Air Velocity (<1.5 m/sec)	High Air Velocity (≥1.5 m/sec)
Light (< 230)	30.0	32.0
Moderate (230–35)	27.8	30.5
Heavy (>350)	26.0	28.9

*A velocity of 1.5 m/sec is "noticeable breeze"; paper blows at .08 m/sec.

Source: Rohles, F. H., and Konz, S. A., 1987. *Climate.* In *Handbook of Human Factors,* G. Salvendy, ed. New York: Wiley. Copyright © 1987. Reprinted by permission of John Wiley and Sons, Inc.

Air Quality

The last environmental stressor we discuss briefly is that resulting from poor air quality, often a consequence of poor ventilation in closed working spaces like mines or ship tanks but also increasingly in environments polluted by smog or carbon monoxide. Included here are the pronounced effects of *anoxia,* the lack of oxygen frequently experience by high altitudes (West 1985). Any of these reductions in air quality can have relatively pronounced negative influences on perceptual, motor, and cognitive performance (Houston, 1987; Kramer, Coyne & Strayer, 1993) and to make matters worse, can sometimes appear insidiously in a way in which the effected operator is unaware of the danger imposed by the degrading air quality.

PSYCHOLOGICAL STRESSORS

The environmental stressors that we discussed in the previous section all had in common the characteristic that some *physical* measure in the environment—such as that recorded by a noise meter, vibration or motion indicator, or thermometer—could be used to assess the magnitude of the stress influence. In contrast, consider two of the stressors on the people described at the beginning of the chapter. The candidate giving her job talk was stressed by the threat of embarrassment; the climber was stressed by the potential injury or even loss of life in the hazardous situation. In neither of these cases is it possible to identify a physical measure that is responsible for the psychological state of stress. Yet in both cases, the negative consequences to performance can be seen, and such consequences are consistent with a great deal of experimental and incident analysis data. Thus, when we talk of *psychological stressors* in this chapter, we are discussing specifically those stressors resulting from the perceived threat of harm or loss of esteem (i.e., potential embarrassment), of something valued, or of bodily function through injury or death.

Cognitive Appraisal

Several factors make the understanding of such stressors more challenging and difficult than is the case with environmental stressors. First, it is difficult to ascertain for each individual what may constitute a threat. The expert climber may perceive circumstances as being an "exciting challenge," whereas the novice may perceive the identical combinations of steep rock and exposure as being a real danger, simply because of the difference in skill level that the two climbers possess to deal with the problem. Second, as noted by Lazarus & Folkman(1984), the amount of stress for a given circumstance is very much related to the person's understanding or *cognitive appraisal* of the situation.

There are several possible reasons for differences in cognitive appraisal. One may fail to perceive the circumstances of risk. For example, the climber may simply be so intent on concentrating on the rock that she fails to notice the deteriorating weather, and she will not feel stressed until she does. One may fail to understand the risk. Here the climber may see the clouds approaching but not appreciate their implications for electrical activity and icy rock. One may be relatively more confident or even *overconfident* (see Chapter 6) in one's ability to deal with the hazard. Finally, if people appraise that they are more in control of the situation, they are less likely to experience stress than if they feel that other agents are in control (Bowers, Weaver, & Morgan, 1995). These facts together thwart the effort to derive hard numbers to predict the "amount of stress" for such psychological stressors in any particular circumstance (although such numbers may indeed be obtained from correlated physiological measures like heart rate).

There are also considerable challenges in doing research in the area of psychological stressors (Wickens, 1996). For clear ethical reasons, it is not always appropriate to put participants in psychological research in circumstances in which they may be stressed by the threat of physical or psychological damage (even though the former may be guaranteed never to occur). This has meant that research in this area must document *in advance* that the benefits to society of the knowledge gained by the research outweigh the potential psychological risks to the participant of being placed in the stressful circumstance. This documentation is often sufficiently difficult to provide that research knowledge in the area of psychological stressors progresses very slowly.

Nevertheless, the collective results of laboratory research and case studies from incident and accident analysis has revealed a general pattern of effects that can be predicted to occur under psychological stress (Broadbent, 1972; Hockey, 1986; Driskell & Salas, 1996), and we consider these below.

Level of Arousal

Stressful circumstances of anxiety and danger produce an increase in *physiological arousal,* which can be objectively documented by changes in a variety of physiological indicators, such as heart rate, pupil diameter, and hormonal chemistry (Hockey, 1986). Concomitant with this arousal increase, investigators have long noted what is characterized as an *inverted U* function of performance shown in Figure 13.2; that is, performance first increases up to a point known as the *optimum level of arousal* and then subsequently declines as stress-induced arousal increases. Also note in the figure that this optimum level of arousal is higher for simpler tasks than for complex ones (or for more highly skilled operators for whom a given task is simpler than for the novice). This function is sometimes referred to as the *Yerkes-Dodson* Law (Yerkes & Dodson, 1908). The cause of the performance increase as arousal increases to the optimum (the left side of the curve) can simply be thought of the facilitory effect of investing effort—"trying harder"; that is, the threat of loss will generally make us more motivated to work harder and perform better. However, the loss in performance above the optimum level of arousal (the right side of the curve) appears to be due to a more complex set of effects of *overarousal* that we describe below.

The Yerkes-Dodson Law may be criticized because it can never specify exactly *where* the OLA is for a particular task, individual, or circumstance. This difficulty is inherent in the inability to specify any physical scale of psychological stress imposed because of differences between people in skill and cognitive appraisal. Nevertheless the law is important in its ability to specify certain specific *information-processing*

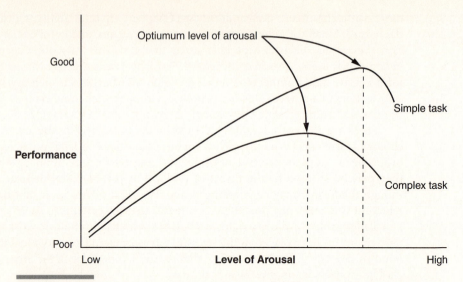

FIGURE 13.2

The Yerkes-Dodson Law showing the relation between level of arousal (induced by stress) and performance.

changes that occur with overarousal, changes that suggest remediations to be taken for operators who may work in such stressful circumstances (e.g., following emergencies or students taking tests).

Performance Changes with Overarousal

Several different changes in information-processing characteristics have been noted to occur as different forms of the sense of danger or threat have been imposed on people. *Perceptual* or *Attentional Narrowing*, sometimes known as *tunneling*, describes the tendency to restrict the range or breadth of attention, to concentrate very hard on only one "thing" (this thing is often the source of stress or information on how to avoid it), and to ignore surrounding information sources. While this strategy of focused attention may be appropriate if the object of tunneling *does* indeed provide the path to safety, it may be highly inappropriate if safety instead requires considering a broader set of less obvious signals, events, or information channels. Thus, the stressed speaker at the beginning of the chapter may have become so focused on the buttons on the video that she fails to notice that the machine is unplugged. Indeed there is evidence that the catastrophe at the Three Mile Island nuclear power plant resulted, in part, because the stress caused by the auditory alert in the nuclear power control room led operators to tunnel on one single indicator (which incorrectly indicated that the water level in the reactor was too high) and fail to perform a wider visual scan that would have allowed attention to be directed to other, correct, indicators (suggesting correctly that the water level was too low; Rubinstein & Mason, 1989, Wickens, 1992).

Just as visual attention can be tunneled to a particular part of the visual environment, so *cognitive tunneling* under stress describes the tendency to focus attention exclusively on one hypothesis of what is going on (e.g., only one failure candidate as the cause of an alarm) and ignore a potentially more creative diagnosis by considering a wider range of options. Thus, our climber at the beginning of the chapter may have focused only on the one solution—"climb upward."

Working memory loss describes just that. Under stress, people appear to be less capable of using working memory to store or rehearse new material or to perform computations and other attention-demanding mental activities (Wickens et al., 1991; Stokes & Kite, 1994; Hockey, 1986). The stressed pilot, panicked over the danger of a failed engine and lost in bad weather, may be less able to remember the air traffic controller's guidance about where he is and where to turn.

While working memory may degrade under stress, a person's *long-term memory* for well-known facts and skills will be little hampered and may even be enhanced. Thus under stress we tend to engage in the most dominant thoughts and actions. The problem occurs when these actions are different from the appropriate response to the stressful situation, for example, when the appropriate and seldom practiced response in an emergency (a condition that will rarely occur) is *incompatible* with the usual response in (frequently encountered) routine circumstances. An example of this is the appropriate emergency response to a skid while driving on an icy road. Under these circumstances, you should first turn *toward* the direction of skid, precisely the opposite of your normal response on dry pavement, which is to turn away from the direction you do not want to go. It is a consequence of this tendency to revert to the dominant habit in emergency that it makes sense to *overlearn* the pattern of behavior appropriate for emergencies.

Finally, there are certain *strategic shifts* that are sometimes observed in stress-producing emergency circumstances. One of these is the tendency to "do something, *now!*"—that is, to take immediate action (Hockey, 1986). The trouble is, as we learned in Chapter 9, fast action often sacrifices accuracy through the *speed-accuracy tradeoff*. Thus, the wrong action might be taken, whereas a more measured and delayed response could be based on more information and more careful reasoning. It is for this reason that organizations may wish to caution operators *not* to take any action at all for a few seconds or even minutes following an emergency, until the appropriate action is clearly identified.

Remediation of Psychological Stress

The previous description of *performance tendencies* following the experience of psychological stress suggests some logical remediations that can be taken (Wickens, 1996). Most appropriately, since these stresses are most likely to occur in emergency conditions, these remediations depend on an analysis of the likely circumstances of emergency and actions that should be taken. Remediations should then proceed with the design of displays, controls, and procedures in a way that *simplifies* these elements as much as possible. For example, emergency instructions should be easy to locate and salient (so that tunneling will not prevent their location or comprehension). The actions to be taken should depend as little as possible on holding information in working memory. As we discussed in Chapter 6, knowledge should be in the world (Norman, 1988). Actions to be taken in emergency should be explicitly instructed when feasible and should be designed to be as compatible as possible with conventional, well-learned patterns of action and compatible mapping of displays to controls (Chapter 9). As discussed in Chapter 5, auditory alerts and warnings should be designed to avoid excessively loud and stressful noises. Finally, training can be employed in two productive directions (Johnston & Cannon-Bowers, 1996). First, as noted above, extensive (and some might say excessive) training of emergency procedures can make these a dominant habit, readily available to long-term memory when needed. Second, generic training of *emergency stress management* can focus both on guidelines, like inhibiting the tendency to respond immediately (unless this is absolutely necessary), and on techniques, such as breathing control, to reduce the level of arousal to a more optimal value.

LIFE STRESS

There is another large category of stressors related to stressful circumstances on the job and in the worker's personal life that can lead to disruption in performance. It has been documented, for example, that industries with financial difficulties may have poorer safety records, or alternatively that workers who are content with labor-management relations (relieving a potential source of job stress) enjoy greater productivity. Correspondingly, stressful life events, like deaths in the family or marital strife (Holmes & Rahe, 1967), have been associated with events such as aircraft mishaps (Alkov et al, 1982), although this relationship is not a terribly strong one; that is, there are lots of people who suffer such life stress events who may be able to cope extremely well on the job.

The cause of both of these types of stress may be related to the different aspects of attention. First, poorer performance by those who are stressed by job-related factors (e.g., poor working conditions, inequitable wages) may be related to the *lack* of attention, resources, or effort put into the job (i.e., low motivation). In contrast, the greater safety hazards of some who suffer life event stress may be related to *distraction* or *diversion* of inattention; that is, attention diverted from the job-related task at hand to thinking about the source of stress (Wine, 1971).

The discussion of remediations for such stresses are well beyond the scope of this book, as they pertain to topics such as psychological counseling or industrial relations. The possibility of removing workers from job settings as a consequence of life stress events is questionable, only because so many people are able to cope effectively with those events and would be unfairly displaced. Perhaps the clearest guidance we can offer here is the need for all to maintain awareness of the possibilities that stress-induced distraction can lead to breakdowns in safety and, hence, the need to clearly understand the possible changes in attention that can result.

WORK OVERLOAD, UNDERLOAD, AND SLEEP DISRUPTION

As shown in Figure 13.3, work overload, underload, and sleep disruption all interact in a fairly complex way. All have negative consequences to performance, can be experienced, and therefore can be adequately defined as stressors. Work overload—having too much to do in too little time—can have negative performance implications on those tasks that are to be accomplished in the limited time; but on the other side of the arousal spectrum, having much too *little* to do except wait and watch for something to happen—the *vigilance task*—also has negative implications for performance of that seemingly simple task.

Both overload and underload situations can be fatiguing, and this fatigue, particularly when coupled with sleep disruption, has negative consequences for *future* performance on tasks of any sort, whether underload or overload (i.e., when performance must be sustained in the face of fatigue and sleepiness). Finally, what we have labeled as sleep disruption can result either from pure *sleep deprivation* or from performance at the "off cycle" of our circadian rhythms. While these concepts are closely linked and interactive, in the following pages we shall deal in sequence first with overload, then fatigue, then underload in the study of vigilance, and finally with the issue of sleep disruption.

Workload

In 1978, an airliner landed far short of the Pensacola Airport runway in Escambia Bay. While flying at night, the flight crew had apparently neglected to monitor their altitude after having to make a faster than usual approach, cramming a lot of the prelanding cockpit tasks into a shorter-than-expected period of time. The high workload apparently caused the pilots to neglect the key task of altitude monitoring. Several years later, an air traffic controller forgot that a commuter aircraft had been positioned on the active runway, and the controller cleared a commercial airliner to land on the same runway. In examining the tragic collision that resulted, the National Transportation Safety Board concluded that, among other causes, the controller had been overloaded by the number of responsibilities and planes that needed to be managed at that time (National Transportation Safety Board, 1992). In the following pages we describe how workload can be predicted and then how it is measured.

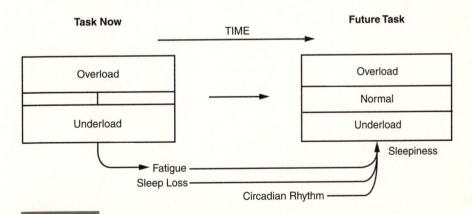

FIGURE 13.3

The relation between overload and underload in performing a current task, as they effect performance of a future task.

The Time-Line Model.   As described above, the concept of workload can be most easily and intuitively understood in terms of a ratio of time required (to do tasks) to time available (to do them in). We can all relate to the high workload of "so much to do, so little time." As we shall see below, the concept of workload is a good deal more sophisticated than this, but the time-ratio concept is a good starting place. Thus, when we wish to calculate the workload experienced by a particular operator in a particular environment, we can begin by laying out a *time line* of when different tasks need to be performed and how long they typically take (Fig. 13.4). Such a time line should be derived on the basis of a careful task analysis, as discussed in Chapter 3. We may then calculate the workload for particular intervals of time as the ratio within that interval of TR/TA (Parks & Boucek, 1989; Kirwan & Ainsworth, 1992). Of course, when calculating these ratios, it is important for the task analyst to include the nonobservable "think time" as part of the time required for tasks (e.g., the cognitively demanding tasks of diagnosis and planning), along with the more visible time during which people are actually looking, manipulating, or speaking.

However, assuming a mean time to complete all tasks and computing the workload on this basis, it is not accurate to assume that "work overload" will occur when the ratio is greater than 1.0. This inaccuracy results from several factors. First, any estimate of the mean time to perform a task (Luczak, 1997) will have a variability from occasion to occasion and person to person. Hence, we must represent these means as *distributions* (Fig. 13.5a). Then, if on some occasion, all of the times happen to be drawn at the long end of the distribution, workload may be excessive, even if mean TR/TA < 1.0. Hence, the measured TR may be more appropriately estimated as the 90th or 95th percentile of the distribution (Fig. 13.5b).

Second, even using the longest time estimates, it is always appropriate to leave a little margin of "spare time" or *spare capacity* in establishing what an overload

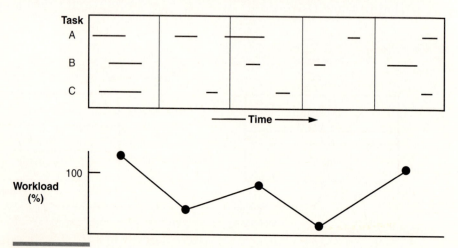

FIGURE 13.4
Time line analysis. The percentage of workload at each point is computed as the average number of tasks per unit time, within each window.

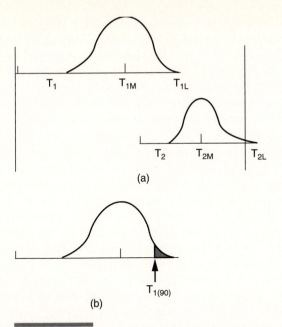

FIGURE 13.5

(a) The mean time for the two tasks within the interval (T_{1m} and T_{2m}) produces a time work-load ratio of less than 1.0. But the longest time for each (T_L) produces a ratio that exceeds 1.0. (b) The estimate of the 90th percentile time is a reasonable "worst case" time estimate.

level of TR/TA should be. This can be assumed to be the spare capacity that might be necessary to handle the unexpected event or emergency without eating into the time necessary to perform the primary tasks. In fact, researchers who have adopted the time-line approach typically recommend that a 20 percent margin of spare capacity be allowed (Kirwan & Ainsworth, 1992), and this view seems to coincide with observations from the aviation domain that pilots begin to make errors when the TR/TA workload ratio exceeds 80 percent (Parks & Boucek, 1989).

A third factor is that if one or two tasks are learned to a high level of automaticity, as discussed in Chapter 6, then they may be fairly easily time shared, and workload would not be considered excessive, even if the TR/TA ratio for the two is close to 200 percent. An example might be steering a vehicle (or walking) while talking.

A final factor concerns the fact that workload may be heavily modulated by the extent to which overlapping tasks on the time line compete for common versus separate resources in the context of multiple resource theory (Wickens, 1992; see Chapter 6).

Time-Stress Effects.   The consequence of imposing time-stress workload (increasing TR/TA) are at one level straightforward: *Something* is likely to suffer. Less predictable, however, is knowing how things will suffer. For example, Edland and Svenson (1993) report any of the following effects to have been found in making decisions under time pressure: more selectivity of input, more important sources of information given more weight, decrease in accuracy, decreasing use of strategies that involve heavy mental computation, and locking onto a single strategy.

Clearly, some of these strategies are more adaptive than others. Hence, it is important to carefully distinguish time stress workload consequences in terms of the degree of *adaptability*. This distinction can be made within the framework of Figure 13.6. An operator will have available multiple channels of information, which are used to perform various tasks. Both the information channels and the tasks can be ordered in terms of *importance*. For example, for pilots, recent weather reports are more important than older ones; it is generally more important for a pilot to monitor altitude information than to monitor fuel information because the former is more likely to vary unpredictably; and it is more important for the pilot to keep the plane in the air (i.e., avoid a stall) than to communicate. Research has shown that when time is short, people will tend to focus more on the tasks *that they believe* to be most important and to attend to the information sources *that they believe* to be most important (Svenson & Maule, 1993; Raby & Wickens, 1994; Chou, Madhavan, & Funk, 1996); that is, the effects of time stress will be to restrict the range of cues and tasks they consider as shown in Figure 13.6. Second, people will also focus more on those information sources that are more *available* (i.e., visible, directly in front, and easy to interpret). Problems result then if the tasks or channels believed to be most important are in reality *not* the most important.

Remediations.   On the basis of these observed trends in behavior, certain remediations are suggested. Most obviously these include task redesign by trying to assign certain time-loading tasks to other operators or to automation (see Chapter 16).

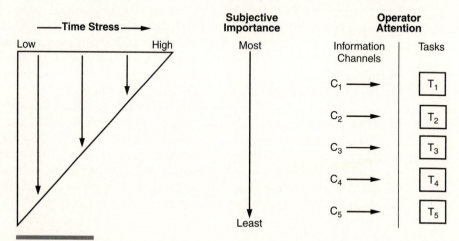

FIGURE 13.6

Relationship between time stress and task optimal task shedding. As time stress increases, depicted at the left, the number of tasks performed (or channels processed) must decrease. However, the order of shedding tasks will be based upon the subjective importance of tasks (or channels). Optimal task shedding results when subjective importance agrees with true importance.

However, they also include developing a display design such that the most objectively important sources are available, interpretable, and salient.

Training for high time-stress workload can focus on either of two approaches. One will be training on the component tasks to try to speed or automate their performance (see Chapter 6). This will mean that tasks will either occupy less time in the time line or will require little attention so that they can be overlapped with others without imposing workload. The other approach is to focus on training of *task management skills* (Chao et al., 1996) and to ensure that operators are properly *calibrated* regarding the relative importance of tasks and information sources (Raby & Wickens, 1994). As an example of this, the nuclear regulatory agency has explicitly stated the policy that in the case of emergency, the operator's first task priority is to try to stabilize the plant (to keep the situation from growing worse), the second is to take steps to ensure safety, and the third is to try to diagnose the cause of the emergency. (Chapter 16).

Effort and Workload.   While time demand is a necessary starting place to understanding workload, there are many circumstances in which changes in workload cannot be uniquely associated with time, and hence the concept of *effort* is used (Kahneman, 1973; Wickens, 1991; Hart & Wickens, 1990). As we noted above, an automated and a nonautomated task may occupy the same space in the time line, but the workload of the automated task will be very much less. As another example, the time required to track a stable velocity control system and an unstable acceleration system may be the same (Chapter 9), but the effort of the second is clearly greater, and it will be more likely to interfere more with other tasks that should be performed at the same time. While it is easy to measure time demands through task time-line analysis, it is far more difficult to predict the amount of effort demands of a task. However, it is clearly easy to specify variables that will increase the effort demanded by a task, as indicated in Table 13.2. The advantage of an approach such as that shown in Table 13.2 is that it will allow the system designer, confronting an environment in which the operator is overloaded, to identify characteristics of the task setting that might be modified to lower the workload. However the actual association of tasks with quantitative workload or effort numbers requires the adoption of workload measurement techniques, an issue we discuss below.

Work Overload Prediction.   With the input of careful task analysis, time-line scales can be used to *predict*, before a system is built, the workload that will be imposed by that system or job environment (Kirwan & Ainsworth, 1992).

Such prediction is relatively easy when (TR/TA) < 100%. However, in many environments, such as driving or flying (Chapter 17) or even taking notes in class while listening to the instructor, when two or more tasks are carried out concurrently and TR/TA > 100%, then predicting differences in workload becomes much more challenging. This is because such prediction must account for differences in task automaticity and in multiple resource competition that will influence performance. Workload models designed to accomplish this are beyond the scope of this text, but are discussed by Sarno and Wickens (1995) and Wickens (1992).

TABLE 13.2 Demand Checklist

Signal/Noise Ratio
Discriminability: Avoid Confusion Between Different Display Symbols
Display Simplicity: (Avoid Clutter)
Display Organization: Reduce Scanning
Compatibility: Display Compatible with Mental Model
Consistency: Of Format Across Displays
Number of Modes of Operation
Prediction Requirements
Mental Rotation
Working Memory Demand (Chunk–Seconds)
Unprompted Procedures
S-R Compatibility
Feedback of Action
   (Intrinsic–Tactile)
   (Extrinsic–Visual)
Precision of Action
Skill–Rule–Knowledge

Mental Workload Measurement

We discussed above the manner in which workload could be defined in terms of TR/TA, and indeed time *is* a major driver of workload (Hendy et al., 1997). However, mental workload can be defined more generally by the ratio of the *resources* required to the *resources* available, where time is one of those resources but not the only one. For example, we know that some tasks are time consuming but not particularly demanding of cognitive resources or effort (e.g., transcribing written text on a keyboard), whereas others may be very effortful but occupy only a short time (e.g., answering a difficult logic question on a test). As we noted above, predictive workload techniques based purely on time lines have limits, and so workload researchers must turn to various forms of assessing or measuring the resource demands of tasks (Lysaght et al., 1989; O'Donnell & Eggemeier, 1986; Tsang & Wilson, 1997).

The assessment of workload can serve two useful functions. First, we have already seen how assessing the workload of *component* tasks can contribute to predictive models of workload. Second, workload assessment after a system has been built (or put in use) can provide a very important contribution to usability analysis because, even though *performance* with the system in question may be quite good (or even satisfactory), if the *workload* experienced while using it is excessive, the system may require improvement. Traditionally, workload has been assessed by one of four different techniques.

Primary Task Measures. Primary task measures are measures of system performance on the task of interest. For example, in assessing an interface for an automated teller machine, the primary task measure may refer to the speed and accuracy with which a user can carry out a transaction. In assessing a prosthetic device for an amputee, it may reflect speed and accuracy measures on certain manipulative tasks. The primary task measure is not really a workload measure per se, but it is often *influenced* by workload and hence assumed to reflect workload (i.e., higher workload will make performance worse). However, this may not always be the case. Furthermore, there are many circumstances in which very good primary task performance is attained but only at a cost of high workload. This means that there will be no margin of reserve capacity if unexpected increases in load occur. It may also mean that users will choose not to use the high-workload device in question when given an option. The amputee, for example, may choose to discard the particular prosthetic device, or the ATM customer may simply choose to go inside the bank to the teller.

Secondary Task Methods. Performance on a secondary or concurrent task provides a method of measuring *reserve capacity*. The assumption is that performance of the primary task takes a certain amount of cognitive resources. A secondary task will use whatever residual resources are left. To the extent that fewer resources are left over from the primary task, performance on the secondary task will suffer. Most researchers using secondary tasks to assess workload have used external secondary tasks or tasks that are not usually part of the job (Tsang & Wilson, 1997; Wierwille & Eggemeier, 1993). In this method, people are asked to perform the primary task as well as possible and then to allocate whatever effort or resources are still available to the secondary task. Increasing levels of difficulty on the primary task will then yield smaller margins of resources for the secondary task, which will ultimately result in diminishing levels of performance on the secondary task. Examples of common secondary tasks are time estimation, tracking tasks, memory tasks, mental arithmetic, and reaction time tasks (Wierwille & Eggemeier, 1993).

Many studies have demonstrated that secondary tasks can show differences in primary task difficulty when primary task performance does not differ. In addition, researchers have shown secondary tasks to be sensitive to differences in automaticity of the primary task (e.g., Bahrick & Shelly, 1958). The use of a secondary task for measuring workload is good because it has high face validity in that it seems like a reasonable measure of demands imposed by the primary task.

However, there are several problems or limitations associated with the use of a secondary task. First, it often seems artificial, intrusive, or both to operators performing the tasks. Because of this, several researchers have suggested the use of *embedded* secondary tasks, which are secondary tasks that are normally part of the job but have a lower priority (Raby & Wickens, 1994; Shingledecker, 1987. See Figure 13.6.). An example might be using the frequency of glances to the rear view mirror as an embedded secondary task measure of driving workload. Second, as we might expect on the basis of multiple resource theory, a given secondary task might be performed at a different level with each of two primary tasks, not because of workload differences but because of the differences in the common resources share between the primary and secondary tasks. Schlegal, Gilliland, & Schlegal (1986) developed a structured set of tasks, the *Criterion Task set*, that access different resource dimensions.

Physiological Measures.   Because of problems with intrusiveness and multiple resources, some researchers have favored using physiological measures of workload (Tsang & Wilson, 1997; Kramer, 1991). In particular, measures of heart rate *variability* have proven to be relatively consistent and reliable measures of *mental* workload, (just as mean heart *rate* has proven to be a good measure of *physical* workload and stress; see Chapter 12). At higher levels of workload, the heart rate (interbeat interval) tends to be more constant over time, whereas at lower workload levels it waxes and wanes from frequencies of around 0.1 Hz to those driven by respiration rate (Tattersall & Hockey, 1995; Roscoe, 1987).

Measures of visual scanning are also useful in understanding the qualitative nature of workload changes. For example, in driving we can measure fixations on the dashboard as a measure of the workload demands (head down time) associated with in-vehicle instrumentations (see Chapter 17). There are many other physiological workload measures associated with variables such as blink rate, pupil diameter, and electroencepholographic (EEG) recording, which will not be described here (See Tsang & Wilson, 1997 and Kramer, 1991 for a fuller discussion). Generally speaking, physiological measures correlate with other measures of workload and hence are valid. The equipment and instrumentation required for many of these, however, may sometimes limit their usefulness.

Subjective Measures.   The most intuitive measure of mental workload, and that which is often easiest to obtain, is to simply ask the operator to rate workload on a subjective scale. The best scales are often anchored by explicit descriptions of the high and low end of the scale. Sometimes they may be associated with a structured decision tree of questions that will guide the rater to a particular number (Wierwille & Casali, 1983). Several researchers have argued that subjective workload should be rated on more than just a single scale because workload is a complex multidimensional construct (Derrick, 1988). For example, the Subjective Workload Assessment Technique (SWAT: Reid & Nygren, 1988) asks users to rate workload on one of three levels on one of three scales. The NASA Task Load Index (TLX; Hart & Staveland, 1989) imposes five different subscales, with seven levels (Wickens, 1992).

While subjective ratings are, as noted, easy to obtain, they also have the limitation that they are, by definition, subjective, and it is a fact of life that people's subjective reports do not always coincide with their performance (Andre & Wickens, 1995). It is also possible to envision raters intentionally biasing their reports to be low (or high) under certain circumstances for motivational reasons.

Workload Dissociations.   The human factors practitioner can well ask, Which method should I use? The fact that most measures (subjective, physiological, and secondary task) generally correlate with each other in discriminating low versus high workload conditions or systems is comforting and often allows the user to select techniques of convenience. Still, multiple measures are recommended where possible. Also, a final concern in workload measurement is that of the dissociation sometimes observed between primary task performance on the one hand and physiological and subjective measures on the other (Hart & Wickens, 1990; Yeh & Wickens, 1988). Dissociation occurs when workload measures are found to increase at the same time that primary task performance is found to improve. To understand the cause of such dissociations, it is important to realize that subjective and physiological workload measures are often good assessments of how much cognitive effort the user invests in a task. It is thus possible to imagine circumstances in which a user invests more effort in a task (for example because of high motivation) whose objective characteristics have not changed. The added effort will signal higher workload but will also improve performance.

Fatigue

High mental workload can have two effects. While performing a task, performance may degrade. But the effects of high and even moderate mental workload are also cumulative in terms of the buildup of *fatigue* in a way that can adversely affect performance on subsequent tasks (Orasanu & Backer, 1996). Mental as well as physical fatigue becomes relevant in scheduling rest breaks or maximum duty cycles in high-workload tasks. For example, the army establishes limits on the amount of helicopter flight time based on the level of workload imposed during flight. Night flying imposes higher workload (and hence shorter duty) than day flight; flight low to the ground imposes higher workload than that at higher altitudes.

The role of fatigue also becomes quite relevant in predicting the consequences of long-duration, sustained operations or continuous performance, such as that which might be observed on a military combat mission (Orasanu & Backer, 1996). Here the effects of fatigue from continuous work are often confounded with those of sleep loss, although their influences are not identical. In these circumstances, studies have revealed that cognitive performance begins to decline within 24 hours, and before the loss of performance involving physical tasks (Haslam, 1985). We return to the issue of sleep loss at the end of this chapter.

Vigilance and Underarousal

At first glance, circumstances in which the operator is "doing little" might seem like less of a human factors problem than circumstances in which the operator is overloaded. Yet a long history of research, as well as accident and incident analysis, reveals that maintaining sustained attention to vigilance tasks in low-arousal environments can be just as fatiguing and just as prone to human vulnerabilities as the high workload situation. For example, Stager, Hameluck, & Jubis (1989) have found that more air traffic control errors typically occur on the low- than on the high-workload parts of the controller's shift, and several studies have found that some quality control inspectors on the assembly line, whose only job is to look for defects, show an alarmingly high miss rate (see Chapter 4). In fact, maintaining sustained, vigilant attention in low-workload situations is both fatiguing and stressful (Hancock & Warm 1989).

Causes of the Vigilance Decrement. The stage for the vigilance problem was set in our discussion of signal detection theory in Chapter 4. There we outlined how signal detection problems were analyzed in terms of the four classes of joint events: hits, correction rejections, misses, and false alarms. The main problem in vigilance appears to be the increased number of misses that occur as the vigil progresses. The years of research that has been carried out on the vigilance problem (Warm, 1984; Warm & Parasuraman, 1987; Davies & Parasuraman, 1982) has identified certain key characteristics of the environment that lead to the loss of performance in detecting the signal or events that are of relevance. The characteristics include:

1. *Time.* The longer duration an operator is required to maintain vigilance, the greater is the likelihood that misses will occur.

2. *Event salience.* Bright, loud, intermittant and other salient events will be easily detected. The event that is subtle, like the typesetting error in the middle of the word, the small gap in the wiring of the circuit board, or the offset of a light will show a larger loss in detection over time.

3. *Signal rate.* When the signal events themselves occur at a relatively low rate, monitoring for their presence will be more effortful, and the likelihood of their detection will be reduced. Part of the reason is because low signal expectancy causes the operator to adopt a more conservative response criterion (producing more misses and fewer false alarms), and part is because the presence (and detection) of events appear to act as "stimulants" that better sustain arousal. When these events are fewer in number, arousal falls.

4. *Arousal level.* A problem with vigilance situations is that there is generally little intrinsic task-related activity to maintain the information-processing system in the state of alertness or arousal to optimize perception. The operator is often at the far left end of the inverted U curve shown in Figure 13.2. As might be expected, anything that will further decrease arousal, like sleep deprivation, will have particularly profound effects on vigilance performance, and we consider the implications of such deprivation in the following section.

Vigilance Remediations.   The four primary factors identified above suggest some appropriate solutions to the vigilance problem discussed in more detail elsewhere (Wickens, 1992). First, watches or vigils should not be made too long, and operators should be given fairly frequent rest breaks. Second, where possible, signals should be made more salient. This is not always easy to achieve, but there are certain techniques of *signal enhancement* that can be cleverly employed in areas such as quality control inspection (Drury, 1982).

Third, if miss rates are high, it is possible to alter the operator's criterion for detecting signals through payoffs (large rewards for detecting signals) or changing the signal expectancy. However, in a situation in which the signals (or events) to be detected occur only rarely, the only way to change signal expectancy effectively (and credibly) is by introducing *false signals* (e.g., put a few known defective parts on the assembly line or concealed weapons in luggage for inspection). Of course, designers and practitioners should always remember that such alterations in the response criterion will invariably produce more false alarms and should therefore assume that the costs of a false alarm to total system performance are less than the benefits of reducing the miss rate.

Fourth, efforts should be made to create or sustain a higher level of arousal. Frequent rest breaks will do this, as will intake of appropriate levels of stimulants such as caffeine. Other forms of external stimulation *may* be effective (e.g., music, noise, or conversation), but caution should be taken that these do not form sources of *distraction* away from the inspected product (or monitored environment). Finally, every effort should be made to ensure that operators are not sleep deprived because of the particular vulnerability of vigilance tasks to fatigue from sleep loss. We turn now to the discussion of sleep disruption.

Sleep Loss

The fatigue resulting from sleep loss can have major negative consequences as any student trying to stay awake while listening to a lecture or taking a test after pulling an "all nighter" can attest. The consequences can sometimes be severe. For example, it is estimated that over 200,000 auto accidents per year are attributed in part to fatigue; impairment on many other sorts of tasks such as medical treatment in the hospital (Asken & Raham, 1983) or performance on the battlefield (Ainsworth & Bishop, 1971) or on the switchboard (Browne, 1949) have been shown to suffer substantially from sleep loss (Huey & Wickens, 1993).

The major cause of sleepiness contributing to these and many other degradations of performance is of course the *deprivation* of sleep during some prior period. This could be from intentional efforts to stay awake, as when the student pulls the all nighter to finish the paper or when the understaffing of a unit, like a ship, forces people to stand longer watches with less sleep time. In addition to voluntarily staying awake, there are causes of sleep disruption when a person is *trying* to sleep that produce sleepiness later on. These include trying to sleep during the daytime (against one's natural circadian rhythms), overcoming the residual effect of too much caffeine, or the aftereffects of stress.

In addition to sleep loss, a second cause of sleepiness is related to the time of the day-night cycle, our phase in the natural *circadian rhythms* (Horne, 1988). These rhythms have a clear physiological base. As shown in Figure 13.7, our body temperature undergoes a natural fluctuation, reaching a minimum in the early hours of the morning, climbing progressively during the day to reach a maximum in the late afternoon/early evening hours before declining again. This is a rhythm of arousal that is then correlated with and "entrained by" the natural day-night cycle on Earth.

There are at least three important variables that are correlated with body temperature, as also shown in the figure. These include *sleepiness* (which can be measured by the *sleep latency test;* how long it takes a volunteer to go to sleep in a dark room on a comfortable bed); the *sleep efficiency,* which measures how long we can sleep (greater at night); and measures of *performance.* Shown in Figure 13.8 are the performance fluctuations observed with four different kinds of tasks; all four show the same consistent drop in performance in the early morning hours, a drop that is mirrored in the real-world observations such as the greater frequency of errors by air traffic controllers (Stager et al., 1989) or accidents by truck drivers (Czeisler et al., 1986; Harris, 1977). It is not surprising that the effects of sleep loss

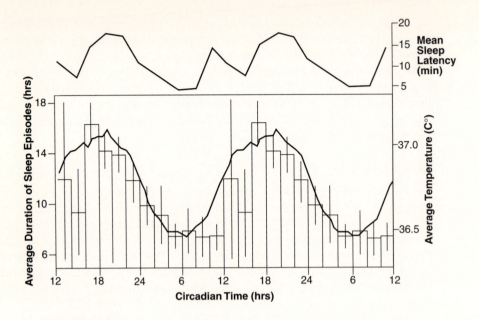

FIGURE 13.7

Graph plotting mean sleep latency (top), circadian rhythms (body temperature), and sleep duration (bottom), against time for two day night cycles. (*Source:* Czeisler, C.A., Weitzman, E.D., Moore-Ede, M.C., Zimmerman, J.C., and Knauer, R.S., 1980. Human sleep: Its duration and organization depend on its circadian phase. *Science,* 210, pp. 1264–1267. Reprinted with permission. Copyright 1980 American Association for the Advancement of Science.)

and circadian cycle essentially add, so that the early morning lows are substantially lower for the worker who has been deprived of sleep during the previous days.

Performance Loss Due to Sleepiness. To some extent, almost all aspects of performance will suffer when a person is sufficiently sleepy, through the combination of sleep loss and low arousal circadian rhythm phase. When we fall asleep, little performance of any kind can be expected! However, short of this, some aspects of performance are more susceptible than others (Huey & Wickens, 1993). Given that sleepiness causes increased blinks, eye closures, and brief durations of "microsleep" (nodding off), it is understandable that tasks depending on visual input will be particularly sensitive to sleep disruption. Furthermore, tasks that are not themselves highly arousing will also be unable to compensate for sleepiness by sustaining operator attention. As we saw in the previous section, this is particularly true of vigilance tasks, which seem to be the first to go when operators are sleep deprived (Farmer & Green, 1985; Horne, Anderson & Wilkinson, 1983).

In addition, researchers have reported that tasks particularly sensitive to sleep disruption are those involving judgment (Krueger et al., 1985), learning or storing new material (Williams et al., 1959), as well as those tasks involving self-initiated cognitive activity, like maintaining situation awareness and planning (Banderet et al., 1981). Not surprisingly, the tasks that are relatively less suscepti-

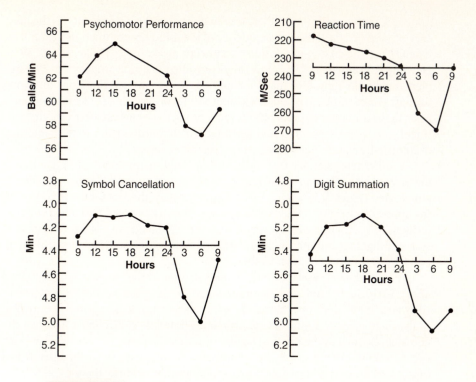

FIGURE 13.8

Graph showing how performance on four kinds of tasks varies as a function of circadian rhythms, shown for a one day cycle. (*Source:* Klein, K.E., and Wegmann, H.M., 1980. *Significance of Circadian Rhythms in Aerospace Operations* [*NATO AGARDograph #247*]. Neuilly sur Seine, France: NATO AGARD.)

ble to sleepiness are those with a great deal of intrinsic arousal, such as those involving a lot of motor activity or highly interesting material.

Remediation to Sleep Disruption. Some of the remediations that can be suggested to combat sleepiness are as obvious as the source of the problem itself: *get more sleep.* In fact, it turns out that even small amounts of sleep, such as 3–4 hours per night, can be quite beneficial in sustaining performance through several days even though such an amount will still not come close to sustaining the performance level of a well-rested individual (Krueger et al., 1985; Orasanu & Backer, 1996).

Napping has by now been well documented as an effective countermeasure. For example, Dinges et al. (1987) found that a single strategically placed 2-hour nap could significantly improve the level of performance of people after 54 hours of sustained wakefulness. Rosekind et al. (1994) have documented the benefits of controlled naps in the cockpit of aircraft on long transoceanic flights. Such naps improve the level of vigilance performance and still allow pilots to get just as good sleep after the flight as if they had not napped at all. In general, a nap should be at least 15 minutes in duration to be effective (Naitoh, 1984). The one possible drawback with naps (or any other sleep in operational environments) is the presence of *sleep inertia.* This is the tendency of the mind not to function with full efficiency for the first 8–10 minutes following awakening (Dinges et al., 1985; Downey & Bonnett, 1987). Hence, any controlled napping strategy must be implemented with allowance made for full recovery of mental functions following the nap. For example, a transoceanic pilot should be awakened at least 10 minutes prior to the initiation of preparations for entering the busier airspace over the continent, and watch keepers should be awakened 10 minutes prior to the beginning of information exchange prior to the watch turnover.

Another remediation can be achieved by building up *sleep credits,* that is, trying to gain extra sleep prior to a mission or period in which sleep deprivation is anticipated (Huey & Wickens, 1993). Unfortunately, this procedure is very often the opposite of reality. For example, Graeber (1988) has noted that pilots will typically sleep *less* than an average amount on the night before a 3–4 day "short haul" series of flights is initiated, a period of time during which sleep is more difficult and fatigue build-up is considerable.

Perhaps the best way of implementing all three of the remediations described above is through implementation of a careful program of *sleep management* (deSwart, 1989). This option may be particularly feasible in relatively controlled units, such as those found in the military. While less controllable in other circumstances, such as the medical facility or industrial factory, it is still feasible for organizations to emphasize the importance of adequate sleep for operational safety, and for example to disapprove of, rather than admire, the individual who may brag of "not sleeping for two nights to get the job done." Clearly, it should be the role of organizations to avoid conditions in which operators must work long hours in life-critical jobs, with little sleep (the pattern often reported by medical students, interns and residents; Asken & Raham, 1983; Friedman et al., 1971).

There are, finally, two remediations that have far less consistent records of success for quite different reasons. First, drugs like caffeine can be used to combat sleepiness in the short run, and these, as well as other motivators, can be used to sustain performance through and after one night's sleep deprivation (Lipschutz et al., 1988). However after two nights, the compensatory ability of such drugs is limited (Horne, 1988). Furthermore, while excessive consumption of caffeine may be adequate in the short run, in the long run it will disrupt the ability to sleep soundly when sleep time *is* available and hence may be counterproductive in reducing overall fatigue.

A second remediation that has only limited success is simply to not require (or to prohibit) work during the late night–early morning hours at the low arousal point of the circadian rhythm. If this is done, then the periods of lowest performance will be avoided, and workers will not be required to sleep during the day when adequate sleep is more difficult to attain. The problem with this remediation is simply that many organizations *must* function round the clock: Ships must sail all night, trucks must drive, and many factories and industrial plants must keep running 24 hours a day to provide services or products. The general issue of *desynchronization* and *shiftwork,* addressing the fatigue patterns of workers who must be on the job during these night hours, concludes our discussion of stress.

Desynchronization

Desynchronization is the term that describes the situation when the circadian rhythms are out of synchrony with the level of activity that a person is trying to maintain. Its major implications are for shiftwork and for long-distance travel.

Shiftwork.   Given that certain jobs must be performed round the clock, some workers will need to be active in the early morning hours when the circadian rhythms are at their lowest level of arousal. There are several possible strategies that can be chosen to deal with the resulting problem. These strategies vary considerably in their effectiveness.

One strategy is simply to assign workers permanently to different shifts, under the assumption that the circadian rhythms of the "night shift" worker will eventually adapt. The problem with this approach is that full adaptation never entirely takes place as long as the worker is exposed to *some* evidence of Earth's natural day-night cycle, evidence which will be desynchronized from the intended circadian cycle. Such evidence will be provided by the omnipresent evidence of sunlight, as well as the natural daytime activity of most of the rest of the population. Another problem with this strategy will be the smaller pool of people who are willing to work the night shift, because of personal preference.

A second strategy, employed for example in shipboard watches, is to maintain a fairly continuous rotation of shifts; a worker might have a night watch one "day," a morning watch the next, an afternoon watch the next, and so forth. Here the problem lies in the fact that desynchronization remains in a continuous state of flux. The circadian rhythms never have a chance to "catch up" to the levels of alertness that the person is trying to obtain via their scheduled shift. Hence, their arousal will never be optimal during the work time (particularly in the early morning hours), nor, for the same reasons, will their sleep be optimal during the off time (Carskadon & Dement, 1975; Huey & Wickens, 1993).

The third, and more successful strategy is to alter the shift periods but to do so relatively infrequently (e.g., following 14–21 days on a given cycle; Wilkinson, 1992). This strategy has the advantage of allowing the circadian rhythm to synchronize with (adapt to) the desired schedule, an adaptation which takes 4–5 days to occur and yet still allows all workers to share in the same inconveniences of night and early morning schedules (Czeisler et al., 1982).

Whether schedules are rotated rapidly or slowly, a second finding that is well documented is that shifts that are *delayed* are more effective than those that are *advanced*. (Barton & Folkard, 1993). A delayed shift is one in which a worker would move, say from a midnight–8 A.M. shift, to an 8:00 A.M.–4:00 P.M. shift, whereas the advanced shift moves from later to earlier. The advantage of delayed shifts appears to be due in part to the fact that the natural circadian rhythms of humans is actually slightly longer than 24 hours. Hence, the rhythms themselves are more naturally attuned to "waiting" and delaying the shift start than to advancing it.

Investigators have reported that shift schedules that adhere to the natural circadian rhythms (infrequent and delayed shifts) are preferred by workers, lead to greater productivity, greater worker health, and reduced turnover (Czeisler et al., 1982).

Jet Lag.   As Figure 13.9 shows, the desynchronization caused by long-duration east or west flights, sometimes referred to as *jet lag,* has effects that are quite analogous to shift changes. A westbound flight (e.g., from San Francisco to Tokyo) is one that makes the day longer and is analogous to a delayed shift. While initially the traveler may be more tired from the longer day, the circadian rhythms will adapt more rapidly, and the total sleep disruption will be less. In contrast, the eastbound flight, with its very rapid day (or night), leads to slow adaptation and considerably greater disruption of sleep patterns (Klein & Wegmann, 1980).

The remediations to these disruptive effects of jet lag are, of course, quite different from those related to shiftwork. Most successful are those remediations that try to bring the body into the local cycle of the destination as rapidly as possible. One way to do this is by waiting till the local bedtime after one has landed rather than napping during the day (Graeber, 1988). A second way to "hurry" the adaptation process along is by exposure to intense light prior to departure at a time that approximates daylight at the destination (Czeisler et al., 1989). Similar effects on

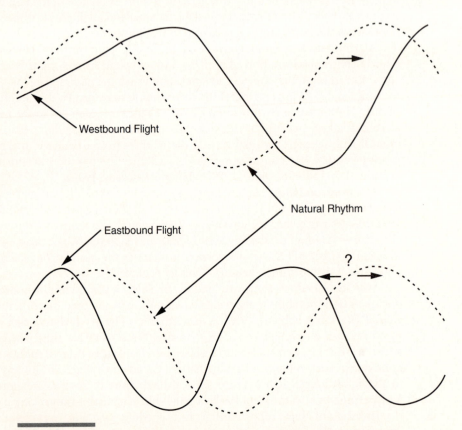

FIGURE 13.9
Graphs showing desynchronization on east- and westbound flights across several time zones. In part, because the body shows uncertainty for how to readjust the rhythms following eastbound flights, adjustment is more difficult.

biochemically adapting the circadian rhythms can be achieved by taking the drug melatonin.

CONCLUSION

In conclusion, stress comes in a variety of different forms from a variety of different causes and symptoms. The one underlying concern for human factors is the potential degradation in performance on tasks that may be otherwise well human factored. Whether the underlying cause is overarousal and overload, as we discussed in the first part of the chapter, or underarousal and underload, as we discussed later, stress reveals the clear vulnerabilities of the human operator. Such vulnerabilities can be a source of accident or error, as we describe in the next chapter, and have led many to advocate the role of computers (Chapter 15) and automation (Chapter 16) to replace the vulnerable stress-sensitive human component. As we shall see however, such solutions have their costs as well as their benefits.

REFERENCES

Ainsworth, L., and Bishop, H.P. (1971). *The effects of a 48-hour period of sustained field activity on tank crew performance.* Alexandria, VA: Human Resource Research Organization.

Alkov, R.A., Borowsky, M.S., and Gaynor, M.S. (1982). Stress coping and the US Navy aircrew factor mishap. *Aviation, Space, and Environmental Medicine, 53,* 1112–1115.

Andre, A.D., and Wickens, C.D. (1995). When users want what's *not* best for them. *Ergonomics in Design,* Oct. 10–13.

Asken, M.J., and Raham, D.C. (1983). Resident performance and sleep deprivation: A review. *Journal of Medical Education, 58,* 382–388.

Bahrick, H.P., and Shelly, C. (1958). Time-sharing as an index of automatization. *Journal of Experimental Psychology, 56,* 288–293.

Banderet, L.E., Stokes, J.W., Farncesconi, R., Kowal, D.M., and Naitoh, P. (1981). The twenty-four hour workday. *Proceedings of a symposium on variations in work-sleep schedule.* Cincinnati: U.S. Dept. of Health and Human Services.

Barton, J., and Folkard, S. (1993). Advanced versus delaying shift systems. *Ergonomics, 36,* 59–64.

Bensel, C.K., and Santee, W.R. (1997). Climate and clothing. In G. Salvendy (ed.), *Handbook of human factors and ergonomics.* New York: Wiley.

Bourne, P.G. (1971). Altered adrenal function in two combat situations in Vietnam. In B.E. Elefheriou and J.P. Scott (eds.), *The physiology of aggression and defeat.* New York: Plenum.

Bowers, C.A., Weaver, J.L., and Morgan, B.B. (1996). Moderating the performance effects of stressors. In J. Driskell and E. Salas (eds.), *Stress and human performance.* Mahwah, NJ: Lawrence Erlbaum.

Broadbent, D.E. (1972). *Decision and stress.* New York: Academic Press.

Browne, R.C. (1949). The day and night performance of teleprinter switchboard operators. *Journal of Occupational Psychology, 23,* 121–126.

Carskadon, M.A., and Dement, W.C. (1975). Sleep studies on a 90-minute day. *Electroencephalogram Clinical Neurophysiology, 39,* 145–155.

Chao, C.D., Madhavan, D., and Funk, K. (1996). Studies of cockpit task management errors. *The International Journal of Aviation Psychology, 6*(4), 307–320.

Czeisler, C.A., Kennedy, W.A., and Allan, J.S. (1986). Circadian rhythms and performance decrements in the transportation industry. In A.M. Coblentz (ed.), *Proceedings of a workshop on the effects of automation on operator performance* (pp. 146–171). Paris: Université René Descartes.

Czeisler, C.A., Kronauer, R.E., Allan, J.S., Duffy, J.F., Jewett, M.E., Brown, E.N., and Ronda, J.M. (1989). Bright light induction of strong (Type O) resetting of the human circadian pace-maker. *Science, 244,* 1328–1333.

Czeisler, C.A., Moore-Ede, M.C., and Coleman, R.M. (1982). Rotating shift work schedules that disrupt sleep are improved by applying circadian principles. *Science, 217* (30 July), 460–462.

Czeisler, C.A., Weitzman, E.D., Moore-Ede, M.C., Zimmerman, J.C., and Knauer, R.S. (1980). Human sleep: Its duration and organization depend on its circadian phase. *Science, 210,* 1264–1267.

Davies, D.R., and Parasuraman, R. (1982). *The psychology of vigilance.* New York: American Elsivier.

Derrick, W.L. (1988). Dimensions of operator workload. *Human Factors, 30*(1), 95–110.

deSwart, J. (1989). Stress and stress management in the Royal Netherlands Army. *Proceedings of the user's stress workshop.* Washington, DC: U.S. Army Health Services Command.

Dinges, D.F., Orne, K.T., Whitehouse, W.G., and Orne, E.C. (1987). Temporal placement of a nap for alertness: Contributions of circadian phase and prior wakefulness. *Sleep, 10,* 313–329.

Dinges, D.F., Orne, M.T., and Orne, E.C. (1985). Assessing performance upon abrupt awakening from naps during quasi-continuous operations. *Behav. Res. Methods, Instruments, & Computers, 17,* 37–45.

Downey, R., and Bonnet, M.H. (1987). Performance during frequent sleep disruption. *Sleep, 10,* 354–363.

Driskell, J.E., and Salas, E. (eds.) (1996). *Stress and human performance.* Mahwah, NJ: Lawrence Erlbaum.

Drury, C. (1982). Improving inspection performance. In G. Salvendy (ed.), *Handbook of industrial engineering.* New York: Wiley.

Edland, A., and Svenson, O. (1993). Judgment and decision making under time pressure: Studies and findings. In O. Svenson and A.J. Maule (eds.), *Time pressure and stress in human judgment and decision making* (pp. 27–40). New York: Plenum Press.

Fanger, P. (1977). *Thermal comfort.* New York: McGraw Hill.

Farmer, E.W., and Green, R.G. (1985). The sleep-deprived pilot: Performance and EEG response. *16th Conference for Western European Association for Aviation Psychology,* Helsinki, 24–285.

Friedman, R.C., Bigger, J.T., and Kornfield, D.S. (1971). The intern and sleep loss. *New England Journal of Medicine, 285,* 201–203.

Funk, K. (1991). Cockpit task management: Preliminary definitions, normative theory, error taxonomy, and design recommendations. *The International Journal of Aviation Psychology, 1*(4), 271–286.

Graeber, R.C. (1988a). Jet lag and sleep disruption. In M.H. Kryger, T. Roth, and W.C. Dement (eds.), *Principles and practice of sleep medicine* (pp. 324–331). Philadelphia: W.B. Saunders Co.

Graeber, R.C. (1988b). Aircrew fatigue and circadian rhythmicity. In E.L. Wiener and D.C. Nagel (eds.), *Human factors in aviation* (pp. 305–344). San Diego: Academic Press.

Griffin, M. (1997). Vibration and motion. In G. Salvendy (ed.), *Handbook of human factors and ergonomics.* New York: Wiley.

Hancock, P.A., and Warm, J.S. (1989). A dynamic model of stress and sustained attention. *Human Factors, 31,* 519–537.

Harris, W. (1977). Fatigue, circadian rhythm, and truck accidents. In R. Mackie (ed.), *Vigilance theory, operational performance, and physiological correlates* (pp. 133–146). New York: Plenum.

Hart, S.G., and Hauser, J.R. (1987). In-flight application of three pilot workload measurement techniques *Aviation, Space, and Environmental Medicine, 58,* 402–410.

Hart, S.G., and Staveland, L.E. (1988). Development of NASA-TLX (Task Load Index): Results of experimental and theoretical research. In P.A. Hancock and N. Meshkati (eds.), *Human mental workload* (pp. 139–183). Amsterdam: North Holland.

Hart, S.G., and Wickens, C.D. (1990). Workload assessment and prediction. In H.R. Booher (ed.), *MANPRINT: An approach to systems integration* (pp. 257–296). New York: Van Nostrand Reinhold.

Haslam, D.R. (1985). Sustained operations and military performance. *Behavior Research Methods, Instruments, and Computers, 17,* 9–95.

Hendy, K., Jian Quiao, L., and Milgram, P. (1997). Combining time and intensity effects in assessing operator information processing load. *Human Factors, 39,* 30–47.

Hockey, G.R.J. (1986). Changes in operator efficiency as a function of environmental stress, fatigue, and circadian rhythms. In K.R. Boff, L. Kaufman, and J.P. Thomas (eds.), *Handbook of perception and human performance, Vol. II* (pp. 44-1–44-49). New York: Wiley.

Holmes, T.H., and Rahe, R.H. (1967). The social readjustment rating scale. *Journal of Psychosomatic Research, 11,* 213–218.

Horne, J.A. (1988). *Why we sleep.* Oxford: Oxford University Press.

Horne, J.A., Anderson, N.R., and Wilkinson, R.T. (1983). Effects of sleep deprivation on signal detection measures of vigilance: Implications for sleep function. *Sleep, 6,* 347–358.

Houston, C. (1987). *Going higher: The story of man at high altitudes.* Boston: Little Brown.

Huey, M.B., and Wickens, C.D. (eds.) (1993). *Workload transition: Implications for individual and team performance.* Washington, DC: National Academy Press.

Johnston, J.A., and Cannon-Bowers, J.A. (1996). Training for stress exposure. In J.E. Driskell and E. Salas (eds.), *Stress and human performance.* Mahwah, NJ: Lawrence Erlbaum.

Kahneman, D. (1973). *Attention and effort.* Englewood Cliffs, NJ: Prentice Hall.

Kirwan, B., and Ainsworth, L. (1992). *A guide to task analysis.* London: Taylor and Francis.

Klein, K.E., and Wegmann, H.M. (1980). *Significance of circadian rhythms in aerospace operations* (NATO AGARDograph No. 247). Neuilly sur Seine, France: NATO AGARD.

Konz, S. (1997). Toxology and human comfort. In G. Salvendy (ed.), *Handbook of human factors and ergonomics.* New York: Wiley.

Kramer, A. (1991). Physiological metrics of mental workload: A review of recent progress. In D. Damos (ed.), *Multiple task performance* (pp. 279–328). London: Taylor and Francis.

Kramer, A.F., Coyne, J.T., and Strayer, D.L. (1993). Cognitive function at high altitude. *Human Factors, 35*(2), 329–344.

Krueger, G.P., Armstrong, R.N., and Cisco, R.R. (1985). *Aviator performance in week long extended flight operations in a helicopter simulator.* Ft. Rucker, AL: U.S. Army Aeromedical Res. Lab.

Lazarus, R.S., and Folkman, S. (1984). *Stress, appraisal and coping.* New York: Springer.

Lipschutz, L., Roehrs, T., Spielman, A., Zwyghuizen H., Lamphere, J., and Roth, T. (1988). Caffeine's alerting effects in sleepy normals. *Journal of Sleep Research, 17,* 49.

Luczak, H. (1997). Task analysis. In G. Salvendy (ed.), *Handbook of human factors and ergonomics.* New York: Wiley.

Lysaght, R.J., Hill, S.G., Dick, A.O., Plamondon, B.D., Linton, P.M. Wierwille, W.W., Zaklad, A.L., Bittner, A.C. Jr., and Wherry, R.J. Jr. (1989). *Operator workload: Comprehensive review and evaluation of workload methodologies* (ARI Technical Report 851). Alexandria, VA: U.S. Army Research Institute for the Behavioral and Social Sciences.

Naitoh, P. (1981). Circadian cycles and restorative power of naps. In L.C. Johnson, D.I. Tepas, W.P. Colquhoun, and M.J. Colligan (eds.), *Biological rhythms, sleep and shift work* (pp. 553–580). New York: Spectrum.

National Transportation Safety Board (1991). *Aircraft Accident Report: Runway Collision of US Air Flight 1493, Boeing 737 and Skywest Flight 5569 Fairchild Metroliner, Los Angeles International Airport* (PB91-910409—NTSB/AAR-91/08). Washington, DC, Feb. 1.

Norman, D.A. (1988). *The psychology of everyday things.* New York: Basic Books.

O'Donnell, R.D., and Eggemeier, F.T. (1986). Workload assessment methodology. In K.R. Boff, L. Kaufman, and J. Thomas (eds.), *Handbook of perception and human performance: Vol. II: Cognitive processes and performance* (Chapter 42). New York: Wiley.

Orasanu, J., and Backer, P. (1996). Stress and military performance. In J. Driskell and E. Salas (eds.), *Stress and human performance.* Mahwah, NJ: Lawrence Erlbaum.

Parks, D.L., and Boucek, G.P,. Jr. (1989). Workload prediction, diagnosis, and continuing challenges. In G.R. McMillan, D. Beevis, E. Salas, M.H. Strub, R. Sutton, and L. Van Breda (eds.), *Applications of human performance models to system design* (pp. 47–64). New York: Plenum Press.

Poulton, E.C. (1976). Continuous noise interferes with work by masking auditory feedback and inner speech. *Applied Ergonomics, 7,* 79–84.

Raby, M., and Wickens, C.D. (1994). Strategic workload management and decision biases in aviation. *International Journal of Aviation Psychology, 4*(3), 211–240.

Reid, G.B., and Nygren, T.E. (1988). The subjective workload assessment technique: A scaling procedure for measuring mental workload. In P.A. Hancock and N. Meshkati (eds.), *Human mental workload* (pp. 185–218). Amsterdam: North Holland.

Roeskind, M.R., Graeber, R.C., Dinges, D.F., Connell, L.J., Rountree, M.S., Spinweber, C.L., and Gillen, K.A. (1994). *Crew factors in flight operations: IX. Effects of pre-planned cockpit rest on crew performance and alertness in long-haul operations* (NASA Technical Memorandum 103884). Moffett Field, CA: NASA Ames Research Center.

Rohles, F.H., and Konz, S.A. (1987). Climate. In G. Salvendy (ed.), *Handbook of human factors* (pp. 696–707). New York: Wiley.

Roscoe, A.H. (1987). In-flight assessment of workload using pilot ratings and heart rate. In *The practical assessment of pilot workload* (AGARD-AG-282) (pp. 78–82). Neuilly sur Seine, France: Advisory Group for Aerospace Research and Development.

Rubinstein, T., and Mason, A.F. (1979). The accident that shouldn't have happened: An analysis of Three Mile Island. *IEEE Spectrum,* Nov., 33–57.

Sarno, K.J., and Wickens, C.D. (1995). The role of multiple resources in predicting time-sharing efficiency: An evaluation of three workload models in a multiple task setting. *The International Journal of Aviation Psychology, 5*(1), 107–130.

Schlegal, R.E., Gilliland, K., and Schlegal, B. (1986). Development of the criterion task set performance database. *Proceedings of the 1986 meeting of the Human Factors Society.* Santa Monica, CA: Human Factors Society.

Shingledecker, C.A. (1987). In-flight workload assessment using embedded secondary radio communications tasks. In *The practical assessment of pilot workload* (AGARDograph No. 282) (pp. 11–14). Neuilly sur Seine, France: Advisory Group for Aerospace Research and Development.

Stager, P., Hameluck, D., and Jubis, R. (1989). Underlying factors in air traffic control incidents. *Proceedings of the 33rd annual meeting of the human factors society.* Santa Monica, CA: Human Factors Society.

Stokes, A.F., and Kite, K. (1994). *Flight stress: Stress, fatigue and performance in aviation.* Brookfield, VT: Ashgate Aviation.

Svenson, S., and Maule, A.J. (eds.) (1993). *Time pressure and stress in human judgment and decision making.* New York: Plenum Press.

Tattersall, A.J., and Hockey, G.R.J. (1995). Level of operator control and changes in heart rate variability during simulated flight maintenance. *Human Factors, 37*(4), 682–698.

Tsang, P., and Wilson, G. (1997). Mental workload. In G. Salvendy (ed.), *Handbook of human factors and ergonomics* (2nd ed.). New York: Wiley.

Warm, J.S. (1984). *Sustained attention in human performance.* Chichester, UK: John Wiley.

Warm, J.S., and Parasuraman, R. (eds.) (1987). Vigilance: Basic and applied. *Human Factors, 29,* 623–740.

Wasserman, D.E. (1987). Motion and vibration. In G. Salvendy (ed.), *Handbook of Human Factors* (pp. 650–669). New York: Wiley.

West, J.B. (1985). *Everest, the testing place.* New York: McGraw-Hill.

Wickens, C.D. (1991). Processing resources and attention. In D. Damos (ed.), *Multiple task performance.* Bristol, CT: Taylor & Francis, pp. 3–34.

Wickens, C.D. (1992). *Engineering psychology and human performance* (2nd ed.). New York: HarperCollins.

Wickens, C.D. (1996). Designing for stress. In J.E. Driskell and E. Salas (eds.), *Stress and human performance.* Mahwah, NJ: Lawrence Erlbaum.

Wickens, C.D., Stokes, A.F., Barnett, B., and Hyman, F. (1991). The effects of stress on pilot judgment in a MIDIS simulator. In O. Svenson and J. Maule (eds.), *Time pressure and stress in human judgment and decision making.* Cambridge, UK: Cambridge University Press.

Wierwille, W.W., and Casali, J.G. (1983). A validated rating scale for global mental workload measurement applications. *Proceedings of the 27th annual meeting of the human factors society* (pp. 129–133). Santa Monica, CA: Human Factors Society.

Wierwille, W.W., and Eggemeier, F.T. (1993). Recommendations for mental workload measurement in a test and evaluation environment. *Human Factors, 35*(2), 263–282.

Wilkinson, R.T. (1992). How fast should night shift rotate? *Ergonomics, 35,* 1425–1446.

Williams, H.L., Gieseking, C.F., and Lubin, A. (1966). Some effects of sleep loss on memory. *Perceptual Motor Skills, 23,* 1287–1293.

Wine, J. (1971). Test anxiety and direction of attention. *Psychological Bulletin, 76,* 92–104.

Yeh, Y.Y., and Wickens, C.D. (1988). Dissociation of performance and subjective measures of workload. *Human Factors, 30,* 111–120.

Yerkes, R.M., and Dodson, J.D. (1908). The relation of strength of stimulus to rapidity of habit formation. *Journal of Comparative Neurological Psychology, 18,* 459–482.

CHAPTER 14

Safety, Accidents, and Human Error

*M*arta loved her new job at the convenience store. One morning, as she was busy restocking some of the shelves, she turned a corner to go down an aisle on the far side of the store. A glare came in through the large window, which is probably why she did not see the liquid that had spilled on the floor. She slipped on the substance and fell, impaling her arm on a blunt metal spike meant to hold chips. Her arm never healed properly, and she had back problems for the remainder of her life.

John walked across a bare agricultural field to where a 6-inch-diameter irrigation pipe came out of the ground. The opening was filled by a large chunk of ice, so John began using a steel pry bar to dislodge the chunk. As the ice chunk broke free, air pressure that had built up underneath in the pipe suddenly drove the ice up against the pry bar. The force sent the bar through John's neck and impaled him backward to the ground. Amazingly, John was taken to the hospital and lived.

Steve and Pete were fighting a canyon forest fire along with several other relatively new firefighters. Suddenly a high wind drove the fire toward them, and all of the men began running to escape the oncoming blaze. Realizing that they would be overtaken at any moment, Steve and Pete quickly set up their survival tents and crawled inside. In the meantime, two other men (who had thrown aside their heavy survival tents in order to run faster) were forced to try to escape by running up a steep hill. The men in the survival tent died, and the men who had to run out made it to safety.

A 4-year-old boy in California climbed up on a new concrete fountain in his backyard to retrieve a ball from the basin area. As he pulled himself up, the fountain toppled over and crushed him to death. His parents successfully sued the manufacturer and landscape company who installed it.

As we saw in Chapter 1, a major goal of human factors is to increase the *health* and *safety* of people in a variety of environments such as work, home, transport systems, and so on. Health and safety are related, but can be distinguished in at least two ways. First, in general, safety concerns itself with injury-causing situations, whereas health is concerned with disease-causing situations. Also, safety focuses on *accidents* resulting from acute (sudden or severe) conditions or events, while health focuses on less intense but more prolonged conditions, such as poor design of a data-entry keyboard (Goetsch, 1996). Hazards in the workplace can lead to health problems, safety problems, or both (noise is one example). In this text, we have focused on hazards that affect health in Chapters 10, 11, and 12, presenting information on the design of physical work environments so as to reduce hazards and decrease long-term ergonomic-based health problems such as cumulative trauma disorders.

In this chapter, we will focus on hazardous conditions or events that may result in more sudden and severe events, causing injury or death. This includes such things as human performance failures, mechanical failures, falls, fires, explosions, and so forth. While the majority of our discussion will center on occupational safety, many of the factors that cause accidents in the workplace are applicable to other more general tasks, such as driving. More specifically, we will review safety and accident prevention by discussing: (1) general factors that contribute to, or directly lead to, accidents, (2) methods for systematically identifying hazards in equipment and the workplace, (3) methods for hazard control, and (4) factors that affect human behavior in hazardous environments.

INTRODUCTION TO SAFETY AND ACCIDENT PREVENTION

All of the scenarios at the beginning of this chapter are based on true stories. They represent just a few of the thousands of ways in which people are injured or killed in accidents every year. Accidents are caused by a variety of factors, including human error, equipment failure, improper equipment design, environmental factors, or a complex interaction between these factors. Safety and accident prevention is a major concern in the field of human factors. One reason is that accidents are the major cause of death in the United States for people under forty-four years of age (National Safety Council, 1993a). In a typical year in the United States, 47,000 people die in motor vehicle accidents, 13,000 die in falls, and 7,000 people die from poisoning. In 1993, there were 10,000 deaths in the workplace alone; Table 14.1 shows the major causes of workplace injury and death as reported by the National Safety Council (1993a). The major causes of injuries are overexertion, impact accidents, and falls. The major causes of death are accidents related to motor vehicles and falls; however, other causes are common as well, such as fire, drowning, poison, and electrical hazards. Finally, the National Institute for Occupational Safety and Health (NIOSH) estimates that over 10 million men and women are exposed annually to hazardous substances that could eventually cause illness (Goetsch, 1996).

In addition to the human tragedy of injury and death, accidents carry a high monetary cost. Table 14.2 shows U.S. accident costs broken down by location. It can be seen that workplace deaths and injuries alone typically produce a cost of $48 billion per year. This reflects factors such as property damage, lost wages, medical expenses, insurance administration, and indirect costs. According to Kohn,

TABLE 14.1 Most Frequent Causes of Workplace Deaths and Injuries

Injury

Overexertion: Working beyond physical limitations

Impact accidents: Being struck by or against an object

Falls

Bodily reaction to chemicals

Compression

Motor vehicle accidents

Exposure to radiation or caustics

Rubbing or abrasions

Exposure to extreme temperatures

Deaths

Motor-vehicle related

Falls

Electrical current

Drowning

Fire related

Air transport related

Poison

Water transport related

Other

Friend, and Winterberger (1996), each workplace fatality costs U.S. society $780,000 per victim, and Goetsch (1996) notes that the total cost of accidents in the workplace represents a cost of $420 per worker in the United States, which can be viewed as the "value-added" required per worker to offset the cost of the deaths and injuries. Statistics such as these show that workplace health and safety is not only a moral concern, but now also an economic one. However, businesses have not always viewed safety as a high priority issue, a fact that becomes most evident by reviewing the history of safety legislation in the United States.

SAFETY LEGISLATION

Safety in the workplace has been strongly impacted by legislation over the last 100 years. It is generally recognized that during the 1800s, workers performed their duties under unsafe and unhealthful conditions. The philosophy of businesses was that of laissez-faire, which means to let things be—letting natural laws operate

TABLE 14.2 Cost of Accidents in Billions for a Typical Year in the U.S.

Motor vehicle accidents	$722.0
Workplace accidents	8.5
Home Accidents	18.2
Public Accidents	12.5

Source: D. L. Goetsch, 1996. *Occupational safety and health.* Engelwood Cliffs, NJ: Prentice Hall. Reprinted with permission of Prentice-Hall, Inc., Upper Saddle River, NJ.

without restriction. Although technically, under common law, employers were expect to provide a safe place to work and safe tools with which to work, in reality the public accepted accidents as inevitable. When an accident occurred, the only means for the employee to obtain compensation was to prove the employer's *negligence*, which was defined as "failure to exercise a reasonable amount of care, or to carry out a legal duty so that injury or property damage occurs to another." The problems was that *reasonable amount of care* was ill-defined. Companies argued that hazardous conditions were normal. In addition, companies could defend themselves by claiming that either: (1) there had been *contributory negligence*—meaning that an injured person's behavior contributed to the accident; (2) a fellow employee had been negligent; or (3) the injured worker had been aware of the hazards of their job and had knowingly assumed the risks (Hammer, 1989). For example, if a fellow employee contributed in any way to an accident, the employer could not be held responsible. As a result of these loopholes favoring businesses, until the early 1900s, working conditions were poor and injury rates continued to climb.

Workers' Compensation and Liability

Between 1909 and 1910, various states began to draft workers' compensation laws. These early laws were based on the concept of providing compensation to workers for on-the-job injuries regardless of who was at fault. The first two such laws were passed in Montana for miners, and in New York for eight highly hazardous occupations. Both laws were thrown out as unconstitutional. Shortly after that, a tragic and highly publicized fire in a shirt factory in New York killed 146 workers and seriously injured 70 more. This increased public demand for some type of legislative protection, and by 1917, the Supreme Court declared that state workers' compensation laws were constitutional. Today there are different workers' compensation laws in each state, with approximately 80 percent of all workers covered by the laws (Hammer, 1989). Overall, the goals of workers' compensation include:

- Provide sure, prompt, and reasonable income and medical benefits to work-accident victims or income benefits to their dependents, regardless of fault.
- Provide a single remedy to reduce court delays, costs, and workloads arising out of personal-injury litigation.
- Eliminate payment of fees to lawyers and witnesses as well as time-consuming trials and appeals.
- Encourage maximum employer interest in safety and rehabilitation through an experience-rating mechanism.
- Promote the study of causes of accidents.

Workers' compensation is a type of insurance, where companies are required to pay premiums just like any other type of insurance. The worker's compensation insurance then pays set rates for benefits, depending on the job and type of injury. To be covered under workers' compensation insurance, an injury must meet three conditions: (1) it arose from an accident, (2) it arose out of the worker's employment, and (3) it occurred during the course of employment.

Under worker's compensation law, workers are not allowed to sue their employer for negligence; however, they are allowed to sue a third party. This can include the manufacturer of the equipment that caused the injury, the driver or company of other involved vehicles, the architect that designed the building, or the safety inspector. Many of the large product liability suits are claims for injuries to industrial workers because it is a way to get benefits beyond the relatively small workers' compensation benefits. As an example, a man in California lost eight fingers in a press that had a defective safety switch. He received $40,000 plus a lifetime disability pension from workers' compensation, but was also awarded $1.1 million in a product liability suit (Hammer, 1989). While claims of negligence are common, claims of *strict liability* are increasing also. Strict liability means that a manufacturer of a product is liable for injuries due to defects without a necessity for the injured party to show negligence or fault.

Establishment of OSHA and NIOSH Agencies

In the 1960s, many people felt that the state legislated laws were still inadequate; many industries still had poor safety and health standards, and injury and death rates were still too high. As a result, in 1970, the federal government acted to impose certain safety standards on industry by signing into effect the Occupational Safety and Health Act. This act established the administrative arm, Occupational Safety and Health Administration (OSHA), under the U.S. Department of Labor. OSHA implements safety programs, sets and revokes health and safety standards, conducts inspections, investigates problems, monitors illnesses and injuries, issues citations, assesses penalties, petitions the courts to take appropriate action against unsafe employers, provides safety training, provides injury prevention consultation, and maintains a database of health and safety statistics (see Goetsch, 1996). OSHA publishes standards for *general industry* (Department of Labor, 1993) and also for specific industries such as construction, agriculture, and maritime. Employers must comply with OSHA regulations through activities such as complying with standards for injury avoidance, keeping records of work-related injuries and death, keeping records of exposure of employees to toxic materials or other hazards, and keeping employees informed on matters of safety and health.

One other federal organization is also important to the human factors profession, the National Institute for Occupational Safety and Health (NIOSH). NIOSH performs research and educational functions. It conducts or reviews research to identify hazardous types of conditions in the workplace. It prepares recommendations that often become provisions of the OSHA standards. Human factors specialists working in the area of workplace design or safety will often use NIOSH standards or recommendations.

Product Liability

While OSHA has resulted in greater industrial safety, there are still numerous problems. As with all large bureaucracies, the agency is cumbersome and slow. OSHA is also heavily influenced by political lobbying, has fines that are ineffectively small, and has too few inspectors. For this and other reasons, safety in both industry and product manufacturing is increasingly influenced by civil and criminal suits.

Whether an injury or death occurs in the workplace or elsewhere, people are increasingly bringing suit against businesses. Most of these suits are *product liability* claims, alleging that a product was somehow defective, and the defect caused the injury or death. Product liability cases usually assume one of three types of defect: a design defect (inherently unsafe), a manufacturing defect, or a warning defect. Also, an increasing number of suits allege improper instruction as well as warning. For example, the suit described earlier for the backyard fountain alleged that the manufacturer failed to properly instruct the retailer on installation of the 500-pound fountain (using adhesive between the fountain tiers) and that both manufacturer and retailer failed to warn the consumer of hazards. The case was tried in California, and a settlement of $835,000 made to the mother of the 4-year old who was killed. The number and size of product liability cases is growing so alarmingly, Congress is attempting to enact a bill limiting the scope and award value of product liability cases.

A critical question that must be answered for each product liability case is whether the product is defective or simply inherently "dangerous." For example, a carving knife is dangerous but would not be considered defective. An important precedent was set by the California Supreme Court in the 1970s. They specified that a product is defective when it "failed to perform safely as an ordinary user would expect when it was used in an intended or reasonably foreseeable manner, or if the risks inherent in the design outweighed the benefits of that design." There are two important implications of this judgment for human factors:

1. The concept of *reasonably foreseeable.* Human factors specialists are often asked to act as expert witnesses to testify concerning what could be considered "reasonably foreseeable." For example, is it reasonably foreseeable that a child would climb on a fountain? Most people would say yes, and this was the verdict in the fountain suit. In another notorious case, a person was injured in the act of using a lawnmower as a hedge trimmer. Is this a reasonably foreseeable use of the equipment?

2. *The trade-off between risk and benefit.* Human factors specialists act as expert witnesses by providing information and analyses relevant to trade-off questions. For a given design, the original designer should have weighed the positive effects of the hazard control against the negative effects such as cost or other disadvantages. Factors considered in assessing the trade-off include the likelihood of injury, the likely severity of injury, possible alternative designs, costs or feasibility of a given design versus alternative designs, the effectiveness of alternative designs, and so forth. A knife can be made safer by making it dull, but the trade-off is that it loses most of its functionality.

A final area where human factors specialists are central to product liability is in helping manufacturers design safer products to avoid litigation in the first place. Professionals trained in hazard and safety analysis work with design teams to ensure that the product is safe for reasonably foreseeable uses. Some of the methods used for such safety analyses will be presented later in this chapter.

Summary

Safety is now legislated at both the state and federal levels. Federal and some state activity centers mostly around OSHA regulations, inspections, and fines; at the state level, workmen's compensation programs require businesses to pay premiums based on their previous safety record. Both state and federal activities have had a positive effect, with businesses becoming more safety oriented. In addition, the increase of safety-related litigation has had an impact on both product design and development of improved instructional materials and warnings.

However, while legislation has done much to reduce death and injury due to accidents in the United States, the data reviewed at the beginning of this chapter makes it clear that there are still numerous problems. People working in the areas of human factors, system safety, industrial safety, and product safety continue to find methods for accident reduction. Such methods include a variety of approaches including equipment redesign, industrial safety programs, development of new guarding or protective equipment, and the use of behavior-change techniques such as warning labels. In order to understand when and why these methods work, it is first necessary to consider the factors that cause or contribute to accidents.

FACTORS THAT CAUSE OR CONTRIBUTE TO ACCIDENTS

A variety of theories and models have been proposed to explain and predict accidents (Firenzie, 1978; Heinrich, Petersen, & Roos, 1980). Most of these only consider some of the factors that contribute to accidents, for example, the social environment. Probably the most comprehensive model, the *systems approach,* is also one that is compatible with the human factors approach. The systems approach assumes that accidents occur because of the interaction between system components (Firenzie, 1978; Slappendel et al., 1993). It is assumed that some factors are closely or directly involved in task performance and therefore are direct causal factors in safety. These factors include characteristics of (a) the employee performing a task, (b) the task itself, and (c) any equipment directly or indirectly used in the task. Other factors will also significantly impact safety. These can be categorized as social/psychological factors and environmental factors. Figure 14.1 shows one particular view of the systems approach proposed by Slappendel et al. (1993).

Some of the factors shown in this model lead directly to hazards and resultant accidents, such as when an employee succumbs to smoke inhalation. Other times, the factors affect performance of the worker more indirectly. For example, one social/psychological factor is the existence of social norms in the workplace. Social norms may support unsafe behavior such as taking off protective gear, using unsafe lifting practices, or walking into unsafe work areas. Construction workers more often than not install roofing without being tied off, as they are supposed to. The predominant reason is that the *social norm* is to not bother with this protective equipment. As another example, many physical environment factors such as heat or noise act as "stressors" that affect how a person performs their job (as reviewed in Chapter 13). When factors do not directly cause an accident, they are said to be *contributing* factors. Table 14.3 shows some of the more important

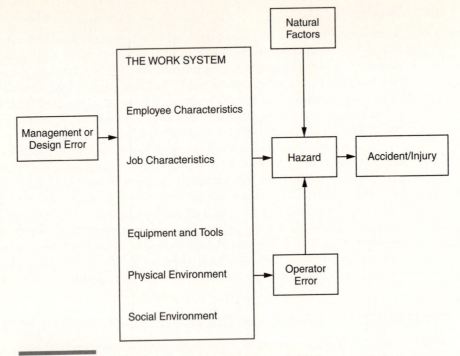

FIGURE 14.1

Model of causal factors in occupational injuries. (*Source:* Slappendel, C., Laird, I., Kawachi, I., Marshall, S., and Cryer, C., 1993. Factors affecting work-related injury among forestry workers: A review. *Journal of Safety Research, 24,* 19-32. Reprinted with permission.)

causal and contributing factors. Notice that many of the causal factors include topics discussed in other chapters of this text. For example:

- Illumination is covered in Chapter 4.
- Noise is covered in Chapter 5.
- Job characteristics are covered in Chapter 13, as well as in Chapters 10–12
- Vibration, temperature, and other environment factors are covered in Chapter 13.
- Mechanical aspects of tools are covered in Chapter 10.
- Training is reviewed in Chapter 18.

It is clear that a concern with safety permeates much if not most of the field of human factors. In the remainder of this section, we will review contributing and causal factors not covered elsewhere; we first discuss the five "work system" factors shown in Figure 14.1 and then briefly discuss operator error. When the material has been covered elsewhere, we will refer to those sections of the text and review the remaining factors as necessary.

TABLE 14.3   Causal and Contributing Factors for Accidents

Task Components

Employees	Job	Equipment and Tools
Age	Arousal, fatigue	Controls & displays
Ability	Physical workload	Electrical hazards
Experience	Mental workload	Mechanical hazards
Drugs, alcohol	Work-rest cycles	Thermal hazards
Gender	Shifts, shift rotation	Pressure hazards
Stress	Pacing	Toxic substance hazards
Alertness, fatigue	Ergonomic hazards	Explosive hazards
Motivation	Procedures	Other component failures
Accident proneness		

Surrounding Environment

Physical Environment	Social/psychological Environment
Illumination	Management practices
Noise	Social norms
Vibration	Morale
Temperature	Training
Humidity	Incentives
Airborne pollutants	
Fire hazards	
Radiation hazards	
Falls	

Personnel Characteristics

There are a number of factors associated with industry personnel that increase the likelihood of accidents. These factors are shown in Figure 14.2. Generally, the factors fall into clusters that affect hazard recognition, decisions to act appropriately, and ability to act appropriately. In this section we will review only some of the more important factors that affect safe behavior.

Age and Gender.   One of the most highly predictive factors for accident rates is age. Research has shown that overall, younger people have more accidents, with accident rates being highest for people between the ages of 15–24 (Bell et al., 1990). Industrial accident rates peak at around age 25. Since this is correlational data, it is difficult to determine why age affects accident rates. Some people speculate that the primary reason is that as people get older, they become more conservative, and their estimations of risk become more conservative; that is, younger people think there is less likelihood of accidents and injury occurring to themselves than older workers (Leonard, Hill, & Otani, 1990). In addition, young males perceive themselves as less at risk and therefore have a greater number of accidents (e.g., Alexander et al., 1990; Lyng, 1990).

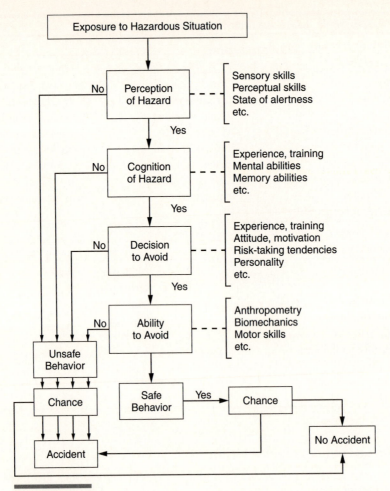

FIGURE 14.2

Operator characteristics that affect various steps in the accident sequence. (Adapted from Ramsey, J., 1985. Ergonomic factors in task analysis for consumer product safety. *Journal of Occupational Accidents, 7,* 113-123.)

However, there are certain exceptions to the general relationship between age and the accident rates; that is, when accidents are tied to the physical and cognitive abilities of the employee, accident rates go up for the elderly (Crowe, 1986; Slappendel et al., 1993). For physically intensive occupations, such as logging, performance may decline at an age as early as 35 (Fibiger, 1981). For perceptual and cognitive abilities, people approaching 50–60 years of age show a decreased "useful field of vision," a slowing in information processing, and more difficulties in encoding ambiguous stimuli. If a job, such as driving, requires information processing capabilities, accident rates will tend to rise.

Job Experience. A second characteristic of employees that predicts accident rate is time on the job, or work experience. A high percentage of accidents (approximately 70%) occur within a person's first 3 years on the job, with the peak at about 2–3 months. This point represents a transition stage, where the person has finished training and is no longer supervised but still does not have the experience necessary for hazard recognition and appropriate response. At this point, workers move out from under supervision and step up their work pace while still working with an incomplete mental model (Slappendel et al., 1993). The best way to mitigate this problem is to make the system less hazardous (by redesign or guarding) and train employees specifically on hazard recognition, appropriate actions, and knowledge of the severity of consequences of doing the wrong thing.

Stress, Fatigue, Drugs, and Alcohol.   Other more temporary characteristics of the employee will affect performance and therefore accident rates. For example, stress, fatigue, or both are factors found to be related to accidents (see Chapter 13). Performance decrements sometimes also result from life stressors outside of work, such as death of a loved one or divorce (e.g., Hartley & Hassani, 1994). These factors can make people more likely to be preoccupied with non-work-related thoughts.

Employees under the influence of drugs or alcohol have been shown to have a higher accident rate (Holcom, Lehman, & Simpson, 1993). Field studies have demonstrated a relationship between drug use and job performance indicators such as injury rates, turnover, and worker's compensation claims (e.g., Lehman & Simpson, 1992; Normand, Salyards, & Mahony, 1990). Many employers are now doing drug testing of employees for this reason. Data show that organizations adopting drug-testing programs are showing a reduction in personal injury rates (Taggart, 1989). While these data imply that drug use directly affects accident rate, this is not necessarily the case. Some theorists believe that drug use simply indicates a general characteristic of employees. It is this characteristic, a sort of "social deviancy," that is the operating mechanism responsible for work-related accidents (Jessor & Jessor, 1978; Holcom et al., 1993). According to this view, drug screening simply reduces the numbers of such people being employed, which results in a lower accident rate.

Holcom et al. (1993) suggest that there are several personality factors that seem to predict accident rates in high-risk jobs, including general deviance, job dissatisfaction, drug use, and depression. This finding is consistent with descriptive research indicating that some people seem to have a greater likelihood of incurring numerous accidents than others (e.g., Mayer, Jones, & Laughery, 1987). Although these employees might be termed *accident prone,* the term is not particularly diagnostic, and we must continue to work toward determining exactly what characteristics make such people more likely to have accidents. Thus, employee assistance programs need to deal with an entire range of psychosocial problems rather than just targeting drug use per se.

Job Characteristics

Many characteristics of the job or task itself can cause difficulties for the operator. Some of these include high physical workload, high mental workload, and other stress-inducing factors such as vigilance tasks that lower physiological arousal levels. Other characteristics associated with an increase in industrial hazards include long work cycles and shift rotation—factors that increase fatigue levels. Job characteristics such as these impair job performance and therefore may increase the likelihood of accidents and injury (see Chapter 13 for a review of these factors).

Equipment

Many of the hazards associated with the workplace are localized in the tools or equipment used by the employee, and as a consequence, much of the safety analysis performed in an industrial environment focuses on hazards inherent in the equipment itself. Other additional hazards may be created by a combination of equipment and environmental conditions. Some factors, such as "heat," could be either equipment or environment depending on the circumstance. While the division between equipment and environment is therefore somewhat arbitrary, it is still helpful to divide factors between these two categories. In the sections below we list the most common industrial hazards.

Controls and Displays.   As we have seen throughout the text, controls and displays can be poorly designed so as to increase the likelihood of operator error (e.g., see Chapter 8 and Chapter 9). While good design of controls and displays is always desirable, any time there are hazards present in the equipment and/or environment, it is especially critical.

Electrical Hazards.   Electric shock is a sudden and accidental stimulation of the body's nervous system by an electric current. The most common hazards are electrical currents through the body from standard household or business currents and being struck by lightning. Electricity varies in current, volts, and frequency. Some levels of these variables are more dangerous than others. The lowest currents, from 0 to 10 milliamperes, are relatively safe because it is possible to let go of the physical contact. However, at a point known as "let-go" current, people lose the ability to let go of the contact. The let-go point for 60-hertz circuits for males is about 9 milliamperes, and for females it is about 6 milliamperes (Hammer, 1989). Above this point, prolonged contact makes the electrical current extremely dangerous due to paralysis of the respiratory muscles. Paralysis lasting over three minutes usually causes death. As the current reaches 200 milliamperes, it becomes more likely to throw the person from the source. This is good, because at this level, any current lasting over 1/4 second is essentially fatal. Thus, we can say that prolonged exposure due to contact generally makes the 10 to 200 milliampere current range the most dangerous. Higher currents stop the heart and cause respiratory paralysis, but the person can often be resuscitated if done immediately.

In general, AC, or alternating current, is more dangerous than DC, direct current, because alternating current causes heart fibrillation. In addition, currents with frequencies of 20 to 200 hertz are the most dangerous. Note that the standard household current is AC, with a 60-hertz current, which is in the most dangerous range. Exposure to such electrical current is damaging after only 25 msec. Home and industrial accidents frequently occur when one person turns off a circuit to make repairs and another person unknowingly turns it back on. Circuits turned off for repairs should be locked out or at least marked with warning tags. Accidents also occur from the degradation of insulating materials. Recent methods to reduce electrical hazards include regulations regarding wiring and insulation; requirements for grounded outlets; insulation of parts with human contact; rubber gloves and rubber mats; and the use of fuses, breakers, and ground-fault circuit interrupts (GFCI). GFCIs monitor current levels, and if a change of more than a few mAmps is noted, the circuit is broken. These mechanisms are now required in most household bathrooms (and are visually distinct).

Mechanical Hazards.   Equipment and tools used in both industrial and home settings often have an incredibly large number of mechanical hazards. At one time, most injuries in industrial plants arose from mechanical hazards (Hammer, 1989). Machines had hazardous components such as rotating equipment, open-geared power presses, and power hammers. More recently, such equipment has been outfitted with safeguards of various types. However, mechanical hazards are still common. Mechanical hazards can result in injuries induced by actual physical contact with a part or component. Examples include the following hazards:

- *Cutting* or *tearing* of skin, muscle, or bone. Typical sources are sharp edges, saw blades, and rough finishes. Tearing can occur when a sharp object pierces the flesh and then pulls away rapidly.
- *Shearing* is most commonly a problem where two sharp objects pass close together. An example is power cutters or metal shears. In industrial plants, workers often position materials in shears and then, realizing at the last moment that the material is not correctly in position, reach in to perform a readjustment. This results in loss of fingers and hands.
- *Crushing* is a problem when some body part is caught between two solid objects when the two objects are coming closer together. These are referred to by OSHA as "pinch points"—any point other than the point of operation at which it is possible for any part of the body to be caught between moving parts.
- *Breaking,* which occurs when crushing is so extreme that bones are broken.
- *Straining* refers to muscle strains, usually caused by workers overexerting themselves, for example, trying to lift more than they are capable. Many workers strain their arms or back by relying too much on those body parts and not enough on the legs. Other common sources of strain are when employees are lifting objects and slip on a wet floor because the attempt to maintain an upright position puts an undue strain on muscles (Hammer, 1989). Chapter 10 discusses these problems in more detail.

As an example of two commonly unrecognized pinch points, consider Figure 14.3. The drawing represents a vacation home dock anchored to two pilings by use of a large U-shaped rings attached to the dock. The dock is made of two units, with a hinge where the components join. The space between the units is large enough for a child's foot to fall through and become pinched between the pieces. To see the second pinchpoint, notice that the U-bolt is large enough so that the dock can move up and down the piling with changes in the water level and passing waves. Now imagine a child swimming next to the dock and becoming tired. The U-bolt appears to be a natural hand hold for resting in the

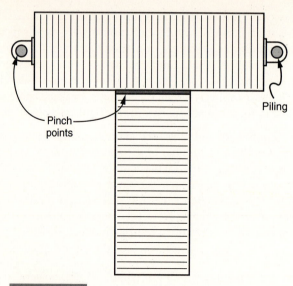

FIGURE 14.3

Pinch points in a standard dock design.

water. Unfortunately, when a wave hits the dock, the dock will be forced against the piling, smashing the fingers or hand in between them.

Guards are commonly used to reduce mechanical hazards, although sometimes people remove them, which defeats the purpose. There are a variety of types of guards, including total enclosures, enclosures with interlocks (if guard is removed the machine is stopped), and movable barriers such as gates (see extensive review in National Safety Council, 1993b). Other common types of safety device are systems that interrupt machine operation if parts of the body are in the hazardous area. This can be accomplished by mechanisms such as optical sensors, electrical fields using wrist wires, two hand controls, and arms that sweep the front of the hazardous area.

According to Hammer (1989), a guard should meet the following criteria:

1. It must be safe under all conditions. If it fails, ceases to operate, or is opened, the machine will immediately and automatically stop.
2. Access to the danger zone must be prevented while the equipment is operating.
3. It must impose no restrictions, discomforts, or difficulties for the worker.
4. It must automatically move into or be fixed in place.
5. It must be designed for the hazard, the machine, and type of operation which will be present.
6. It must not require delicate adjustment for use or move out of alignment easily.
7. It must be impossible for an operator to bypass or inactivate it without simultaneously inactivating the equipment on which it is mounted.

8. It should require minimum maintenance.
9. It should not itself constitute a hazard.
(Hammer, 1989, p. 292)

In addition, Hammer suggests that (1) all operators should be given instructions on hazards, safeguards, and appropriate actions; (2) each operator should know the location of *stop* or *emergency* buttons; (3) equipment should be inspected regularly; (4) operators should be instructed against removing guards; and (5) repairs requiring removal of guards should be performed only by trained and authorized personnel.

Pressure and Toxic Substance Hazards.   The most common problems associated with pressure are vessel ruptures. In many industrial settings, liquids and gases are contained in pressurized vessels. When the liquid or gas expands, the vessel, or some associated component, ruptures and employees may be injured. These can be considered "hidden hazards" because employees may not be aware of the inherent dangers. The factors that typically cause vessels to rupture are direct heat (such as fire), heat from the sun or nearby furnaces, overfilling, and altitude changes. When pressurized liquids or gases are released, injuries may be sustained from the contents themselves, fragments of the vessel, or even shock waves. An example of hazards associated with pressurized vessels is the use of compression paint sprayers. Paint sprayers aimed at a human have enough pressure to drive the paint molecules directly into the skin causing toxic poisoning, a hazard of which many people are unaware. Steps that should be taken to deal with pressure hazards include safety valves, depressurizing vessels before maintenance activities, marking vessels with contents and warning labels, use of protective clothing, and so on (see Hammer, 1989).

Toxic substances may or may not be contained within pressurized vessels. There is an increasing concern with exposure to toxic substances as we begin to see an increase in long-term effects on health. The effects of toxic substances depend on several factors including the size of the dose, duration of the dose, route into the body, degree of substance toxicity, rate of absorption, and temperature of the environment. All other things being equal, the most serious effects are engendered when the route into the body core is relatively direct, such as injection into the tissues or bloodstream, entry through cuts and wounds, and entry through the respiratory system. For this reason, protective clothing and respirators are critical for employee protection.

Toxic substances tend to fall into classes depending on how they affect the body. *Asphyxiants* are gases that create an oxygen deficiency in the blood causing asphyxiation. Examples include carbon dioxide, methane, and hydrogen. Natural gas is a "hidden hazard," because it is normally odorless and colorless. Sometimes odorants are added to act as a warning mechanism. *Irritants* are chemicals that inflame tissues at the point of contact, causing redness, swelling, blisters, and pain. Obviously these substances are particularly problematic if they are inhaled or ingested. *Systemic poisons* are substances that interfere with organ functioning. Examples include alcohol and other drugs. *Carcinogens* are substances that cause cancer after some period of exposure. Because of the length of time to see effects of carcinogens, they are particularly difficult to study in an industrial setting.

Hazardous substances have become a focus of federal concern, and since 1987, OSHA has required all employers to inform workers about hazardous materials. The purpose of the OSHA Hazard Communication Standard is to ensure that information about chemical hazards is communicated to employees by means of "comprehensive hazard communication programs, which are to include container labeling and other forms of warning, material safety data sheets and employee training" (OSHA Hazard Communication Standard 29 CFR 1910.1200). Because the category of toxic substances includes materials such as bleach, ammonia, and other cleaners, the OSHA standard applies to almost every business.

The Physical Environment

Illumination. We have discussed the need for proper lighting in several previous chapters. Lighting most directly affects safety by making it relatively easy or difficult to perform tasks. However, there are other factors that are important for safety. Probably the biggest one is the discrepancy between illumination of task areas versus surrounding areas (ambient lighting). If a high illumination contrast exists between task and ambient lighting, people will suffer from the effects of transient adaptation as they visually move back and forth between the two areas (a lag in light/dark adaptation). Another problem related to differences between task and ambient light conditions is the problem of *phototropism*. This refers to our tendency to move our eyes toward a brighter light. Not only does this take our attention away from the central task area but may cause transient adaptation, making it more difficult to see once our attention does return to the task area. Large windows are especially problematic in this regard. In the case of the convenience store slip and fall case described earlier, phototropism may have been a contributing factor if the employee's visual attention was temporarily drawn toward the brighter window area. Finally, glare has been previously mentioned as a problem that can cause not only discomfort but also performance decrements that may affect safety under some circumstances. As noted, the effects of glare can be minimized by mounting the sources of light as far as possible away from the normal task line of sight.

Noise and Vibration. Noise and vibration are two factors associated with equipment that can be hazardous to workers. Noise can have an impact as either a loud and sudden occurrence or as a health hazard over time (as discussed in Chapter 5). Vibration can result in several different types of hazards that affect health and/or safety. First, as discussed in Chapter 13, vibration can negatively impact manual dexterity and control, thus making some jobs more hazardous due to poor performance. Vibration can also cause health problems in limbs, or in the body as a whole (termed whole-body vibration).

Temperature and Humidity. Working conditions that are either too hot or too cold pose serious safety hazards either directly by impacting body health or indirectly by impairing operator performance (see Chapter 13). The effects of external temperatures are moderated by other factors, including humidity and airflow.

Humidity and airflow significantly impact the body's ability to heat or cool itself. Clothing is also a key factor in the body's ability to transfer or maintain heat. It is important to note that many types of *protective clothing* designed to guard the operator from other hazards may exacerbate the problems of thermal regulation by limiting airflow over the body, making the cooling mechanisms of vasodilation and sweating less effective.

Fire Hazards. In order for a fire to start, there must be a combination of three elements: fuel, an oxidizer, and a source of ignition. Common fuels include paper products, cloth, rubber products, metals, plastics, process chemicals, coatings such as paint or lacquer, solvents and cleaning fluid, engine fuel, and insecticides. These materials are considered flammable under normal circumstances, meaning they will burn in normal air. Oxidizers mean any substance that will cause the oxidation-reduction reaction of fire. Atmospheric oxygen is the most common oxidizer, but others include pure oxygen, fluorine, and chlorine. Some of these are powerful oxidizers and great care must be taken that they do not come in contact with fuels.

Ignition is the "energizing of molecules of fuel and oxidizer in a mixture so they collide with each other with suffcent velocity and force to initiate a reaction" (Hammer, 1989). The activation energy for ignition is usually in the form of heat; however, light can sometimes also be an ignition source. Typical fire ignition sources include open flames, electric arcs or sparks (including static electricity), and hot surfaces (such as cigarettes, metals heated by friction, overheated wires, etc.). In spontaneous reaction or combustion, materials gradually absorb atmospheric gases such as oxygen and, due to decomposition processes, become warm. This is especially common for fibrous materials that have oils or fats on them. If materials are in an enclosed location, such as a garbage bin, the heat buildup from oxidization cannot be dissipated adequately. The heat accumulated from the numerous reactions in the materials eventually provides the ignition source. The length of time required for oily rags or papers to combust spontaneously can range from hours to days, depending on temperatures and the availability of oxygen. Preventing spontaneous combustion requires frequent disposal in airtight containers (thus eliminating the oxidizer). In industrial settings, there are numerous standard safety precautions to prevent hazardous combinations of fuel, oxidizers, and ignition sources (see Hammer, 1989).

Radiation Hazards. Certain combinations of neutrons and protons result in unstable atoms, which then try to become stable by giving off excess energy in the form of particles or waves (radiation). These unstable atoms are thus said to be "radioactive." *Radioactive material* is any material that contains radioactive (unstable) atoms. Some types of radiation have enough energy that the particles actually ionize a neutral atom by ejecting an electron into it. Ionizing radiation causes damage to human tissue and includes radiation such as cosmic rays (from the sun or outer space), terrestrial radiation (from rocks or soil), and radioactivity within the human body. These types of ionizing radiation generally have levels of energy that are too low to be considered a hazard. Nuclear power plants or transportation systems for nuclear fuels or nuclear waste have high levels of energy and are considered to be the major sources of radiation hazards.

The criticality of exposure to radiation depends on several factors including the type of radiation (x-rays, gamma rays, thermal neutrons, etc.), the strength of the radiation (REM), and the length of exposure. These factors all affect the "dose," which is the amount of radiation actually absorbed by human tissue. Damage to human tissue occurs because atoms in the body cells are ionized and molecules fall apart. When this happens, the molecules may either rejoin to become the same molecule, or they may rejoin to become a *different* molecule. This new molecule formation is the primary hazard of radiation. New molecule formation can sometimes be repaired with no permanent physical damage. Other times it causes serious cell deterioration. Damage to body cells can therefore range from slight damage, to damage that is repairable, to damage that causes improper cell operation, and finally to cell death.

Biological effects of radiation can occur in a one-time acute exposure or from chronic long-term exposure. Chronic low levels of exposure can actually be safer than acute exposure because of the body's ability to repair itself. However, as chronic levels increase, long-term damage such as cancer will occur. Acute doses of radiation are extremely hazardous. At moderate levels of exposure (100 REM), the body will experience nausea and some injury to organs such as bone marrow, spleen, and lymphatic tissues. At levels over 125 REM, the injury becomes more severe. At 300 REM, 50 percent of people exposed will die within 50 days if they receive no medical treatment, suffering damage to the gastrointestinal tract and the central nervous system (Hammer, 1989). The best defense against radioactivity is an appropriate shield (e.g., plastic or glass for beta particles, lead and steel for gamma rays).

Falls.   Falls resulting in injury or death are relatively common. The most common type of injury is broken bones, and the most serious is head injury (Hammer, 1989). Unfortunately, falls can be more serious than most people realize. According to one estimate, 50 percent of all persons impacting against a surface at a velocity of 18 mph will be killed (see Hammer, 1989). This represents a fall of only 11 feet. People can fall and sustain injuries in a number of ways, including slipping on wet flooring and falling, falling from one floor to another, falling from an natural elevation or building, falling from a ladder, and falling from a structural support or walkway. Falls from ladders are so common that there are now OSHA precautionary regulations for the design and use of various types of ladders.

The Social Environment

There are a number of contextual factors that indirectly affect accident rates. Researchers are beginning to realize that hazard controls at the equipment level are not always successful because human behavior occurs within a social context. A ship captain may not see warning lights if he or she is in the next room having a drink. A construction worker will not wear safety equipment on the third story roof because his boss told him that none of the crew "bothers with that stuff." The social environment can provide extremely powerful influences on human behavior.

The list of social factors shown in Table 14.3 identified some of the major contributing factors to accidents, including management practices, social norms, morale, training, and incentives. Each of these factors affects the likelihood that an employee will behave in a safe manner. For example, management can implement incentive programs to reward safe behavior. Feedback concerning accident reduction has also been shown to reduce the rate of unsafe behaviors (e.g., Fellner & Sulzer-Azaroff, 1984). Training is also an important consideration, because this is one of the primary ways that people learn about hazards, what behaviors are appropriate or safe, and the consequences of unsafe behavior. In addition, as we will see in Chapter 19, group performance and decision making can be enhanced through training, and this reduces the incidence of human error.

Finally, social norms refer to the attitudes and behavior of an employee's peers. People are extremely susceptible to social norms; they are likely to engage in safe or unsafe behaviors to the extent that others around them do so (e.g., Wogalter, Allison, & McKenna, 1989). For example, if no one else wears protective goggles on the shop floor, it is unlikely that a new employee will do so for very long. In the section below on implementing safety programs, we review some of the methods to facilitate safe behavior by affecting these social factors. Chapter 19 also addresses this subject as it relates to macroergonomics.

Human Error

Many of the causal factors that contribute to accidents can be viewed as different "types" of *human error*. Human error can be defined as inappropriate human behavior that lowers levels of system effectiveness or safety, which may or may not result in an accident or injury. Technically the term *human error* could include mistakes made by humans operating a system, humans who designed the equipment, who supervise the worker, and who trained or advised the worker. However, the term is most frequently used to refer to *operator error,* the inappropriate behavior of the person directly working with the system. Because we have already discussed problems associated with equipment and the broader work context, we will now focus on "operator error," a central focal point in human factors because it is a common cause of accidents (Heinrich, 1959; Petersen, 1984; Rouse, 1990; Sanders & Shaw, 1988).

In reality, most accidents are caused by an unusual *combination* of multiple factors, only some of which are human error. Consider the analysis performed by Wagenaar and Groeneweg (1988), who evaluated 100 accidents at sea that were heard by the Dutch Shipping Council. They estimated that the total number of causal factors underlying the accidents was 2,250, or an average of 22 per case. While only 345 of these causal factors were human error, it is more informative to consider the fact that only 4 of the 100 accidents occurred without human error being a causal factor; that is, "in 96 out of 100 cases the people involved could and should have prevented the accident, but did not" (Wagenaar & Groeneweg, 1988). Operator errors can occur for many reasons, including inattentiveness, poor work habits, lack of training, poor decision making, personality traits, social pressures, and so forth. In the example of accidents at sea, half of the human errors consisted of false hypotheses (see Chapter 8), and another 35 percent were human errors based on poor training (Wagenaar & Groeneweg, 1988). These data are consistent with other research on the role of human error in accidents (Reason, 1990).

There have been several attempts to classify the types of errors that people make during task performance. These classification schemes are then used to design "fail-safe" systems or to develop methods to improve human performance. One such scheme that is frequently used is a simple dichotomy between errors of omission and errors of commission. *Errors of omission* are instances where the operator fails to perform one or more procedural step that is necessary for the particular circumstance they are facing. Errors of omission can be caused by a number of events or conditions. People may be confused or having communication problems (Rouse, 1990). Distraction or diversion of attention is often the source of errors of ommission. An inadequate mental model of a complex system can lead to errors of omission when the system experiences a malfunction. Errors of omission are particularly prevalent (and often have serious consequences) in maintenance tasks, when a single step like tightening a screw or retrieving a tool is neglected as the maintenance job is being completed.

Errors of commission refer to errors in which the operator performs extra steps that are incorrect or performs a step incorrectly. An example would be the incident of using a pry bar to dislodge the ice chunk in the irrigation pipe. Errors of commission also include instances where the operator performs a sequence of steps in the wrong order or performs a step too quickly or too slowly. Errors of commission are caused by a number of factors. Often they reflect inadequate training of procedures, poor instruction or job aids (Chapter 18), or an employee being unaware of hidden hazards associated with equipment or the environment.

A second distinction of error types that is also useful is Norman's (1981) distinction between the operator's intentions and his or her actual behavior; that is, when someone steps down a ladder and misses the rung and falls, the person does not intend to miss the rung. Whereas when people press a computer key and then lose the file they were working on, they may have intended to perform the action, but they did not intend for it to have the consequence it did (the whole file). If the intention is correct for the situation, but the execution is incorrect, this is termed a *slip*. Slips include errors resulting from inattention, misperceptions, losing track of one's place, and so on. (Reason & Mycielska, 1982). Whereas when the person has an inappropriate intention and then carries it out, this is considered a *mistake.* If a person intentionally turns onto a one-way street going the wrong way, this is a mistake. Mistakes occur at Rasmussen's level of *knowledge-based processing* (Chapter 6) and result from human processing limitations, incorrect knowledge, or unwillingness to invest the effort necessary to formulate intentions more carefully. Mistakes are also invited by poor displays that do not offer a coherent picture of the situation.

There have been a number of attempts to model more formally and predict human errors. The work on *human reliability assessment* has focused on (a) development of systematic methods for identifying potential human errors, and (b) quantification of error likelihood (Kirwan, 1990, 1992a). A well-known example is Technique for Human Error Rate Prediction (THERP) (Swain & Guttmann, 1983). THERP provides extensive guidelines for an analyst to identify errors that might occur at each point in a task analysis (such as an act carried out too early) and assign probabilities to each error. Some of the more successful human reliability assessment efforts have been based on formal models such as Rasmussen's SRK model (see review in Chapter 7). Two such methods are the Systematic Human Error Reduction and Prediction Approach (SHERPA) (Embry, 1986), and Generic Error Modeling System (GEMS) (Reason, 1987). SHERPA specifies potential psychological error mechanisms and then identifies the behavioral error that would be the result. The behavioral errors include the following:

- Action omitted
- Action too early
- Action too late
- Action too much
- Action too little
- Action too long
- Action too short
- Action in wrong direction
- Right action on wrong object
- Wrong action on right object
- Misalignment error
- Information not obtained/transmitted
- Check omitted
- Check on wrong object
- Wrong check
- Check mistimed

In using SHERPA, the analyst uses a tabular format to list the tasks from a task analysis, external error type (from list above), psychological mechanism that caused the error, potential recovery steps, and consequences. GEMS focuses more on rule- and knowledge-based behavior, with the error analysis an expansion of the slip/mistake dichotomy. In an extensive qualitative assessment of various methodologies, Kirwan (1992b) reports that none of the human reliability assessment methods can be deemed "best." All of the methods reviewed showed problems of poor comprehensiveness and tended to rely heavily on the ability of the person using the method. Kirwan suggests that analysts strive to use more than one method.

Human errors and their negative consequences are decreased in one of three ways: personnel selection, training, or system design. For system design, errors can be reduced by making it impossible for a person to commit an error, making it difficult to commit an error or making the system *error tolerant* so that when errors occur, the negative consequences are avoided (Rouse, 1983). Error tolerance can be achieved by methods such as feedback to the operator about current consequences, feedback about future consequences, and monitoring actions for possible errors. Design features can be included so that erroneous actions can be reversed (if they are noticed) before they have serious consequences on system performance. Computer systems now typically give the user a "second chance" before permanently deleting a file (e.g., by asking "are you sure you want to delete?" or by providing an "undo" key; see Chapter 15). Performance can also be supported using the methods suggested at the end of Chapter 8 in the discussion of decision support systems. Finally, when system design or information support cannot be used, then selection and training methods should be designed to minimize operator error. In the next section, we provide additional information on methods for enhancing system safety.

APPROACHES TO HAZARD CONTROL

In general, safety engineers adhere to the philosophy that hazard control should be approached from an optimization standpoint. This means that, first, in a facility or system with multiple hazards, the most critical or "high-risk" hazards should receive top priority. Second, in controlling hazards, there are certain methods that are considered more optimal and reliable than others. Consider the first issue: What does it mean to say that a hazard is critical or high-risk?

Criticality and Risk

There have been many operational definitions of hazard *criticality*. It is often considered synonymous with risk, which is a combination of the *probability* and *severity* of the event or accident. Probability is the likelihood of an event taking place. Probability is measured in a number of ways and is often referred to as "frequency." Sometimes it is precisely quantified by using accident frequency rates for the task in a particular environment. For example, a particular injury might occur in a plant at the rate of 5.0 per million man-hours. Sometimes probability must be estimated because of the lack of adequate accident data. When probability is estimated, it is often categorized in a ranked scale of Frequent, Probable, Occasional, Remote, and Improbable (Roland & Moriarity, 1990). Severity is usually scaled according to the severity of the injury. As an example, Military Standard MIL-STD-882B (Department of Defense, 1984) uses the following categories: Catastrophic, Critical, Marginal, or Negligible. These categories correspond to death or loss of a system, severe injury or major damage, minor injury or minor system damage, and no injury or system damage (Department of Defense, 1984).

One way of combining these two factors into a single *criticality* scale has been provided in MIL-STD-882B. A matrix is used that combines the frequency and severity categories described in the previous paragraph. By using the hazard-assessment matrix (shown in Table 14.4), the hazard can be assigned a numerical value ranging from 1 to 20, with one representing the highest criticality and 20 the lowest.

TABLE 14.4 Hazard Matrix for Combining Frequency and Severity into a Single "Criticality" Variable

	Severity			
	Catastrophic	Critical	Marginal	Negligible
Frequency				
Frequent	1	3	7	13
Probable	2	5	9	16
Occasional	4	6	11	18
Remote	8	10	14	19
Improbably	12	15	17	20

Source: Adapted from Department of Defense MIL–STD–882B, 1984.

Hazard Control Priority

Hazards associated with a tool or piece of equipment can be thought of as originating at a source and move along some path to a person. The reduction of hazards should be prioritized as follows:

- Source
- Path
- Person
- Administrative controls

The best hazard reduction is to eliminate it at the "source." This is also called *designing out* a hazard. An example would be eliminating a sharp edge on a piece of equipment. Designing out hazards should always be attempted before other methods of hazard control. However, it is possible that the tool or equipment cannot function with the hazard designed out. An automobile can be designed to go only 2 miles per hour, eliminating the hazard of injuring a person on the inside and significantly reducing the likelihood of injury to someone on the outside. While a hazard has been designed out, the functionality has been designed out also.

After designing out, the next best solution is to provide a hazard control on the "path." This usually means providing a barrier or *safeguard* of some sort. This method is considered less optimal because it is more likely to fail to control the hazard. As an example, consider a worker in a paper plant who is responsible for bringing large rolls of paper (weighing thousands of pounds) into a piece of equipment for wrapping. The paper rolls are moving through the area and, due to their size and weight, constitute a hazard to the worker. A "path" hazard control would keep the worker from entering the area where the paper rolls are moving, unless operations are stopped first. However, such a barrier could conceivable by overridden by the employee. Another example would be where maintenance personnel must enter an environment with airborne toxins and *personal protective equipment* is worn to keep the hazard from reaching the person. However, as with other types of guarding, personal protective equipment is not failproof, because it can be removed by the person. Hazard control through guarding is generally problematic to the extent that it can be made ineffective by the person. For example, the choice to wear protective gear is highly dependent on a number of factors that affect risk-related decisions (as discussed below).

It is sometimes not possible to either design out or guard against a hazard. In this case, the hazard control must consist of trying to control the hazard at the point of the "person," changing their behavior. This approach usually depends on *warning* or *training* and is considered even less reliable for hazard control than guarding. An example would be training workers not to place their hands near a pinch point. The workers may be well intentioned, but human error could still result in an accident. Another example is the plastic bags from dry cleaners. Consumers will naturally come into contact with such objects. However, they pose a serious suffocation hazard for children. Since guarding is not possible, the next best hazard control is at the point of the person, warning or training them about the hazards associated with the plastic bag.

A final method of hazard control is through administrative procedures or *legislation*. In industry, administrative procedures might include shift rotation, mandatory rest breaks, sanctions for incorrect and risky behavior, and so forth. Federal and state legislation has already been discussed. In addition to laws and regulations for industry, there are general public laws or regulations such as requirements to use seat belts, requirements for motorcyclists to use helmets, and so on. The problem is that like training or warning, theses methods are meant to impact the behavior of a person. Since people ultimately do as they wish (including suffer the consequences), these methods are less reliable than design or even guarding. In addition, there appears to be evidence that legislative methods are generally less effective than warning or training methods of behavior change (e.g., Lusk, Ronis, & Kerr, 1995).

How does an engineer or safety expert identify possible methods of hazard reduction? Safety texts and articles are one source of information. For example, Hammer (1989) provides a fairly complete discussion of methods for reducing the various types of hazard listed earlier (fire, pressure, toxic, etc.). In addition, the National Safety Council publishes texts and documents (such as *Safeguarding Concepts Illustrated*, 6th ed., 1993), numerous publishers print texts specializing in Health and Safety (e.g., Mansdorf, 1993; Moran, 1996), and there are a number of journal and conference sources in the field of industrial safety.

SAFETY ANALYSIS FOR PRODUCTS AND EQUIPMENT

Safety can be enhanced through a number of general approaches. First, designers can consider safety issues and attempt to identify potential hazards when a product, tool, or piece of equipment is first designed. For each significant hazard, controls are evaluated and selected. Second, facilities or operational systems can be evaluated in a proactive manner for identify hazards and control them before accidents occur. Third, facilities or operational systems can be evaluated in a reactive manner by evaluating accidents and remediating the hazards that caused them. In this section, we briefly review a limited number of methods for the first process, considering hazards in the design of a product or piece of equipment. There are numerous methods for analyzing the safety of a simple system or piece of equipment, and a complete review is not feasible in this text (see Kirwan & Ainsworth, 1992, for a review). Instead, we will describe several complementary analysis methods that, when used together properly, will yield a majority of the hazards associated with tools and equipment.

System safety analysis consists of identifying potential hazards and making recommendations for hazard reduction. One sequence for this work has been suggested by Weinstein et al. (1978):

1. *Task Analysis.* Delineate the scope of product uses.
2. *Environment Analysis.* Identify the environments within which the product will be used.
3. *User Analysis.* Describe the user population.
4. *Hazard Identification.* Postulate all possible hazards, including estimates of probability of occurrence and seriousness of resulting harm.
5. *Generate Methods for Hazard Control.* Delineate alternative design features or production techniques, including warnings and instructions, that can be expected to effectively mitigate or eliminate the hazards.
6. *Evaluate Hazard Control Alternatives.* Evaluate such alternatives relative to the expected performance standards of the product.
7. *Select Hazard Controls.* Decide which features to include in the final design.

This design sequence is similar to the design sequence outlined in Chapter 3. In that chapter, we reviewed common methods for performing task analysis. For safety and hazard analysis, the task analysis should include the major tasks and subtasks, organized hierarchically. For tasks of any complexity (such as operating a lawnmower or power saw), there should be at least two or three levels of detail, and the task analysis can be represented either in a table format or in a graph hierarchy. It is important to include the conditions under which the person does alternative actions, the correct action sequences (when appropriate), and possible or definite consequences of the actions. During or before completion of the task analysis, the designer specifies the different user populations for the product and possible environmental conditions. This is necessary because these variables may affect how the task is performed in some cases, and also consequences of the actions. After the task, user, and environment analyses are completed, the designer uses this material for hazard identification.

Hazard Identification

In designing equipment, one should ideally look for every possible hazard that could occur during each step in the operator's job. This must be done for all environmental conditions and for every possible foreseeable use of the equipment. In addition, the equipment must be analyzed as it will exist in combination with other equipment and with other possible environmental hazards. There are several complementary methods that are used for identifying potential hazards.

Preliminary Hazards Analysis.   The most simple method for hazard analysis, a preliminary hazards analysis, is often done before other more detailed methods, early in the conceptual design phase (Hammer, 1989). In a preliminary hazards analysis, the specialist evaluates the combinations of task actions, potential users, and environments to develop a list of the most obvious hazards that will be associated with a system (preliminary hazard, analyses are usually presented in a columnar table format). For example, if a power tool is being designed, the engineer will know that all standard electrical hazards must be considered. After each hazard is listed, columns are used to specify the cause of each hazard and the most likely effect on the system. The engineer then uses whatever data or knowledge is available to estimate the likelihood that an accident would occur as a result of the hazard and perhaps estimate the severity of the consequences. Potential corrective measures are then listed for each hazard. The problem with performing a preliminary hazards analysis is that the analyst may let it suffice and never complete the more thorough analyses.

Failure Modes and Effects Criticality Analysis (FMECA).   FMECA is an extension of a traditional method known as FMEA, which focused on the hazards associated with physical components of a system (Henley & Kumamoto, 1981). A FMEA begins with a breaking down of the physical system into subassemblies. For example, an automobile would be broken down into engine, cooling system, brake system, and so forth. Next, each subassembly is broken down into constituent components, and the analyst studies each individual component to identify the different ways that it could break down or function incorrectly, the *failure modes*. After this step, *effects* of the component failure on other components and on other subassemblies are estimated. As an example, the component of an automobile fuel tank might be evaluated for the failure mode of "punctured." This would result in fuel leakage. The analyst would evaluate the *effects* of a fuel leak on other components in the fuel system, other subassemblies, and the entire system. This process is done for every system and environmental condition, including whether the automobile is running, outdoor temperature, and other factors such as potential surrounding heat sources. Many FMEAs also include a cause for each failure mode, and also corrective measures to control the failure or its effects (Kirwan & Ainsworth, 1992).

The FMECA is essentially an FMEA, but with an added factor. Once the component is analyzed for its effect on the system, the hazard is also given a score representing the hazard criticality of the effect. Consider Table 14.5 which illustrates part of a FMECA. The first column lists the component, the second column lists each possible failure mode for the component. The third column describes the effect of the failure mode on other individual components, and the fourth shows the effect on the overall system. Because of the many possible combinations, a FMECA can have several pages of possible failure modes and effects for even just one system component. The next column describes the criticality of the effect on the system. Criticality can be defined however the analyst wishes. A simple system might use simple broad categories, such as "1 = catastrophic, 2 = critical, 3 = marginal, and 4 = nuisance or negligible." A more de-

TABLE 14.5 Example of Items from FMECA for Lawnmower

Component	Failure Mode	Effect on other components	Effect on system/subsystem	Criticality	Comments
Blade	Come loose	Damage housing	• Damage to surrounding parts • Uneven cut	6	Not as severe as broken blade, but is somewhat likely and can cause significant damage
	Break Fracture	Severe vibration from imbalance can cause engine components to fall off or come loose	• Severe vibration could make mower difficult to control • Uneven cut • Flying metal pieces	4	
	Dent Dull				

scriptive and useful method for assigning criticality would be to use the MIL-STD 882B 20-point scale shown in Table 14.4.

While traditionally FMEAs have not focused on humans and human error, it is possible and desirable to extend the FMECA to analysis of the human system, that is, operator performance (Kirwan & Ainsworth, 1992). Instead of listing components and their failures, the analyst evaluates each step within the task analysis; that is, for each step, the engineer can list the types of errors that might occur (omission, incorrect performance, and so forth) and the possible effects of the error on the system. For example, if a person omitted the step of putting the gas cap back on a lawnmower, what would be the effects on system components and the system in general? How critical would those effects be? In this way, failures in human performance are analyzed for effects on the system in much the same way as failure of physical components. It is important to include foreseeable misuse in this analysis. An example of part of a FMECA focusing on human error is shown in Table 14.6.

Fault Tree Analysis. While FMECAs begin with a molecular view of the system and its components and work in a "bottom up" fashion, other methods work in the opposite direction. One such analysis technique is *fault tree analysis,* which works from the "top down" from an incident or undesirable event down to possible causes (Green, 1983; Kirwan & Ainsworth, 1992). These causes could be conditions in the physical system, events, human error, or some combination. For each identified

TABLE 14.6 **Example of "Human Error" Components for FMECA for Lawnmower**

Human Error Component	Failure Mode	Effect on Component(s)	Effect on System/Subsystem	Criticality	Comments
Set blade torque	Torque set too high	Bolt experiences undue stress, breaks	Blade comes off mower	6	
	Torque set too low				
Check mower blade	Fail to see blade cracks				

event or condition, the analyst works downward to identify all possible causes of *that* event. This is continued, and branches of the fault tree are added downward.

Fault trees show combinations of causal factors that result in the next level of event or condition through the use of Boolean AND/OR logic to represent the causal relationships. As an example, recall that a fire requires a fuel, oxidizer, and ignition source. All three must be present for a fire to occur. The fault tree would represent this as fuel AND oxidizer AND ignition source (see Figure 14.4.) As another example, Figure 14.5 shows part of a fault tree that focuses on combinations of system conditions and human error. The example shows three possible reasons for why a visual alarm is not seen, which would lead to the visual alarm not "perceived." Since each of these reasons could independently contribute to the failure, they are linked by an OR gate. Where possible, bottom-level events can be associated with probability estimates.

Fault trees are extremely powerful methods of hazard identification. One advantage of fault tree analysis is that it systematically identifies single causes and also multiple interacting causes of accidents. Single causes, known as *single-point failures,* are usually more likely to occur than combinations of conditions or events, and therefore high in priority for controlling. Single-point failures are causes that pass upward or propagate through OR gates rather than AND gates. Because they are relatively difficult to build in isolation, fault trees are usually used in conjunction with other methods, such as FMECA.

Hazard Controls

The next step in the safety analysis is to develop a list of hazard controls. Analyses such as FMECAs or fault trees will yield a number of hazards, which can then be listed in the first column of a *hazard controls* table. A second column can show the criticality of each hazard. The focus is then to generate all possible controls for each hazard, making sure *first* to try to generate controls that design the hazard out and then to generate ways to guard against the hazard. Different means of controlling each hazard should be generated if possible. Once the control methods are generated, they must be evaluated in terms of cost-benefit trade-offs. Factors to consider include:

- Other hazards that may be introduced by the various alternatives

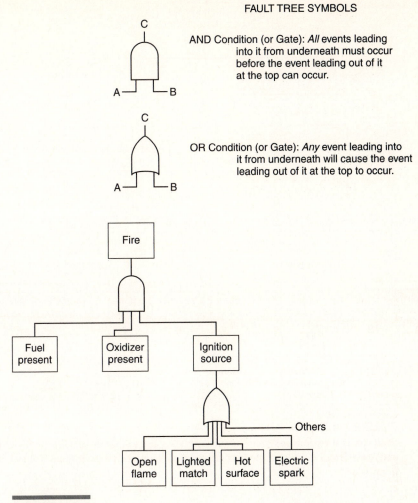

FAULT TREE SYMBOLS

AND Condition (or Gate): *All* events leading into it from underneath must occur before the event leading out of it at the top can occur.

OR Condition (or Gate): *Any* event leading into it from underneath will cause the event leading out of it at the top to occur.

FIGURE 14.4
Part of fault tree diagram that represents combinations of events that lead to a fire.

- Effects of the control on the subsequent usefulness of the product
- Effect of the control on the ultimate cost of the product
- A comparison to similar products (What control methods do they use?)

If necessary, the designer will have to consult with others for information on factors such as manufacturing costs related to the hazard controls. Notes on the relative advantages and disadvantages of each alternative control should be made in the next column or in a separate document (for liability reasons). Finally, the designer should choose one control method and list it in a final "recommended control" column. Once a product or system is designed to include the hazard

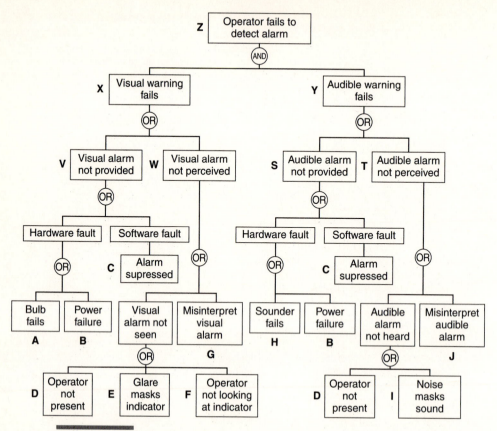

FIGURE 14.5

Fault tree that represents system component faults and human error. (*Source:* Kirwan, B., and Ainsworth, L.K. 1992. *A guide to task analysis.* London: Taylor & Francis. Reprinted with permission.)

controls identified, the design team should do a final check to make sure the design does not have any defects that have historically led to litigation. Hammer (1989) provides a reasonably complete although generic checklist of design defects that can be used for this purpose (see Table 14.7).

FACILITY SAFETY

Safety in industry is promoted in a number of ways. As we have just seen, one is through proper design of equipment and facilities. Others include safety management work at specific facilities through activities such as assessing facility safety, taking remedial actions to enhance safety, and performing formal accident or incident investigations. In this section, we briefly summarize some methods for safety management in a company or facility.

TABLE 14.7 Design Defects That Lead to Accidents and Litigation

Design deficiencies may result because a designer or design:

Creates an unsafe characteristic of a product.

Is faulty so it causes an accident.

Is faulty so the product or operation will not take place as envisioned.

Does not envision, consider, or determine the consequences of an error, failure, action, or omission.

Fails to foresee an unintended use of a product or its consequences.

Fails to properly prescribe or evaluate an operational procedure where a hazard might be present.

Procedure is incomplete, in error, or confusing.

Violates normal tendencies or capabilities of a worker or user.

Places an unreasonable stress on the operator.

Fails to minimize or eliminate possibilities of human error or leads to errors.

Creates an arrangement of operating controls and indicating meters that are inducive to errors or increase reaction time in an emergency.

Leaves safety of a product up to its user to avoid an accident.

Fails to warn of a hazard.

Fails to provide adequate protection in workers' personal protective equipment.

Is faulty in that worker will not wear safety equipment because it is too heavy, cumbersome, restricts breathing or movement, interferes with work, or has any other adverse feature.

Provides a warning, such as by a label, instead of providing a safe design to eliminate it.

Fails to provide a suitable safety device where a hazard exists in that the:

a. safety device is inadequate and does not provide service intended when required.

b. safety device is located where it is inaccessible in an emergency.

c. safety device can easily be removed or bypassed by an operator or user.

Fails to provide adequately against an adverse environment.

Fails to avoid use of a toxic or other hazardous material without providing adequate safeguards.

Source: W. Hammer, 1989. *Occupational safety management and engineering* (4th ed.). Englewood Cliffs, NJ: Prentice Hall. Reprinted with permission of Prentice-Hall, Inc., Upper Saddle River, NJ.

Safety Programs

A person rarely has to go in and set up an entire safety program in a business from scratch, but occasionally it does happen. A safety program should involve the participation of both management and staff. Many studies have demonstrated that employee involvement makes a significant difference in the effectiveness of a safety program (e.g., Robertson, Bowman, & Rosenberg, 1986). Manning (1996) suggests the following three stages:

1. *Identify risks to the company.*
2. *Develop and implement safety programs.*
3. *Measure program effectiveness.*

We will briefly describe some of the methods that can be used in each phase. Readers are referred to Manning (1996) and Kohn et al. (1996) for excellent and in-depth treatment of effective methods for implementing safety programs.

Identifying Risks.   A full assessment should first be conducted to evaluate existing hazards, hazard controls, accident frequency, and company losses due to accident/incident claims. A safety officer would usually begin by analyzing appropriate company documents including accident/incident reports, safety records, training materials, and so on. Information from these documents should be tabulated for the different jobs or tasks, and according to OSHA injury categories:

Struck by	*Fall/slip/trip*
Body mechanics	*Caught-in-between*
Laceration/cut/tear/puncture	*Struck against*
Contact with temperature extremes	*Eye*
Miscellaneous	

After document analysis, the safety officer conducts interviews with supervisors and employees and performs observational analysis via walk-throughs (see Hammer, 1989). The purpose of this activity is to look for equipment or behavior-based hazards associated with task performance. A facility walk-through should also be conducted using a safety checklist based on OSHA General Industry Standard 1910 (Table 14.8 shows part of a typical checklist). Complete checklists can be found in Hammer (1989), Goetsch (1996), and Manning (1996).

From these activities, the safety officer or analyst can begin to develop a list of hazards. In addition to this "reactive" approach, the analyst should use a "proactive" approach by using the system safety analysis methods described above and also by using the analysis methods described in Kohn et al. (1996). One particularly valuable method is *job safety analysis,* a method that relies on supervisors and employees to identify hazards associated with a particular job. The major advan-

TABLE 14.8   Examples of Checklist Items for Identifying Industrial Hazards

Fall-Related Hazards	*Electrical Hazards*
Are foreign objects present on the walking surface or in walking paths?	Are short circuits present anywhere in the facility?
Are there design flaws in the walking surface?	Are static electricity hazards present anywhere in the facility?
Are there slippery areas on the walking surface?	Are electrical conductors in close enough proximity to cause an arc?
Are there raised or lowered sections of the walking surface that might trip a worker?	Are explosive/combustible materials stored or used in proximity to electrical conductors?
Is good housekeeping being practiced?	Does the facility have adequate lightning protection?
Is the walking surface made of or covered with a nonskid material?	Etc.
Etc.	

tages to this approach include: (1) the heavy involvement of employees, a factor that has been shown to have substantial effects of safety program effectiveness (Kohn et al., 1996; Ray, Purswell, & Bowen 1993), (2) the long-term benefits of having employees more knowledgeable about hazards, and (3) the efficiency of having employees working to identify hazards. Finally, the analyst should evaluate ergonomic factors that reflect potential hazards to long-term health, such as repetition and excessive force requirements (see Chapter 10).

The final result of this stage should be a table of hazards for each job, piece of equipment, and facility location, with hazard prioritization according to criticality scores. The analysis should also identify those hazards that result in large numbers of accidents and produce the greatest financial (or potential financial) loss.

Implementing Safety Programs.   Safety programs should be developed with the assistance and "buy-in" of management and employees (Robertson, Bowman, & Rosenberg, 1986). Safety programs usually include the following elements:

Management Involvement. Involve executive management from the beginning, and have supervisors attend or be responsible for conducting monthly safety meetings. Develop procedures for management receiving and acting on labor suggestions. Develop and distribute a general safety policy signed by the chief officer.

Accident/Incident Investigation. Ensure that investigation procedures are in place, identify routing for investigation reports, and train personnel responsible for accident investigation.

Recommendations for Equipment, Environment, Job Changes. Develop recommendations for hazard control of high priority hazards and make all facility changes necessary for OSHA compliance.

Safety Rules. Develop general safety rules and job task rules; develop a plan for yearly evaluation of safety rules, and post safety rules in conspicuous places; cover safety rules in new employee orientation; and develop policies for safety rule violation.

Personal Protective Equipment (PPE). Write standards for use of PPE, compliance criteria, and policies for PPE violations. Develop and implement training on use of PPE.

Employee Training. Develop training for job tasks, new employee orientation, hazard awareness, knowledge, and hazard avoidance behavior. Begin regular safety meetings, and develop employee manual to include safety rules and other safety information.

Safety Promotion: Feedback and Incentives. Display safety posters, notices, memos; display data on frequency of safe behavior and accidents and injury rates; and provide individual and group recognition or other incentives (incentive programs are effective over long periods as long as they are not dropped permanently at some point).

Suggestions and guidelines for implementing these components can be found in sources such as Goetsch (1996), Kohn et al. (1996), Manning (1996), Manuele

(1993), and the Department of Labor (1990). After changes have been implemented, safety checklists can be used for "walk-throughs" to check for OSHA compliance (e.g., see Davis, Grubbs, & Nelson, 1995). Research to date suggests that the most effective means for increasing safety, after design and guarding methods, are to: (1) use a participatory approach involving management and employees (Robertson et al., 1986), (2) providing training for knowledge of hazards, safe behavior, and belief/attitude change, and (3) use behavior change methods such as feedback and incentives (Ray, Purswell, & Bowen, 1993).

Measuring Program Effectiveness.   After initial collection of baseline data (e.g., accidents, injury, monetary losses, etc.), it is important to continue to collect such data. Program effectiveness is usually evaluated by looking at changes in safe behaviors, accident/incident rates, number of injuries or death, and number of days off due to injury. OSHA logs (which are to be kept by the safety officer) are valuable for this purpose because they contain data on the type and number of injuries for each worker.

Accident and Incident Investigation

OSHA requires investigation of all accidents and for some industries, such as petrochemical plants, also requires investigation of *incidents* (OSHA Rule 29 CFR1910.119). An incident is the occurrence of some event that could have resulted in injury or death but did not. A near miss is considered an incident. There are some relatively standardized procedures for performing an accident or incident investigation. The sequence of steps shown in Table 14.9 represents a typical accident or incident investigation process (from McCallister, 1993).

It can be seen that, like a police investigation, accident investigations often require careful securing of evidence, extensive interviewing, information collection, analyses of evidence, and drawing of conclusions. Training programs just for performing accident or incident investigations are becoming common.

RISK-TAKING AND WARNINGS
Risk-Taking as a Decision Process

When hazards are not designed out or guarded, people are ultimately responsible for safe behavior. Examples include proper use of ladders, following correct job procedures, cautious driving behavior, and use of seat belts. Even when safeguards are employed, people frequently have the option of overriding them, such as in the choice not to use personal protective equipment. The choice between safe and unsafe behavior is initially a knowledge-based decision process; eventually, it may become rule-based behavior or simply automatic. One area of research in human factors considers the factors that affect the decision to act safely. If we look back at Figure 7.4 and its associated discussion in the text, we can see that the *decision* to act safely will be a function of the factors that affect the top area of the diagram, people must know a hazard exists (diagnosis), know what actions are available (generation of alternative actions), and know the consequences of the safe behavior versus alternative behaviors in order to make a wise decision (evaluate alternative actions).

TABLE 14.9 Prototypical Tasks for Incident Investigation

Step 1. Secure the incident scene and request that all evidence be preserved.

Step 2. Define the scope of the investigation and establish the investigation team.

Step 3. Obtain necessary security clearances and provide for the safety of the team.

Step 4. Obtain record-keeping materials.

Step 5. Collect evidence and obtain background information:
- Walk the incident site.
- Identify and preserve evidence.
- Identify and interview witnesses.
- Review records including other relevant accident reports.

Step 6. Analyze facts:
- Obtain and review applicable standards and codes to identify requirements applicable to the incident.
- Obtain and review any relevant hazard analyses.
- Obtain and review audits.
- Obtain and review safety information applicable to the incident.
- Obtain and review standard operating instructions, operating procedures, and social norms (typical behavior) relevant to the incident.
- List findings pertinent to the incident.

Step 7. Integrate facts and draw conclusions:
- Establish the chain of events and contributing factors.
- Conduct an analysis of change which specifies the incident situation, a comparable incident-free situation, and an analysis of the differences.
- Conduct a barrier analysis if appropriate.
- Group findings into categories.
- Write findings.

Step 8. Validate conclusions:
- Check to determine whether each conclusion is supported by findings.
- Check to identify any missing information.

Step 9. Make recommendations:
- Will recommendations fix the contributing factors?
- If not, go back to Step 8.
- Is each recommendation supported by one or more conclusions?
- Are there missing conclusions?

Step 10. Write and submit the investigation report.

Source: McCallister, D.R., 1993. Unpublished paper, University of Idaho. Used with permission.

The view of choosing to act safely as an analytical knowledge-based decision suggests that people might sometimes use simplifying heuristics such as satisficing and other times use more extensive decision analysis. In the first case, satisficing the individual would consider an action and then evaluate the consequence of that one action. If the consequence is seen as positive to some criterion level, the action will be carried out. For example, a person wants to cut a piece of wood with a circular saw. The cord does not reach an outlet so this person gets out an extension cord and connects it to the tool. This individual might briefly try to think of the positive and negative consequences associated with the action. On the positive side, the tool is now operable, and he or she does not really think of any negative consequences that would be very likely. Thus, based on satisficing, the person would go ahead and use the equipment. Taking this view, decision making relative to use of hazardous tools or equipment would depend heavily on the processes of "generation of an action" and "evaluation of the action." If the person performs the evaluation via running a mental model, the quality of evaluation will depend on the quality and completeness of the person's knowledge base plus the availability of different types of information in memory.

We might also assume that in some cases, people perform a decision analysis to evaluate alternative choices. If this were the case, we would expect subjective expected utility theory to be applicable to behavioral data (DeJoy, 1991), and in fact, several researchers have demonstrated that both expected frequency of consequences and severity of consequences affect decisions or intentions to act safely (e.g., Wogalter, Desaulniers, & Brelsford, 1987). However, it appears that *severity* of injury has a greater effect than *likelihood* on risk perception (Young, Wogalter, & Brelsford, 1992) and that other variables impact the decision process as well. For example, Young and Laughery (1994), as well as Schacherer (1993), found that intentions to behave in a safe manner were affected by three psychological components: (1) variables related to perceived severity of the hazard/injury, (2) the *novelty* of the hazard and whether exposure was *voluntary*, and (3) how *familiar* the product or item was to the person.

In understanding the choice to act safely, it is helpful to think of the action selection process as involving two closely related cognitive stages—risk perception and action choice (DeJoy, 1991). *Risk perception* is the process of determining the likelihood and severity of injury to one's self and may be closely determined by the *availability* of risk in memory. For example, if a vehicle driver has recently suffered a rear end collision, this event will be available and hence judged as more likely. The perceived risk of tailgating will be greater. After this estimate, the person chooses between the "safe" and alternative actions by considering the subjective costs and benefits of each behavior outcome. For example, wearing safety goggles while mowing the yard would have the benefit of eliminating possible eye injury but might also have costs such as finding the goggles, wearing them with associated discomfort, not being able to see as well, and looking silly to the neighbors. We refer to these factors collectively as the *cost of compliance*. The alternative, not wearing goggles, has the cost of possible eye injury, but also benefits such as comfort and being able to see well. A variety of studies have shown that people do, in fact, seem to weigh these types of consideration in making their decisions. For example, the *costs of compliance* associated with safe behavior such as wearing personal protective equipment, have an extremely strong, negative effect on the frequency of safe behavior (Wogalter, Allison, & McKenna, 1989). Greater costs are tolerated for behaviors only where probability and particularly the severity of injury are perceived to be relatively high.

Written Warnings and Warning Labels

We saw that hazard control often relies on instruction or warning about hazards. Especially in the area of consumer products, warnings are becoming increasingly common. One of the reasons for this is that manufacturers have found that warnings are the easiest and cheapest means of protecting themselves against product liability suits, as discussed earlier in the chapter. Unfortunately, to be defensible, warnings must be targeted for every foreseeable use of a tool or piece of equipment, which is not usually feasible. As a result, there is often disagreement, even among human factors experts, about the number and type of warning labels that should be placed on products.

Written warnings are meant to convey the hazards of a product or piece of equipment. Their goal is to affect people's intentions and behavior so that their actions do not bring about an accident, injury, or death. As we noted earlier, warnings and warning labels should only be used when design and safeguard hazard controls are not feasible. Most guidelines suggest that a warning should include a signal word plus information pertaining to the hazard, consequences, and necessary behavior (Wogalter et al., 1987):

- *Signal Word* conveying the seriousness, such as Danger, Warning, or Caution
- *Description of the Hazard*
- *Consequences* associated with the hazard
- *Behavior Needed* to avoid the hazard

An example including these elements is given by Strawbridge (1986):

DANGER:
Contains Acid
To avoid severe burns, shake well before opening.

Another example using both the standard caution icon and a pictograph is shown in Figure 14.6.

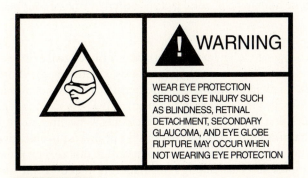

FIGURE 14.6

Warning label with pictograph, caution icon, and hazard information. (*Source:* Dingus, T.A., Hathaway, J.A., and Hunn, B.P., 1991. A most critical warning variable: Two demonstrations of the powerful effects of cost on warning compliance. *Proceedings of the Human Factors Society 35th Annual Meeting* [pp. 1034–1038]. Santa Monica, CA: Human Factors Society.)

In designing warning labels, one must remember several factors. First, people may not see or read a warning label. Therefore, designers should attempt to make such labels as noticeable as possible. One way this is currently being accomplished is by the use of bright orange in all or part of the warning or placing the warning next to a part of the equipment that the user *must* look at to operate (e.g., the power switch). Gaining a persons attention is the first goal. Second, people must actually read the words and interpret any pictures or icons. This means the warning must use legible font size and contrast (see Chapter 4), short and relatively simple text (Chapter 6), and easily interpreted pictures or icons (Chapter 8). Traditionally, designers use different *signal words* to convey different degrees of hazard severity:

- *Danger:* An immediate hazard that would likely result in severe injury or death.
- *Warning:* Hazards that could result in personal injury or death.
- *Caution:* Hazards or unsafe practices that could result in minor personal injury or property damage.

However, there has been some recent research indicating that the public is not particularly good at interpreting the difference between the three signal words (e.g., Wogalter, Jarrard, & Simpson, 1992), and people especially seem to have difficulty recognizing differences in meaning for WARNING and CAUTION (Kalsher et al., 1995). When in doubt, designers are usually encouraged to provide more rather than less information on warnings and warning labels. The problem is that a hazardous tool such as a table saw could end up with hundreds of warning labels, each with a considerable amount of information. At some point, the labels are ignored and become ineffective.

Third, people must *comply* with the warning. Compliance will be encouraged by clear articulation of the consequences and the behavior needed, but in the workplace, compliance can also be supported by administrative controls and enforcement, as we discuss in the context of highway safety in Chapter 17. But of course, compliance can never be assured to the extent that someone intentionally chooses to engage in hazardous behavior. Figure 14.7 summarizes , in terms of a fault tree, many of the human behavioral factors underlying hazardous behavior.

Conclusion

In conclusion, achieving safe behavior is a critical but complex goal of human factors. It depends on identifying and analyzing hazards, identifying the shortcomings of design (both inanimate components and human factors) that may induce those hazards, and finally, proposing (and implementing) the various remediations or "fixes" which will reduce hazards and accidents. While the surest means is to eliminate the hazards itself, we know that this is not always possible, given the hazards to which humans are inevitably exposed in certain tasks of environments. Thus, the most complex and challenging remediation is to address the human's choice to engage in safe versus unsafe behavior. Psychologists' knowledge of this, and other choice processes as discussed in Chapter 7, still remains far from mature, but the contributions such knowledge can make to the human factors of safety are potentially quite large.

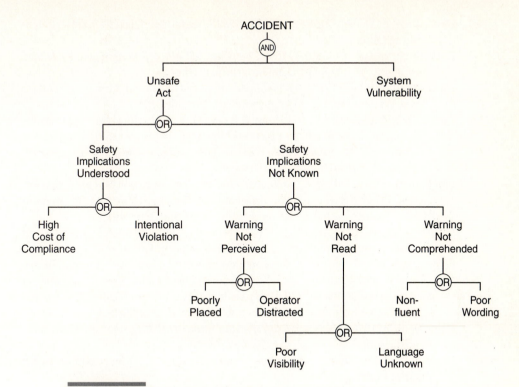

FIGURE 14.7

Fault tree analysis showing the causes of an accident. The unsafe act must be committed at a time when the system is vulnerable (thus, the AND gate). The unsafe act might be committed when its safety implications are understood but dismissed either because the cost of compliance is too high or for other intentional reasons. Alternatively the safety implications may not be known, as a result of a series of possible breakdowns in the effectiveness of warnings, as described in the text.

REFERENCES

Alexander, C.S., Kim, Y.J., Ensminger, M., and Johnson, K.E. (1990). A measure of risk taking for young adolescents: Reliability and validity assessments. *Journals of Youth and Adolescence, 19(6), 559–569.*

Bell, C.A., Stout, N.A., Bender, T.R., Conroy, C.S., Crouse, W.E., and Meyers, J.R. (1990). Fatal occupational injuries in the United States, 1980 through 1985. *JAMA, 263,* 3047–3050.

Crowe, M.P. (1986). Hardwood logging accidents and counter-measures for their reduction. *Australian Forestry, 49(1),* 44–45.

Davis, W., Grubbs, J.R., and Nelson, S.M. (1995). *Safety made easy: A checklist approach to OSHA compliance.* Rockville, MD: Government Institutes.

DeJoy, D.M. (1991). A revised model of the warning process derived from value-expectancy theory. *Proceedings of the Human Factors Society 335th Annual Meeting* (pp. 1043–1047). Santa Monica, CA: Human Factors Society.

Department of Defense (1984). *MIL-STD-882B.* Washington, DC: U.S. Government Printing Office.

Department of Labor (1990). *OSHA Compliance Manual: Recordkeeping guidelines.* Washington, DC: U.S. Government Printing Office.

Department of Labor (1993). *Occupational safety and health standards for general industry.* Washington, DC: U.S. Government Printing Office.

Dingus, T.A., Hathaway, J.A., and Hunn, B.P. (1991). A most critical warning variable: Two demonstrations of the powerful effects of cost on warning compliance. *Proceedings of the Human Factors Society 35th Annual Meeting* (pp. 1034–1038). Santa Monica, CA: Human Factors Society.

Embry, D.E. (1986). *SHERPA: A systematic human error reduction and prediction approach.* Paper presented at the International Topical Meeting on Advances in Human Factors in Nuclear Power Systems, Knoxville, Tennessee.

Fellner, D.J., and Sulzer-Azaroff, B. (1984). Increasing industrial safety practices and conditions through posted feedback. *Journal of Safety Research, 15(1),* 7–21.

Fibiger, W. (1981). Physiological cost and physical working capacity: Criterion for tree fallers. In W.H. Gladstone (ed.), *Ergonomics and the disabled person: Proceedings of the 18th Annual Conference of the Ergonomics Society of Australia and New Zealand* (pp. 223–230). Canberra: The Ergonomic Society of Australia and New Zealand.

Firenzie, R.J. (1978). *Industrial safety: Management and Technology.* New York: Kendall/Hunt.

Goetsch, D.L. (1996). *Occupational safety and health* (2nd ed.). Englewood Cliffs, NJ: Prentice Hall.

Green, A.E. (1983). *Safety systems reliability.* Chichester, UK: John Wiley.

Hammer, W. (1989). *Occupational safety management and engineering* (4th ed.). Englewood Cliffs, NJ: Prentice Hall.

Hartley, L.R., and Hassani, J.E. (1994). Stress, violations and accidents. *Applied Ergonomics, 25(4),* 221–231.

Heinrich, H.W. (1959). *Industrial accident prevention* (4th ed.). New York: McGraw-Hill.

Heinrich, H.W., Peterson, D., and Roos, N. (1980). *Industrial accident prevention* (5th ed.). New York: McGraw-Hill.

Henley, J., and Kumamoto, J. (1981). *Reliability engineering and risk assessment.* New York: Prentice Hall.

Henrich, H.W., Petersen, D., and Roos, N. (1980). *Industrial accident prevention* (5th ed.). New York: McGraw-Hill.

Holcom, M.L., Lehman, W.E.K., and Simpson, D.D. (1993). Employee accidents: Influences of personal characteristics, job characteristics, and substance use in jobs differing in accident potential. *Journal of Safety Research, 24,* 205–221.

Jessor, R., and Jessor, S.L. (1978). Theory testing in longitudinal research on marijuana use. In D.B. Kandel (ed.), *Longitudinal research on drug use: Empirical findings and methodological issues* (pp. 41–71). Washington, DC: Hemisphere.

Kalsher M.J., Wogalter, M.S., Brewster, B.M., and Spunar, M.E. (1995). Hazard level perceptions of current and proposed warning sign and label panels. *Proceedings of the Human Factors and Ergonomic Society 39th Annual Meeting* (pp. 351–355), Santa Monica, CA: Human Factors and Ergonomics Society.

Kirwan, B. (1990). Human reliability assessment. In J.R. Wilson and N. Corlett (eds.), *Evaluation of human work* (pp. 706–754). London: Taylor & Francis.

Kirwan, B. (1992a). Human error identification in human reliability assessment. Part 1: Overview of approaches. *Applied Ergonomics, 23*(5), 299–318.

Kirwan, B. (1992b). Human error identification in human reliability assessment. Part 2: Detailed comparison of techniques. *Applied Ergonomics, 23*(6), 371–381.

Kirwan, B., and Ainsworth, L.K. (1992). *A guide to task analysis.* London: Taylor & Francis.

Kohn, J.P., Friend, M.A., and Winterberger, C.A. (1996). *Fundamentals of occupational safety and health.* Rockville, MD: Government Institutes.

Lehman, W.E.K., and Simpson, D.D. (1992). Employee substance use and on-the-job behaviors. *Journal of Applied Psychology, 77*(3), 309–321.

Leonard, S.D., Hill, G.W., and Otani, H. (1990). Factors involved in risk perception. *Proceedings of the Human Factors Society 34th Annual Meeting* (pp. 1037–1041). Santa Monica, CA: Human Factors Society.

Lusk, S.L., Ronis, D.L., and Kerr, M.J. (1995). Predictors of hearing protection use among workers: Implications for training programs. *Human Factors, 37*(3), 635–640.

Lyng, S. (1990). Edgework: A social psychological analysis of voluntary risk-taking. *American Journal of Sociology, 95*(4), 851–886.

Manning, M.V. (1996). *So you're the safety director: An introduction to loss control and safety management.* Rockville, MD: Government Institutes.

Mansdorf, S.Z. (1993). *Complete manual of industrial safety.* Englewood Cliffs, NJ: Prentice Hall.

Manuele, F.A. (1993). *On the practice of safety.* New York: Van Nostrand Reinhold.

Mayer, D.L., Jones, S.F., and Laughery, K.R. (1987). Accident proneness in the industrial setting. *Proceedings of the Human Factors Society 31st Annual Meeting* (pp. 196–199). Santa Monica, CA: Human Factors Society.

McCallister, D.R. (1993). *Investigation of industrial incidents: An instructional program.* Salt Lake City, UT: Salt Lake City Business Unit.

Moran, M.M. (1996). *Construction safety handbook: A practical guide to OSHA compliance and injury prevention.* Rockville, MD: Government Institutes.

National Safety Council (1993a). *Accident facts.* Chicago, IL: National Safety Council.

National Safety Council (1993b). *Safeguarding concepts illustrated* (6th ed.). Chicago, IL: National Safety Council.

Norman, D.A. (1981). Categorization of action slips. *Psychological Review, 88*, 1–15.

Normand, J., Salyards, S.D., and Mahony, J.J. (1990). An evaluation of preemployment drug testing. *Journal of Applied Psychology, 75*, 629–639.

Petersen, D. (1984). *Human-error reduction and safety management.* New York: Aloray.

Ray, P.S., Purswell, J. L., and Bowen, D. (1993). Behavioral safety program: Creating a new corporate culture. *International Journal of Industrial Ergonomics 12*, 193–198.

Reason, J. (1987). Generic error-modelling system (GEMS): A cognitive framework for locating common human error forms. In J. Rasmussen, K. Duncan, and J. Leplat (eds.), *New technology and human error* (pp. 63–83). New York: Wiley.

Reason, J. (1990). *Human error.* Cambridge, England: Cambridge University Press.

Reason, J., and Mycielska, K. (1982). *Absent minded: The psychology of mental lapses and everyday errors.* Englewood Cliffs, NJ: Prentice Hall.

Robertson, M.M., Bowman, J.D., and Rosenberg, S.M. (1986). Evaluating employee participation programs addressing health, safety, and ergonomic issues in the

United States. *Proceedings of the Human Factors Society 30th Annual Meeting* (pp. 1111–1115). Santa Monica, CA: Human Factors Society.

Roland, H.E., and Moriarty, B. (1990). *System safety engineering and management* (2nd ed.). New York: Wiley.

Rouse, W.B. (1983). Elements of human error. In N. Moray and J.W. Senders (eds.), *Preprints of NATO Conference on human error.*

Rouse, W. B. (1990). Designing for human error: Concepts for error tolerant systems. In H.R. Booher (ed.), *Manprint: An approach to systems integration* (pp. 237–255). New York: Van Nostrand Reinhold.

Sanders, M., and Shaw, B. (1988). *Research to determine the contribution of system factors in the occurrence of underground injury accidents.* Pittsburgh, PA: Bureau of Mines.

Schacherer, C.W. (1993). Toward a general theory of risk perception. *Proceedings of the Human Factors and Ergonomics Society 37th Annual Meeting* (pp. 984–988). Santa Monica, CA: Human Factors Society.

Slappendel, C., Laird, I., Kawachi, I., Marshall, S., and Cryer, C. (1993). Factors affecting work-related injury among forestry workers: A review. *Journal of Safety Research, 24,* 19–32.

Strawbridge, J. (1986). The influence of position, highlighting, and imbedding on warning effectiveness. *Proceedings of the Human Factors Society 30th Annual Meeting* (pp. 716–720). Santa Monica, CA: Human Factors Society.

Swain, A.D., and Guttmann, H.E. (1983). *A handbook of human reliability analysis with emphasis on nuclear power plant applications.* USNRC-Nureg/CR-1278, Washington, DC.

Taggart, R.W. (1989). Results of the drug testing program at Southern Pacific Railroad. In S.W. Gust and J.M. Walsh (eds.), *Drugs in the workplace: Research and evaluation data* (NIDA Research Monograph No. 91). Washington, DC: U.S. Government Printing Office.

Wagenaar, W.A., and Groeneweg, J. (1988). Accidents at sea: Multiple causes and impossible consequences. In E. Hollnagel, G. Mancini, and D.D. Woods (eds.), *Cognitive engineering in complex dynamic worlds* (pp. 133–144). San Diego, CA: Academic Press.

Weinstein, A., Twerski, A., Piehler, H., and Donaher, W. (1978). *Products liability and the reasonably safe product.* New York: Wiley.

Wogalter, M., Allison, S., and McKenna, N. (1989). Effects of cost and social influence on warning compliance. *Human Factors, 31*(2), 133–140.

Wogalter, M.S., Desaulniers, D.R., and Brelsford, J.W. (1987). Consumer products: How are the hazards perceived. *Proceedings of the Human Factors Society 31st Annual Meeting* (pp. 615–619). Santa Monica, CA: Human Factors Society.

Wogalter, M.S., Jarrard, S.W., and Simpson, S.N. (1992). Effects of warning signal words on consumer-product hazard perceptions. *Proceedings of the Human Factors Society 36th Annual Meeting* (pp. 935–939). Santa Monica, CA: Human Factors Society.

Young, S.L., and Laughery, K.R. (1994). Components of perceived risk: A reconciliation of previous findings. *Proceedings of the Human Factors and Ergonomics Society 38th Annual Meeting* (pp. 888–892). Santa Monica, CA: Human Factors Society.

Young, S.L., Wogalter, M.S., and Brelsford, J.W. (1992). Relative contribution of likelihood and severity of injury to risk perceptions. *Proceedings of the Human Factors and Ergonomics Society 36th Annual Meeting* (pp. 1014–1018). Santa Monica, CA: Human Factors Society.

CHAPTER 15

Human– Computer Interaction

Ray Cox was a 33-year-old man who was visiting the East Texas Cancer Center for radiation treatment of a tumor in his shoulder. He had been in several times before and found that the sessions were pretty short and painless. He laid chest-side down on the metal table. The technician rotated the table to the proper position and went down the hall to the control room. She entered commands into a computer keyboard for the PDP-11 that controlled the radiotherapy accelerator. There was a videocamera in the treatment room with a television screen in the control room, but the monitor was not plugged in. The intercom was inoperative. However, Mary Beth viewed this as normal; she had used the controls for the radiation therapy dozens of times and it was pretty simple.

The Therac-25 radiation therapy machine had two different modes of operation, a high-power x-ray mode using 25 million electron volt capacity, and a relatively low-power "electron beam" mode that could deliver about 200 rads to a small spot in the body for cancer treatment. Ray Cox was to have treatment using the electron beam mode. Mary Beth pressed the "x" key (which was for the high-power x-ray mode) and then realized that she had meant to enter "e" for the "electron beam" mode. She quickly pressed the "up" arrow key to select the edit function. She then pressed the "e" key. The screen indicated that she was in the "electron beam" mode. She pressed the return key to move the cursor to the bottom of the screen. All actions occurred within 8 seconds. When she pressed the "b" to fire the electron beam, Ray Cox felt an incredible pain, as he received 25 million volts in his shoulder. In the control room, the computer screen displayed the message "Malfunction 54." Mary Beth reset the machine and pressed "b." Screaming in pain, Ray Cox received a second high-powered proton beam. He died 4 months later of massive radiation poisoning. It turned out that similar accidents had happened at other treatment centers because of a flaw in the software. When the edit

451

function was used very quickly to change the "x-ray" mode to "electron beam" mode the machine displayed the correct mode but incorrectly delivered a proton beam of 25,000 rads with 25 million electron volts. (A true story adapted from S. Casey, Set phasers on stun and other true tales of design, technology, and human error, *1993).*

There is now little doubt that computers are having a profound impact on all aspects of life, whether at work or in the home environment. We have already seen the computer revolutionize the way people perform office tasks such as writing, communicating with co-workers, analyzing data, keeping databases, and searching for documents. Computers are increasingly being used to control manufacturing processes, medical devices, and a variety of other industrial equipment. Computers are becoming so small that they can be implanted in the human body to sense and transmit vital body statistics for medical monitoring. Because the application of computers is spreading so rapidly, we must assume that much, if not most, of human factors work in the future will deal with the design of complex computer software and hardware.

Human factors work related to computers can roughly be divided into topics related to hardware design and topics related to the design of the software interface. Software interface refers to the information provided by the computer that we see or hear and the control mechanisms for inputting information to the computer. Currently, for most computers, this means the screen display, keyboard, and mouse.

On the hardware side, computer workstations should be designed to maximize task performance and minimize ergonomic problems or hazards, such as cumulative trauma disorders. Chapter 10 discussed some of the more well-known methods for design of computer workstations and specific hardware components such as keyboards or video display terminals. Chapter 9 discussed various methods for system control with common input devices for computers.

Good software interface design must take into account the cognitive and perceptual abilities of humans, as outlined in Chapters 4, 5, and 6. Interface design also requires the application of display principles as described in Chapter 8. And finally, the human-computer interaction process will affect and/or be affected by other factors such as fatigue, mental workload, stress, and anxiety. Clearly, most of the material in this text is relevant to the design of the software interface to one extent or another. While we can successfully apply general human factors principles and guidelines to interface design, there is also a solid line of research and methodology that is unique to human-computer interaction (HCI). A variety of books and journals are written exclusively on this topic (e.g., *Human-Computer Interaction* and *International Journal of Human-Computer Interaction*), and annual meetings result in proceedings reflecting the cutting-edge views and work, such as *Computer-Human Interaction (CHI)*. Given the expanding role of human-computer interaction in the field of human factors, it is appropriate to include a chapter that presents some of the basic concepts and principles from the subspecialty of HCI.

SOFTWARE USABILITY

Computers are relatively new tools; because they change rapidly and tend to be complex, they are high on most peoples' list of "things that are difficult to use." The fact that computer software is sometimes poorly designed and therefore difficult to use causes a variety of negative consequences. First, user performance suffers; researchers have found the magnitude of errors to be as high as 46 percent for commands, tasks, and transactions in some applications (Galitz, 1993). Other consequences follow, such as confusion, panic, boredom, frustration, incomplete use of the system, system abandonment altogether, modification of the task, compensatory actions, and misuse of the system (Galitz, 1993). In studying office software, Hiltz (1984) found a system abandonment rate of 40 percent, although this is improving now with more recent types of interface design.

We stated earlier that human factors designers strive to maximize the ease, efficiency, and safety of products and environments. These goals all apply to software interface design. As Shneiderman (1992) notes, the well-designed software interface can have a sizable impact on learning time, performance speed, error rates, and user satisfaction. In industry, this often translates into large monetary savings, and in consumer products these factors can mean success or failure. Finally, when the software controls life-critical systems such as air traffic control systems, power utilities, and medical instruments (such as a device for delivering x-rays), the usability of the software can quickly and easily become a matter of life and death. Usability is thus one of the greatest concerns for those working on software interface design.

Usability Criteria

A number of researchers have specified factors that define or at least suggest high system usability. One well-known set of factors or criteria has been suggested by Nielson (1993); learnability, efficiency, memorability, low error rate, and user satisfaction. Although these criteria were developed to evaluate software interfaces, note that they can be applied to any system with controls and displays (e.g., our camera controls and displays described in Chapter 6).

Learnability refers to the speed with which novice users can learn to use a system. Some complex systems (such as nuclear power plants) might typically take some time to learn, but most users in the everyday world want systems that are "walk up and use" to some extent from the beginning. For many people, learnability is practically synonymous with usability.

Efficiency refers to the degree to which the system supports user performance after they have become familiar with it. A system that has poor usability will result in slow or inefficient task performance. Efficiency is normally measured by having experienced users perform a variety of tasks, and evaluating whether the tasks are successfully carried out within a reasonable period of time and with a minimal number of steps (see below).

Memorability is important because many products, especially computer software, are used by casual users. A *casual user* is someone who uses a product intermittently with relative long periods of time between uses. The camera for nonprofessionals is a good example of product design for the casual user. It is important that once the person learns how to use the system, the acquired knowledge will stay with them for a long time. It is relatively easy to measure memorability. Users are asked to use the product/system for a variety of tasks. They are then brought back after a sufficient length of time (usually this should be at least several weeks) and are then tested on the extent to which they remember things such as: What do the various displays mean? How do they accomplish major goals? and so on.

Errors are frequently the signpost of poor usability. Consider the example of the push-bar door. People make errors by pushing on the wrong side. Measuring errors in system use is probably the most common method for measuring usability. Representative groups of users are asked to perform a variety of tasks with the system or prototype. The number and type of errors are recorded. These are usually expressed as percentages of the total number of times the task is performed. Implications for design changes are then identified.

We should point out that while it seems, on the surface, quite clear how to measure errors, it is sometimes not that straightforward. For example, if we are measuring the performance of an F-16 pilot using a new cockpit display, what constitutes an error? If he chooses one particular mode of operation for the radar that is not "ideal," is that an error, or is he just trying a new way of doing things? If he switches back to a "better" mode almost immediately, did he commit an error? Design teams must be careful in defining errors, and the user on the design team is often very helpful in this process.

Finally, *satisfaction* is a subjective quality that is also important, especially from a marketing point of view. The most common method for determining whether users are satisfied with the product/system is to simply ask them. This can be done through open-ended questions (i.e., How well did you like the product?) or more quantitatively oriented questions, such as rating scales.

The five usability criteria should be used both as design goals and as final evaluative criteria with which to judge the success of the interface. While designers should evaluate all five criteria, it is important to note that sometimes certain criteria will have either greater or lower priority than others depending on the characteristics of users and the task. This idea is briefly examined in the next section.

Task and User Characteristics

Software varies from performing very simple functions such as basic arithmetic to extremely complex functions such as control of functions in a chemical processing plant. The *functionality* of a system generally refers to the number, complexity, or both of the things the computer system can do. Software designers usually strive to build in as much system functionality as is feasible. However, as a rule of thumb, the greater the functionality, the more difficult it is to design the interface to be "usable" or "user-friendly." If the functions are complex, the interface will have numerous displays, display formats, control systems, and many levels or groups of interface functions. The goal of the human factors specialist is to help create a system that has both high functionality and high usability, a system that is actually used to its potential. Imagine designing an interface to the information superhighway in such a way that any literate person could sit down and successfully use the interface to search for whatever item they happen to need at the moment.

Complex software requires a complex interface with many functions. This will, almost by definition, mean some learning time for the user. The reality is that each designer must strive to find the correct balance between making the system usable and expecting the user to expend some effort on learning to use the software. Three of the considerations central to this balancing act between functionality and ease of use are: (1) the frequency of task performance using the particular software, (2) mandatory versus discretionary use, and (3) the knowledge level of the user.

Some computer-based tasks, such as word processing, might be done by a user 8 hours a day, every day. Other tasks, such as making a will, might be done only once or twice in a lifetime. *Frequency of use* has important implications for the software interface design for several reasons. For example, people who will be using a software system frequently are more willing to invest initial time in learning; therefore, performance and functionality can take precedence (to some degree) over initial ease of learning (Mayhew, 1992). In addition, users who perform tasks frequently will have less trouble remembering interactive methods such as commands from one use to the next. This means that designers are able to place efficiency of operation over memorability (Mayhew, 1992).

There is also a difference between mandatory use of software and *discretionary* use, where people use a system because they want to, not because they are required to. Discretionary users are people who use a particular software program somewhat frequently but are not broadly knowledgeable as in the case of an expert. Santhanam and Wiedenbeck (1993) describe discretionary users as having expertlike characteristics on a small number of routine tasks, but they may know little regarding anything beyond those tasks. Mayhew (1992) suggests that for high frequency of use or mandatory use, designers should emphasize ease of use. However, for low or intermittent frequency of use or for discretionary users, ease of learning and remembering should have priority over ease of use.

Finally, users may range from *novice,* or users who have little experience with the system, to *expert* users, who have accumulated a great deal of system knowledge. Shneiderman (1992) describes three common classes of users:

Novice users: People who know the task but have little or no knowledge of the system.
Knowledgeable intermittent users: People who know the task but because of infrequent use may have difficulty remembering the syntactic knowledge of how to carry out their goals.
Expert frequent users: Users who have deep knowledge of tasks and related goals, and the actions required to accomplish the goals.

Design of software for novice users tends to focus on ease of learning and low reliance on memory. Vocabulary is highly restricted, tasks are easy to carry out, and error messages are constructive and specific. Sometimes systems that are built for first-time users, and that are extremely easy to use, are termed "walk up and use" systems. Currently, the technologies predominantly being used for novice users rely heavily on the use of icons, menus, short written instructions, and a *graphical user interface* (GUI). Users select items from menus or groups of icons rather than typing in commands, thus reducing the load on long-term memory or the need to look things up. Input commands are often achieved by manipulating objects on the screen with a mouse. For example, a portion of text can be marked, and then "moved" on the screen from one section of the document to another. In addition to reducing memory load, this makes the task easier because it maps onto how the task might be done without a computer (e.g., cut a section out and move it to a different section of the document).

Reducing the load on memory is especially critical for *intermittent* users, whether they are expert or not. Such users may have a good idea of how the software works but be unable to recall the specific actions necessary to complete a task. However, typing in commands is often preferred by experts, especially if they are frequent users, giving them a feeling of control and quick performance (Shneiderman, 1992). This point demonstrates the difficulty of designing one software interface to meet the needs of multiple types of users. To deal with this problem, a software interface might have features that accommodate several types of user, as in the case of software that has input *either* from clicking on buttons *or* from typed-command entry. However, research has shown that once people use a graphical user interface such as menus, even when they become experienced, they will not be prone to switching to the more efficient command entry format. For this reason, adaptive interfaces are often desirable, automatically monitoring performance and prompting the user to switch entry styles as particular tasks become familiar (e.g., Gong & Salvendy, 1994).

Initial ease of learning and memorability are often less important for systems that will be primarily used by *experts.* For a nuclear power control panel, the designer will strive to develop an interface that provides information and input mechanisms that map onto the task. If the task is complex, then learning the software interface will probably take a period of time. In addition, for life-critical systems or hazardous equipment, designers may perceive that error rates are by far the most important of the five criteria listed above; that is, longer training periods are acceptable but should result in fast, efficient, and error-free performance. However, while designers may occasionally lower the priority for ease of learning, it is still generally the case that software interface design strives to maximize all five of the usability criteria listed above.

THEORIES, MODELS, AND METAPHORS

Contemporary researchers strive to provide guidance to software designers so that design can be something more than sheer intuition. This guidance for designers falls into several categories; high-level theories and models, basic principles and guidelines, and methods for development and testing. In this section, we review a few of the more commonly used theories and models. Such theories or models provide a general framework for designers to conceptualize their problem and discuss issues, using a language that is application independent. We will also show how the concepts of mental models and metaphors are used to enhance software design.

Theoretical Models of Human-Computer Interaction

If we can develop a theory of how people interact with computers, then we can design software that facilitates that interaction. Several such theories have been suggested, although all are still relatively abstract. While these theories do not provide specific guidelines for interface design, they do help designers develop an overall idea or mental model of the user, including a description of the kinds of cognitive activity taking place during software use.

Seven Stages of Action.   One model that has been useful in guiding user-oriented interface design is Norman's (1986) *seven stages of action* model. This model suggests that no matter what the task, users will progress through a series of activities that can be divided roughly into seven steps or stages:

1. Establish the goal

CARRY OUT AN ACTION BY:
2. Forming the intention
3. Specifying the action sequence
4. Executing the action

ASSESS THE EFFECTS OF THE ACTION BY:
5. Perceiving the system state
6. Interpreting the state
7. Evaluating the system state with respect to the goals and intentions

The user first establishes a psychological goal, such as sending an e-mail to a friend. If the person feels that this goal is something that he or she might be able to accomplish using the system, the user forms an intention to carry out actions required to accomplish the goal. Next the user identifies the action sequence necessary to carry out the goal. It is at this point that a user may have the first difficulties. Users must translate their psychological goals and intentions into the desired system events and states and then determine what input actions or physical manipulations are required. The discrepancy between psychological variables and system variables and states may be difficult to bridge. Even if the user successfully identifies needed input actions, the input device may make them difficult to carry out physically. For example, the "hot" portion of a small square to be clicked using a mouse might be so small that it is difficult to be accurate. Norman notes that the entire sequence must move the user over the "gulf of execution" (see Fig. 15.1). A well-designed interface makes that translation easy or apparent to the user, allowing him or her to bridge the gulf. A poorly designed interface will result in the user not having adequate knowledge and/or the physical ability to make the translation and therefore be unsuccessful in task performance.

Once the actions have been executed, users must compare the system events and states with the original goals and intentions. This means perceiving system

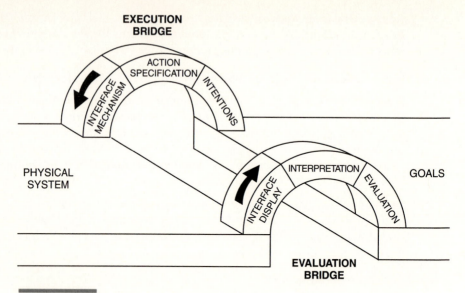

EXECUTION BRIDGE

ACTION SPECIFICATION

INTERFACE MECHANISM

INTENTIONS

PHYSICAL SYSTEM

INTERFACE DISPLAY

INTERPRETATION

EVALUATION

GOALS

EVALUATION BRIDGE

FIGURE 15.1

Bridging the gulf of execution and gulf of evaluation. (*Source:* Norman, D., 1986. Cognitive engineering. In D.A. Norman and S.W. Draper (eds.), *User-Centered System Design.* Hillsdale, NJ: Lawrence Erlbaum. Copyright © 1986. Reprinted by permission of Lawrence Erlbaum Associates.)

display components, interpreting their meaning with respect to system events and current state, and comparing this interpretation with the goals. The process moves the user over the "gulf of evaluation." If the system displays have been designed well, it will be relatively easy for the user to identify the system events and states and compare them with original goals. As a simple example, consider a user who is trying to write a friend via e-mail. This user has composed a letter and is now ready to send it. The goal is to "send letter," and the user clicks on the button marked "send." Note this is a relatively straightforward mapping allowing easy translation of goal into action. However, after the button is pressed, the button comes up and the screen looks like it did before the user clicked on it. This makes evaluation difficult because the user does not know what system events occurred (i.e., did the letter get sent?). Viewed in terms of this model, system design will support the user by making two things clear—what actions are needed to carry out user goals, and what events and states resulted from user input.

GOMS.   A similar model that centers around goals and actions but is more specific is the *goals, operators, methods, and selection rules* (GOMS) model developed by Card, Moran, and Newell (1983) and extended by Kieras (1988a). This model assumes that users formulate goals (such as write e-mail) and subgoals (make blank page to write on) that they achieve by way of methods and selection rules. A method is a sequence of steps that are perceptual, cognitive, or motor operators. Since there are often several methods that can be used to accomplish a goal or subgoal, selection rules must be postulated to identify the conditions under which a user will use one method or another. As an example, consider the goal of printing a document using a typical Windows type of word-processing system. The person could use the *method* of:

1. Using the mouse to move the cursor over the button with the printer symbol
2. Quickly depressing and releasing the left-upper area of the mouse one time.

Or alternatively, the user could use the *method* of:

1. Using the mouse to move the cursor over the word *File* at the top of the screen
2. Quickly depressing and releasing the left-upper area of the button
3. Using the mouse to move the cursor down to the word *Print*
4. Quickly depressing and releasing the left-upper area of the button, and so forth.

There are also other methods for printing the document, such as using keyboard input instead of the mouse. Selection rules would specify the conditions under which the user would choose each of the methods. Note that different users might have varying selection rules, and these might be different from what the software designers would consider to be the "best" selection rules.

The GOMS model has been useful to designers in a number of ways. Probably the most common is use of the GOMS language for describing software functionality and interface characteristics (e.g., Irving, Polson, & Irving, 1994). This supports a systematic analysis of potential usability problems. Designers generally do the following: (1) explicitly identify and list users' goals and subgoals; (2) identify all of the alternative methods (sequences of operators) that could be used for achieving each goal/subgoal; and (3) write selection rules, specifying the conditions under which each method should be used. Evaluation of the GOMS structure reveals problems such as: there are too many methods for accomplishing a particular goal; similar goals are supported by inconsistent methods; and there are methods that rely too heavily on long-term memory (e.g., see Gong & Kieras, 1994). When there are multiple methods to accomplish one goal, designers may realize that one method is so clearly preferable that there will be no conditions under which a person would choose the alternative. This alternative can then be altered or dropped altogether. Designers may also realize that users will not ever notice that an alternative method exists or be able to infer the correct selection rules to discriminate between different methods. One recent solution to both of these problems is the idea of "helpful hints." For example, a word-processing program might open with a different Helpful Hint box each day, suggesting new and easier methods for accomplishing a task or conditions under which the person might choose one method over another.

Other researchers have developed computer models of software systems using the GOMS notation. For example, Kieras and Polson (1985) used production rules to specify the conditions and actions in an interactive text editor. They found that the number and complexity of production rules predicted actual user performance with respect to both learning time and performance time. Thus, the GOMS model provides a language and structure for modeling of interactive software. This allows designers to make modifications to the software interface and predict the impact of such changes on performance time. Finally, some experts have studied the weaknesses of on-line help systems and developed design principles based on the use of specific GOMS elements for presenting information to users (Elkerton, 1988).

Mental Models and Metaphors

In designing a system, the analyst begins with a general conceptual model of how the software will look and act. A *conceptual model* is "the general conceptual framework through which the functionality is presented" (Mayhew, 1992). Once a conceptual model is identified, the designer begins to translate the model into interactive strategies at a rather general or semantic level. Finally, the exact input actions and display components are designed using a detailed syntax (Phillips et al., 1988; Shneiderman, 1992). Often the success of a system hinges on the quality of the original conceptual model. For example, the success of the "cut-and-paste" feature in many programs is due to the simple but functional conceptual model of this component (cut and paste) and the fact that required computer input allows a person to continue thinking of the task in relatively the same way as performance with real paper.

Identifying a good conceptual model for a new software system often hinges on understanding and applying the concept of a *mental model*. Because this is a critical concept in design, we will review some basic characteristics and then look at how mental models are relevant to software interface design. Recall from Chapters 6 and 7 that mental models are internal psychological representations of a person's conceptualization and understanding of a system (Gentner & Stevens, 1983; Kieras, 1988b; Mayhew, 1992). A mental model is a dynamic model of system components, how the system works, how components are related, what the internal processes are, and how they affect the components (Carroll & Olson, 1988). Many researchers also include the cognitive processes that allow the model to be "run" in order to derive predictions of future system behavior (Kieras, 1988b). For example, we have a mental model of our television set, what the buttons are, how it works, what will happen if we do certain actions, and so on. This mental representation provides an internal system of understanding that we can use to generate alternative actions or problem solutions by running the model to see what would happen under various "what if" scenarios. Research has demonstrated that, to varying degrees, peoples' mental models are incomplete, erroneous, unstable, and fragmented (e.g., Norman, 1987; Gordon & Gill 1989; Masson, Hill, & Conner 1988; Rosson, 1983). In addition, people may have several mental models of a single system (Rouse & Morris, 1986; Wilson & Rutherford, 1989) where each of the models represents different facets of the system.

On the one hand, when we can visually *look* at an entire system and see its components working together, such as in a bicycle, we can use this visual information to develop our internal representation or mental model. Designers frequently refer to such a system as being *transparent*. In general, when systems are transparent, our mental model of the system is more complete and accurate than when the system is not transparent (as in a car engine or refrigerator cooling system). When we perform actions on the system, we can see the effects or string of effects so that our mental model correctly represents components and their causal relationships. On the other hand, we must sometimes develop a mental model of a system that has invisible or hidden components, for example, when we learn to use a VCR. In such a case, we form a mental model based on *inferences* about system parts and functions. We can only hypothesize some of the likely relationships between the invisible parts and processes of the system and the visible parts and processes (Casner & Lewis, 1987; Mayhew, 1992). Novice users typically have very incomplete, fragmented, and erroneous mental models of a system. In fact, with some systems, such as a programmable VCR, even long-time users may have a very incomplete or inaccurate mental model of the system.

As Mayhew (1992) notes, "Users always have mental models and will always develop and modify them, regardless of the particular design of a system." Given that users will always have a mental model of the software system they are using, the goal of designers should be to facilitate the user developing an *effective* mental model. An effective mental model is one that is relatively complete, accurate, and supports the required tasks and subtasks. It allows the user to predict correctly the results of various actions or system inputs. The development of effective mental models can be facilitated by system designers. This is done by making the conceptual model of the system explicit or "transparent." Mayhew (1992) suggests this can be done in a number of ways, including:

> *Making invisible parts and processes visible to the user.* For example, clicking on an icon that depicts a file and dragging it to a trash can makes an invisible action (getting rid of a file) visible to the user.
>
> *Providing feedback.* When an input command is given, the system can report to the user what is happening (e.g., loading application, opening file, searching, etc.).
>
> *Building in consistency.* People are used to organizing their knowledge according to patterns and rules. If a small number of patterns or rules are built into the interface, it will convey a simple yet powerful conceptual model of the system.
>
> *Presenting functionality through a familiar metaphor.* Designers can make the interface look and act similar to a system with which the user is familiar. This approach uses a *metaphor* from the manual real world with which the user is supposedly familiar.

Metaphor is the process of using objects and events in a software system that are taken from a noncomputer domain (Wozny, 1989). The use of a metaphor provides knowledge about what actions are possible, how to accomplish tasks, and so forth. Many of the GUI interfaces currently in use are strongly based on well-known metaphors. As examples, we see "desktop" metaphors where the user manipulates files, calendars, clocks, and so on, publishing metaphors with actions such as "cut and paste" and spreadsheet metaphors with matrix-structured data (Carroll, Mack, & Kellogg, 1988). Even the use of a mouse to move objects around in physical space is loosely based on the real-world metaphor of "putting things" in different physical places. Another example of a powerful metaphor is that of "rooms." The Internet has different types of rooms, including "chat rooms" where people can "go" to "talk." Obviously, none of these actions are literal, but the use of the concepts provides some immediate understanding of the system. People then only need to refine their mental model or add a few specific rules.

Sometimes designers identify several metaphors that would work for a particular application. For example, Perkins and Rollert (1994) discuss a case study where the prototype interface for an on-line service being developed by Ziff-Davis Interactive went from a relatively unsuccessful "channel changer" metaphor to a more conventional "file folder" metaphor and back again to a much improved version of the channel changer metaphor. Sometimes the success of a metaphor depends as much on *how* the metaphor is carried out as it does on the identity of the metaphor per se. Finally, use of a metaphor can have adverse consequences as well as positive benefits (Halasz & Moran, 1982; Mayhew, 1992). For example, overreliance on a physical metaphor can cause users to overlook powerful capabilities available in the computer because they simply do not exist in the manual world. In addition, there are always differences between the metaphorical world and the software system. If these differences are not made explicit, they can cause errors or gaps in users' mental models of the software system (Halasz & Moran, 1982). For example, researchers demonstrated that anywhere between 20 percent and 60 percent of novice errors on a computer keyboard could be attributed to differences between the typewriter metaphor and actual editor functions (Douglas & Moran, 1983; Alwood, 1986).

In summary, users will invariably develop a mental model of the software system. Designers must try to make the conceptual model of the system as explicit as possible, and this is sometimes aided by the use of real-world metaphors. Mayhew (1992) provides thirteen clear and explicit guidelines for facilitating "the development by users of useful, efficient mental models." Although Mayhew believes that it is possible to present a conceptual model without exploiting existing mental models, Carroll et al. (1988) state that people will always draw some type of comparison with an existing metaphor. This idea is supported by the strong notion in cognitive psychology that understanding of something occurs by applying existing prior knowledge.

DESIGN PRINCIPLES AND GUIDELINES

Theoretical models, such as those described above, are helpful tools for generating the conceptual design or *semantic* level of the software system. These models are relatively widely used because there really are no specific guidelines for how to design an effective software system at the conceptual stage. However, when designers are ready to translate the conceptual model into the *syntactic* components, which are the actual interface elements, there are a large number of design principles and guidelines available to enhance the effectiveness and usability of software interfaces (e.g., Mayhew, 1992; Nielson, 1993; Shneiderman, 1992; Smith & Mosier, 1986; Willeges, Willeges, & Elkerton, 1987). Several computer-based tools have been developed to provide access to these guidelines (e.g., Iannella, 1995).

Some guidelines concern the content and formatting of a single screen, some relate to the use of color or other graphical elements, and some provide direction for the interactive or "dialog" elements of the interface. All share the goal of optimizing usability in one way or another. Several good resources are now available for readers who will be involved in the design of software interfaces, including the Macintosh Human Interface Guidelines, 1992; the Unix OSF/Motif styleguide; Mayhew, 1992; Nielson, 1993, 1994a; Shneiderman, 1992; and Smith and Mosier, 1986.

Basic Screen Design

Most interaction with computers at this point in time consists of using various *manual* input methods (as opposed to voice or other means) and viewing text or graphic displays on a monitor. Although there is a great deal of dynamic interaction, designers still must focus heavily on the components and arrangement of *static* screen design, that is, what each screen looks like as a display panel (Galitz, 1985). Most current screen layout and design focuses on two types of elements, output displays (information given by computer) and input displays (buttons, slider switches, or other input mechanisms that may be displayed directly on the screen). For information related to output displays, see Chapter 8 of this text.

Guidelines for basic screen design have also been developed specifically within the field of HCI. For example, Mayhew (1992) divides screen layout and design principles into five categories: general layout, text, numbers, coding techniques, and color. By reviewing research and published applications, she identified a number of design principles relevant to each of these categories. The principles are summarized in Table 15.1.

These principles are reiterated or expanded by software companies such as Microsoft, SunSoft, and Bellcore. For example, while novice designers tend to overuse color, most professional designers suggest that, because of factors such as the prevalence of color-blindness, one should always design the interface program in achromatic black and white (e.g., Mayhew, 1992; Nielson, 1993; Shneiderman, 1992). Nielson (1993) also recommends using light gray or light colors for background. Color should then be used conservatively and only as redundant coding. The coding principles provided in Table 15.1 are minimal, and readers are referred back to relevant chapters of this text for more in-depth consideration of coding principles. While Table 15.1 does not focus specifically on text layout, a number of researchers and designers have given more detailed rules and guidelines (e.g., see Galitz, 1985, 1993; Tullis, 1988).

Principles to Increase Usability

Usability means that a system is easy to learn, easy to use, efficient, causes few errors, and allows error recovery. What characteristics would lead to increased usability? Based on Norman's (1986) view (see Fig. 15.1), we could say that the interface should have the following characteristics:

> At any given time, users should understand what is being presented, what they are required to do or have the option of doing, what they must do to accomplish their current goal, what would happen if they chose a particular option, and what the system is currently doing (e.g., saving a file), if anything.

Many sets of usability guidelines have been published in an effort to help designers accomplish these general goals (e.g., Mayhew, 1992; Smith & Mosier, 1986).

TABLE 15.1 Screen Layout Design Principles and Guidelines

General Layout

Include *only* information essential to the task.

Include *all* information essential to the task.

Start in the upper-left corner.

Design formatting standards and follow them consistently in all screens within a system. Group items logically.

Provide symmetry and balance through the use of adequate white space.

Avoid heavy use of all-uppercase letters.

Distinguish captions and fields.

Text

Messages should be brief and concise.

Text or messages should be simple, specific, and comprehensible or clear.

Design the level of detail according to users' knowledge and experience.

Express messages in the affirmative.

Messages should be constructive, not critical.

Messages should imply that the user is in control.

When messages imply a necessary action, use words in the message that are consistent with that action (e.g., Use "Put landing gear down," not "Landing gear is not down.")

Place instructional prompts when and where they will be needed.

Phrase prompts in the active voice.

Avoid negatives.

Order prompts chronologically.

Format prompts using white space, justification, and visual cues for easy scanning.

Use consistent terminology.

Numbers

Right justify integers.

Decimal-align real numbers.

Avoid leading zeros when they are unnecessary and nonstandard.

Break up long numbers into groups of three to four digits. Use standard separators when they apply; otherwise use spaces.

Coding Techniques

Use attention-getting techniques appropriately. For example, use blinking, bold, reverse video, and underlining sparingly.

Limit size coding to five or less sizes.

Use two to four different character types (fonts, etc.) for coding.

Use shapes to convey certain types of information, such as a triangle for warning.

Use borders to help group items together.

Color

Use color sparingly. Design the interface in monochrome first.

Use color to draw attention, communicate organization, and indicate status.

Use color to support search tasks, and as task-related coding.

Don't use color without some other redundant cue (for example when using color to convey an error message, also present the message in an error message box).

TABLE 15.1 (continued)

Use colors consistently, with each color always used for the same purpose and consistent
   with the job and culture.

Limit color coding to eight colors (four or less is preferable).

Avoid using saturated blues for text or other small, thin line symbols.

Choose color combinations carefully. ISO (1988) standards suggest color images on an
   achromatic background or achromatic images on a color background.

Source: Mayhew, D. J., 1992. *Principles and guidelines in software user interface design.* Englewood Cliffs,
NJ: Prentice Hall. Adapted by permission of Prentice-Hall, Inc., Upper Saddle River, NJ.

Sometimes the guidelines are written to be used during the design process, and
other times they are written as *usability heuristics.* Usability heuristics are a set of
guidelines to be used during *heuristic evaluation,* a process of evaluating the early
interface design with respect to a fairly broad set criteria (Nielson, 1994b; Nielson
& Molich, 1990). In general, the same types of guidelines that are used for design
can also be used for heuristic evaluation (Nielson, 1994a).

   Nielson (1994a) recognized that some usability guidelines might be more
predictive of common user difficulties than others. In order to assess this possibility, he conducted a study evaluating how well each of 101 different usability
heuristics explained usability problems in a sample of eleven projects. Besides
generating the predictive ability of each individual heuristic, Nielson performed
a factor analysis and successfully identified a small number of usability factors that
"structured" or clustered the individual heuristics and that accounted for most of
the usability problems. Table 15.2 shows the general usability principles identified
by Nielson (1994a), with some of the individual usability heuristics that formed
the basis of the factor analysis. These usability principles provide direction to a design team developing software, and can also be used as the basis for simple usability checklists after prototypes have been developed.

   The first principle, matching the system to the real world, should sound familiar to readers. This is the idea that the software interface should use concepts,
ideas, and metaphors that are well known to the user, and map naturally onto the
user's tasks and mental goals. Familiar objects, characteristics, and actions cannot
be used unless the designer has a sound knowledge of what these things are in the
user's existing world. Such information is gained through performing a task analysis, as discussed in Chapter 3. This is not to say that the interface should only reflect the user's task *as the user currently performs it.* Computers can provide new
and powerful tools for task performance that move beyond previous methods
(Gentner & Grudin, 1990; Nielson, 1994c). The challenge is to map the new interface onto general tasks required of the user, while still creating new computer-
based tools to support performing the tasks more effectively and efficiently.

   The second principle is to make the interface consistent, both internally and
with respect to any existing standards. *Internal consistency* means that design elements are repeated in a consistent manner throughout the interface: The same type
of information is located in the same place on different screens, the same actions
always accomplish the same task, and so forth (Nielson, 1989). An application

TABLE 15.2 User Principles Based on Heuristics

Match between system and real world

Speak the user's language.

Use familiar conceptual models and/or metaphors.

Follow real-world conventions.

Input cues map onto user's goals.

Consistency and standards

Express the same thing the same way throughout the interface.

Use color coding uniformly.

Use a uniform input syntax (e.g., require the same actions to perform the same functions).

Show similar information at the same place on each screen.

Functions should be logically grouped and consistent from screen to screen.

Conform to platform interface conventions.

Visibility of system status

Keep user informed about what goes on (status information).

Show that input has been received.

Features change as user carries out task.

Provide feedback for all actions.

Indicate progress in task performance.

Make feedback timely and accurate.

Use direct manipulation: visible objects, visible results.

User control and freedom

Forgiveness: Obvious way to undo and redo actions.

Clearly marked exits.

Ability to reorder to cancel tasks.

Allow user to initiate/control actions.

Avoid modes when possible.

Error prevention, recognition, and recovery

Prevent errors from occurring in the first place.

Help users recognize, diagnose, and recover from errors.

Use clear, explicit error messages.

Memory

Use see-and-point instead of remember-and-type.

Make the repertoire of available actions salient.

All user needs should be available through the GUI.

Provide lists of choices and picking from lists.

Direct manipulation: Visible objects, visible choices.

Evoke goals in the user.

Flexibility and efficiency of use

Provide shortcuts and accelerators.

User tailorable to speed up frequent actions.

System should be efficient to use (Also, ability to initiate, reorder, or cancel tasks).

TABLE 15.2 (continued)

Simplicity and aesthetic integrity

Things should look good with a simple graphic design.

Use simple and natural dialog; eliminate extraneous words or graphics.

Avoid clutter.

All information should appear in a natural and logical order.

Source: Nielson, J. *Enhancing the explanatory power of visability heuristics.* Chi '94 Proceedings. New York: Association for Computing Machinery.

should also be consistent with any platform standards on which it will run. For example, a Windows application must be designed to be consistent with standardized Windows icons, groupings, colors, dialog methods, and so on. This consistency acts like a mental model—the user's mental model of "Windows" allows the user to interact with the new application in an easier and quicker fashion than if the application's interface components were entirely new.

The third principle, visibility of system status, should also sound familiar. The goal is to support the user's development of an explicit model of the system—making its functioning transparent. Features important in this category are: showing that input has been received, showing what the system is doing, and indicating progress in task performance. Sometimes this can be accomplished fairly easily with the right metaphor. For example, showing the cursor dragging a file from one file folder to another provides feedback regarding what the user/system is doing. However, showing the cursor dragging a short dotted line from one file folder to another is making system functioning slightly less visible.

The principle of *user control and freedom* centers around the idea that users need to be able to move freely around in an interface. They need to be able to undo actions that may have been incorrect, get out of somewhere they accidentally "entered," cancel tasks midpoint, go to a different point in their task hierarchy, put away a subtask momentarily, and so forth. Exits can be provided in the form of "undo" commands that put the user back to the previous system state (Abowd & Dix, 1992; Nielson, 1993). The interface should provide alternative ways of navigating through screens and information and alternative paths for accomplishing tasks.

This brings us to a closely related category, errors and error recovery. It is a basic fact of life that computer users will make errors, even minor ones such as hitting the wrong key. Software should be designed first to minimize user error. The next best thing is to minimize the negative consequences of errors or to help users recover from their errors (Nielson, 1993). Such *error tolerant* systems rely on a number of methods. First, systems can provide "undo" facilities as discussed previously. Second, the system can monitor inputs (such as "delete file") and verify that the user actually meant it. Third, a clear and precise error message can be provided, prompting the user to (1) recognize that he or she has made an error, (2) successfully diagnose the nature of the error, and (3) determine what must be done to correct the error. Shneiderman (1992) suggests that error messages should have the following characteristics:

- They should be clearly worded and avoid obscure codes.
- They should be precise and specific rather than vague or general.
- They should constructively help the user solve the problem.
- They should be polite and not intimidate the user (e.g., "ILLEGAL USER ACTION").

The accident described in the beginning of this chapter occurred because: (1) the software system had a bug that went undetected, (2) there was not good error prevention, and (3) there was not good error recognition and recovery. As an example, when the operator saw the term "Malfunction 54," she assumed the system had failed to deliver the electron beam, so she reset the machine and tried again.

As we have seen in earlier chapters, human memory is not particularly reliable. Working memory cannot accommodate much information, and long-term memory often fails to yield information, especially if it is in the form of small and relatively meaningless chunks of information. For novice, infrequent, or casual users, a see-and-point type of input will be much easier than a remember-and-type kind of input (such as command lines). This is why so many current software products are based on a GUI environment. Sometimes even having visible icons as buttons to click may not be enough. For example, recent Windows applications have the added feature of a drop-down label appearing when the cursor is held briefly over a button. That way, if the user forgets what the button does, he or she simply needs to hold the cursor over it for a short time to be reminded. It is also important to keep working-memory and mental workload limitations in mind when designing the interface.

While the previous guidelines are aimed mostly at the novice or infrequent user, expert users need to be accommodated with respect to efficiency and error-free performance. Principle seven, *flexibility and efficiency of use,* refers to the goal of having software match the needs of the user. For example, software can provide shortcuts or accelerators for frequently performed tasks. Shortcuts and accelerators include facilities such as function keys or command keys that capture a command in a single keypress, having buttons available to access important functions directly from screens where they are likely to be most needed, and using system defaults (Greenberg, 1993; Nielson, 1993). In other words, they are any technique that can be used to shorten or automate tasks that users perform frequently or repeatedly in the same fashion.

One common tendency among designers is to provide users with a vast assortment of functions, meeting every possible need in every possible circumstance. While this "creeping featurism" may seem to be providing a service to users, it may be doing more harm than good. Facing a complex interface is often overwhelming and confusing to users. Designers must remember that users do not bring rich knowledge and understanding to their perception of the system in the way that designers do. An interface that presents lots of information and lots of options will simply seem difficult. The ultimate design goal is to provide a broad functionality through a simple interface (Mayhew, 1992). One common way to accomplish this is to layer the interface so that much of the functionality is not immediately apparent to the novice. System defaults are an example of this approach. Once users become more familiar with the system, they can go in and change defaults to settings they prefer. An example is the typical graphical word-processing software with "invisible" defaults for page layout, font, style, alignment, and so on. Design goals of simplicity and consistency will pay off in software that users find easy to learn and easy to use. This in return will make them more likely to appreciate and use its unique functionality.

Dialog Styles

Given that computers are information-processing systems, people engage in a *dialog* with computers, where that dialog consists of iteratively giving and receiving information. Computers are not yet technologically sophisticated enough to use unrestricted human natural language, so the interface must be restricted to a dialog that both computer and user can understand. There are currently several basic dialog styles that are used for most software interfaces. These dialog styles include:

> *Menus:* Provide users with a list of items from which to choose one or many
> *Fill-in forms:* Provide blank spaces for users to enter alpha or numeric information
> *Question/answer:* Provides one question at a time, and user types answer in field
> *Command languages:* At prompt, user types in commands with limited, specific syntax
> *Function keys:* Commands are given by pressing special keys or combinations of keys
> *Direct manipulation:* Users perform actions directly on visible objects
> *Restricted natural language:* Computer understands and outputs limited language

While it is sometimes difficult to distinguish perfectly between these dialog styles, it is still convenient to categorize them as such for design purposes. Some dialog styles are suited to specific types of application or task, and a number of dialog styles are frequently combined in one application. Although research in the area of human-computer interaction is still relatively new, it is still possible to draw some inferences about which dialog styles are best for particular types of activity. Mayhew (1992) describes such guidelines in great depth, a few of which are included in the following discussion. For further information, see Mayhew (1992), Smith and Mosier (1986), Nielson (1993), Helander (1988), and Shneiderman (1992).

Menus. Menus have become very familiar to anyone who uses the Macintosh or Windows software environment. Menus provide a list of "actions" to choose from, and they vary from menus that are permanently displayed to pull-down or multiple hierarchical menus. Figure 15.2a shows a combination of menus from

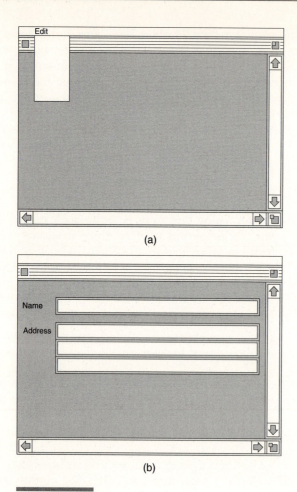

(a)

(b)

FIGURE 15.2

Examples of dialog styles. (a) Permanent and pull-down menus in Microsoft Word interface. (b) Fill-in form dialog style.

Microsoft Word; one menu across the top (file, edit, etc.) is permanently displayed, and another menu has been "pulled down by the user" to display a variety of editing options.

Menus should be used as a dialog style when users have one or more of the following: negative attitudes, low motivation, poor typing skills, little computer or task experience. It is especially appropriate for tasks that are discretionary or are infrequently performed. Menus should be designed so that the items and structure match the task. Mayhew (1992) provides the following guidelines (among others):

- Use graying out of inactive menu items.
- Create logical, distinctive, and mutually exclusive semantic categories.
- Menu choice labels should be brief and consistent in grammatical style.

- Distinguish between "choose one" and "choose many" menus.
- Order menu choices by convention, frequency of use, order of use, functional groups, or alphabetically, depending on the particular task and user preferences.

Menus that have a large number of options can be designed to have few levels with many items per level or to have many levels with few items per level. In general, usability is higher with fewer numbers of levels with more items in each category.

Fill-In Forms.   Fill-in forms are like paper forms: They have labeled spaces, termed *fields,* for users to fill in alphabetical or numeric information. Like menus, they are good for users who have a negative to neutral attitude, low motivation, and little system experience. However, they should be reasonably good typists and be familiar with the task. Otherwise, very strong guidance is needed for filling out the form spaces. Fill-in forms are useful because they are easy to use, and a "form" is a familiar concept to most people.

Like menus, fill-in forms should be designed to reflect the content and structure of the task itself. An example would be a form filled out by patients visiting a doctor's office (Fig. 15.2b). The form could look very similar to the traditional paper forms, asking for information about the patient's name, address, medical history, insurance, and reason for the visit. Having the patient type this information on a computer in the waiting room would alleviate the need for a receptionist to type the information for the patient's file. Fill-in forms should be designed in accordance with the following basic principles:

- Organize groups of items according to the task structure.
- Use white space and separate logical groups.
- Minimize the number of screens for high-frequency users.
- Support forward and backward movement.
- Keep related and interdependent items on the same screen.
- Indicate whether fields are optional.
- Keep input fields short.
- Prompts should be brief and unambiguous.
- Provide direct manipulation for navigation through fields.

Question-Answer.   In this dialog style, the computer displays one question at a time, and the user types an answer in the field provided. The method is good for users who have a negative attitude toward computer technology, low motivation, little system experience, and relatively good typing skills. It is appropriate for tasks that have low frequency of use, discretionary use, and low importance.

Question-answer methods must be designed so that the intent of the question and the required response is clear: (1) use visual cues and white space to clearly distinguish prompts, questions, input area, and instructions; (2) state questions in clear and simple language; (3) provide flexible navigation; and (4) minimize typing requirements.

Command Languages.   At a prompt, such as >, the user types in commands that require use of a very specific and limited syntax (such as C+ or Basic). Command languages are appropriate for users who have a positive attitude toward computer use, high motivation, medium- to high-level typing skills, high computer literacy, and high task-application experience. Designers who are creating a command language should strive to make the syntax as natural and easy as possible; make the syntax consistent; avoid arbitrary use of punctuation; and use simple, consistent abbreviations (see Mayhew, 1992, for additional guidelines).

Function Keys.   In this dialog style, users press special keys or combinations of keys to provide a particular command. An example is pressing/holding the control button and then pressing the "B" key to change a highlighted section of text to boldface type. The use of function keys as input mechanisms in computer dialog is declining, probably because they are arbitrary and taxing on human memory. However, for users who perform a task frequently, want application speed, and have low-level typing skills, function keys are extremely useful.

Because of their arbitrary nature and demands on memory, design of function key commands is tricky. Designers should follow the following guidelines, among others:

- Reserve the use of function keys for generic, high-frequency, important functions.
- Arrange in groups of three to four and base arrangement on semantic relationships or task flow.
- Label keys clearly and distinctly.
- Place high-use keys within easy reach of home row keys.
- Place keys with serious consequences in hard to reach positions and not next to other function keys.
- Minimize the use of "qualifier" keys (e.g., alt, ctrl, command, etc.).

Direct Manipulation.   Direct manipulation refers to performing actions directly "on visible objects" on the screen. An example is using a mouse to position the cursor to a file title or icon, clicking and holding the mouse button down, "dragging" the file to a trash can icon by moving the mouse, and "dropping" the file in the trash can by letting up on the mouse key. Direct manipulation dialog styles are becoming extremely popular because they map well onto a users mental model of the task, are easy to remember, and do not require typing skills. Direct manipulation is a good choice for users who have a negative to moderate attitude toward computers, low motivation, low-level typing skills, and moderate to high task experience. Mayhew (1992) provides the following design guidelines, among others:

- Minimize semantic distance between user goals and required input actions.
- Choose a consistent icon design scheme.
- Design icons to be concrete, familiar, and conceptually distinct.
- Accompany the icons with names if possible.

Direct manipulation interface design requires a strong understanding of the task being performed and high creativity to generate ideas for metaphors or other means of making the direct manipulation interface make "sense" to the user.

Natural Language.   Finally, natural language is an interface dialog style that currently has some limited applications. In this method, users speak or write a constrained set of their natural language. Because it is a natural rather than artificial style for human operators, natural language can be thought of as the "interface of choice." As technology improves, this dialog style will become more common. However, the technology required to enable computers to understand human language is quite formidable, and progress has been slower than computer scientists first imagined.

USER SUPPORT

It is a worthwhile goal to make computer software so "intuitive" that people require no training or help to be able to use it. Unfortunately, much of the time this goal cannot be entirely achieved. Like other complex equipment, many software systems have features that are ultimately useful for task performance but require time and learning from the user. This means that as people begin to use a software system, they will need assistance or "user support" from time to time. User support refers to a variety of assistance mechanisms, which may include:

- Software manuals
- On-line help
- Stand-alone tutorials
- On-line or context-sensitive tutorials
- Human help (such as a help desk or help line).

There is also variety even within this array of user support services. For example, on-line help methods may include keyword help (Houghton, 1984), command prompting (Mason, 1986), context-sensitive help (Fenchel & Estrin, 1982; Magers, 1983), task-oriented help (Magers, 1983; Finin, 1982), and intelligent on-line help (Aaronson & Carroll, 1987; Dix et al., 1993; Elkerton, 1988). All of these methods provide users with information concerning how to use the interface to accomplish tasks. Dix et al. (1993) suggest that help systems should be: (1) accessible at any point during software use and not require quitting the application; (2) complete, up-to-date, and accurate; (3) reliable and able to provide the user with error handling when needed; (4) flexible, adapting to the specific context, task, and ability level of the user; and (5) unobtrusive, not intruding on the user's work in terms of screen space or interruption of task performance.

In the sections below, we briefly consider the two most commonly used support mechanisms—manuals and on-line help. Readers are also referred to Chapter 18, which reviews material relevant to manuals and tutorials.

Software Manuals

Most software systems are sufficiently complex to require a manual and possibly on-line help systems. The difficulty in writing manuals is that users do not read them as instructional texts ahead of time as much as they use them as reference manuals when they need immediate help (Nielson, 1993; Rettig, 1991). Because of this type of use, manuals should have well-designed, task-oriented, search and look-up tools. Writers should keep in mind that users will be using search words based on their *goals* and *tasks,* not on system components or names.

Note that the software manual is a system in and of itself. For that reason, it should be designed using standard human factors principles and guidelines to maximize efficiency and effectiveness. Software manuals can be subjected to usability testing just like any other system. Table 15.3 gives some general guidelines for designing software manuals, and readers are also referred to Adams and Halasz (1983), Gordon (1994), Gottfredson and Guymon (1989), Sheppard (1987), and Weiss (1991).

On-line Help Systems

Hard-copy manuals are the default help system for software, but many designers are realizing the advantages of offering on-line help systems. Among other things, having help on-line can offer the following:

- Easy to find information (where hardcopy manuals may be lost or loaned out).
- Can be context-sensitive.
- Users do not have to find available work space to open manuals.
- Information can be electronically updated.
- Given the right search terms, electronic search is faster than manual.
- On-line systems can include graphics, sound, color, and other techniques that might be useful.
- On-line help systems can include powerful search mechanisms such as string search, multiple indices, electronic bookmarks, hypertext navigation, and backward tracing.

Because of these advantages, most commercial interfaces now come packaged with some type of on-line help system in addition to the paper manual.

Search effectiveness and efficiency is a general difficulty for on-line help systems. For example, in one study, Egan et al. (1989) found that it took almost 50 percent longer for users to find information in an on-line help system than it took to find the information in a hard-copy manual (7.6 min versus 5.6 min). This longer search time was finally reduced to a smaller amount than the hard-copy manual only after extensive usability testing and iterative design. Other problems that may be associated with on-line help systems are:

- Text may be more difficult to read on a computer screen.
- Pages may overlap with task information and therefore interfere with the task.
- Pages on the computer may contain less information than hard-copy manuals.
- Pages may take longer to scroll through on a computer screen.
- People are used to finding information in manuals, whereas navigation may be more difficult in on-line help systems.

Careful design can reduce many of these problems. For example, powerful browsing systems can make access to on-line manuals successful. In addition, a well-designed table of contents can help users locate information. Shneiderman (1992)

TABLE 15.3 General Guidelines for Writing Software Manuals

Guideline	Example
Make information easy to find	
Let the user's tasks guide organization: base the labeling, entry names, and sequencing on user goals and tasks rather than system components	Base labeling and entries on terms such as "send letter," "open mail," etc. rather than "distribution list" or other system labels.
Include entry points that are easy to locate by browsing	Have each text section name shown in boldface, arrange sections alphabetically, and put the terms at the top of each page as headers.
Use both table of contents and index. Include entries based on both the system components and user goals, and have both types of entries indexed at back of manual along with extensive synonyms.	Use system and user task terms such as *format callout button* and *create a callout.*
Make information easy to understand Keep it simple and concrete.	Poor: The system will find the solution after the F3 key is pressed.
Put it naturally and use direct action words. Show clear examples; use sample sessions in complex scenarios.	Better: To solve, press F3.
Use numbered sequences of steps.	
Use system overviews or diagrams.	
Make information task-sufficient	
Include all information that is needed.	
Make sure information is correct.	
Exclude what is not needed.	
Indicate how user can tell whether the operation was successful.	
Include list of error messages.	

suggests a properly designed table of contents that stays on the screen when text is displayed and the use of an expanding/shrinking table of contents. Like any other software system, design of on-line help should follow principles of good design and should be subjected to extensive usability testing and iterative design.

THE DESIGN PROCESS

Development Life Cycle

In Chapter 3, we outlined a basic method for system design used by human factors specialists to enhance system effectiveness and safety. In human-computer interaction, a similar type of design method is used. In the design sequence, the critical components will include: (1) use of guidelines and principles, (2) involvement of typical users throughout the design life cycle, and (3) iterative usability testing beginning early in the design process. While there are many models or prescriptions for software interface design, most include steps such as those suggested by Mayhew (1992), shown in Table 15.4. One important aspect of the design process is that users are heavily involved at each step. For example, in step #4, users are interviewed as part of the task analysis.

Nielson (1993) suggests asking users to identify goals, information they need to achieve goals, steps that must be accomplished, and the various outcomes or reports that are produced. Hierarchical task analysis structures can be developed using simple questioning techniques. For example, each time the user indicates a task/subtask, the interviewer can ask "Why do you do it?" (to relate the task to higher level goals), "How do you do it?" (to decompose the task into lower level subtasks), "Why do you not do it in *x* fashion?" and "Do errors ever occur when you do this?" (Gordon & Gill, 1992; Graesser, Lang, & Elofson, 1987; Nielson et al., 1986). Some software design teams incorporate users as actual members of the design team from beginning to end, an approach termed *participatory design*

TABLE 15.4 Typical Steps for Software Interface Design

Phase 1: Scoping

   1. Develop project plan which specifies scope and schedule.

   2. Develop a user profile, describing user characteristics.

   3. Define hardware and software platform, and list interface techniques supported by the platform.

Phase 2: Functional Specification

   4. Perform task analysis.

   5. Set user interface goals, which should include minimum acceptable performance levels.

   6. Define training and documentation.

Phase 3: Design

   7. User interface mockup: Generate initial design ideas in storyboard form or using rapid prototyping methods. User feedback is obtained and used to modify designs.

   8. Develop style guide. The high-level design identified through step 7 is documented in a specification termed a style guide.

   9. Perform detailed user interface design, including screen layout, error messages, etc.

  10. Develop interface prototype.

  11. Write prototype user interface test plan.

  12. Perform prototype user interface testing. Test prototypes, make design changes, and retest.

Phase 4: Development

  13. Develop training and documentation.

  14. Develop user interface test plan, which specifies testing of the full system against the ease of user and ease of learning goals identified in step 5.

Phase 5: Testing/Implementation

  15. User interface testing. Testing and redesign are conducted iteratively until the ease of use and ease of learning goals are achieved.

  16. Evaluate final user interface.

Source: Mayhew, D.J., 1992. *Principles and guidelines in software user interface design.* Engelwood Cliffs, NJ: Prentice Hall. Adapted by permission of Prentice-Hall, Inc., Upper Saddle River, NJ.

(Dayton, McFarland, & White, 1994). However, as Nielson (1993) cautions, users working with design teams become steeped in the designers' ways of thinking and familiar with the software system. A different set of users must be brought in for system usability testing.

In the earlier stages involving actual design, such as step #12, designers can conduct *usability tests* with low-fidelity mock-ups or prototypes (Carroll, 1995). Many iterations of design should be expected, so it is not efficient to worry about details of screen design or making the screens look elegant. At later stages, such as step #15, usability tests are conducted multiple times as the interface design goes through modifications. Also, while the steps are listed sequentially, the realities of interface design are that the steps themselves are usually iterative; that is, designers might have to go back and repeat work of earlier steps (such as hardware specification) based on the results of later steps. Readers are referred to texts such as Wiklund's (1994) *Usability in Practice: How Companies Develop User-Friendly Products* for descriptions of case studies on interface design and enhancing usability.

Another issue for designers is the kind of prototypes to use for usability testing. While it may seem that all usability testing would be done with screens that look much like the final software, this is not the case. Most usability specialists use a variety of "prototypes" which may range in fidelity, with low-fidelity methods including index cards, stickies, paper and pen drawings, and storyboards. *Storyboards* are a graphical depiction of the outward appearance of the software system, without any actual system functioning. High-fidelity methods would include fully interactive screens, having the look and feel of the final software. Many people believe that low-technology prototypes should be used early in the design process (e.g., Dayton et al., 1994; Salasoo et al., 1994; Wilson et al., 1994). There are actually several good reasons for this practice including: (1) it is often faster, easier, and can be modified more easily *during* usability testing; (2) since designers are less invested in work, they are more willing to change or discard ideas; (3) users give more substantive feedback to prototypes that are obviously low fidelity; and (4) users focus more on the functionality and less on the graphical design per se (Carroll, 1995). As Salasoo et al. (1994) write when describing the use of paper and pen technique, "Several people can work at once (collaboratively) and . . . users have as much access to the prototype medium as product team members." The goal is to move through different design ideas until one is identified that works well for users. Once the interface has gone through several loops of iterative design, the prototype is then moved to computer screens for more advanced usability testing (see phases above).

Usability Metrics

When designers are conducting usability testing, whether early in the low-fidelity prototyping stages or late in the design lifecycle, they must identify *what* they are going to measure, often referred to as *usability metrics.* Usability metrics tend to change in nature and scope as the project moves forward. In early conceptual design phases, usability can be done with a few users and focuses on qualitative assessment of general usability (can the task even be accomplished using the system) and user satisfaction. Low-fidelity prototypes are given to users who then imagine performing a very limited subset of tasks with the materials or screens (Carroll, 1995). Note that at this point, there is usually little to no quantitative data collection; simply talking with a small number of users can yield a large amount of valuable information.

As the design takes on more specific form, usability testing becomes more formalized and often quantitative. The most commonly used metrics for later stages of usability testing are number of errors, time to perform tasks and subtasks, and user subjective reactions. Table 15.5 shows some of the more common usability metrics related to the usability categories of effectiveness, efficiency, and subjective satisfaction (from Mayhew, 1992; Nielson, 1993; Whiteside, Bennett, & Holtzblatt, 1988). To collect data on these measurements, a fully functioning prototype is built, and users are given a set of task scenarios to perform as they would under normal circumstances (e.g., see Carroll, 1995; Neale & Kies, 1996). In addition to collecting quantitative measures such as those shown in Table 15.5, designs ask users to think aloud during task performance and answer questions from the designer. The goal is to find a prototype design that users like, learn easily, and can use to successfully perform tasks. Observation of users gives the designers insight into difficulties with controls, navigation, general conceptual models, and so on.

For example, consider the usability testing performed by a GE Team (Stimart, 1994). The software was Business Talk 2000, a Windows-based software product

---

TABLE 15.5 Examples of Software Usability Metrics (with usability defined in a broad sense)

Effectiveness

Percent of tasks completed

Ratio of successes to failures

Number of features or commands used

Workload (not excessive for user and other concurrent task performance)

Efficiency

Time to complete a task

Time to learn

Time spent on errors

Percent or number of errors

Frequency of help or documentation use

Number of repetition of failed commands

User Satisfaction

Rating scale for usefulness of the software

Rating scale for satisfaction with functions/features

Number of times user expresses frustration or dissatisfaction

Rating scale for user vs. computer control of task

Perception that the software supports tasks as needed by user

designed to perform an assortment of electronic messaging and business communication functions. The tasks given to sixteen users included receiving new mail, sending mail, deleting mail, attaching a file, and so forth. Each task was presented in a short scenario, such as:

> "You have just returned to the office. Check to see if you have any new messages. If you have received any new mail messages, please read them aloud."

Users are asked to use the software to perform the task. They may be videotaped, observed, and/or timed on task performance. The task times and number of errors are then compared to goals originally identified by the design team. After task performance, users can be given rating scales with which to indicate their reaction to the software. An example would be a scale ranging from 1 = extremely difficult to use, to 9 = extremely easy to use. However, it is important to note that sometimes user satisfaction or liking does not predict which software is best at supporting task performance (Kissel, 1995; Bailey, 1993). Finally, the interface design is modified until time, error rates, and subjective reaction are all within the acceptable limits of the team and project managers.

Comments

In summary, good interface design requires the use of knowledge and principles from the fields of HCI and human factors. It also requires the designer to be willing to consider many possible design ideas and be open to the possibility that his or her initial designs will not work very well for users. Finally, designers must buy into the concept that the purpose of the software is to support the user in some task, not to provide all kinds of great features that are fun, interesting, handy, useful once in a lifetime, or that might be used by 1 percent of the population. User-centered design requires a concerted effort to make the software fit the user, not count on the user adapting to the software. Having users highly involved or even on the design team can make it easier to stay focused on the true purpose of the project. For more specific guidelines on interface design and usability testing, readers are referred to Dix et al. (1993), Mayhew (1992), Nielson (1993), or Whiteside et al. (1988). Finally, it is important to point out that good interface design goes beyond the usability of the software interface per se (e.g., see Dix et al., 1993). Computers are being used to support an ever widening array of tasks, including complex cognitive functioning (see Chapter 7), group work such as problem solving and decision making (see Chapter 19), scientific visualization, database management, and so on. One just has to look at the growing use of the Internet to understand the complexities and challenges we face in designing software. It is important for human factors specialists to design and evaluate the system so that it works effectively for the user in the sense of "deep" task support, as well as usability at the superficial interface level. This requires full evaluation of cognitive, physical, and social functioning of users and their environment during task performance.

INFORMATION TECHNOLOGY

Although the computer was originally designed as a traditional computational device, one of the greatest emerging potentials is in the handling of information. Currently, computers can make vast amounts of information available to users in a manner that is potentially far more efficient than was previously possible. Large library databases can be accessed on a computer, eliminating trips to the library and long searches through card catalogs. As suggested in Chapter 7, diagnostic tests and troubleshooting steps can be called up in a few key presses, instead of requiring the maintenance technician to page through large and cumbersome maintenance manuals containing out of date, or even missing, pages. And physicians can rapidly access the records of hundreds of cases of a rare disease to assess the success of various treatments. All of these uses require people to be able to interact with the computer in order to search for information. Supporting information search and retrieval is a critical emphasis in human factors and software interface design. In the sections below, we briefly consider some of the issues involved in designing information systems.

Hypertext and Hypermedia

Many computer-based documents now make use of computational power by linking one information "chunk" to another, changing the traditional linear text format to a nonlinear one. This technique of linking chunks of information is termed *hypertext*. The most common example of hypertext occurs when certain words in text are highlighted and the user clicks on the highlighted area to see additional information. Sometimes clicking on the highlighted material brings up a pop-up screen, and other times it simply "moves" to user to a different part of the document.

Hypertext essentially stores all text and graphics as chunks of information, called nodes, in a network. The chunks are electronically linked together in whatever manner the designer chooses. Although hypertext was originally designed for use on static text and graphics, it has now been extended to linking chunks of any information, including text, audio clips, video clips, animation, and so forth. Because this information is *multimedia,* the technique of linking these types of material is called *hypermedia.* Hypermedia is the basic principle behind a variety of information networks, such as the Internet.

Networks of information are arguably the fastest growing computer application today. Scientists studying hypermedia estimate that somewhere between 40 and 50 million people use the Internet on a regular basis, and this number is growing rapidly (e.g., Fenn & Maurer, 1994). The World Wide Web (WWW) is an extremely successful application of hypermedia on the Internet. It has a relatively easy to use interface, Mosaic, that allows wide-ranging forays to distant sites and documents. While e-mail, direct document transfers, and WWW browsing are the most common uses of the Internet, other more interactive applications are the real growth areas. For example, thousands of businesses are currently working on putting advertising, job performance support materials, and training programs onto the Internet.

Although hypermedia is a powerful search mechanism, it also has a serious and well-documented drawback. That is the tendency for users to have difficulties finding their way around the hypermedia networks. Many of us have experienced the problems with a poorly designed hypertext interface—becoming lost, disoriented, and unable to move in the desired direction. The phrase "lost in hyperspace" has been coined to describe this phenomenon (Utting & Yankelovich, 1989; Billingsley, 1982; Wickens & Baker, 1995). Because of this phenomenon, most information systems that use hypertext have a "home" button so users can get back to the top of the network hierarchy. Becoming lost and having to go "home" to start over can be frustrating and greatly increases time required to perform search tasks. Researchers are evaluating various support mechanisms, such as maps, to overcome these types of navigation problem (Beard & Walker, 1990; Mukherjea, Foley, & Hudson, 1995).

Information Database Access

As computers become more technologically sophisticated, we are using them to access increasingly large and complex databases. However, while the computer holds the potential to allow users to access, search, and manipulate extremely large information databases, it is less apparent how computers should be designed to support these processes. This question represents an important aspect of human-computer interaction (Wickens & Seidler, 1995).

As with any other domain of human factors, a fundamental first step is to perform a task analysis (Chapter 3). What are the tasks, or user needs, in interacting with an information database? We can list at least four general kinds of needs that vary along the degree to which the user can specify the information needed from the database in advance:

1. The user knows a precise label for a piece of information that needs to be retrieved; for example, a telephone operator needs to retrieve the phone number of a person whose name is known.

2. The user knows some general characteristics of the desired item but will only be able to identify it positively when he or she sees it; for example, you know the general topic of the particular book you want, but you can remember neither the specific author nor title.

3. The user wants to learn what exists in the database regarding a general area but wishes initially to browse through that area, searching opportunistically for certain items that may be of interest, and does not know in advance if they are there. For example, you may be searching an accident database for particular cases, and are not aware of the existence of what turns out to be a very relevant class of accidents until you encounter them in the database.

4. The user simply wants to understand the overall structure of the database: what cases exist, what ones do not, and how certain classes of cases relate to others. For example, the epidemiologist may wish to examine the occurrence of a disease over space and time to gain some understanding of its transmission.

While specific applications for document retrieval interfaces will require more elaborate task analysis than this simple categorization scheme (e.g., Belkin, Marchetti, & Cool, 1993; Terveen, 1993), the four types of search listed above will serve to illustrate the important trade-offs between different database interaction techniques. Across the four classes, there are different dialog interface methods that may be better suited for one than another, as we discuss below.

Mediated Retrieval.   When the nature of information required can be precisely specified in advance, a command language or keyword search is often an adequate technique for directly retrieving the information. Much as one uses an index to look up a precise piece of information in a book, one formulates a list of keywords to specify, as uniquely as possible, the attributes of the desired piece of information (fact, book, passage, etc.). In designing interfaces for such direct retrieval systems, it is important for designers to label the index or keyword terms according to standard conventions within the domain, using semantic labels that users will be most likely to generate.

This principle may be somewhat difficult to carry out if one interface must be designed for multiple classes of users. It turns out that people use an extremely diverse set of terms when looking for the same object; some estimates suggest that the chances of two people choosing the same term for a familiar object are less than 15 percent (Furnas, et al., 1987). For example, if you are an engineering student, access to topics in human factors may be most likely through more familiar engineering terminology (e.g., displays, controls, manual control). However, for psychologists, similar topics may be more familiarly accessed through psychological terms like *perception, response,* or *tracking.* The key to good keyword access is to provide *multiple routes* to access the same entities. Such a design may not produce the shortest, most parsimonious index or keyword list, but it will greatly reduce the frustration of users.

Even with well-designed multiple access routes, keyword searches are not always satisfactory from a user's point of view for two primary reasons. First, it is sometimes difficult for users to specify precisely the queries or combinations of keywords that identify their needs. In particular, people are not very good at using the Boolean logic that forms the backbone of most query systems. (Mackinlay, Rao, & Card, 1995). An example of such a query might be: "All the information on people with incomes above a certain level, that live in a certain region *and* incomes above a different level, who live in a different region and are female."

The second problem, somewhat related to the first, is that users are not always fully satisfied with the results of such keyword searches (Muckler, 1987). For example, in searching a library database, large numbers of documents that are irrelevant to the target search may be retrieved (false alarms) and large numbers of relevant documents may well remain unretrieved (misses). To compound this possibility, users may have more confidence in the exhaustiveness of the search than is warranted, as they have no way of assessing the rate of misses (they don't know what they don't know) (Blair & Maron, 1985).

Intelligent Agents.   Because people often have difficulties finding the information they want or need, a new approach under development is the concept of a computer-based helper to act as an interface agent between the user and the information database (Maes, 1994). These intelligent agents take input in the form of general needs and goals of the user. A detailed knowledge about the organization of the information database as well as access mechanisms allows the intelligent agent to search for the most relevant and useful information. The agent "goes to get" information, and then displays either the information itself (as in decision aids) or a listing of the information that has been obtained. Intelligent agents are essentially one type of interface that provides an expert assistant to users. This has the advantage of users being saved from having to do their own search. However, the other side of the coin is that it also eliminates users from being able to "browse" the database themselves.

Spatially Organized Databases. While strides are being made to provide more computer power to translate and interpret user queries (Maes, 1994) and therefore offer more user satisfaction to verbally mediated information searches, an alternative approach is to rely on a spatial representation of the information space to support search processes (e.g., Fowler, Fowler, & Wilson, 1991). Good arguments can be made for dialogue interfaces that support *navigation* or *travel* through the database or information space rather than direct retrieval. Because navigation and travel are spatially relevant terms, we describe these as *spatially organized databases* (Lund, 1994). Such organization is logical, in part because the items in many databases bear analog similarity relations to each other; that is, certain items are more similar to each other than to others, perhaps because they share more common keywords, or are more related to the same task. A spatial organization also makes sense because space and navigation are such natural metaphors, coming from interaction with the everyday environment (Hutchins, Hollan, & Norman, 1985).

Different kinds of spatially organized databases or information spaces have different ways of defining *proximity,* or "near" and "far" (Durding, Becker, & Gould, 1977). For example, in a menu structure (Fig. 15.3a), proximity is typically defined by the lowest common ancestor in the hierarchy. Thus, in the figure, X is "closer" to Y than to Z. In a network information space, like a communications network defining "who talks to who" on the Internet, proximity may be defined in terms of the number of links joining a pair of nodes (Fig. 15.3b). In a matrix database (Fig. 15.3c), like a spreadsheet, proximity may be defined simply in terms of the nearness of cells (rows and columns) to each other. Euclidean spaces, like those in Figure 15.3d, define distance or proximity in terms that are directly equivalent to those used to describe natural 3-D space. Such spaces may often be used for depicting scientific data which itself is often located at different Euclidean coordinates (e.g., a severe thunderstorm, geological strata, or the spread of pollution).

Spatially defined databases have both benefits and costs. The benefits are first that they will generally position task-related elements close together and hence allow the user to consider these elements "in a single glance," or at least with little time spent traveling from one to the other (e.g., comparing two related entries to see which is more relevant or tagging a set of related entries for later retrieval). Hence, like the principles of good display layout discussed in Chapter 8, a spatially defined database can adhere to the layout principles of relatedness and sequence of use (Seidler & Wickens, 1992; Wickens & Seidler, 1997). The second benefit is that such databases can allow the user to better understand the full structure of the database by examining a broad "map" of its elements.

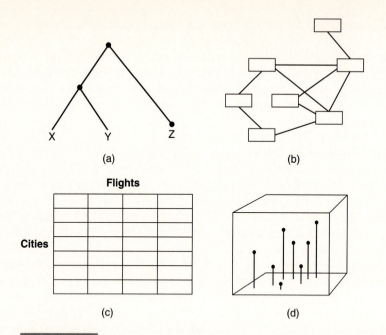

Flights

Cities

FIGURE 15.3

Four examples of spatially organized databases: (a) menu structure, (b) information network, (c) spreadsheet, (d) Euclidian space.

Against these benefits, we can identify at least three potential costs, which careful design should strive to minimize:

1. *Travel time.* Just as it will be easy to traverse the information space between related items, it may be more difficult (or time consuming) to travel between unrelated ones. Consider, for example, the number of keystrokes that might be required to travel between page X and page Z in the database menu shown in Figure 15.3a. To guard against this problem, users may be given the option of direct access, via keywords, to any item in the database. In menu systems, they should also be given clear instructions on how to "pop up" to the top of the menu directly, thereby saving upward steps (Wickens & Seidler, 1997).

2. *Getting lost.* As databases become more complex and populated, an emerging problem is that of getting lost in the information space, as was noted when we discussed hypertext interfaces. There are several specific solutions that can be offered to remedy this problem. First, the database should be spatially organized in a manner that is consistent with the user's mental model (Roske-Hofstrand & Paap, 1986; Seidler & Wickens, 1992). In this case, navigation becomes more characteristic of traveling through a familiar world than an unfamiliar one. Second, users should be provided with an overall "map" of the space (Vicente & Williges, 1988; Beard & Walker, 1990) that is either continuously viewable on the screen or, if screen space is at a premium, can be rapidly and easily called up on a window.

The design of this map can be a challenging exercise when the information space is large and multidimensional. It may well capitalize on familiar metaphors like rooms and walls (Robertson, Card, & MacKinlay, 1993; Seligmann, Mercuri, & Edmark, 1995). Figure 15.4 provides some examples. Third, users should be allowed an option to "recover" when they are lost, allowing them to "backtrack" to the previous item (Nielson, 1987) or perhaps by making readily available the same "pop-up" option to the top of the menu (or any other well-known landmark within the space). Fourth, it is often useful to provide a historical record of where one has recently been within the space. Many systems offer "bookmarks" that can label entries one may want to rapidly revisit (Bernstein, 1988).

3. *Update rate.* Even in normal computer use, we can easily become frustrated by long (and variable) computer responses to our inputs. However, two features of spatially organized databases or information spaces make these particularly vulnerable to frustrating delays. First, the screen graphics of such systems are often very complex. If such spaces are also 3-D and have a certain level of pictorial realism, then the time required to "redraw" the depicted space as, for example, a user "moves through" it, can be long enough to interfere with the perception of motion. Second, if a direct manipulation interface is provided to allow the user to "travel" through the space, the delays encountered in this tracking task can be devastating to control stability, as we learned in Chapter 9. The user can easily overshoot targets, turn too far, and so forth, thus defeating the very purpose of interactivity. What is important to realize about the update-rate problem is that users may quickly become frustrated with such a system and simply chose not to use it at all.

The solutions to update-rate problems lie both in hardware and software. Of course, many computers are becoming more powerful, particularly with regard to their graphic engines, and hence can address some aspects of the problem. But software system designers must be aware that not all users will possess the sufficient connection speed, memory, and graphics capability to allow rapid-image updating. Courseware, for example, that is intended to be used remotely by a variety of students over the World Wide Web or some other network may unfairly penalize students in the class who do not have access to the necessary computing power.

The other solution is for designers to think very carefully about what aspects of image complexity or system interactivity are really necessary for users. For example, in many cases photo images are not the most effective instructional tools because they contain too much visual complexity. Color and three-dimensional graphics are also often unnecessary or even intrusive. In particular, the full level of "immersed" interactivity provided by virtual reality may sometimes even be counterproductive for effective task performance (Wickens & Baker, 1995). For example, users can more effectively understand the structure of the database from an outside-in, less interactive perspective. An interface designer who understands what information is and *is not* important for a user's task should be able to work closely with computer engineers to create compromise designs that still support interactivity without imposing great delays. As an example of such a solution, much of the precision of many images in an information space need not be rendered while a user is traveling. Only when the user stops to inspect would fine details of an image be drawn. Hence, one can define a separate "travel" and an "inspection" mode.

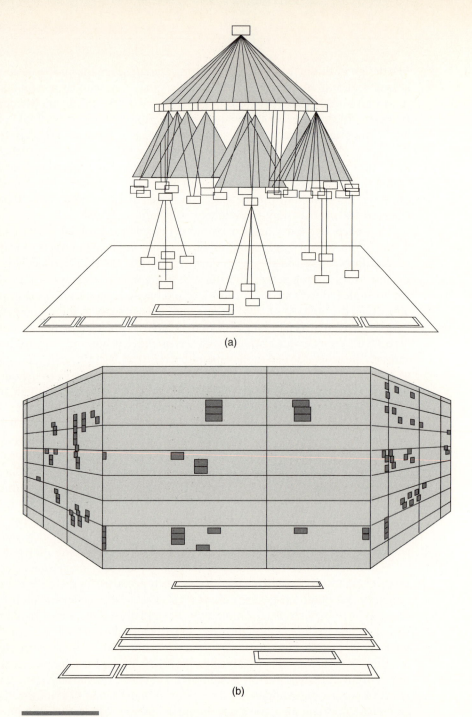

(a)

(b)

FIGURE 15.4

Different ways of visualing information databases. (a) Cone tree visualization tool for hierarachical data. Interactive device can "rotate" the tree. (*Source*: Robertson, G.G., Card, S.K., and Mackinlay, J. D., 1993. Information visualization using 3D interactive animation, *Communications of the ACM, 36*[4], 57–71.) (b) Perspective wall for linearly structured information spaces. (*Source*: Robertson, Card, and Mackinlay, 1993. The next generation of GOIs, *Communications of the ACM, 36*[4], 57–71.)

Virtual Reality

It is but a short leap from our discussions of interactive spatial databases to those involved in virtual reality (VR) interfaces. The latter are certainly examples of human computer interaction, in which the computer is expected to be extremely powerful, and render the user's experience as closely as possible to direct interaction with the natural world; that is, the computer interface should be entirely "transparent" to the user. We have discussed other issues of the human factors of virtual reality elsewhere in this book (see also Durlack & Mavor, 1995; Barfield & Furness, 1995, for good treatments of this topic). Here we wish only to reemphasize two points made above: (1) designers should ensure that the *task* for which a VR interface is designed is, in fact, one that is best suited for full immersion; (2) designers should be extremely sensitive to the negative effects of delayed updates. Such lags become progressively more disruptive (and likely) the more immersed is the environment, and the more richly the designer tries to create a visual reality. It is important to understand that simpler images, updated more frequently, are usually far more effective in an interactive VR environment than are complex images, updated with longer lags (Wickens & Baker, 1995). We discuss other issues related to virtual reality in Chapters 4 and 8.

REFERENCES

Aaronson, A., and Carroll, J.M. (1987). Intelligent help in a one-shot dialogue: A protocol study. In *Proceedings of CHI + GI 1987* (pp. 163–168). New York: Association for Computing Machinery.

Abowd, G.D., and Dix, A.J. (1992). Giving undo attention. *Interacting with Computers, 4*(3), 317–342.

Adams, K.A., and Halasz, I.M. (1983). *Twenty-five ways to improve your software user manuals.* Worthington, OH: Technology Training Systems.

Alwood, C.M. (1986). Novices on the computer: A review of the literature. *International Journal of Man-Machine Studies, 25,* 633–658.

Andre, A.D., and Wickens, C.D. (1995, Oct.). When users want what's *not* best for them: A review of performance-preference dissociations. *Ergonomics in Design,* 10–13.

Bailey, R.W. (1993). Performance vs. preference. *Proceedings of the Human Factors and Ergonomics Society 37th Annual Meeting* (pp. 282–286). Santa Monica, CA: Human Factors and Ergonomics Society.

Barfield, W., and Furness, T.A., III (eds.) (1995). *Virtual environments and advanced interface design.* New York: Oxford University Press.

Beard, D.V., and Walker, J.Q. (1990). Navigational techniques to improve the display of large two-dimensional spaces. *Behavior & Information Technology, 9*(6), 451–466.

Belkin, N.J., Marchetti, P.G., and Cool, C. (1993). BRAQUE: Design of an interface to support user interaction in information retrieval. *Information Processing and Management, 29*(3), 325–344.

Bernstein, M. (1988). The bookmark and the compass. *ACM SIGOIS Bulletin, 9*(4), 34–45.

Billingsley, P.A. (1982). Navigation through hierarchical menu structures: Does it help to have a map? *Proceedings of the 26th Annual Meeting of the Human Factors Society* (pp. 103–107). Santa Monica, CA: Human Factors Society.

Blair, D.C., and Maron, M.E. (1985). An evaluation of retrieval effectiveness for a full-text document-retrieval system. *Communications of the ACM, 28*(3), 289–299.

Card, S., Moran, T.P., and Newell, A. (1983). *The psychology of human-computer interaction.* Hillsdale, NJ: Lawrence Erlbaum Associates.

Carroll, J.M. (ed.) (1995). *Scenario-based design: Envisioning work and technology in system development.* New York: Wiley.

Carroll, J.M., Mack, R.L., and Kellogg, W.A. (1988). Interface metaphors and the user interface design. In M. Helander (ed.), *Handbook of human-computer interaction* (pp. 67–85). Amsterdam: North-Holland.

Carroll, J.M., and Olson, J.R. (1988). Mental models in human-computer interaction. In M. Helander (ed.), *Handbook of human-computer interaction* (pp. 45–65). Amsterdam: North-Holland.

Casey, S. (1993). *Set phasers on stun and other true tales of design, technology and human error.* Santa Barbara, CA: Aegean Publishing.

Casner, S., and Lewis, C. (1987). Learning about hidden events in system interactions. *CHI '87 Proceedings* (pp. 197–204). New York: Association for Computing Machinery.

Dayton, T., McFarland, A., and White, E. (1994). Software development: Keeping users at the center. *Exchange: Information technology at work, 10*(5), 12–17.

Dix, A., Finlay, J., Abowd, G., and Beale, R. (1993). *Human-computer interaction.* New York: Prentice Hall.

Douglas, S., and Moran, T.P. (1983). Learning text editor semantics by analogy. *Proceedings CHI '83: Human factors in computing systems* (pp. 207–211). New York: Association of Computing Machinery.

Durding, B.M., Becker, C.A., and Gould, J.D. (1977). Data organization. *Human Factors, 19,* 1–14.

Durlach, N.I., and Mavor, A.S. (eds.) (1995). *Virtual reality: Scientific and technological challenges.* Washington, DC: National Academy Press.

Egan, D.E., Remde, J.R., Gomez, L.M., Landauer, T.K., Eberhardt, J., and Lochbaum, C.C. (1989). Formative design-evaluation of SuperBook. *ACM Transactions on Information Systems, 7*(1), 30–57.

Elkerton, J. (1988). Online aiding for human-computer interfaces. In M. Helander (ed.), *Handbook of human-computer interaction* (pp. 345–364). Amsterdam: North-Holland.

Fenchel, R.S., and Estrin, G. (1982). Self-describing systems using integral help. *IEEE Transactions on Systems, Man, and Cybernetics, SMC-12,* 162–167.

Fenn, B., and Maurer, H. (1994). Harmony on an expanding net. *Interactions: New visions of human-computer interaction, 1*(4), 29–38.

Finin, T.W. (1982). *Help advice in task oriented systems.* Philadelphia: The Moore School, Department of Computer and Information Science, University of Pennsylvania, Technical Report MS-CIS-1982-22.

Fowler, R.H., Fowler, W.A.L., and Wilson, B.A. (1991). Integrating query, thesaurus, and documents through a common visual representation. *Proceedings of CHI '91* (pp. 142–151). New York: Association for Computing Machinery.

Furnas, G.W., Landuaer, T.K., Gomez, L.M., and Dumais. S.T. (1987). The vocabulary problem in human system communication. *Communications of the ACM, 30*(11), 964–971.

Galitz, W.O. (1985). *Handbook of screen format design.* Wellesley Hills, MA: QED Information Sciences.

Galitz, W.O. (1993). *User-interface screen design.* New York: Wiley.

Gentner, D.R., and Grudin, J. (1990). Why good engineers (sometimes) create bad interfaces. *CHI '90 Proceedings* (pp. 277–282). New York: Association for Computing Machinery.

Gentner, D., and Stevens, A.L. (1983). *Mental models.* Hillsdale, NJ: Erlbaum.

Gong, R., and Kieras, D. (1994). A validation of the GOMS model methodology in the development of a specialized, commercial software application. *CHI '94* (pp. 351–357). New York: Association for Computing Machinery.

Gong, Q., and Salvendy, G. (1994). Design of skill-based adaptive interface: The effects of a gentle push. *Proceedings of the Human Factors and Ergonomics Society 38th Annual Meeting* (pp. 295–299). Santa Monica, CA: Human Factors and Ergonomics Society.

Gordon, S.E. (1994). *Systematic training program design: Maximizing effectiveness and minimizing liability.* Englewood Cliffs, NJ: Prentice Hall.

Gordon, S.E., and Gill, R.T. (1989). The formation and use of conceptual structures in problem solving domains. Technical Report for the Air Force Office of Scientific Research, grant #AFOSR-88-0063.

Gordon, S.E., and Gill, R.T. (1992). Knowledge acquisition with question probes and conceptual graph structures. In T. Lauer, E. Peacock, and A. Graesser (eds.), *Questions and information systems* (pp. 29–46). Hillsdale, NJ: Lawrence Erlbaum Associates.

Gottfredson, C.A., and Guymon, R.E. (1989). *Style guide for designing and writing computer documentation.* Alpine, UT: The Gottfredson Group.

Graesser, A.C., Lang, K.L., and Elofson, C.S. (1987). Some tools for redesigning system-operator interfaces. In D.E. Berger, K. Pezdek, and W.P. Banks (eds.), *Applications of cognitive psychology: Problems solving, education, and computing* (pp. 163–181). Hillsdale, NJ: Lawrence Erlbaum Associates.

Greenberg, S. (1993). *The computer user as toolsmith: The use, reuse, and organization of computer-based tools.* Cambridge, UK: Cambridge University Press.

Halasz, F., and Moran, T.P. (1982). Analogy considered harmful. *Human Factors in Computer Systems Proceedings* (pp. 383–386). Washington, DC: National Bureau of Standards.

Helander, M. (ed.) (1988). *Handbook of human-computer interaction.* Amsterdam: North-Holland.

Hiltz, S.R. (1984). *Online communities: A case study of the office of the future.* Norwood, NJ: Ablex Publishers.

Houghton, R.C. (1984). Online help systems: A conspectus. *Communications of the ACM, 27,* 126–133.

Hutchins, E.L., Hollan, J.D., and Norman, D.A. (1985). Direct manipulation interfaces. *Human-Computer Interaction, 1*(4), 311–338.

Iannella, R. (1995, April). HyperSAM: A management tool for large user interface guideline sets. *SIGCHI* (pp. 42–45). New York: Association for Computing Machinery.

Irving, S., Polson, P., and Irving, J.E. (1994). A GOMS analysis of the advanced automated cockpit. *CHI '94* (pp. 344–350). New York: Association for Computing Machiner.

Kieras, D.E. (1988a). Towards a practical GOMS model methodology for user se interface design. In M. Helander (ed.), *Handbook of human-computer interaction* (pp. 135–157). Amsterdam: North-Holland.

Kieras, D.E. (1988b). What mental models should be taught: Choosing instructional content for complex engineering systems. In J. Psotka, L. Massey, and S. Mutter (eds.), *Intelligent tutoring systems: Lessons learned* (pp. 85–112). Hillsdale, NJ: Lawrence Erlbaum Associates.

Kieras, D., and Polson, P.G. (1985). An approach to the formal analysis of user complexity, *International Journal of Man-Machine Studies, 22,* 365–394.

Kissel, G.V. (1995). The effect of computer experience on subjective and objective software usability measures. *Human Factors in Computing Systems: CHI '95 Conference Companion* (pp. 284–285). New York: Association for Computing Machinery.

Lund, A.M. (1994). Navigating on the information highway. *Proceedings of the Human Factors and Ergonomics Society 38th Annual Meeting* (pp. 271–274). Santa Monica, CA: Human Factors and Ergonomics Society.

Mackinlay, J.D., Rao, R., and Card, S.K. (1995). An organic user interface for searching citation links. *CHI '95* (pp. 67–73). New York: Association for Computing Machinery.

Maes, P. (1994). Agents that reduce work and information overload. *Communications of the ACM, 37*(7), 31–40.

Magers, C.S. (1983). An experimental evaluation of on-line HELP for non-programmers. In *Proceedings of CHI '83: Human Factors in Computing Systems* (pp. 277–281). New York: Association for Computing Machinery.

Mason, M.V. (1986). Adaptive command prompting in an online documentation system. *International Journal of Man-Machine Studies, 25,* 33–51.

Masson, M.E.J., Hill, W.C., and Conner, J. (1988). Misconceived misconceptions? *Proceedings of CHI '88* (pp. 151–156). New York: Association for Computing Machinery.

Mayhew, D.J. (1992). *Principles and guidelines in software user interface design.* Englewood Cliffs, NJ: Prentice Hall.

Muckler, F.A. (1987). The human-computer interface: The past 35 years and the next 35 years. In G. Salvendy (ed.), *Cognitive engineering in the design of human-computer interaction and expert systems: Proceedings of the 2nd International Conference on Human-Computer Interaction.* Amsterdam: Elsevier Science Publishers.

Mukherjea, S., Foley, J.D., and Hudson, S. (1995). Visualizing complex hypermedia networks through multiple hierarchical views. *CHI '95* (pp. 331–337). New York: Association for Computing Machinery.

Neale, D.C., and Kies, J.K. (1996). Scenario-based design for human-computer interface development. *Proceedings of the Human Factors and Ergonomics Society 40th Annual Meeting* (pp. 338–342). Santa Monica, CA: Human Factors and Ergonomics Society.

Nielson, J. (1987). Using scenarios to develop user friendly videotex systems. *Proceedings of NordDATA '87 Joint Scandinavian Computer Conference* (pp. 133–138), Trondheim, Norway, June 1987.

Nielson, J. (1989). Executive summary. In J. Nielson (ed.), *Coordinating user interfaces for consistency* (pp. 1–7). Boston, MA: Academic Press.

Nielson, J. (1993). *Usability engineering.* Cambridge, MA: AP Professional.

Nielson, J. (1994a). Enhancing the explanatory power of usability heuristics. *Chi '94 Proceedings* (pp. 152–158). New York: Association for Computing Machinery

Nielson, J. (1994b). Heuristic evaluation. In J. Nielsen and R.L. Mack (eds.), *Usability inspection methods* (pp. 25–64). New York: Wiley.

Nielson, J. (1994c). As they may work. *Interactions: New Visions of Human-Computer Interaction* (October, pp. 19–24). New York: Association for Computing Machinery.

Nielson, J., Mack, R.L., Bergendorff, K.H., and Grischkowsky, N.L. (1986). Integrated software in the professional work environment: Evidence from questionnaires and interviews. *Proceedings of the ACM CHI '86 Conference* (pp. 162–167). New York: Association for Computing Machinery.

Nielson, J., and Molich, R. (1990). Heuristic evaluation of user interfaces. *CHI '90 Proceedings* (pp. 249–256). New York: Association for Computing Machinery.

Norman, D.A. (1986). Cognitive engineering. In D.A. Norman and S.W. Draper (eds.), *User centered system design: New perspectives on human-computer interaction* (pp. 31–61). Hillsdale, NJ: Lawrence Erlbaum Associates.

Norman, D.A. (1987). Some observations of mental models. In R.M. Baecker and W.A.S. Buxton (eds.), *Readings in human-computer interaction* (pp. 241–244). Los Altos, CA: Morgan Kaufmann Publishers.

Perkins, R., and Rollert, D. (1994). Interchange, an online service for people with special interests. In M.E. Wiklund (ed.), *Usability in practice: How companies develop user-friendly products* (pp. 427–456). Cambridge, MA: AP Professional.

Phillips, M.D., Bashinski, H.S., Ammerman, H.L., and Fligg, C.M. (1988). A task analytic approach to dialogue design. In M. Helander (ed.), *Handbook of human-computer interaction* (pp. 835–857). Amsterdam: North-Holland.

Rettig, M. (1991). Nobody reads documentation. *Communications of the ACM, 34*(7), 19–24.

Robertson, G.G., Card, S.K., and Mackinlay, J.D. (1993). Information visualization using 3D interactive animation. *Communications of the ACM, 36*(4), 57–71.

Roske-Hofstrand, R.J., and Paap, K.R. (1986). Cognitive networks as a guide to menu organization: An application in the automated cockpit. *Ergonomics, 29,* 1301–1311.

Rosson, M.B. (1983). Patterns of experience in text editing. *Proceedings of the CHI-83 Conference on Human Factors in Computing* (pp. 171–175). New York: Association for Computing Machinery.

Rouse, W.B., and Morris, N.M. (1986). On looking into the black box: Prospects and limits in the search for mental models. *Psychological Bulletin, 100,* 349–363.

Salasoo, A., White, E.A., Dayton, T., Burkhart, B.J., and Root, R.W. (1994). Bellcore's user-centered design approach. In M.E. Wiklund (ed.), *Usability in practice: How companies develop user-friendly products* (pp. 489–515). Boston, MA: AP Professional.

Santhanam, R., and Wiedenbeck, S. (1993). Neither novice nor expert: The discretionary user of software. *International Journal of Man-Machine Studies, 38*(2), 201–229.

Seidler, K.S., and Wickens, C.D. (1992). Distance and organization in multifunction displays. *Human Factors, 34,* 555–569.

Seligmann, D.D., Mercuri, R.T., and Edmark, J.T. (1995). Providing assurances in a multimedia interactive environment. *Proceedings of the ACM CHI '85 Conference* (pp. 250–256). New York: Association for Computing Machinery.

Sheppard, S.B. (1987). Documentation for software systems. In G. Salvendy (ed.), *Handbook of human factors* (pp. 1542–1584). New York: Wiley.

Shneiderman, B. (1992). *Designing the user interface: Strategies for effective human-computer interaction* (2nd ed.). Reading, MA: Addison-Wesley Publishing Company.

Smith, S.L., and Mosier, J.N. (1986). *Guidelines for designing user interface software* (Technical Report NTIS No. A177 198). Hanscom Air Force Base, MA: USAF Electronic Systems Division. (NTIS No. AD.)

Stimart, R.P. (1994). GE information services. In M.E. Wiklund (ed.), *Usability in practice: How companies develop user-friendly products* (pp. 517–557). Boston, MA: AP Professional.

Terveen, L.G. (1993). Interface support for data archaeology. In *Proceedings of the Second International Conference on Information and Knowledge Management* (pp. 356–363). New York: Association for Computing Machinery.

Tullis, T.S. (1988). Screen design. In M. Helander (ed.), *Handbook of human-computer interaction* (pp. 377–411). Amsterdam: North-Holland.

Utting, K., and Yankelovich, N. (1989). Context and orientation in hypermedia networks. *ACM Transactions on Information Systems, 7*(1), 58–84.

Vicente, K.J., and Williges, R.C. (1988). Accommodating individual differences in searching a hierarchical file system. *International Journal of Man-Machine Studies, 29,* 647–668.

Weiss, E.H. (1991). *How to write usable user documentation* (2nd ed.). Phoenix, AZ: Oryx Press.

Whiteside, J., Bennett, J., and Holtzblatt, K. (1988). Usability engineering: Our experience and evolution. In M. Helander (ed.), *Handbook of human-computer interaction* (pp. 791–817). Amsterdam: North-Holland.

Wickens, C.D., and Baker, P. (1995). Cognitive issues in virtual reality. In W. Barfield and T.A. Furness III (eds.), *Virtual environments and advanced interface design* (pp. 515–541). New York: Oxford University Press.

Wickens, C.D., and Seidler, K.S. (1985). Information access, representation and utilization. In R. Nickerson (ed.), *Emerging needs and opportunities for human factors research.* Washington, DC: National Academy of Sciences.

Wickens, C.D., and Seidler, K.S. (1997). Information access in a dual task context. *Journal of Experimental Psychology: Applied, 3,* 1–20.

Wiklund, M.E. (ed.) (1994). *Usability in practice: How companies develop user-friendly products.* Boston, MA: AP Professional.

Willeges, R.C., Willeges, B.H., and Elkerton, J. (1987). Software interface design. In G. Salvendy (ed.), *Handbook of human factors* (pp. 1416–1449). New York: Wiley.

Wilson, C.E., Loring, B.E., Conte, L., and Stanley, K. (1994). Usability engineering at Dun & Bradstreet Software. In M.E.Wiklund (ed.), *Usability in practice: How companies develop user-friendly products* (pp. 389–425). Boston, MA: AP Professional

Wilson, J. R., and Rutherford, A. (1989). Mental models: Theory and application in human factors. *Human Factors, 31*(6), 617–634.

Wozny, L.A. (1989). The application of metaphor, analogy, and conceptual models in computer systems. *Interacting with Computers, 1*(3), 273–283.

CHAPTER 16

Automation

The pilots of the China Airlines transport were flying high over the Pacific, allowing their autopilot to direct the aircraft on the long, routine flight. Gradually, one of the engines began to lose power, causing the plane to tend to veer toward the right. As it did, however, the autopilot appropriately steered the plane back to the left, therefore continuing to direct a straight-flight path. Eventually, as the engine continued to lose power, the autopilot could no longer apply the necessary countercorrection. As in a "tug of war" when one side finally loses its resistance and is rapidly pulled across the line, so the autopilot eventually "failed." The plane suddenly rolled, dipped, and lost its airworthiness, falling over 30,000 feet out of the sky before the pilots finally regained control just a few thousand heart-stopping feet above the ocean (National Transportation Safety Board, 1986; Billings, 1996). Why did this happen? In analyzing this incident, investigators concluded that the autopilot had so perfectly handled its chores during the long routine flights that the flight crew had been lulled into a sense of "complacency," not monitoring and "supervising" its operations as closely as they should have. Had they done so, they would have noted early on the gradual loss of engine power (and the resulting need for greater autopilot compensation), an event they clearly would have detected had they been steering the plane themselves.

Automation characterizes the circumstances when a machine (nowadays usually a computer) assumes a task that is otherwise performed by the human operator. As the aircraft example above illustrates, automation is somewhat of a mixed blessing and hence is characterized by a number of ironies (Bainbridge, 1983). When it works well, it usually works *very* well indeed—so well in fact that we sometimes trust it more than we should. Yet on the rare occasions when it does fail, those failures may often be more catastrophic, less forgiving, or at least more frustrating than would have been the corresponding failures of a human in the same circumstance. Sometimes, of course, these failures are relatively trivial and benign—like my copier, which keeps insisting that I have placed the book in an orientation that I do not want (when that's exactly what I *do* want). At other times, however, as with the aircraft incident discussed above, or a host of recent aircraft crashes that have been attributed to automation problems (Dornheim, 1995; Billings, 1996; Sarter & Woods, 1995), the consequences are severe.

If the serious consequences of automation resulted merely from failures of their software or hardware components, then this would not be a topic in the study of human factors. However, it turns out that the system problems with automation are distinctly and inexorably linked to human issues of perception and cognition in *dealing* with the automated system in its normally operating state, when the system that the automation is serving has failed, and when the automated component itself has failed (Parasuraman & Riley, 1997). Before addressing these problems, we will first consider why we automate and describe some of the different kinds of automation that exist. Then, after discussing the various human performance problems with automation and suggesting their solution, we conclude by discussing automation issues in industrial process control and manufacturing. While both of these systems have many human factors implications that extend beyond automation, we chose to treat them here because their current and future functions are so closely linked to automation.

WHY AUTOMATE?

The reason designers develop machine replacements for human performance are varied but can be roughly placed into four categories.

1. Some processes are automated because it is either dangerous or impossible for humans to perform the equivalent tasks. In Chapter 9, we learned that teleoperation, or robotic handling of hazardous material (or material in hazardous environments), was a clear example. As another example, certain mathematical or reasoning processes are so complex as to exceed the capabilities of the human brain to perform in a timely fashion (calculate the square root of a six-digit number or carry out a factor analysis). Thus, automated calculation is pretty much a necessity. Also, there are many circumstances in which automation can serve the particular needs of special populations whose disabilities may leave them unable to carry out certain skills without assistance. Examples here would include automatic guidance systems for the quadriplegic or automatic readers for the visually impaired.

2. Other processes, while not impossible, may be very challenging for the unaided human operator, such that humans carry out the functions poorly. (Of course, the border between "impossible" in category 1 and "difficult" is somewhat fuzzy). Here again, mathematical operations are examples. The calculator "automatically" multiplies digits that can be multiplied in the head. But the latter is generally more effortful and error producing. Robotic assembly cells automate highly repetitive and fatiguing human operations. Workers can do these things but often at a cost to fatigue, morale, and sometimes safety. Autopilots on aircraft provide more precise flight control and can also unburden the fatiguing task of continu-

ous control over long-haul flights. As another example, we have learned in Chapters 4 and 13 that humans are not very good at *vigilant monitoring*. Hence, automation is effective in monitoring for relatively rare events, like the "idiot light" that appears when your oil pressure or fuel level is low in the car. Of course, sometimes the automation itself can impose more vigilant monitoring tasks on the human, an example of which we saw in the airplane incident over the Pacific. This is one of the many "ironies of automation," (Bainbridge, 1983).

3. Sometimes automated functions may not replace but may simply *aid* humans in doing things in otherwise difficult circumstances. For example, we have seen in Chapter 6 that human working memory is vulnerable to forgetting. Automated aids that can supplement memory will be useful. Consider an automated telephone operator that can directly print the desired phone number on a small display on your telephone or directly dial it for you (with a $.17 service charge). Predictive displays, discussed in Chapter 8, are examples of automation that relieve the human operator of some cognitively demanding mental operations. Automated planning aids have a similar status (Layton et al., 1994), and pilots report that autopilots can be quite useful in temporarily relieving them from duties of aircraft control when other task demands temporarily make their workload extremely high.

4. Finally, sometimes functions are automated simply because the technology is there and inexpensive, even though it may provide little or no value to the human user. I have gone through painfully long negotiations with automated "phone menus" to get answers that would have taken me only a few seconds with a human operator on the other end of the line. But I am sure the company has found that a computer operator is quite a bit cheaper. Many household appliances and vehicles have a number of automated features that provide only minimal advantages, that may even present costs and, because of their increased complexity and dependence on electrical power, are considerably more vulnerable to failure than are the old manually operated systems they replaced. It is unfortunate when these features are marketed because to their purported "technological sophistication," when they have no real usability advantages.

Classes of Automation

Automated devices can be classified in a number of ways. One useful way is in terms of the kinds of human processes that they are designed to replace (Wiener & Curry, 1981). In this regard we may think of three important categories relating to perception, cognition, and control.

Perception.   Several automated devices have been created to replace human perceptual capabilities. We have seen the potential value of automated monitors, such as the "idiot lights" in cars. Successful examples of automated monitors have been created in aviation, in the form of both the *ground proximity warning system (GPWS),* and the *traffic alert and collision avoidance system* (TCAS; Chappell, 1990). These systems monitor the aircraft's position and trend with respect to the ground and to other aircraft, respectively, alerting the pilot if there is a dangerous potential for collision. The positive influence of the GPWS on safety has been well documented (Diehl, 1991). We saw in Chapter 5 that a major issue in the design of automated monitoring (and alerting) systems is in the establishment of the appropriate level of alarm sensitivity so that "false alarms" do not lead to greater mistrust.

More challenging for technology than the development of simple monitoring and detection functions are automated devices that replace much of the very natural human *perceptual* processes of *pattern recognition*. We generally take for granted the automaticity with which we read text and understand speech. Yet as we saw in Chapter 9, efforts to develop automated speech recognizers have encountered severe challenges, and similar challenges have been confronted in the development of devices to recognize handwriting, even as simple as the address label on an envelope.

Cognition.   Just as human thought and decision making may be viewed as more complex than human perception, so the development of automated devices to replace (or assist) these functions has also presented a substantially greater challenge. An important category of such devices, discussed in Chapter 15, is that concerning *expert systems,* which typically provide intelligent reasoning about a particular restricted domain of knowledge (Chignell & Peterson, 1988). Examples might include reasoning about the infectious diseases that may cause certain symptoms in a patient, recommendations of risk regarding bank loans, or the cause of a malfunction in a complex nuclear power plant. Expert systems are closely related to *decision aids* (discussed in Chapter 7), such as those that might recommend the appropriate course that an aircraft should take in avoiding weather, the wisest investment of money in the market, the appropriate location for oil drilling, or the appropriate sequence of scheduling jobs. In many intelligent automated devices, the joint functions of *diagnosing* the state of affairs and *recommending* a course of action, may be inexorably linked. This, for example, might occur if an intelligent tutor system automatically diagnoses a learner's needs and then presents the appropriate level or type of information.

Control.   Automation may serve to replace different levels of the human's action or control functions. As we learned in Chapter 9, control necessarily depends on the perception of desired input information, and therefore control automation also includes the automation of certain perceptual functions. (These functions usually involve *sensing* position and trend, rather than *categorizing* information.) Autopilots in aircraft, cruise control in driving, and robots in industrial processing represent clear examples of control automation.

Typically, control automation can be characterized by the *level* at which desired intentions are stated by the human operator. For example, in the automated vehicle of the future, some designers envision that a driver may specify the goal destination and allow the car to do all of the driving and navigating to reach that destination. At a lower level of control, the driver may assume control at all intersections but allow the autopilot to navigate curves on the road segments where there are no choice points. At a still lower level, typical of today's vehicles, the automation may only control the gas pedal to maintain the speed to a desired level, while steering control and speed adjustment are carried out manually. Several corresponding levels of aircraft automation exist currently in the *flight management system* of today's modern transport aircraft (Sarter & Woods, 1994, 1995).

PROBLEMS IN AUTOMATION

Whatever the reason chosen for automation, and no matter which kind of function (or combination of human functions) are being "replaced," the history of human interaction with such systems has revealed certain shortcomings. In discussing these shortcomings, however, it is important to stress that they must be balanced against the number of very real *benefits* of automation. There is little doubt that the ground proximity warning system in aircraft, for example, has contributed to the saving of many lives by alerting pilots to possible crashes they might otherwise have failed to note (Diehl, 1991). Autopilots have contributed substantially to fuel savings in aircraft; robots have allowed workers to be removed from unsafe and hazardous jobs; and computers have radically improved the efficiency of many human communications, computations, and information-retrieval processes. Still, there is room for improvement, and the direction of those improvements can be best formulated by understanding the nature of the remaining, or emerging, *problems* that result when humans interact with automated systems.

Automation Reliability

To the extent that automation can be said to be reliable, it does what the human operator expects it to do. The cruise control will hold the car at the set velocity. The automated copier will faithfully reproduce the number of pages requested and so forth. It turns out however that what is important for human interaction is not the reliability per se but the perceived reliability. There may be at least three reasons why automation may be perceived as unreliable.

First, it may itself be unreliable: a component may fail or have been misprogrammed. In this regard, it is noteworthy that automated systems typically are more complex and have more components than their manually operated counterparts and therefore contain more components that *could* go wrong at any given time (Wickens, 1992), as well as working components that are incorrectly signaled to have failed. The nature of these "alarm false alarms" was addressed in Chapter 5.

Second, the human operator who "sets up" the automation system may have made an error. The accidental flight of a Korean Airlines jet over Soviet airspace some years back, creating an incident in which the plane was shot down and all passengers were lost, appears to have resulted when the pilots misprogrammed the automation inertial navigation system (Stein, 1983). The plane faithfully went where it was told to go. But the latter instruction was apparently programmed in error. Thus, automation is often described as "dumb and dutiful."

Third, there are circumstances when the automated system does exactly what it is supposed to do, but the logic behind the system is sufficiently complex and poorly understood by the human operator that it *appears* to the operator to be acting erroneously. Sarter and Woods (1994, 1995; Woods, 1996) have observed that these "automation induced surprises" appear relatively frequently with the complex *flight management systems* in modern aircraft. The automation triggers certain actions, like an abrupt change in air speed or in altitude, for reasons that may not be readily apparent to the pilot. If pilots perceive these events to be failures and try to intervene inappropriately, disaster can result.

Trust: Calibration and Mistrust

The concept of *perceived* automation reliability is critical to understanding the human performance issues because of the relation between reliability and *trust*. As we know, trust in another human is related to the extent to which we can believe that he or she will carry out actions that are expected. Trust has a similar function in a human's belief in the actions of an automated component (Muir, 1987; Lee & Moray, 1992). Ideally, when dealing with any entity, whether a friend, a salesperson, a witness in a court proceeding, or an automated device, trust should be *calibrated*. This means our confidence in the agent, whether human or computer, should be in direct proportion to its reliability. As our confidence goes down, we should be better prepared to act ourselves and more receptive to other sources of advice or information than that provided by the mistrusted agent. While this relation holds true to some extent (Lee & Moray, 1992; Parasuraman, Mouloua, Molloy, & Hilburn, 1996; Kantowitz et al., 1997), there is also some evidence that human trust in automation is not entirely well calibrated: sometimes it is too low, sometimes too high. For example, in some circumstances humans trust their own performance better than that of a computer, even when both are performing at precisely the same level of accuracy (Liu, Fuld, & Wickens, 1993). Mistrust in automation may also result from a failure to understand the nature of the automated algorithms that function to produce an output, whether that output is a perceptual categorization, a decision or diagnostic recommendation, or a controlled action.

The consequences of mistrust are not necessarily severe, but they may lead to inefficiency, when mistrust leads people to reject the good assistance that automation can offer. For example, a pilot who mistrusts a flight management system and prefers to fly the plane by hand may become more fatigued and may fly routes that are less efficient in terms of fuel economy. Many times "doing things by hand" rather than, say, using a computer can lead to slower performance that may be less accurate, when the computer-based automation is of high reliability. As we have noted, mistrust of faulty automated warning systems can lead to the real danger of ignoring legitimate alarms (Sorkin, 1988).

Overtrust and Complacency

In contrast to mistrust, *overtrust* of automation, sometimes referred to as *complacency,* can have severe negative consequences if the automation is less than fully reliable (Parasuraman, Molloy, & Singh, 1993; Parasuraman et al., 1996). We saw at the beginning of the chapter the incident involving the airline pilot who trusted his automation too much, became complacent in monitoring its activity, and nearly met disaster. The cause of complacency is probably an inevitable consequence of the human tendency to let *experience* guide our expectancies. Most automated systems that are marketed *are* quite reliable. (They would not last long in the marketplace if they were not.) Hence, it is likely that many people using a particular system may not ever encounter failures, and hence, their perception of the reliability of the automation is that it is perfect (rather than the high, but still less than 100 percent number that would characterize all operations of the system in question). Perceiving the device to be of perfect reliability, a natural tendency would be for the operator to cease monitoring its operation or at to least monitor it far less vigilantly than is appropriate. This situation is exacerbated by the fact that, as we learned in Chapter 3, people make pretty poor monitors in the first place, when they are doing nothing *but* monitoring (Parasuraman, 1986; Warm, Dember, & Hancock, 1996).

Of course the real problem with complacency, the failure to monitor adequately, only surfaces in the infrequent circumstances when something *does* fail (or is perceived to fail) and the human must (or feels a need to) intervene. Automation then has three distinct implications for human intervention related to detection, situation awareness, and skill loss.

1. *Detection.* In the first place the complacent operator will likely be slower to *detect* a real failure (Wickens & Kessel, 1980). As we have noted in Chapters 4 and 13, detection in circumstances in which events are rare (the automation is reliable) is generally poor since this imposes a vigilance monitoring task. Indeed, the more reliable is the automation, the rarer the "signal events" become, and the poorer is their detection (Parasuraman et al., 1996).

2. *Situation awareness.* It is by now understood that people are better aware of the state of processes in which they are active participants than when they are passive monitors of someone (or something) else carrying out those processes (Cowan, 1988; Endsley, 1996; Hopkin, 1996). Hence, independent of their ability to detect a failure in an automated system, they will be less likely to intervene correctly and appropriately if they are out of the loop and do not fully understand the system's momentary state. This can be particularly problematic if the system is designed with poor feedback regarding the ongoing state of the automated process.

3. *Skill loss.* A final implication of being out of the loop has less to do with failure response than with the long-term consequences. Wiener (1988) has described *deskilling* as the gradual loss of skills an operator may experience by virtue of not having been an active perceiver, decision maker, or controller during the time that automation assumed responsibility for the task. Such a loss of skill may have two implications. First, it may make the operator less trustful of his or her own performance and hence *more* likely to continue to use automation (Lee & Moray, 1992). Second, it may degrade still more the operator's ability to intervene appropriately should the system fail. The relation between trust and these features of automation is shown in Figure 16.1.

Indeed, another one of the ironies of automation is that the very circumstances in which some automated devices fail are those in which they are confronted by problems or challenges so difficult that they cannot handle them. Such was the case with the failed engine in our story at the beginning of the chapter. These circumstances may also occur with decision aids that are programmed to handle ordinary problems but must "throw up their hands" at very complex ones. It is, of course, in these very circumstances that the automated system may

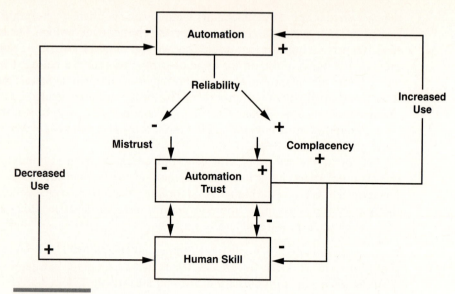

FIGURE 16.1

Elements of automation reliability and human trust. The "+" and "−" indicate the direction of effects. For example, increased (+) automation reliability leads to increased (+) trust in automation, which in turn leads to increased (+) use and a decrease (−) in human skill.

"hand off" the problem to its human counterpart (Hopkin & Wise, 1996). But now the latter, who will be out of the loop and may have lost skill, will be suddenly asked to handle that problem of the *most* difficult, challenging nature, hardly a fair request for one who may have been complacent and whose skill might have been degraded.

Automation and Workload

Automation is often introduced with the goal of reducing operator workload (see Chapter 13). For example, an automated device to control lane keeping or headway maintenance in driving may be assumed to reduce driving workload (Hancock et al., 1996; see Chapter 17) and hence allow mental resources to be used for other tasks. However, in practice, sometimes the workload is reduced by automation in environments when workload is already too low and loss of arousal, rather than high workload, is the most important problem (e.g., driving at night). In fact, it is probably incorrect to think that vigilance tasks are low workload at all, if attention is adequately allocated to them so that event detection will be timely (Warm, Dember, & Hancock, 1996). Indeed, the effective monitoring of automated systems can be a task of both high workload and high stress.

Loss of Human Cooperation

In nonautomated, multiperson systems, there are many circumstances in which subtle communications, achieved by nonverbal means or voice inflection, can provide valuable sources of information (Chapter 19; Bowers et al., 1996). The air traffic controller can often tell if a pilot is in trouble by the sound of the voice, for example. Sometimes automation may eliminate these valuable channels. For example, in the digital *datalink* system (Kerns, 1991), which is proposed to replace air-to-ground radio communications with digital messages that are typed in and appear on a display panel, such information will be gone. Furthermore, there are often circumstances in which a spirit of negotiation between humans, necessary to solve nonroutine problems, may be eliminated by automation. Many of us have undoubtably been frustrated when trying to interact with an uncaring, automated phone menu in order to try to get a question answered that was not foreseen by those who developed the automated logic.

Job Satisfaction

The issues noted above have primarily addressed *performance* problems associated with automated systems. But the issue of job satisfaction goes well beyond performance (and beyond the scope of this book) to consider the morale implications of the worker who is being replaced by automation. In reconsidering the reasons of "why automate" discussed earlier in the chapter, we can imagine that automation that will improve safety or unburden the human operator will be well received. But automation which is introduced merely because the technology is available or which increases the job efficiency may not necessarily be well received. Many operators are highly skilled and proud of their craft. Replacement by robot or computer will not be well received. If the unhappy, demoralized operator then is still asked to remain in a potential position of resuming control, an unpleasant situation could result.

HUMAN-CENTERED AUTOMATION

Correction of the several problems with automation discussed above can potentially be achieved by incorporating the principles of *human-centered automation* (Billings, 1996). Of course there are a number of things that can be meant by the phrase human-centered automation. It can refer to keeping the human more closely "in touch" with the process being automated, to giving the human more authority over the automation, to choosing a level of human involvement that leads to the best performance, or to creating the worker's maximum satisfaction with the workplace. In fact, all of these characteristics are important human factors considerations, despite the fact that they may not always be totally compatible with each other. We present below our own list of five human-centered automation features that we believe will achieve the goal of maximum harmony between human, system, and automation.

1. *Keeping the human informed.* However much authority automation assumes in a task, it is important for the supervisor to be informed of what the automation is doing and why, via good displays. As a positive example, the pilot should be able to see the amount of thrust delivered by an engine, as well as the amount of compensation that the autopilot might have to make to keep the plane flying straight. A negative example here is a small feature that contributed to the catastrophe at the Three Mile Island nuclear power plant (Rubinstein & Mason, 1979). Among the myriad displays, one in particular signaled to the crew that an

automatic valve had closed. But in fact the display only reflected that the valve had received a signal to close; the valve had become stuck and did *not* actually close, hence continuing to pass liquid and drain coolant from the reactor core. Because the operator only saw the signal "closed" and was not informed of the processes underlying the automation, the status of the plant coolant was misdiagnosed, and the radioactive core was eventually exposed.

A more positive example of keeping informed lies with the evolution of the TCAS system, alerting pilots to potential midair collisions, as discussed earlier in this chapter. The system not only *commands* the pilot how to maneuver (an automated decision process) but offers a *status* display of the location of the nearby aircraft, thereby allowing the pilot to be informed of the reasons for the command.

Of course, however, as pointed out in Chapter 7, merely presenting information is not sufficient to guarantee that it will be understood. Coherent and integrated displays are also necessary to attain that goal. A criticism of the current level of automation in the flight deck management system is that the integrated picture of what the FMS is doing must be gleaned by scanning across three separate panels to capture information that is represented digitally or symbolically, not spatially (Sarter & Woods, 1992). Parasuraman et al. (1996) have shown how attention to designing more integrated displays can help keep the automation monitor better able to detect and respond to failures.

2. *Keeping the human trained.* As long as any automated system might conceivably fail or require rapid human intervention, it is essential that the human's skill in carrying out the automated function be maintained at as high a level as possible. (In fact, it could be argued that it is *more* critical for the human to possess high skill levels, given the unexpected circumstances in which manual intervention may be required.) In this regard, it is certainly helpful if the pilot has plenty of manual skill before being introduced to the automation. Hence, aircraft pilots learn to "hand fly" an aircraft before being introduced to its autopilots. It is also useful for the operator to have lots of training in "exploring" the automation's various functions and features in an interactive fashion (Irving, Polson, & Irving, 1994). But even these steps may be inadequate if the operator subsequently uses automation extensively, while the manual skills are forgotten (Wiener, 1988. See Figure 16.1). Thus, so long as reversion to manual performance remains a possibility, some form of continued recurrent training in the manual mode is critical, whether this training is accomplished by sessions of manual control or by adapting the *level of automation* to one in which the operator continues to exercise some manual control skills, an issue we consider next.

3. *Keeping the operator in the loop.* This is one of the most challenging goals of human-centered automation. How does one keep the operator sufficiently in the control loop so that awareness of the automated state is maintained without reverting fully to manual control so that the valuable intentions of automation (e.g,. to reduce workload when needed) are defeated. Endsley and Kiris (1995) have defined five levels of involvement on a continuum of automation, shown in Fig. 16.2. At the top, the human does everything. At the bottom, nothing. When these levels were implemented and compared in an automated vehicle navigational task, the authors found indeed that the highest levels of automation degraded the driver's situation awareness and their ability to jump back into the control loop if the system failed. There was, however, some evidence that performance was equivalent across the three middle conditions; that is, as long as the human maintained some involvement in decision making regarding whether to accept the automation suggestions (by vetoing unacceptable solutions at level 4), then adequate levels of situation awareness were maintained even as workload was reduced.

Nevertheless, in general, there is an inherent dilemma for the system designer whenever automation is intended to unburden the user. Greater unburdening will usually lead to greater loss of awareness. The dilemma may be solved in part by selectively introducing higher automation levels, only when they are needed. This is the human-centered issue of flexible and adaptive automation that we turn to next.

4. *Making the automation flexible and adaptive.* A conclusion that can be clearly drawn from studies of automation is that the *amount* of automation needed for any task will be likely to vary from person to person and within a person will vary over time. Hence, a flexible automation system, in which the level could vary along the dimension of Figure 16.2, would appear to be preferable over one that is fixed and rigid. Flexible automation then simply means that different levels are possible. One driver may choose to use cruise control, the other may not. This flexibility seems to be a wise goal to seek.

Adaptive automation, however, goes one step further than flexible automation, by implementing the level of automation based on some particular characteristics of the environment-user-task (Rouse, 1988; Scerbo, 1996; Fig. 16.3). For example, an adaptive automation system would be one in which the level of automation would increase as either the workload imposed on the operator increased or the operator's capacity decreased (e.g., because of fatigue). While such systems have proven effective (Rouse, 1988; Parasuraman et al., 1993), for example, in environments like the aircraft flight deck in which there are wide variations in workload over time, they should be implemented only with great caution because of their potential pitfalls (Wickens 1992). Because such systems are adaptive closed-loop systems, they may fall prey to problems of negative feedback, closed-loop instability, as discussed in Chapter 9. Humans do not always easily deal with rapidly changing

Level of Automation		Roles	
		Human	System
None	1	Decide, Act	———
Decision Support	2	Decide, Act	Suggest
Consensual AI	3	Concur	Decide, Act
Monitored AI	4	Veto	Decide, Act
Full Automation	5	———	Decide, Act

FIGURE 16.2

Continuum of shared responsibility between human and computer (*Source:* Endsley, M.R., and Kiris, E.O., 1995. The out-of-the-loop performance problem and level of control in automation. *Human Factors,* 37[2], pp. 381–394. Reprinted with permission. Copyright 1995 by the Human Factors and Ergonomics Society. All rights reserved.)

system configurations. Remember that *consistency* is an important feature in design (Chapter 8). Finally, as Rouse (1988) has noted, computers may be good at *assuming* automation (e.g., on the basis of measuring degraded performance by the human in the loop) but are not always good at giving back control to the human.

5. *Maintaining a positive management philosophy.* A worker's acceptance and appreciation of automation can be greatly influenced by the management's philosophy (McClumpha & James, 1994). If, on the one hand, workers view that automation is being "imposed" because it can do the job better than they can, their attitudes toward it will probably be poor. On the other hand, if automation is introduced as an aid to improve human-system performance and a philosophy can be imparted in which the human remains the master and automation the servant, then the attitude will be likely to remain more accepting (Billings, 1991, 1996). This can be accompanied by good training of what the automation does and how it does its task. Under such circumstances, a more favorable attitude will also probably lead to better understanding of automation, better appreciation of its strengths, and more effective utilization of its features. Indeed studies of the introduction of automation into organizations have revealed several features of management that have made this process successful (Bessant et al., 1992).

AUTOMATION-BASED COMPLEX SYSTEMS
Industrial Manufacturing and Process Control

There are a wide variety of tasks confronting today's worker, in which the human operator must control an industrial process in order to make some product. Some of the products are distinct and discrete manufactured units, like automobiles,

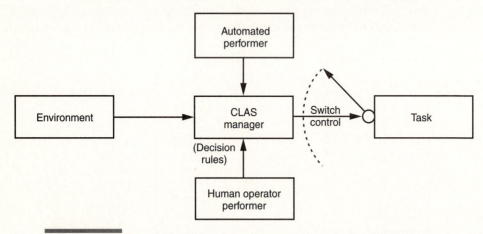

FIGURE 16.3

Adaptive automation. The choice of assigning the task between the human or the automated system is based upon some intelligent agent that considers environmental demands and capabilities of both human and agent. (*Source:* Wickens, C.D., 1992. *Engineering Psychology and Humand Performance* (2nd ed.) New York: HarperCollins. Reprinted by permission of Addison-Wesley Educational Publishers, Inc.)

computers, and so forth (manufacturing). Other kinds of products are not so much distinct entities but rather continuous ones, like the production of electrical or nuclear power, the distillation of chemicals, or the refinement of petroleum products (Meshkati, 1996; Moray, 1997).

In both cases, there is usually a human operator responsible for the process. However, because of both the complexity of and the delays in the processes involved, it is often the case that the operator does not directly control the process, as in the closed-loop tracking tasks that we discussed in the last chapter. Rather, the control is often mediated by some forms of automation, which is why we consider these processes in the present chapter, and not Chapter 9.

Of course there are a large number of important human factors issues related to industrial process control that are "generic" in the sense that they are relevant to all chapters discussed in this book. For example, many workstations are poorly laid out, with displays that are not readily visible or controls that may be confusing or may require awkward and dangerous postures to reach. The climate may be noisy or poorly ventilated, and work shifts may be structured in a way that fatigue and sleep disruption are serious problems (Chapter 13). While all of these are critical issues, their treatment can be found in other chapters. Here we focus on the specific features of the process control task itself that have important human factors implications.

Process Control

In process control, energy exchange and chemical mixture are usually critical elements. As noted, many of these processes are slow, or lagged, a feature that we saw in the Chapter 9, makes human control quite challenging. In addition, of course, the processes are often complex, involving a combination of many processes with many different entities (fuel, heat, water, steam, etc.). The combination of lags and complexity, coupled with the hazardous nature of many of these processes (e.g., toxic or superheated), often requires high levels of automation to accomplish the goals. Finally, because of the hazards involved, there are very high risks associated with the operations. When things go wrong, incidents of the magnitude of the Three Mile Island, Bhopal, or Chernobyl disasters are very real possibilities (Reason, 1990; Meshkati, 1996; Read, 1993).

All of these features of process control influence different aspects of the human supervisor's performance of three different phases of the task: Transients (start-up and shutdown), steady-state operations, and fault management. Each of these phases have somewhat different characteristics and impose different demands on the human operator (Wickens, 1992; Moray, 1997).

During transients, many processes are highly volatile and unstable. The operator workload demands are high, and many aspects of the task approximate a higher order tracking task, in that variables are manipulated to bring some lagged quantity (the system output, like energy level) through a carefully defined trajectory to a target value (the command input). The process is sometimes made more difficult because this phase is encountered rarely and displays that are designed for steady-state operation do not always give a coherent picture of whether the start up is behaving normally. (As a simple example, look at all the warning "idiot lights" that light up on your car dashboard for the first few seconds after you turn the ignition.) Because of the sluggish nature of many of these processes, we are not surprised to hear that predictive displays (see Chapter 8) are very useful features (Woods & Roth, 1988).

During steady-state operations, which are in effect almost all of the time, the life of the supervisor often becomes very routine and occasionally boring, involving only constant monitoring of plant state, record keeping, and occasional "trimming" (minor adjustment of control variables). Hence, during this period, many of the issues of automation monitoring discussed earlier in the chapter become relevant. (Parasuraman, 1986) How do we keep the operator actively involved in updating his or her situation awareness or mental picture of the system when there is little to do, a goal that is particularly challenging during the middle of the night (see Chapter 13)?

The reason such monitoring is critical is because of the rare but extremely dangerous circumstances in which there is a fault or failure within the plant that must be *managed.* This is the third phase we discuss. Fault management actually has three related components: (1) Safety must be ensured; (2) damage to the plant must be minimized, and the efficiency of operation should be preserved; and (3) ideally the nature of the fault should be diagnosed. These goals are, of course, not always compatible with each other. Too much concern for diagnosis, for example, may lead the operator to forego operations that are necessary just to restore the plant to a safe operation.

Most plants are equipped with sufficient sensors and warning systems so that if something serious goes wrong within the plant, the operator will easily know it. Hence, using the terminology of signal detection theory discussed in Chapter 4, the hit rate of *detection* of faults is not a problem. However, there are real concerns for false alarms. As discussed in Chapter 5, there may be instances in which a warning indicates a possible fault when there is none simply because the "setpoint" of some parameter indicator has been set to an overly sensitive level. Under such circumstances, if an operator has safety as her *only* concern and shuts down the process, this could unnecessarily lead to large costs to the company or inconveniences to the customer. Hence, information must be sufficiently comprehensive so that the operator can go beyond noting that just a single indicator is out of bounds and will be able to diagnose the nature and seriousness of the initial symptoms of a problem.

In this regard, however, many process control plants present another problem. Many display arrays are not designed to provide a comprehensive picture of the nature of an underlying fault. Because of the complex interactions between the underlying system components, a given fault (like a stuck valve or a broken pipe) may rapidly cascade to bring a large number of parameters above a warning region on their display, leading, perhaps within a few seconds, to a confusing array of flashing lights (Grimm, 1976). The operator's efforts to interpret this confusing picture, discussed at the opening of Chapter 8, may well be further hindered by a loud and stress-inducing alarm sound (see Chapter 5).

Considering this scenario, which may well have contributed to the deteriorating situation at both Three Mile Island and Chernobyl, it is understandable that important human factors contributions can and should be made in two directions. The first is designing comprehensive and integrated system displays that present information in a manner consistent with the operator's mental model of the plant (Vicente & Rasmussen, 1992; Vicente, 1992; Vicente et al., 1996). Thus, for example, the mimic display shown in Figure 16.4, proposed for a pasteurizer plant, portrays the variables in a manner that is laid out according to the spatial and caused flow of matter and energy. We also saw in Chapter 8 (Figure 8.12) how the use of integrated displays could foster an understanding of the relation between plant variables.

The second direction is through the development of automation supports for diagnosis. Such supports typically involve expert systems (see Chapter 15) that can integrate symptomatic information (i.e., parameters that are out of their normal range) and provide educated diagnoses of the source of the fault. As we have noted above, however, this level of automation brings to the fore the critical issues of trust (Lee & Moray, 1992). With what level of accuracy can the expert system be expected to operate, particularly because the evidence itself on which the di-

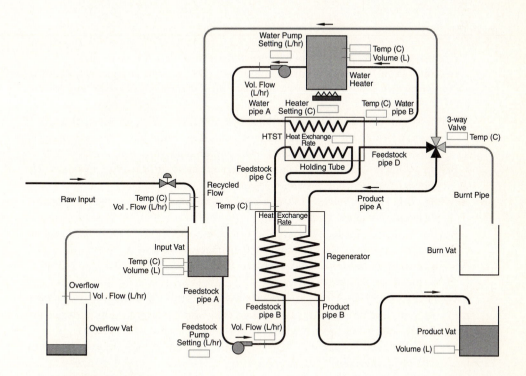

FIGURE 16.4

Example of a functional mimic display. (*Source:* Courtesy of Dal Vernon Reising.)

agnosis is based may be fuzzy? And if an automation-suggested diagnosis is incorrect, is there a danger that this might lead the operator down the wrong path (i.e., to a sense of overtrust)? Many of these issues are challenges that await the contributions of good human factors research.

Automated Manufacturing

A somewhat different form of automation appears in the automated manufacturing station, where the product is more typically "assembled" by mechanical (often robotic) means rather than generated by thermochemical means. Issues of robotic control and supervision are of course relevant here, as discussed in Chapter 9. However, in *flexible manufacturing* systems (Sanderson, 1989), there are important added issues of scheduling. A flexible manufacturing system is one in which a given unit may possibly be reconfigured and employed for different tasks over time, depending on the changing needs. As a consequence, this flexibility may impose heavy cognitive demands on the supervisor's scheduling and predictive abilities (Biard & Salvendy, 1994). Hence, it is not surprising again that effective and accurate predictive displays can support this process well (Sanderson, 1989, 1991).

REFERENCES

Bainbridge, L. (1983). Ironies of automation. *Automatica, 19*(6), 775–779.

Bessant, J., Levy, P., Ley, C., Smith, S., and Tranfield, D. (1992). Organization design for factory 2000. *The International Journal of Human Factors in Manufacturing, 2*(2), 95–125.

Biard, S., and Salvendy, G. (1994). Analytical modeling and experimental study of human workload in scheduling of advanced manufacturing systems. *The International Journal of Human Factors in Manufacturing. 4*, 205–234.

Billings, C.E. (1991). Toward a human-centered aircraft automation philosophy. *The International Journal of Aviation Psychology, 1*(4), 261–270.

Billings, C.E. (1996). *Aviation automation: The search for a human-centered approach.* Mahwah, NJ: Lawrence Erlbaum.

Bowers, C.A., Oser, R.L., Salas, E., and Cannon-Bowers, J.A. (1996). Team performance in automated systems. In R. Parasuraman and M. Mouloua (eds.), *Automation and human performance: Theory and applications* (pp. 243–263). Mahwah, NJ: Lawrence Erlbaum.

Chappell, S.L. (1990). Pilot performance research for TCAS. *Managing the modern cockpit: Third human error avoidance techniques conference proceedings* (SAE 902357; pp. 51–68). Warrendale, PA: Society of Automotive Engineers.

Chignell, H.J., and Peterson, J.G. (1988). Strategic issues in knowledge engineering. *Human Factors, 30*, 381–394.

Cowan, N. (1988). Evolving conceptions of memory storage, selective attention, and their mutual constraints within the human information processing system. *Psychological Bulletin, 104*(2), 163–191.

Diehl, A.E. (1991). Human performance and systems safety considerations in aviation mishaps. *International Journal of Aviation Psychology, 1*(2), 97–106.

Dornheim, M.P. (1995). Dramatic incidents highlight mode problems in cockpit. *Aviation Week and Space Technology.* (Jan 30) 55–59.

Endsley, M.R., and Kiris, E.O. (1995). The out-of-the-loop performance problem and level of control in automation. *Human Factors, 37*(2), 381–394.

Endsley, M.R., and Rodgers, M.D. (1996). Attention distribution and situation awareness in air traffic control (pp. 82–85). *Proceedings of the 40th Annual Meeting of the Human Factors & Ergonomics Society.* Santa Monica, CA: Human Factors and Ergononics Society.

Erzberger, H., Davis, T.J., and Green, S. (1993). Design of center-TRACON automation system. AGARD Conference Proceedings 538: Machine intelligence in air traffic management (pp. 11-1–11-12). Neuilly sur Seine, France: Advisory Group for Aerospace Research and Development.

Grimm, R. (1976). Autonomous I/O-colour-screen-system for process-control with virtual keyboards adapted to the actual task. In T.B. Sheridan and G. Johannsen (eds.), *Monitoring behavior and supervisory control.* New York: Plenum Press.

Hancock, P.A., Parasuraman, R., and Byrne, E. A. (1996). Driver-centered issues in advanced automation for motor vehicles. In R. Parasuraman and M. Mouloua (eds.), *Automation and human performance: Theory and applications* (pp. 337–364). Mahwah, NJ: Lawrence Erlbaum.

Hopkin, D. (1996). *Human factors of air traffic control.* London: Taylor & Francis.

Hopkin, V.D., and Wise, J.A. (1996). Human factors in air traffic system automation. In R. Parasuraman and M. Mouloua (eds.), *Automation and human performance: Theory and applications* (pp. 319–336). Mahwah, NJ: Lawrence Erlbaum.

Irving, S., Polson, P., and Irving, J.E. (1994). A GOMS analysis of the advanced automated cockpit. *CHI-94 Conference Proceedings.* New York: Association of Computing Machinery.

Kantowitz, B.H., Hanowski, R.J., and Kantowitz, S.C. (1997). Driver acceptance of unreliable traffic information. *Human Factors, 2,* pp. 164–176.

Kerns, K. (1991). Data-link communication between controllers and pilots: A review and synthesis of the simulation literature. *The International Journal of Aviation Psychology, 1*(3), 181–204.

Layton, C., Smith, P.J., and McCoy, E. (1994). Design of a cooperative problem-solving system for enroute flight planning: An empirical evaluation. *Human Factors, 36*(10), 94–119.

Lee, J., and Moray, N. (1992). Trust, control strategies and allocation of function in human-machine systems. *Ergonomics, 35*(10), 1243–1270.

Liu, Y., Fuld, R., and Wickens, C.D. (1993). Monitoring behavior in manual and automated scheduling systems. *International Journal of Man-Machine Studies, 39,* 1015–1029.

McClumpha, A.M., and James, M. (1994). Understanding automated aircraft. In M. Mouloua and R. Parasuraman (eds.), *Human performance in automated systems: Current research and trends* (pp. 183–190). Hillsdale, NJ: Lawrence Erlbaum.

Meshkati, N. (1996). Orgaizational and safety factors in automated oil and gas pipeline systems. In R. Parasuraman and M. Mouloua (eds.), *Automation and human performance: Theory and applications* (pp. 427–446). Mahwah, NJ: Lawrence Erlbaum.

Moray, N. (1997). Human factors in process control. In G. Salvendy (ed.), *The handbook of human factors and ergonomics* (2nd ed.). New York: Wiley.

Muir, B. (1987). Trust between humans and machines, and the design of decision aids. *International Journal of Man-Machine Studies, 27,* 527–549.

National Transportation Safety Board (1986). China Airlines B-747 Northwest of San Francisco, Cal. 2/09/85 (NTSB Report # AAR-86/03. Washington, DC.

Parasuraman, R. (1986). Vigilance, monitoring and search. In K. Boff, L. Kaufman, and J. Thomas (eds.), *Handbook of perception and performance* (*Vol. 2,* pp. 43.1–43.39). New York: Wiley.

Parasuraman, R., Molloy, R., and Singh, I.L. (1993). Performance consequences of automation-induced complacency. *International Journal of Aviation Psychology, 3*(1), 1–23.

Parasuraman, R., Mouloua, M., Molloy, R., and Hilburn, B. (1996). Monitoring of automated systems. In R. Parasuraman and M. Mouloua (Eds.), *Automation and human performance: Theory and applications* (pp. 91–115). Mahwah, NJ: Lawrence Erlbaum.

Parasuraman, R., and Riley, V. (1997). Humans and automation: Use, misuse, disuse, abuse. *Human Factors.*

Read, P.P. (1993). *Ablaze: The story of the heroes and victims of Chernobyl.* New York: Random House.

Reason, J. (1990). *Human error.* New York: Cambridge University Press.

Rouse, W.B. (1988). Adaptive aiding for human/computer control. *Human Factors, 30*(4), 431–443.

Rubinstein, T., and Mason, A.F. (1979). The accident that shouldn't have happened: An analysis of Three Mile Island. *IEEE Spectrum,* Nov., pp. 38–40.

Sanderson, P.M. (1989). The human planning and scheduling role in advanced manufacturing systems: An emerging human factors domain. *Human Factors, 31,* 635–666.

Sanderson, P.M. (1991). Toward the model human scheduler. *International Journal of Human Factors in Manufacturing. 1,* 195–219.

Sarter, N.B., and Woods, D.D. (1992). Pilot interaction with cockpit automation: Operational experiences with the flight management system. *The International Journal of Aviation Psychology, 2*(4), 303–321.

Sarter, N.B., and Woods, D.D. (1994). Pilot interaction with cockpit automation II: An experimental study of pilots' model and awareness of the flight management system. *The International Journal of Aviation Psychology, 4*(1), 1–28.

Sarter, N.B., and Woods, D.D. (1995). "How in the world did we get into that mode?" *Human Factors, 37*(1), 5–19.

Scerbo, M.W. (1996). Theoretical perspectives on adaptive automation. In R. Parasuraman and M. Mouloua (eds.), *Automation and human performance: Theory and applications* (pp. 37–64). Mahwah, NJ: Lawrence Erlbaum.

Sorkin, R. (1988). Why are people turning off our alarms? *Journal of Acoustial Society of America, 84,* 1107–1108.

Sperandio, J.C. (1976). From the plane space to the air mobile space: Experimental comparison between two displays of spatio temporal information. *Le Travail Humain, 30,* 130–154.

Stein, K.J. (1983). Human factors analyzed in 007 navigational error. *Aviation Week and Space Technology,* 165–167.

Vicente, K.J. (1992). Multilevel interfaces for power plant control. *Nuclear Safety, 33*(3), 381–397.

Vicente, K.J., Moray, N., Lee, J.D., Rasmussen, J. Jones, B.G., Brock, R., and Djemil, T. (1996). Evaluation of a Rankine Cycle display for nuclear power plant monitoring and diagnosis. *Human Factors, 38*(3), 506–522.

Vicente, K.J., and Rasmussen, J. (1992). Ecological interface design: Theoretical foundations. *IEEE Transactions on Systems, Man, and Cybernetics, 22*(4), 589–606.

Warm, J.S., Dember, W.N., and Hancock, P.A. (1996). Vigilance and workload in automated systems. In R. Parasuraman and M. Mouloua (eds.), *Automation and human performance: Theory and applications* (pp. 183–199). Mahwah, NJ: Lawrence Erlbaum.

Wickens, C.D. (1992). *Engineering psychology and human performance* (2nd ed.). New York: HarperCollins.

Wickens, C.D., and Kessel, C. (1980). The processing resource demands of failure detection in dynamic systems. *Journal of Experimental Psychology: Human Perception & Performance, 6,* 564–577.

Wiener, E.L. (1988). Cockpit automation. In E.L. Wiener and D.C. Nagel (eds.), *Human factors in aviation* (pp. 433–461). San Diego, CA: Academic Press.

Wiener, E.L., and Curry, R.E. (1980). Flight deck automation: Promises and problems. *Ergonomics, 23*(10), 995–1011.

Woods, D.D. (1996). Decomposing automation: Apparent simplicity, real complexity. In R. Parasuraman and M. Mouloua (eds.), *Automation and human performance: Theory and applications* (pp. 3–17). Mahwah, NJ: Lawrence Erlbaum.

Woods, D.D., and Roth, E. (1988). Aiding human performance: II. From cognitive analysis to support systems. *Le Travail Humain, 51,* 139–172.

CHAPTER 17

Transportation Human Factors

Every day, millions of people travel by land, water, and air. There are certain features of vehicles that make them stand apart from several of the other systems with which human factors is concerned and hence call for a separate chapter. Tracking and continuous manual control are normally a critical part of any human-vehicle interaction. Navigational issues also become important when travel is undertaken in unfamiliar environments. Furthermore, those environments may change dramatically across the course of a journey from night to day, rain to sunshine, or sparse to crowded conditions. Such changes have major implications for human interaction with the transportation system. The advent of new technologies, such as the satellite-based global positioning system, and the increased power of computers are in the process of revolutionizing many aspects of ground and air transportation. Finally, because aircraft and ground vehicles are often moving at high speeds, the safety implications of transportation systems are tremendously important. Indeed in no other system than the car do so many people have access to such high-risk systems and particularly a system in which their own lives are critically at risk. Every year, 500,000 people worldwide lose their lives in auto accidents, and around 40,000 lives per year are lost in the United States alone (Evans, 1996), while the cost to the U.S. economy of traffic accident–related injuries is typically well over $100 billion per year.

In this chapter, we place greatest emphasis on the two most popular means of transportation: the automobile (or truck) and the airplane; these have received the greatest amount of study from a human factors perspective. However, we also consider briefly some of the human factors implications of public ground transportation, both with regard to the operators of such vehicles and to the potential consumer, who may choose to ride with public transportation rather than use a personally owned vehicle.

AUTOMOTIVE HUMAN FACTORS

The incredibly high rate of accidents on the highways and their resulting cost to insurance companies and to personal well-being of the accident victims (through injuries) makes highway safety an issue of national importance; the fact that the human is a participant in most accidents and that a great majority of these (as high as 90 percent) are attributable to human error bring these issues directly into the domain of human factors. Many of the human factors issues relevant to highway safety are dealt with elsewhere in the book. But here we integrate them all, as they pertain to the task of driving a vehicle, often at high speeds along a roadway. In this section we first present a task analysis of the vehicle roadway system and then proceed to treat critical issues related to *visibility, hazards and collisions, impaired drivers, training and selection,* and *automation.*

At the outset, it is important to note that driving typically involves two somewhat competing goals, both of which have human factors concerns. *Productivity* involves reaching one's destination in a *timely* fashion, which may lead to speeding. *Safety* involves the avoidance of accidents (to oneself and others), which is sometimes compromised by speeding. Our emphasis in this chapter will be predominantly on the safety aspects. Safety itself can be characterized by a wide range of statistics (Evans, 1991, 1996), including fatalities, injuries, accidents, citations, or nonevasive measures of speeding.

Two aspects of interpreting these statistics are important to remember. First, figures like fatality *rates* can be greatly skewed by the choice of *baseline.* For example, a comparison of fatalities per year may provide very different results from a comparison of fatalities per passenger mile. In the United States, the former figure has increased or remained steady over the past decade, while the latter has declined (Evans 1996). Second, statistics can be heavily biased by certain segments of the population. For example, as we will see, accident statistics including the full population may be very different from those that do not include young drivers, male drivers, or young male drivers.

Task Analysis of the Vehicle Roadway System

The Tracking Task.   As shown in Figure 17.1, the vehicle driver performs in a multitask environment. At the core of this environment, shown at the top, is the two-dimensional tracking task of vehicle control. Using the terminology introduced in Chapter 9, the lateral task of maintaining lane position can be thought of as a second-order control task with preview (the roadway ahead) and a predictor (the heading of the vehicle). The "longitudinal" task is that of speed keeping, with a command input either given by the internal goals (travel fast but do not lose control or get caught for speeding) or by the behavior of the vehicles, hazards, or traffic control signals in front. Thus, the tracking *display* presents three channels of command visual information to be tracked along the two axes: Lateral tracking is commanded by the roadway; longitudinal tracking is commanded by a distributed set of inputs—the flow of motion along the roadway, the location or distance of hazards, or traffic control devices and the speedometer. The quality of this visual input may be degraded by poor visibility conditions (night, fog) or by momentary scans away from the roadway.

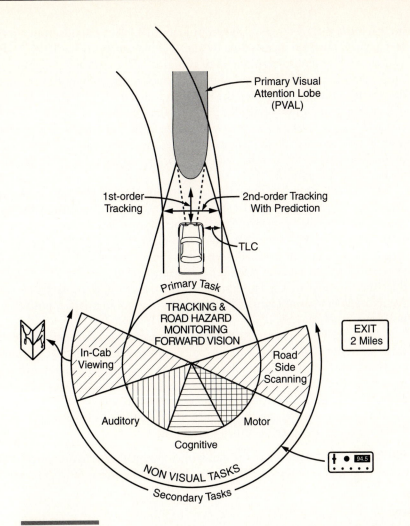

Primary Visual
Attention Lobe
(PVAL)

1st-order
Tracking

2nd-order Tracking
With Prediction

TLC

Primary Task

TRACKING &
ROAD HAZARD
MONITORING
FORWARD VISION

In-Cab
Viewing

Road
Side
Scanning

EXIT
2 Miles

Auditory

Motor

Cognitive

NON VISUAL TASKS

Secondary Tasks

FIGURE 17.1

Representation of the driver's information-processing tasks. The top of the figure depicts
the tracking or vehicle control tasks involved with lane keeping and hazard avoidance. The
bottom of the figure presents the various sources of competition for resources away from
vehicle tracking. These may be thought of as secondary tasks.

Research has indicated that the best measure of lateral tracking performance
is not a measure of error, but a measure of *time to lane crossing*, or TLC, which provides a direct estimate of the average amount of time a driver has available before
the goal (of staying within the lane or on the roadway) is lost (Godthelp et al.,
1983), given the current heading and distance from the lane edge.

The Multitask Environment. The driving task is also defined by a series of component tasks, varying in their degree of importance (see Chapters 6 and 13). We
can define the primary task as that of lane keeping and roadway hazard monitoring. Both of these depend critically on the *primary visual attention lobe* (PVAL) of

information, a shaded region shown in Figure 17.1 that extends from a few meters to a few hundred meters directly ahead (Mourant & Rockwell, 1972). Figure 17.2 shows side and forward views of this area. Most critical for highway safety (and a force for human factors design concerns) are any competing tasks that will draw *visual attention* away from the PVAL. Indeed a study by Malaterre (1990) indicated that *inattention* was the leading human error cause of accidents. The most critical resource diversions of course are those from other competing visual tasks. But multiple resource theory tells us that *any* concurrent task (auditory, cognitive, motor) can create some conflict with monitoring and processing and information in the PVAL (Chapter 6).

The visual secondary tasks that act as sources of distraction, shown in the middle of Figure 17.1, may relate to scans to the side of the roadway for signs or scans inside the vehicle at maps, radio controls, or other devices (Dingus et al., 1988; Table 17.1). From the standpoint of highway safety, the most common denominator of all of these visual attention traps is the amount of time that visual resources are diverted away from the PVAL (Benel, Huey, & Lerner, 1995). When this time is more than some minimum value, a dangerous circumstance is created. For a variety of reasons discussed below the amount of this danger is directly proportional to vehicle speed.

While the visual channel is thus the most important channel for the driver, there are nontrivial concerns with secondary motor activity related for example to adjusting controls, dialing cellular phones, or reaching and pulling, which can compete with manual resources for effective steering. Similarly as noted in our discussion of multiple resources in Chapter 6, intense cognitive activity or auditory information processing can compete for perceptual/cognitive resources with the visual channels necessary for efficient scanning.

The Cabin Environment.   From the standpoint of vehicle safety, it is apparent that one of the best ways to minimize the dangerous distracting effects of "eyes in" time is to

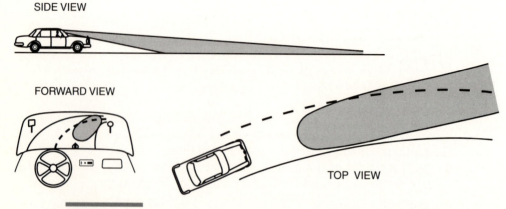

FIGURE 17.2
Representation of the primary visual attention lobe (PVAL) from the forward view, top view, and side view.

create the simplest, most user-friendly design of the internal controls and displays that is possible, using the many principles described earlier in the book. Controls should be consistently located, adequately separated, and compatibly linked to their associated displays (Chapter 9); displays should be of high contrast (Chapter 4), interpretable, and easy to read (Chapter 8); and design of the task environment within the vehicle should strive toward simplicity by avoiding unnecessary features and gizmos.

Visibility

Great care in the design of motor vehicles must be given to the visibility of the critical PVAL for vehicle control and hazard detection. Four main categories of visibility issues can be identified.

Anthropometry. First, the application of good human factors requires that attention be given to the anthropometric factors of *seating,* discussed in Chapter 10. Can seat adjustments easily allow a wide range of body statures to be positioned so that the eye point provides adequate visibility down the roadway, or will drivers with the smallest seated eye height be unable to see hazards directly in front of their cars? (Such anthropometric concerns must also address the *reachability* of different controls.) Vehicles provide a clear example of where the philosophy of "design for the mean" is *not* appropriate. However in creating various flexible options for seating adjustment to accommodate individual differences in body stature, great care must be given to making adjustment controls both accessible (so they can and *will* be used) and interpretable (i.e., compatible) so that they will be used *correctly* (Fig. 17.3).

FIGURE 17.3
Compatible seating control. Note the spatial congruence between the control interface and the area of seat to be controlled. (*Source:* Anthony D. Andre, Interface Analysis Associates, San Jose, CA.).

Illumination.   Second, as we noted in Chapter 4, putting information visible within the line of sight does not guarantee that it will be sensed and perceived. In vehicle control, the darkness of night driving presents one of the greatest safety concerns, as darkness may obscure both the roadway and the presence of hazards like pedestrians, parked cars, or potholes. Schwing and Kamerud (1988) provide statistics that allow one to infer that the relative fatality risk is nearly ten times greater for night than for day driving (although we see below that this higher risk is only partly related to visibility). Important gains to visibility and therefore to highway safety can be attained by adequate highway lighting. For example, an analysis of thirty-one thoroughfare locations in Cleveland, Ohio, revealed that placing overhead lights reduced the number of fatalities from 556 during the year before illumination to 202 the year after (Sanders & McCormick, 1993). Corresponding gains in safety of vehicle control at night can be obtained by adequate reflectors that mark both the center of the lane and the lane's edges. The latter should be textured or broken rather than smooth, since much of our ability to judge both literal position and the speed with which we move through an environment is obtained by processing the flow of texture down the visual field, in both foveal and peripheral vision (Warren & Wertheim, 1990; see Chapter 4).

Signage.   A third visibility issue pertains to signage (Dewar, 1993; Lunenfeld & Alexander, 1990). As we noted, both searching for and reading critical highways signs can be a source of visual distraction. Hence, there is an important need for highway designers to: (1) *minimize visual clutter* from unnecessary signs, (2) *locate* signs consistently, (3) *identify* sign classes distinctly (a useful feature of the redundant color, shape, and verbal coding seen, for example, in the stop sign), and (4) *allow* verbal signs to be *read efficiently* by giving attention to issues of contrast sensitivity and glare, as discussed in Chapter 4. An important issue in roadway design is the manner in which a large number of road guidance signs can create a high level of visual workload for the driver. To the extent that several guidance and exit signs are bunched together along the highway, this can create a profile of visual load demands that are added to the steady-state level of primary task tracking, to create potentially dangerous overload situations (Benel, Huey, & Lerner, 1995; Lunenfeld & Alexander, 1990). Signage should be positioned in ways along the road such that visual workload is evenly distributed.

We will note below how all of the above visibility issues can become amplified by deficiencies in the eyesight of the viewer (Klein, 1991; Shinar & Schieber, 1991). Contrast will be lost, accommodation may be less optimal, and so forth.

Resource Competition.   The fourth visibility issue pertains to the serious distraction of in-cab viewing and other activity. This may be the result of distraction from radios, switches, maps (Dingus & Hulse, 1993, Dingus et al., 1988; Table 17.1), or auxiliary devices such as cellular phones (Violanti & Marshall, 1996; Redelmeier & Tibshirani, 1997), a distraction that may result from the manual and cognitive components of the activities as well as their visual components.

Visibility issues have been dealt with in a number of ways. In addition to simplicity of in-cab controls and displays, more technological design solutions have considered possibilities of using *auditory displays* to replace (or augment) critical nav-

TABLE 17.1 Total Required Display Glance Time (Seconds) for Each Task

Task	Mean	Standard Deviation
Speed	0.78	0.65
Following Traffic	0.98	0.60
Time	1.04	0.56
Vent	1.13	0.99
Destination Direction	1.57	0.94
Remaining Fuel	1.58	0.95
Tone Controls	1.59	1.03
Information Lights	1.75	0.93
Destination Distance	1.83	1.09
Fan	1.95	1.29
Balance	2.23	1.50
Sentinal	2.38	1.71
Defrost	2.86	1.59
Fuel Economy	2.87	1.09
Correct Direction	2.96	1.86
Fuel Range	3.00	1.43
Temperature	3.50	1.73
Cassette Tape	3.23	1.55
Heading	3.58	2.23
Zoom Level	4.00	2.17
Cruise Control	4.82	3.80
Power Mirror	5.71	2.78
Tune Radio	7.60	3.41
Cross Street	8.63	4.86
Roadway Distance	8.84	5.20
Roadway Name	10.63	5.80

Source: Dingus, T.A., Antin, J.F., Hulse, M.C., and Wierwille, W., 1988. Human factors associated with in-car navigation system use. *Proceedings of the 32nd Annual Meeting of the Human Factors Society.* Santa Monica, CA: Human Factors Society, pp. 1448–1453. Copyright 1988 by the Human Factors and Ergonomics Society. All rights reserved.

igational guidance information (i.e., maps), a design feature that has proven advantages for vehicle control (Dingus & Hulse, 1993; Parkes & Coleman, 1990; Srinivasan & Jovanis, 1997). However, it should be remembered that even auditory information is not interference-free. Auditory tasks will still compete for perceptual resources with visual ones, leading to some degree of interference (Alm & Nilsson, 1995). Tactile displays on the steering wheel also offer some promise (Schumann, 1994).

Automotive designers have also proposed using *head-up displays* to allow information such as speedometers to be viewed without requiring a scan downward to the dashboard (Fig. 8.9; Kaptein, 1994; Kiefer, 1995; Kiefer and Gellatly, 1996; Sojourner and Antin, 1990). Visual scanning measures indicate that less time is spent scanning downward when information is presented on the HUD (Kiefer, 1995) and that response time to peripheral events is faster (Srinivasan & Jovanis, 1997). Some other measures of lane keeping and speed keeping also reflect a HUD advantage (Kiefer, 1995; Kaptein, 1994). There is, however, some concern that any advantages created by reduced scanning, could be offset by the potentially dangerous costs that could result if roadway hazards were masked by HUD symbology (Wickens, 1997; see Chapter 8). If images are simple, such as a digital speedometer, HUD masking does not appear to present a problem (Kiefer & Gellatly, 1996). However this masking may be more serious to the extent that more complex imagery is considered for head-up display location.

Although technological advances such as the use of auditory guidance displays may sometimes reduce the competition for the critical forward visual channel, it is also the case that many of these advances, designed to provide *more* information to the driver, may also induce a *greater* distraction from the critical eyes-out viewing. For example, the negative safety implications of in-cab cellular phones are by now well established (Violanti & Marshall, 1996; Redelmeier & Tibshirani, 1997), and it may be the case that electronic maps or other navigational aides discussed later in the chapter will be just as distracting as are paper maps (Dingus & Hulse, 1993). When such electronic aids are introduced, it becomes critical that human factors features are incorporated that facilitate easy and immediate interpretation (Lee, Morgan, Wheeler, Hulse and Dingus, 1997). These include such properties as a "track-up" map rotation and a design that minimizes clutter (see Chapter 8).

Hazards and Collisions

Nearly all serious accidents that result in injury or death result from one of two sources: loss of control at high speed (a failure of lateral tracking) or collision with a roadway hazard (a failure of longitudinal tracking or speed control). The latter in turn can result from a failure to detect the hazard (pedestrian, parked vehicle, turning vehicle) or from an inappropriate judgment of the rate of closure with (or time to contact) a road obstacle or intersection.

Control Loss.   Loss of control can result from several factors: Obviously slick or icy road conditions are major culprits, but so also are narrow lanes and momentary lapses in attention away from lateral guidance, which may cause a lane violation. A lane violation followed by a rapid overcorrection (a high-gain response) can lead to unstable oscillations, as we saw in Chapter 9. In all of these cases, the likelihood of a loss of control is directly related to the *bandwidth* of correction which, in turn, is related to vehicle speed. The faster one travels, the less forgiving is a given error, the more immediate is the need for correction; but the more rapid the correction at higher speed, the greater is the tendency to overcorrection, instability, and possible loss of control (e.g., rollover).

Human factors solutions to the problems of control loss come in several varieties. Naturally any feature that will keep vision directed outward will be useful, as will anything that will prevent lapses of attention (e.g., caused by fatigue, see Accident Solutions, below). Correspondingly, wider lanes will lessen the likelihood of control loss. Two-lane rural roads are eight times more likely to produce fatalities than are interstate highways (Evans, 1996). Speed is such a critical variable that it will be dealt with extensively below; hence, speed limits that are adjusted for the curvature of the road can help. However, most critical are any feedback devices that provide the driver with natural intrinsic feedback of high speed. Visible marking of lane edges (particularly at night) will be useful, as will "passive alerts" such as the "turtles" dividing lanes or "rumblestrips" on the berm that warn the driver via the auditory and tactile sense of an impending loss of control (Godley et al., 1997)

Hazard Response.   The failure to detect hazards results from a breakdown of visual monitoring because of either poor visibility or inattention. In understanding hazard response, a key parameter is the estimated *time to react* to unexpected objects, which is sometimes called the perception-reaction time. On the basis of actual on-the-road measurements, this value has been estimated to be around 2–4 seconds for the average driver with a mean of around 2.5 seconds (Summala, 1981; Dewar, 1993; AAHSTO, 1990; Henderson, 1987). This is a value that is well above the reaction-time values typically found in psychology laboratory experiments. It is also important to note that the 2.5 second value is a mean, and estimates of variability suggest that a safe value to use for design purposes should be well above this, in the range of 3–4 seconds, to accommodate those drivers (or conditions) that delay the response time (Dewar, 1993; Triggs & Harris, 1982). It is elevated because it applies here to the detection of (and response to) objects that are often unexpected (see Chapter 9), and it is the lack of expectancy that is probably the greatest contribution to hazard collisions (Evans, 1991).

Once a hazard is detected, an *avoidance response* must be implemented. Depending on the circumstances, this might be either a swerve or a braking response, although some data suggest that people tend to bias toward the latter (Hale et al., 1988). The ability to execute either of these maneuvers successfully in a timely fashion is heavily dependent on the inertia (mass and speed) of the vehicle in question.

Speeding.   High vehicle speed provides a quadruple threat to driver safety (Evans, 1996): (1) It increases the likelihood of control loss; (2) it decreases the probability that a hazard will be detected in time; (3) it increases the distance traveled before a successful avoidance maneuver can be implemented; and (4) it increases the damage at impact. These factors are illustrated in Figure 17.4, which shows how the time to contact a hazard (closure time) will diminish with faster speeds. Driving should be done so that this time is less than an allowable time available, creating a positive safety margin.

Why then do people speed? Obviously this tendency is sometimes the result of consciously formed goals, for example, the rush to get to a destination on time after starting late. But there are also other reasons why drivers tend to "overspeed," relative to their braking capabilities (Wasielewski, 1984; Evans, 1991, 1996; Summala, 1988). For example, Wasielewski (1984) found that the average separation between cars on a busy freeway is 1.32 seconds, despite the fact that the *minimum* separation value recommended for safe stopping is 2 seconds! The sources of such a bias may be perceptual (i.e., underestimating true speed) or cognitive (i.e., overestimating the ability to stop in time). Perceptual biases, for example, were seen in the study by Eberts and MacMillan (1985) discussed in Chapter 4, in which small cars were found to be more likely to be hit from behind because of biased size distance judgments (the small cars were perceived as farther away than

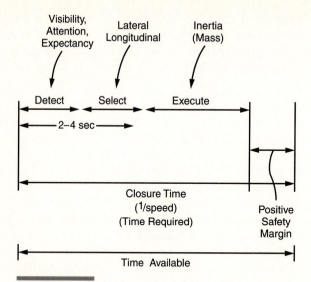

FIGURE 17.4

Illustrates the components of the hazard response time, which is the time required to stop before contacting a hazard, the influences on these components, and the need to maintain a positive safety margin between the time required and the time available.

in reality). Any factors that reduce the *apparent* sense of speed (quieter engines, higher seating position above the ground, less visible ground texture) will lead to a bias to overspeed (Evans, 1991). Adaptation level also plays a role. Drivers who drive for a long period of time on a constant road environment will eventually perceive their speed to be lower than it really is and hence may overspeed for example, when reaching the off-ramp of an interstate highway or motorway. In contrast, any techniques that will artificially create a perceptual illusion of higher (or increasing) speed can be used to induce a more cautious (and desirable) slowing, as was observed by Denton (1980) in his study of road markers at a Scottish traffic circle (Godley et al., 1997; see Chapter 4). While speed may be directly perceived, vehicle *inertia* and the kinetic energy carried by a vehicle, which depends on vehicle mass and also affects stopping time, is not (Owens et al., 1993).

Equally important to the perceptual biases but less easily quantifiable are the *cognitive biases* that can lead to overspeeding. Such biases are induced by the driver's feeling of *overconfidence* that hazards will not suddenly appear or that if they do, he or she will be able to stop in time; that is, overconfidence yields an underestimation of *risk* (Brown, Groeger, & Biehl, 1988; Summala, 1988; see Chapter 14). Psychologists have noted overconfidence in a wide variety of human phenomena, such as the belief of drivers that they are less likely to be involved in an accident than "the average driver" (Svenson, 1981). We may ascribe some aspect of this bias in risk perception to the simple effects of *expectancy,* discussed in Chapters 4 and 8; that is, most drivers have *not* experienced a collision with an obstacle in front, and so their mental model of the world portrays this as a highly improbable or perhaps "impossible" alternative (Summala, 1988; Evans, 1991). For example, the normal driver simply does not entertain the possibility that the vehicle driver in front will suddenly slam on the brakes or that a vehicle will be stationary in an active driving lane.

Accident Solutions

Compliance.   Intuitively, an ideal solution to problems of collisions would be to have everyone drive more slowly. Indeed the safety benefits of lower speed limits have been clearly established (Summala, 1988; McKenna, 1988; Evans, 1996). Yet despite these benefits, public pressure in the United States led to a decision first to increase the national limit to 65 miles per hour, causing an increase in fatalities of 10–16 percent and then to remove the national speed limit altogether. Several states have chosen to raise it well above the value of 65 mph that was in effect nationwide. Effective enforcement of speed limits can of course make some difference. While "scare" campaigns about the dangers of high speeds are less effective than actual compliance enforcement (Summala, 1988), a more positive behavior-modification technique that proved effective was based on posting signs that portrayed the percentage of drivers complying with speed limits (Van Houten & Nau, 1983). Another study of drivers, in Nova Scotia, revealed the success of a campaign by which police issued a greater frequency of nonpunitive warnings, relative to the more traditional approach of issuing fewer (because of their time consumption) speeding tickets (Evans, 1991).

Protective Devices.   A different approach is to reduce the *consequence* of an accident (rather than reducing accident frequency per se) through mandatory requirements of collision restraints (seat belt laws, airbags). The effectiveness of such devices is now well established. (Evans, 1996) For example, the failure to use lap/shoulder belts is associated with a 40 percent increase in fatality risk (Evans, 1991), and airbags have a corresponding protective value (Status Report, 1995). Of course, the mere availability of active restraints like seat belts does not guarantee that they will be used. As a consequence, mandatory seat belt laws have been introduced in several states, and their enforcement is clearly documented to be associated with increases in both compliance and safety (Campbell et al., 1988). Correspondingly, safety gains are associated with passage and enforcement of motorcycle helmet laws (Evans, 1991). The combined effects of seat belt laws and enforcement served to increase compliance in North Carolina from 25 percent to nearly 64 percent (Fig. 17.5) and was estimated to reduce fatalities by 11.6 percent and serious injuries by 14.6 percent (Reinfurt, Campbell, Stewart, & Stutts, 1990). One interesting study that used the "carrot" rather than the "stick" approach found that if police officers randomly *rewarded* drivers with cash or coupons if seat belts were being worn, this increased the proportion of people using seat belts in the area and provided more enduring behavioral changes than pure enforcement (Mortimer, Goldsteen, Armstrong, & Macrina, 1990).

Sensing.   It is apparent that speed limit enforcement can have little influence on the behavior of "tailgaters," who follow too closely (since safe separation can be violated at speeds well below the limit) nor on those drivers whose inattention or

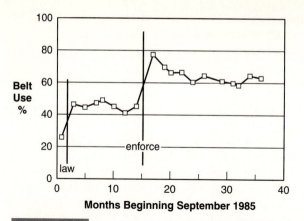

FIGURE 17.5

Indicates the impact of the North Carolina seat belt law introduction and subsequent enforcement on compliance (*Source:* Campbell, B.J., Stewart, J.R., and Campbell, F.A., 1988. *Changes with death and injury associated with safety belt laws 1985–1987.* Chapel Hill, NC: University of North Carolina Highway Safety Research Center Report HSRC-A138, Dec.)

lack of relevant visual skills do not enable them to perceive closure with the vehicle in front. Since rear-end collisions account for at least 25 percent of all motor vehicle accidents (NHTSA, 1990), the potential human factors payoffs in this area are evident. Here, human factors research has revealed some modest success of the high mounted brake lights that can make the sudden appearance of a braking vehicle more perceptually evident (Kahane, 1989; McKnight & Shinar, 1992; Mortimer, 1993). Other "passive" systems can make inferences about the leading vehicle in a pair. For example, a "trilight" system will enable the lights of the leading vehicle to turn amber if the accelerator is released but the brake not applied because this condition may forecast a future braking. Shinar (1996) has reported the success of a system that will provide advanced brake light information to the following driver, if the leader suddenly releases his foot from the accelerator, in a pattern suggestive of immediate (and emergency) braking response.

More active sensor solutions, depending on integrating information within the following vehicle, involve direct sensors of the rate of closure. If this rate is high, it can then be relayed directly to the following driver by either visual, auditory, or kinesthetic signals (Dingus et al., 1997). In the latter case, the accelerator is suddenly increased in its resistance to depression.

Cognitive Factors in Driving: Expectancy, Prediction, and Risk.   A point that we have made previously in this book is that people perceive and respond rapidly to things that they expect on the basis of past experience but do *not* do so on the basis of the unexpected. The role of expectancy is critical in driver perception (Theeuwes & Hagenzieker, 1993). Hence, design should capitalize on expectancy. For example, standardization of roadway layouts and sign placements by traffic engineers will lead drivers to expect certain traffic behaviors and information sources (Theeuwes & Godthelp, 1995). However, the design of highways and traffic control devices should also ensure that the *unexpected* is well forecast to the driver in advance. Using this philosophy, there are a series of solutions that can help drivers anticipate needed decision points through effective and visible signage in a technique known as *positive guidance* (Alexander & Lunenfeld, 1975; Dewar, 1993; Benel, Huey, & Lerner, 1995). While these points (i.e., turnoffs, traffic lights, intersections) are not themselves hazards, a driver who is not prepared for their arrival may well engage in hazardous maneuvers—sudden lane changes, overspeeding turns, or running a red light are examples. The human factors design of signage and traffic control devices should take into account the human perceptual variables of expectancy. As one example, a shorter-than-expected green light will lead the driver to fail to anticipate the change, say, from green to yellow to red, and hence increase the possibility of delayed braking and running through the red light (Van Der Horst, 1988). Light cycles must be standardized according to the speed with which the typical driver approaches the intersection in question.

Expectancy and standardization also applies to sign location and intersection design. For example, left exits off a freeway (in all countries outside of Great Britain) are so unexpected that they represent accident invitations. So too are sharper-than-average curves or curves whose radius of curvature decreases during the turn (i.e., which "spiral inward").

The driver's *own* expectancy of events or incidents, when coupled with the expected costs of these incidents defines the concept of *risk*. Several researchers have pointed out the extent to which drivers underestimate driving risks (the probability that a dangerous event could occur) (McKenna, 1988; Evans, 1991), particularly as driving becomes more automated with high levels of skill (Summala, 1988). The cause of this underestimation can be understood if we assume that the driver in question has never been in a serious accident (most of us have not). Based on actual experience then, the driver's subjective probability of the accident happening may be set to zero, leading driving to be faster than it should be or leading safety margins (i.e., in car following separation) to be reduced well below their safe level.

As such, risk-based solutions must address ways of leading people to better appreciate the probability of these low-frequency events and hence better *calibrating* their perceived risk level to the actual risk values (e.g., publishing cumulative likelihood of fatality over a lifetime of not wearing a seat belt; Fischhoff & MacGregor, 1982). Drivers should be encouraged to adopt an attitude of awareness, to "expect the unexpected" (Evans, 1991).

The concept of driving risk has been incorporated into a model explaining why innovations designed to improve traffic safety do not always realize their full benefits. According to the *risk homeostasis* model (Wilde, 1988), drivers seek to maintain their risk at a constant rate. Hence, when such safety features as antilock brakes or four-lane highways are introduced, people simply take advantage of these features to drive faster and less cautiously, thereby negating any advantages to safety.

In fact, highway safety data appear to be only partially consistent with this viewpoint (Evans, 1991; Summala, 1988). On the one hand, Evans argues that drivers are rarely conscious of any *perceived* risk of an accident (in such a way that they might use this value to adjust their driving speed). Instead, driving speed is dictated by either the direct motives for driving faster (i.e., rush to get to the destination) or simply force of habit. On the other hand, Evans points out that different safety-enhancing features can actually have quite different effects on safety. Some of those that actually improve vehicle *performance* (e.g., antilock brakes) may indeed have a less than expected benefit (Farmer et al., 1997; Wilde, 1988). But others, such as widening highways from two to four lanes have clear and unambiguous benefits on safety (Evans, 1996), as do those features like protection devices that have no effect on driving performance but address safety issues of crashworthiness.

The Impaired Driver

Vehicle drivers who are drunk, fatigued, angry (Simon & Corbett, 1996), or otherwise impaired will present a hazard to themselves as well as others on the highway.

Fatigue. Along with poor roadway and hazard visibility, fatigue is the other major contributor to the lower safety of night driving (Summala & Mikkola, 1994). The late-night driver may not only be in the lower portion of the arousal curve driven by circadian rhythms (see Chapter 13) but also may well be fatigued at the end of a very long and tiring stretch of driving initiated during the previous daylight period. As we noted in Chapter 13, the kind of task that is most impaired under such circumstances is that of *vigilance:* monitoring for low-frequency (and hence unexpected) events. In driving, these might involve the low-visibility hazard in the roadway or even the nonsalient "drift" of the car toward the edge of the roadway.

For drivers of personal vehicles there are few solutions other than the obvious ones discussed in Chapter 13, designed to foster a higher level of arousal (adequate sleep, concurrent stimulation from radio, caffeine, etc.). For long-haul truck drivers, more administrative procedures are being imposed to limit driving time during a given twenty-four-hour period and to enforce rest breaks. Highway-safety researchers have also examined the feasibility of "fitness for duty" tests, that can be required of long-haul drivers at inspection stations or geographical borders (Miller, 1996; Gilliland & Schlegel, 1995). Such tests, perhaps involving a "video game" that requires simultaneous tracking and event detection, could be used to infer that a particular driver needs sleep before continuing the trip.

A proposed future solution to fatigue problems is embodied in *driver monitoring systems* (Brookhuis & de Waard, 1993) that can monitor parameters both within the vehicle (e.g., steering behavior) and within the driver (e.g., blink rate, EEG; Stern, Boyer, & Schroeder, 1994) and can then infer a pending loss of arousal. Following such an inference, the system could alert the driver accordingly via an auditory warning.

Alcohol. Alcohol has been found to be involved in around 50 percent of fatal highway accidents in this country, and the effects of alcohol on driving performance are by now well known: With blood alcohol content as low as 0.05%, drivers react more slowly, are poorer at tracking, are less effective at time-sharing, and show impaired information processing (Evans, 1991). All of these changes create a lethal invitation for a driver who may be overspeeding at night, who will be less able to detect hazards when they occur, and who are far slower in responding to those hazards appropriately. Exhortations and safety programs appear to be only partially successful in limiting the number of drunk drivers, although there is good evidence that states or countries that are least tolerant have a lower incidence of "driving under the influence" (DUI) accidents (Evans, 1991). A dramatic illustration of the effect of implementing strict driving-under-the-influence laws on traffic fatalities in England is provided by Ross (1988), who observed that the frequency of serious injuries on weekend nights was reduced from 1200/month to approximately 600/month in the months shortly thereafter. Beyond consistent enforcement of DUI laws, Evans notes that the most effective interventions may involve "social norming," changing the way in which society views drinking and driving, in the same manner that such societal pressures have successfully influenced the perceived glamour and rate of smoking.

One solution that has been proposed to DUI problems has been the implementation of *interlock* systems. These are behind-the-wheel tests that must be accomplished by the driver to a certain performance criterion in order to allow the vehicle to be started or driven (e.g., tracking error must be below some value, problems must be solved within some time limit; Voas, 1988; Allen, Stein, & Jex, 1984). While effective in screening a substantial proportion of alcohol-impaired drivers, two limitations of such techniques are evident. First, it is possible for them to be disengaged or "shortcutted," for example, by having another person perform the test. Second, as with any such screening tests, there may be sober drivers who are unable to pass the test. Should they too be temporarily "locked out" of driving?

Age.   Although age is not in itself an impairment, it does have a pronounced influence on driving safety, as shown in Figure 17.6, with safety increasing till the midtwenties and then decreasing again above the midfifties. It is apparent that the reasons for the higher accident rates at the younger and the lower end of the scale are very different and so shall be treated separately. Younger drivers may be less skilled and knowledgeable, simply because of their lack of training. Furthermore, the younger driver will have a greater sense of overconfidence (or a greater underestimation of dangers and risks; Brown, Groeger, & Biehl, 1988). For example, the younger driver will drive faster and will be more likely to drive at night (Waller, 1991) and while under the influence of alcohol.

Starting at the very beginning, statistics show that the brand new driver of age sixteen is *particularly* at risk; a characteristic that is probably heavily related to the lack of driving skill and increased likelihood of driving errors (Status Report, 1994). For example, such drivers have a greater proportion of fatalities from rollover loss-of-control accidents, suggesting driving-skill deficiency. The sixteen year old is also much more likely to suffer a fatality from speeding (Status Report 1994). After age seventeen, however, the still-inflated risk (particularly of males) is due to other factors. The driver at this age (1) is more exposed to risky conditions (e.g., driving fast, at night, while fatigued, or under the influence; Waller, 1991; Summala & Mikkola, 1994; Brown, 1994); (2) is more likely to experience risk as intrinsically rewarding (Fuller, 1988); (3) has greater overconfidence (Brown,

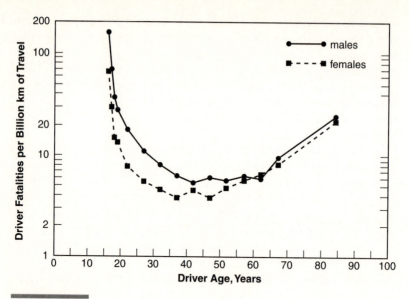

FIGURE 17.6

Fatality rate as a function of age and gender. (*Source:* Evans, L., 1988. Older driver involvement in fatal and severe traffic crashes. *Journal of Gerontology: Social Sciences, 43*[5], 186–193. Copyright © The Gerontological Society of America.)

Groeger, & Biehl, 1988); and (4) has not sufficiently acquired more subtle safe-driving strategies (as opposed to the pure perceptual motor skills; Evans, 1991).

While the younger (particularly male) driver presents a greater hazard to others on the highway, in contrast, the increased accident (and fatality) rate of much older drivers is only a hazard to them and not to others on the highway. In contrast to the skill differences and the risk-exposure differences of the younger driver, it is the *information-processing impairments* of the older driver that represent the source of greater hazard (Barr & Eberhard, 1991; Evans, 1988). Increasing age leads to slower response times; to a more restricted field of attention (Ball, Owsley, Sloan, Roenker, & Bruni, 1993) and reduced time-sharing abilities (Brouwer et al., 1991; Kortelling, 1994); and of course, to reduced visual capabilities, particularly at night and imposed by glare (Shinar & Schieber, 1991; see Chapter 4). Most older drivers are able to compensate fully these degraded capabilities in normal driving conditions simply by driving more slowly and cautiously, or by avoiding high-risk driving environments (Waller, 1991).

The safety hazards presented by the younger driver may be addressed, in part, through legislation and effective enforcement. For example, the only state to raise the minimum driving age to seventeen (New Jersey) receives a corresponding benefit to traffic safety (as do most European countries in which the age minimum is eighteen), and increases in the minimum drinking age in this country has been associated with a significant 13 percent reduction in driving fatalities (NHTSA, 1989).

The issue of how to address the safety hazards imposed by the older driver is a more difficult one (Nicolle, 1995). Clearly, the requirement for more frequent driving tests above a certain age can effectively screen the age-impaired driver, and yet because they adopt a compensating conservative behavior described above (drive more slowly, avoid darkness), many older drivers who might fail performance tests would not show higher risk behavior on the road. At the same time, deprivation of independent vehicle mobility can severely degrade the quality of life of many older residents (Waller, 1991).

Training and Selection

In the previous section, we saw that some aspects of higher accident rates were related to both limited skills (for the very young driver) and limited information-processing abilities (for the elderly). These are both limitations addressed by human factors solutions of training and selection (see Chapter 18). In driver education programs the two solutions are carried out to some extent in parallel. Driver's tests include both declarative knowledge (the written test) and procedural knowledge (the "behind-the-wheel" test), sandwiched around a period of "driver's ed" training, much of which involves actual behind-the-wheel driving. However, despite its mandatory nature, there is little evidence that driver's training programs actually serve to improve driver safety (Evans, 1991; Mayhew et al., 1997), and these might actually have a safety-retarding influence if they allow drivers to be licensed at a younger age. Certain aspects of training and selection call for improvement. In terms of selection, for example, research has found that the standard visual acuity test, an assessment of 20/40 corrected vision, has very little relevance for driving (Wood & Troutbeck, 1994). Unlike the static visual acuity tests given at the testing stations, the visual demands of driving are much more relevant for viewing *dynamic* events, often represented by *lower spatial frequencies than that tested by the acuity test* (see Chapter 4) and often *at night.* Furthermore, driver selection tests fail to examine critical abilities related to visual attention skills (Ball & Owsley, 1991).

We learn also in Chapter 18 that actual "behind-the-wheel" navigation in a vehicle may not be the best environment for all forms of learning. Such an environment may be stressful, performance assessment is generally subjective, and the ability of the instructor to create (and therefore teach a response to) emergency conditions will of course be very limited. It is for this reason that increasing attention is being given to the development of effective driving simulators (Green, 1995; Kaptein, Theeuwes, & Van Der Horst, 1996). The design of simulators that are both useful training devices and somewhat cost effective, however, is not a trivial task. For example, certain kinds of skill training benefit considerably from having both a motion base and high-fidelity dynamic visual characteristics (Kaptein, Theeuwes, & Van Der Horst, 1996), although other aspects of judgment skills can be taught with lower levels of simulator fidelity.

It is important to emphasize that the pure perceptual-motor components of driving skill are but a small component of the skills that lead to safe driving. For example, professional race car drivers, who are surely the most skilled in the perceptual-motor aspects, have an accident and moving violation rate in normal highway driving that is well above the average for a control group of similar age (Williams & O'Neill, 1974; Evans, 1996).

Automobile Automation

The previous sections have described several automation components that might conceivably address problems in highway safety. We can consider, for example, the concepts of collision monitors, automated navigation systems, driver monitors, and so forth. Collectively many of these are being developed under the auspices of the *Intelligent Vehicle Highway System* or *IVHS* (Owens et al., 1993). The development of the various tools within this system depends on a number of advances in technology. For example, automated navigation aids depend on in-vehicle computer knowledge of the vehicle's momentary location, a capability that must utilize either the satellite-based *global positioning system,* or intelligent roadway sensors (that can inform the passing vehicle of its momentary location). Collision warning devices must also incorporate accurate sensing devices to detect rate-of-closure with vehicles ahead, and intelligent route planners must be equipped with an accurate updated estimate of the state of nearby highway traffic.

The introduction of automated devices such as these raises two sorts of issues. First, as we discuss in Chapter 16, the introduction of automation must be accompanied by considerations of user *trust* and complacency (Stanton & Marsden, 1996; Kantowski et al., 1997). Suppose, for example, that an automated collision warning device becomes so heavily trusted that the driver ceases to carefully monitor the vehicle ahead and removes his or her eyes from the roadway for longer periods of time. In one study of automated braking, for example, Young and Stanton (1997) found that many drivers would intervene too slowly to prevent a rear-end collision should the automated brake fail to function. Will the net effect be a compromise rather than an enhancement of safety? If the automated systems become *so* good that the reliability is extremely high, might not this lead to still more complacency?

Second, for the kinds of automation that provide secondary information, such as navigation or trip planning aids, there is a danger that attention may be drawn more heavily into the vehicle, away from the critical primary visual attention lobe, as the potentially rich automated information source is processed (Dingus et al., 1988 Lee et al. 1997). Is the answer to display such information "head up"? Such a decision should be made only if it is certain that information at that location does not obscure hazards on the roadway.

These cautions do not mean that automobile automation is a bad idea. As we have seen, many of the safety-enhancing possibilities are clearly evident. But as we pointed out in Chapter 16, automation must be carefully introduced within the context of a *Human-Centered Philosophy.*

Conclusion

Vehicle driving remains a very hazardous undertaking compared to most other activities both in and outside of the workplace. Following a comprehensive review of the state of various highway-safety enhancement programs, accident statistics, and safety interventions, Evans (1991) attempts to identify where greatest safety benefits to this serious problem can be realized. He argues primarily that interventions into the human infrastructure will be more effective than into the engineering infrastructure. The ordering within these two categories is also based on his inferred ordering of effectiveness; it is apparent that the most effective solutions will be those that address social norms—emphasizing the "noncost" dangers of driving with alcohol and the fact that fast driving has the potential of killing many innocent victims. Legislation can help in this direction, but society's pressure must somehow exert more gradual but enduring change.

Finally, it can be argued that American society should be investing more research dollars into ways to improve this glaring safety deficiency. As Table 17.2 shows, the ratio of preretirement life lost to research dollars expended is vastly inflated for highway-safety deaths compared to deaths from cancer or heart/stroke ailments (Evans, 1991).

PUBLIC GROUND TRANSPORTATION

Statistically, it is far safer to take the bus (30 times), train (7 times), or subway than it is to drive one's own vehicle (National Safety Council, 1989). Bus drivers are more carefully selected and trained than automobile drivers, and rail-based carriers are, of course, removed from the hazardous roadways. Their added mass makes them considerably more "survivable" in high-speed crashes. As an added benefit, the increased use of public ground transportation is much more kindly toward the environment because the amount of pollution per passenger mile is much less than it is with personal vehicles. Finally, as any city commuter will acknowledge, it is sometimes much more efficient to take public transportation than to sit immobile in traffic jams during rush hour.

As a consequence of these differences in safety, efficiency, and environmental pollution, it is apparent that one of the important human factors issues in public ground transportation lies in the efforts to induce *behavioral changes* of the traveling and commuting public—making this segment of the population more aware of the lower risks, lower costs, and greater efficiency of public transportation (Nickerson & Moray, 1995; Leibowitz, Owens, & Helmreich, 1995). Equally important are systemwide efforts to improve the *accessibility* of public transportation by designing schedules and routings in accordance with people's travel needs, and so on.

In addition to the above issues unique to public transportation, many of the same driving safety issues are present that affect the automobile or truck driver.

TABLE 17.2 **Relation Between Research Expenditure and Fatalities**

	Research Expenditures (Million $)	Years of Preretirement Life Lost (Millions)
Cause:		
Traffic Injuries	112	4.1
Cancer	998	1.7
Heart Disease & Stroke	624	2.1

Source: Evans, L., 1991. *Traffic safety and the driver.* New York. Van Nostrand Reinhold.

Because the consequence of accidents are typically far greater than those for personal vehicles (since there are more passengers onboard), there is of course a correspondingly greater emphasis on training and selection for public transportation drivers. Furthermore, because the vehicles are larger, the *control inertia* characteristics for hazard avoidance discussed in the section on Hazards and Collisions also become more critical. A long train, for example, may travel as long as a mile before it can come to a full stop following emergency braking and elaborate energy-based displays can help the train engineer compute optimal speed management on hilly tracks. Trucks are much more susceptible to closed-loop instability than are cars.

Unlike buses and other road vehicles, subways and trains depend much more on a fully operating infrastructure. Tracks and roadbeds must be maintained, and railway safety is critically dependent on track switch and signal management. Recent major train accidents have resulted because of possible failures of ground personnel to keep tracks in the right alignment or to signal switches in appropriate settings. Because trains and subways can operate more autonomously from other ground vehicles (and their unpredictable behavior) than can highway vehicles, these rail-based transportation modes have a greater potential for full computer automation. One sees this already on the little subways that operate between terminals at major airports. Finally, fatigue, circadian rhythms, and shift work, discussed in Chapter 13, remain a major concern for many railroad workers.

AVIATION HUMAN FACTORS

The number of pilots is far smaller than the number of drivers, and aircraft crashes are much less frequent than auto accidents. Statistically the chances of dying while riding in a motor vehicle are 30–50 times greater than while riding in a commercial aircraft (as estimated by deaths per passenger mile; Evans, 1991).[1] However, the number of people who fly as passengers in aircraft is large enough, and the cost of a single air crash is sufficiently greater than that of a single car crash that the human factors issues of airline safety are as important as those involved with ground transportation. In the following section, we discuss the aircraft pilot's task, the social context in which the pilot works, and the implications of stress and automation on aviation human factors (Wiener & Nagel, 1988; O'Hare & Roscoe, 1990).

The Tasks

The task of the aircraft pilot, like that of the vehicle driver can be described as a primary multiaxis tracking task, embedded within a multitask context in which resources must be shared with other tasks. As compared with car driving, the pilot's tracking task is in most respects more difficult, involving higher order systems,

---

[1]Note that such statistics are biased by the high automobile risk of young male drivers. For the forty-year-old male driver wearing seat belts, the chances of being killed on a 300-mile freeway trip are no greater than on an airline flight of equivalent distance (Evans, 1991).

more axes and more interactions but in some respects less difficult, involving a lower bandwidth (more slowly changing) input and a somewhat greater tolerance for deviations than the car driver experiences on a narrow roadway. The competing tasks involve maintaining *situation awareness* for hazards in the surrounding airspace, *navigating* to three-dimensional points in the sky, following *procedures* related to aircraft and airspace operations, and *communicating* with air traffic control and other personnel on the flight deck. Much of the competition for resources is visual (see Chapter 6), but a great deal more involves more general competition for perceptual, cognitive, and response-related resources. Depending on the nature of the aircraft, the mission, and the conditions of flight, pilot workload will range the extreme gamut from underload conditions (transoceanic flight) to conditions of extreme overload (e.g., military combat missions, helicopter rescue missions, single pilots in general aviation aircraft flying in bad weather).

Tracking and Flight Control.   To understand the considerable tracking demands of flying, the reader may wish to review the material covered in Chapter 9. As Figure 17.7 shows at the top, the aircraft has 6 degrees of freedom of motion. It can rotate around three axes of rotation (curved white arrows), and it can translate along three axes of displacement (straight black arrows). Conventionally rotational axes are described by *pitch, roll (or bank), and yaw.* Translational axes are described by lateral, vertical, and longitudinal (airspeed or "along track") displacement. (Actually, lateral displacement is accomplished, as in driving, by controlling the heading of the vehicle.) All six axes are normally characterized by some target or command input, and tracking is perturbed away from these inputs by disturbance inputs, usually winds and turbulence. In controlling these degrees of freedom (a six-axis tracking task), the pilot has two primary goals. One is keeping the plane from *stalling* by maintaining adequate air flow over the wings, which produces lift. This is accomplished through careful control of the airspeed and the *attitude* of the aircraft (pitch and roll). The other goal is to *navigate* the aircraft to points in the 3-D airspace. If these points must be reached at precise *times,* as is often the case in commercial aviation, then the task can be described as *4-D* navigation.

In order to accomplish this set of tasks, the pilot manipulates three controls shown at the top of the figure: the *yoke* controls the elevators and ailerons, which control the pitch and bank, each via first-order dynamics (i.e., yoke position determines the rate of change of bank and of pitch). The *throttle* controls airspeed, and the *rudder pedals* are used to help coordinate turning and heading changes. These direct control links are shown by the solid thin arrows at the top of Figure 17.7.

There are three facets that make this multielement tracking task a much more difficult one than that involved in driving: the displays, the control dynamics, and the interactions between the six axes.

The Displays.   The information displayed in the traditional flight instruments (bottom of Fig. 17.7) does not always correspond directly to the axis goals that need to be tracked. For example, although airspeed, pitch, and bank are directly displayed, there is no direct indication of how close the combination of these variables is to reaching a critical stall state, and although heading will determine

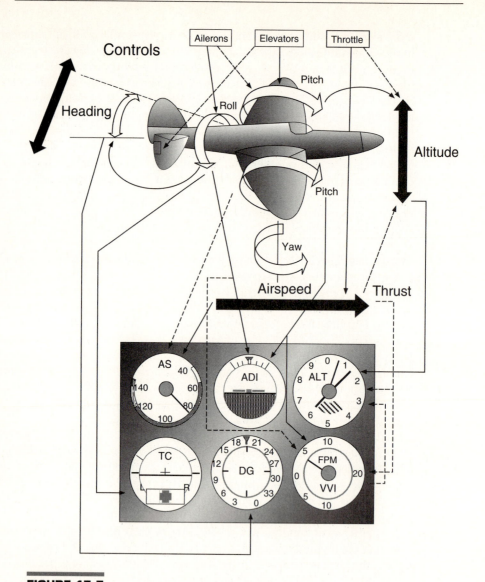

FIGURE 17.7

Representation of flight control dynamics; controls (top), and primary flight displays (bottom). The thin lines represent causal influences.

the future lateral deviation from the flight path, on many aircraft there is no direct display of the latter variable. While the automobile driver can get nearly all of the information needed to control the vehicle from a fixation down the roadway ahead (using peripheral vision to assist in the task), the pilot must collect this information from repeated fixations across the small instruments, often needing to acquire information with very high acuity demands.

The Control Dynamics.   Many of the variables to be controlled are quite sluggish because of the high inertia in some large aircraft and because of the high control order of some axes. The control of heading and altitude are second-order tracking tasks (displacement of the yoke affects the acceleration of heading and altitude), while the control of lateral position is a *third-order* task (and we learned in Chapter 9 how hard second-order tracking was). Because of the lags imposed by this higher order sluggishness, the need for prediction and anticipation is very critical in aircraft flying. If pilot anticipation is not adequate (i.e., the pilot "flies behind" the aircraft), then closed loop instability can result in *pilot-induced oscillations.* For example, the aircraft may overshoot and then undershoot its desired altitude.

Axis Interactions.   As seen by the dashed arrows in Figure 17.7, different aspects of the aircraft dynamics interact with each other and with the different pilot goals. For example, changes in pitch (accomplished by the elevators) will affect not only altitude but airspeed. Changes in roll (aileron control), intended to change heading in order to reduce a lateral deviation, will change pitch and may also increase the likelihood of stalling. The skilled pilot must form a very accurate *mental model* of these flight dynamics to achieve effective control (Bellenkes et al., 1997).

Conventionally, the difficult task of learning to control the aircraft has been addressed through many hours of training both in flight simulators and in the air to move the declarative knowledge of flight dynamics to effective procedural knowledge. However, with the development of more computer-based displays, to replace the old electromechanical "round dial" instruments in the cockpit (Figure 17.7), aircraft designers have been moving toward incorporating human factors display principles of *proximity compatibility, the moving part,* and *pictorial realism* (Roscoe, 1968; see Chapter 8) to design more "user-friendly" displays. One may compare, for example, the standard instrument display shown at the bottom of Figure 17.7 with the current display in many advanced transport aircraft (Fig. 17.8a) and with even more integrated displays proposed for future design (Fig. 17.8b).

Given the sluggish nature of aircraft dynamics, a valuable feature on almost every advanced display is the availability of *prediction* (of future aircraft position) and *preview* (of future command input) (Jensen, 1981; Haskell & Wickens, 1993). Farther in the future and less well established in terms of its benefits is the implementation of *3-D* displays, such as that shown in Figure 17.8b. In spite of their promise, the advantages of such displays, in terms of their ability to integrate three axes of space, may sometimes be offset by their costs, in terms of the ambiguity with which they depict the precise spatial location of aircraft relative to ground and air hazards (Wickens, Liang, Prevett, & Olmos, 1996; Wickens, 1995; see Chapter 8).

Maintaining Situation Awareness.   Piloting takes place in a very dynamic environment. To a far greater extent than in driving, much of the information that is relevant for safety is not directly visible in its intuitive "spatial" form. Rather, the pilot must depend on an *understanding* or *awareness* of the location and

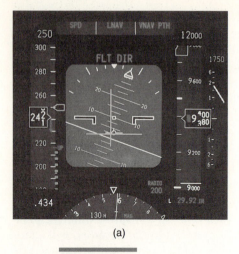
(a)

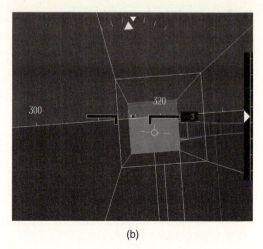
(b)

FIGURE 17.8

(a) Flight displays for modern commercial aircraft (*Source:* Courtesy of the Boeing Corporation); (b) Flight display envisioned for future aircraft. Note the preview "tunnel in the sky." (*Source:* Theunissen, E., Delft University of Technology, Faculty of Electrical Engineering, The Netherlands.)

future implications of hazards, relative to the current aspect of the aircraft; that is, the pilot must achieve an awareness of "the situation" (*Human Factors,* 1995; Garland & Endsley, 1995). Is she aware that an aircraft six miles to the side and below is on a possible collision course? Is she aware of the high point in the terrain below, invisible through the clouds, and so forth? Equally important to awareness of hazards outside the aircraft is the awareness of the state of automated systems within the aircraft itself (Sarter & Woods, 1995). The topic of situation awareness has received an expanded amount of recent research, addressing its characteristics not only in aviation but in other domains such as medicine, air traffic control, driving, and process control (Adams, Tenney, & Pew, 1995; Endsley, 1995; Garland & Endsley, 1995; Sarter & Woods, 1994; Wickens 1995; Gugerty, 1997).

The most direct human factors solutions to achieving situation awareness in aviation can be achieved through display design, providing the right information, in the right form, at the right time. For example, *head-up displays* (Weintraub & Ensing, 1992) can allow the pilot to monitor critical flight instruments without needing to bring the eyes away from monitoring the outside world (see Chapter 8, Figure 8.9). This outside scan is necessary to maintain visual awareness of potential air traffic or of command inputs (such as the position of the runway on a final approach). However, as with automobiles, it is possible for head-up displays to become too cluttered with unnecessary information and thereby mask critical unexpected targets in the airspace outside (Wickens & Long, 1995).

Integrated electronic displays, such as that shown in Figure 17.9, can allow the pilot to visualize a much broader view of the world surrounding the aircraft than can the more restricted conventional flight instruments. However, as with head-up displays, there are potential human factors costs associated with more "panoramic" displays. They may need to occupy more display "real estate" (a requirement that imposes a nontrivial engineering cost), and they must also depict the aircraft's position and its movement with smaller resolution, thus possibly lessening the degree of precision with which the pilot can track. As we noted above and in Chapter 8, when such displays are portrayed in 3-D perspective, they can make the precise judgments of where things are in space difficult because of the ambiguity of projecting a 3-D view onto a 2-D (planar) viewing surface (McGreevy & Ellis, 1986).

Following Procedures. To a much greater extent than in driving, the aircraft pilot *must* reliably accomplish a series of actions at specified points in a flight. Sometimes these actions are fairly routine because they are always required (like lowering the landing gear or setting the flaps), and sometimes they are novel or contingent on unpredictable circumstances (e.g., dealing with a closed runway or an engine failure). Neglect of procedures of either sort can be deadly. In 1987, pilots on an airliner taking off from Detroit Metropolitan Airport neglected to set the flaps on the wing, an essential ingredient for achieving ad-

FIGURE 17.9
Integrated panoramic 3-D display for aviation, supporting situation awareness.

equate lift on takeoff. The airplane hit a ground obstacle and crashed, causing many fatalities (NTSB, 1988).

The procedures that the pilot must follow are embodied in vast numbers of documents of declarative knowledge (FAA Regulations and aircraft operating manuals). This is far more information than the pilot can be expected to retrieve reliably from memory when it is needed. To assist the pilot's *prospective memory* (remembering to do the right things at the right time; Chapter 6), aircraft designers support the pilot by providing *knowledge in the world* in the form of checklists (Degani & Wiener, 1993; see Figure 17.10). There are large numbers of these, each devoted to different phases of flight (e.g., preflight, taxi, takeoff, etc.) and to different operating conditions (e.g., normal, engine out, fire).

As we have noted elsewhere, however, following checklists (e.g., Set switch A to "on") can be susceptible to two kinds of errors. First, as discussed in Chapter 8, top-down processing (coupled with time pressure) may lead the pilot to "see" the item in its appropriate (expected) state, even if it is not. Second, as discussed in Chapters 6 and 13 the distractions of a multitask environment can lead the pilot to skip a step in the checklist; that is, the distraction may divert the pilot's attention away from the checklist task, and attention will return to it at a later step than the one pending when the distraction occurred. Indeed it appears that this might have been the case in the Detroit Airport crash. The pilot's attention was diverted from the checklist by a procedural change called for by air traffic control, and attention apparently returned to the checklist at a point just after the critical "set flaps" item.

Human factors solutions to procedures following must address the design issues related to readability, discussed in Chapter 4 (Degani & Wiener, 1993). Issues of top-down processing and distraction can be addressed in one of two ways. First, the *redundant* participation of two members of the flight crew facilitates the more accurate adherence to and following of the list. In the "challenge and response" method, one crew member challenges the other to check the list item and does not proceed to the next until the verbal response is given. Second, there are possible benefits associated with *automation* that can redundantly check (and actively report) the status of switches and things on board the aircraft, whose state can easily be sensed (Palmer & Degani, 1991; Bresley, 1995). Automation can easily keep the pilot in the loop by simply reminding the pilot if certain key steps in the list (that can be sensed) have not yet been carried out. Electronic lists may also require the pilot to actively enter the "completed" status so that the completion status can be monitored.

The Social Context

Most pilots carry out their tasks as a member of two and sometimes three "teams": a team joining them with other members of the flight deck, a team joining them with the air traffic controller within whose sector they are flying, and sometimes a team joining them with personnel performing other missions onboard the air-

■ INTERMEDIATE STOP ITEMS
▲ S/O'S FUNCTION
NO CHALLENGE

B-727 PILOT'S CHECKLIST
(– 232 & –247 Modified)

▲ DELTA

FAA APPROVED
DATE: 3-15-88

FIRST FLIGHT OF DAY CHECK THE FOLLOWING:

STANDBY RUDDER	FLIGHT DIRECTORS
ANTI-SKID	STAB TRIM
ANTI-ICE	AUTOPILOT
PITOT HEAT	

BEFORE START

■ A/C STATUS & LOGBOOK	CK
■ FUEL REQD	ON BOARD
OXY MASK/REG/INTERPHONE	CK
STANDBY RUDDER	OFF
FLIGHT CONTROL SWITCHES	ON
ANTI-SKID	OFF
STALL WARNING	CK
INSTRUMENT COMPARATOR	CK
EMERGENCY EXIT LIGHTS	ARMED
#2 ENG ACCESS DOOR LIGHT	OFF
ENGINE START SWITCHES	OFF
■ SEAT BELT & NO SMOKING	ON
■ WINDOW HEAT	ON
ANTI-ICE	CLOSED
PITOT HEAT	OFF
INTERIOR & EXTERIOR LIGHTS	SET
■ NAVIGATION LIGHTS [247]	ON
■ ENGINE FIRE WARNING SYSTEMS	CK
ALT & FLT INSTS	SET/CROSSCK
COMPASS SELECTORS	SLAVED
GPWS	CK
STATIC SOURCE SELECTORS	NORMAL
MACH AIRSPEED WARNING	CK
INDICATOR LIGHTS & APD	CK
ENGINE INSTRUMENTS	CK
LANDING GEAR	DOWN, IN, 3 GREEN
■ RADAR & TRANS	CK & SET
FLIGHT DIRECTORS	STBY
SPEED BRAKE	DETENT
REV. THROTTLES & START LEVERS	
	DOWN, CLOSED & CUTOFF
FLAPS	UP
STAB TRIM	NORMAL
AUTOPILOT	OFF
■ RADIOS & NAV INSTS	CK & SET
■ RUDDER & AILERON TRIM	ZERO
STANDBY POWER	CK
■ CABIN & S/O PREFLIGHT	COMPLETE
■▲ AUTOPILOT TEST SW	NORMAL
■▲ CIRCUIT BREAKERS	CK
■ DEPARTURE BRIEFING	COMP

BEFORE DISPATCH

▲ #2 SYS B HYD PUMP	ON
▲ APU & BATT CHARGER	START & CK
▲ PACK(S)	AS REQD

ENGINE START

▲ DOOR WARNING LIGHTS	CK
▲ PACKS	BOTH OFF
▲ GALLEY POWER	OFF
▲ FUEL SYSTEM	SET
BEACON	ON
PARKING BRAKE	AS REQD
PNEUMATIC PRESSURE	PSI

AFTER START

▲ ELEC SYSTEM	CK & SET
▲ EXTERNAL POWER & AIR	REMOVE
▲ GALLEY POWER	ON
▲ FUEL SYSTEM	SET
▲ SYS A & B HYD PUMPS	CK & ON
▲ ENG 2/APU BLEEDS	AS REQD
▲ PACKS	AS REQD
▲ COCKPIT DOOR	LOCKED (PRIOR TO T/O)
ENGINE INSTRUMENTS	CK
ENGINE ANTI-ICE	AS REQD

TAXI

T/O DATA COMPUTED RWY	USING RWY
AUTO PACK TRIP LT	REQD OR NOT REQD
PITOT HEAT	ON
AIRSPD & EPR BUGS	SET/CROSSCK
AIRSPD WARN SWS	SET, 3 (A OR B)
ALT & FLT INSTS	SET/CROSSCK
STAB TRIM	UNITS

When Delayed Start is Desired

DELAYED ENGINE START

▲ PACKS	BOTH OFF
▲ GALLEY POWER	OFF
▲ FUEL SYSTEM	SET
PNEUMATIC PRESSURE	PSI

DELAYED AFTER START

▲ ELEC SYSTEM	CK & SET
▲ GALLEY POWER	ON
▲ FUEL SYSTEM	SET FOR TAKEOFF
▲ SYS A HYD PUMPS	CK & ON
▲ ENG 2/APU BLEEDS	CLOSE
▲ PACKS	ON
ENGINE INSTRUMENTS	CK
ENGINE ANTI-ICE	AS REQD

TAXI (CONTINUED)

▲ FUEL HEAT	AS REQD
▲ FLT GRD SWITCH	FLT
▲ F/O ALT VIBRATOR C/B [232]	IN
SHOULDER HARNESS	ON
FLAPS	GREEN LIGHT
FLIGHT CONTROLS	CK
NAV INSTRUMENTS	SET

BEFORE TAKEOFF

TAKEOFF BRIEFING	COMP
FLIGHT ATTENDANTS	NOTIFIED/ACKD
ANTI-SKID	ON
CONTINUOUS IGNITION [232]	ON
START SWITCHES [247]	FLT START
NAV LIGHTS [232]/STROBE[247]	ON
TRANSPONDER	ON
▲ APU MASTER SWITCH	OFF
▲ FUEL HEAT	OFF
▲ APU LIGHT	OFF
▲ AUTO PACK TRIP SWITCH	NORMAL
▲ CSD OIL COOLER [247]	GROUND OFF

Figure 1. *Delta Air Lines Flight 1141 checklist (Source: NTSB, 1989).*

FIGURE 17.10

Typical aircraft checklist. (*Source:* Degani, A., and Wiener, E.L., 1993. Cockpit checklists: Concept, design, and use. *Human Factors,* 35(2), 345–360. Copyrighted 1989 by the National Transportation Safety Board.)

craft. For commercial flight this third team will be the cabin crew of flight attendants; for EMS operations it will be medical personnel on board; for military flight it may consist of a number of other operators engaged in combat, supply, surveillance, or rescue-related activity.

As in all teamwork, the issue of communications (usually via voice) is of critical importance. It has been estimated that over half of the incidents in flying relate to a breakdown in information transfer (Nagel, 1988). We have noted in Chapter 5 how important it is to consider the vulnerability of voice communications to both bottom-up and top-down (expectancy-driven) errors. However, during the early 1980s, human factors researchers began to realize that many communications breakdowns resulted not because statements were heard incorrectly but because key information was not relayed at all (Foushee, 1984). Many of these breakdowns occurred in circumstances such as those in which a junior inexperienced copilot or flight engineer would feel reluctant to "speak up" to a gruff senior captain and point out to the captain (typically a male) an error in his ways or identify to him a condition of which he should have been aware. In these circumstances, both parties are responsible for the breakdown: the junior for failing to be assertive and the senior for creating a climate in which the sharing of valuable information is not perceived as welcome.

In response to these concerns and to the accidents resulting from such breakdowns, the airlines working in conjunction with NASA have developed programs to train flight deck *teams* in the details of *cockpit resource management* or CRM (Wiener, Kanki, & Helmreich, 1993). Such training programs include familiarization with case studies where communications have broken down, team exercises in which participants can have their own behavior critiqued (e.g., in handling unexpected emergencies in a simulated flight), and teaching of series of guidelines is to be followed. These guidelines emphasize the necessity of creating an open climate in which information is shared both up and down the chain of command. They also point to the necessity of clear and unambiguous communications in both directions. Pilots would be encouraged to say, for example: "I note that your altitude is too low" rather than "Have you checked your altitude recently?"

The concept of cockpit resource management has often been defined more broadly as *crew resource management* to broaden its scope in two directions. First, *CRM* becomes a term that now includes teams of any sort and so is equally relevant to the cabin crew of flight attendants, to air traffic controllers, as well as to team operations in domains other than aviation (e.g., the medical operating room). Second, the concept of *resources* has been broadened so that resources are not just "other people" but may include automated agents and the pilot's own "attentional resources." As such, CRM addresses important issues of *task management*, discussed briefly in Chapter 13. Does the pilot delegate tasks appropriately to other crew members when the workload gets high? If certain tasks must be "shed," are they the ones of lower priority (Raby & Wickens, 1994; Schutte & Trujillo, 1996)?

Recent safety data provide a clear indication that CRM programs are effective. For example, when accident frequency data of large aviation organizations are

TABLE 17.3 ADM/CRM Operational Evaluations

Organization/Subjects	Materials	Accident Rates
PHI/Commercial Pilots	ADM & CRM	54% Decrease
BHTI/All Jetranger Pilots	ADM*	36% Decrease
BHTI/U.S. Jetranger Pilots	ADM	48% Decrease
USN/Helicopter Crew Members	CRM	28% Decrease
USN/ A 6 / EA 6 Crew Members	CRM	81% Decrease
USAF/ Transport Crew Members	CRM	51% Decrease

Source: Diehl, A. The Effectiveness of Training Programs for Preventing Aircrew Error. In *Proceedings 7th International Symposium on Aviation Psychology,* R. Jensen, ed. Columbus, OH; Ohio State University.
*ADM: Aeronautical Decision Making.

compared before and after the introduction of CRM programs, noticeable and significant drops in accident rates are observed (Diehl, 1991; Table 17.3). We discuss teams further in Chapter 19.

Stress and Impairments

The training and licensing qualifications for flying are much more stringent than they are for driving, and the perceived risk is much higher. As a result, problems of alcohol, fatigue, and age-related impairments are far less prevalent in the air than they are on the ground. On the other hand, the aircraft environment is loaded with the potential for both physical and psychological stressors that can have both direct and indirect effects on performance (O'Hare & Roscoe, 1990; Chapter 13).

For student pilots in the high-risk high-hazard environment, the source of psychological stress from the potential dangers of crashing is obvious, and such stress will be amplified during early solo flights (Baker, Lamb, Li, & Dodd, 1996). Hence, the student pilot appears to be particularly vulnerable to breakdowns in information-processing skills related to the higher levels of stress, and those skills are particularly vulnerable for the student pilot because they are not well learned. Many of the sources of accidents in student flying can be directly associated with the kinds of cognitive breakdowns discussed in Chapter 13. The need for extensive use of flight training simulators to bring many emergency management skills to a level of automaticity is a direct implication of these circumstances.

Depending on the nature of the aircraft and mission, there are many other stressors that can negatively influence performance of pilots at all levels of skill. For example, military pilots must perform combat missions with the added threat of danger from hostile forces. They are also subjected to high gravitational forces that can restrict vision and motor movement. Pilots in light aircraft can be quite stressed by motion sickness (Chapter 5) and by the closely associated state of spatial disorientation (O'Hare & Roscoe, 1990). Both of these unpleasant states are most likely to occur when the pilot is flying "in the clouds" and when the horizon line is thus invisible. Spatial disorientation can lead pilots to put the aircraft into a dangerous stall attitude if they fail to appreciate which way is "up." High workload is a mission-related stressor that is often imposed on single pilots flying in bad weather, on military pilots in combat, on all pilots just prior to landing, and on helicopter pilots carrying out missions low to the ground (i.e., hovering). For the latter, physical stress will be enhanced by vibration, noise, and possibly heat (Hart, 1988).

Aircraft Automation

Paralleling our discussion of general issues of automation in Chapter 16, aircraft automation can take on several forms: autopilots can assist in the tracking task, route planners can assist in navigation, collision avoidance monitors can assist in traffic and terrain monitoring, and more elaborate *flight management systems* can assist in optimizing flight paths (Sarter & Woods, 1995). Some automated devices have been introduced because they reduced workload (autopilots), others because they replaced monitoring tasks that humans did not always do well (collision alerts), and still others like the flight management system were introduced for economic reasons: they allowed the aircraft to fly shorter, more fuel-conserving routes.

As we noted in Chapter 16, many of the human factors issues in automation were directly derived from accident and incident analysis in the aviation domain, coupled with laboratory and simulator research. From this research has evolved many of the guidelines for introducing *human-centered automation* (Billings, 1996) that were discussed in that chapter.

AIR TRAFFIC CONTROL

The pilot is supported on the ground by the air traffic controller. The task of air traffic control (ATC) has as many elements in common with that of industrial process control, as discussed in Chapter 16, as with the pilot. Like the process controller, the air traffic controller is responsible for *controlling* something, in this case, the aircraft passing through the air space. As with process control, the control process of ATC is a complex one. There are multiple entities (aircraft, rather than process variables) that may each have their own unique dynamic-sand dynamic interrelationships. Also, just as the process controller had multiple goals that are not entirely compatible with each other (safety, diagnosis, profit), so the air traffic controller is confronted with the multiple, sometimes conflicting goals of "maintaining the *safe* and *expeditious* flow of aircraft through the airspace" (Luffsey, 1990). These two goals are conflicting in the sense that maximum safety would be obtained if planes never flew (hence, no expedience), and the safest flights (from the point of view of avoiding potential conflicts) will only occur if there is very wide separation between aircraft. This sort of separation will, of course, greatly reduce the efficiency of the national air system in terms of its ability to get the greatest number of planes from takeoff to landing in the shortest time. Finally, like process control, there are many human factors issues related to ATC that have relatively little to do with either control or automation but touch on nearly all of the other chapters in this book (Wickens, Mavor, & McGee, 1997; Hopkin, 1995). As we describe the task of the air traffic controller in more detail below, we see the nature of these connections to other topics, even as we focus most directly first on the control process and then on its relevance to future automation.

There are basically three kinds of air traffic controllers (Hopkin, 1995; Luffsey, 1990). Tower controllers work in "the tower" where they can usually see (and control) aircraft as they taxi, take off, and land. Terminal radar approach controllers (TRACON) typically work in a dimly lit area in which they control the aircraft, displayed on radar, in a region of 20–50 miles surrounding most large or midsize airports. En route controllers manage the flow of traffic along the cross-country airways between the various TRACON areas, again interacting through radar displays. TRACON and en route controllers typically have "sectors" of the air space within which they are responsible for all traffic.

The actual "control" that all controllers exercise is quite different from the typical manual control that we discussed in Chapter 9. Air traffic control is neither manual nor continuous but is typically verbal and discrete, issued in terms of instructions or "clearances" to the pilots (and acknowledged verbally by the pilots). As such, control effectiveness depends critically on the human factors of voice communications systems, discussed extensively in Chapter 5.

As we learned in Chapter 9, most control is based upon some sort of input signal, usually displayed visually, as well as a set of goals, usually defined in terms of minimizing or maximizing some quantities. For the air traffic controller, the goals are to maximize the flow of traffic in and out of a controller's sector, while adhering to various strict criteria for minimum separation (to ensure safety). The inputs to the ATC task are complex and represent the full array of aircraft within the sector of responsibility for a controller (or approaching the sector). Most of these aircraft are prominently displayed either on a radar scope (Fig. 17.11a; for the TRACON and en route controller) or by direct vision (for the tower controller) and in terms of a visual-verbal categorical representation on "flight strips" (see Fig. 17.11b) for all categories of controllers. To a much greater extent than traditional manual control, the air traffic controller cannot base the control clearances *directly* on visual input but rather must first interpret this input in terms of a visual-spatial mental model or image of the air space, an image that is sometimes known as "the big picture" (Hopkin, 1995; Wickens et al., 1997). The sources of input to the big picture are not just that which is presented on the radar display but also include information gleaned from the flight strips, from radio communications with the pilot, and from knowledge of airplane characteristics and capabilities.

Another feature shared with process control is the inherent *sluggishness* of the system. A control issued to an aircraft to speed up, slow down, or change its altitude or heading may not be seen to occur for a few minutes. As a result of this sluggishness it should not be surprising that a tremendously important aspect of the controller's task is related to *prediction, anticipation,* and *planning.* These cognitive processes, for example, are relevant in answering the typical question: "What do I need to do now to get these three converging aircraft lined up so that when

(a)

1 DAL542 **DC9/A** **T468 G555** **16 16** **486 09**	**7HQ** **1827**	**30** **18** PXT	**330**		**FLL J14 ENO 00D212** **00D PHL**	**2575** ***ZCN**

(b)

▬▬▬▬▬▬▬▬
FIGURE 17.11
(a) Typical radar display for air traffic control. (*Source:* Monkmeyer Press Photo Service. Photograph by Gerard Fritz, © MONKMEYER/Fritz.); (b) flight data strips for air traffic control. (*Source:* Federal Aviation Administration.)

they leave my sector in about 10 minutes they will be all at the same altitude and five miles apart?" Because of these predictive demands, it is apparent that predictor displays represent a valuable augmentation to an air traffic controller's task (Erzberger et al., 1993).

Two final aspects of air traffic control deserve mention because they stand in partial contrast to the world of the process controller. First, even more than the process controller, the air traffic controller is an integral part of two teams. One team is defined by the controller and the pilots of all aircraft in his or her sector. The other team membership is defined by all controllers at a facility, who must communicate with each other as they "hand off" aircraft from one sector to the next, who must share duties and responsibilities and be ready to lend a hand when one controller encounters a particularly difficult problem. In this regard the aspects of team or group human factors, discussed in Chapter 19, become particularly critical.

The second source of difference from much of process control concerns workload. Process control has sometimes been described as "hours of boredom punctuated by a few minutes of pure hell" (transients and fault management); that is, a great proportion of the process controller's time may be spent in a low-workload environment. In contrast, the workload of the air traffic controller is much more likely to be at a sustained and fairly high level. Although there are still many periods of light traffic during a controller's shift, these are often accompanied by a reduction in staffing by giving a controller responsibility for more air space so that the number of planes/controller is kept relatively constant.

Because workload in air traffic control is a key issue, there are a number of concerns for both the causes of high workload (more aircraft, more variability of aircraft types, more "complex" airspace) as well as the effects of that workload. These effects can either be adaptive (controllers change their strategy in dealing with aircraft; Sperandio, 1976) or maladaptive (the failure to notice an impending loss of separation; Endsley & Rodgers, 1996), and workload can also have consequences the on controller's experience of stress (Chapter 13).

On the whole, the air traffic control system may be viewed as remarkably safe, given what it has been asked to do—move millions of passengers/year through the crowded skies at speeds of several hundred miles per hour. This safety can be attributed to the considerable redundancy built into the system, along with the high level of the professional ATC work force. Yet arguments have been made that the high record of safety, achieved with a system that is primarily based on *human* control, has sacrificed efficiency, leading to longer than necessary delays on the ground and wider-than-necessary (to preserve safety) separations in the air. A consequence has been a considerable amount of pressure exerted by the air carriers to automate many of the functions traditionally carried out by the human controller under the assumption that intelligent computers can do this more accurately and efficiently than their human counterparts (Wickens, Mavor & McGhee, 1997).

Such automation includes some straightforward "assistance," like computer updating of the flight strips (Manning, 1995) or replacement of some vulnerable human functions (electronic data-link can support the potentially vulnerable voice communications channel or predictive displays can support human prediction Kerns, 1991). However, some proposed ATC automation includes replacement of key perceptual and cognitive functions. Automated devices now in place can predictively warn of pending loss of separation. More controversial are automated systems proposed to suggest and perhaps implement aircraft flight path changes in order to avoid conflicts and maximize route efficiency (Erzberger et al., 1993). It should be apparent from our discussions in Chapter 16 that great caution should be exercised in implementing these solutions because of the possible human factors (and system performance) costs of being out of the loop should unexpected circumstances suddenly occur (Hopkin & Wise, 1996; Wickens et al. 1997).

CONCLUSION

The human factors of transportation systems is a complex and global issue. An individual's choice to fly, drive, or take public ground transportation is dictated by a complex set of forces related to risk perception, cost perception, and expediency. The consumer's choice for one influences human factors issues in each of the others. For example, if more people choose to fly, fewer automobiles will be on the road and unless people drive faster as a result, highways will become safer. However, the airspace will become more congested and its safety will be compromised. Air traffic controllers will be more challenged in their jobs. In the continuing quest for more expediency, demands will appear (as they have now appeared) for either greater levels of air traffic control automation or for more responsibility to be shifted from air traffic control to the pilots themselves for route selection and for maintaining separation from other traffic (Planzer & Jenny, 1995). The technology to do so becomes more feasible with the availability of the global positioning system. Collectively, if they are not well managed, all of these factors may create a more hazardous airspace, inviting the disastrous accident that can shift risk perceptions (and airline costs) once again.

It should be apparent that such global economic issues related to consumer choice (itself a legitimate topic for human factors investigation) will impact the conditions in which vehicles travel and the very nature of those vehicles (levels of automation, etc.) in a manner that has direct human factors relevance to design.

REFERENCES

Adams, M.J., Tenney, Y.J., and Pew, R.W. (1995). Situation awareness and the cognitive management of complex systems. *Human Factors, 37*(1), 85–104.

Alexander, G., and Lunenfeld, H. (1975). *Positive guidance in traffic control.* Washington, DC: Federal Highway Administration.

Allen, R.W., Stein, A.C., and Jex, H.R. (1984). Field test of a drunk driving warning system (DDWS). *American Association for Automotive Medicine, 28th Annual Proceedings* (pp. 262–272).

Alm, H., and Nilsson, L. (1995). The effects of a mobile telephone task on driver behaviour in a car following situation. *Accid. Anal. and Prev., 27*(5), 707–715.

American Association of State Highway and Transportation Officials (1990). *A policy on geometric design of highways and streets.* Washington, DC: Author.

Baker, S.P., Lamb, M.W., Li, G., and Dodd, R.S. (1996). *Crashes of instructional flights: Analysis of cases and remedial approaches* (DOT/FAA/AM-96/3). Washington, DC: Office of Aviation Medicine, Federal Aviation Administration.

Ball, K., and Owsley, C. (1991). Identifying correlates of accident involvement for the older driver, *Human Factors, 33*(5), 583–596.

Ball, K., Owsley, C., Sloan, M., Roenker, D.L., and Bruni, J.R. (1993). Visual attention problems as a predictor of vehicle crashes among older drivers. *Investigate Ophthalmology and Visual Science, 34*(11), 3110–3123.

Barr, R.A., and Eberhard, J.W. (eds.) (1991). Safety and mobility of elderly drivers, Part 1. *Human Factors Special Issue, 33*(5).

Bellenkes, A.H., Wickens, C.D., and Kramer, A. (1997). Visual scanning and pilot expertise: The role of attentional flexibility and mental model development. *Aviation, Space, and Environmental Medicine, 68* #5 pp 1–11.

Benel, D.C.R., Huey, R.W., and Lerner, N.D. (1995). *Driver information overload (conceptual model description)* (Technical Report NCHRP 3-50). Silver Spring, MD: COMSIS Corporation.

Billings, C. (1996). *Toward a human centered approach to automation.* Englewood Cliffs, NJ: Lawrence Erlbaum.

Bresley, B. (1995). 777 flight deck design. *Airliner,* 1–9 (Apr.–Jun.).

Brookhuis, K.A., and de Waard, D. (1993). The use of psychophysiology to assess driver status. *Ergonomics, 36,* 1099–1110.

Brouwer, W.H., Waternik, W., Van Wolffelaar, P.C., and Rothengatter, T. (1991). Divided attention in experienced young and older drivers: Lane tracking and visual analysis in a dynamic driving simulator. *Human Factors, 33*(5), 573–582.

Brown, I.D. (1994). Driver fatigue. *Human Factors, 36*(2), 298–314.

Brown, I.D., Groeger, J.A., and Biehl, B. (1988). Is driver training contributing enough towards road safety? In J.A. Rothergatter, and R.A. de Bruin (eds.), *Road users and traffic safety* (pp. 135–156). Assen/Maastricht, Netherlands: Van Corcum.

Campbell, B.J., Stewart, J.R., and Campbell, F.A. (1988). *Changes with death and injury associated with safety belt laws 1985–1987* (Report HSRC-A138). Chapel Hill, NC: University of North Carolina Highway Safety Res. Ctr.

Degani, A., and Wiener, E.L. (1993). Cockpit checklists: Concept, design, and use. *Human Factors, 35*(2), 345–360.

Denton, G.G. (1980). The influence of visual pattern on perceived speed. *Perception, 9,* 393–402.

Dewar, R. (1993). Warning: Hazardous road signs ahead. *Ergonomics in Design,* July. pp. 26–31.

Diehl, A.E. (1991). The effectiveness of training programs for preventing aircrew error. In R.S. Jensen (ed.), *Proceedings of the 6th International Symposium on Aviation Psychology* (pp. 640–655). Columbus, OH: Dept. of Aviation, Ohio State University.

Dingus, T.A., Antin, J.F., Hulse, M.C., and Wierwille, W. (1988). Human factors issues associated with in-car navigation system usage. *Proceedings of the 32nd Annual Meeting of the Human Factors Society* (pp. 1448–1453). Santa Monica, CA: Human Factors Society.

Dingus, T.A., and Hulse, M.C. (1993). Some human factor design issues and recommendations for automobile navigation information systems. *Transportation Research 1C,*(2), 119–131.

Dingus, T.A., McGehee, D.V., Manakkal, N., Johns, S.K., Carney, C., and Hankey, J. (1997). Human factors field evaluation of automobile headway maintenance/collision warning devices. *Human Factors, 39,* 216–229.

Eberts, R.E., and MacMillan, A.G. (1985). Misperception of small cars. In R.E. Eberts and C.G. Eberts (eds.), *Trends in ergonomics/human factors II* (pp. 33–39). North Holland, The Netherlands: Elsevier Science Publishers, B.V.

Endsley, M.R. (1995). Measurement of situation awareness in dynamic systems. *Human Factors, 37*(1), 65–84.

Endsley, M.R., and Rodgers, M. (1996). Attention distribution and situation awareness in air traffic control. In *Proceedings 40th Annual Meeting of the Human Factors Society.* Santa Monica, CA: Human Factors. pp. 82–86.

Erzberger, H., Davis, T.O., and Green, S. (1993). Design of the Center-TRACON Automation System. In *Proceedings of the AGAARD Guidance & Control Panel 56th Symposium on Machine Intelligence in Air Traffic Control.* Berlin, Germany.

Evans, L. (1988). Older driver involvement in fatal and severe traffic crashes. *Journal of Gerontology: Social Sciences, 43*(5), 186–193.

Evans, L. (1991). *Traffic safety and the driver.* New York: Van Nostrand.

Evans, L. (1996). A crash course in traffic safety. *1997 Medical and Health Annual* Chicago: Encyclopaedia Britannica.

Farmer, C.M., Lund, A.K., Trempel, R.E., and Brover, E.R. (1997 in press). Fatal crashes of passenger vehicle systems before and after adding antilock braking systems. *Accident Analysis and Prevention.*

Fischhoff, B., and MacGregor, D. (1982). Subjective confidence in forecasts. *Journal of Forecasting, 1,* 155–172.

Foushee, H.C. (1984). Dyads and triads at 35,000 feet: Factors affecting group process and aircrew performance. *American Psychology, 39,* 885–893.

Fuller, R. (1988). Psychological aspects of learning to drive. In J.A. Rothergatter and R.A. de Bruin (eds.), *Road users and traffic safety* (pp. 527–537). Assen/Maastricht, Netherlands: Van Gorcum.

Garland, D.J., and Endsley, M.R. (eds.) (1995). *Experimental analysis and measurement of situation awareness: Proceedings of the international conference.* Daytona Beach, FL: Embry-Riddle Aeronautical University Press.

Gilliland, K., and Schlegal, R.E. (1995). Readiness to perform testing and the worker. *Ergonomics and Design, 3* January, 14–19.

Godley, S., Fildes, B.N., and Triggs, T.J. (1997). Perceptual counter measures to speeding. In D. Harris (ed.), *Engineering psychology and cognitive ergonomics.* London England: Ashgate.

Godthelp, H., Milgram, P., and Blaauw, T.S. (1983). Driving under temporary visual occlusion. *Proceedings 3rd European Conference on Human Decision Making & Manual Control.* pp. 357–370. Roskilde, Denmark.

Green, P. (1995). Automotive techniques. In J. Weimer (ed.), *Research techniques in human engineering,* 165–201. San Diego, CA: Academic Press.

Gugerty, L.J. (1997). Situation awareness during driving: Explicit and implicit knowledge in dynamic spatial memory. *Journal of Experimental Psychology: Applied, 3*(1), 42–66.

Hale, A., Quist, A., and Stoop, J. (1988). Errors in routine driving tasks. *Ergonomics, 31,* 631–641.

Hart, S.G. (1988). Helicopter human factors. In E.L. Wiener and D.C. Nagel (eds.), *Human factors in aviation* (pp. 591–638). San Diego, CA: Academic Press.

Haskell, I.D., and Wickens, C.D. (1993). Two- and three-dimensional displays for aviation: A theoretical and empirical comparison. *International Journal of Aviation Psychology, 3*(2), 87–109.

Henderson, R.L. (ed.) (1987). *Driver performance data book.* Washington, DC: National Highway Traffic Safety Administration.

Hopkin, V.D. (1995). *Human Factors in Air Traffic Control.* London: Taylor & Francis.

Hopkin, V.D., and Wise, J.M. (1996). Human factors in air traffic control automation. In R. Parasuraman and M. Mouloua (eds.), *Human Performance in Automated Systems.* Hillsdale, NJ: Lawrence Erlbaum.

Jensen, R.S. (1982). Pilot judgment: Training and evaluation. *Human Factors, 24,* 61–74.

Kahane, C.J. (1989). *An evaluation of center high mounted stop lamps based on 1987 data* (DOT HS 807 442). Washington, DC: National Highway Traffic Safety Administration.

Kaptein, N.A. (1994). *Benefits of in-car head-up displays* (Technical report #TNO-TM 1994 B-20). Soesterberg, The Netherlands: TNO Human Factors Research Institute.

Kaptein, N.A., Theeuwes, J., and Van Der Horst, R. (1996). *Driving simulator validity: Some considerations* (Report 96-13 38). Transportation Research Board 75th Annual Meeting, Washington, DC, Jan. 7–11.

Kerns, C. (1991) Data link communications between controllers and pilots. *International Journal of Aviation Psychology 1,* 187–204.

Kiefer, R.J. (1995). Defining the "HUD benefit time window." In *Vision in vehicles VI Conference.* Amsterdam: Elsevier Science Publishers B.V.

Kiefer, R. and Gellatly, A.W. (1996). Quantifying the consequences of the "Eyes on the Road" benefit attributed to Head Up Displays. Society of Automative Engineers Publication 960946. Warrendale, PA.: Society for Automotive Engineers.

Klein, R. (1991). Age-related eye disease, visual impairment, and driving in the elderly. *Human Factors, 33*(5), 521–526.

Kortelling, J.E. (1994). Effects of aging, skill modification and demand alternation on multiple task performance. *Human Factors 36,* 27–43.

Lee, J.D., Morgan, J., Wheeler, W.A., Hulse, M.C. and Dingus, T.A. (1997). Development of Human Factors Guidelines for Advanced Traveler Information Systems. US Federal Highway Administration Report FHWA-RD-95-201. Washington, DC.

Leibowitz, H.W., Owens, D.A., and Helmreich, R.L. (1995). Transportation. In R. Nickerson (ed.), *Emerging needs and opportunities for human factors research* (pp. 241–261). Washington, DC: National Academy Press.

Luffsey W.S. (1990). *How to become an FAA Air Traffic Controller.* New York: Random House.

Lunenfeld, H., and Alexander, G. (1990). *A user's guide to positive guidance* (3rd ed.). Washington, DC: Federal Highway Administration.

Malaterre, G. (1990). Error analysis and in-depth accident studies. *Ergonomics, 33,* 1403–1421.

Manning, C. (1995). Empirical Investigation of the use of flight strips. In R. Jensen (ed). *Proceedings 8th International Symposium on Aviation Psychology.* Columbus OH: Ohio State.

Mayhew, D.R., Simpson, H.M., Williamson, S.R., and Ferguson, S.A. (1997, in press) Effectiveness and role of driver education in a graduated licensing system. *Journal of Public Health Policy.*

McGreevy, M.W., and Ellis, S.R. (1986). The effect of perspective geometry on judged direction in spatial information instruments. *Human Factors, 28,* 439–456.

McKenna, F.P. (1988). What role should the concept of risk play in theories of accident involvement? *Ergonomics, 31,* 469–484.

McKnight, A.J., and Shinar, D. (1992). Brake reaction time to center high-mounted stop lamps on vans and trucks. *Human Factors, 34*(2), 205–213.

Miller, J. (1996). Fit for duty? *Ergonomics in design.* 4 April 11–17.

Mortimer, R.G. (1993). The high mounted brake lamp: A cause without a theory. *Proceedings of the 37th Annual Meeting of the Human Factors & Ergonomics Society* (pp. 955–959). Santa Monica, CA: Human Factor and Ergonomics Society.

Mortimer, R.G., Goldsteen, K., Armstrong, R.W., and Macrina, D. (1990). Effects of incentives and enforcement on the use of seat belts by drivers. *Journal of Safety Research, 21,* 25–37.

Mourant, R.R., and Rockwell, T. H. (1972). Strategies of visual search by novice and experienced drivers. *Human Factors, 14,* 325–335.

National Highway Traffic Safety Administration (1989). *Interim report on the safety consequences of raising the speed limit on rural interstate highways.* Washington, DC.

National Highway Traffic Safety Administration (1990, Dec.). *General estimates system 1989: A review of information on police reported traffic crashes in the United States* (DOT-HS-807-665). Washington, DC: U.S. Department of Transportation.

National Traffic Safety Council (1989). *Accident Facts,* Chicago.

National Transportation Safety Board (1988). *Northwest Airlines. DC-9-82 N312RC, Detroit Metropolitan Wayne County Airport. Romulus, Michigan, August 16, 1987* (Aircraft Accident Report, NTSB/AAR-88/05). Washington, DC.

Nagel, D.C. (1988). Human error in aviation operations. In E.L. Wiener and D.C. Nagel (eds.), *Human factors in aviation* (pp. 263–303). San Diego, CA: Academic Press.

Nickerson, R.S., and Moray, N.P. (1995). Environmental change. In R. Nickerson (ed.), *Emerging needs and opportunities for human factors research* (pp. 158–176). Washington, DC: National Academy Press.

Nicolle, C. (1995). Design issues for older drivers. *Ergonomics in Design, 3* 14–18 July.

O'Hare, D., and Roscoe, S.N. (1990). *Flightdeck performance: The human factor.* Ames, IA: Iowa State University Press.

Owens, D.A., Helmers, G., and Sivak, M. (1993). Intelligent vehicle highway systems: A call for user-centered design. *Ergonomics, 36,* 363–369.

Palmer, E., and Degani, A. (1991). Electronic checklists: Evaluation of two levels of automation. *Proceedings of the sixth International Symposium on Aviation Psychology.* Columbus, OH: Ohio State University, Department of Aviation.

Parkes, A.M., and Coleman, N. (1990). Route guidance systems: A comparison of methods of presenting directional information to the driver. In E.J. Lovesey (ed.), *Contemporary ergonomics 1990* (pp. 480–485). London: Taylor & Francis.

Planzer, N., and Jenny, M.T. (1995). Managing the evolution to free flight. *Journal of ATC,* Jan.–Mar., 18–20.

Raby, M., and Wickens, C.D. (1994). Strategic workload management and decision biases in aviation. *International Journal of Aviation Psychology, 4*(3), 211–240.

Redelmeier, D.A., and Tibshirani, R.J. (1997). Association between cellular-telephone calls and motor vehicle collisions. *New England Journal of Medicine, 336,* 453–502.

Reinfurt, D.W., Campbell, B.J., Stewart, J.R., and Stutts, J.C. (1990). Evaluating the North Carolina safety belt wearing law. *Acid Anal & Prev, 22*(3), 197–210.

Roscoe, S.N. (1968). Airborne displays for flight and navigation. *Human Factors, 10,* 321–332.

Ross, H.L. (1988). Deterrence-based policies in Britain, Canada, and Australia. In Lawrence, M.D., Stortum, J.R., and Zimrig, F.E. (eds), *Social control of the drinking driver* (pp. 64–78). Chicago, IL: University of Chicago Press.

Sanders, M.S., and McCormick, E.J. (1993). *Human factors in engineering and design.* New York: McGraw Hill.

Sarter, N.B., and Woods, D.D. (1994). Pilot interaction with cockpit automation II: An experimental study of pilots' model and awareness of the flight management system. *The International Journal of Aviation Psychology, 4*(1), 1–28.

Sarter, N.B., and Woods, D.D. (1995). How in the world did we ever get into this mode? Mode error and awareness in supervisory control. *Human Factors, 37*(1), 5–19.

Schumann, J. (1994). *On the use of discrete proprioceptive tactile warning signals during manual control.* Münster, Germany/New York: Waxman.

Schutte, P.C., and Trujillo, A.C. (1996). Flight crew task management in non-normal situations. *Proceedings of the 40th Annual Meeting of the Human Factors Society* (pp. 244–248). Santa Monica, CA: Human Factors and Ergonomics Society.

Schwing, R.C., and Kamerud, D.B. (1988). The distribution of risks: Vehicle occupant fatalities and time of the week. *Risk Analysis, 8,* 127–133.

Shinar, D., and Schieber, F. (1991). Visual requirements for safety and mobility of older drivers. *Human Factors, 33*(5), 507–520.

Shinar, D., Rotenberg, E., and Cohen, T. (1997). Crash reduction with an advanced brake warning system: a digital simulation. *Human Factors, 39,* 296–302.

Simon, F., and Corbett, C. (1996). Road traffic offending, stress, age, and accident history among male and female drivers. *Ergonomics, 39*(5), 757–780.

Sojourner, R.J., and Antin, J.F. (1990). The effect of a simulated head-up display speed meter on perceptual task performance, *Human Factors, 32,* 329–340.

Sperandio J.C. (1976). Variation of operator's strategies and regulating effects on workload. *Ergonomics, 14* 571–577.

Srinivasan, R. and Jovanis, P.P. (1997). Effect of selected in-vehicle route guidance systems on driver reaction times. *Human Factors, 39,* 200–215.

Stanton, N.A., and Marsden, P. (1996). From fly-by-wire to drive-by-wire: Safety implications of automation in vehicles. *Safety Science.*

Status Report (Dec 17, 1994). All the 16-year-olds didn't make it home. *29.* #13. Arlington, VA: Insurance Institute for Highway Safety.

Status Report (March 18, 1995). Airbags Save Lives. *30* #3. Arlington, VA: Insurance Institute for Highway Safety.

Stern, J.A., Boyer, D., and Schroeder, D. (1994). Blink rate: A possible measure of fatigue. *Human Factors, 36*(2), 285–297.

Summala, H. (1981). Driver/vehicle steering response latencies. *Human Factors, 23,* 683–692.

Summala, H. (1988). Zero-risk theory of driver behaviour. *Ergonomics, 31,* 491–506.

Summala, H., and Mikkola, T. (1994). Fatal accidents among car and truck drivers: Effects of fatigue, age, and alcohol consumption. *Human Factors, 36*(2), 315–326.

Svenson, O. (1981). Are we less risky and more skillful than our fellow drivers? *Acta Psychologica, 47,* 143–148.

Theeuwes, J., and Godthelp, H. (1995). Self-explaining roads. *Safety Science, 19,* 217–225.

Theeuwes, J., and Hagenzieker, M.P. (1993). Visual search of traffic scenes: On the effect of location expectations. In A.G. Gale et al. (eds.), *Vision in vehicles-IV* (pp. 149–158). Amsterdam: Elsevier Science Publishers B.V.

Triggs, T., and Harris, W.G. (1982). *Reaction time of drivers to road stimuli* (Human Factors Report HFR-12). Clayton, Australia: Monash University.

Van Der Horst, R. (1988). Driver decision making at traffic signals. In *Traffic accident analysis and roadway visibility* (pp. 93–97). Washington, DC: National Research Council.

Van Houten, R., and Nau, P.A. (1983). Feedback interventions and driving speed: A parametric and comparative analysis. *Journal of Applied Behavior Analysis, 16*, 253–281.

Violanti, J.M., and Marshall, J.R. (1996). Cellular phones and traffic accidents: An epidemiological approach. *Accid Anal and Prev, 28*(2), 265–270.

Voas, R.B. (1988). Emerging technologies for controlling the drunk driver. In M.D. Laurence, J.R. Snortum, and F.E. Zimring (eds.), *Social control of the drinking driver* (pp. 321–370). Chicago, IL: University of Chicago Press.

Waller, P.F. (1991). The older driver. *Human Factors, 33*(5), 499–506.

Warren, R., and Wertheim, A.H. (1990). *Perception and control of self-motion.* Hillsdale, NJ: Lawrence Erlbaum.

Wasielewski, P. (1984). Speed as a measure of driver risk: Observed speeds versus driver and vehicle characteristics. *Accident Analysis and Prevention, 16*, 89–103.

Weintraub, D.J., and Ensing, M.J. (1992). *Human factors issues in head-up display design: The book of HUD* (SOAR CSERIAC State of the Art Report 92-2). Dayton, OH: Crew System Ergonomics Information Analysis Center, Wright-Patterson AFB.

Wickens, C.D. (1997) Attentional issues in head up displays. In D. Harris (ed.), *Engineering Psychology and Cognitive Ergonomics.* VT: Ashgate.

Wickens, C.D. (1995). The tradeoff of design for routine and unexpected performance: Implications of situation awareness. In D.J. Garland and M.R. Endsley (eds.), *Situation Awareness Analysis and Measurement: Proceedings of the International Conference.* Daytona Beach, FL: Embry-Riddle Aeronautical University Press.

Wickens, C.D., Liang, C.C., Prevett, T., and Olmos, O. (1996). Electronic maps for terminal area navigation: Effects of frame of reference and dimensionality. *International Journal of Aviation Psychology, 6*(3), 241–271.

Wickens, C.D., and Long, J. (1995). Object- vs. space-based models of visual attention: Implications for the design of head-up displays. *Journal of Experimental Psychology: Applied, 1*(3), 179–194.

Wickens, C.D., Mavor, A., and McGee, J. (1997). *Flight to the future. Human factors in Air Traffic Control.* Washington, DC.: National Academy of Sciences.

Wiener, E.L., Kanki, B.G., and Helmreich, R.L. (eds.) (1993). *Cockpit resource management.* San Diego, CA: Academic Press.

Wiener, E.L., and Nagel, D.C. (1988). *Human factors in aviation.* San Diego, CA: Academic Press.

Wilde, G.J.S. (1988). Risk homeostasis theory and traffic accidents: Propositions, deductions and discussion of dissension in recent reactions. *Ergonomics, 31*(4), 441–468.

Williams, A.F., and O'Neill, B. (1974). On-the-road driving records of licensed race drivers. *Accident Analysis and Prevention, 6*, 263–270.

Wood, J.M., and Troutbeck, R. (1994). Effect of visual impairment on driving. *Human Factors, 36*(3), 476–487.

Young, M., and Stanton, N. (1997). Automotive automation: Effects, problems and implications for driver mental workload. In D. Harris (ed.), *Engineering psychology and cognitive ergonomics.* London, UK: Ashgate.

CHAPTER 18

Selection and Training

$\mathbf{M}$idwestern Gas and Electric had a problem common to many large companies: supervisors who failed to fill out performance appraisal forms correctly. To address this problem the newly hired training director coordinated development of a multimedia training package. This computer-based training program was self-paced and began with a short video clip introducing the goals and general method for conducting performance appraisals. The supervisor/ trainee then saw interviews with several "video mentors"—real supervisors sharing their thoughts about performance appraisals: how they did them, factors that were important, and how to deal with difficult situations. The computer-based training program then walked the supervisor/trainee through filling out an evaluation form. At each section where rules or regulations were relevant, the section was highlighted and a brief verbal message was used to explained the regulation and how the section should be filled out in order to conform with policies. Sometimes a humorous remark was added at the end of the message. Supervisors were also provided with a printed policy manual with three examples of filled-out appraisal forms in the back. The multimedia program contained several example cases, where trainees watched video clips of employee behavior and then practiced filling out appraisals. In addition to this training program, supervisors were told that they would receive a bonus for every appraisal form completed in a thorough manner. A year later, evaluation of the program showed that annual performance appraisals were more thorough and accurate than before. Supervisors also reported feeling more confident in their ability to perform the task.

In pursuing their goals to optimize system performance and enhance human health and safety, ergonomists tend to focus the optimization process on the machine and environment components (as opposed to the human component). However, technological or design innovations do not always guarantee increased job performance or safety, because characteristics of the operator, or of the organizational environment itself, may still create problems (e.g., Imada & Feiglstok, 1990; Hendrick, 1986; Root, 1993). As an example, consider safety in home construction. While well-designed harnesses and ropes could be provided free of charge to workers doing roof construction, they still might not use them because of existing attitudes or "peer pressure" among the workers. This example illustrates the fact that, while equipment and the environment should certainly be designed to fit the physical and cognitive attributes of people, there are still factors strictly relevant to the human "component" that will affect system performance.

In her discussion of human performance problems, Rossett (1992) noted that there are four types of factors that lead to poor performance:

1. *The environment is in the way.* Employees do not have the tools, equipment, space, information, or other things needed to perform the job successfully.
2. *Employees lack skill or knowledge.* People are motivated to do well but simply do not have the ability to do the task or subtasks being asked of them. This category might also include lack of knowledge related to feedback, where the employee does not know that the behavior is important or that he or she is failing to live up to standards (Rummler, 1983).
3. *There are no, few, or improper incentives.* There are either no consequences of doing the job well, or even worse, there are negative consequences of doing the job well. For example, janitors in a large organization who do a particularly good job in their building might be "rewarded" by being upgraded to a larger or more difficult building (a true example told by a janitor while explaining the reason he was not motivated to perform well).
4. *Employees are not internally motivated.* If employees are performing a boring or menial task (such as frying french fries), they may have difficulty in finding much pride or meaning in their work; that is, how important will doing a good job actually be to them?

We can see that the first cause, inadequate equipment, the environment, or both is essentially the focus of this text up to this point. In this chapter, we switch gears somewhat and consider ways to amend problems related to #2, lack of skills or knowledge. The most commonly used strategies to enhance knowledge and skills are selection, performance support, and training. Finally, in Chapter 19, we will briefly consider a new area termed macroergonomics, an approach that strives to address problems associated with #3, external rewards, and #4, internal motivation.

We might point out before beginning our discussion of these topics that economic competitiveness and other factors have caused a renewed interest in all types of performance enhancement, especially that of employee training. There are a number of fields focusing on human performance, including human factors, organizational development, and instructional design, to name just a few. However, one relatively new interdisciplinary field is *solely* concerned with improving human performance, the field of *human performance technology* (Stolovitch &

Keeps, 1992; Druckman & Swets, 1988; Druckman & Bjork, 1994). Like human factors, human performance technology is a systematic and scientific approach to performance improvement. The intervention methods include selection strategies, performance support, job aids, instruction manuals, training, process or job re-design, incentive programs, and motivational strategies. The topics of selection, performance support, and training overlap substantially with traditional human factors. It is also interesting to note that many emerging topics in human factors, such as macroergonomics, are areas central to the field of human performance technology. Thus, we can expect to find an increasing overlap between the two fields in the future.

PERSONNEL SELECTION

Personnel selection is chronologically the first approach taken to maximize the skills and knowledge needed by an employee to perform a job. It is a problem-solving process with the primary goal being to identify those people who will be most likely to succeed at their job. Selection has been a critical concern for government agencies such as the armed forces, and a long tradition of research in areas such as personnel psychology has grown out of this concern. The major focus of selection research is to identify reliable means of predicting future job performance. There are a number of methods used today to select employees for a particular job; such methods include interviews, work histories, background checks, tests, references, and work samples. Some use techniques that have been scientifically developed and validated; others use methods that are informal and depend heavily on intuition. A long line of research has demonstrated that, in general, the best techniques for selection include tests of skills and abilities and job-related work samples. The poorest methods (although they are still widely used) are interviews and references from previous employers (Osburn, 1987; Smither, 1994; Ulrich & Trumbo, 1965). Smither (1994) describes several interesting reasons for the poor predictive ability but widespread use of interviews and references. Probably the strongest factor currently biasing references is past employers' fear of litigation (Liebler & Parkman, 1992).

Selection can be conceptualized in terms of signal detection theory (see Chapter 4); where:

hit = hiring a person who will be good at the job
miss = not hiring someone who would do a good job
false alarm = hiring someone who ends up being unacceptable or doing a poor job
correct rejection = not hiring someone who, in fact, would not do a good job if they had been hired

Framed this way, selection is usually performed using any means possible to maximize the number of employee "hits" (successes) and minimize the number of "false alarms." Employers have traditionally been less concerned with the people that they do not hire. However, recent Equal Employment Opportunity (EEO) laws require that all individuals have equal opportunity with regard to employment. While no employer is required to hire individuals who cannot do the work, neither can they arbitrarily refuse to hire those who can. Obviously, this means that employers must be careful to use selection procedures that are valid and fair; that is, the selection criteria are *directly related* to job skills and abilities. Selection using irrelevant criteria is considered employment discrimination. As an example, firefighters cannot be selected on the basis of gender alone. However, a selection test could require applicants to lift and move 100 pounds of coiled fire hose, if that task is considered part of the normal job.

Basics of Selection

Identifying people who will successfully perform a job first requires a thorough analysis of the duties or behaviors that define a job, a process termed *job analysis.* Job analysis (which is closely related to task analysis) is the basis of many related activities, such as selection, training, performance appraisal, and setting salary levels. Job analysis can be accomplished in a number of ways (e.g., Smither, 1994), but usually includes specifying the tasks normally accomplished, the environments in which the tasks are performed, and the related knowledge, skills, and abilities required for successful task performance.

Once the job knowledge, skills, and abilities have been identified, employers must prioritize them with respect to which knowledge and skills are essential for job entry and which are desirable but not essential. Employers then look for applicants who either (a) already have the task-specific knowledge and skills required for a job or (b) show evidence of having basic knowledge and abilities (such as mathematical ability or psychomotor skills) that would eventually lead to successful job performance. Many businesses, as well as government agencies such as the armed forces, face high numbers of cases in the second category. This is because students directly out of college rarely have enough specific job skills to allow selection on the basis of job skills alone. Instead, employers must select people based on criteria that are not measures of job skills per se but are measures of basic abilities that are fundamental to eventual job performance.

A measure that is highly correlated with ultimate job performance is said to have high criterion-related validity. A measure with high validity is extremely useful for selection because employers can assume that applicants receiving a high score on the test will probably perform well on the job. Obviously, the higher the correlation coefficient, the more confidence the employer can have that high scores are predictive of high job performance. No test scores are perfectly related to job performance, and thus employers must deal with uncertainty. Figure 18.1 shows this problem in the context of a signal detection analysis. It can be seen that the employer must select a score cutoff for the predictive measure that will maximize selection success (hits). This is relatively easy if there are enough applicants with high scores to eliminate the people falling in the lower-right quadrant (false alarms). However, when the applicant pool is relatively small, setting the cutoff level so high may not be possible. This gives us some insight into why the armed forces seem to recruit so vigorously and offer big dividends for enlistment.

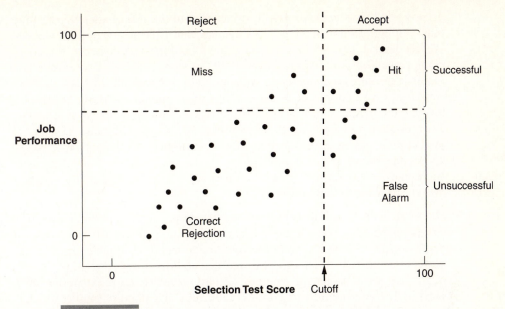

FIGURE 18.1

Hypothetical relationship between selection test and eventual job performance.

Selection Tests and Procedures

Not all selection procedures are equally effective, and this can translate into thousands or millions of dollars lost for an organization (e.g., it costs over $1 million to train a competent fighter pilot). Selection errors result in problems such as more training time and expense than necessary, supervisors or other staff having to compensate for inadequate performance, and supervisors having to spend time on reviews, feedback, and documentation of problems. In addition, poor selection can result in low employee moral, resentment, and complaints. This section describes some of the commonly used selection tests and procedures and notes those that seem to be most predictive of job performance.

Measures of Cognitive Ability. Many commonly used selection tests are standardized tests of cognitive or information-processing abilities. People have numerous abilities, which are used in various combinations for task performance. Typical categories of cognitive ability measured for selection include general ability, verbal ability, numerical ability, reasoning or analytical ability, perceptual speed, memory, and spatial-mechanical abilities (Osburn, 1987). Schmidt and Hunter (1981) presented evidence that cognitive ability tests are valid predictors of job performance, usually more valid than other assessment procedures. In addition, Hunter and Hunter (1984) found that tests of verbal and numerical ability were better predictors for jobs with high complexity, while tests of motor coordination and manual dexterity were better predictors for jobs with low complexity.

Some jobs may have additional or more restricted requirements for information-processing capabilities. For example, some researchers have suggested that driving and flying tasks rely heavily on abilities in the area of selective attention (e.g., Gopher & Kahneman, 1971; Kahneman, Ben-Ishai, & Lotan, 1973; Gopher, Weil, & Baraket, 1994). Measures of selective attention could therefore be used for employment decisions (e.g., Avolio et al., 1981; Gopher, 1982). Finally, certain jobs require a complex combination of skills, and selection methods should reflect this complexity. For example, in the aerospace domain, Hunter and Burke (1994) performed an analysis using 68 published studies of methods for pilot selection. They found that a battery of several measures of cognitive ability was best able to predict pilot success, including tests of verbal and numerical ability, mechanical knowledge, spatial ability, perceptual speed, and reaction time. Similarly, Stokes and Bohan (1995) found that dual-task performance and spatial ability were predictive of success in flight programs.

Measures of Physical Ability and Psychomotor Skills. Some jobs require physical strength in particular muscle groups, physical endurance, manual dexterity, and/or psychomotor skills. It is therefore common and legally acceptable to select employees on the basis of tests measuring these abilities. Physical ability measures often include static strength, dynamic strength, trunk strength, extent flexibility, gross body coordination, gross body equilibrium, and stamina. Besides measuring these variables, alternative approaches are simply to select people whose maximum aerobic power and or physical strength is great enough so that they can perform the job without excessive fatigue (see also discussions in Chapters 10–12). Other tests focus on motor abilities such as manual dexterity, finger dexterity, and arm-hand steadiness (Osburn, 1987). Finally, some tests are intended to target psychomotor skills such as reaction time or control precision. As an example, selection tests for pilots often include various types of tracking tasks (such as continuous pursuit tracking) because tracking is a key skill in that job.

Personality Assessment. Personality assessment has become more popular for selection in recent years. For selection purposes, there are generally two different types of standardized personality measures. The first is what might be termed "clinical" measures because they primarily identify people with mental illness or behavioral disorders. Examples include the well-known Minnesota Multiphasic Personality Inventory (MMPI). Such traditional personality tests are not particularly appropriate for employee selection; they have not proven to be valid for prediction of success (Newcomb & Jerome, 1995), and they are often troublesome from a legal point of view (Burke, 1995a).

The other type of personality test measures "personality dimensions" that are found in one degree or another in all people. Examples of tests that measure general personality characteristics include Cattell's 16PF (Cattell, Eber, & Tatsuoka, 1970), and the Eysenck Personality Inventory (Eysenck & Eysenck, 1964). Recent work on using personality measures for selection has indicated that five basic personality factors or clusters are useful in predicting job performance (Barrick & Mount, 1991; Pedersen et al., 1992):

Neuroticism: cluster of traits such as anxiety, depression, impulsiveness, and vulnerability

Extroversion: cluster of traits such as warmth, gregariousness, activity, and positive emotions

Openness: includes feelings, actions, ideas, values

Agreeableness: cluster of traits including trust, altruism, compliance, straightforwardness

Conscientiousness: includes competence, order, dutifulness, achievement striving, self-discipline.

A detailed description of these factors is provided in McCrae and Costa (1985). Barrick and Mount (1991) found that the *conscientiousness* factor was effective in predicting performance in a wide array of jobs including police, managers, salespeople, and skilled or semiskilled workers. Consistent with this finding, researchers evaluating the potential of personality tests for pilot selection have found that conscientiousness is the most strongly predictive measure (Bartram, 1995a; Pettitt & Dunlap, 1995). However, other trait clusters such as high *extroversion* and low *anxiety/neuroticism* are also predictive of pilot success in training programs (Bartram & Dale, 1982; Jessup & Jessup, 1971), a finding that appears to be consistent across commercial and military applicants, as well as four different nationalities (Bartram, 1995b). It is interesting to note that commercial pilot selection measures include personality tests, whereas U.S. military selection batteries do not (Damos, 1995).

Work Samples.   Work sampling typically requires applicants to complete a sample of work they would normally be required to perform on the job. Examples include a driving course for forklift operators, a typing test for secretaries, and an "in-basket test" where management candidates must respond to memos frequently found in a manager's mailbox. Work samples have shown a history of relatively strong predictive validity as a selection method (Campion, 1972; Hunter & Burke, 1995). A new and fairly inexpensive method for conducting work sampling is the use of video assessment (Smither, 1994). Video assessment is essentially a low-technology work simulation. Videotapes are shown to the job candidate, which portray workers in situations that require a decision. The applicants see a short scenario and then are asked how they would respond in the situation. Some evaluations have shown that video assessments are often more predictive than more traditional paper-and-pencil tests (e.g., Scott, McIntire, & Burroughs, 1992). Finally, when possible, more realistic simulations can be used to obtain work samples either for individuals or for jobs requiring teamwork (Burke, 1995b; Hunter & Hunter, 1984; Reilly & Chao, 1982; Steuffert, Pogash, & Piasecki, 1988).

Work samples are most useful for those jobs where applicants are expected to already have the appropriate knowledge and skills. However, there are some variations of this method that can be used in instances where applicants are to be hired and then trained for a substantial portion of the job. An example is *miniature job training,* where the assumption is that "a person who can demonstrate the ability to learn and perform on a job sampling will be able to learn and perform on the total job" (Siegel, 1983). The method, while not widely known, has been shown to have strong predictive validity (Reilly & Chao, 1982; Siegel, 1983).

Structured Interviews. While interviews have relatively poor predictive validity (Smither, 1994), they can be made more predictive by using certain structuring methods (Friedman & Mann, 1981). At a minimum, questions should be based on and related to knowledge and skills identified in the job analysis. Other methods for structuring the interview focus on asking applicants to describe previous work behaviors. For example, Hendrickson (1987) suggests using the "critical behavior interview" approach. With this method, applicants are asked to discuss recent occasions when they felt they were performing at their best. They are asked to describe the conditions, what they said or did, and so on. The interviewer looks for and scores behaviors that are consistent with job-related selection criteria. Interviews that culminate in scoring procedures are generally more valid than those which only result in a yes/no overall evaluation (Liebler & Parkman, 1992).

Future Trends

There are several trends in human performance intervention that will affect the nature of selection and training in the next decade. As described by Brandenburg and Binder (1992), four of these are:

- Accelerating turnover of knowledge, especially in the scientific and engineering worlds
- Rapid advances in information technology
- An increasingly diverse work force, with respect to entering skills, personal values, and learning needs
- Increasing international business competition, with a resulting emphasis on productivity and quality

These factors demand that new methods be found to enhance both selection and training of business and government employees. As an example, consider the changing tasks performed by pilots or air crew members. Their jobs now involve highly complex equipment with an increased focus on cognitive performance and teamwork and a decreasing focus on simply psychomotor skills such as tracking. This change is mirrored in the fact that the traditional selection tests for pilots (e.g., spatial ability, mechanical aptitude, gross motor dexterity, perceptual speed) are gradually declining in predictive ability (Hunter & Burke, 1994).

The changing nature of jobs will require a change in selection measures. As Damos (1995) notes, the only effective way to develop appropriate and effective selection tests and/or procedures is to first perform detailed analyses of the jobs as they exist now and are expected to be in the near future. These analyses must include cognitive task analysis, as well as analyses focusing on newer areas such as communication skills, relational skills (i.e., fitting into an organization, being able to work constructively and positively within the social and business environment), and teamwork skills (Burke, 1995; Damos, 1995; Salas et al., 1992; Smith, 1994).

PERFORMANCE SUPPORT AND JOB AIDS

Jobs have become increasingly complex, and the knowledge and skills needed for successful job performance are changing rapidly. It is difficult to provide enough training for employees to cope with the volume and rapid turnover of information and technology related to their tasks. As an example, imagine trying to provide training for the phone-in help service operators of a computer software company. These people need to either know a vast amount of information, or at least know where to find it within a matter of seconds. The amount of information required for many jobs is simply too large to impart through traditional training methods such as classroom instruction.

Because of the increasingly poor fit between job needs and standard training methods, such as seminars or instructional manuals, performance technology specialists are moving toward a direct *performance support* approach. This philosophy assumes that information and training activities (such as practice) should be provided on an *as-needed* basis, shifting a "learn-and-apply" cycle to a "learning-while-applying" cycle (Brandenburg & Binder, 1992; Rosow & Zager, 1990; Vazquez-Abad & Winer, 1992). It is considered more efficient to allow the person to access information (and learn) while they are doing a task rather than to try to teach them a large body of knowledge and assume they will retrieve it from memory at some later time. Performance support is the process of providing a set of information and learning activities in a context-specific fashion *during* task performance (an example is given below). Performance support is frequently viewed as the method of choice (Geber, 1991; Gery, 1989; Layton et al., 1995; Vazquez-Abad & Winer, 1992); it is more efficient, and often preferred by employees because it is less taxing on memory (training in one context does not have to be remembered and carried over to the job context).

This "efficiency" point view is often applied to instruction of software users (e.g., Spool & Snyder, 1993). Figure 18.2 illustrates a continuum of methods used by software interface designers for helping users learn new software. The right side shows the most desirable circumstance, where system "affordances" make the software inherently easy to use. It wastes the least time for users, and does not rely on user capabilities and motivation. The least desirable support is the traditional "learn ahead-of-time" classroom instruction because it is so dependent on learner motivation, comprehension of the material, and retention of information. Also consistent with this view, researchers in human factors are arguing more forcibly against traditional training that imparts a large body of declarative knowledge before people do the tasks in which the knowledge is used (e.g., Mumaw & Roth, 1995).

Types of Performance Support and Job Aids

Performance support methods range from simple to complex and go by a variety of names, as illustrated in Table 18.1. We will broadly use the traditional term of *job aid* to refer to short documents such as checklists or procedural guides; the term *performance support system* to refer to more complex systems that provide

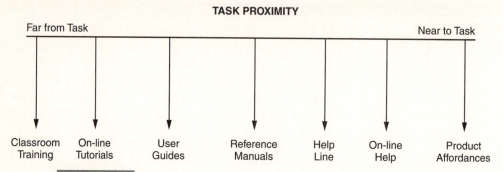

FIGURE 18.2

Continuum of computer interface training methods.

advanced functions such as information databases, expert systems, complex procedural support, or decision support systems (Carr, 1992), and the term *performance aid* to refer to any system that uses information to support task performance at the time of task.

Instructions

Traditionally, an important form of job aid for performance support is the instruction manual—often but not necessarily on paper. Psychologists know a fair amount about effective instructions, much of it drawn from material on comprehension (as discussed in Chapter 6), and effective display design (discussed in Chapter 8). Wright (1977) has outlined a particularly effective and compelling set of empirically based guidelines for printed technical instructions. Such guidelines include the caution against using prose (or prose alone) to present very complex sets of relationships or procedures and the recommendation that such prose can often be replaced by well-designed flow charts. Wright's guidelines also highlight the effective use of pictures that are redundant with, or related to words in conveying instructions, as illustrated in Figure 18.3. This is another illustration of the benefits of redundancy gain described in Chapter 8 (see Booher, 1975; Wickens, 1992b). Wright also notes the importance of locating pictures or diagrams in close proximity to relevant text, an example of the proximity-compatibility principle.

The phrasing of any text should of course be straightforward, as discussed in Chapter 6, and illustrations should be clear. In this regard it is important to emphasize that clarity does not necessarily mean photo realism (Spencer, 1988). In fact, in instructions such as emergency procedures in passenger aircraft evacuation, well articulated line drawings may be better understood than photographs (Schmidt & Kysor, 1987). Finally, with voice synthesis becoming increasingly available as an option for multimedia instructions, it is important to note that research indicates an advantage for voice coupled with pictures when presenting instructions (Nugent, 1987). With this combination, words can be used to provide information related to pictures, but in contrast to print, the eyes do not have to leave the pictures as the words are being processed.

TABLE 18.1 Systems That Support Performance at the Time of Task Performance

Term	Definition
Performance Support System	Any "information" system that directly supports the user in performance of a task (at the time of task performance).
Job Aid	Any product, on or off the computer, that provides assistance or support to a person performing a task. Job aids are usually very short and succinct. Examples include checklists, procedure guides, technical documentation, references, etc.
Electronic Performance Support System (Gery, 1991), also termed Integrated Information System (Johnson, Norton, & Utsman, 1992)	A computer-based integration of one or more of the following: information databases, on-line reference, learning experiences and simulations, assessment systems, productivity software, and expert advisory systems.
Aiding* (Rouse, 1991)	Any functionality that is separate from, and added to, the basic system. Examples are an airplane autopilot, automobile automatic transmission, expert system to aid decision making, etc. It is any secondary system designed to help or enhance human performance.
Adaptive Aiding (Rouse, 1991)	Aiding that changes in nature and/or degree from one task to another and from one user to another.
Intelligent Support System	Computer-based system that has an internal representation of the domain as well as the user to provide expert assistance to the user performing essentially any type of task.
Decision Aiding, Decision Support System	Computer-based system that supports information access, evaluation, and decision making or judgment.

* While Rouse defines aiding as any system that supports performance (such as an automatic transmission), he generally restricts his discussions to aiding systems that are computer-based and informational or advisory in nature.

Source: Gordon, S.E., *Systematic training program design: Maximizing effectiveness and minimizing liability* (Englewood Cliffs, NJ: P T R Prentice Hall, 1993), p. 5. Copyright 1993 by P T R Prentice Hall. Reprinted by permission.

Job Aids

A job aid is a device or document that guides the user in doing a task while the user is performing it (Swezey, 1987). In either paper or computer-based form, it should be available when and where the user needs it. Examples of job aids are the daily to-do list, a recipe, note cards for a speech, a computer keyboard template, instructions for assembling a product, or a procedural list for filling out a form (tax forms come with extensive job aids). A job aid can be a few words, a picture, a series of pictures, a procedural checklist, or an entire book. A well-designed job aid

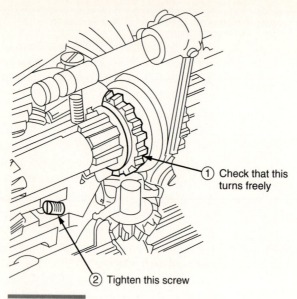

① Check that this
turns freely

② Tighten this screw

FIGURE 18.3

Advantage of partially redundant combination of pictures and words. (*Source:* Wright, P.,
1977. Presenting technical information: A Survey of Research Finding. *Instructional Science.*
6, 93–134. Reprinted by permission of Kluwer Academic Publishers.)

promotes accurate and efficient performance by taking into account the nature
and complexity of the task, as well as the capabilities of the user.

While job aids are often the right performance support solution, they are not
without their shortcomings. Recent reviews have indicated that misuse of checklists was partially responsible for several major airline accidents (e.g., Degani &
Wiener, 1993), and checklist problems have been identified in other industries as
well (Swain & Guttmann, 1983). Checklists used by flight crews are relatively
lengthy and are divided into separate checklists for different flight segments, such
as preflight, taxi, takeoff, and so on. Degani and Wiener (1993) describe a number of human errors associated with the use of such checklists, such as overlook-
ing an item in a long checklist, thinking that a procedure on the checklist had been
completed when in actuality it had not, and being temporarily distracted from
checklist performance. The authors also provide a set of design principles for development of any checklist that is relatively long and that involves complex system
operation. In general, checklists should follow sound human factors principles:
provide information that is needed, leave out superfluous information, use chunking, use consistent and logical sequencing, and so on.

Electronic Performance Support

Performance support systems are frequently computer-based, in which case they
may be termed *electronic performance support systems* (Gery, 1989, 1991). Gery
(1989) defines an electronic performance support system as "an integrated elec-

tronic environment which is available to and easily accessed by each employee and is structured to provide immediate, individualized on-line access to the full range of information, software, guidance, advice and assistance, data, images, tools and assessment and monitoring systems to permit him or her to perform his or her job with a minimum of support and intervention by others" (p. 65). These systems pull together a number of common stand-alone technologies such as information databases, expert systems, help systems, adaptive aiding, and computer-based training. An example of a typical electronic performance support system is described by Varnadoe and Barron (1993). This system provides support for intermediate maintenance technicians. The system components are:

Job Aid: The job aid is a comprehensive set of procedural descriptions for equipment repair, maintenance, and troubleshooting. The procedures are shown in graphical flowcharts where necessary. Within the job aid component, users can access a technical manual, glossary, or videos of the procedure.

Training: The training system component has a computer-based training module with lessons that can be accessed at any time. In addition, when "training" is selected from within the job aid, a walk-through of the step depicted in the job aid is shown.

Illustrated Parts Breakdown: This section includes CAD drawings of the various assemblies and subassemblies and includes textual information such as government standards, part numbers, descriptions, and so forth. This information is linked to job aid steps and the technical manual.

It can be seen that in this particular case, most of the performance support system is simply a complex information database with hyperlinks. However, if designed correctly, this type of system can be highly useful for information intensive tasks. More advanced electronic performance support systems have a greater degree of "intelligence" and adaptiveness built into the modules. Finally, many are designed as mobile computers for employees such as maintenance technicians and field personnel. The current state of computer technology results in serious limitations (i.e., battery life) for such mobile systems, which makes effective system design even more challenging (Layton et al., 1995).

A final question involves knowing when to use performance support, training, or a combination of both. Most instructional design models have a step where this decision is made (e.g., see below). Some guidelines also exist to help designers with this decision. Table 18.2 lists a number of guidelines provided by various researchers (e.g., Gordon, 1994); however, keep in mind that these suggestions assumed relatively basic performance support systems and may be less applicable for advanced displays or intelligent agents.

TRAINING PROGRAM DESIGN

In spite of our technological advances in system design and performance support, training is still at the heart of efforts to increase employee knowledge and skills. An example is driving a car—even the most ergonomically sound interior and

---

TABLE 18.2 Factors Indicating Use of Performance Support Systems or Training

Use Performance Support Systems When:

The job or tasks allow sufficient time for a person to look up the information.

The job requires use of large amounts of information and/or complex judgments and decisions.

Task performance won't suffer from the person reading instructions or looking at diagrams.

The job or task requires a great number of steps that are difficult to learn or are difficult to remember.

Safety is a critical issue, and there are no negative repercussions of relying on a job aid.

The task is performed by a novice, or the person performs the job infrequently.

The job involves a large employee turnover rate.

The job is one where employees have difficulty obtaining training (due to distance, time, etc.).

Use Training Systems When:

The task consists of steps performed quickly and/or in rapid succession.

The task is performed frequently.

The task must be learned in order to perform necessary higher-level tasks (e.g., read sheet music in order to play an instrument).

The person wishes to perform the task unaided.

The person is expected to perform the task unaided.

Performance of the task would be hindered by attending to some type of aid.

The task is psychomotor or perceptual, and use of a job aid is not feasible.

---

dashboard systems do not alleviate the need to spend time learning to control the vehicle and drive in traffic among hundreds of other vehicles.

There are many different ways to teach a person how to perform tasks. There are different types of media, such as lecture or text, and there are other considerations as well, such as how much and what type of practice is most efficient for learning skills. Like other topics in this book, training program design is really an entire course in itself. Here, we will just skim the surface and describe some of the most prevalent concepts and issues in human factors. Before describing these concepts and issues, we will first review a general design model for developing training programs and the major types of training media that training specialists combine together in designing a training program.

A Training Program Design Model

The majority of professionally designed business and government training programs are developed using a systematic design method termed *Instructional System Design,* or *ISD* (Andrews & Goodson, 1980; Catalina & Bills, 1993; Gordon, 1994; Reigeluth, 1989). ISD models are similar to human factors design models (see Chapter 3); they typically include a front-end analysis phase, design and development phase (or phases), implementation, and a final system evaluation phase. ISD models are also used to develop job aids and performance support systems (Gordon, 1994). Most professional instructional designers agree that the process used for designing the training program can be just as important as the type of program or the media chosen (e.g., video, computer-based training, etc.).

A number of studies have demonstrated that use of systematic design methods can result in more effective training programs than less systematic methods, such as simply asking a subject matter expert to provide training (Goldstein, 1986).

An instructional program is a product or system and can therefore be designed using an "ergonomic" approach. Gordon (1994) modified a generic ISD model by incorporating methods derived from cognitive psychology and human factors. This model, shown in Figure 18.4, still has the traditional ISD phases of front-end analysis, design and development, and system evaluation. However, it also includes less traditional methods such as early usability testing. The design model can be used for developing job aids, instructional manuals, and performance support systems, in additional to more traditional training programs. The model contains four basic procedures or phases described below: front-end analysis, design and development, full-scale development, and final evaluation.

Front-End Analysis. Like other types of design, training program design begins with an analysis of needs. In this model, front-end analysis is accomplished by performing an organizational analysis, task analysis, and trainee analysis. The information collected in the analyses is then used to determine whether training or some other intervention is needed and to define requirements and constraints for design of the training system.

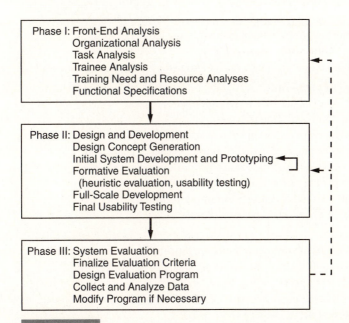

FIGURE 18.4
Instructional system design model. (*Source:* Gordon, S.E., 1993. *Systematic Training Program Design: Maximizing Effectiveness and Minimizing Liability.* Englewood Cliffs, NJ: Prentice Hall, p. 12. Copyright 1993 by Prentice Hall. Reprinted by permission.)

The *organizational analysis* is an information-collection activity that looks at the broad context of the job or task; the goal is to identify any factors that would bear on the need for, and success of, a training program. Such factors include future company changes such as job redesign or acquisition or new technology, management attitude toward the job duties, and so on. In this analysis, one tries to answer questions such as those shown in Table 18.3 (see Gordon, 1994, for a complete discussion). The information can be collected through a combination of methods such as document analysis, interviews, questionnaires, job tests, and observation (Wexley & Latham, 1991). The answers to the questions in Table 18.3 determine whether training would be desirable and consistent with organizational and employee goals and values.

Task analysis is performed to identify the knowledge, skills, and behaviors required for successful task performance. Task analysis for front-end analysis can be performed using the same methods that are used for other types of human-factors analysis (see Chapter 3). Some commonly used methods for the data collection are structured interviews, verbal protocol analysis, and observation. Data representation methods vary, ranging from tables to flow charts to conceptual

---

TABLE 18.3   Typical Questions to Answer in Performing Organizational Analysis

The Organization

What are the goals of the organization as a whole?
What are the methods by which the organization hopes to accomplish its goals?
What are the values of the industry in general?
What are the organizational policies that are relevant to the job in question?
What are the trends in the organizational structure?
What are some of the relevant performance-related problems within the organization?

The Employee's Organizational Unit

What are the goals and values of the unit or unit managers?
What are the unit written and unwritten policies?
What is the job performance level expected by management?
What are the managers' perceptions of actual employee job performance levels?
What are trends in the target job (and/or jobs above or below the target job)?
What are unit policies regarding performance enhancement and/or training?
What are managers attitudes toward training and/or performance support?
What are implicit and explicit expectations of employees?

Job Performance

What is the performance level of which employees are capable?
What is the performance level at which employees are currently working?
What are performance levels expected by employees and their peers?
What are the performance levels employees perceive that they could conceivably attain, and what
   circumstances would support or facilitate those levels?
What are the factors that managers feel interfere with job performance?
What are the factors that employees feel interfere with job performance?
What are some stories or anecdotes about an employee or others who have had difficulties in
   task performance?

graphs (e.g., Gordon, 1994). Hierarchical graph formats are often useful because they reveal the inherent organization in the material, which can be valuable for later instructional design. Contents of the task analysis are used to define contents of the training program. Careful task analysis is also useful to determine the types of knowledge and strategy required for successful job performance because these factors determine the overall *type* of training program utilized.

After completion of the task analysis, a brief *trainee analysis* is performed. This process identifies: (1) *prerequisite* knowledge and skills that should be possessed by trainees in order to begin the training program (e.g., eighth-grade English to take beginning course for auto mechanics); (2) *demographics* such as age, physical capabilities, primary language, background, etc.; and (c) *attitudes* toward training methods if not done as part of organizational analysis.

Results from the organizational, task, and trainee analyses are used in a *training needs analysis* to determine whether the most appropriate performance improvement approach is task redesign, performance support, or develop a training program (if motivation is the problem, none of these would be used).[1]

It is not always easy to determine whether the performance intervention should be a human factors redesign, performance support, or training. For example, consider training a forklift operator. Safety training videotapes have traditionally warned operators of the hazards associated with lifting heavy loads too high. Because of the leverage effect of a forklift, raising heavy loads too high in the front has the potential to bring the rear wheels off the ground. Operators needed to learn when the load was being lifted too high, which was dependent on the load weight. On the one hand, training operators to know this information and consistently apply it would be a challenge. On the other hand, an equipment redesign could more effectively solve the problem. Examples might include such things as (1) design the forklift so that weight was measured and some type of feedback or warning device used to provide information to the operator, or (2) design the forklift so that load weight was measured and the vehicle would not move in any direction if the load was higher than what was safe.

Finally, there are many occasions when a combination of job aid and training program is identified as the best solution. The scenario described at the beginning of the chapter is an example of such a combination, where the multimedia training program was augmented by a hard-copy job aid of company rules and regulations.

At this point, *functional specifications* are written that include the training program goal, training objectives, system performance requirements, and development constraints. Performance requirements are important because they include the characteristics to be possessed by the training program from an instructional design and human factors standpoint, such as desirable instructional strategies and interface requirements for ease of use, or ease of learning (see Baird, Schneier,

---

[1]Some researchers use the term *training need analysis* to refer to identification of the specific medium to be used for training (such as classroom instruction, computer-based training, etc.). Note that this is not the meaning of the term in this model.

& Laird, 1983; Fisk, 1989; Gordon, 1994; Holding, 1987; Jonassen, 1988; Keller & Suzuki, 1988). Table 18.4 shows some commonly used instructional strategies that might be specified for training system performance requirements. In addition, designers can specify tasks that should be trained to the point of automaticity (e.g., for jobs with high mental workload or stress) and suggest "mental models" that should be supported in training because of their centrality to task performance (Cannon-Bowers et al., 1991; see Chapter 6). Functional specifications act as a blueprint for the remainder of the design process and also help protect training program designers from professional liability resulting from accident or injury (Gordon, 1994).

Design and Development.   The second phase, design and development, is where the analyst chooses a training program method or combination of methods and proceeds with further design and development while also performing formative evaluation. The steps for this phase are listed below in a given sequence, but often there is iteration back through the steps many times. This is considered standard practice for most ISD models.

TABLE 18.4 Instructional Strategies for Enhancing Training Effectiveness

Acquiring Declarative Knowledge

Make information meaningful and relevant to learner's existing knowledge.

Tie new information to previously learned information.

Provide specific examples or abstract concepts and principles.

Use memorable types of information to act as retrieval cues.

Use video and/or animation to present declarative knowledge that involves dynamic systems.

Use advance organizers: Before presenting a learning segment, provide a general structure.

Promote active, generative learning by having trainees solve problems, generate examples, etc.

Acquiring Procedural Knowledge

For pattern-recognition or perceptual learning (perception-action rules), use a wide range of examples as well as a number of nonexamples (e.g., a wide variety of x-rays that *are* tumors and x-rays that *are not* tumors).

In practicing examples and nonexamples, try to make the critical situational cues or features salient.

For complex skills, carefully define and provide a range of examples and problems to solve so that the trainee develops correct rules.

When learners are first acquiring procedural-skill knowledge, provide relevant declarative knowledge or prompt the learner to retrieve it.

Teach and test for required subskills before higher-level skills.

Use repetition of tasks or subtasks spaced over time for maximum retention.

Emphasize realistic practice under varied circumstances.

Provide feedback after performance, preferable for each subtask being learned.

Use part-task training where subtasks are independent and whole-task training would result in too much demand on cognitive resources.

Make use of both visual and auditory channels of communication when appropriate.

By considering the information contained in the functional specifications, the designer generates a number of *design concepts* that would work for the problem. If there is more than one possible solution, the alternatives can be compared by using a cost-benefit analysis in a matrix table format. By using such a table, the designer can choose the best overall design solution or, alternatively, complementary methods that can counteract the other's disadvantages. Once the design concept has been chosen, a project plan is written, including budget, equipment, personnel, and task time line. In some cases, a cost-benefit analysis is performed to make sure that the proposed design solution will be adequately cost-effective (Marrelli, 1993).

A prototype is used for *formative evaluation* of the design concept. The prototype is used to gain management approval and peer (human factors or instructional designer) approval and to perform usability testing. In the latter case, representative trainees are asked to review the prototype and provide comments on its acceptability, perceived effectiveness, weaknesses, and so forth. As more fully functional prototypes are developed, trainees "use" the system prototype in the same way that standard "usability" evaluations are conducted, something now made possible by the use of *rapid prototyping* techniques (e.g., Wilson & Rosenberg, 1988).

Full-Scale Development.   After formative evaluation and usability testing has been accomplished, the full-scale development can proceed. Material is taken from the task analysis and translated into instructional units using instructional design guidelines such as those given by Clark (1989), Romiszowski (1984), or Merrill (1983). An example of a rather traditional guide is Merrill's component-display theory (Merrill, 1983), a system that suggests a list of instructional strategies to be used depending on the type of concepts or skills being taught. Information is taught by combining *primary methods* and *secondary methods.* For example, general concepts and principles are taught by presenting the main idea and then asking questions about the idea. Secondary methods would then be added by using activities such as relating general principles to examples and nonexamples (an example of something that does *not* embody the principle), presenting an alternative representation (such as a paraphrase or diagram), presenting an analogy, and providing a context for examples.

While these "building block" methods provide a useful checklist of instructional design strategies, they are mostly based on the rather outmoded view of learners as passive recipients of knowledge. We now realize that instruction based on this viewpoint is not particularly efficient (Gordon, 1994). As a result, many researchers are focusing on instructional systems that have learners actively doing things rather than passively receiving information (e.g., Chandler, 1996; Gordon et al., 1994; Mumaw and Roth, 1995; Salzman, Dede, & Loftin, 1995).

As the system is developed, the design team should periodically perform additional formative evaluation. This prevents any unanticipated and unpleasant surprises at the end, when changes are more costly. Evaluation should focus on whether the training program appears to be acceptable to trainees and effective in meeting its goals and objectives. If possible, the training program should be used with several naive trainees who have not been part of the design process. They should receive the training program and be tested on knowledge and skill acquisition both immediately after training and after a period of time similar to that expected to occur after training on the fielded system. Trainees should be asked questions via interview or questionnaire regarding their subjective reactions to the system (Gordon, 1994).

Program Evaluation.   The fielded training program or performance aid should be evaluated for system effectiveness and then periodically monitored. The evaluation process is carried out much like the evaluation processes described in Chapter 3. Goals of the evaluation process are to answer questions such as (Goldstein, 1986):

- Has a change occurred in trainee task performance?
- Is the change a result of the instructional program (as opposed to some other factor such as a change in management or incentive programs)?
- Would the change occur with other trainees besides those in our sample?
- Would the change occur in other contexts or for other tasks?

To answer these questions, we design an evaluation plan by specifying *what* criteria (variables) to measure, *when* to measure the criteria, *who* (which trainees) to use in measuring the criteria, and *what context* to use. You can see that these are the same types of question involved in development of the research designs discussed in Chapter 2. While training programs are often not systematically evaluated, evaluation of a fielded training program should be performed by using either a pretest-posttest experimental design (with one group measured before and after training) or a control group design with one group of randomly selected trainees receiving the old training method (or none at all), and the other group receiving the training program being evaluated. Program evaluators strive to: (1) conduct the evaluation in an environment as similar to the ultimate performance environment as possible; (2) conduct the knowledge and skill tests after a realistic period of time; and (3) base the evaluation on tasks and task conditions that are representative of the ultimate job (Gordon, 1994).

In addition to evaluation of trainee job performance, it may sometimes be desirable to evaluate the impact of a training program on an organization's productivity and performance levels. This is achieved by performing a longitudinal systematic evaluation incorporating multiple measures. An example in the area of team training is a study conducted by Robertson, Stelly, and Wagner (1995) to evaluate an aviation maintenance team training program. As one of the various measures, the study evaluated overall maintenance performance for 6 months before and 26 months after the training program. Measures included variables such as dependability of on-time airplane departures and "lost time" injuries.

Training Media

Although we often think of "training" as an activity performed by a person in a classroom setting, there are actually a large number of ways to deliver training programs, including lecture, text, videotape, and computer-based training. Businesses use more classroom lecture type of training than anything else, but this is quickly changing to a more predominant use of computer-assisted instruction and performance support systems. Jobs that require psychomotor skills, such as flying a jet, are often trained using computer-based simulators. Table 18.5 lists some of the major training methods, along with some of their associated advantages and disadvantages.

One of the biggest trends in training, besides the use of performance support, is to move toward a greater use of computer-based training or computer-assisted instruction (including Web-based training). *Computer-assisted instruction* (CAI) can be loosely defined as a computer-based instructional system that relies on some combination of information presentation, testing, opportunity for skill practice, and individualized feedback. Various forms of computer-assisted instruction, or computer-based training (CBT) as it is sometimes called, have been used in business and government training for many years, allowing considerable evaluation of the efficacy of this method (e.g., Kulik & Kulik, 1991; Niemiec & Walberg, 1987). Reviews and meta-analyses show that CAI appears to enhance learning, reducing training time by up to 30 percent, and increasing test scores by up to 10–15 percent (Kulik & Kulik, 1991). However, there are numerous cases where lower-technology training methods such as job aids can be just as effective as CAI (e.g., Swezey, Perez, & Allen, 1988; Williams, Wickens, & Hutchinson, 1994). One conclusion common among instructional designers is that training effectiveness will be strongly impacted by the overall quality of the instructional design process (Goldstein, 1986).

Another trend that is growing within the area of computer-assisted instruction is the use of *multimedia systems* (Ambron & Hooper, 1990; Batra, Bishu, & Donohue, 1995; Chandler, 1996; Jonassen & Mandl, 1990; Nix & Spiro, 1990). Multimedia systems allow diverse links between units of knowledge and procedural skills and allow audio/video to be blended seamlessly into a computer-based tutorial system. It allows the learner to go much closer to the job environment in which they will eventually be performing their tasks. However, like other hypertext or hypermedia systems, multimedia training programs can cause users to have difficulty with navigation and experience disorientation (Clibbon, 1995; see Chapter 15). This is problematic in learning programs because it takes *cognitive resources* away from the primary learning task. Software usability testing of the instructional program is critical to prevent such problems.

Simulations are artificial re-creations of a some real-world system or environment. As computer technology advances, simulations are being used with increasing frequency because of their ability to provide a learning environment that approximates the eventual job environment (Lierman, 1994). This facilitates development of skills that transfer to the employee's job (see later section on transfer of training). Simulations are an ideal environment to train: tasks that have a large perceptual or pattern-recognition component; skills that require interpersonal tasks such as managerial leadership; tasks that have a large cognitive decision-making or problem-solving component; tasks that require teamwork skills or group problem solving; and tasks that are too dangerous or expensive to be performed in the real world. Simulations can be efficient by presenting a wide variety of scenarios in an optimal order for learning. Lierman (1994) notes that simulations can reduce training time by as much as 85 percent.

One issue concerning simulations that has received a fair amount of attention is the question of *fidelity* (e.g., Bothwell & Lacey, 1993; Druckman & Bjork, 1995).

TABLE 18.5 **Most Frequently Used Training Methods with Their Relative Advantages and Disadvantages**

Text

Advantages

Low development and delivery cost, relatively easy to modify later.

Learners familiar with the medium, can control pace.

Can provide graphic information, answer questions, act as a job aid later.

Disadvantages

Not interactive, can be boring, not capable of diagnosing student error.

Doesn't provide dynamic, visual, auditory information.

More difficult to modify than lecture or tutoring.

Lecture

Advantages

Easy and inexpensive to develop, easy to modify.

Motivating, somewhat adaptive to trainees, potential for being interactive.

Captive audience, may be important for areas such as safety.

Disadvantages

Students and instructor must meet in one location, delivery can be expensive.

Less adaptive to individual than tutoring or OJT.

Passive learning, trainees have little control over pace, location.

Audiovisual Methods

Advantages

Can potentially be interesting and motivating.

Relatively easy and inexpensive to deliver.

Can present dynamic material, learners can control the pace.

Disadvantages

Somewhat difficult and costly to develop.

Not interactive, can't adapt to level of learner.

No testing and remediation, no opportunity to practice and/or receive feedback.

Computer-Assisted Instruction (CAI)

Advantages

Moderately easy to develop, convenient and easy delivery.

Potential for high level of interactivity, adaptation to trainee.

Improves confidence, potentially interesting, motivating.

Speed of response and feedback, efficient learning.

Can be multimodal, potential for topic coverage, practice, and testing (more than OJT).

Disadvantages

Depending on application, can be resource-intensive to develop.

Development requires specialized knowledge.

Requires predicting learning needs.

Some skills are not amenable to practice on computer.

TABLE 18.5 (continued)

Simulations and Intelligent Tutoring Systems

Advantages
Provide realistic job context, breadth of practice examples, and feedback.
Highly interactive, interesting, motivating.
Can be less dangerous, expensive, etc. than OJT.
Potential for dynamic, audiovisual information.

Disadvantages
Difficult, costly, and time-consuming to develop and modify.
More difficult and/or expensive to deliver.
May not be appropriate for teaching concepts/principles.
Task performance may not be similar to actual job (e.g., CPR).

On-The-Job Training (OJT)

Advantages
It's easy and inexpensive to implement; doesn't require instructor or special equipment.
There are no extra operating costs, the content is flexible and changes with the job.
There is opportunity to apply declarative knowledge, and high transfer of training.
It makes use of audio/visual channels, provides opportunity for active learning.

Disadvantages
They are usually not systematically designed and implemented.
Trainer is worker, not professional instructor, leaving opportunity to learn poor
    methods.
Trainer usually must continue with job, making it difficult and causing resentment.
Trainer usually doesn't cover adequate breadth of required knowledge and skills.
There is usually too little practice and too few different types of scenario or situations.

A training simulation with high fidelity has a high level of similarity to the actual job task and job environment. A flight simulator with high fidelity means that elements such as the flight controls and displays, the cockpit and seat, and the "feel" of the simulator are all very similar to those of the actual aircraft. It is important to know how much fidelity is required for training simulators to be effective because more fidelity almost always means higher cost. Most researchers now believe that fidelity is required for the perceptual cues that are directly relevant to the task, or combination of tasks, at hand (e.g., Mumaw & Roth, 1995; Rouse, 1991). For example, if a pilot must fly a plane and learn to use a new weapons system at the same time, the controls and displays directly relevant to those tasks must be relatively high in fidelity. However, factors such as the actual seat itself or the overall feel of the aircraft are less important because they are not part of the cue set in the "rules" being acquired.

The use of simulations for training is increasing at a rapid rate, and one interesting new twist is the use of *virtual reality* for education and training. Many people believe that educational virtual realities will become powerful teaching and training tools in the relatively near future (Bricken & Byrne, 1993; Heeter, 1993; Salzman et al., 1995). Salzman and colleagues (1995) suggest that virtual reality is an ideal training tool because it supports direct experience, is three-dimensional, facilitates "multiple frames of reference," and is physically immersive. Virtual reality educational environments will be effective given that designers can make them *usable* and capture the relevant perceptual cues necessary for learning (Wickens, 1992a). It is important to remember too that many aspects of task learning are *not* perceptual-motor but require a higher level of conceptual or verbal abstraction, for which virtual reality may not be the best learning tool (Wickens, 1992a).

Intelligent tutoring systems are computer-based instructional systems that act much as a human tutor would, monitoring performance, answering questions, and so on (Livergood, 1991; Psotka, Massey, & Mutter, 1988). Because they require substantial artificial intelligence components, intelligent tutoring systems are generally difficult to develop and are still in the early research stages. An especially promising method that is becoming more widely used is the combination of simulation systems with a relatively constrained *intelligent tutoring system.* These tutoring systems provide practice trials tailored to individual student needs, monitor performance, provide advice and feedback by comparing performance with an expert model, and demonstrate correct task performance (e.g., Farr & Psotka, 1992; Gordon et al., 1994; Mark & Greer, 1995; Mitchell & Govindaraj, 1991; Smith et al., 1991). This approach overcomes one drawback of simulations, the need for some type of explicit "instructional" support. Brown and VanLehn (1980) suggest that procedural learning is motivated by two situations: the learner attempting to do something and finding it did not work, and the learner finding a task tedious and wondering if there is a better way to do it. Tutoring systems embedded in a simulation can provide the necessary guidance at these learning points (Tait, 1994).

On-the-job training (OJT) is typically an informal procedure whereby an experienced employee shows a new employee how to perform a set of tasks. There are rarely specific guidelines for the training, and effective training depends highly on the ability of the person doing the training. OJT, as normally performed, has been shown to be much less effective than other training methods. However, if the training is done using ISD methods, with strong guidance to the trainer, this method can be very effective (Goldstein, 1986).

Finally, another type of instruction, *embedded training,* combines computer-based training with on-the-job performance. Evans (1988) defines embedded training as "training that is provided by capabilities built into or added into the operational system to enhance and maintain skill proficiency necessary to maintain or operate the equipment." Embedded training is most appropriate for jobs that rely at least partially on computers because the training is computer-based. This type of training is especially useful for people who just need occasional refresher training to keep up their skills. Embedded training should be considered for tasks when the task is critical with regard to safety concerns or when the task is moderate to high in cognitive complexity (Evans, 1988).

It is easy to see that each training method has its own unique advantages and disadvantages. For this reason, many training programs are based on some mix of the methods listed in Table 18.5 and also often rely on job aids or performance support systems as well. As an example of a successful combination, Manpower, a company that provides temporary workers, developed computer-based training programs named SKILLWARE—with one computer program for each piece of hardware or software to be learned by employees (Rosow & Zager, 1990). After completion of the training program, employees received a small pocket-size "Operator Support Manual," written in a style similar to the training program. This could be used for brush-up training or even as a job aid.

Recent work has demonstrated that certain types of instruction and combinations of instruction essentially work against the way we learn best. For example, Mumaw and Roth (1995) note that the typical training sequence of presenting requisite knowledge and theory before training with simulators is ineffective and inefficient. One reason is that teaching via lecture or text requires using rote memory for large amounts of declarative knowledge. This knowledge is not tied to its function in task performance and thus becomes "inert" (see Chapter 7). When trainees begin task performance in simulations or on-the-job training, they must often relearn the factual information. A more effective and efficient method for training jobs with relatively high cognitive complexity is the use of several tracks or "strands" throughout the training from beginning to end (Mumaw & Roth, 1995). In the beginning of training, operators acquire small amounts of declarative knowledge, watch operators in a real-world environment, and perform task exercises on highly pared down simulations so that important perceptual cues are salient. As training progresses, the simulations become more complex with higher fidelity, and the trainee also begins doing simple tasks in the actual operational environment. Figure 18.5 shows a schematic for this approach with the "strands" listed in the far-left column: simulation, presentation of component skills and knowledge, and apprenticeship in the real operational environment. Recent research findings on active learning support this approach to learning in the task context from the beginning.

TRAINING CONCEPTS AND ISSUES

In this section, we will briefly consider some of the training-related topics that are of primary concern to human factors practitioners. You will be able to see that some of these derive from the fact that human factors specialists have historically been heavily involved in military work, and in this case, military training issues.

Transfer of Training

Transfer of training generally refers to how well the learning that has occurred in one environment, such as a training simulator, enhances performance in a new environment. As Holding (1987) words it: "When learning a first task improves the scores obtained in a second task (B), relative to the scores of a control group learning B alone, the transfer from A to B is positive" (p. 955). The concept of *positive transfer of training* is important because it is a major goal of any training program, and measures of transfer of training are often used to evaluate training

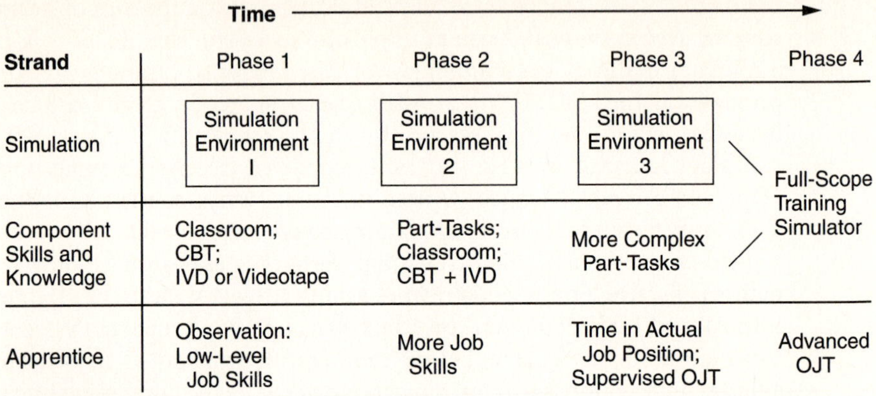

Time →

Strand	Phase 1	Phase 2	Phase 3	Phase 4
Simulation	Simulation Environment I	Simulation Environment 2	Simulation Environment 3	Full-Scope Training Simulator
Component Skills and Knowledge	Classroom; CBT; IVD or Videotape	Part-Tasks; Classroom; CBT + IVD	More Complex Part-Tasks	
Apprentice	Observation: Low-Level Job Skills	More Job Skills	Time in Actual Job Position; Supervised OJT	Advanced OJT

FIGURE 18.5

Use of concurrent training strands in the functional context approach to training. (*Source:* Mumaw, R. J., and Roth, E. M.,1996, Training complex tasks in a functional context. *Proceedings of the Human Factors and Ergonomics Society 39th Annual Meeting*, Santa Monica, CA: Human Factors and Ergonomics Society. Copyright 1996 by the Human Factors and Ergonomics Society. All rights reserved.)

program effectiveness. While there are a variety of qualitative measures for transfer of training, a commonly used approach is to express the variable as a percentage of time saved by using the training program as compared to a no-training control group:

$$\% \text{ transfer} = \frac{(\text{control time—transfer time})}{\text{control time}} \times 100 = \frac{\text{savings}}{\text{control time}} \times 100$$

As applied for training programs, "control time" is the amount of performance time it takes for the untrained operators to come up to perform at some criterion level on Task B in the new environment, and "transfer time" is the amount of performance time it takes for trained operators to come up to the performance criterion. Thus, when put in the real job environment, it might take the control group an average of 10 hours to come up to expected performance levels, and it might take the trained group 2 hours. This would be a transfer savings of 80 percent. Notice, however, that this variable does not take into account the fact that the training itself takes time. If the training program required 8 hours, the savings would be nullified. The ratio of savings/training time is called the *transfer effectiveness ratio* (Povenmire & Roscoe, 1973). Finally, it is important to point out that training in environments other than the real world can be desirable for reasons other than transfer savings, including factors such as safety, greater variety of practice experiences, operational costs, and so forth. For example, use of a high-fidelity flight simulator costs only a fraction of the operating cost for an F-16. For this reason, training systems may be quite desirable even if the transfer effectiveness ratio is less than 1.0.

A related concern is the possibility of *negative transfer* (Wickens, 1992b). Negative transfer occurs when task performance in one environment causes performance to be worse in the second environment, as compared to performance without the prior experience. This can be thought of as a type of "interference" effect. For example, a person who is used to typing on a computer with the backspace key in one location might make more errors with a new system (where the key has a different location) than a person who has no prior keyboarding experience and begins with the new system. Most changes among tasks tend to result in positive transfer. However, occasionally we do find negative transfer. This seems to occur most frequently when the two situations have highly similar stimulus (i.e., display or environmental) cues, but different responses are required. The more similar the set of stimulus characteristics, the more likely will be the accidental use of the old response rather than the new (Singley & Anderson, 1989).

Human factors practitioners strive to promote positive transfer when designing training programs by insuring that the stimulus cues that are associated with a response in the real-world task are correctly replicated in the training environment. In addition, the potential for negative transfer must be carefully assessed. As an example, imagine that police officers are trained in realistic and stressful circumstances to draw their weapons and fire accurately. For safety reasons, they are instructed to keep the firearm safety on until they are ready to fire. Given the situational cues, they become accustomed to releasing the safety just before firing. When they are in a real event, they are to release the safety and be ready to fire. Given the time constraints of the task, the difference in response required under the same circumstances may cause negative transfer and substantial interference with performance. Negative transfer of training is problematic not only for training programs but also when operators move from an old system to a new design. Numerous fatal accidents have occurred because system operators showed negative transfer when using a new system.

Methods for Enhancing Training

The human factors practitioner is usually concerned with three issues: The method that provides the best training in the shortest time, leads to the longest retained knowledge and skill retention, and is cheapest. Training programs that result in the best learning and job performance for the least time and expense are *efficient* and therefore desirable. In this section, we consider some of the concepts and principles that have been studied because of their effects on training effectiveness and efficiency.

Practice and Overlearning. Our discussion in Chapter 6 stressed that training for declarative knowledge is qualitatively different than for procedural knowledge. Practice is especially necessary to acquire procedural (perceptual or rule-based) knowledge. In addition, research has shown that practice effectiveness is maximized by providing informative *feedback* to trainees relatively soon after task performance and by spacing the practice out over time with rest breaks between sessions (Baddeley & Longman, 1978; Salmoni, Schmidt, & Walter, 1984). In addition to practice, there are numerous specific instructional strategies for promoting positive transfer of training, such as maximizing the similarity between the training situation and the job situation (even with psychological factors such as stress) (e.g., see Wexley & Latham, 1991).

One important application of the distinction between learning declarative and procedural information is training for emergency situations. Recall from Chapter 13 that physical or psychological stress can reduce capabilities for cognitive processing. Tasks that are performed using conceptual or declarative knowledge tend to require more working memory and cognitive resources and are very susceptible to effects of stress. Emergency procedures should be practiced so that they become proceduralized, or rule based. This makes them easier to recall and apply under adverse conditions. As an example, consider that you are training elderly people in California to perform emergency evacuation procedures in the event of an earthquake. You might tell them to keep shoes next to their bed and put them on if there is an earthquake (due to possible broken glass on the floor). They could pass a test assessing their memory for this information. However, the likelihood of remembering to put their shoes on under such a circumstance is unlikely. A more effective way to train this behavior would be to simulate an earthquake and have learners actually put their shoes on—thereby associating the situational cues with the action (as illustrated in the middle cognitive-processing level of Figure 7.3). To be even more effective, learners should practice this skill over time (see next paragraph on rate of forgetting). This is the idea behind fire drills in elementary schools.

We also know that practice leads to continued improvement for an extensive period of time, although the amount of improvement will gradually decrease (Newell & Rosenbloom, 1981). Learning is therefore said to show an exponential function (see Figure 18.6). Performance accuracy for some tasks may eventually reach error-free levels, and the question then becomes one of whether further practice will yield any additional benefits. Sometimes further practice beyond error-free performance, termed *overlearning*, does have training benefits. First, overlearning results in a continued improvement in *speed* of performance, whether cognitive or motor control. Overlearning would therefore be important in jobs where speed is critical. In addition, overlearning has shown to decrease the *rate of forgetting* and increase the ease with which a task can be relearned after some period of time (Anderson, 1990; Fisk & Hodge, 1992). In some jobs, a skill that is critical in emergency or unusual situations might not be practiced on a routine basis. In these cases, overlearning is desirable so that when the emergency occurs, the operator is more likely to remember how to perform the task.

Automaticity. Continued practice may also lead to *automaticity* of the skill characterized in particular by a reduced resource demand (see Chapter 6 for review of controlled vs. automatic processing). However, mere practice may not lead to automatic processing. Automatic processing requires practice where stimulus cues are *consistently mapped* to a response (Fisk, 1989; Schneider, 1985). That is, the same cues always lead to the same response. Automaticity does not develop as readily where the cues are associated with one response in one case and another response in another case. For example, driving two different manual transmission cars with two different gear-shift patterns will inhibit development of automatic processing. Development of automatic processing is a very useful training procedure (Schneider, 1985). An increasing number of jobs require people to perform

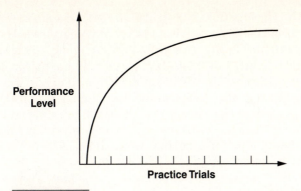

FIGURE 18.6
General shape of relationship between practice and performance.

complex cognitive tasks, frequently performing several tasks concurrently (e.g., air traffic controllers). If some tasks can be assumed to always require performance in a consistent manner, they can be trained to a level of automatic processing. This will then free up cognitive resources for performing other tasks that are variable and therefore not amenable to automatization. In addition, tasks trained to automation have been shown to be very long-lived, even with disuse over a period of many years (Cooke, Durso, & Schvaneveldt, 1994).

Above Real-Time Training.   Another method for training tasks that require high-speed skills is the use of *above real-time training*, ARTT (Guckenberger et al., 1993; Vidulich, Yeh, & Schneider, 1983). With this method, tasks that require fast performance, such as flying fighter jets and engaging in air-to-air combat, are trained in a simulated environment that functions at a faster rate than normal task time (Guckenberger et al., 1993). For example, an air maneuver that would normally take approximately 5 minutes would be compressed into 2 or 3 minutes. Notice that this approach is a departure *away* from the usual goal of high fidelity in the training environment. This approach originated with anecdotal comments from pilots at NASA flight centers saying that simulator time felt "slower" than real aircraft time. Experimentation with a simulator revealed that 1.5 times the normal speed made the simulator feel equivalent to real flight maneuvers (Guckenberger et al., 1993). The theoretical explanation for this phenomenon is that (simplified) a person's state of arousal affects their perception of the speed of time passing (Parasuraman, 1986; Skelly, 1993). As an example, imagine the passage of time while standing in line versus playing an exciting video game. Since the early 1970s, the use of "fast-time" simulators has been both endorsed by government agencies and studied experimentally. A number of studies have shown that ARTT results in more accurate performance for tasks such as pilot maneuvers and emergency procedures than does real-time training (Guckenberger, Uliano, & Lane, 1992; Guckenberger et al., 1993; Vidulich et al, 1983).

Part-Task Training.   There is some evidence that breaking a task down into its component subtasks and training the subtasks separately results in more efficient training (Fisk, 1987; Lesgold & Curtis, 1981; Mane, 1984). An example would be learning a piece of piano music for each hand before combining them. However, some reviews of the literature indicate that such *part-task* training is not always superior to *whole-task* training, a method where all subtasks are trained at once (Cream, Eggemeier & Klein, 1978; Wightman & Lintern, 1985). In fact, some studies indicate a superiority for whole-task training in terms of transfer effectiveness ratio (e.g., Goettl, 1995; Connelly et al., 1987). Wightman and Lintern (1985) suggest that one factor that affects the success of part-task training is how the task is broken down for part-task training, which can be done in one of two ways, segmentation or fractionation.

The most successful use of part-task training is *segmentation*, where a task is partitioned on the basis of nonoverlapping temporal components, which are then trained separately. This procedure makes sense if one or more (but not all) of the segments are very difficult. Then, by segmenting the whole task relatively more time can be allocated to training the difficult segment(s), without spending time training the easier segment(s). One segmentation technique that has proven to be effective in a number of domains is *backward chaining* (e.g., Wightman & Sistrunk, 1987). With this approach, learners initially practice on the terminal segment of the whole task and then progressively work backward through the task. Wightman and Sistrunk (1987) had learners use a flight simulator to learn carrier landing procedures. Learners performed segments of the carrier landing task beginning at 2,000 feet from touchdown (16 practice trials), then at 4,000 feet from touchdown, then from 6,000 feet from touchdown.

A less successful use of part-task training is when a complex task is broken down into component tasks that are normally performed simultaneously, termed *fractionation*. This would be like training on the left and right hand of a piano piece separately. Training consists of teaching only a subset of the components at first. Apparently, fractionated part-task training may or may not be successful depending on which subtasks are chosen for training (Wightman & Lintern, 1985). Anderson (1990) suggests that if subtasks are independent of one another in total task performance, they are amenable to part-task training. This may be particularly true if the whole task is overwhelmingly complex in its information-processing demands, as in a task like flying (see Chapter 17). Here, at least in early phases of practice, part-task training can prove beneficial, particularly if parts can be trained to automaticity. However, if the component parts are quite interdependent the advantage of part-task training is eliminated. This interdependence occurs if performance on one of the part tasks depends on or affects performance of the other when combined. There has been some success with using systematic task decomposition methods for identifying critical independent subtasks for part-task training (Frederiksen & White, 1989; Mane, Adams, & Donchin, 1989).

Guided and Adaptive Training

One training strategy with intuitive appeal is to make the task easy early in training and then increase its demands as the skill develops. There are two ways of accomplishing this. In *adaptive training*, the level of difficulty is adapted to the level of skill of the learner. For example, in training driving skill in a simulator, the simulated speed of vehicle travel could be gradually increased as skill proficiency develops. In *guided training,* which adopts a "training wheels" approach (Cotrambone & Carroll, 1987), various constraints are imposed so that mistakes cannot be made by the learner, producing "error-free" learning. (The analogy to training wheels on a bicycle is direct.) These constraints are then withdrawn gradually or abruptly as the skill is mastered.

An argument for both guided and adaptive training can be made on the basis of the assertion that errors are nonproductive and should not be a part of training because those errors might be learned. A second argument is similar to that made for part-task training; that is, at early stages of learning, a complex task can be overwhelming, and all three techniques serve to reduce the complexity somewhat.

While some success for both guided and adaptive training has been observed (Mane et al., 1989; Cotrombone & Carroll, 1987; Druckman & Bjork, 1995), particularly when, in adaptive training, increasing time pressure has served as an adaptive training variable (Mane et al., 1989), there are two factors that mitigate against unqualified acceptance of the techniques. First, it should be noted that error prevention only makes good sense to the extent that errors are relatively *catastrophic* (e.g., a training session must be restarted from the beginning if an error is performed or equipment is damaged) or if the training regime allows errors to be *repeated* without corrective feedback. However, it is a myth to assume that error-free performance during training will produce error-free performance (or even, necessarily, effective performance) on transfer to the real skill (Druckman & Bjork, 1995). Indeed there are many advantages for learners to be allowed to *commit* errors during training, if part of the training focuses on *learning how to correct* those errors, since the error-correction skill will undoubtedly be important after the skill is transferred out of the training environment.

The second factor is that both adaptive and guided training can lead to learning of a skill in a way that is inappropriate and will transfer negatively to the real world. To go back to our training wheels example, the learning cyclist may learn to depend on the training wheels as a balancing aid and hence may never learn the critical skill of self-balancing on a single wheel. Correspondingly, learning to fly a simulated aircraft with simplified (and therefore easier) flight dynamics that are gradually adapted to the more difficult ones (adaptive training) will not be successful because the response habits with the simpler dynamics do not transfer to the more complex ones. It is perhaps for this second reason related to negative transfer that the most successful adaptive training regimes seem to be those in which the qualitative nature of the task is not altered as training progresses, but the adaptive variable is simply the time pressure imposed on the learner (Mane et al., 1989).

Conclusion: Learning as Information Processing

We note in conclusion that the learning supported by training tools, particularly at the critical early stages, depends very much on the information-processing skills discussed in Chapter 6. These involve perception (of displays, of the environment, and of any feedback that is offered) and working memory (involved in chunking to transfer material to long-term memory, in processing feedback, and in discovering and pondering contingencies in the learning environment).

Because of these simultaneous demands on perception and working memory, the learning process places very heavy demands on the learner's *cognitive resources,* and if these are overloaded, effective learning cannot progress. Thus some of the training strategies, such as adaptive and part-task training, can be effective at early stages of learning to the extent that they accomplish this (Schneider, 1985). In addition, concerns about resource scarcity during learning suggest three additional guidelines:

1. Feedback, while important to be delivered in a timely fashion, should not be offered *while* attention is concurrently allocated to performing very difficult components of the skill. At best, the feedback may be ignored by the learner as resources are allocated to the skill; and if it is ignored, it will not be processed. At worst, if the skill is learned in a risky environment (e.g., driving behind the wheel), diversion of resources to feedback processing could compromise safety.
2. Close attention should be paid to designing training tools in such a way that extraneous elements do not divert resources from the material to be learned (Chandler & Sweller, 1991). Examples might be a poor user interface for computer-based learning tool, poorly worded and complex examples (cognitive resources are expended understanding what the examples say rather than how they are relevant), or text in a training manual that is far removed from the pictures which it describes, a violation of the proximity compatibility principle discussed in Chapter 8.
3. Concern must be directed to inducing the learner to invest adequate resources or effort into the material to be learned. This, in part, is a basis for designing learning tools that are intrinsically interesting (note the use of humor in the example at the beginning of the chapter). However, such concern raises issues of learner motivation that go well beyond the focus of the current textbook.

In summary, the designer of training modules must adopt a systems perspective and view the human as the most critical element of the system. Relevant then is not just the content of information to be delivered to the human learner, but the matter in which the constraints on and qualities of human information processing, discussed elsewhere in this text, can greatly effect the acquisition and storage of that information.

REFERENCES

Ambron, S., and Hooper, K. (eds.) (1990). *Learning with interactive multimedia: Developing and using multimedia tools in education.* Redmond, WA: Microsoft Press.

Anderson, J. (1990). *Cognitive psychology and its implications* (3rd ed.). New York: W.H. Freeman and Company.

Andrews, D.H., and Goodson, L.A. (1980). A comparative analysis of models of instructional design. *Journal of Instructional Development, 3(4),* 2–16.

Avolio, B.J., Alexander, R.A., Barrett, G.V., and Sterns, J.L. (1981). Designing a measure of selective attention to assess individual differences in information processing. *Applied Psychological Measurement, 5,* 29–42.

Baddeley, A.D., and Longman, D.J.A. (1978). The influence of length and frequency of training session on the rate of learning to type. *Ergonomics, 21,* 627–635.

Baird, L.S., Schneier, C.E., and Laird, D. (eds.) (1983). *The training and development sourcebook.* Amherst, MA: Human Resource Development Press.

Barrick, M.R., and Mount, M.K. (1991). The big five personality dimensions and job performance: A meta-analysis. *Personnel Psychology, 44,* 1–26.

Bartram, D. (1995a). The predictive validity of the EPI and 16PF for military flying training. *Journal of Occupational and Organizational Psychology,* 68(3), 219–236.

Bartram, D. (1995b). Personality factors in pilot selection: Validation of the Cathay Pacific Airways selection procedures. *Proceedings of the Eighth International Symposium on Aviation Psychology* (pp. 1330–1335). Columbus, OH: Ohio State University.

Bartram, D., and Dale, H.C.A. (1982). The Eysenck Personality Inventory as a selection test for pilots. *Journal of Occupational Psychology, 55,* 287–296.

Batra, S., Bishu, R., and Donohue, B.J. (1995). The potential of computerized interactive training in manufacturing. *Proceedings of the Human Factors and Ergonomic Society 39th Annual Meeting* (pp. 1294–1298). Santa Monica, CA: Human Factors and Ergonomics Society.

Booher, H.R. (1975). Relative comprehensibility of pictorial information and printed words in proceduralized instructions. *Human Factors, 17,* 266–277.

Bothwell, R.L., and Lacy, J.W. (1993). Low-cost cockpit trainer design: Challenges and solutions. *Proceedings of the Interservice/Industry Training Systems and Education Conference* (pp. 650–658). Washington, DC.

Brandenburg, D.C., and Binder, C. (1992). Emerging trends in human performance interventions. In H.D. Stolovitch and E.J. Keeps (eds.), *Handbook of human performance technology* (pp. 651–671). San Francisco, CA: Jossey-Bass.

Bricken, M., and Byrne, C.M. (1993). Summer students in virtual reality. In A. Wexelblat (ed.), *Virtual reality: Applications and explorations* (pp. 199–218). New York: Academic Press.

Brown, J.S., and VanLehn, K. (1980). Repair theory: A generative theory of bugs in procedural skills. *Cognitive Science, 44,* 379–415.

Burke, E. (1995a). Pilot selection I: The state-of-play. *Proceedings of the Eighth International Symposium on Aviation Psychology* (pp. 1341–1346). Columbus, OH: Ohio State University.

Burke, E. (1995b). Pilot selection II: Where do we go from here? *Proceedings of the Eighth International Symposium on Aviation Psychology* (pp. 1347–1353). Columbus, OH: Ohio State University.

Campion, M.A. (1972). Work sampling for personnel selection. *Journal of Applied Psychology, 56,* 40–44.

Cannon-Bowers, J.A., Tannenbaum, S.I., Salas, E., and Converse, S.A. (1991). Toward an integration of training theory and technique. *Human Factors,* 33(3), 281–292.

Carr, C. (1992). Performance support systems: A new horizon for expert systems. *AI Expert, 7*(5) 44.

Catalina, B.H., and Bills, C.G. (1993). Applying the instructional system development (ISD) process in U.S. Air Force system defense system acquisition. *Proceedings of the 15th Interservice/Industry Training Systems and Education Conference* (pp. 406–413). Washington, DC.: National Security Industrial Association.

Cattell, R.B., Eber, H.W., and Tatsuoka, M. (1970). *Handbook for the Sixteen Personality Factor Questionnaire (16PF).* Champaign, IL: Institute for Personality and Ability Testing.

Chandler, P., and Sweller, J. (1991). Cognitive load theory and the format of instruction. *Cognition and Instruction, 8*(4), 293–332.

Chandler, T.N. (1996). Star: Situating the work experience through storytelling and multimedia techniques. *Proceedings of the Human Factors and Ergonomic Society 40th Annual Meeting* (pp. 1087–1091). Santa Monica, CA: Human Factors and Ergonomics Society.

Clark, R.C. (1989). *Developing technical training: A structured approach for the development of classroom and computer-based instructional materials.* Reading, MA: Addison-Wesley.

Clibbon, K. (1995). Conceptually adapted hypertext for learning. *Proceedings of CHI '95* (pp. 224–225).

Connelly, J.G., Wickens, C.D., Lintern, G., and Harwood, K. (1987). Attention theory and training research. *Proceedings of the Human Factors Society 31st Annual Meeting* (pp. 648–651). Santa Monica, CA: Human Factors Society.

Cooke, N.J., Durso, F.T., and Schvaneveldt, R.W. (1994). Retention of skilled search after nine years. *Human Factors, 36*(4), 597–605.

Cotrambone, R., and Carroll, J.M. (1987). Learning a word processing system with training wheels and guided exploration. *Proceedings of CHI and GI Human Factors in Computing Systems and Graphics Conference* (pp. 169–174). New York: ACM.

Cream, B.W., Eggemeier, F.T., and Klein, G.A. (1978). A strategy for the development of training devices. *Human Factors, 20,* 145–158.

Damos, D. (1995). Issues in pilot selection. *Proceedings of the Eighth International Symposium on Aviation Psychology* (pp. 1365–1368). Columbus, OH: Ohio State University.

Degani, A., and Wiener, E.L. (1993). Cockpit checklists: Concepts, design, and use. *Human Factors, 35*(2), 345–359.

Druckman, D., and Bjork, R. (1994). *Learning, remembering, believing: Enhancing human performance.* Washington, DC: National Academy Press.

Druckman, D., and Swets, J. (1988). *Enhancing human performance.* Washington, DC: National Academy Press.

Evans, D.C. (1988). Developing embedded training (ET) design and integration concepts for the all source analysis system/enemy situation correlation element (ASAS/ENSCE). *Proceedings of the Human Factors Society 32nd Annual Meeting* (pp. 1256–1260). Santa Monica, CA: Human Factors Society.

Eysenck, H.J., and Eysenck, S.B.G. (1964). *Manual of the Eysenck Personality Inventory.* London: University of London Press Limited.

Farr, M.J., and Psotka, J. (eds.) (1992). *Intelligent instruction by computer: Theory and practice.* New York: Taylor & Francis.

Fisk, A.D. (1987). High performance cognitive skill acquisition: Perceptual/rule learning. *Proceedings of the Human Factors Society 31st Annual Meeting* (pp. 652–656). Santa Monica, CA: Human Factors Society.

Fisk, A.D. (1989). Training consistent components of tasks: Developing an instructional system based on automatic/controlled processing principles. *Human Factors, 31*(4), 453–463.

Fisk, A.D., and Hodge, K.A. (1992). Retention of trained performance in consistent mapping search after extended delay. *Human Factors, 34*(2), 147–164.

Frederiksen, J.R., and White, B.Y. (1989). An approach to training based upon principled task decomposition. *Acta Psychologica, 71,* 89–146.

Friedman, B.A., and Mann, R.W. (1981). Employee assessment methods assessed. *Personnel, 58*(6), 69–74.

Geber, B. (1991). HELP! The rise of performance support systems. *Training, 28,* 23–29.

Gery, G.J. (1989). Training versus performance support: Inadequate training is now insufficient. *Performance Improvement Quarterly, 2*(3), 51–71.

Gery, G. (1991). *Electronic performance support systems.* Boston, MA: Weingarten.

Goettl, B.P. (1995). Part-task training of complex tasks: Utility of backward transfer. *Proceedings of the Human Factors and Ergonomics Society 39th Annual Meeting* (pp. 1345–1349). Santa Monica, CA: Human Factors and Ergonomics Society.

Goldstein, I.L. (1986). *Training in organizations: Needs assessment, development, and evaluation* (2nd ed.). Monterey, CA: Brooks/Cole.

Gopher, D. (1982). A selective attention test as a predictor of success in flight training. *Human Factors, 24,* 173–183.

Gopher, D., and Kahneman, D. (1971). Individual differences in attention and the prediction of flight criteria. *Perceptual and Motor Skills, 33,* 1335–1342.

Gopher, D., Weil, M., and Baraket, T. (1994). Transfer of skill from a computer game trainer to flight. *Human Factors, 36*(3), 387–405.

Gordon, S.E. (1994). *Systematic training program design: Maximizing effectiveness and minimizing liability.* Englewood Cliffs, NJ: Prentice Hall.

Gordon, S.E., Babbitt, B.A., Bell, H.H., and Sorensen, H.B. (1994). Development of a real-time simulation with intelligent tutoring capabilities. *Proceedings of the Human Factors and Ergonomics Society 38th Annual Meeting* (pp. 1247–1251). Santa Monica, CA: Human Factors and Ergonomics Society.

Guckenberger, D., Uliano, K.C., and Lane, N.E. (1992). The application of above real-time training for simulators: Acquiring high performance skills. *Proceedings of 14th Interservice/Industry Training Systems and Education Conference* (pp. 928–935).

Guckenberger, D., Uliano, K.C., and Lane, N.E., and Stanney, K. (1993). The effects of above real-time training (ARTT) on three tasks in an F-16 part-task simulator. *Proceedings of 15th Interservice/Industry Training Systems and Education Conference* (pp. 99–108).

Heeter, C. (1993). The thin line: Hypermedia meets virtual reality. *Ed Tech Review,* Spring/Summer, 37–46.

Hendrick, H.W. (1986). Macroergonomics: A conceptual model for integrating human factors with organizational design. In O. Brown Jr. and H. W. Hendrick (eds.), *Human factors in organizational design and management II* (pp. 467–477). Amsterdam: North Holland.

Hendrickson, J. (1987). Hiring the right stuff. *Personnel Administrator, 32*(11) 70–74.

Holding, D.H. (1987). Concepts of training. In G. Salvendy (ed.), *Handbook of human factors* (pp. 939–962). New York: Wiley.

Hunter, D.R., and Burke, E.F. (1994). Predicting aircraft pilot training success: A meta-analysis of published research. *The International Journal of Aviation Psychology, 4,* 1–12.

Hunter, D.R., and Burke, E.F. (1995). *Handbook of pilot selection.* Aldershot, UK: Avebury Aviation.

Hunter, J.E., and Hunter, R.F. (1984). Validity and utility of alternative predictors of job performance. *Psychological Bulletin, 96,* 72–98.

Imada, A.S., and Feiglstok, D.M. (1990). An organizational design and management approach to improving safety. In K. Noro and O. Brown Jr. (eds.), *Human factors in organizational design and management* (pp. 4799–482). Amsterdam: North Holland.

Jessup, G., and Jessup, H. (1971). Validity of the Eysenck Personality Inventory in pilot selection. *Occupational psychology, 21,* 158–169.

Jonassen, D.H. (ed.) (1988). *Instructional design for microcomputer courseware.* Hillsdale, NJ: Lawrence Erlbaum.

Jonassen, D., and Mandl, H. (eds.) (1990). *Designing hypermedia for learning.* New York: Springer Verlag.

Kahneman, D., Ben-Ishai, R., and Lotan, M. (1973). Relation of a test of attention to road accidents. *Journal of Applied Psychology, 58,* 113–115.

Keller, J.M., and Suzuki, K. (1988). Use of the ARCS motivation model in courseware design. In D.H. Jonassen (ed.), *Instructional designs for microcomputer courseware* (pp. 401–434). Hillsdale, NJ: Lawrence Erlbaum.

Kulik, C.L.C., and Kulik, J.A. (1991). Effectiveness of computer-based instruction: An updated analysis. *Computers in Human Behavior, 7,* 75–94.

Layton, C.F., Christodoulou, M.J., Jackson, J.T., and Turner, J.L. (1995). Lessons learned in the development of mobile electronic performance support systems. *Proceedings of the Human Factors and Ergonomics Society 39th Annual Meeting* (pp. 268–272). Santa Monica, CA: Human Factors and Ergonomics Society.

Lesgold, A.M., and Curtis, M.E. (1981). Learning to read words efficiently. In A.M. Lesgold and C.A. Perfetti (eds.), *Interactive processes in reading.* Hillsdale, NJ: Lawrence Erlbaum Associates.

Liebler, S.N., and Parkman, A.W. (1992). Personnel selection. In H.D. Stolovitch and E.J. Keeps (eds.), *Handbook of human performance technology* (pp. 259–276). San Francisco, CA: Jossey-Bass.

Lierman, B. (1994). How to develop a training simulation. *Training & Development,* February, 50–52.

Livergood, N.D. (1991). From computer-assisted instruction to intelligent tutoring systems. *Journal of Artificial Intelligence in Education, 2*(3) 39–50.

Mane, A.M. (1984). Acquisition of perceptual-motor skills: Adaptive and part-whole training. *Proceedings of the Human Factors Society 28th Annual Meeting* (pp. 522–526). Santa Monica, CA: Human Factors Society.

Mane, A.M., Adams, J.A., and Donchin, E. (1989). Adaptive and part-whole training in the acquisition of a complex perceptual-motor skill. *Acta Psychologica, 71,* 179–196.

Mark, M.A., and Greer, J.E. (1995). The VCR tutor: Effective instruction for device operation. *The Journal of the Learning Sciences, 4*(2), 209–246.

Marrelli, A.F. (1993). Determining costs, benefits, and results. *Technical and Skills Training,* November/December, 8–14.

McCrae R.R., and Costa, P.T. (1985). Updating Norman's "Adequate Taxonomy": Intelligence and personality dimensions in natural language and in questionnaires. *Journal of Personality and Social Psychology, 49,* 710–721.

Merrill, M.D. (1983). Component display theory. In C.M. Reigeluth (ed.), *Instructional-design theories and models: An overview of their current status* (pp. 279–334). Hillsdale, NJ: Lawrence Erlbaum.

Mitchell, C.M., and Govindaraj, T. (1991). Design and effectiveness of intelligent tutors for operators of complex dynamic systems: A tutor implementation for satellite system operators. *Interactive Learning Environments, 1*(3), 193–229.

Mumaw, R.J., and Roth, E.M. (1995). Training complex tasks in a functional context. *Proceedings of the Human Factors and Ergonomics Society 39th Annual Meeting* (pp. 1253–1257). Santa Monica, CA: Human Factors and Ergonomics Society.

Newcomb, L.C., and Jerome, G.C. (1995). A statistical model for predicting success in aviation. *Proceedings of the Eighth International Symposium on Aviation Psychology* (pp. 1113–1116). Columbus, OH: Ohio State University.

Newell, A., and Rosenbloom, P.S. (1981). Mechanisms of skill acquisition and the law of practice. In J.R. Anderson (ed.), *Cognitive skills and their acquisition* (pp. 1–55). Hillsdale, NJ: Erlbaum.

Niemiec, R., and Walberg, H.J. (1987). Comparative effects of computer-assisted instruction: A synthesis of reviews. *Journal of Educational Computing Research, 3,* 19–37.

Nix, D., and Spiro, R. (eds.) (1990). *Cognition, education, & multimedia.* Hillsdale, NJ: Lawrence Erlbaum.

Nugent, W.A. (1987). A comparative assessment of computer-based media for presenting job task instructions. *Proceedings of the 31st Annual Meeting of the Human Factors Society* (pp. 696–700). Santa Monica, CA: Human Factors Society.

Osburn, H.G. (1987). Personnel selection. In G. Salvendy (ed.), *Handbook of human factors* (pp. 911–938). New York: Wiley.

Parasuraman, R. (1986). Vigilance, monitoring, and search. In K.R. Boff, L. Kaufman, and J.P. Thomas (eds.), *Handbook of perception and human performance: Volume II: Cognitive processes and performance* (pp. 43-1–43-39). New York: Wiley.

Pedersen, L.A., Allan, K.E., Laue, F.J., and Siem, R. (1992). *Personality theory and construction in selection and classification* (Tech. Report AL-TR-1992–0021). Brooks Air Force Base, San Antonio, TX: Armstrong Laboratory.

Pettitt, M.A., and Dunlap, J.H. (1995). Psychological factors that predict successful performance in a professional pilot program. *Proceedings of the Eighth International Symposium on Aviation Psychology* (pp. 1122–1126). Columbus, OH: Ohio State University.

Povenmire, H.K., and Roscoe, S.N. (1973). Incremental transfer effectiveness of a ground-based general aviation trainer. *Human Factors, 15,* 534–542.

Psotka, J., Massey, L.D., and Mutter, S.A. (eds.) (1988). *Intelligent tutoring systems.* Hillsdale, NJ: Lawrence Erlbaum.

Reigeluth, C.M. (1989). *Instructional design theories and models: An overview of their current status.* Hillsdale, NJ: Lawrence Erlbaum Associates.

Reilly, R.R., and Chao, G.T. (1982). Validity and fairness of some alternative employee selection procedures. *Personnel Psychology, 35,* 1–62.

Robertson, M.M., Stelly, J.W., and Wagner, R. (1995). A systematic training evaluation model applied to measure the effectiveness of an aviation maintenance team training program. *Proceedings of the Eighth International Symposium on Aviation Psychology* (pp. 631–636). Columbus, OH: Ohio State University.

Romiszowski, A.J. (1984). *Producing instructional systems: Lesson planning for individualized and group learning activities.* New York: Nichols Publishing.

Root, R.W. (1993). Growing a styleguide: Macroergonomic strategies for achieving consistent user interface design. *Proceedings of the Human Factors and Ergonomics Society 37th Annual Meeting* (pp. 882–885). Santa Monica, CA: Human Factors and Ergonomics Society.

Rosow, J.M., and Zager, R. (1990). *Training—The competitive edge.* San Francisco, CA: Jossey-Bass.

Rossett, A. (1992). Analysis of human performance problems. In H.D. Stolovitch and E.J. Keeps (eds.), *Handbook of human performance technology: A comprehensive guide for analyzing and solving performance problems in organizations* (pp. 97–113). San Francisco, CA: Jossey-Bass.

Rouse, W.B. (1991). *Design for success: A human-centered approach to designing successful products and systems.* New York: Wiley.

Rummler, G.A. (1983). Human performance problems and their solutions. In L.S. Baird, C.E. Schneider, and D. Laird (eds.), *The training and development sourcebook* (pp. 7–14). Amherst, MA: Human Resource Development Press.

Salas, E., Dickinson, T. L., Converse, S. A., and Tannenbaum, S. I. (1992). Toward an understanding of team performance and training. In R. Sweezey and E. Salas (eds.), *Teams: Their training and performance* (pp. 3–29). Norwood, NJ: Ablex Publishing.

Salmoni, A.W., Schmidt, R.A., and Walter, C.B. (1984). Knowledge of results and motor learning: A review and critical reappraisal. *Psychological Bulletin, 95,* 355–386.

Salzman, M.C., Dede, C., and Loftin, R.B. (1995). Usability and learning in educational virtual realities. *Proceedings of the Human Factors and Ergonomics Society 39th Annual Meeting* (pp. 486–490). Santa Monica, CA: Human Factors and Ergonomics Society.

Schmidt, F.L., and Hunter, J.E. (1981). Employment testing: Old theories and new research findings. *American Psychologist, 36*(10), 1128–1137.

Schmidt, J.K., and Kysor, K.P. (1987). Designing airline passenger safety cards. *Proceedings of the 31st Annual Meeting of the Human Factors Society* (pp. 51–55). Santa Monica, CA: Human Factors Society.

Schneider, W. (1985). Training high-performance skills: Fallacies and guidelines. *Human Factors, 27,* 285–300.

Scott, D.R., McIntire, S.A., and Burroughs, W.A. (1992). Improving performance and retention through video assessment: A longitudinal study. Paper presented at the annual meeting of the American Psychological Association, Washington, DC.

Siegel, A.I. (1983). The miniature job training and evaluation approach: Additional findings. *Personnel Psychology, 36,* 41–56.

Singley, M.K., and Anderson, J.R. (1989). *The transfer of cognitive skill.* Cambridge, MA: Harvard University Press.

Skelly, J. (1993). The role of event time in attenuating. *Time and Society, 2*(1), 107–128.

Smith, M. (1994). A theory of the validation of predictors in selection. *Journal of Occupational and Organizational Psychology, 67,* 13–32.

Smith, P.J., Miller, T.E., Gross, S., Guerlain, S., Smith, J.W., Svirbely, J., Rudmann, S., and Strohm, P. (1991). The transfusion medicine tutor: Methods and results from the development of an interactive learning environment for teaching problem-solving skills. *Proceedings of the Human Factors Society 35th Annual Meeting* (pp. 1408–1411). Santa Monica, CA: Human Factors Society.

Smither, R.D. (1994). *The psychology of work and human performance* (2nd ed.). New York: HarperCollins.

Spencer, K. (1988). *The psychology of educational technology and instructional media.* London: Routledge.

Spool, J.M. and Snyder, C. (1993). *Product usability: Survival techniques.* Tutorial presented for IBM Santa Teresa Laboratory. Andover, MA: User Interface Engineering.

Steuffert, S., Pogash, R., and Piasecki, M. (1988). Simulation-based assessment of managerial competence: Reliability and validity. *Personnel Psychology, 41,* 537–557.

Stokes, A.F., and Bohan, M. (1995). Academic proficiency, anxiety, and information-processing variables as predictors of success in university flight training. *Proceedings of the Eighth International Symposium on Aviation Psychology* (pp. 1107–1112). Columbus, OH: Ohio State University.

Stolovitch, H.D., and Keeps, E.J. (eds.) (1992). *Handbook of human performance technology: A comprehensive guide for analyzing and solving performance problems in organizations.* San Francisco, CA: Jossey-Bass.

Swain, A.D., and Guttmann, H.E. (1983). *Handbook of human reliability analysis with emphasis on nuclear power plant applications* (NUREG/CR-1278). Washington, DC: Nuclear Regulatory Commission.

Swezey, R.W. (1987). Design of job aids and procedural writing. In G. Salvendy (ed.), *Handbook of human factors* (pp. 1039–1057). New York: Wiley.

Swezey, R.W., Perez, R.S., and Allen, J.A. (1988). Effects of instructional delivery system and training parameter manipulations on electromechanical maintenance performance. *Human Factors, 30*(6), 751–762.

Tait, K. (1994). DISCOURSE: The design and production of simulation-based learning environments. In T. de Jong and L. Sarti (eds.), *Design and production of multimedia and simulation-based learning material* (pp. 111–131). The Netherlands: Kluwer Academic.

Ulrich, L., and Trumbo, D. (1965). The selection interview since 1949. *Psychological Bulletin, 63,* 100–116.

Varnadoe, S., and Barron, A.E. (1993). Designing electronic performance support systems. *Proceedings of the 15th Interservice/Industry Training Systems and Education Conference* (pp. 748–754). Washington, DC: National Security Industrial Association.

Vazquez-Abad, J., and Winer, L.R. (1992). Emerging trends in instructional interventions. In H.D. Stolovitch and E.J. Keeps (eds.), *Handbook of human performance technology* (pp. 672–687). San Francisco, CA: Jossey-Bass.

Vidulich, M., Yeh, Y.Y., and Schneider, W. (1983). Time compressed components for air intercept control skills. *Proceedings of the Human Factors Society 27th Annual Meeting* (pp. 161–164). Santa Monica, CA: Human Factors Society.

Wexley, K.M., and Latham, G.P. (1991). *Developing and training human resources in organizations (2nd ed.)*. New York: HarperCollins.

Wickens, C.D. (1992a). Virtual reality and education. *Proceedings of the IEEE International Conference on Systems, Man, and Cybernetics, 1* (pp. 842–847). New York: IEEE Press.

Wickens, C.D. (1992b). *Engineering psychology and human performance (2nd ed.)*. New York: HarperCollins.

Wightman, D.C., and Lintern, G. (1985). Part-task training for tracking and manual control. *Human Factors, 27*(3), 267–283.

Wightman, D.C., and Sistrunk, F. (1987). Part-task training strategies in simulated carrier landing final-approach training. *Human Factors, 29*(3), 245–254.

Williams, H.P., Wickens, C.D., and Hutchinson, S. (1994). Fidelity and interactivity in navigational training: A comparison of three methods. *Proceedings of the Human Factors and Ergonomics Society 38th Annual Meeting* (pp. 1163–1167). Santa Monica, CA: Human Factors and Ergonomics Society.

Wilson, J., and Rosenberg, D. (1988). Rapid prototyping for user interface design. In M. Helander (ed.), *Handbook of human-computer interaction* (pp. 859–875). Amsterdam: North-Holland.

Wright, P. (1977). Presenting technical information: A survey of research findings. *Instructional Science, 6*, 93–134.

CHAPTER 19

Social Factors

George entered the meeting room Monday morning at 7:25, thinking that he could get a lot more accomplished without these 7:30 A.M. weekly meetings. His boss, Stuart, would already be there, ready and waiting with the two-page agenda. He could see the meeting play out already. By the second or third project item, the department critic, Martin Jones, would be going into a long lecture about all the problems associated with whatever they happened to be discussing. Last time, it was that the project had too many problems, they should not have ever taken it on, it was causing everyone to put in too much time, and on and on. Martin seemed to perpetually dominate the discussions, keeping anything from really getting accomplished. George wished they had some magic tool that could make the meetings a little more productive.

Ergonomic interventions in business and industry usually focus on changing the workstation or equipment characteristics for the *individual* worker. For example, attempts to increase system safety might result in redesigning displays, adding alarms, or changing how a task is performed. However, as we noted in the previous chapter, there are factors that sometimes affect human performance that are larger than, or outside of, the envelope of the person-equipment system. Most notably, individual behavior is a function of the *social context,* referring to the attitudes and behavior of co-workers and others in the work environment and a function of the *organizational context,* which includes variables such as management structure, reward or incentive systems, and so forth.

In this chapter, we review some of the human factors topics that pertain to the larger social context. Because organizational re-engineering is increasing the amount of time that people are working together in either groups or teams, we first consider how the use of groups and teams interacts with human performance. We also look at some of the concepts being applied in the emerging area of team training. Next, we will consider how technology is being used to support work done by groups or teams who may be separated in time or space, an area termed computer-supported cooperative work. Finally, we will briefly review some of the ways that ergonomic intervention in industry is changing as a function of broader social and organizational ergonomic perspectives.

GROUPS AND TEAMS

Because businesses must operate in a rapidly dynamic economic environment, recent trends in organizational design are placing a strong emphasis on the "flattening" of management structures, decentralized decision making (where workers at lower levels are making more important management decisions), and the use of work groups or teams for increased efficiency and flexibility (Hammer & Champy, 1993). Teams are also becoming more common as a way to respond to increasing job complexity and the associated cognitive demands placed on workers (Salas, Dickinson, Converse, & Tannenbaum, 1992; Sundstrom, De Meuse, & Futrell, 1990). All indications suggest that the use of teams and work groups will be a long-term trend in industry (Shea & Guzzo, 1987). Johnson (1993) reports that 27 out of 35 surveyed companies responded that the use of work teams had resulted in favorable or strongly favorable results. In addition, 31 of the 35 organizations said that work-team applications were likely to increase in their company.

Why would human factors specialists be concerned with the behavior of groups or teams of workers? One reason is that just as individuals vary with respect to performance and error, so do teams. In a growing number of industries, including the aviation industry, investigators have found that a large number of accidents have been caused primarily by a breakdown in team performance (Helmreich & Foushee, 1993). Human factors specialists are attempting to address this phenomenon as part of their traditional focus on safety and human error. They are therefore attempting to identify the skills responsible for successful teamwork, and develop new methods that can efficiently and effectively train those skills. In this section, we will briefly define and contrast the concepts of groups, teams, and crews. We will also review a few of the basic concepts and findings concerning group performance and teamwork.

Characteristics of Groups and Teams

Sociologists and social psychologists have studied group processes for fifty years but have only recently become seriously interested in teams (i.e., in the mid-eighties). Most of the groups and teams described in the literature are "small," with less than twelve members. However, teams can technically be quite large; for example, in the military, a "combat team" might have hundreds of members. As another example, the new business re-engineering efforts are resulting in self-regulating work teams of all sizes. Peters (1988) suggested that organizations "organize every function into ten- to thirty-person, largely self-managing teams."

All teams are groups, but not all groups are teams. Groups are aggregations of people who "have limited role differentiation, and their decision making or task performance depends primarily on individual contributions" (Hare, 1992).

Examples include a jury, board of directors, or a college entrance committee. A team, however, is a small number of people with complementary skills and specific roles or functions (high role differentiation), who interact dynamically toward a common purpose or goal for which they hold themselves mutually accountable (Katzenbach & Smith, 1993; Salas et al., 1992). Teams tend to have the following characteristics (Sundstrom & Altman, 1989):

- Perception of the group as a work unit by members and nonmembers
- Interdependence among members with respect to shared outcomes
- Role differentiation among members
- Production of a group-level output
- Interdependent relations with other groups and/or their representatives

There are numerous definitions of teams, but they all seem to center around the concepts of a *group goal* or output attained by *multiple people* working in an *interdependent* manner. As compared to groups, teams have more role differentiation and more coordination required for their activities (Hare, 1992). Group decision making is therefore not necessarily the same as teamwork.

Several researchers have focused on the characteristics or preconditions that must exist for a team to be successful or effective. These include the following types of requirement (from Bassin, 1988; Patten, 1981; Katzenbach & Smith, 1993):

- A vision; a common, meaningful purpose; a natural reason for working together
- Specific performance goals and/or a well-defined team work-product
- A perceived, dependent need; members are mutually dependent on each others' experience and abilities
- Commitment from every member to the idea of working together as a group
- Commitment to a common approach, built from group discussion and consensus building
- Leadership that embodies the vision and transfers responsibility to the team members
- Coordination; effective use of resources and the team members' skills
- Team members who assume social roles that promote success by supporting, interpreting, challenging, remembering, leading, etc.; these roles may change with each new situation
- Shared team accountability; the group must feel and be accountable as a unit within the larger organization

Patten (1981) states that the key to group performance is communication within the group: "There has to be a singleness of mission and a willingness to cooperate." In considering the nature of teams and teamwork, Critchley and Casey (1984) suggested that the use of teams is most appropriate in situations involving high uncertainty and maximum choice in problem solving.

If a team is a group of interdependent members, how is this distinguished from the concept of a *crew?* The term *crew* is typically reserved for a group of persons or team that manages some form of technology, usually some type of transportation system such as ships, airplanes, spacecraft, and so forth. Human factors specialists seem to be particularly interested in crew performance (e.g., Sukhia & Funk, 1995), possibly partly because of the strong emphasis in the airline industry on aircrew performance and training (e.g., Cannon-Bowers et al., 1989; Gregorich & Wilhelm, 1993; Helmreich & Foushee, 1993; Helmreich & Wilhelm, 1991; Hormann et al., 1995). In addition to the research specifically targeted toward crew performance, we can probably assume that any findings or principles based on the study of team performance is equally applicable. In addition, teams and crews are groups by definition, and often do "group" tasks that are not necessarily interdependent in nature.

Group Performance

In many group tasks, the individuals often do some work (such as making a decision or performing problem solving), then have discussions and share information with the others. Some research on groups has focused on comparing the performance productivity level of the group with that of individuals trying to answer the question of whether groups help people do a better job. Overall, groups are found to be better at tasks than the *average* of the individuals but not better than the best individual (Hare, 1992; Hill, 1982). In terms of output or work productivity, a group will generally yield less than the sum of the individuals. This difference is increased to the extent that people feel their efforts are dispensable, their own contribution cannot be distinguished, there is shared responsibility for the outcome, and/or motivation is low. Even in the well-known method known as "brainstorming," the number of ideas produced by a group is less than the number produced by the members working individually (Street, 1974).

Certain characteristics will tend to make a group more productive. For example, if groups have members with certain personalities that allow them to take initiative, work independently, and act compatibly with others, productivity will increase. Groups will also be more productive if they have a high level of cohesiveness, have appropriate or adequate communications, have needed information, and have adequate time and resources (Hare, 1992). For a job requiring discussion, the optimal group size is five (Bales, 1954; Yetton & Bottger, 1983), and some researchers have argued that a consensus model is ultimately better for group productivity than a majority decision model (Hare, 1982). Finally, it is usually best to have a leader to coordinate group subtask performance, communicate group goals, and summarize constraints.

Team Performance

Successful team performance begins with the selection of an appropriate combination of members. Team members should be chosen where the leader has a style that fits the project, individuals have the necessary complementary taskwork skills and teamwork skills, and creation of a team that is not so large that communication becomes difficult (Hackman & Oldham, 1980; Heenefrund, 1985).

The choice of team members and their associated skills depends on the type of work team being assembled. Sundstrom and colleagues (1990) evaluated the concept of work teams and determined that teams can be placed in four categories of application. The categories are defined by factors such as whether the teams have high or low role differentiation, the work pace is externally or internally controlled, and the team process requires high or low synchronization with outside units (Sundstrom et al., 1990):

- *Advice/involvement groups.* Examples include review panels, boards, quality control circles, employee involvement groups, and advisory councils. These groups are characterized by *low* role differentiation, *low* demands for external synchronization, work cycles that may be brief, and work cycles that may not be repeated.
- *Production/service groups.* Examples include assembly teams, manufacturing teams, mining teams, flight attendant crews, data-processing groups, and maintenance crews. This category of group activity is characterized by *low* role differentiation, *high* demands for external synchronization with other people or work units, external pacing because of synchronization with other units, and work cycles that are typically repeated continuously.
- *Project/development groups.* Examples include research and development groups, planning teams, architect teams, engineering teams, development teams, and task forces. The teams are typically characterized by *high* role differentiation, *low* to medium external synchronization and pacing related to outside units (although the work might require a large amount of communication with outside units).
- *Action/negotiation groups.* Examples include surgery teams, cockpit crews, production crews, negotiating teams, combat units, sports teams, and entertainment groups. The work requires high role differentiation (with frequently long team life spans), high levels of synchronization with outside units, externally imposed pacing, and repetitive work cycles that are often brief and take place under new or changing conditions.

Each of the four types of teams will need different organizational support in order to be effective. For example, action/negotiation teams require a high degree of expertise among members and synchronization with outside people. This usually means that training and technology will play a major role in determining team effectiveness.

While the development of work teams is usually carried out with optimism, there are a number of problems that may interfere with team performance, including (Blake, Mouton, & McCanse, 1989):

- Problems centering around power and authority
- Lack of shared norms or values
- Poor cohesion or morale
- Poor differentiation or problems of team structure
- Lack of shared and well-defined goals and task objectives
- Poor or inadequate communication
- Lack of necessary feedback or critique

One reason that teams often perform below the initial expectations of management is that there has been an inadequate amount of training and team-building in advance. Responding to this problem, a number of researchers in organizational development have developed methods for giving team-building workshops and seminars (e.g., George, 1987; Nanda, 1986).

Effective teams require that members have *taskwork* skills, which pertain to correct subtask performance, and also *teamwork* skills, which pertain to interpersonal skills such as communication (Morgan et al., 1986). Teamwork skills include a variety of behaviors that seem to cluster around the ability to cooperate and communicate effectively with other team members. For example, Morgan et al. (1986) suggest that teamwork skills include behaviors reflecting the following general categories of activity: cooperation, coordination, communication, adaptibility, giving suggestions or criticisms, acceptance of suggestions or criticism, and showing team spirit.

When teams must perform tasks in a complex, dynamic environment with safety issues, such as an air traffic control room or hospital operating room, there is an even greater need to perform smoothly and effectively. In such environments, periods of stressful, fast-paced work activity lead to cognitive overload, and under most circumstances, the overall impact on teams appears to be a decline in communication and job performance (Bogner, 1994; Kleinman & Serfaty, 1989; Urban et al., 1996; Volpe et al., 1996; Williges, Johnston, & Briggs, 1966; Xiao et al., 1996).

It appears that team members' reduced ability to communicate during periods of high workload and stress can negatively impact team performance in several ways. First, the members do not have the opportunity to build a common mental model of the current problem and related environmental or equipment variables (Orasanu & Salas, 1993). Second, the members may not have the time and cognitive resources to communicate plans and strategies adequately. Third, members may not have the cognitive resources available to ask others for information they need. Some researchers have found that highly effective teams are able to overcome this problem by making good use of the "downtime" between periods of high workload (Orasanu, 1990; Pepitone, King, & Murphy, 1988). That is, effective teams use low workload time to share information regarding the situation, plans, emergency strategies, member roles, and so forth. This way, when they actually encounter emergencies, they can use the shared information for *implicit* coordination that does not require extensive communication.

Some preliminary work suggests that communication among team members has a strong impact on performance (e.g., Donchin et al., 1995). Successful performance relies on adequate information from the environment and communication of information between group members in an "anticipatory" mode. Teams perform well when members have a *shared mental model* of the task. This provides them with a common understanding of who is responsible for what task and the information needs of others (Cannon-Bowers, Salas, & Converse, 1993; Orasanu, 1990; Orasanu & Salas, 1993; Stout, 1995; Stout, Cannon-Bowers, & Salas, 1994). Individuals use their mental models to state relevant task information before or as it is needed by others, rather than waiting for it to be requested (Johannesen, Cook, & Woods, 1994). Other researchers have noted the importance of variables such as team coordination, information flow, situation awareness, problem solving, planning and decision making, time management, and stress management (Hanson et al., 1995; Hormann et al., 1995; Jentsch et al., 1995; Salas et al., 1995; Stout, 1995; Volpe, 1993).

Team Training

Although traditional training programs focus on taskwork skills, more recent research and development activities in human factors have emphasized the acquisition of teamwork skills (e.g., Stout & Salas, 1993; Salas et al., 1992; Salas et al., 1995; Serfaty et al, 1993). For example, training programs for flight crew resource management have attempted to enhance factors such as communication and stress management (e.g., Hormann et al., 1995). According to Serfaty et al. (1993), "Well-trained teams cope with stress through internal mechanisms of decision strategy adaptation, coordination adaptation, and structural reconfiguration, in an effort to maintain stress below an acceptable level while keeping team performance at a required level" (p. 1229).

The implication is that, at least for certain types of teams, team training must go beyond the usual organizational development "team-building" activities. Effective training to acquire teamwork skills must promote (1) the development and use of shared mental models and (2) strategies for effective communication, adaptation to stress, maintenance of situational awareness, group decision making, and coordinated task performance (Orasanu & Salas, 1993; Robertson et al., 1995; Salas et al., 1995; Serfaty et al., 1993; Stout, 1995; Volpe, 1993). A variety of team training methods are being evaluated including the use of *job cross-training* to enhance knowledge of team members' information needs and increase the use of shared mental models (Volpe et al., 1996). Preliminary research has demonstrated that using simulated exercises to give team members experience in other members roles can increase knowledge about appropriate or necessary communications (Salas, Cannon-Bowers, & Johnston, 1997).

Finally, researchers are beginning to develop taxonomies of teamwork that can be used to identify the optimal instructional strategies for team training. As an example, Armstrong and Reigeluth (1991) developed the Team Instructional Prescriptions (TIP) theory of instructional design that specifies the type of instructional method to be used depending on key characteristics of the team and its tasks. These three characteristics are:

1. *Team Development Stages:* forming stage, performing I stage, and performing II stage
2. *Task Process:* interdependent serial subtasks or independent subtasks
3. *Task Variability:* procedural tasks (tasks are essentially always the same) or transfer tasks (where task performance will have to be modified according to the situation)

The training program is designed by first determining where the team and tasks fit in these categories. The trainer then uses rules provided by the TIP model (see

Armstrong & Reigeluth, 1991) to identify the instructional methods (e.g., role playing, simulations, etc.) most appropriate for the combination of characteristics in that particular circumstance.

COMPUTER-SUPPORTED COOPERATIVE WORK

The increasing use of groups and teams in the workplace, combined with rapid technological advances in the computer and communications industries, is resulting in a trend for group members to work separately and communicate via computer. As an example, control room displays are moving from large single-screen displays toward individual "cockpit" workstations for each operator or team member (Stubler & O'Hara, 1995). These people may be in the same room working at different stations or might even be in entirely separate locations. The individual workstations rely on a computer-based graphical interface to combine and coordinate functions such as controls, displays, procedural checklists, communication support, decision aids, and so on (O'Hara & Brown, 1994; Stubler & O'Hara, 1995; Woods, Roth, Stubler, & Mumaw, 1990).

The process of using computers to support group or team activity is termed *computer-supported cooperative work (CSCW)*, and the software that supports such activity is termed *groupware*. CSCW is a broad term that includes a number of different types of activities, including decision making, problem solving, design, procedural task performance, and so forth. These activities and their associated functions can be broken down or classified in a number of ways. In the sections below, we first consider basic decision making and some of the research findings relevant to CSCW. We then discuss CSCW as it pertains to team and crew task performance. While the potential for computers to support group process is enormous, we will focus predominantly on the interpersonal aspects; that is, computers can support a number of task activities, such as scientific visualization, but we will address issues that pertain only to interpersonal or teamwork factors, such as communication and coordination.

Decision Making Using Groupware

Kraemer and Pinsonneault (1990) distinguish between two types of support for group process: group communication support systems, and group decision support systems. *Group communication support systems* are information systems built primarily to support the communication among group members regardless of the task. Examples of communication support systems include teleconferencing, electronic mail, electronic boardrooms, and local group networks (Kraemer & King, 1988). *Group decision support systems* are targeted mostly toward increasing the quality of a group decision by reducing noise in the decision process or by decreasing the level of communication barriers between group members (DeSanctis & Gallupe, 1987). Therefore decision support systems can be thought of as communication systems plus other aids to provide functions such as eliminating communication barriers, structuring the decision process, and systematically directing the pattern, timing, or content of discussion (DeSanctis & Gallupe, 1987;

Nopachai & Casali, 1994). They support decision making or problem solving through the use of mechanisms such as:

- providing anonymity
- imposing structure on the process
- providing word-processing functions for synthesis of writing
- providing work space for generating ideals, decisions, consequences, and so on
- reducing counterproductive behavior such as disapproval
- reducing authority and control problems exhibited by a minority of group members

This list demonstrates that much of the functionality of these systems resides in counteracting negative interpersonal dynamics of group meetings and decision processes, such as the problem described at the beginning of this chapter.

Effects of Decision Support Systems.   Analyses of group decision support systems have resulted in a number of relatively consistent findings. Most studies indicate that these systems increase group members' depth of analysis (Steeb & Johnson, 1981; Gray, 1983), increase group communication and efforts to achieve clarification (Gray, 1983; Sharda, Barr, & McDonnell, 1988), increase member participation (George, Northcraft, & Nunamaker, 1987; Nunamaker, Applegate, & Konsynski, 1987), decrease the domination by a few people (Nunamaker, et al., 1987), and increase the consensus building of the group (Steeb & Johnson, 1981).

In addition, when looking at output, decisions seem to usually (although not always) be of higher quality for groups using group-decision support systems (Bui, et al., 1987; George, et al., 1987; Sharda, et al., 1988; Steeb & Johnson, 1981). It should be noted that the advantages of these systems could be caused by the promotion of more positive interaction among the group members, or by the provision of specific decision aids such as computer-aided decision-tree analysis (e.g., Steeb & Johnson, 1981). Other benefits include the findings that use of a decision support system increases the confidence of group members in the decision (Steeb & Johnson, 1981), and increases the satisfaction of group members with the decision (Steeb & Johnson, 1981).

Effects of Communication Support Systems.   The study of communication support systems has resulted in some general findings regarding their benefits over person-to-person interaction. Some of these results happen to pertain to work output or decision-making measures, which is important because they show the impact of systems with *only* communication support per se, without the decision support functions.

Communication support systems have been found to (1) increase the level of participation and effort expended by group members, (2) increase the depth of analysis, (3) decrease domination of the group by a few members, and (4) increase decision times (Gallupe, DeSanctis, & Dickson, 1988; Kraemer & Pinsonneault, 1990; Zigurs, Poole, & DeSanctis, 1987). However, they have also been shown to decrease overall cooperation and consensus building (e.g., Turoff & Hiltz, 1982).

Apparently group members become more invested in the task but do not necessarily converge well on a consensus (Kraemer & Pinsonneault, 1990). Finally, while they increase the quality of decisions, they often decrease the confidence and satisfaction of group members (e.g., Bui & Sivasankaran, 1987; Gallupe et al, 1988).

Computer-Supported Team Performance

Some computer-supported groups are engaged in team performance activities such as cockpit management, maintenance tasks, or process control. Teams working via groupware are sometimes referred to as "virtual teams" (Cano & Kleiner, 1996). Note that for group ware to support these types of collaborative task performance, the software functions must usually be much more elaborate than the basic communication and decision support systems discussed in the previous section. This type of group ware is likely to support task performance via controls and displays, system status information, information concerning what other team members are doing, procedural checklists, and other types of support, such as those discussed in Chapter 7. Stubler and O'Hara (1995) have recently evaluated some of the more critical display elements for group ware that support complex task performance, referring to the displays for these systems as *group-view displays*. Stubler and O'Hara (1995) have proposed that group-view displays should provide the following categories of support:

1. *Provide a status overview.* The display should provide information that conveys a high-level status summary to inform all personnel about important status conditions. Such displays should provide information about changes in process status and equipment status.

2. *Direct personnel to additional information.* The display should direct team members to other information that would be helpful or necessary but that is not currently displayed. Systems that do not provide this help have been criticized by users (Reiersen et al., 1987). The displays should generally follow human factors display design principles and guidelines, such as supporting easy manual retrieval of information (e.g., O'Hara et al., 1995; Woods, 1984; Woods et al., 1990).

3. *Support collaboration among crew members.* When crew members are sharing the same task (and do not have role differentiation), it is important that their collaboration is supported. Supporting collaboration is accomplished by activities such as recording actions of different personnel, providing whiteboard or other space for collaborative problem-solving or brainstorming, displaying previous activity or highlights, and so forth. In face-to-face collaboration, the use of gestures, facial expressions, and body language is an important part of the communication process (Tang, 1991). If crew members are working remotely, their communication must be supported by some other means.

4. *Support coordination of crew activities.* Some team and crew members have highly differentiated roles and will therefore be doing different but related tasks. In this case, the group ware should support coordination of the work performed by the various crew members. Such support would

facilitate a common understanding of each person's goals, activity, and information requirements. It would also support activities such as identifying and resolving errors, exchanging information, one person providing assistance to another, and monitoring the activity of others.

These suggestions illustrate the need for group ware to support the numerous interpersonal activities critical for successful teamwork.

Earlier in this chapter, we noted that groups or teams usually engage in one of four types of activity; (1) Advice/involvement, (2) Production/service, (3) Project/development, and (4) Action/negotiation (from Sundstrom et al., 1990). Each of these activities can be supported by group ware in a number of ways. The different activities are defined by characteristics such as whether the group members have role differentiation and whether work is externally paced.

These characteristics have implications for the types of function that would be provided by group ware. In addition, groups or teams performing computer-supported cooperative work can be working either together in the same space, termed *local,* or working in different rooms, buildings, or cities, termed *remote* (Preece, 1994). Table 19.1 shows the four types of groups or teams, divided by whether the members are working in a local or remote manner. The right-hand column lists the types of support that would likely be provided by group ware for the specific group activity in either a local or remote manner of work. By considering the content of this table, we can see that the suggestions made by Stubler and O'Hara (1995) for collaborative and coordination support will be applicable to most team and crew activities.

Difficulties in Remote Collaboration

Finally, some researchers studying real-world collaborative computer-based work environments have focused on the disadvantages imposed by CSCW used by participants working remotely (e.g., Benford et al, 1995). As an example, there is evidence that people working in the same location use facial expressions and their bodies to communicate information implicitly and explicitly about factors such as task activity, system status, attention, mood, identity, and so forth (e.g., Benford et al., 1995; Tang, 1991). Inzana, Willis, and Kass (1994) found that collocated teams were more cohesive and outperformed distributed teams.

If we evaluate the difficulties of team performance under high workload or stress, we can assume that remote team performance would result in problems such as: (1) increased difficulty in collaboration—knowing who is doing what, (2) increased difficulty in communication because of the loss of subtle cues from eye contact and body language, and (3) increased difficulty in maintaining situation awareness because of a decrease in communication. Researchers performing field studies have confirmed many of these assumptions. For example, in studying crew communication in the cockpit, Segal (1994) found that crew members watch each other during teamwork and rely heavily on nonverbal information for communication and coordination. Other field studies have also shown the use of visual information for task coordination and communication (e.g., Burgoon, Buller, & Woodall, 1989; Hutchins, 1990) and have demonstrated that reducing available

TABLE 19.1 Functions Provided by Groupware Depending on the Type of Group Activity and the Location of Group Members.*

Advice/Decision Groups
(examples include committees, advisory boards, review panels)

Local	Decision support
Remote	Above plus the following:
	Communication support
	Identity support
	Visual feedback

Project/Development Groups
(examples include engineering teams, architectural teams, task forces)

Local	Task performance support (e.g., provide a structure for the design process, answer queries, support statistical modeling, etc.)
	Collaboration support
	Coordination support
Remote	Above plus the following:
	Communication support
	Identity support
	Occasional visual feedback

Production/Service Groups
(examples include assembly teams, flight attendant crews, maintenance crews)

Local	Task performance support (e.g., provide a status overview, direct operator to additional information, answer queries, record actions, events, etc.)
	Collaboration support
	Coordination support (in instances when members have differentiated roles)
Remote	Above plus the following:
	Communication support

Action/Negotiation Groups
(examples include surgery teams, negotiating teams, cockpit crews)

Local	Task performance support (e.g., provide controls and displays, status reports, etc.)
	Collaboration support
	Coordination support
Remote	Above plus communication support

*_Local_ indicates that people are in the same room. _Remote_ is when people are in different rooms or buildings.

visual access significantly impacts group dynamics (e.g., Chapanis et al., 1972; Heath & Luff, 1992).

When collaborative team members must work remotely via a computer-supported collaborative environment, they lose a great deal of information. People become "disembodied," known only through their actions, which Benford and colleagues (1995) suggest is analogous to the concept of poltergeists. Their conclusion is that group members should somehow be visible to one another. One low-technology method for accomplishing this is the use of a video system. Ishii, Kobayashi, and Arita (1994) describe a collaborative work environment for drawing and design. The system uses video cameras to capture live face images of each group member, as well as desktop surface images and hand gestures as work progresses. In this system, the computer display shows the team member faces on the right side of the screen and a working drawing on the left. Each team member's hand gestures and drawing activity is *overlaid* onto the working drawing so that everyone can see (and hear) what others are doing in real time. Further in the future is the use of a collaborative virtual reality environment where members are "directly visible to themselves and to others through a process of direct and sufficiently rich embodiment" (Benford et al., 1995). It is clear that the groupware methodologies are in their infancy, and as hardware technologies advance, the types of support provided by groupware will increase in power and sophistication. Whether the advances will be able to completely overcome the disadvantages of distance collaboration is not clear.

MACROERGONOMICS AND INDUSTRIAL INTERVENTION

Traditional ergonomic interventions in industry have focused on making changes in the workstation or physical environment for individual workers, an approach that has been referred to as *microergonomics* (Hendrick, 1986). Experience in industrial intervention has taught us that sometimes microergonomic changes are unsuccessful because they address performance and safety problems at the physical and cognitive levels but do not address problems at the social and organizational levels (Hendrick, 1986, 1994; Nagamachi & Imada, 1992). For this reason, we are beginning to see a new emphasis on re-engineering work systems whereby the analyst takes a larger perspective, addressing the social and organizational factors that impact performance as well as the more traditional human factors considerations (Alexander, 1991; Carroll, 1994; Dray, 1985; Getty, 1993; Hendrick, 1994, 1995; Noro & Imada, 1991; Imada & Hubert, 1993; Monk & Wagner, 1989). The *macroergonomic* approach addresses performance and safety problems by including analysis of the organization's personnel, social, technological, and economical subsystems (Brown, 1990; Hendrick, 1986; Meshkati, 1991); that is, it evaluates the larger system as well as the person-machine system for the individual worker.

Macroergonomics represents a "top-down sociotechnical systems approach to the design of organizations, work systems, jobs, and related human-machine, user-system, and human-environment interfaces" (Hendrick, 1986, 1992, 1995). The purpose of macroergonomics analysis is to combine jobs, technological systems, and worker abilities/expectations to harmonize with organizational goals and structure (Hoffman, Lowe, & Wilson, 1993). After the initial analysis, macroergonomic *solutions* and interventions also focus on larger social and organizational factors, including actions such as increasing employee involvement, changing communication patterns, restructuring reward systems, and integrating safety into a broad organizational culture (Imada & Feiglstok, 1990). As Carroll (1994) notes when discussing accidents in high-hazard industries, "Decisions must be understood in context, a context of information, procedures, constraints, incentives, authority, status, and expectations that arise from human organizations" (p. 924). Because these are human social factors, they cannot necessarily be addressed with conventional engineering design solutions. The general goal of integrating technological systems with social systems is similar to goals of fields such as organizational development and industrial psychology. For this reason, human factors may begin to overlap with these fields more than it has done so in the past.

The most common method for taking a macroergonomic approach to industrial problems and issues is to perform an analysis similar to the one described in Chapter 3, only performed on a more companywide basis (e.g., Imada & Nagamachi, 1990); that is, systematic analyses are performed for organizational structure and goals, jobs and how they interrelate, organizational climate and norms, safety concerns, and so on (Carroll, 1994). Programs are developed that address the entire range of causal factors. These may include employee training, incentive programs, safety programs including job and equipment redesign, management education about program changes, and other macro-level changes.

One of the most commonly used methods for taking a macroergonomic approach is the use of *participatory ergonomics,* a method whereby employees are centrally involved from the beginning (e.g., Getty, 1993; Imada, 1991; King, 1994; Noro & Imada, 1991). They are asked to help with the front-end analysis, to do problem solving in identifying ergonomic or safety problems, to participate in generating solutions, and to help implement the program elements. Imada provides three reasons for using a participatory ergonomics approach: (1) employees know a great deal about their job and job environment, (2) employee and management ownership enhances program implementation, and (3) end-user participation causes flexible problem solving. Employee familiarity with the problems, what works and what does not, and the implicit social dynamics of the workplace allow them to see issues and think of design solutions that an outsider might not consider. It has also been widely noted that strong involvement and "ownership" of employees from the beginning of the intervention process tends to make the changes more successful and long-lasting (e.g., Brown, 1995; Dunn & Swierczek, 1977; Hendrick, 1995; Huse & Cummings, 1985).

Ergonomic interventions represent a type of change in the workplace. Unfortunately, intervention efforts and their associates changes are often difficult to bring about for a number of reasons, often referred to as *organizational barriers.* Organizational barriers are common, and include factors such as the following:

- Interventions, such as training, may be costly (or perceived as costly)
- Stockholders put pressure on top managers to pay dividends rather than reinvesting money
- Managers may resist change because they feel that they would lose power and decision-making authority
- The company has powerful norms and culture(s)
- Many people just have a general tendency to resist change
- Reward structures do not support change

These are all reasons for using the participatory approach because strong management and employee participation tend to overcome these barriers (Brown, 1995).

Some strategies for changing employee behaviors related to safety come from general models of behavior and attitude change. For example, Peters (1991) reviewed the following five strategies for promoting employee self-protective behavior: (1) use of individual or group incentives, (2) use of disciplinary actions, (3) fear messages, (4) behavior modeling of others, and (5) employee surveys. After assessing the research literature, Peters concluded that each of these methods is effective under some circumstances but not others. He provides a limited set of suggestions for using the methods and notes that more research is needed on intervention methods for promoting workplace safety.

REFERENCES

Alexander, D.C. (1991). Macro-ergonomics: A new tool for the ergonomist. In M. Pulat and D. Alexander (eds.), *Industrial ergonomics: Case studies* (pp. 275–285). Norcross, GA: Industrial Engineering and Management Press.

Armstrong, R.B., and Reigeluth, C.M. (1991). The TIP Theory: Prescriptions for designing instructions for teams. *Performance Improvement Quarterly, 4*(3), 13–40.

Bales, R. (1954). In conference. *Harvard Business Review, 32,* 44–50.

Bassin, M. (1988). Teamwork at General Foods: New and improved. *Personnel Journal, 67*(5), 62–70.

Benford, S., Greenhalgh, C., Bowers, J., Snowdon, D., and Fahlen, L.E. (1995). User embodiment in collaborative virtual environments. *Chi '95: Human Factors in Computing Systems* (pp. 242–249). New York: Association for Computing Machinery.

Blake, R.F., Mouton, J.S., and McCanse, A.A. (1989). *Change by design.* Reading, MA: Addision-Wesley.

Bogner, M.S. (ed.) (1994). *Human error in medicine.* Hillsdale, NJ: Erlbaum.

Brown, O., Jr. (1990). Macroergonomics: A review. In K. Noro and O. Brown, Jr. (eds.), *Human factors in organizational design and management III* (pp. 15–20). Amsterdam: North-Holland.

Brown, O., Jr. (1995). The challenge: Strategies for overcoming obstacles to change. *Proceedings of the Human Factors and Ergonomics Society 39th Annual Meeting* (pp. 771–774). Santa Monica, CA: Human Factors and Ergonomics Society.

Bui, T., and Sivasankaran, T.R. (1987). *GDSS use under conditions of group task complexity.* Monterey, CA: The U.S. Naval Postgraduate School.

Bui, T., Sivasankaran, T.R., Fijol, Y., and Woodbury, M.A. (1987). Identifying organizational opportunities for GDSS use: Some experimental evidence. *DSS-87,* 68–75.

Burgoon, J.K., Buller, D.B., and Woodall, W.G. (1989). *Nonverbal communication: The unspoken dialogue.* New York: Harper & Row Publishers.

Cannon-Bowers, J.A., Prince, C., Salas, E., Owens, J.M., Morgan, B.B., Jr., and Gonos, G.H. (1989, November). Determining aircrew coordination training effectiveness. *Proceedings of the 11th Annual Meeting of the Interservice/Industry Training Systems Conference* (pp. 128–136). Ft. Worth, TX.

Cannon-Bowers, J.A., Salas, E., and Converse, S.A. (1993). Shared mental models in expert team decision making. In N.J. Castellan, Jr. (ed.), *Current issues in individual and group decision making* (pp. 221–246). Hillsdale, NJ: Erlbaum.

Cano, A.R., and Kleiner, B.M. (1996). Sociotechnical design factors for virtual team performance. *Proceedings of the Human Factors and Ergonomics Society 40th Annual Meeting* (pp. 786–790). Santa Monica, CA: Human Factors and Ergonomics Society.

Carroll, J.S. (1994). The organizational context for decision making in high-hazard industries. *Proceedings of the Human Factors and Ergonomics Society 38th Annual Meeting* (pp. 922–925. Santa Monica, CA: Human Factors and Ergonomics Society.

Chapanis, A., Ochsman, R.B., Parrish, R.N., and Weeks, G.D. (1972). Studies in interactive communication: I. The effects of four communication modes on the behavior of teams during cooperative problem-solving. *Human Factors, 14*(6), 487–509.

Critchley, B., and Casey, D. (1984). Second thoughts on team building. *Management Education and Development, 15*(2), 163–175.

DeSanctis, G., and Gallupe, R.B. (1987). A foundation for the study of group decision support systems. *Management Science, 33*(5), 589–609.

Donchin, Y., Gopher, D., Olin, M., et al. (1995). A look into the nature and causes of human errors in the intensive care unit. *Critical Care Medicine, 23*, 294–300.

Dray, S.M. (1985). Macroergonomics in organizations: An introduction. In I.D. Brown, R. Goldsmith, K. Coombes, and M.A. Sinclair (eds.), *Ergonomics International 85* (pp. 520–522). London: Taylor & Francis.

Dunn, W., and Swierczek, F. (1977). Planned organizational change: Toward grounded theory. *Journal of Applied Behavioral Science, 13*(2), 135–157.

Gallupe, R.B., DeSanctis, G., and Dickson, G. (1988). Computer-based support for group problem finding: An experimental investigation. *MIS Quarterly, 12*(2), 277–296.

George, J.F., Northcraft, G.B., and Nunamaker, J.F. (1987). *Implications of group decision support system use for management: Report of a pilot study.* Tucson, AZ: College of Business and Public Administration, University of Arizona.

George, P.S. (1987). Team building without tears. *Personnel Journal, 66*(11), 122–129.

Getty, R.L. (1993). The integration of ergonomics in a safety improvement program: Design and implementation of an ergonomics initiative. *Proceedings of the Human Factors and Ergonomics Society 37th Annual Meeting* (pp. 891–895). Santa Monica, CA: Human Factors and Ergonomics Society.

Gray, P. (1983). Initial observation from the decision room project. *DSS-83 Transactions*, 135–138.

Gregorich, S.E., and Wilhelm, J.A. (1993). Crew resource management training assessment. In E.L. Wiener, B.G. Kanki, and R.L. Helmreich (eds.), *Cockpit resource management* (pp. 173–198). San Diego, CA: Academic Press.

Hackman, J.R., and Oldham, G.R. (1980). *Work redesign.* Reading, MA: Addison-Wesley.

Hammer, M., and Champy, J. (1993). *Reengineering the corporation.* New York: HarperCollins.

Hanson, M.A., Hedge, J.W., Logan, K.K., Bruskiewicz, K.T., and Borman, W.C. (1995). Application of the critical incident technique to enhance crew resource management training. *Proceedings of the Eighth International Symposium on Aviation Psychology* (pp. 568–573). Ohio State University.

Hare, A.P. (1982). *Creativity in small groups.* Beverly Hills, CA: Sage.

Hare, A.P. (1992). *Groups, teams, and social interaction: Theories and applications.* New York: Praeger.

Heath, C., and Luff, P. (1992). Media space and communicative asymmetries: Preliminary observations of video-mediated interaction. *Human-Computer Interaction, 7.* Hillsdale, NJ: Lawrence Erlbaum Associates.

Heenefrund, W. (1985). The fine art of team building. *Association Management, 37*(8), 98–101.

Helmreich, R.L., and Foushee, H.C. (1993). Why crew resource management? Empirical and theoretical bases of human factors training in aviation. In E.L. Wiener, B.G. Kanki, and R.L. Helmreich (eds.), *Cockpit resource management* (pp. 3–45). San Diego, CA: Academic Press.

Helmreich, R.L., and Wilhelm, J.A. (1991). Outcomes of Crew Resource Management training. *The International Journal of Aviation Psychology, 1,* 287–300.

Hendrick, H.W. (1986). Macroergonomics: A conceptual model for integrating human factors with organizational design. In O. Brown, Jr. and H.W. Hendrick (eds.), *Human factors in organizational design and management II* (pp. 467–477). Amsterdam: North-Holland.

Hendrick, H.W. (1992). A macroergonomic approach to work organization for improved safety and productivity. In S. Kumar (ed.), *Advances in industrial ergonomics and safety* (pp. 3–10). London: Taylor and Francis.

Hendrick, H.W. (1994). Macroergonomics as a preventative strategy in occupational health. In G.E. Bradley and H.W. Hendrick (eds.), *Human factors in organizational design and management—IV* (pp. 713–718). Amsterdam: North-Holland.

Hendrick, H.W. (1995). Humanizing re-engineering for true organizational effectiveness: A macroergonomic approach. *Proceedings of the Human Factors and Ergonomics Society 39th Annual Meeting* (pp. 761–765). Santa Monica, CA: Human Factors and Ergonomics Society.

Hill, G.W. (1982). Group versus individual performance: Are N + 1 heads better than one? *Psychological Bulletin, 91,* 517–539.

Hoffman, M.S., Lowe, C.K., and Wilson, K.S. (1993). Macroergonomics research methodology: Determining future job requirements of a customer service representative (CSR) in a bank. *Proceedings of the Human Factors and Ergonomics Society 37th Annual Meeting* (pp. 877–881). Santa Monica, CA: Human Factors and Ergonomics Society.

Hormann, H., Goeters, K., Maschke, P., and Schiewe, A. (1995). Implementation and initial evaluation of the DLR/LH CRM-training. *Proceedings of the Eighth International Symposium on Aviation Psychology* (pp. 591–596). Ohio State University.

Huse, E.F., and Cummings, T.G. (1985). *Organizational development and change* (3rd ed.). St. Paul, MN: West.

Hutchins, E. (1990). The technology of team navigation. In J. Galegher, R. Kraut, and C. Edigo (eds.), *Intellectual teamwork: Social and technical bases of cooperative work* (pp. 191–220). Hillsdale, NJ: Lawrence Erlbaum Associates.

Imada, A.S. (1990). Ergonomics: Influencing management behaviour. *Ergonomics, 33,* 621–628.

Imada, A.S. (1991). The rationale and tools of participatory ergonomics. In K. Noro and A.S. Imada (eds.), *Participatory ergonomics* (pp. 30–49). London: Taylor & Francis.

Imada, A.S., and Hubert, R.J. (1993). Physical and psychological factors in perceived safety: A macroergonomic case study. *Proceedings of the Human Factors and Ergonomics Society 37th Annual Meeting* (pp. 901–904). Santa Monica, CA: Human Factors and Ergonomics Society.

Imada, A.S., and Feiglstok, D.M. (1990). An organizational design and management approach for improving safety. In K. Noro and O. Brown, Jr. (eds.), *Human factors in organizational design and management III* (pp. 479–482). Amsterdam: North-Holland.

Imada, A.S., and Nagamachi, M. (1990). Improving occupational safety and health: Nontraditional organizational design and management approaches. In K. Noro and O. Brown, Jr. (eds.), *Human factors in organizational design and management III* (pp. 483–486). Amsterdam: North-Holland.

Inzana, C.M., Willis, R.P., and Kass, S.J. (1994). The effects of physical distribution of team members on team cohesiveness and performance. *Proceedings of the Human Factors and Ergonomics Society 38th Annual Meeting* (p. 953). Santa Monica, CA: Human Factors and Ergonomics Society.

Ishii, H., Kobayashi, M., and Arita, K. (1994). Iterative design of seamless collaborative media. *Communications of the ACM, 37*(8), 83–97.

Jentsch, F.G., Sellin-Wolters, S., Bowers, C.A., and Salas, E. (1995). Crew coordination behaviors as predictors of problem detection and decision making times. *Proceedings of the Human Factors and Ergonomics Society 39th Annual Meeting* (pp. 1350–1353). Santa Monica, CA: Human Factors and Ergonomics Society.

Johannesen, L.J., Cook, R.I., and Woods, D.D. (1994). Cooperative communications in dynamic fault management. *Proceedings of the Human Factors and Ergonomics Society 38th Annual Meeting* (pp. 225–229). Santa Monica, CA: Human Factors and Ergonomics Society.

Johnson, S.T. (March-April 1993). Work teams: What's ahead in work design and rewards management. *Compensation and Benefits Review,* 35–41.

Katzenbach, J.R., and Smith, D.K. (1993). *The wisdom of teams: Creating the high-performance organization.* Boston, MA: Harvard Business School Press.

King, P.M. (1994). Participatory ergonomics: A group dynamics perspective. *Work, 4*(3), 195–200.

Kleinman, D.L., and Serfaty, D. (1989). Team performance assessment in distributed decision making. In R. Gilson, J.P. Kincaid, and B. Goldiez (eds.), *Proceedings of the Interservice Networked Simulation for Training Conference* (pp. 22–27). Orlando, FL.

Kraemer, K.L., and King, J. (1988). Computer-based systems for cooperative work and group decision making. *Computing Surveys, 20,* 115–146.

Kraemer, K.L., and Pinsonneault, A. (1990). Technology and groups: Assessments of the empirical research. In J. Galegher, R.E. Kraut, and C. Egido (eds.), *Intellectual teamwork: Social and technical foundations of cooperative work* (pp. 375–405). Hillsdale, NJ: Lawrence Erlbaum Associates.

Meshkati, N. (1991). Macroergonomics and technology transfer. *Proceedings of the 11th Congress of the International Ergonomics Association* (pp. 1184–1186). Paris: Taylor & Francis.

Monk, T. H., and Wagner, J.A. (1989). Social factors can outweigh biological ones in determining night shift safety. *Human Factors, 31*(6), 721–724.

Morgan, B.B., Glickman, A.S., Woodward, E.A., Blaiwes, A.S., and Salas, E. (1986). *Measurement of team behaviors in a navy environment* (Tech. Report NTSC TR-86-014). Orlando, FL: Naval Training Systems Center.

Nagamachi, M., and Imada, A.S. (1992). A macroergonomic approach for improving safety and work design. *Proceedings of the Human Factors Society 36th Annual Meeting* (pp. 859–861). Santa Monica, CA: Human Factors Society.

Nanda, R. (1986). Training in team and consensus building. *Management Solutions, 31*(9), 31–36.

Nopachai, S., and Casali, S.P. (1994). The impact of group decision support systems on group consensus processes and outcomes. *Proceedings of the Human Factors and Ergonomic Society 38th Annual Meeting* (pp. 215–219). Santa Monica, CA: Human Factors and Ergonomics Society.

Noro, K., and Imada, A.S. (1991). *Participatory ergonomics.* London: Taylor & Francis.

Nunamaker, J.F., Applegate, L.M., and Konsynski, B.R. (1987). Facilitating group creativity: Experience with a group decision support system. *Journal of Management Information Systems, 3*(4), 6–19.

O'Hara, J., and Brown, W. (1994). *Advanced human system interface design review guideline* (NUREG/CR-5908). Washington, DC: U.S. Nuclear Regulatory Commission.

O'Hara, J., Brown, W., Stubler, W., Wachtel, J., and Persensky, J. (1995). *Human system interface design review guideline* (Draft NUREG-0700, Rev 1.). Washington, DC: U.S. Nuclear Regulatory Commission.

Orasanu, J. (1990). *Shared mental models and crew decision making* (Tech. Report 46). Princeton, NJ: Princeton University, Cognitive Sciences Laboratory.

Orasanu, J., and Salas, E. (1993). Team decision making in complex environments. In G. Klein, J. Orasanu, and R. Calderwood (eds.), *Decision making in action: Models and methods* (pp. 327–345). Norwood, NJ: Ablex.

Patten, T.H., Jr. (1981). *Organizational development through teambuilding.* New York: Wiley.

Pepitone, D., King, T., and Murphy, M. (1988). *The role of flight planning in aircrew decision performance* (Society for Automotive Engineers Technical Paper Series #881517).

Peters, R.H. (1991). Strategies for encouraging self-protective employee behavior. *Journal of Safety Research, 22,* 53–70.

Peters, T.J. (1988). *Thriving on chaos.* New York: Knopf.

Preece, J. (1994). *Human-computer interaction.* Reading, MA: Addison-Wesley.

Reiersen, C., Baker, S., Marshall, E., Verle, A., and Gertman, D. (1987). *Further evaluations exercises with the integrated process status overview—IPSO* (Tech. Report HWR-184). Halden, Norway: Halden Reactor Project.

Robertson, M.M., Taylor, J.C., Stelly, J.W., and Wagner, R. (1995). A systematic training evaluation model applied to measure the effectiveness of an aviation maintenance team training program. *Proceedings of the Eighth Symposium on Aviation Psychology* (pp. 631–636). Columbus, OH.

Salas, E., Cannon-Bowers, J.A., and Johnston, J.H. (1997). How can you turn a team of experts into an expert team?: Emerging training strategies. In C. E. Zsambok and G. Klein (eds.), *Naturalistic decision making* (pp. 359–370). Mahwah, NJ: Erlbaum.

Salas, E., Dickinson, T.L., Converse, S.A., and Tannenbaum, S.I. (1992). Toward an understanding of team performance and training. In R. Sweezey and E. Salas (eds.), *Teams: Their training and performance* (pp. 3–29). Norwood, NJ: Ablex Publishing.

Salas, E. Prince, C., Baker, D. P., and Shrestha, L. (1995). Situational awareness in team performance: Implications for measurement and training. *Human Factors, 37*(1), 123–136.

Segal, L.D. (1994). Actions speak louder than words: How pilots use nonverbal information for crew communications. *Proceedings of the Human Factors and Ergonomics Society 38th Annual Meeting* (pp. 21–25). Santa Monica, CA: Human Factors and Ergonomics Society.

Serfaty, D., Entin, E.E., and Volpe, C. (1993). Adaptation to stress in team decision-making and coordination. *Proceedings of the Human Factors and Ergonomics Society 37th Annual Meeting* (pp. 1228–1232). Santa Monica, CA: Human Factors and Ergonomics Society.

Sharda, R., Barr, S.H., and McDonnell, J.C. (1988). Decision support system effectiveness: A review and an empirical test. *Management Science, 34,* 139–159.

Shea, G.P., and Guzzo, R.A. (1987). Group effectiveness: What really matters? *Sloan Management Review, 3,* 25–31.

Steeb, R., and Johnson, S.C. (1981). A computer-based interactive system for group decision-making. *IEEE Transactions, 11,* 544–552.

Stout, R.J. (1995). Planning effects on communication strategies: A shared mental model perspective. *Proceedings of the Human Factors and Ergonomics Society 39th Annual Meeting* (pp. 1278–1282). Santa Monica, CA: Human Factors and Ergonomics Society.

Stout, R.J., and Salas, E. (1993). The role of planning in coordinated team decision making: Implications for training. *Proceedings of the Human Factors and Ergonomics Society 37th Annual Meeting* (pp. 1238–1242). Santa Monica, CA: Human Factors and Ergonomics Society.

Stout, R., Cannon-Bowers, J.A., and Salas, E. (1994). The role of shared mental models in developing shared situational awareness. In R.D. Gilson, D.J. Garland, and J.M. Koonce (eds.), *Situational awareness in complex systems* (pp. 297–304). Daytona Beach, FL: Embry-Riddle Aeronautical University Press.

Street, W. (1974). Brainstorming by individuals, coacting and interacting groups. *Journal of Applied Psychology, 59,* 433–436.

Stubler, W.F., and O'Hara, J.M. (1995). Group-view displays for enhancing crew performance. *Proceedings of the Human Factors and Ergonomics Society 39th Annual Meeting* (pp. 1199–1203). Santa Monica, CA: Human Factors and Ergonomics Society.

Sukhia, C., and Funk, K. (1995). Functional model of crew performance: A systems engineering perspective. *Proceedings of the Eighth International Symposium on Aviation Psychology* (pp. 522–527). Ohio State University.

Sundstrom, E., and Altman, I. (1989). Physical environments and work-group effectiveness. *Research in Organizational Behavior, 11,* 175–209.

Sundstrom, E., De Meuse, K. P., and Futrell, D. (1990). Work teams: Applications and effectiveness. *American Psychologist, 45,* 120–133.

Tang, J.C. (1991). Findings from observational studies of collaborative work. In S. Greenberg (ed.), *Computer-supported cooperative work and groupware* (pp. 11–28). San Diego, CA: Academic Press.

Turoff, M., and Hiltz, S.R. (1982). Computer support for group versus individual decisions. *IEEE Transactions on Communications, COM-30*(1), 82–90.

Urban, J.M., Weaver, J.L., Bowers, C.A., and Rhodenizer, L. (1996). Effects of workload and structure on team process and performance: Implications for complex team decision making. *Human Factors, 38*(2), 300–310.

Volpe, C.E. (1993). Training for team coordination and decision making effectiveness: Theory, practice, and research directions. *Proceedings of the Human Factors and Ergonomics Society 37th Annual Meeting* (pp. 1226–1227). Santa Monica, CA: Human Factors and Ergonomics Society.

Volpe, C.E., Cannon-Bowers, J.A., Salas, E., and Spector, P.E. (1996). The impact of cross-training on team functioning: An empirical investigation. *Human Factors, 38*(1), 87–100.

Willeges, R.C., Johnston, W.A., and Briggs, G.E. (1966). Role of verbal communication in teamwork. *Journal of Applied Psychology, 50,* 473–478.

Woods, D.D. (1984). Visual momentum: A concept to improve the cognitive coupling of a person and computer. *International Journal of Man-Machine Studies, 21,* 229–244.

Woods, D.D., Roth, E.M., Stubler, W.F., and Mumaw, R.J. (1990). Navigating through large display networks in dynamic control applications. *Proceedings of the Human Factors Society 34th Annual Meeting* (pp. 396–399). Santa Monica, CA: Human Factors Society.

Xiao, Y., Hunter, W.A., MacKenzie, C.F., Jefferies, N.J. (1996). Task complexity in emergency medical care and its implications for team coordination. *Human Factors, 38*(4), 636–645.

Yetton, P., and Bottger, P. (1983). The relationships among group size, member ability, social decision schemes, and performance. *Organizational Behavior and Human Performance, 32,* 145–159.

Zigurs, I., Poole, M.S., and DeSanctis, G. (1987). *A study of influence in computer-mediated decision making.* Minneapolis, MN: MIS Department, Curtis I. Carlson School of Management, University of Minnesota.

Author Index

Subject Index